Lecture Notes in Computer Science

Lecture Notes in Computer Science

Edited by G. Goos and J. Hartmanis

122

Algorithms in Modern Mathematics and Computer Science

Proceedings, Urgench, Uzbek SSR
September 16–22, 1979

Edited by A.P. Ershov and D.E. Knuth

Springer-Verlag
Berlin Heidelberg New York 1981

AMS Subject Classifications (1980): 01, 03, 68
CR Subject Classifications (1979): 1.2, 2.1, 5.21, 5.25, 5.27

ISBN 3-540-11157-3 Springer-Verlag Berlin Heidelberg New York
ISBN 0-387-11157-3 Springer-Verlag New York Heidelberg Berlin

Printing and binding: Beltz Offsetdruck, Hemsbach/Bergstr.
2145/3140-543210

Foreword

SOME TIME AGO a group of mathematicians and computer scientists (including the editors of this volume) thought of making a scientific pilgrimage to the birthplace of al-Khwârizmî, the outstanding ninth-century mathematician who gave his name to the word "algorithm". As his name indicates, al-Khwârizmî came from the Khorezm oasis, a celebrated center of civilization that has given mankind a whole constellation of remarkable philosophers, scientists, and poets. We had learned not only that al-Khwârizmî's famous writings eventually led to our word algorithm, but that the word "algebra" also stems from the title of his major work—thereby accounting for both algebra and algorithms, two of the most important concepts in all of mathematics and computer science. So we felt that a visit to this site would be a special experience for every mathematician, whether he works on abstract or concrete questions, whether he studies philosophical foundations or applications to modern society.

After discussing this idea with a wider circle of scientists, and also consulting with the Academies of Science in the Soviet Union and in the Uzbek S.S.R., our dreams became a reality: An international symposium on the theme *Algorithms in Modern Mathematics and Computer Science* was held during the week October 16–22, 1979, in the city of Urgench, the modern center of the Khorezm region in Uzbekistan. The symposium was organized by the Academy of Sciences of the Uzbek S.S.R., with the support of the Soviet Academy and its Siberian branch.

In order to help prepare for a fruitful pilgrimage, we had written the following letter to potential participants during the planning stages:

> It seems to us that this is a splendid opportunity for a truly unique and fruitful conference, an unforgettable experience. Instead of having just another "ordinary" symposium at which we read prepared papers, we prefer to have mutual discussions about fundamental problems of mathematics and computer science. We believe that the desert setting and the atmosphere of history that pervades the conference site will provide us with a special opportunity to take our minds away from the everyday work that fills our lives at home; it should help inspire us to thoughts of a more penetrating, far-sighted, and philosophical nature. Nevertheless, we don't believe that the work of the symposium will succeed if people come completely unprepared, expecting an entirely spontaneous discussion; some serious preliminary study will enable us to work better and to learn better during the time we are together. The attendees will no doubt be specialists in a variety of disciplines with a variety of different modes of thinking, and we certainly don't expect that a sudden unifying consensus of opinion will be reached about the intrinsic nature of algorithms; yet we do feel that the symposium will be an important experience leading to future progress.

It gives us great pleasure now to look back and see that our high hopes for an unforgettable week were indeed fulfilled and surpassed.

The following tentative suggestions for discussion topics, representing problems of common interest about which the participants at the symposium might wish to reach a mutual understanding, were sent out before the meeting:

1. Is there a fundamental distinction between "algebraic" and "algorithmic" methods in mathematics?

2. What is the best way to communicate algorithms between people?

3. What should one do when confronted with a special case of a problem that is algorithmically unsolvable in general?

4. What is the right way to synthesize computer programs containing, say, more than a million instructions?

5. How would the original work of al-Khwârizmî be expressed in modern notation?

6. What sorts of non-algorithmic languages for programming are desirable?

7. Do algorithms provide ideal models for the organization of specific branches of knowledge (e.g., biological sciences, physical sciences, social sciences, music, or mathematics itself)?

Of course, these questions were merely intended to indicate the flavor of the discussions we hoped to incite, rather than to set up strict boundaries about what topics would be treated.

Several of the potential participants added additional comments that helped to set the theme of our meeting. For example:

> Is it possible to formulate an appropriate generalization of the Church thesis that would embrace computability in arbitrary object domains and, particularly, computability with probabilistic and nondeterministic devices?　　[D. Skordev]

> Your ideas for a symposium in the Khowarizm region sound very good. Too many researchers work on problems simply because the problems have been proposed as interesting by others. The result is a large number of competent papers leading nowhere. Some reflection on why particular problems are important and what type of advances are possible is much needed. ... You might add to the list of topics one on mathematical notation. I have often wondered why natural problems so often turn out to be complete for some class. One would expect that the probability of a problem being complete is vanishingly small. There must be something about our notation that forces us into considering only nice problems.　　[J. Hopcroft]

> What are algorithms on real numbers?　　[N. N. Nepeivoda]

> I am interested in various relationships of the concept of algorithm with other mathematical notions: algorithms vs. enumerable sets, algorithms in logic, algorithms and automata and other processes, algorithms and problems with a high degree of complexity, relative computability.　　[G. S. Tseytin]

> I am especially interested in 'How to create an algorithm'.　　[E. H. Tyugu]

> There is a view in which 'algorithmic' and 'algebraic' approaches look almost identical. Maybe the real alternative is 'algorithmic' vs. 'set-theoretical'? Can the concept of algorithm be defined in terms of other standard (say, set-theoretic) mathematical notions or is it essentially independent and primary?　　[V. A. Uspensky]

> What would be a good course on algorithms and logic to be taught at computer science departments? Is it worth while to look for an invariant characterization of computable functions, algorithms, processes of computation?　　[A. P. Ershov]

It was necessary to limit the size of the symposium to comparatively few delegates in order to keep it from being unwieldy, but we soon realized that the discussions would be stimulating and valuable to a large number of people. Therefore most of the proceedings were subsequently written down, and they are presented here in English. We hope that many readers will now be able to share at least partly in the excitement of that week.

The participants of the symposium are deeply grateful to their Uzbek hosts who showed extraordinary hospitality—what a joy it was for all of us! Special thanks are due to S. Kh. Sirazhdinov, vice president of the Uzbek Academy of Sciences and chairman of the organizing committee; to R. I. Ishchanov, chairman of the executive committee of the Khorezm region; to V. K. Kabulov, director of the Institute of Cybernetics of the Uzbek Academy and co-chairman of the organizing committee; and to K. Š. Babamuradov, division manager of the Institute of Cybernetics and vice-chairman of the organizing committee.

We also are grateful to the many wonderful people we met in the city and in the surrounding countryside, who gave us a warm welcome that we will always remember. Tours were arranged by which we were able to visit historical sites as well as modern schools, farms, and industries. We were impressed that so many people showed great interest in the work of our symposium, following its progress in the newspapers and on television. A public monument in the center of Urgench was dedicated to al-Khwârizmî's memory in a special ceremony when we arrived. It pleases us very much to know that the tradition of al-Khwârizmî lives on in his home territory.

—A. P. Ershov and D. E. Knuth

TABLE OF CONTENTS

AL-KHOREZMI

His Background, His Personality

His Work and His Influence

Paper read at the Symposium on "Algorithms in Modern
Mathematics and Computer Science", dedicated to Al-Khorezmi
in Urgench (Khorezm Region, Uzebk S.S.R.), September 16 - 22, 1979

by
Prof. Dr. Heinz Zemanek, Vienna
IBM Fellow

This is a short version of an
extensive work to be published later

INTRODUCTION

We have assembled here in this symposium, in one of the most famous
and most unknown countries of the world, to celebrate one of the most
famous and most unknown mathematicians. This is a symposium on the
algorithm, one of the most commonly used terms in the computing
world, but it is almost unknown that this term is derived from the
name of a mathematician and his country: al-Khorezmi and Khorezm.

In a medieval manuscript the formula DIXIT ALGORIZMI, the Latin
equivalent of the Arabic formula QALA AL-KHOREZMI (in German we
would say ALSO SPRACH AL-KHOREZMI) was a hallmark which guaranteed
clarity and reliability. Al-Khorezmi was considered an ultimate
authority. I wish to show how this came about. In doing so I shall
use the ancient formula - in this paper all quotations of
al-Khorezmi will begin with DIXIT ALGORIZMI.

Al-Khorezmi certainly did not invent the algorithm - everyone who
talks about Euclid's algorithm realises that - and even the Greeks
were not the inventors. The history of mathematics provides
sufficient evidence that much of Greek mathematics and science was
based on or taken from older sources - Babylonian, Egyptian, and
others unknown to us. Al-Khorezmi was definitely neither the only
nor necessarily the greatest mathematician of his time. I hope to
show you in this paper why he deserves to have his name immortalized
in the algorithm and to be treated as the most excellent representative of Arab mathematics and to be celebrated here.

Let me start by expressing my gratitude to two specific men and to
a group of people - a distinguished selection from the many
people who have contributed to and supported my work. These two
men are Academicians A.A. DORODNICYN and V.K. KABULOV, who made it
possible for me, three years ago, to visit Urgench and Khiva. This
visit is unforgettable for me and was the spark that triggered off
my investigations into al-Khorezmi. Yet the visit had something
of a misprint. When one looks up Khorezm in an encyclopedia, one
finds that Khorezm and Khiva are identical. I wanted to see Khiva
and bothered the Academician for years by telling him that if I
went to Tashkent I wanted also to go to Khiva. In fact Khorezm is
not the same as Khiva, but during four centuries the Khanat of Khiva

3

covered more or less the historic oasis along the big river called Khorezm. Khiva had probably existed much longer than can be proved at the moment by archaelogical evidence, evidently since the 6th century, but it did not become the capital of Khorezm until 1511. Before that date, the capital was *Kath* and later *Djordjaniya*, now called *Kunya (old) Urgench*. The cities in this part of the world have been destroyed frequently; only some of them were rebuilt, and even then very often in different places. Hardly any other part of the world has such a live history and geography.

While preparing for my trip to Tashkent I began to realize what a jewel I had selected as the heart of my dreams - possibly the only remaining complete ensemble of Central Asian architecture. My first visit to Khiva, thanks to and in the company of Academicians KABULOV and DORODNICYN, developed into one of the greatest adventures of my life and when you see Khiva this week you will understand why I immediately stopped any other historical work and engaged in al-Khorezmi research.

The group of people I have to thank are the librarians of many cities and institutions who helped me to gain access to the knowledge I have now collected. There is, of course, nothing new one can discover about Khorezm, the Khorezmians and al-Khorezmi. Moreover, my knowledge of the ancient languages required for primary investigation - Arab, Greek, Latin, Hebrew, and a couple of others - is very close to zero.

What I could do was to read as much secondary material as I could find. Thanks to my friends, the librarians, this amounted to quite a lot. There is, of course, no way to be satisfied about the completeness, but I believe I can present a picture which is as reliable as presently possible. It might become much better when all Arab libraries have edited and published their treasures so that some missing areas of the picture are completed.

ROMAN EMPIRE (GERMAN)	BYZANTINE EMPIRE	AL-KHOREZMI	CALIPHS
		780	
	CONSTANTINE VI	790	
CHARLEMAGNE	IRENE	800	HARUN AR-RASHID
	NICEPHORUS I	810	
	MICHAEL I		AL-AMIN
	LEO V	820	AL-MAMUN
LOUIS I	MICHAEL II	830	
	THEOPHILUS	840	AL-MUTASIM
			AL-WATHIK
LOTHAIR I	MICHAEL III	850	AL-MUTAWAKKIL

KHOREZM

As I have already said, you are now in a country that can be described - in terms of European education - as one of the oldest and
still most unknown countries of the world. In a certain sense, you
are now in the hub of the old world. Hindu astronomy used the city
of Arin (today Ujjain) at 76° east (23° north) as the zero meridian
for their tables, because they assumed Arin to be located in the
midpoint of the hemisphere which extends from the Ocean in the
West to the Ocean in the East. Khorezm is even better fitted to
be the center point because it is really the heart of the Eurasian
continent: a circle with a radius of 5000 km, i.e. a quadrant of
the earth, touches Mogadiscio, Toledo, Dublin, Spitsbergen, Yakutsk,
Nanking, Hong Kong, Bangkok, and closes south of India and Ceylon.

When Alexander the Great of Macedonia and his army occupied Central
Asia, they conquered Baktra and in the spring of 328 B.C. the King
of Khorezm came to meet them and to conclude an alliance with
Alexander, offering the support of the 1500 horsemen he had brought
with him to defeat one of his eastern enemies. This was typical
Khorezmian cunning. It was successful. Alexander and his army
never penetrated into Khorezm, but turned northeast from Baktra
and the Iaxartes river and the southeast towards India. From the
report of Alexander's campaign we know the spelling Χορεσμια
and today, 2300 years later, the Russian spelling is Хоресм and
the car plates show the letters X 3.

While we have heard about Samarkand and Buchara, we generally know
nothing about Khorezm and even specialists have little information.
Furthermore, since the European maps down to the 17th century did
not show Lake Aral and had the rivers Oxus and Iaxartes flowing
into the Caspian Sea, there was for a long time a basic geographic
distortion in European knowledge. This distortion gave substance
to an ancient legend, which said that the river Oxus had deviated
and run to the Caspian Sea for some 200 years. I will come back
to this story later on.

Khorezm was very probably the country into which Zarathustra
travelled from the mountains and is thus the homecountry of Awesta
and Mithras; indeed there is in the Awesta - originally written

in a language very similar to the Khorezmian language - the description of a building combining the elements of fortress, city and farm which is exactly the same type of building that has been excavated in Khorezm. The old Khorezmian language was an eastern Iranian - and therefore Indoeuropean - language written in letters related to the Arameic alphabet. Although we know very little at the moment we may be sure that the remains of a high culture are hidden under hundred of sandhills that cover the ruins of cities and fortresses.

I will not go into details and can only mention that in 712 A.D., one year after the Muslim conquest of Spain, Khorezm was conquered by the Arabs. Later reports about the killing of all priests and scientists and the burning of all books by the Arab conquerors are probably a fiction - the old habits and books simply lost their meaning and use in the Arab culture and disappeared gradually, but not completely. The centralized power of the early years of Arab rule was gradually taken over by local rulers: Khorezm slowly became independent and the ancient title of the Khorezm Shah was revived. Between 1100 and 1200 the country was a superpower; the Khorezm Shahs dominated Persia and even part of Arabia. Khorezm's economic basis at this time was based on its being at the crossroad of Asia.

In 1220 the Khorezmians killed - without any plausible reason - a delegation sent by the ruler of the Mongols. It is not impossible that this murder incited the Mongols to go west. In any case, Khorezm was the first country to be destroyed by the Mongols; under the leadership of the famous Djingis Khan cities were annihilated and people murdered. The country and its culture never recovered from this catastrophe. The Mongols continued their raids. Between 1237 and 1241 they devastated Europe, and in 1258 they destroyed Baghdad. Several generations later, Tamerlane united the Mongols again; in 1379 he destroyed Khorezm, and although he rebuilt some cities in 1391 the country from then on continuously declined. From 1511 to 1917 it was ruled from Khiva and subsequently called the Khanat of Khiva. The Khans repeatedly used the title of Khorezm Shah - a unique case in Central Asia of a pre-islamic title maintaining its glamour until the early 20th century. In the course of the Russian Revolution, the Khan was removed from power and an

independent Soviet Republic established. The only distinction Lenin
ever accepted was a Khorezmian order. Since 1924, when Central Asia
was reorganized on ethnic principles, Khorezm has been a region
(oblast) of the Uzbek Soviet Republic with 9 districts (rayons) of
more than 500 000 inhabitants, bordered by the Turkmenian SSR in the
south and the Karakalpakian ASSR in the north, and is, in fact,
smaller than the ancient Khorezm. In flying here you will have seen
that the once ruined canals have been rebuilt and that Khorezm is
again a green oasis along the lowest part of the Amu Darya river.
The canals are as important as 1000 years ago: the Uzbek flag
shows them in a symbolic shape. The history of Khorezm is now being
extensively studied and since 1937 excavations under the direction
of Academician S.P. TOLSTOV have slowly been bringing to light what
sand and dust have covered for centuries. Unfortunately, none of the
scientific reports are available in any western language; however,
I obtained a German translation of a more popular book which is a
kind of notebook of TOLSTOV's trips and ideas, of his adventures and
findings.

We are of course interested in the Khorezm of al-Khorezmi's time.
There are two descriptions of the Khorezmians which I want to quote.
The first is by ISTAKHRI, the second by MOKADASSI; both were written
about the year 1000.

> DIXIT ISTAKHRI: *Khorezm is the name of a country which is cut off*
> *from Khorassan and Transoxania since it is enclosed by the desert.*
> *In the north and in the west it borders the region of the Turks*
> *(Ghozziya). It has many cities on both shores of the Djaihun.*
> *Its capital, Kath ("The Castle"), is on the northern bank, but on*
> *the southern side there is also a big city, al-Djordjaniya (today*
> *Kunya Urgench), a market for the Turks and a junction of caravan*
> *routes.*
>
> *Khorezm is a prosperous country, rich in grain and tree fruits.*
> *Textiles made of wool and cotton are exported into all directions.*
> *Of all people in Central Asia, the Khorezmians travel most. There*
> *is no big city without a strong Khorezmian community. They have*
> *their own language which is spoken nowhere else. Their usual*
> *dress is a characteristic jacket called Kortah and a hat bent back*
> *in a special manner. They are courageous and know how to keep*
> *the Turks in check.*

DIXIT MOKADASSI: I have rarely seen an Imam teaching law, humanities and the Koran and not having one or more Khorezmians among his pupils surpassing the others and distinguishing themselves. But Khorezmians are reserved and somehow lack spirit, adroitness and the glamour of finest education. They like to entertain their guests, but they are voracious themselves.

In short, they have many remarkable properties.

The Khorezm of Arab times had many cities. ISTAKHRI mentions the capital Kath with its already empty citadel Fyr. The river with its trend to the right had already eroded it and would soon undermine the whole city. So the second-biggest city, Djordjaniya, was slowly overtaking Kath in importance. Other cities mentioned are Tahiriya and Hazarasp (Hundred Horses, still the same name), Khiva and Ardakoshmithan, Git and Madhminiya.

As I have already mentioned, the European maps down to the 17th century did not show Lake Aral so that the rivers Oxus and Iaxartes, today Amu Darya and Syr Darya, are shown flowing into the Caspian Sea. Thus Khorezm, though it appears frequently on maps, was not correctly placed. After 1717, an ancient legend was accepted as being scientifically correct, which again led to confusion. In several versions, this ancient legend says that the Oxus river (the Amu Darya) changed its course twice, in about 1400 and 1575, that it deviated into the Caspian Sea and after some time turned back into Lake Aral. There is indeed a dry bed almost all the way from Khorezm down to the Balkhan Mountains on the Caspian Sea, seen by several explorers from 1717 onwards. The Czar had the idea of connecting the Gold Valley of Serafshan to the Volga river and thus having a waterway connection to India by redeviating the Amu Darya into the Caspian Sea: this dream inspired people and politicians for many decades. In a very detailed publication of 1875, the Dutch orientalist de Goeje deduced from literature what Academician TOLSTOV confirmed on October 6, 1947, by viewing the dry bed systematically from an aircraft: the dry bed dates back to prehistoric times and there is not the slightest trace of ancient settlements. The mythical stories can only refer to a local event when one of the branches of the river brought water to Lake Sarykamysh, a little more than 100 km west of Kunya Urgench.

SKIZZE der OASE von KHIVA

nach russischen Quellen entworfen von P. Lerch.

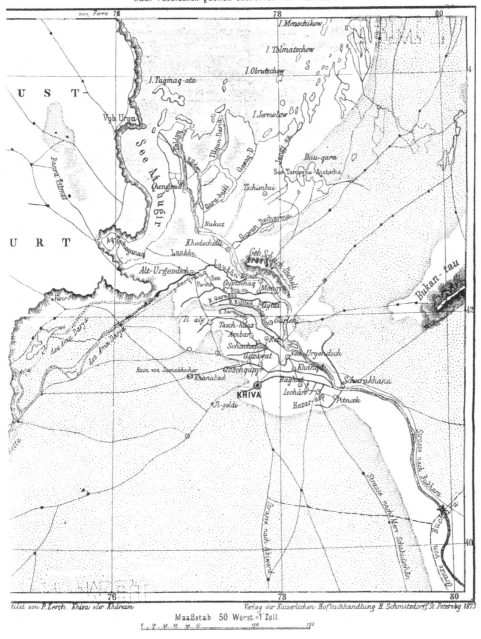

Maaßstab 50 Werst = 1 Zoll.

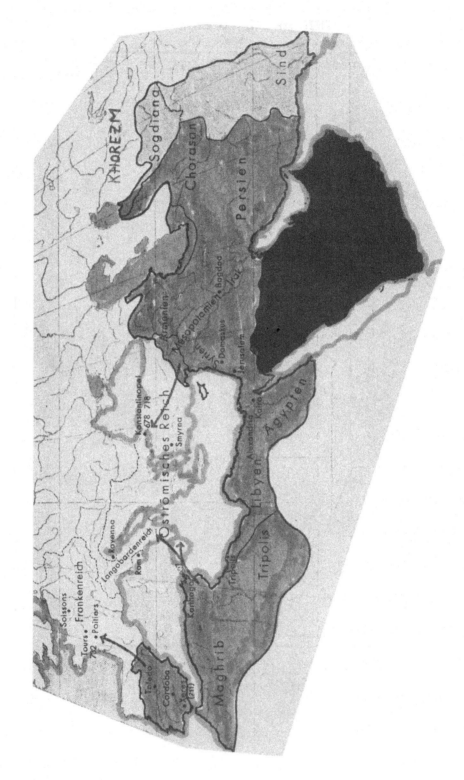

The Arab Exploration

It is principally the unprotected situation of the Khorezmian oasis
between desert and steppe which accounts for the stormy and violent
history of Khorezm and the poor information flow concerning Khorezm
into the general consciousness of world history.

This symposium gives us the opportunity of bringing a better understanding of the home country of al-Khorezmi into the world of
information processing.

View of the town of Khiva

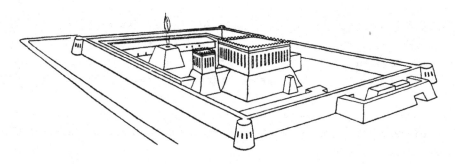

Reconstructions of Old-Khorezmian
Fortresses

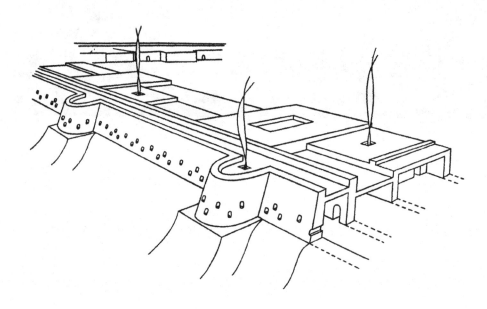

THE ABBASID CALIPHS AND THEIR CAPITAL

The migration of Mohammed on July 15, 622 A.D. from Mekka to Yatri,
subsequently called Medina (the City of the Caliph) marked the
starting point of one of the most important periods in history -
the founding of the Muslim faith and the development of the Islamic
Empire ruled by the caliphs. At this stage I must rely on your
knowledge of history, or else I would have to give a third lecture -
and even that might not be sufficient to provide the background
to the al-Khorezmi story.

After the first dynasty of the caliphs, the Ummayads (661 - 749),
came the dynasty of the Abbasids. For science, three Abbasid
caliphs were of great importance:

Abu Djafar al-Mansur (the Victorious), caliph from 754 to 775, who
founded Baghdad, prepared for the development of Arabic science
and started a library at the court; his grandson

Harun ar-Rashid (the Righteous), caliph from 786 to 809. Famous
in Europe because of the delegation he sent to Charlemagne and the
stories of the Arabian Nights. He expanded the library into an
Academy of Sciences and started the development of Arabic science;
and his second son,

Abd Allah al-Mamun (the Trustworthy), caliph from 813 to 833, who
brought the Academy to its zenith and added an observatory to it. He
also launched and protected the most rapid advances in Arabic science,
and attached al-Khorezmi to the Academy.

All three caliphs are reported to have had automata in their palaces;
the delegation which ar-Rashid sent to Charlemagne confirmed these
reports by bringing a waterclock as a present, which created a
sensation in the Occident.

Baghdad, the Arabic capital, was founded as an artificial city,
modelled on the ancient oriental circular fortress cities.

DIXIT ALGORIZMI
(in his Chronicle):
The year 145 A.H. (762 A.D.) began on Thursday, the first of Nisan 1073 Seleucid Era. In it al-Mansur began the construction of Baghdad which is called Madinat-as-Salam, the City of Peace.

The year 146 A.H. (763 A.D.) began on Monday, the twentyfirst Adar 1074 Seleucid Era. In it al-Mansur completed the construction of the Round City and he dwelled there with his servants and officials.

The year 149 A.H. (766 A.D.) began on Sunday, the sixteenth Shebat 1077 Seleucid Era. In it the walls of Baghdad as well as the construction of the whole city were completed.

We know from his records that al-Mansur spent more than 4 million dragmas on the construction of the Round City. This was equivalent to the state income of five years, but the city was worth the expenditure.

We have fabulous descriptions of Baghdad. The Round City, about 2500 m in diameter, was protected by a wall 34 m high, 50 m wide on the ground and 14 m wide at the top, a defense circle 20 m wide and a moat 57 m deep and 20 m wide filled with water, and a second, smaller wall. The Round City was called Madinat-as-Salam, the City of Peace: and that peace was maintained under the strong control of an efficient administration and a powerful police force. The city had four gates and four quarters; it may be an exaggeration that Baghdad had 100 000 mosques, 80 000 bazars, 60 000 baths and 12 000 mills, but it is very probable that it had 2 million inhabitants. It was an international city in which the major groups were Arabs, Persians, Chorasanians, and Khorezmians; later on the Turks were also recorded. The markets were full of goods from these nations and from India, China and Africa. The importance of Baghdad as a center of Arab commerce, culture and science was not reduced by the removal of the residence to Samarra from 835 to 883, and neither by the caliphs' turning away from science nor the slow but constant decline of the Caliphate. In 1258 the city was destroyed by Hulagu, grandson of Djingis Khan. Today's map of Baghdad shows a railway area in the place of the ancient Round City.

The peace of Madinat-as-Salam did not last very long. After its
glorious period under the caliph Harun ar-Rashid, whose reputation
is greater than is justified by his personality, civil war hit the
city so badly in 812 that all chroniclers recorded a decline of the
Round City from which it never recovered. But the outcome of the
Civil War was of tremendous importance for the development of science.

Harun ar-Rashid had three sons: al-Amin from the Arab princess
Zubeida, al-Mamun from a Persian slave girl called Maradjil, and
al-Mutasim. Harun had carefully arranged the succession, but
when al-Amin tried to outplay al-Mamun, the tension between the
traditional Arabic mentality and the Persian culture (based on centuries of ancient Persian empires) suddenly surfaced in the rivalry
of the half-brothers: al-Amin as the representative of the Arabic and
al-Mamun as the representative of the Persian party. It soon became
apparent which party was stronger: al-Amin lost his power step by
step and was killed when he tried to get out of the hopeless situation
in the Round City which had been besieged for 14 months by a general
devoted to al-Mamun.

AL-MAMUN

The caliph al-Mamun, the discoverer and patron of al-Khorezmi,
warrants closer description. Again we can start out from al-Khorezmi's
characterization.

> *DIXIT ALGORIZMI*
> *(in his introduction to the Algebra):*
> *That fondness for science, by which God has distinguished the Imam*
> *Al-Mamun, the Commander of the Faithful, (besides the Caliphat which*
> *He has vouchsafed unto him by lawful succession in the robe of which*
> *He has invested him, and with the honours of which He has adorned him),*
> *that affability and condescencsion which he shows to the learned, that*
> *promptitude with which he protects and supports them in the elucidation*
> *of obscurities and in the removal of difficulties, has encouraged me*
> *to compose a short work on Algebra.*

Al-Mamun was as extraordinary in his personality as al-Khorezmi.
This caliph was a philosopher and scientist himself, well-educated,
with both Arabic and Persian education, and with a sharp mind.
Many stories illustrate this. For instance, when a widow came and
complained about having received only one dragma as inheritance,
al-Mamun needed only to hear one sentence to compute immediately
the entire partition of the estate, thus proving to the widow that
she had been treated correctly and in conformity with Muslim law.

Al-Mamun's reign was like a period of enlightenment for the Islamic
world. His patronage of science and literature had tremendous
consequences for the Arab culture and - three hundred years later -
for the rise of European science.

The Exploration of the Great Pyramid

An example well-suited to describing the energy and spirit of
al-Mamun was the exploration of the Great Pyramid. This venture
preceded later scientific enterprises by many centuries. When the
Arabs captured Alexandria in 640 A.D., they found that they had
conquered a large city with 1000 palaces, 4000 baths and 400 theaters.
However, there was no library worth of mention.

Al-Mamun was informed that the Great Pyramid contained a secret

chamber with maps and tables of celestial and terrestrial spheres.
Although they were supposed to have been drawn up in the remote
past, they were said to be very accurate. The chamber was also
reputed to contain treasure and strange articles such as *arms which
would not rust and glass which might be bended and not break.*

In the year 820 the caliph collected together a large group of
scientists, architects, builders and stonemasons to attack the pyramid. For days they searched the steep polished surfaces (which, as
you know, were removed in later centuries in order to build mosques
and houses in Cairo and elsewhere), but they could not find a trace
of the secret entrance. Al-Mamun decided to enter the Pyramid by
force. He ordered a fire to be lit so that the blocks got red-hot,
and then they were doused with vinegar until they cracked. Battering
rams knocked out the broken stone. For over 100 feet al-Mamun's men
tunnelled into the solid core of the pyramid. Al-Mamun was on the
point of giving up when a workman heard the muffled sound of something heavy falling somewhere deep in the pyramid. Renewing their
efforts, the workers finally broke into a hollow way, *exceedingly
dark, dreadful to look at and difficult to pass.* They had discovered the
original secret descending passage, which led upwards to the hidden
entrance and downwards to an unfinished, roughly hewn chamber which
contained nothing but debris and dust.

But what the workmen had heard falling was a large prismatic stone
which had covered a heavy plug. So they knew the direction in which
to advance further to a passage up in the body of the pyramid which
had never been mentioned in the old sources. They had to chisel
around several plugs. Al-Mamun hoped to have discovered the secret
kept since the original construction of the pyramid. What they
found, however, after scrambling up 150 feet of dark, slippery
passage-way with a slope of 26° and a low horizontal passage was
the Queen's Chamber (a misnomer). After further efforts they found
the King's Chamber which contained nothing of interest or value;
there was only a large, empty sarcophagus. It is reported that
al-Mamun smuggled a treasure of gold into the pyramid during the
night in order to pacify his disappointed men.

18

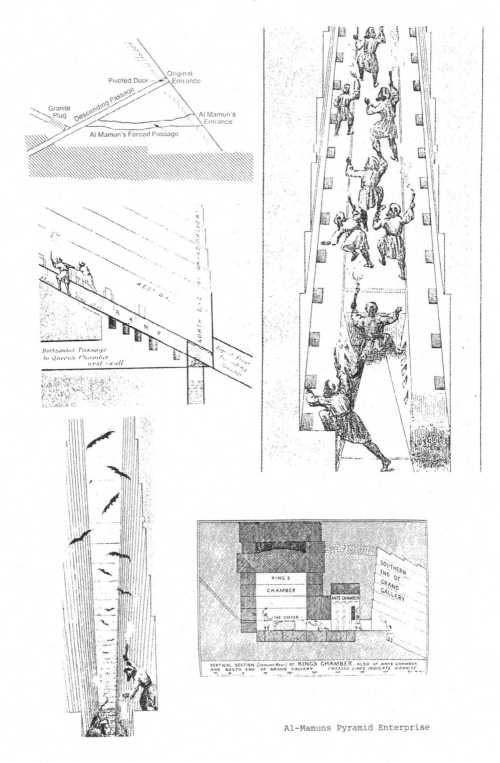

Al-Mamuns Pyramid Enterprise

THE HOUSE OF WISDOM

How did the Arab rulers, at the beginning not very different from
all the other kings and princes of their time, develop their interest
in science? Here were the sons of the desert, used to a hard and
wild life, suddenly settled on a throne that offered all the oriental
abundance in food and pleasure, entertainment and luxury. Mind and
body were able to adjust to the new conditions with one exception -
the stomach, which could not cope with the rich food. The caliphs
were very often seriously ill. Help came from Syrian, mostly
Christian, doctors whose medical knowledge was based on Greek science.
Elias of Nisibis does not quote al-Khorezmi, but Pethion on this
matter:

> *DIXIT ELIAS*
> *(in chapter 8 of part II of his Chronicle):*
> *In the year 148 A.H. (765 A.D.) al-Mansur fell ill; his stomach*
> *was upset. He sent for George, the first medical doctor of*
> *Beth-Lapat (Djundai-Sabur or Gundaisapur), and he let him come.*
> *When George came, the Caliph honoured him. And after a few*
> *days the Caliph recovered and was cured.*
>
> *In the year 151 A.H. (768 A.D.) the Caliph sent George (obviously*
> *for another cure) three beautiful Greek slave girls and 3000 denars.*
> *George accepted the denars and sent the girls back, telling the*
> *Caliph: "With such I do not live in the house, since it is not per-*
> *mitted for Christians to have more than one wife, and I have my*
> *wife in Beth-Lapat." When the Caliph heard this, he praised him and*
> *took kindly to him.*

It is not surprising that Greek science achieved a miraculous
reputation in the eyes of the Arab leading class. It became a mystical
and practical goal and the hobby of the caliphs. In successive
stages they built up an institution which can be called a workshop
for the production of Arab science: the Baghdad Academy of Sciences,
called Bayt al-Hikma, the House of Wisdom. Its director had the
title *Sahib Bayt al-Hikma* and his rank was only inferior to that of a
minister. The core of the House of Wisdom was the library, which
was a well-planned organization designed to collect, translate,
write, copy and distribute scientific books. At the beginning

the main source was Greek science. Whenever the caliphs of the 8th
and 9th centuries won an important victory over the Byzantine Empire
the peace treaties contained a clause which stipulated the surrender
of a certain number of old Greek books; the Byzantine emperors had
a hard time locating some of these books which were kept in
monasteries in all corners of the Empire.

When the caliph decided to have a book translated, he appointed an
editor-in-chief who coordinated the translators, writers, illustra-
tors and copiers. In the Bayt al-Hikma al-Mamun had a large team
of scientists, mathematicians, astronomers, astrologers, geographers
and historians. Most of them were of course universalists with
knowledge of all disciplines and working in all of them. However,
they might establish special reputations in their chosen field. They
were on duty round the clock for the caliph. When he needed information or a horoscope, when he wanted to impress visitors and amba-
sadors, or when he was in the mood for philosophical discussion, he
would call for certain members of the House of Wisdom. So besides
working in their Academy they also lived there most of the time.
The caliph ordered them to carry out many types of work or duties,
which were often carried out in well-organized teamwork. Translation
of books was a continuing team activity, but there were also special
projects.

Measurement of the Degree

One of these special teamwork projects was al-Mamun's measurement
of the degree in 827. The scientists of the House of Wisdom
obviously knew of the measurements of Eratosthenes and Posidonius.
The caliph ordered these measurements to be checked. Under the
leadership of Khalid ibn Abd al-Malik al Marwarrudi and Ali ibn Isa
two groups of scientists were organized - and it is highly probable
that al-Khorezmi al-Asturlabi was a member of one of them; we do
not know the names of the team members. One group worked in the
plain west of Baghdad near Sinear and the other in the plain of
Palmyra (which had already been destroyed), close to Aleppo.

The measurement principle was to fix by means of an astronomical
device two points on the same meridian 1 degree apart from each
other, and then measure the distance between the two points. The
astronomical device was the astrolabium which had supposedly been

invented by Hipparchus and was the forerunner of the sextant and the theodolite. It was considerably improved by the Arabs. Such instruments are still in existence, although not from the time of al-Mamun, but from two centuries later. The distance was measured by means of wooden rods that were laid out flat on the ground and kept in a straight line by putting up marking poles.

The results obtained by the two teams were 56 and 56 2/3 Arabic miles to the degree. so they averaged 56 1/3. Unfortunately there is no agreement on the length of the Arabic mile and so it is hard to judge the precision of the measurement. Moreover, there is an apparently contradictory statement in al-Khorezmi's TABLES.

> DIXIT ALGORIZMI
> (in his Tables):
> Know that conforming to the Chaldeans 4000 camel paces make a mile
> and that 33 1/3 miles on earth correspond to half a degree in the
> sky, so that the circumference of the earth is 24 000 miles. The
> reason for this is that if one goes from any place correctly to
> the south, one will observe after 66 2/3 miles that a star, ob-
> served at the same time, will stand exactly one degree higher.

And there is a second contradictory statement:

> DIXIT ALGORIZMI
> (refers an Arab scholar):
> that the circumference of the earth is 7000 farsangs or 21000
> Arab miles.

This would be 58 1/3 miles to the degree instead of 56 1/3.

First of all, the miles of the TABLES, the miles of different quotations and the miles of the actual measurement are not likely to be the same. Secondly, the TABLES had been revised at least once without any indication as to what had been modified. But altogether there is no reason why al-Mamun's scientists should not have reached a precision of a couple of percent: if 20 400 miles is accurate to 5%, then an Arabic mile should measure something between 1867 m and 2060 m, and this is well within the range of conjectures for the Arabic mile from different sources.

The Imago Mundi

Another teamwork project ordered by al-Mamun was his map of the
world, which probably decorated one of the big halls of the caliph's
palace. The scientists of the House of Wisdom started out from a
Greek source; it was known that Ptolemy had drawn a map of the
world and there were records of its coordinates. A closer investigation of the data of al-Mamun's map indicates that the members of
the Academy used Ptolemy's coordinates, but not exclusively so.
Wherever they knew better, and that was of course mainly the case
with the geography of the Arab Empire, they made corrections and
entries. More details of the map will be given in the second part
of this report, because a protocol was written by al-Khorezmi.

AL-KHOREZMI

Having established the background, we can now turn to al-Khorezmi
himself. The starting point for any investigation of an Arab scientist
from that time is a glance into the Arabic Who's Who of the 10th century,
which is known as "Fihrist". This is a list of Arab scientists with
short characterizations written in 987 by an-Nadin. The manuscript
of this work is in Leiden and the German orientalist FLÜGEL edited
it in 1872; an English translation by Bayard DODGE appeared in 1970.

The section on al-Khorezmi reads as follows:

> *His name was Mukhammad ibn Musa. His origin was in Khorezm. He
> was attached to the House of Wisdom of al-Mamun. He was one of the
> masters of the science of the stars. Both before and after obser-
> vation, people relied upon his first and second astronomical tables
> known as Sindhind. Among his books were Astronomical Tables in
> two editions, the first and the second, the Sun Dial, Operating with
> the Astrolabe, Making the Astrolabe, and the Chronicle.*

The most astonishing fact is that the main works of al-Khorezmi, his
ARITHMETIC and his ALGEBRA, do not appear in this list although
several commentaries on the ALGEBRA are included in the Fihrist
which means that an-Nadin must have known of it. It has been suggested
that the copier moved down several titles of al-Khorezmi into the
next entry, but then it turned out that that scholar wrote all the
books listed in his entry. So the conclusion is that the Fihrist is
incomplete like any Who's Who and that the copiers may have lost more
than we can complete.

The Fihrist, moreover, gives little detail on al-Khorezmi's biography.
This is normal for Arab scholars. Only in rare exceptions do we know
more about their life; most facts must be collected from indirect
sources and the rest are conclusions or assumptions on a more or less
weak basis.

His Life

From the Fihrist it is clear that al-Khorezmi established his reputation through his TABLES, of which even two editions appeared, and
which were written before the other works, i.e. quite some time before
820. This is confirmed by statements of various Arab scholars; one
of them says that the TABLES were written before al-Mamun became
caliph. So it is not impossible that al-Khorezmi was already in Merv
in the service of the Crown Prince in about 810. In any case, he must
have been more than 20 years old at that time; it is generally
assumed that he was born around 780. We could take a vote that it
was in 779 and celebrate his 1200th birthday today.

According to the Fihrist, he was attached to the House of Wisdom during
the caliphate of al-Mamun, and in all probability he stayed there till
the end of his life.

We have a little story which indicates that he was still alive in 847.
In this year, the caliph al-Watiq, a grandson of ar-Rashid and nephew
of al-Mamun, fell very ill. He called for his scientists and asked
for a horoscope to find out how long he still had to live. (Even
horoscopes were produced by teamwork.) The scientists came to the
conclusion that the caliph had more than 50 years to live. Ten days
later he was dead. The chronicler of this story, at-Tabari, writes
not without irony and provides - with a certain touch of malice - the
name of the Academy team, including al-Khorezmi. So it is generally
assumed that he died around 850.

His Travels

There are notes on three journeys made by al-Khorezmi, one to Afgha-
nistan, one to the country of the Khazars, and one into the Byzantine
Empire. They are not very reliable, but, on the other hand, not totally
improbable. Names can be easily confused and, in particular, there
were several Mukhammad ibn Musas and several Khorezmians. So we cannot
be sure whether or not he really made those journeys.

It was very natural for the caliph to send a Khorezmian into the
country of the Khazars - his language would come in very useful.
When Khorezm had been conquered a hundred years earlier by the Arabs,
many Khorezmians fled to the Khazars who had a very well-organised

and influential empire (khanat) between the Volga, the Don and the
Caucasus, and which stopped the Arab advance to the north.

The Khorezmians were received in a friendly fashion by the Khazars.
Gradually they got more influential positions and finally they took
over command of the Khazar empire and the Khan was reduced to a merely
religious position. It is not entirely clear what role the Khorezmians
played in the conversion of the Khazars to the Jewish religion in the
9th century. There is no doubt that there was a Jewish community
in old Khorezm and it can be assumed that most of them fled to the
Khazars; the open question is whether it was a political consideration
of constituting the third power between the Christians Byzantines and
the Muslim Arabs. The Khazars were a superpower for two centuries,
before their empire was destroyed in 965 by Prince Svyatoslav of Kiev.
But this did not mean the end of their national existence though there
is almost nothing known about their history in the following centuries.
A line of scholars has, since the 19th century, developed the theory
that the Eastern European Jews are descendants of the Khazars and
Khorezmians rather than of one of the twelve tribes; Arthur KOESTLER
consequently named his book on the Khazars "The Thirteenth Tribe".
And if this rather controversial story is true, then there is still
quite some Khorezmian blood around in our day.

We do not have any report on al-Khorezmi's journey to the Khazars,
but there *is* a short report in two versions on the second journey and
this story has puzzled me a good deal.

When al-Khorezmi was sent to collect books from the Byzantines, so
says the report, the caliph ordered him to inspect the Cave of the
Seven Sleepers that was close to his route anyway. When I searched
for the keyword "Seven Sleepers" I found that it was an early Christian
legend of presumably Syrian origin, and that the key location was
Ephesos.

Ephesos is the domain of the Austrian archeologists, so I went over
to the university to see them. They very proudly handed me a large
and impressive book: the report on the Austrian excavation of the
basilica of the Seven Sleepers which confirms that the first part of
the basilica was built in the 5th century, that it was then abandoned
and fell into ruin. The report also contains the Roman version of

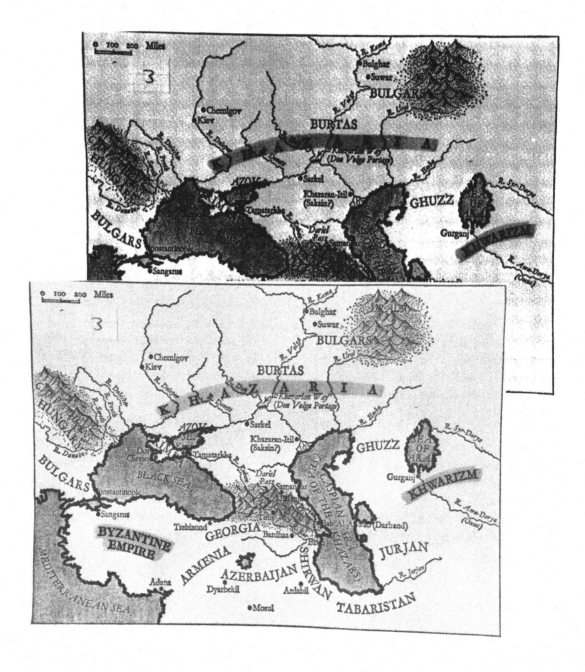

the legend which goes as follows:

Seven young men at the court of the Roman Emperor Decius (250) in Ephesos had become Christians and refused to give up their faith; they hid instead in a cave which the Emperor ordered to be closed up by a wall. The seven young men slept until 448 when the wall was torn down because a stable was to be built. They gave testimony before the Byzantine Emperor Theodosius and then died.

The legend found its way to Arabia and Mohammed mentions it in the Koran; surah 18 concerns the men in the cave. So I thought I had cleared up the story until I realized that neither the geographical description of al-Khorezmi's trip nor the description of the cave fits the report of the Austrian excavation. Let me give you the al-Khorezmi travel report.

They had to travel up the Euphrates river and pass the border to the Byzantine Empire south of the fortress of Qurrah (Greek: Κορον). They arrived at the cave after a two days' trip from Qurrah. The custodian tried to prevent al-Khorezmi from entering the cave by telling him frightening stories. Since al-Khorezmi insisted and could show the permit of the Byzantine Emperor, the custodian prepared torches and a meal and they went into the cave. There they found seven bodies wrapped up in rough linen which fell to dust when it was touched. The bodies were well-conserved, the skin dry and the hair felt like wire when they touched it. When the custodian offered them a meal after they had finished their inspection, they could not stand it and could not help but vomit. There was some danger, says the report, that the custodian would try to kill the visitors because he was afraid of the negative effects of the visit (he had maintained that the bodies were life-like), but al-Khorezmi managed to leave the place safely.

Further research has convinced me that this cave was not in Ephesos but in Amorion, a town in Central Turkey; the sanctuary there has, however, not yet been located with any degree of certainty and other authors maintain that the correct place is Afşin in Eastern Turkey. The title of this section of the book I am going to write will therefore be: *The 14 Seven Sleepers*. I might add that I have visited many places in Europe with churches devoted to these saints, whose commemoration

a) The names of the Seven Sleepers around that of their dog Qiṭmīr; Turkey 1318/1900.

The Saint Seven Sleepers - Arab Tradition

day is June 27 or July 27; a weather rule states that if it rains
on June 27 it will rain for the next seven weeks. The most beautiful
of these churches is in Bavaria near the Austrian border and the most
impressive sanctuary is near Lannion in French Brittany where a prehistoric monolithic cave still attracts a pilgrimage in which Arabs
participate every third Sunday in July. But that is another story.

Al-Khorezmi certainly went on a large number of journeys - you remember
Istakhri - "the Khorezmians travel most". He may have accompanied his
caliph when he went abroad or when a war broke out; he may also have
been used for diplomatic missions; and he may have visited scientists
in other countries. We do not know. We have only one extensive
testimony: the books which al-Khorezmi wrote.

His Work

If we assemble the works of which we have manuscripts and translations,
those quoted in the Fihrist and those of which we have excerpts or
quotations, the following list is the result:

1.   The TABLES - Kitab az-zij al-sindhind,
     of which we have a Latin translation (of a slightly adapted
     version) in Oxford. The TABLES are based on Indian astronomy and
     consist of tables and commentaries for their use. In addition
     to the astronomic content, there is a chronology with calendar
     algorithms and there are the first known tables of the sine and
     cotangent functions. The astronomic tables almost instantly
     established al-Khorezmi's fame and reputation.

2.   The ARITHMETIC - (probably) Kitab hisab al-'adad al-hindi,
     in Latin called 'Algorithmi de numero Indorum'. The earliest
     form we have is an incomplete Latin translation, probably of a
     revised Arabic version, in Oxford, but the original can be detected
     in many later manuscripts. This work introduces the Indian
     number system and the algorithms to calculate with them, i.e. to
     perform the basic arithmetic operations adding and subtracting,
     doubling, halving, multiplying, dividing and finding the root.
     This is the most successful of al-Khorezmi's treatises - the
     vehicle, one can say, by which the Indian number system was
     introduced first into the Arabic world and subsequently into
     Europe. For medieval mathematics, arithmetic became identified

with his name in the word 'Algorismus'. And now information
processing commemorates his name whenever the word algorithm
is used.

3. The ALGEBRA - Kitab al-muhtasar fi hisab al-gabr w'al-muqabalah
    A compact introduction to calculation using rules of completion
    and reduction. We have several Arabic manuscripts (in Oxford,
    Cairo and Berlin), and several incomplete Latin translations. The
    only complete translation into English was written by Rosen in
    1831 and has a number of shortcomings. Is is a shame that no
    improved edition and revised translation of this treatise has been
    made. The chapters in this book deal with linear and quadratic
    euqations, business calculations, i.e. regula de tri (Bab al-
    mu'amalat), geometry (Bab al-misahat), and computation of legacies
    (Kitab al-wasaya). Whilst Arab scholars state that al-Khorezmi
    was the first to write on this subject, this does not, of course,
    mean that he invented or founded algebra. Even if there were
    earlier exponents, al-Khorezmi's treatise is still the groundstone
    of development on which influential later authors based their
    work. The word al-gabr in its title became (or it was already)
    the name for the science of computing unknowns. Soon many other
    treatises on algebra were written, often with similar titles
    and new additional contents. Thus al-Khorezmi's influence on
    algebra is not as discernible as in arithmetics, but his paramount
    importance as the first major author is unquestioned.

    The Arithmetic, the Algebra and the Trigonometric Tables have been
    translated into Russian and commented on by Yu. Kh. Kopelevich
    and B. A. Rozenfel'd (Tashkent 1964).

4. The JEWISH CALENDAR - Istakhraj tarikh al-Yahud
    Written in 823. There is an Arabic manuscript in Bankipore, India,
    which describes the Jewish calendar and gives algorithms for the
    transformation of dates.

5. The CHRONICLE - Kitab at-tarikh,
    of which we have only a set of quotations in the Chronicle of the
    Archbishop of Nisibis (today Nusaybin) written in both Arabic and
    Syrian. Unfortunately, the most interesting section, the pages
    concerning the years 786 to 877, the lifetime of al-Khorezmi,
    are missing in the manuscript which is in the British Museum.

Al-Khorezmi's CHRONICLE is often mentioned and there are scholars
who consider al-Khorezmi as one of the earliest historians.

6.   The GEOGRAPHY - Kitab surat al-ard,
     The Picture of the World or Imago Mundi.
     Written in 817. We have an Arabic manuscript in Strasbourg. It
     is a record of al-Mamun's implementation of the map of the world
     giving the geographic coordinates of cities, mountains, rivers
     and coast lines. It was edited and translated by the Viennese
     orientalist Hans von Mžik.

7. and 8. The MAKING OF THE ASTROLABE and THE USE OF THE ASTROLABE -
     Kitab 'amal al-astrolab, Kitab al-'amal bi'l-astrolab.
     We have only an Arabic excerpt from the treatise On the Use of
     the Astrolabe; this manuscript is in Berlin. It was translated
     into German by Josef Frank in Erlangen in 1922.

9.   The SUNDIAL - Kitab ar-rukhamakh
     This book is lost.

10. The ASTROLOGY,
     of which we know only indirectly. Al-Khorezmi is reported to have
     investigated whether the birth date of Mohammed was likely to
     have had an influence on his becoming a prophet; I have dis-
     covered a manuscript in Paris dealing with the magic power of
     the Arabic letters when making a talisman or an amulet. This
     also provides one quotation and a little original information.

His Name (and the name Khorezm)

It is necessary to explain the meaning of the names Khorezm and
al-Khorezmi and their different spellings. On the meaning of "Chorezm"
there have, from Arabic times onwards, been a number of wrong explanations in the literature. From the linguistic point of view, the
second part of the word is absolutely clear: 'zem' is the land, as
one knows from Novaya Zemlya, the island north of the Ural mountains.
'Zem' is a common word of all Slavic and Iranian languages. My own
name has the same root: 'zem' also means 'land' in the Czech language
from which my name is derived, and 'zemán' (I was baptized by a
priest of Czech origin who restored the accent on my name which my

father had already lost in Vienna;   I use it only in Czechoslovakia:
who wants his name to be misspelled?)   is the man who works on the land.
This is the same as 'farmer' in English, 'Bauer' in German, and 'George'
in Greek - indeed one can deduce the proper translation of 'George'
from general knowledge.   Many years ago a Bulgarian student of mine
pointed this out to me to my perplexion: 'geos' is known from geography, and 'erg' from the unit 'erg' and from 'energy'.

'Khor' is not so unambiguous.   It might be derived from a tribe, the
Khorras;   it might mean the land of the sun - the smile of a blue sky
throughout many months in this country between the deserts (and for
the friendly population of today the 'country of the smile' would be
an appropriate name):   it might mean the 'Eastern Country' - which
would put Khorezm in a similar situation to Austria, whose name means
Eastern Land (Öster-reich).   But the most probable and most widely
accepted root is 'khor' meaning 'low' or 'nether' - indeed the geographical situation along the lowest part of the Amu Darya river
supports the translation 'the Central Asian Netherlands' and the number
and the economic importance of the canals make Khorezm a real counterpart of Holland.   So the name al-Khorezmi means 'the Netherlander'
and that connects him to Professor van Wijngaarden (whose first name
Aadrian, as he remarked, Hadrian, means 'the cultivator of the land'
and so relates him to 'zem').

The classic Arabic languages, in contrast to the Iranian ones, do not
contain the vowel 'o'.   The form 'Mohammed', containing 'o' and 'e'
is of Western and later origin.   The Eastern and classic old Arabic
has only three vowels a, i and u.   The general transcription of 'o' by
Arabic letters is UA (WA) which explains all forms like Khwarizm, Khu-
warizm, etc.   There may be an ancient Iranian pronunciation with VA, WA
or UWA, but not only the Greek Χορεσμια and the Russian spelling Хоресм
prove the correctness of the 'o' - the main proof is, of course, the word
'algorithm'.   When the scientists of the 12the century took this term
from their Arab colleagues languages were not learned from books as
was done in the 19th century when the incorrect spelling al-Khowarizmi
was introduced: at that time Arabic was learned by speaking with the
Arabs in Spain and so the correct 'o' was used.   Due to the freedom
of spelling throughout the centuries and to different transliterations
from the Arabic many vairations developed, and there is hardly any
other scientist whose name has been written in so many different ways.

The German orientalist Julius Ruska has discussed this in a footnote
and collected many variants, and in the Museum of Samarkand there is a
table listing such variations by countries. Here is a combinatorial
chart of the possibilities:

A	L	KH	O			R	E	Z	-	M	I
E	U	GH	U	W	A		A	S	E	N	-
		CH	A	V			I	TH	I		
		K	-	-	-			X	Y		
		G	AU								
		H									
		J									

Select a stochastical path through the chart - many of them will
yield actually occurring variations.

The Universalist

Al-Khorezmi was universal not only in his scientific knowledge and
writings, but also in his blend of cultural background. In the introduction to his ALGEBRA, he himself gives an idea of his philosophy
and mentality.

DIXIT ALGORIZMI
(in the introduction to his Algebra):
The learned in times which have passed away, and among nations which have
ceased to exist, were constantly employed in writing books on the several
departments of science and on the various branches of knowledge, bearing
in mind those that were to come after them, and hoping for a reward pro-
portionate to their ability, and trusting that their endeavours would
meet with acknowledgement, attention and remembrance - content as they
were even with a small degree of praise - small, if compared with the
pains which they had undergone and the difficulties which they had en-
countered in revealing the secrets of science.

An additional characterization can be demonstrated by considering his
full name. Arabic names consist of the given name, the father's name,
the son's name and of further terms, called nisbah, which express
properties, nationality or birth town or similar characteristics.

His full name is

Mukhammad ibn Musa abu Abdallah (or abu Djafar) al-Khorezmi al-Madjusi
al-Qutrubulli

Mukhammad: As can be seen from several of the introductions of
              his writings, he was a devoted Muslim who though matched
              the liberal attitude of his caliph in that spirit of
              enlightenment which characterized the reign of al-Mamun.

Ibn Musa: Moses was a common Muslim name, but it appears symbolic
              that he inherited this Jewish name from his father.
              His book on the Jewish calendar proves his intimate
              knowledge of the Jewish culture; one can also detect
              an underlying interest in the Babylonian culture -
              the Jewish calendar was an inheritance of the Hebrews'
              stay in Babylon.

Abu Djafar or Abu Abdallah: Two versions of his son's name occur in
              different places. This ambiguity symbolizes the
              mysterious aspect of al-Khorezmi. Did he lose his
              first son? Is it simply a copying error? Or are we
              dealing with two persons under one name? The latter
              possibility is small since al-Khorezmi's reputation
              appears genuine, being the natural result of such a
              unique personality. The only source of suspicion to me
              is the remark of Mžik stating that the text of the geo-
              graphy is written in rough, even barbaric Arabic which
              does not at all match the fine and careful language of
              the ALGEBRA. There is a basic open-endedness in our
              knowledge of al-Khorezmi.

Al-Khorezmi: He was known as a Khorezmian and it was the tolerance
              of the Baghdad court which permitted him to identify
              himself during his lifetime with the conquered country;
              it seems that al-Mamun, probably due to the influence
              of his Persian mother, had a special interest in Iranian
              scientists. For example, when Musa-ibn-Shakir, another
              renowned Iranian scientist, died leaving three boys,
              al-Mamun made one of the scientists their godfather and
              arranged for them to stay and be educated in the House
              of Wisdom. The brothers, the 'Banu Musa', themselves

became famous, important scientists and rich men
who were often given political tasks. The oldest of
the three brothers, Mukhammad ibn Musa, is often confused with al-Khorezmi and some of the al-Khorezmi
stories, such as the trip to the Khazars or the
horoscope for al-Watiq might as well be his stories.
The second brother, Akhmad, was the initiator of Arabic
technology; he wrote the major share of a book written
by the three brothers, the kitab al-hijal, the Book
on Ingenious Devices.

Al-Qutrubbuli (al-Qatrabbuli): This part of the name seems to occur
only in the horoscope story. But it is a highly important addendum. For Qutrubbul was the district of
Baghdad inhabited by the Khorezmians, famous for its
restaurants and cellars (where people certainly, in
spite of the Prophet's rules, drank wine), famous for
its music and singing, a district preferred by artists
and poets. It causes the picture of Grinzing in Vienna
to rise before my eyes. Al-Khorezmi may have had a
country house out there. It was probably inherited from
his father or a gift from al-Mamun and he may have
retired there from the House of Wisdom when his service
permitted him to do so.

Al-Madjusi: This means the magician or the son of the magician,
and occurs also only once in the same quotation.
Who would not think of the Magicians who visited Bethle-
hem when Christ was born? The Viennese astronomer
Ferrari d'Ochieppo has assembled all the scientific
evidence supporting the Biblical report. There was
an extremely rare conjunction (occurring once every
350 years) of Jupiter and Saturn in the Fishes,
culminating on November 12, in the year 7 B.C., which
the Babylonian magicians might have computed: archeologists have found cuneiforms of the astronomic tables
and even of the formulae which were used in Babylon at
that time. The magicians of the Biblical episode
no longer represented a powerful state, but they were
witness to the wisdom and science conserved in Babylon

which may have survived for several centuries more
in Persia and Khorezm; it is very likely that
al-Khorezmi inherited much of what still existed at
his time.

The universalist al-Khorezmi was opposed to one-sided views, and we
can imagine him as a kind of leader against the one-sided admiration
of Greek science that was as common in Baghdad as it was and still
is in our Western world. Al-Khorezmi was definitely not an enemy of
Greek mathematics and science - he used them in his works - but he
was probably the one who continuously propagated the importance of
including the knowledge of other nations, of confronting Greek science
with the science of the East. We can assume with little risk that he
read and even spoke many languages; apart from Arabic, in which of
course he wrote his works, he certainly spoke his Khorezmian language
and therefore also Persian; we have already mentioned his knowledge
of the Jewish culture, so he may have at least read Hebrew. Some
scholars are convinced that he spoke and read some Indian language,
probably Sanskrit. Syrian and Greek as well as Turkish are further
possibilities.

The Practitioner

Al-Khorezmi's universal knowledge and philosophy was complemented by
a natural practical orientation. He never lost himself in theory,
because he kept the practical needs in sight. All the works we have
were meant for general use. More than any other author of that time
he supported his algorithms by practical examples. And it is from
these examples, as we shall see later on, that he got the inspiration
to demonstrate his algorithms by drawings which illustrated the
relationship: he was obviously the inventor of analytical geometry
in a preliminary form.

The Man

When one carries out research on one person for a long time, this
person slowly becomes more than an entity in the mind of the observer.
One also gets a feeling for many details of the character of the
person in question. And so it is for me with al-Khorezmi. Not all
of this can be expressed in words.

Let me select one quotation only which may say more about the
mentality of al-Khorezmi. While the opening reference to Allah
and the caliph may be a formula, a convention and a necessary acknowledgement of the system of power in which he was forced to live, he
comes back to a personal statement at the end of his introduction to
his ALGEBRA which can only be seen as a personal declaration before
he ends with the words which again seem to signify a return to convention.

> DIXIT ALGORIZMI
> (at the end of the introduction to the Algebra)
> Relying on the goodness of my intention therein
> (namely in the book)
> and hoping that the learned will reward it,
> by obtaining for me, through their prayers,
> the excellence of divine mercy,
> in requital of which, may the choiciest blessings
> and the abundant bounty of God be theirs!
> My confidence rests in God,
> in this as in everything,
> and in Him I put my trust.
> He is the Lord of the Sublime Throne.
> May his blessing descend
> upon all his prophets, and heavenly messengers!

The first part of this paper has tried to establish a background for
the understanding of the personality, the time and the work of
al-Khorezmi. The second part discusses the extant treatises of
al-Khorezmi and their influence on the development of European
mathematics. In principle, the chapters have the following structure:

A The Manuscript
B The Content
C Special Stories
D The Influence

1. THE TABLES - Kitab az-zij al-sindhind

1.A. The Manuscripts

As we know not only from the Fihrist, two editions of the TABLES
established the reputation and fame of al-Khorezmi during his
lifetime. For this book as for most of the works of al-Khorezmi
it is practically impossible to establish the year in which it
was written.

It is not clear how much of the structure and of the personnel
of the House of Wisdom al-Mamun had established while he was
crown prince at his residence Merv (Mary) in Khurasan, and how
much he inherited from his father ar-Rashid in Baghdad. It is
possible that al-Khorezmi was in the services of al-Mamun already
in Merv; this is indicated in one of the quotations.

The TABLES were certainly started long before 819, and very
probably al-Khorezmi continued to improve them for quite some
time. As their name indicates, they are based on the Indian
tables and on Indian astronomy which had arrived with the Indian
number system in Baghdad fifty years earlier. Unfortunately, no
manuscript of the original TABLES is extant. What we have is a
Latin translation, presumably written by Adelard of Bath around
1126, of an Arabic text which is a revision of al-Khorezmi's
Tables by Maslama ibn Ahmad al-Majriti (fl. 1000). This revision
in essence follows the original, but transforms certain astronomical data from a reference to Baghdad into a reference to Madrid.
What other changes, omissions, additions and improvements
al-Majriti has made cannot be established in detail. Robert of
Chester rearranged these tables some time later, and Hermann of
Carinthia (Hermannus of Dalmatia) seems to have made another
translation, which explains the difference in the various existing
manuscripts.

But we have, on the other hand, a commentary on al-Khorezmi's
TABLES written by Ibn al-Muthanna in the 10th century, the
original of which is also lost, but of which we have a Latin
(three manuscripts in Oxford and Cambridge) and a Hebrew translation (two manuscripts in Parma and in Oxford).

Al-Khorezmi's Tables, version by al-Madjriti
Latin Translation, Madrid Manuscript

The TABLES, in al-Majriti's version, have been carefully edited, translated and commented by Bjørnbo, Suter and Neugebauer.

1.B. The Contents

I shall not deal with astronomy at the moment. The manuscripts have neither headlines nor any other visible chapter order so that we shall follow the order given by Goldstein in his edition of al-Muthanna's commentary.

1.   Chronology
2.   Planetary Theory
3.   Trigonometry
4.   Seasonal Hours and Gnomons
5.   Planetary Latitude
6.   Conjunction and Opposition
7.   First Visibility of the Lunar Crescent
8.   Diameters of the Sun, Moon and Shadow
9.   Lunar Eclipses
10.   Solar Eclipses
11.   Excess of Revolution

1.C.1.   The Julian Day and the Julian Year

It was normal to begin tables with a chronology. This was nece sary because the difference in time indications and calendars would otherwise have made the tables ambiguous. It was also normal to idealize the chronology; an old tradition of Indian astronomy chose a moment of creation in which all the planets were in one line, having the same latitude of $0°$. The next fixed point was the Flood. Mixing different years, however, did not bother the ancient scholars too much; there were various tradi- tions of counting in certain periods Egyptian years of 365 days and in other Julian years of 365.25 days (being 1461 days to 4 years). It was known for scholars to ignore the difference in computation.

Al-Khorezmi, in his chronology, writes a sentence which can be seen as the basis of an insight and of a chronological order which he did not, however, arrange in a system; this was only

JULIAN YEAR

CHRISTIAN YEAR	JULIAN YEAR	SUN CYCLE	MOON	INDICT
4713 BC	0001	01	01	01
4712 BC	0002	02	02	02
4711 BC	0003	03	03	03
2 BC	4712	08	19	02
1 BC	4713	09	01	03
1 AD	4714	10	02	04
2 AD	4715	11	03	05
1900 AD	6613	05	01	13
1979 AD	6692	28	04	02
3267 AD	7980	28	19	15

JULIAN DAY

MO	1 JAN 4713 BC	0000000	SCALIGER ERA
FR	18 FEB 3102 BC	0588466	FLOOD (IND KALYUGA)
MO	1 OCT 312 BC	1607739	SELEUCID ERA
DO	12 NOV 7 BC	1719182	VISIT MAGICIANS
SA	1 JAN 1 AD	1721424	CHRISTIAN ERA
FR	30 APR 30 AD	1732112	CRUCIFICATION
DO	15 JUL 622 AD	1948439	MOHAMMEDAN ERA
DI	16 JUN 632 AD	1952063	JEZDEGERD ERA
Do	4 OCT 1582 AD	2299160	END JULIAN CAL IN ROME
FR	15 OCT 1582 AD	2299161	BEGIN GREG CAL IN ROME
MI	17 NOV 1858 AD	2400001	MJD = 00000
MO	1 JAN 1979 AD	2443875	MJD = 43874
MO	18 SEP 1979 AD	2444135	MJD = 44134

accomplished in the renaissance, but it remained useful for chronology and astronomy, and was revived during the Geophysical Year 1954 for the purpose of space research.

> DIXIT ALGORIZMI
> (in his Tables):
> If now someone wishes to know how many Arabic years are
> evenly contained in how many Roman years, he may resolve
> both into days: then their correspondence will become evident.

The day is certainly the phenomenon that can actually be counted with no margin of arbitrariness. The day is the natural unit of time, seconds and calendar years are artificial. The second, for instance, does not exist as such; what can be done is to build a beat-generator, count its beats and compare them to the day in order to get a precise second. With the advent of quartz and molecular clocks, we now have beat-generators of such precision that the solar system appears irregular and we have changed the definition of a second onto a molecular basis - with the result that the owners of such clocks and watches proclaim leap seconds for the New Year's night just as the ancient Chaldeans proclaimed leap months.

Al-Khorezmi's principle of placing calendar calculations on a basis of days was formed into a system by the renaissance scholar Joseph Scaliger (1540 - 1609) who introduced a chronology with the epoch - epoch is the first day in the chronology - on 1 JAN 4713 B.C. He chose this year because, when the years are counted from this epoch, the remainders of the year number when divided by 28, 19 and 15 yield the value of the solar cycle, the moon cycle or the golden number and the indiction or Roman fiscal number. Mathematically speaking it is a residual class number system with a period of 28 x 19 x 15 = 7980 years, so covering history for all purposes. The year 1979 is the Julian Year 6692; the remainders are 28 (solar circle), 4 (golden number), and 2 (Roman fiscal number). Monday, 1 JAN 4713 B.C. is day number zero in Scaliger's system of Julian days (JD), with 0.25 at 6 a.m., and 0.75 at 6 p.m., and today, 18 SEP 1979, is Julian Day 2 444 135. This number easily yields the day of the week: if divided by seven, the remainder gives it. (Remainder 0 - day of the week - Monday; 1 - Tuesday, 2 - Wednesday, etc.) 2 444 135 : 7 = 349 162, remainder 1: 18 SEP 1979 was a Tuesday.

Once the Julian Day of an event is established, there is no more
doubt when the event happened. Transformation to and from different calendars can be performed by means of algorithms similar
to the one al-Khorezmi describes for the transformation between
Roman and Arab dates, only today they are written in a programming
language (see ACM Communications, August 1963). The first scientists to generally introduce Scaliger's Julian Day were the
astronomers who tabulated celestial events versus the Julian Day
and its decimal fractions. However, they did not like to change
the observation day at midnight, as Scaliger's system requires,
and so they shifted the origin for 0.5 - which of course helped
only in the case of Europe. In the Geophysical Year, mainly on
account of space research, the Julian Day was standardized as the
universal time scale, simplifying its use by suppressing the first
two places and moving the origin back to Greenwich midnight, but
in such a way that there is now a full day's difference and the
modified Julian Day (MJD) is 2 400 001 less than Scaliger's
Julian Day, , and so we have for today 2 444 135 - 2 400 001 =
44 134. This MJD you will find, for instance, used in the tables
giving the retrospective corrections for the high-precision time
broadcast stations.

1.C.2.   How to write a sine table without a minus sign, decimal
          fractions and Indian numbers

For all we know, al-Khorezmi produced the first sine table, but he
did not have all the tools which seem so ordinary to us: negative
numbers, decimal fractions and Indian numbers. So the three
questions that arise are: how do we write a sine table without

          (a) a minus sign?
          (b) decimal fractions?
          (c) Indian numbers?

(a) No minus sign and no negative number is the simplest problem
to solve. For this we must turn to astrology. There the full
circle of the sky is subdivided into 12 houses corresponding to
the 12 signs of the zodiac. Al-Khorezmi's tables have 3 sections
from 1 to 30 degrees; each section stands for 4 houses, and the
houses are numbered from 0 to 11. By means of a little sketch
al-Khorezmi resolved the problems of directions. The medieval
translators numbered from I to XII: the horror of the zero was

C 72ʳ, O 129ᵛ,
N 38ᵛ.

Tabula elgeib (O)
[Tabula sinus]

Semitae numerorum (CO) Lineae numeri (N)								Elgeib (CO) Sinus (N)		
Sig.	Gr.	Sig.	Gr.	Sig.	Gr.	Sig.	Gr.	Part.	Min.	Sec.
2	1	3	29	8	1	9	29 .	52	28	38
2	2	3	28	8	2	9	28	52	58ᵃ)	37ᵇ)
2	3	3	27	8	3	9	27	53	27	37
2	4	3	26	8	4	9	26	53	55	40
2	5	3	25	8	5	9	25	54	22	42
2	6	3	24	8	6	9	24	54	48	46
2	7	3	23	8	7	9	23	55	13	49
2	8	3	22	8	8	9	22	55	37c)	52
2	9	3	21	8	9	9	21	56	0	53
2	10	3	20	8	10	9	20	56	22	54
2	11	3	19	8	11	9	19	56	43	52
2	12	3	18	8	12	9	18	57	3	48
2	13	3	17	8	13	9	17	57	22	42
2	14	3	16	8	14	9	16	57	40	32
2	15	3	15	8	15	9	15	57	57	20
2	16	3	14	8	16	9	14	58	13	4
2	17	3	13	8	17	9	13	58	27	44
2	18	3	12	8	18	9	12	58	41	20
2	19	3	11	8	19	9	11	58	53	51
2	20	3	10	8	20	9	10	59	5	13
2	21	3	9	8	21	9	9	59	15	41
2	22	3	8	8	22	9	8	59	24	58
2	23	3	7	8	23	9	7	59	33	11
2	24	3	6	8	24	9	6	59	40	16
2	25	3	5	8	25	9	5	59	46	19 d)
2	26	3	4	8	26	9	4	59	51	14
2	27	3	3	8	27	9	3	59	55	4
2	28	3	2	8	28	9	2	59	57	49
2	29	3	1	8	29	9	1	59	59	27
3	0	3	0	9	0	9	0	60	0	0

Tabula umbrarum (CO)
Gedval adhel (C)

C 75ᵛ, O 133ʳ.

Numerus ipsius artifa[1]	Umbra		Numerus ipsius artifa[2]	Umbra		Numerus ipsius artifa[3]	Umbra	
	Digiti	Dak.		Digiti	Dak.		Digiti	Dak.
1	687	29ᵃ)	31	19	58	61	6	39
2	343ᵇ)	38	32	19	13	62	6	24
3	228c)	58d)	33	18	29o)	63	6	7
4	171e)	36	34	17	47	64	5	51
5	137f)	10g)	35	17	8p)	65	5	36h)
6	114	10	36	16	30	66	5	21
7	97	44	37	15	55	67	5	6u)
8	85	22	38	15	21	68	4	51
9	75	45	39	14	49q)	69	4	36
10	68	3h)	40	14	18	70	4	22
11	61	44	41	13	48	71	4	9
12	56	27	42	13	20r)	72	3	54
13	51	58	43	12	52	73	3	40
14	48	9	44	12	25	74	3	26
15	44	47	45	12	0	75	3	13
16	41	51	46	11	35	76	2	59
17	39	15	47	11	11	77	2	46
18	36	55	48	10	48	78	2	32
19	34	51l)	49	10	25	79	2	19
20	32	58k)	50	10	4	80	2	6
21	31	15	51	9	43	81	1	54
22	29	42l)	52	9	22	82	1	41
23	28	16	53	9	2	83	1	28
24	26	57m)	54	8	44	84	1	15
25	25	44	55	8	24	85	1	2
26	24	36	56	8	5	86	0	50
27	23	33	57	7	47	87	0	37
28	22	34	58	7	29	88	0	25
29	21	39n)	59	7	13s)	89	0	12v)
30	20	47	60	6	55	90	0	0

too strong. Al-Khorezmi did use in his table a sign for zero that denoted an empty entry in the table.

> DIXIT ALGORIZMI:
> When (in a subtraction) nothing is left over, then write a little circle so that the place does not remain empty.

The novelty of the zero was not the character, but its use for the place system, on which al-Khorezmi continues:

> DIXIT ALGORIZMI:
> The little circle has to occupy the position, because otherwise there would be fewer places, so that the second might be mistaken for the first.

(b) The second question can be easily answered because you use the method yourself, but only for two entities, for the angle and for the time, in other words for degrees and hours. It is the subdivision into minutes and seconds. Since al-Khorezmi's tables give the sine only for entire numbers of degrees, the minutes and seconds appear on the - for us - wrong side of the table, namely where we expect to find the decimal places.

This principle is very old, dates back at least to Chaldean mathematics and can be continued to terzes, quarts, quints etc.

As an example, π is here expressed in this system:

$$\pi = 3^o \ 8^m \ 29^s \ 44^t \ 0^{qua} \ 47^{qui} \ 25^{sex} \ 25^{sep}$$

Al-Khorezmi did not base the sign on a hypothenusis of 1. In al-Masudi's version the radius is 60; al-Khorezmi had used - as we know from old quotations - the ancient Indian value of 150. With this radius and minutes and seconds, the precision of the tables is theoretically one in a million, i.e. they correspond to a six-place table. As an example, let us look at the sine of 60, which is 60 . sine 60, expressed in the Latin copy as

LX	‖	LI	|	LVII	|	XLI	
60	‖	51	|	57	|	41	= 51+57/60+41/3600

Reduced to radius 1, this becomes 0.8660231, while the correct value is 0.8660254 - there are 5 correct places.

(c) The third question requires a most unexpected and the longest answer. It could be assumed that al-Khorezmi would have used Roman numbers which were old enough in his time and must have been known, since the Roman Empire had extended to the northern part of the Arabic peninsula. But al-Khorezmi and all the Arab mathematicians had a much better and a much older system: the Phoenician letter code. Let me give his own explanation:

DIXIT ALGORIZMI
(at the beginning of his ALGEBRA):
When I considered what people generally want in calculating,
I found that it always is a number.

I also observed that every number is composed of units, and
that any number may be divided into units.

Moreover, I found that every number, which may be expressed
from one to ten, surpasses the preceding one by one unit:
afterwards the ten is doubled or tripled, just as before the
units were: thus arises twenty, thirty, etc., until a
hundred; then the hundred is doubled and tripled in the
same manner as the units and the tens, up to a thousand;
then the thousand can thus be repeated at any complex number;
and so forth to the utmost limit of numeration.

That means that to the different letters are attached in alphabetic order the numeric values from 1 to 9, then from 10 to 90 and finally from 100 to 900; this requires 27 letters, and if there is a 28th, then the value 1000 can be attached. More common is some syntactic symbol for the thousands. There is, moreover, the same ancient sequence for the Phoenician, Hebrew, Greek, Syrian, Arabic and Georgian (Grusinian) alphabets. I could not, however, discover any Latin tradition, though I suspect that it did exist in the earliest period, and so I have added a Latin sequence, leaving the Roman sequence unchanged and only inserting the German so-called sharp 'ß' between 'n' and 'o'. In the Greek alphabet, there are the ancient letters digamma (f), quoppa (q), and sanpi,

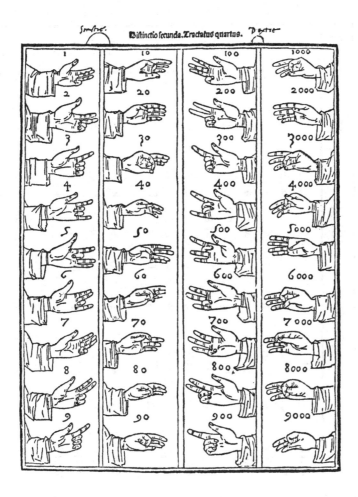

Finger Code and Arabic Letter Code

1	ا	10	ى	100	ق	1000	غ	10 000	يغ	100 000	قغ
2	ب	20	ك	200	ر	2000	بغ	20 000	كغ	200 000	رغ
3	ج	30	ل	300	ش	3000	جغ	30 000	لغ	300 000	شغ
4	د	40	م	400	ت	4000	دغ	40 000	مغ	400 000	تغ
5	ه	50	ن	500	ث	5000	هغ	50 000	نغ	500 000	ثغ
6	و	60	س	600	خ	6000	وغ	60 000	سغ	600 000	خغ
7	ز	70	ع	700	ذ	7000	زغ	70 000	عغ	700 000	ذغ
8	ح	80	ف	800	ض	8000	حغ	80 000	فغ	800 000	ضغ
9	ط	90	ص	900	ظ	9000	طغ	90 000	صغ	900 000	ظغ

ZAHL	HEBREW	SYRIAN	ARABIC	GEORGIAN	GREEK	LATIN	ZAHL
1	ALEPH	ALAPH	ALIF	AN	ALPHA	A	1
2	BETH	BETH	BA'	BAN	BETA	B	2
3	GIMEL	GAMAL	JIM	GAN	GAMMA	C	3
4	DALETH	DALATH	DAL	DON	DELTA	D	4
5	HE	HE	HA'	ENI	E PSILON	E	5
6	WAW	WAU	WAW	WIN	DI GAMMA	F	6
7	ZAIN	ZAIN	ZA	ZEN	ZETA	G	7
8	KHETH	KHETH	HA	KHE	ETA	H	8
9	THETH	THETH	TA	THAN	THETA	I	9
10	YODH	YODH	YA'	IN	IOTA	J	10
20	KAPH	KOPH	KAF	KAN	KAPPA	K	20
30	LAMEDH	LAMADH	LAM	LAS	LAMBDA	L	30
40	MEM	MIM	MIM	MAN	MY	M	40
50	NUN	NON	NUN	NAR	NY	N	50
60	SAMEKH	SEMKATH	SIN	JE	XI		60
70	AYIN	E	'AIN	ON	O MIKRON	O	70
80	PE	PE	FA'	PAR	PI	P	80

ZAHL	HEBREW	SYRIAN	ARABIC	GEORGIAN	GREEK	LATIN	ZAHL
90	SSADHE	SSADHE	SAD	SHAN	QOPPA	Q	90
100	QOPH	QOPH	QAF	RAE	RHO	R	100
200	RESH	RESH	RA'	SAN	SIGMA	S	200
300	SHIN	SHIN	SHIN	TAN	TAU	T	300
400	TAW	THAU	TA'	UN	Y PSILON	U	400
500	KAF		THA	PHAR	PHI	V	500
600	MEM		KHA	KHAN	KHI	W	600
700	NUN		DHAL	GHAN	PSI	X	700
800	FE		DAD	QAR	O MEGA	Y	800
900	SADE		ZA	SHIN	SANPI	Z	900
1000			GHAIN	CHIN			1000

which disappeared in early Greek times. The letter code, however, was used in the Greek culture until a few centuries ago, and can be seen on old Greek buildings, on churches for instance.

The same grouping from 1 to 9, 10 to 90, and 100 to 900 (and 1000) is used in the finger-number system.

In order to display the handiness of this system and its superiority to the Roman number system, there is a multiplication table below which not only shows a lot of regularities, but is also more efficient from an information-theoretical point of view, because the more frequent numbers require fewer letters. The table expresses by 489 letters what we would express by 654 numerics and the gain is even greater if probability is considered, because the more frequent round values are given by one or two letters.

ß ‖ na | ng | ma   instead of   LX ‖ LI | LVII | XLI

and ß would actually be b$|^{\circ}$ because the angle is given in houses and degress.

It must be remembered, however, that the Arabic alphabet is the least suited for the letter code, since it has relatively many letters which are distinguished only by small diacritical signs. A lost point is usually harmless in the redundant context of sentences, but in a redundancy-free functions table a missing point is catastrophic. The copiers of Arabic mathematical works made many mistakes - and the same things happened in al-Khorezmi's Geography, as will be seen.

1.D. Early European Tables

Already in al-Khorezmi's time his TABLES were by no means the only ones. Al-Mamun had ordered the composition of tables which were named after him. I have not yet been able to find out whether anything can be said about the relation between al-Mamun's and al-Khorezmi's tables. In the observatory in the House of Wisdom in Shammashiya, a tradition of protocolled observation was developed, a standardized procedure to increase the reliability of observation records, and this, of course, led to a continuous improve

in the Arabic tables. Most of this material is lost today, but
the improved tables found their way into Europe.

In the 11th century, Arab scholars composed the Toledan Tables,
using al-Khorezmi's and al-Battani's Tables - another proof, by
the way, of the continuous impact of al-Khorezmi - transforming
certain data from the Baghdad reference to the Toledo reference.
At this time a very sudden interest in astronomy and astrology
sprang up in Europe and gave rise to a need for tables. Thus
Christian tables were derived from the Arab Toledan Tables, and
many copies were made and transported all over Europe. Ernst
Zinner, a German authority on the Toledan Tables, has listed
52 manuscripts of them, and he says that this is an incomplete
list. Only very few of them, by the way, have been edited and
published in modern times.

At the end of the 13th century, astronomic knowledge had considerably increased and the Toledan Tables accordingly met with growing
criticism; therefore Alfons X. of Castile, another scientist on
the throne called "el Sabió" (the Wise, 1221 - 1284), financed
the production of new tables that were named after him. The
producing team, headed by Rabbi Issak ben Said, called Hassan,
finished the Tables in 1252; they were printed several times from
1483 on in Venice and there is another print of 1488 in Augsburg.

2.   THE ARITHMETIC - Kitab Hisab al-'Ada al-hindi
                  sive: Algorthmi de numero indorum

2.A. The Manuscript

If the TABLES established al-Khorezmi's fame and reputation during
his lifetime and in his Arabic environment, his ARITHMETIC has
connected him forever with the history of mathematics, made him
an often quoted authority in medieval mathematics and stored his
name in the term 'algorithm'. His person, however, disappeared
behind the science and the term, and very soon nobody knew any
longer that Algorismus had been a person. And up to our time it
is safe to state that the majority of people using the term
'algorithm' know nothing about its relation to a person and a
still existing country.

In a note to the French Academy of Sciences of 1858, Michel Chasles
adds the following comment to the manuscript of the ARITHMETIC
just discovered by the Italian historian of mathematics Prince
Baldassare Boncampagni and published under the title: "Algoritmi
de numero indorum": *"This work seems to offer a real interest. It throws
a live light on the still uncertain origin of the word 'algorismus'. It is
known that this word has become, during the 13th century, the name of our
arithmetic; it is conveyed also in the algebra with another meaning."* In the
explanation which he offers to the Academy Michel Chasles says:
*"This text seems to be a translation of an Arabic work, being the first one
which can be seen with some certainty as a translation from the Arabic original.
The work is attributed to Algoritmi, obviously the name of an Arab author,
and one thinks immediately of the famous geometrician Abu Djafar Mukhammad
ibn Musa."* The confirmation is given by a self-quotation of
al-Khorezmi (who indeed quotes his ALGEBRA in the ARITHMETIC),
and by a passage in the "Library of Philosophers" reported by
Casiri, which says that *"al-Khorezmi had made known to the Arabs a treatise
of arithmetic in the Indian system surpassing all others by its compactness
and easiness."*

The origin of the place number system is certainly India, but
very little is known about its early history. This is not the
place to go into history of early Indian mathematics (and I have
had no time to do more than read a few books).

We know from several - different and slightly contradictory -
reports that in the time of al-Mansur, in about 772, an Indian
mathematician and astronomer came to Baghdad, who was experienced
in the calculus called Sindhind and in the movement of the stars
as well as in the computation of eclipses. He had tables with
steps of half a degree of angle and one minute of time.
All of this was contained in a book to be translated into Arabic.
This task was entrusted to al-Fazari. His translation was in use
until al-Khorezmi rewrote the TABLES. It can be assumed that
his ARITHMETIC is based on the same source.

The knowledge of the Indian number system was thus about 50 years
old at al-Khorezmi's time. Why, then, was it al-Khorezmi who
wrote the treatise that should introduce this system first into
the caliph's empire and then into European mathematics? Very
obviously, he succeeded in explaining the new idea in a form

readable and acceptable for both very learned and less learned
people of his or later times, and in a form demonstrating the value
of such a basic change in the writing of numbers.

A revolution in science is a rare event. The work of any scientist
is based on the bulk of previous work, on the achievements of many
generations. Science and technology, often qualified as revolutionary powers, indeed can become revolutionary by their consequences, but their philosophy of progress is terribly disciplined.
First of all, whoever dares to propose or to experiment a change
in the views or methods of the past, requires the solid ground of
the secured tradition in order to begin. Secondly, unless he is
able to present all the necessary proofs, he will be attacked,
ridiculed or ignored. No scientist and no engineer likes people
who threaten to turn inherited methods upside down. Counter-
revolution defines its position as long as possible and
it is easy to recognize that stability is indeed the first requirement for realiable work. Therefore, every scientist who makes
an important step forward must come to grips with the counter-
active effects. Even worse: real scientists of good character
regard their own achievements very critically and try to prove
their new findings as conveniently and even as falsely as possible.
Max Planck is known to be a good example for this kind of behaviour,
while Galilei failed terribly in this respect.

Al-Khorezmi had no such problems as far as we know. He must have
proceeded very carefully. His innovation was opposed to a
historically established way of writing numbers, and it has been
shown in Chapter 1 that the letter coding system for numbers was
not all that bad - in particular for tables; in any case it was
much better than the Roman number code system into which the
medieval scholars translated the early Arabic mathematics and
tables. Was it al-Mamun who recognized the value of the Indian
system for the spreading of arithmetical skills in his empire, or
did al-Khorezmi convince the caliph? In any case, al-Khorezmi
must have been given strong protection and support, otherwise his
treatise could not have spread through all the Arabic countries.

Unfortunately, the Arabic original of the ARITHMETIC has not
survived; even the title has been reconstructed and is not
authentic. We have only one manuscript of a Latin translation,

probably written in the 13th century in the Abbey Bury St. Edmunds near Bedford, from where it was brought into the Cambridge University Library. This manuscript has been carefully edited (but not translated) by the German orientalist and historian of mathematics Kurt Vogel.

The Latin translations usually omit the introduction, because the Arabic treatises begin with a reference to Allah and his Prophet. The translators - Christian monks - could not include this reference but did not want to alter the text. So they left the introduction untranslated and we do not know whether the introduction to the ARITHMETIC is similar to the introduction to the ALGEBRA, in which the caliph is thanked for his encouragement, or whether a different motivation was mentioned.

I must skip here the story of the acceptance of the Arabic numbers and the history of their shapes; it would be a long, complicated and confusing report.

2.B. The Contents

1. Introduction of Indian figures and position values
2. Addition and subtraction
3. Halving and doubling
4. Multiplication
5. Division
6. Fractions and the hexagesimal system
7. Multiplication of fractions
8. Division of fractions
9. Arrangement of fractions
10. Multiplication of fractions
11. Division of fractions
12. Radix

2.D. Influence

It is the general impression, not only in Central Europe, that the renaissance knowledge of Greek philosophy, mathematics and science was brought into Europe by the crusaders, by diplomatic and scientific relationships to the Byzantine Empire and finally by the refugees from the conquered Byzantium (1453). All the

evidence from what have studied indicates that these sources are,
if at all, of only minor importance. The knowledge of Greek
authors came from the Arabs via Spain. When the Spaniards started
to push the Moors back and conquered city after city in Spain, a
large population of Arab scientists obviously remained, and in
the periods of peace in between there was an intensive exchange
of information between Arab scientists and Christian scientists
who had learned the Arabic language. The main place was Toledo
and the majority of the translators were English monks.

Three Ways

So the main way in which the Indian number system spread through
Europe began in Spain and England and continued from monastery to
monastery. Kurt Vogel gives his opinion on the flow of events
and the relationships between early European manuscripts of the
ARITHMETIC in the form of a flow-diagram in which al-Khorezmi
manuscripts follow the center line while the two flanks are
constituted by two groups of treatises: the Liber Ysagorum
Alchorizmi, The Book of Introduction into the Algorismus, to
the left, and the Liber Alghoarismi by Johannes Hispalensis to
the right.

The second way in which the Indian numbers were propagated in
Europe was opened by Fibonacci or Leonardo of Pisa by his Liber
Abbaci of 1204.   Leonardo of Pisa was the son of a merchant who
had a number of agencies in the Arab countries around the Medi-
terranean. Being interested in mathematics, Leonardo succeeded
in collecting a lot of Arabic mathematical knowledge and, as one
can see from the resulting scientific compendium, the Liber Abbaci,
he found the traces of al-Khorezmi's treatise; such traces are
also found in the treatises of other mathematicians down to the
times of Adam Ries.

There may be a third way which, in my opinion, has not yet been
sufficiently investigated. During the 12th century the German
Hohenstaufen ruled Germany and Italy, and had their court in
Sicily where they kept a large staff of court employees, including
scientists. Some of them were highly interested in mathematics
and science and well able to conduct discussions with visiting
Arab guest scientists. It would be amazing if this interaction

did not result in a lot of oral and written information flowing into Germany. The recent Stauffer exhibition in Stuttgart was, however, extremely poor in its mathematical and scientific content. My research has not yielded any indication of such traces, but, as I have already pointed out, I have only had the chance to look at secondary material: what we need is further primary research. It seems to be generally true for historians and even more so for orientalists that many documents presently stored remain untouched since there is no one to take an interest in them. It is very possible that new discoveries and better views of the early history of European mathematics lie before us. A key device to help is the fast copier which is only slowly becoming an inexpensive tool and is equally often used in the humanities as it is in technology.

Formal Notation

It would be very inviting to describe here the development of mathematics in Europe during the 13th to 16th centuries and show the influence of al-Khorezmi's work on this development. I can make only a few remarks. For a long time, teaching of mathematics at European universities consisted only of the Computus, the calculation of the calendar including the correct date of Easter. The first full-time professors of mathematics appear late in the university annals.

Another amazingly late development in mathematics is formal notation.

The German historian of mathematics Nesselmann distinguished three historical stages in the development of mathematical notation. The first stage may be called rhetorical algebra or reckoning by complete words. The second stage is syncopated or contracted algebra, still essentially rhetoric, but making use of certain symbolic abbreviations for a few recurring operations and quantities. The third stage is the symbolic algebra as we know it; the Hindus made some use of it, but the actual introduction into mathematics does not happen before the middle of the 17th century. Thus symbolic algebra is not much older than 300 years.

While Diophantus - whose work al-Khorezmi obviously did not know (there is not a single example out of his works and Diophantus was translated into Arabic only some 100 years later) - belongs to the syncopated stage, al-Khorezmi belongs to the rhetoric stage. This was not a step backwards. Al-Khorezmi is a representative of the rhetorical stage of the ancient Egyptian and Babylonian system of algebra (here I quote Soloman Gandz), a great scholar of the old type, like the ancient Egyptian priests or Chaldean scribes.

3. The ALGEBRA

3.a. The Manuscripts

Al-Khorezmi's ALGEBRA is the earliest Arabic book on mathematics so far preserved and accessible. In the middle of the 12th century its first two chapters were twice translated into Latin, by Gerhard of Cremona and by Robert of Chester. With regard to this second translation, the American historian of mathematics, George Sarton, stated: *"The importance of this particular translation can hardly be exaggerated. It may be said to mark the beginning of the European algebra."* Solomon Gandz calls al-Khorezmi's ALGEBRA *"the foundation and cornerstone of this science"*.

At the end of the 18th century, mathematicians began to study the history of their subject. In 1797, Pietro Cassali wrote a paper with the title "Origin, Transportation to Italy and First Progress There of the Algebra". He praises al-Khorezmi, but he knew of very few manuscripts of his work, if any. The ARITHMETIC was discovered by the Italian historian of mathematics Baldassare Boncampagni in 1857, the ALGEBRA was in the Bodleian Library much earlier and was translated into English by the German Frederick Rosen, who lived in England, in 1831. This is the first and so far the only translation of the whole book.

The Latin translations exist in many manuscripts in the main libraries of Europe: Paris, Oxford, Cambridge, Dresden, the Vatican, Vienna, Tübingen and others. None of them includes Chapter 4, most give only Chapter 1.

As I have said, it would be desirable that an improved translation

Al-Khorezmi's Algebra - Page with Pythagoras of Oxford Latin
Manuscript (Negative)

based on a synopsis of all existing manuscripts would be made.

There has been an extensive discussion about the origins of al-Khorezmi's ALGEBRA, whether the contents come from Greek, Hindu, Hebrew or Babylonian sources. All one-sided views do not stand closer critical investigation. Al-Khorezmi was a universalist in many respects and amalgamated whatever he found for his purpose, because he was, moreover, extremely pragmatic.

3.B. The Contents

The contents of the ALGEBRA will be described in the same structure as al-Khorezmi's book which is composed of four relatively independent chapters - so independent that we might consider them four different books if we did not have al-Khorezmi's introduction which proves that he saw the whole work as an entity.

The four chapters are:

(1) The Solution of Equations
(2) Business Calculation
(3) Geometry
(4) Algebra of Legacies

Chapter I: The Solution of Equations

DIXIT ALGORIZMI:
I found that the numbers required for the calculation by completion and reduction are of three kinds: roots, powers and simple numbers.

The root is an amount which is to be multiplied by itself.
The power is the amount of the root multiplied by itself.
The simple number is any number which may be pronounced without reference to root or power.

DIXIT ALGORIZMI:
Sex autem sunt modi di quibus quantum ad numerum sufficienter diximus.

We have observed that every question which requires
equation or reduction for its solution will refer you
to one of the six cases which I have proposed in this
book.

These quotations set the stage for Chapter I. Al Khorezmi's
ALGEBRA is restricted to equations with one unknown of first
or second degree.

In his ALGEBRA, following an ancient tradition, the unknown,
the square of the unknown, and the constant have names.

(1) The root (al-jadhr), sometimes called the "Thing" (shay)
     is the appearance of the unknown. The Latin translation
     used radix, res or cause.
(2) The power (al-mal), which also means capital, possession or
     wealth, is the other appearance, so sometimes the word 'mal'
     is also used in the sense 'the unknown'. The Latin trans-
     lations used the word 'census'.
(3) The simple number, in Latin 'numerus', is usually made a
     named value by giving it in dragmas (dirham).

What we in our symbolic algebra write as

$$x^2 + 10\,x = 39$$

al-Khorezmi expresses by the sentence:

"A power and ten roots of the same amount to thirty-nine dragmas".

The step forward al-Khorezmi made - and there are indications
that this is his personal contribution to mathematics, was to
replace the old Babylonian set of little tricks by a standard
system. Whatever the original statement of the problem is, he
says, it can be transformed into one of six cases. Six forms are
sufficient, he says.

These six forms are a logical consequence of the fact that
al-Khorezmi does not consider negative values as entities; values
may be subtracted, but a negative quantity is not real. With

this restriction, the six cases are the 'realistic' subset of
the twelve possibilities we would see today:

$$a.x^2 + b.x + c = 0$$

a	b	c	equation	comment	venerable example
+	+	+	$a.x^2+b.x+c = 0$	impossible	
+	+	0	$a.x^2+b.x\ \ = 0$	impossible	
+	+	-	$a.x^2+b.x-c = 0$	(4)	$x^2 + 10x = 39$
+	0	+	$a.x^2\ \ \ +c = 0$	impossible	
+	0	0	$a.x^2\ \ \ \ = 0$	impossible	
+	0	-	$a.x^2\ \ \ -c = 0$	(2)	$5x^2 = 80$
+	-	+	$a.x^2-b.x+c = 0$	(5)	$x^2 + 21x = 10$
+	-	0	$a.x^2-b.x\ \ = 0$	(1)	$x^2 = 5x$
+	-	-	$a.x^2-b.x-c = 0$	(6)	$x^2 = 3x + 4$
0	+	+	$b.x+c = 0$	impossible	
0	+	0	$b.x\ \ = 0$	impossible	
0	+	-	$b.x-c = 0$	(3)	$4x = 20$

For the forms (1) to (3) al-Khorezmi gives simple examples showing
the algorithm. For the forms (4) to (6) he gives again examples
and the algorithm and then returns to the latter three forms and
shows a drawing which illustrates and proves the computation.

The already mentioned equation $x^2 + 10x = 39$, a venerable equation,
because thousands of Arab and European students have had to learn
it and the way to its solution since the time of al-Khorezmi
throughout the centuries belongs to category (4). Al-Khorezmi's
method is the following: we know that x^2 is a square of unknown
size. Let us draw it. This square should be increased by ten
roots; so let us put up five roots each on two adjacent edges of
the square. Then we see that if we complete the area, of which
we know that it is 39, by a square of the edge 5, i.e. by 25, we
have a bigger square the area of which is 39 + 25 or 64. Of this
square we know that the edge is 8, and since 5 is coming from
the completion, the missing difference of 3 is the value of the
unknown. We have carried out an algorithm which we can handle
mechanically once we master it well enough, but at any time we
can go back to the drawing and understand why the algorithmic
process is as described. Al-Khorezmi's algorithm is as elegant

as it is transparent.

One might object that al-Khorezmi misses the second root, -13.
But this negative value does not exist for him. 13 is the solution
of a different equation, namely

$$x^2 = 10x + 39$$

belonging to group (6).

At this point I want to insert a remark on the meaning of the
word 'algebra'. The title of al-Khorezmi's book "al-ǧabr
wa'l-muqābalah" has been translated in many ways, e.g. as
"completion and reduction" or "restauration and comparison",
distinguishing two kinds of operations, the removal of negative
quantities from the equation and the removal of positive quantities on both sides of the equation.

Since al-Khorezmi does not expressly explain these two kinds of
operations, he was reproached for having used a title without
telling the reader what the title meant.

I am inclined to follow Solomon Gandz in his view that the word
'al-ǧabr' is an Arabic version of the ancient Babylonian word
'gabru', which means the art of solving equations, and that
'al-muqābalah' is the Arabic transcription of the same word.
Both words together designated for the Arabs the art of solving
equations so that al-Khorezmi's title was absolutely clear for
any of his contemporary readers.

Chapter II: On Business Calculations

DIXIT ALGORIZMI:
Know that all business affairs of people - all that concerns buying and
selling, barter and renting - are covered by two variants of questions
asked by the questioner and by four numbers pronounced by the questioner,
namely al-musa''ar, the quantity of the statement, at-taman, the quan-
tity of the question, as-si'r, the price of the statement, and al-mu-
tamman, the price of the question. The quantity of the statement
is opposite to the price of the question and the price

of the statement is opposite to the quantity of the question. Of these four numbers three are always known and one is unknown. And the rule here is: you look on the three known numbers and there is no other way out than that you multiply the two known opposite numbers, each of it with its companion, and what results, divide it by the last known number the companion of which is unknown. And what you get is the unknown number for which the questioner has asked, and it is the opposite to the number by which you have divided.

Al-Khorezmi immediately attaches a set of examples. Let me quote the first.

DIXIT ALGORIZMI:

Decam cafficii sunt pro sex dragmis.
Quot ergo pervenit tibi pro quatuor dragmis?

Ten caffices (a unit of capacity) cost six dragmas.
How much do you get for four dragmas?

Al-Khorezmi's wisdom can be seen from the following example: A man is hired to work for 30 days in a vineyard for 10 dragmas. He works for 6 days. How much of the amount agreed upon should he receive? This example is so simple that one can see the answer immediately. But it opens the way to what even today is still a problem for the student: the transition from a situation in real life, expressed in ordinary language, to the mathematical formulation.

DIXIT ALGORIZMI:
With these two variants, one can solve all problems - without error, if God will.

And this seems to be all that must be said in this chapter.

Chapter III: Geometry

Contents: area, triangles, rhombus, circle, segment, prism, pyramid and cone, theorem of Pythagoras, rectangle, more about the triangle, circle and cone, truncated pyramid, and how to inscribe a square into an equilateral triangle.

DIXIT ALGORIZMI:

Know that in each rectangular triangle, if each of the two shorter edges is multiplied by itself and if the two products are added, this sum is equal to the product of the longest side with itself.

Al-Khorezmi does not have a general proof, he gives only a drawing for the symmetrical rectangular triangle where the proof is easy to see.

Al-Khorezmi gives three different values for π, each in the form of an algorithm how to compute the circumference from the diameter, and the values are

$$22/7, \quad \sqrt{10} \quad \text{and} \quad 62843/20000$$

These are Indian values, and al-Khorezmi makes the reader understand that all three are approximations.

Two generations after him, Thabit ibn Qurra, a student of the three sons of Musa whom we have mentioned earlier, found a proof which al-Khorezmi certainly would have liked to include in his book, although the practical treatise had no intention to load the algorithm with proofs. I like this proof not only because of its simplicity, but also because I discovered it myself when I was an undergraduate in the German military service, a teacher of military electronics in Salonica. Was it the daily sight of Mount Olympus that gave birth to this idea? I sent my proof to my teacher of mathematics at the University of Vienna, who commented laconically: "Very good, young man, but this proof has been known since the 10th century!" The question I could never ask my teacher, who was killed at his desk by a shell in the last days of the battle of Vienna, is: Why do students not learn this proof?

I showed this proof also to Edsger Dijkstra, and he gave me another one. If the Thabit ibn Quarra proof is one for the child, then this one is for the learned. It consists only of the triangle with the height drawn in. There are three similar triangles. In similar figures, corresponding straight lines have equal ratios; and areas are related like the squares of the corresponding lines. Therefore, since the sum of the two smaller triangles is equal to the big triangle, the same must be true for the squares over their hypothenuses.

3.G. Khorezmi's Geometry: A Hebrew Mishna of 150 A.D.?

Ancient Jewish scholars like Rashi, Yalqut, Ibn Ezra and others quote a book called Mishnat of the 49 Middot. The quotations relate to geometric theorems and to the measures of the Temple. In 1862, the German orientalist Moritz Steinschneider discovered the manuscript of a very old Hebrew geometry in Munich, written in 1480 in Byzantium, with the title Mishna ha-Middot. This manuscript confirmed only those quotations related to geometry, not those related to the measures of the Temple.

Twenty years later, the German mathematician Schapira published an improved translation, and he was the first to point out the astonishing correspondence between this manuscript and al-Khorezmi's Geometry. A scientific discussion was started which will probably never find a solution: have Jewish scholars copied al-Khorezmi's chapter or has al-Khorezmi copied a Jewish mishna? Solomon Gandz worked on this problem between 1925 and 1932, and he concluded that it was a mishna of about 150 A.D. He had a second manuscript, a fragment, which included paragraphs on the Temple measures and confirmed the name Mishnat of 49 Middot.

The correspondence is really startling. The differences are not much more than a different arrangement of the chapters. I have had a discussion with one of the most prominent scholars for ancient Jewish literature, Professor Scholem, who supports the conclusions of Gandz because of the very old and typical language.

It is difficult to carry out proofs on the copies of copies of
copies. Many arguments speak for, many against the Jewish priority.
I think that al-Khorezmi would merely smile. He had enough opportunity to get old manuscripts, and there were many Jewish scholars
at al-Mamun's court and at the Academy. If this text suited his
purpose, why should he not use it? And if the Hebrew scholars
used his text to produce a Jewish introduction to geometry by
rearranging his treatise - what is wrong about it? Al-Khorezmi
would smile and leave us to our doubts. A secret of this kind
is of no harm.

Chapter IV: The Algebra of Legacies

Contents: Many examples of inheritance cases where the simple
partition of the inheritance is complicated by the existence of a
legacy.

Al-Khorezmi applied a system throughout this chapter, as Gandz
has pointed out, which has four sections:

(1) Facts and data on the legal heirs and the stipulated legacies
listed.
(2) The computation method begins with finding a common denominator for the shares, some entire number.
(3) Then the computation is developed further by including the
stipulation of the legacies, which leads either to a higher
common denominator or to the introduction of an unknown
which must be resolved.
(4) The solution then consists of two parts. The first is the
determination of the amounts for legacies, and, secondly,
the remainder must be divided among the heirs in conformance
with the Muslim rules of inheritance.

Al-Khorezmi in all cases omits the trivial computation steps - the
chpater is a treatise for advanced students, and this is very
appropriate: al-Khorezmi could assume that his readers were people
who had learned the basic rules of the partition of inheritances
in the Koran schools.

This very simple situation had very negative consequences for
al-Khorezmi. One thousand years after his death he was accused
of having been a mediocre mathematician.

Defamation and Rehabilitation of al-Khorezmi

Any important and famous man runs the danger of being attacked or
defamated. Al-Khorezmi seems to have been, during his lifetime,
in the center of those fights and arguments which are natural for
a group of learned people. But he was also attacked after his
death, because we know of books which defend and rehabilitate him.

But that a scientist is defamated one thousand years after his
death is a rare case and seems typical for the unique position of
al-Khorezmi. The reason for this is, amazingly enough, the fact
that his ALGEBRA was translated fairly early, namely already in
1831. His translator, Frederick Rosen, a German living in
England, praises al-Khorezmi for his style and his didactic qua-
lities, although he notes that al-Khorezmi cannot be considered
the inventor of the ALGEBRA he wrote. It is in the introductory
note to the fourth chapter that he makes the defamating remark:
The solutions which the author has given of the remaining problems of this
treatise are, mathematically considered, for the most part i n c o r r e c t.
It is not that the problems, when once reduced into equations, are incorrectly
worked out; but in reducing them to equations, arbitrary assumptions are made
which are foreign and contradictory to the data first announced, for the
purpose, it should seem, of forcing solutions to accord with established rules
of inheritance, as expounded by Arab lawyers. The object of the lawyers in
their interpretations, and of the author in his solutions, seems to have been
to favour the heir or next of kin.

Now such a remark, says Solomon Gandz, is certainly apt to considerably impair the reputation of al-Khorezmi as a mathematician
and a scientist. How can al-Khorezmi be one of the greatest
scientists of his race, the greatest mathematician of his time
and one of the greatest of all times, if the above accusations
are true? And Rosen's remark was well understood in its negative
sense: one finds degrading comments on al-Khorezmi in the literature based on Rosen's remark, but not only on Rosen's remark,
because the defamation was continued. Moritz Cantor and Herman
Hankel in their books on the history of mathematics soften the

reproaches by speaking of contradictory requirements which
al-Khorezmi had brought under one umbrella by contradictory tricks.
But the German scientists Ruska and Wieleitner - the first is an
Arabist, the latter a mathematician - confirm the attack and say
that *the arbitrary assumptions are bigger in the previous chapters, because
also many of the earlier examples would both have been resolvable without
such assumptions which do not occur in the text.*

So al-Khorezmi was fully under the suspicion of having manipulated
the problems where he was unable to give a correct solution. The
rehabilitation was undertaken by Solomon Gandz and published in
1936. *Some philosophers,* he begins, *maintain that the arbitrariness does
not exist, its source being our own ignorance. If we are not aware of the
deeper causes of our actions, we believe to act arbitrarily. In our case, the
alleged arbitrariness of al-Khorezmi is due entirely to the ignorance of his
critics.*

The starting point of the defamation was that Rosen and the other
critics did not know the simple rules of inheritance partition which
al-Khorezmi presupposed and was justified in presupposing.

*Since the legal conditions, on which the problems rely, appear only from the
solution,* says critic Wieleitner, *the problems are often perplexing (ver-
blüffen die Auggaben häufig).* But, says Gandz, *al-Khorezmi would be "ver-
blüfft", perplexed and startled, to learn that people take up the algebra of
inheritance before studying the law of inheritance, and that they merely try to
guess and infer the provisions of the law from his solutions.*

And then Gandz gives proof after proof that all examples of
al-Khorezmi are not only correctly worked out once they are in the
form of an equation, but that they are equally correct in the
transformation from the verbal statement of the problem to the
draft of the equations.

Of course, the language difficulties in all such translation work
are enormous. Rosen, for instance, was not a mathematician at all,
he had only a mathematician friend to advise him (the one who had
talked him into undertaking the translation), and Rosen certainly
did not know anything about the Arabic Koran laws. I suspect that
his knowledge of Arabic was not necessarily that of the classic
Arabic required for al-Khorezmi's book.

In summary, it can be said that al-Khorezmi's "Algebra of Legacies" is as clear and correct as all the other treatises he wrote. The defamation was actually a consequence of the missing knowledge on the part of the translators. The hard words of Karl Kraus *"Übersetzung ist Unfug"* (translation is misdemeanor) have been confirmed once more.

Let me make a final remark on the "Algebra of Legacies". I had expected when I first heard of this chapter that the legal complications of the Muslim law of inheritance stem from the institution of polygamy. Just imagine four wives of different legal status and consequently four kinds of children - that would be a difficult mathematical problem. But in all the eighty examples of al-Khorezmi there is not a trace of it. There is always only one wife or widow.

The chapter on legacies has had, of course, almost no influence on European medieval mathematics. It was not translated into Latin, and was only rediscovered in the 19th century. But the first three chapters mark the beginning of European mathematics. Directly or indirectly, al-Khorezmi has formed European mathematics by his popular and pragmatic, abdridged treatise more than the bulk of much more scientific books by al-Khorezmi's colleagues.

Of the ARITHMETIC and the ALGEBRA as well as of the trigonometric section of the TABLES there exists a Russian translation.

4.   THE JEWISH CALENDAR - Fi istakhraj ta'rikh al yahud
4.A.   The Manuscript

> *DIXIT ALGORIZMI:*
> *Since knowledge concerning it is possessed by only a few of the*
> *Jews, I have written for anyone who has occasion to use it.*

This manuscript was found in the Library of Bankipore near Patra in India and was published by the Oriental Publications Bureau in Hyderabad in 1948. F.S. Kennedy has summarized and commented this treatise. He feels that the internal evidence in the text supports the attribution to al-Khorezmi and he concludes by saying that by the early 9th century a body of doctrine concerning the cyclic religious calendar was widely accepted by the Jewish

community, of which we have so far recovered only part. Of the
three sources, Maimonides, al-Birmi and al-Khorezmi, the latter is
the oldest one. A date used in the treatise falls in 823/824;
it is reasonable to regard it as that of the composition of the
treatise.

4.B. The Contents

The treatise consists of the following sections: after an introduction noting the scriptural injunctions upon which the calendar
is based, there is a list of the names of the months and the
number of their days. The synodic month is given as 29 days,
12 hours and 793 helek; this is a well-known Babylonian parameter
and the helek is the Hebrew time unit of 1/1080 of an hour. The
decimal equivalent is 29.53059 and this value is precisely the
one we are using today, while the length of the year given a
little later with 365.24682 is 0.00462 or a thousandth of a percent
too long. Then the rules are given to compute the day of the
New Year, first Tishri, and the length of the varying months. A
chronological statement on the time between the creation of Adam
and the year 1135 of the Alexandrian era is 4582, which fixes
the time scale for the following sets of planetary positions. Then
there is a rule for the computation of the mean longitudes of the
sun and the moon at any given time and the last section is a rule
for the computation of the time since the last new moon. All
those algorithms explain how the calendar of any year is established. All algorithms ensure that only operations with integers
are required.

5.   THE CHRONICLE - Kitab at-tarikh

The CHRONICLE of al-Khorezmi has not survived. There is only the
Chronicle of the Archbishop (metropolite) of Nisibis, Elias Bar
Shinaya, which was written in 1019 A.D. and of which we have only
the manuscript in the British Museum. Nisibis is today Nusaybin,
a station on the railway Istanbul - Baghdad at the Turkish-Syrian
border, on the Turkish side. At the time of Elias, it was an
important Christian center. The CHRONICLE is a fragment with
many missing and damaged sheets, and from it we can get an idea
of what al-Khorezmi's CHRONICLE may have looked like, because
Elias very scrupulously annotated from which sources he had

compiled his text.

It seems that al-Khorezmi's CHRONICLE began with the death of
Mohammed - this is where the entries taken from his work start -
but since the pages on the most interesting and decisive years from
786 to 877 are missing in this unique manuscript, we do not know
when al-Khorezmi's CHRONICLE began and how he had recorded his own
time.

To give an example of the quotations, I selected an entry of 74 A.H.

> *DIXIT ALGORIZMI*
> *(in his Chronicle):*
> *The year 74 began on Tuesday, 13 Ijar 1004. In it was an eclipse*
> *of the sun, so that the stars became visible on 29 Djamadi or*
> *5 Tishri I.*

The 13 Ijar 1004 of the Seleucid era is May 13, 693 A.D.   The
eclipse can be found in the Tables of R. Schram.   29 Djamadi I in
the Arab calendar is 5 Tishri I in the Syrian calendar and corresponds to October 5, 693, JD 1974454.   In Baghdad, the middle of
the eclipse was at 11 a.m. local time.

6.   THE GEOGRAPHY
6.A. The Manuscript

When Wilhelm Spitta, called Spitta-Bey, a German orientalist, pur-
chased a manuscript in Cairo in October 1878 which he then studied
more closely and thought it to be an Arabic transcription of an
excerpt of Ptolemy's Geography. It consisted of 45 sheets, some
of them in very bad shape, broken and repaired; in the whole
manuscript many punctuation marks had been left out by the copiers.
For the names this is very annoying, but for the coordinates, which
were of course in the Phoenician letter code, it is catastrophic.
The Viennese orientalist Hans von Mžik edited and published the
manuscript of the GEOGRAPHY in 1928.   He made an enormous effort
to restore the correct punctuation, considering many aspects of the
problem and comparing the data with the other (later) sources.

The manuscript remained what it was for Spitta-Bey, a unique
treasure, but further investigation showed that this GEOGRAPHY was

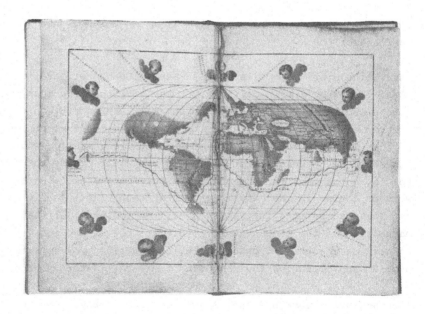

Old World Maps
Lake Aral is missing

a work of its own, related to Ptolemy's data, but recording a very
different kind of map.

6.B. The Contents

There is no introduction, and after the formula "In the name of
God the Gracious and Merciful" there are the tables giving the
geographical positions - longitude and latitude - of 537 cities,
209 mountains (beginning and end points of the mountain ranges as
well as the colour - not their natural colour but obviously the
colour on al-Mamun's map), the contour points and shape indications
of 5 oceans, many lakes and islands and finally a list of rivers.

Each chapter is arranged according to the ancient (Greek) notion
of the seven climata, i.e. strips parallel to the equator with
the limits

$$
\begin{array}{ll}
(1) & 16^{\circ}\ 27' \\
(2) & 24^{\circ} \\
(3) & 30^{\circ}\ 22' \\
(4) & 36^{\circ} \\
(5) & 41^{\circ} \\
(6) & 45^{\circ} \\
(7) & 48^{\circ}
\end{array}
$$

Originally, the distinction was based on the length of the day in
the region, but al-Khorezmi has a classification or rather a set
of borderlines of his own.

It is a pity that the map was nowhere produced after the record.
It would be an outstanding object for any museum. From ancient
Arabic maps we can get an idea what al-Mamun's show-piece might
have looked like. Arab maps were highly abstract, closer to
topology than to photography. And we can imagine how proudly
al-Mamun showed the world and his empire to the visitors of the
palace.

6.C. The Image of the World

Knowledge of the image of the world grew very slowly. Three
pictures demonstrate the increase in detail from 517 B.C. to
Ptolemy.

A special example is the description of the Caspian Sea. The re-
production out of a thesis by Daunicht, Bonn 1968, shows a very
strange distortion of the shape.

One could assume that the Arabs were prone to making the same
errors as the Europeans, namely that Lake Aral did not exist or was
only an eastern part of the Caspian Sea. But al-Khorezmi's list
does give coordinates for Lake Aral, although without details of
the shape; on the other hand, the mouths of both Oxus and Iaxartes
(Amu Darya and Syr Darya) are listed. Apart from a certain distortion, the map gives the right image. And we have little reason
to depreciate the value of the geographic work of the Arabs. As
an example an 18th century map of the province around Vienna shows
Lake Neusiedl, which actually has a shape very similar to that of
the Caspian Sea, and which on the map is distorted almost exactly
as on al-Khorezmi's map. No connoisseur of old maps would criticize this distortion, and indeed the map serves very well for
orientation purposes. The same is true of al-Mamun's masterpiece.

If this distortion is acceptable, understandable and therefore
pardonable, the misrelations of the cities of Central Asia, of the
part of the world in which we are at present, are not. Any caravan
leader could have estimated the distances better than al-Mamun's
geographers - and this is hard to understand. Are all these errors
copying errors? Maybe; as I have said, the Arab letter code, in
which the protocol is of course written, is prone to errors since
one missing diacritical mark may make a city jump over hundreds
of miles. But I have found no explanation and I do not understand
why so many errors should occur just in this part of the world.
I have already thought that the Khorezmians distorted the map on
purpose, as a measure to protect their country in case of war,
but this is no better explanation than the other; it is at least
equally improbable.

There are further intriguing facts in the Strasbourg manuscript.
It is there that al-Khorezmi's name includes a different son's
name. But the most disturbing thing for me is a remark by Hans
von Mzik, the Viennese orientalist who edited and translated the
Strasbourg manuscript. He says, I quote, that the language of the
Kitab surat is a quite barbaric and clumsy Arabic (p. XXIX), and
this is contradictory to the quality of expression we see in

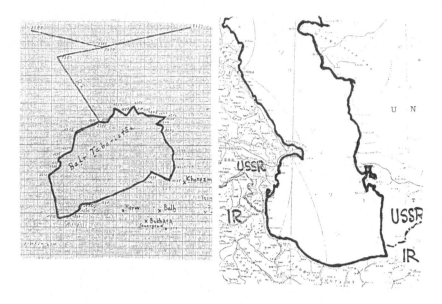

Al-Khorezmi's Caspian Sea versus real shape

18th century map of Lake Neusiedl near Vienna
versus real shape

al-Khorezmi's other books. This work would deserve further and detailed investigation. After its edition by Hans von Mžik a dissertation was written in 1968, but that seems to be all.

7. THE ASTROLABE

DIXIT ALGORIZMI:

The first one needs when using an astrolabe is the determination of the height of the sun. In order to determine it, turn the astrolabe with its back to you and let it hang from your right hand; the sun should be opposite to your left shoulder. Then direct the ninety lines, i.e. the grade scale, which is on the back of the astrolabe, to the sun. Hereupon elevate the alhidade slowly until you see the sun through both holes. Then read on which of the ninety parts located on the back of the astrolabe the pointer on the alhidade, being its sharp end, falls. This is the height of the sun at this hour. Keep it in mind!

This is the style in which al-Khorezmi teaches the use of the astrolabe. This instrument is the forerunner of the theodolite and the sextant. It has of course no lens. It consists of a reference plate and one or more moving units, the alhidade, which has two holes for fixing the direction of a line of sight. Since the instrument is held hanging down on a thread, the angle read from the scale refers to the zenith of the observer. But the astrolabe is more than a measuring device for observing angles; it appears as an analog computer for astronomical functions. Sine and tangent can be found - with the radii of 60 and 12 as mentioned in the chapter on the TABLES. Other astronomical values or lists can be engraved so that it can also serve as a compact handbook.

We have an instrument almost from the time of al-Khorezmi and there are many books on the astrolabe. The book of al-Khorezmi is, however, the oldest text we know. It was translated into German by Josef Frank in Erlangen and published in 1922.

Al-Khorezmi's Work on the Astrolabe
Arabic Manuscript (Berlin)
Schematic of Astrolabe

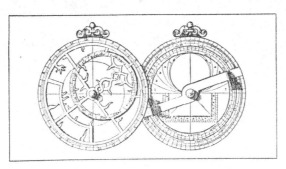

CONCLUSION

The first sine table, the introduction of the Indian number system and
the systematization of quadratic equations and of business calculations
is a list of achievements which is long enough to justify calling
al-Khorezmi one of the most important and influential mathematicians in
history. He deserves to be mentioned with the same respect as the
Greek mathematicians of whom we hear so much in High School.

But I want to emphasize a few conclusions drawn from my research into
al-Khorezmi and his work which are closely related to the subject of
the symposium - the algorithm.

In his ALGEBRA and ARITHMETIC and wherever else it appeared practical,
e.g. in calendar calculations, al-Khorezmi expressed the concept and
methodology of the algorithm in an extraordinarily clear language. His
style, as is true of most of ancient mathematics, is a digital style,
a computer-oriented style in the sense that the processing is restricted
to digital expressions and numbers: rather than getting involved in
operations with complicated fractions, values are transformed into
minutes, seconds, terces, etc., as if a device with stones or pins or
impulses had to be operated.

Al-Khorezmi's work is the beginning of a practical mathematical abstraction, of an abstraction very different from the Greek philosophy which
remained intensively connected to the real, sensual nature, while
al-Khorezmi's abstractions are as operational and goal-oriented as the
abstractions which are used for and are running the computers of our
century.

And this principle of abstraction invites two lines of thought. The
first one is comprehension and illustration. Al-Khorezmi was familiar
with the Indian method of demonstration and proof which avoided wordy
explanations by showing a picture plus the single word: *LOOK!* The proof
of Pythagoras I have shown is a perfect example for this. Al-Khorezmi's
method for solving all quadratic equations by one of six algorithms
is systematically connected to six drawings where the abstract procedure is compensated by optical *INSIGHT* in the fundamental sense of the
word. *LOOK* at the drawing and you understand the algorithm.

I think that we computer scientists of the 20th century, in particular the algorithmic community, have quite a lot to learn from al-Khorezmi's method and success: not allowing our listeners and readers to get lost in the purely mechanical derivations, elaborations and computations, but expanding on the abstract bones by a second piece of information to which our only comment can be the simple and old Indian word *LOOK!* - and our listener or reader can absorb the essence of the message, the entity of what we want to communicate and to be used.

This may not be possible or make sense in certain instances. Generally speaking, the computer is a devastating device due to its ability to swallow the most complicated structures and processes in space and time dimensions and remove them far from human perception and, therefore, from their place of origin, the human mind. No word is more useless in front of a computer than the word *LOOK!* Looking is possible only in documents, into computer descriptions and printouts, whether on paper or on the screen, but how seldom is it appropriate with our documentation to show it to the user and simply say *LOOK!*

And that leads to a second line of thought. Nobody can watch, under the circumstances described above, the structures and processes in our machines. Many of them are already so complicated that no single person, even provided with ideal documentation, could say he knows all of it. The richness of detail has outwitted the single person. We must trust in the correctness of what happens in information processing, and there is more hearsay than we are ready to admit.

The methodological consequence of this situation is aimed towards perfection. Algorithmic thinking has developed since al-Khorezmi to an ideal of perfection which al-Khorezmi himself would have rejected. We often behave as if we had already reached total perfection, total prediction, procedural omnipotence and algorithmic conscience. He knew better. We also know better. We are inclined to think we have reached them because we have reached them in certain contexts. What for al-Khorezmi still was a science bordering on the unknown, namely the science of quadratic equations, has for us become so crystal clear that we are entitled to say that as far as quadratic equations are concerned we *are* omniscient. We know at the same time that this perfection is not even true for the theory of the algorithm. Goedel, Turing and Markov have shown the irreparable imperfection of this theory. Since then we have started to aim at correctness proofs. And of course reality has shown us that in principle the same open-ended recursivity applies: correctness proofs of correctness proofs of correctness proofs etc. ad infinitum is not a chain that ends. However perfect the mechanics of the computer may be, its scope extends into imperfection. And the unavoidable symbiosis of man and computer is not only connected to "some imperfection", it can easily be a million times amplified human imperfection.

Al-Khorezmi teaches the programmer humbleness a thousand years before Dijkstra and reminds us that we are servants of our society just as he was a servant of the caliph. In the metropolis of Baghdad not only many nations cooperated for a common goal; certain men, like al-Khorezmi, achieved an alloy of cultures, the fruit of which survived the centuries even if the creative men themselves faded out of history and had to wait - or are still waiting - for rediscovery. We can end here with only one wish: that in a thousand years our rediscoverers will look at what has remained of us with the same respect with which we are looking back today on al-Khorezmi and his colleagues in the House of Wisdom.

Algorithms in Modern
Mathematics and Computer Science

DONALD E. KNUTH

Department of Computer Science, Stanford University, Stanford, CA 94305, USA

MY PURPOSE in this paper is to stimulate discussion about a philosophical question that has been on my mind for a long time: What is the actual rôle of the notion of an algorithm in mathematical sciences?

For many years I have been convinced that computer science is primarily the study of algorithms. My colleagues don't all agree with me, but it turns out that the source of our disagreement is simply that my definition of algorithms is much broader than theirs: I tend to think of algorithms as encompassing the whole range of concepts dealing with well-defined processes, including the structure of data that is being acted upon as well as the structure of the sequence of operations being performed; some other people think of algorithms merely as miscellaneous methods for the solution of particular problems, analogous to individual theorems in mathematics.

In the U.S.A., the sorts of things my colleagues and I do is called Computer Science, emphasizing the fact that algorithms are performed by machines. But if I lived in Germany or France, the field I work in would be called *Informatik* or *Informatique*, emphasizing the stuff that algorithms work on more than the processes themselves. In the Soviet Union, the same field is now known as either *Kibernetika* (Cybernetics), emphasizing the control of a process, or *Prikladnaſa Matematika* (Applied Mathematics), emphasizing the utility of the subject and its ties to mathematics in general. I suppose the name of our discipline isn't of vital importance, since we will go on doing what we are doing no matter what it is called; after all, other disciplines like Mathematics and Chemistry are no longer related very strongly to the etymology of their names. However, if I had a chance to vote for the name of my own discipline, I would choose to call it Algorithmics, a word coined about 16 years ago by J. F. Traub [27, p. 1].

The site of our symposium is especially well suited to philosophical discussions such as I wish to incite, both because of its rich history and because of the grand scale of its scenery. This is an ideal time for us to consider the long range aspects of our work, the issues that we usually have no time to perceive in our hectic everyday lives at home. During the coming week we will have a perfect opportunity to look backward in time to the roots of our subject, as well as to look ahead and to contemplate what our work is all about.

I have wanted to make a pilgrimage to this place for many years, ever since learning that the word "algorithm" was derived from the name of al-Khwârizmî, the great ninth-century scientist whose name means "from Khwârizm." The Spanish word *guarismo* ("decimal number") also stems from this root. Khwârizm was not simply a notable city (Khiva) as many Western authors have thought, it was (and still is) a rather large district. In fact, the Aral Sea was at one time known as Lake Khwârizm (see, for example, [17, Plates 9–21]). By the time of the conversion of this region to Islam in the seventh century, a high culture had developed, having for example its own script and its own calendar (cf. al-Bîrûnî [21]).

Catalog cards prepared by the U.S. Library of Congress say that al-Khwârizmî flourished between 813 and 846 A.D. It is amusing to take the average of these two numbers, obtaining 829.5, almost exactly 1150 years ago. Therefore we are here at an auspicious time, to celebrate an undesesquicentennial.

Comparatively little is known for sure about al-Khwârizmî's life. His full Arabic name is essentially a capsule biography: Abu Ja'far Muhammad ibn Mûsâ al-Khwârizmî, meaning "Mohammed, father of Jafar, son of Moses, the Khwârizmîan." However, the name does not prove that he was born here, it might have been his ancestors instead of himself. We do know that his scientific work was done in Baghdad, as part of an academy of scientists called the "House of Wisdom," under Caliph al-Ma'mûn. Al-Ma'mûn was a great patron of science who invited many learned men to his court in order to collect and extend the wisdom of the world. In this respect he was building on foundations laid by his predecessor, the Caliph Harûn al-Rashîd, who is familiar to us because of the *Arabian Nights*. The historian al-Ṭabarî added "al-Quṭrubbullî" to al-Khwârizmî's name, referring to the Quṭrubbull district near Baghdad. Personally I think it is most likely that al-Khwârizmî was born in Khwârizm and lived most of his life in Quṭrubbull after being summoned to Baghdad by the Caliph, but the truth will probably never be known.

The Charisma of al-Khwârizmî

It is clear in any event that al-Khwârizmî's work had an enormous influence throughout the succeeding generations. According to the *Fihrist*, a sort of "Who's Who" and bibliography of 987 A.D., "during his lifetime and afterwards, people were accustomed to rely upon his tables." Several of the books he wrote have apparently vanished, including a historical Book of Chronology and works on the sundial and the astrolabe. But he compiled a map of the world (still extant) giving coordinates for cities, mountains, rivers, and coastlines; this was the most complete and accurate map that had ever been made up to that time. He also wrote a short treatise on the Jewish calendar, and compiled extensive astronomical tables that were in wide use for several hundred years. (Of course, nobody is perfect: Some modern scholars feel that these tables were not as accurate as they could have been.)

The most significant works of al-Khwârizmî were almost certainly his textbooks on algebra and arithmetic, which apparently were the first Arabic writings to deal with such topics. His algebra book was especially famous; in fact, at least three manuscripts of this work in the original Arabic are known to have survived to the present day, while more than 99% of the books by other authors mentioned in the *Fihrist* have been lost. Al-Khwârizmî's *Algebra* was translated into Latin at least twice during the twelfth century, and this is how Europeans learned about the subject. In fact, our word "algebra" stems from part of the Arabic title of this book, *Kitâb al-jabr wa'l-muqâbala*, "The Book of Aljabr and Almuqâbala." (Historians disagree on the proper translation of this title. My personal opinion, based on a reading of the work and on the early Latin translation *restaurationis et oppositionis* [3, p.2], together with the fact that *muqâbala* signifies some sort of standing face-to-face, is that it would be best to call al-Khwârizmî's algebra "The Book of Restoring and Equating.")

We can get some idea of the reasons for al-Khwârizmî's success by looking at his *Algebra* in more detail. The purpose of the book was not to summarize all knowledge of the subject, but rather to give the "easiest and most useful" elements, the kinds of mathematics most often needed. He discovered that the complicated geometric tricks previously used in Babylonian and Greek mathematics could be replaced by simpler and more systematic methods that rely on algebraic manipulations alone. Thus the subject became accessible to a much wider audience. He explained how to reduce all nontrivial quadratic equations to one of three forms that we would express as $x^2 + bx = c$, $x^2 = bx + c$, $x^2 + c = bx$ in modern notation, where b and c are positive numbers; note that he has gotten rid of the coefficient of x^2 by dividing it out. If he had known about negative numbers, he would have been delighted to go further and reduce these three possibilities to a single case.

I mentioned that the Caliph wanted his scientists to put all of the existing scientific knowledge of other lands into Arabic texts. Although no prior work is known to have incorporated al-Khwârizmî's elegant approach to quadratic equations, the second part of his *Algebra* (which deals with questions of geometric measurements) was almost entirely based on an interesting treatise called the *Mishnat ha-Middot*, which Solomon Gandz has given good reason to believe was composed by a Jewish rabbi named Nehemiah about 150 A.D. [4]. The differences between the *Mishnat* and the *Algebra* help us to understand al-Khwârizmî's methods. For example, when the Hebrew text said that the circumference of a circle is $3\frac{1}{7}$ times the diameter, al-Khwârizmî added that this is only a conventional approximation, not a proved fact; he also mentioned $\sqrt{10}$ and $\frac{62832}{20000}$ as alternatives, the latter "used by astronomers." The Hebrew text merely stated the Pythagorean theorem, but al-Khwârizmî appended a proof. Probably the most significant change occurred in his treatment of the area of a general triangle: The *Mishnat* simply states Heron's formula $\sqrt{s(s-a)(s-b)(s-c)}$ where $s = \frac{1}{2}(a+b+c)$ is the semiperimeter, but the *Algebra* takes an entirely different tack. Al-Khwârizmî wanted to reduce the number of basic operations, so he showed how to compute the area in general from the simpler formula $\frac{1}{2}(\text{base} \times \text{height})$, where the height could be computed by simple algebra. Let the perpendicular to the largest side of the triangle from the opposite corner strike the longest side at a distance x from its end; then $b^2 - x^2 = c^2 - (a-x)^2$, hence $b^2 = c^2 - a^2 + 2ax$ and $x = (a^2 + b^2 - c^2)/(2a)$. The height of the triangle can now be computed as $\sqrt{b^2 - x^2}$; thus it isn't necessary to learn Heron's trick.

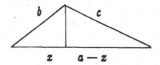

Unless an earlier work turns up showing that al-Khwârizmî learned his approach to algebra from somebody else, these considerations show that we are justified in calling him "the father of algebra." In other words, we can add the phrase "abu-aljabr" to his name! The overall history of the subject can be diagrammed roughly thus:

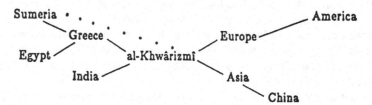

(I have shown a dotted line from Sumeria to represent a plausible connection between ancient traditions that might have reached Baghdad directly instead of via Greece. Conservative scholars doubt this connection, but I think they are too much influenced by obsolete attitudes to history in which Greek philosophers were regarded as the source of all scientific knowledge.) Of course, al-Khwârizmî never took the subject beyond quadratic equations in one variable, but he did make the important leap away from geometry to abstract reckoning, and he made the subject systematic and reasonably simple for practical use. He was unaware of Diophantus's prior work on number theory, which was even more abstract and further removed from reality, therefore closer to modern algebra. It is difficult to rank either al-Khwârizmî or Diophantus higher than the other, since they had such different aims. The unique contribution of Greek scientists was their pursuit of knowledge solely for its own sake.

The original Arabic version of al-Khwârizmî's small book on what he called the Hindu art of reckoning seems to have vanished. Essentially all we have is an incomplete 13th-century copy of what is a probably a 12th-century translation from Arabic into Latin; the original Arabic may well have been considerably different. It is amusing to look at this Latin translation with modern eyes, because it is primarily a document about how to calculate in Hindu numerals (the decimal system) but it uses Roman numerals to express numbers! Perhaps al-Khwârizmî's original treatise was similar in this respect, except that he would have used the alphabetic notation for numbers adapted from earlier Greek and Hebrew sources to Arabic; it is natural to expect that the first work on the subject would state problems and their solutions in an old familiar notation. I suppose the new notation became well known shortly after al-Khwârizmî's book appeared, and that might be why no copies of his original are left.

The Latin translation of al-Khwârizmî's arithmetic has blank spaces where most of the Hindu numerals were to be inserted; the scribe never got around to this, but it is possible to make good guesses about how to fill in these gaps. The portion of the manuscript that survives has never yet been translated from Latin to English or any other Western language, although a Russian translation appeared in 1964 [16]. Unfortunately both of the published transcriptions of the Latin handwriting ([3],[28]) are highly inaccurate; see [18]. It would surely be desirable to have a proper edition of this work in English, so that more readers can appreciate its contents. The algorithms given for decimal addition, subtraction, multiplication, and division—if we may call them algorithms, since they omit many details, even though they were written by al-Khwârizmî himself!—have been studied in detail by Îushkevich [9] and Rosenfel'd [16]. They are interesting because they are comparatively unsuitable for pencil-and-paper calculation, requiring lots of crossing-out or erasing; it seems clear that they are merely straightforward adaptations of procedures that were used on an abacus of some sort, in India if not in Persia. The development of methods more suitable for non-abacus calculations seems to be due to al-Uqlîdisî in Damascus about two centuries later [22].

Further details of al-Khwârizmî's works appear in an excellent article by G. J. Toomer in the *Dictionary of Scientific Biography* [26]. This is surely the most comprehensive summary of what is now known about Muḥammad ibn Mûsâ, although I was surprised to see no mention of the plausible hypothesis that local traditions continued from Babylonian times to the Islamic era.

Before closing this historical introduction, I want to mention another remarkable man from Khwârizm, Abû Rayḥân Muḥammad ibn Aḥmad al-Bîrûnî (973–1048 A.D.): philosopher, historian, traveler, geographer, linguist, mathematician, encyclopedist, astronomer, poet, physicist, and computer scientist, author of an estimated 150 books [12]. The term "computer scientist" belongs in this list because of his interest in efficient calculation. For example, al-Bîrûnî showed how to evaluate the sum $1 + 2 + \cdots + 2^{63}$ of the number of grains of wheat on a chessboard if a single grain is placed on the first square, two on the second, twice as many on the third, etc.: using a technique of divide and conquer, he proved that the total is $\left(\left(\left(16^2\right)^2\right)^2\right)^2 - 1$, and he gave the answer 18,446,744,073,709,551,615 in three systems of notation (decimal, sexagesimal, and a peculiar alphabetic-Arabic). He also pointed out that this number amounts to approximately 2305 "mountains", if one mountain equals 10000 wâdîs, one wâdî is 1000 herds, one herd is 10000 loads, one load is 8 bidar, and one bidar is 10000 units of wheat [20; 21, pp. 132–136; 23].

Some Questions

Will Durant has remarked that "scholars were as numerous as the pillars, in thousands of mosques," during that golden age of medieval science. Now here we are, a group of scholars with a chance to be inspired by the same surroundings; and I would like to raise several questions that I believe are important today. *What is the relation of algorithms to modern mathematics?* Is there an essential difference between an algorithmic viewpoint and the traditional mathematical world-view? *Do most mathematicians have an essentially different thinking process from that of most computer scientists?* Among members of university mathematics departments, why do the logicians (and to a lesser extent the combinatorial mathematicians) tend to be much more interested in computer science than their colleagues?

I raise these questions partly because of my own experiences as a student. I began to study higher mathematics in 1957, the same year that I began to work with digital computers, but I never mixed my mathematical thinking with my computer-science thinking in nontrivial ways until 1961. In one building I was a mathematician, in another I was a computer programmer, and it was as if I had a split personality. During 1961 I was excited by the idea that mathematics and computer science might have some common ground, because BNF notation looked mathematical, so I bought a copy of Chomsky's *Syntactic Structures* and set out to find an algorithm to decide the ambiguity problem of context-free grammars (not knowing that this had been proved impossible by Bar-Hillel, Perles, and Shamir in 1960). I failed to solve that problem, although I found some useful necessary and sufficient conditions for ambiguity, and I also derived a few other results like the fact that context-free languages on one letter are regular. Here, I thought, was a nice mathematical theory that I was able to develop with my computer-science intuition; how curious! During the summer of 1962, I spent a day or two analyzing the performance of hashing with linear probing, but this did not really seem like a marriage between my computer science personality and my mathematical personality since it was merely an application of combinatorial mathematics to a problem that has relevance to programming.

I think it is generally agreed that mathematicians have somewhat different thought processes from physicists, who have somewhat different thought processes from chemists, who have somewhat different thought processes from biologists. Similarly, the respective "mentalities" of lawyers, poets, playwrights, historians, linguists, farmers, and so on, seem to be unique. Each of these groups can probably recognize that other types of people have a different approach to knowledge; and it seems likely that a person gravitates to a particular kind of occupation corresponding to the mode of thought that he or she grew up with, whenever a choice is possible. C. P. Snow wrote a famous book about "two cultures," scientific vs. humanistic, but in fact there seem to be many more than two.

Educators of computer science have repeatedly observed that only about 2 out of every 100 students enrolling in introductory programing courses really "resonate" with the subject and seem to be natural-born computer scientists. (For example, see Gruenberger [8].) Just last week I had some independent confirmation of this, when I learned that 220 out of 11000 graduate students at the University of Illinois are majoring in Computer Science.

Since I believe that Computer Science is the study of algorithms, I conclude that roughly 2% of all people "think algorithmically," in the sense that they can rapidly reason about algorithmic processes.

While writing this paper, I learned about some recent statistical data gathered by Gerrit DeYoung, a psychologist-interested-in-computer-science whom I met at the University of Illinois. He had recently made an interesting experiment on two groups of undergraduate students taking introductory courses in computer science. Group I consisted of 135 students intending to major in computer science, while Group II consisted of 35 social science majors. Both courses emphasized non-numeric programming and various data and control structures, although numerical problems were treated too. DeYoung handed out a questionnaire that tested each student's so-called quantitative aptitude, a standard test that seems to correlate with mathematical ability, and he also asked them to estimate their own performance in class. Afterwards he learned the grades that the students actually did receive, so he had three pieces of data on each student:

$A =$ quantitative aptitude;

$B =$ student's own perception of programming ability;

$C =$ teacher's perception of programming ability.

In both cases B correlated well with C (the coefficient was about .6), so we can conclude that the teachers' grading wasn't random and that there is some validity in these scores. The interesting thing was that there was *no* correlation between A and B or between A and C among the computer science majors (Group I), while there was a pronounced correlation of about .4 between the corresponding numbers for the students of Group II. It isn't clear how to interpret this data, since many different hypotheses could account for such results; perhaps psychologists know only how to measure the quantitative ability of people who think like psychologists do! At any rate the lack of correlation between quantitative ability and programming performance in the first group reminds me strongly of the feelings I often have about differences between mathematical thinking and computer-science thinking, so further study is indicated.

I believe that the real reason underlying the fact that Computer Science has become a thriving discipline at essentially all of the world's universities, although it was totally unknown twenty years ago, is *not* that computers exist in quantity; the real reason is that the algorithmic thinkers among the scientists of the world never before had a home. We are brought together in Computer Science departments because we find people who think like we do. At least, that seems a viable hypothesis, which hasn't been contradicted by my observations during the last half dozen or so years since the possibility occurred to me.

My goal, therefore, is to get a deeper understanding of these phenomena; the "different modes of thought" hypothesis merely scratches the surface and gives little insight. Can we come up with a fairly clear idea of just what algorithmic thinking is, and contrast it with classical mathematical thinking?

At times when I try to come to grips with this question, I find myself almost convinced that algorithmic thinking is really like mathematical thinking, only it concentrates on more "difficult" things. But at other times I have just the opposite impression, that somehow algorithms hit only the "simpler" kinds of mathematics.... Clearly such an approach leads only to confusion and gets me nowhere.

While pondering these things recently, I suddenly remembered the collection of expository works called *Mathematics: Its Content, Methods, and Meaning* [1], so I reread what A. D. Aleksandrov says in his excellent introductory essay. Interestingly enough, I found that he makes prominent mention of al-Khwârizmî. Aleksandrov lists the following characteristic features of mathematics:

- Abstractness, with many levels of abstraction.
- Precision and logical rigor.
- Quantitative relations.
- Broad range of applications.

Unfortunately, however, all four of these features seem to be characteristic also of computer science. Is there really no difference betwen computer science and mathematics?

A Plan

I decided that I could make no further progress unless I took a stab at analyzing the question "What is mathematics?"—analyzing it in some depth. The answer, of course, is that "Mathematics is what mathematicians do." More precisely, the appropriate question should probably be, "What is good mathematics?" and the answer is that "Good mathematics is what good mathematicians do."

Therefore I took nine books off of my shelf, mostly books that I had used as texts during my student days but also a few more for variety's sake. I decided to take a careful look at page 100 (i.e., a "random" page) in each book and to study the first result on that page. This way I could get a sample of what good mathematicians do, and I could attempt to understand the types of thinking that seem to be involved.

From the standpoint of computer science, the notion of "types of thinking" is not so vague as it once was, since we can now imagine trying to make a computer program discover the mathematics. What sorts of capabilities would we have to put into such an artificially intelligent program, if it were to be able to come up with the results on page 100 of the books I selected?

In order to make this experiment fair, I was careful to abide by the following ground rules: (1) The books were all to be chosen first, before I studied any particular one of them. (2) Page 100 was to be the page examined in each case, since I had no a *priori* knowledge of what was on that page in any book. If somehow page 100 turned out to be a bad choice, I wouldn't try anything sneaky like searching for another page number that would give results more in accord with my prejudices. (3) I would not suppress any of the data; every book I had chosen would appear in the final sample, so that I wouldn't introduce any bias by selecting a subset.

The results of this experiment opened up my eyes somewhat, so I would like to share them with you. Here is a book-by-book summary of what I found.

Book 1: Thomas's Calculus

I looked first at the book that first introduced me to higher mathematics, the calculus text by George B. Thomas [25] that I had used as a college freshman. On page 100 he treats the following problem: *What value of x minimizes the travel time from $(0, a)$ to $(x, 0)$ to $(d, -b)$, if you must go at speed s_1 from $(0, a)$ to $(x, 0)$ and at some other speed s_2 from $(x, 0)$ to $(d, -b)$?*

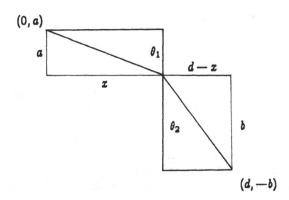

In other words, we want to minimize the function

$$f(x) = \sqrt{a^2 + x^2}/s_1 + \sqrt{b^2 + (d-x)^2}/s_2.$$

The solution is to differentiate $f(x)$, obtaining

$$f'(x) = \frac{x}{s_1\sqrt{a^2 + x^2}} - \frac{d-x}{s_2\sqrt{b^2 + (d-x)^2}} = \frac{\sin\theta_1}{s_1} - \frac{\sin\theta_2}{s_2}.$$

As x runs from 0 to d, the value of $(\sin\theta_1)/s_1$ starts at zero and increases, while the value of $(\sin\theta_2)/s_2$ decreases to zero. Therefore the derivative starts negative and ends positive; there must be a point where it is zero, i.e., $(\sin\theta_1)/s_1 = (\sin\theta_2)/s_2$, and that's where the minimum occurs. Thomas remarks that this is "Snell's Law" in optics; somehow light rays know how to minimize their travel time.

The mathematics involved here seems to be mostly a systematic procedure for minimization, based on formula manipulation and the correspondence between formulas and geometric figures, together with some reasoning about changes in function values. Let us keep this in mind as we look at the other examples, to see how much the examples have in common.

Book 2: A Survey of Mathematics

Returning to the survey volumes edited by Aleksandrov et al. [1], we find that page 100 is the chapter on Analysis by Lavrent'ev and Nikol'skiĭ. It shows how to deduce the derivative of the function $\log_a x$ in a clever way:

$$\frac{\log_a(x + h) - \log_a x}{h} = \frac{1}{h}\log_a\frac{x+h}{x} = \frac{1}{x}\log_a\left(1 + \frac{h}{x}\right)^{x/h}.$$

The logarithm function is continuous, so we have

$$\lim_{h\to 0}\frac{1}{x}\log_a\left(1 + \frac{h}{x}\right)^{x/h} = \frac{1}{x}\log_a\lim_{h\to 0}\left(1 + \frac{h}{x}\right)^{x/h} = \frac{1}{x}\log_a e,$$

since it has already been proved that the quantity $(1 + \frac{1}{n})^n$ approaches a constant called e, when n approaches infinity through integer or noninteger values. Here the reasoning involves formula manipulation and an understanding of limiting processes.

Book 3: Kelley's General Topology

The third book I chose was a standard topology text [10], where page 100 contains the following exercise: "*Problem A. The image under a continuous map of a connected space is connected.*" No solution is given, but I imagine something like the following was intended: First we recall the relevant definitions, that a function f from topological space X to topological space Y is continuous when the inverse image $f^{-1}(V)$ is open in X, for all open sets V in Y; a topological space X is connected when it cannot be written as a union of two nonempty open sets. Thus, let us try to prove that Y is connected, under the assumption that f is continuous and X is connected, where $f(X) = Y$. If $Y = V_1 \cup V_2$, where V_1 and V_2 are disjoint and open, then $X = f^{-1}(V_1) \cup f^{-1}(V_2)$, where $f^{-1}(V_1)$ and $f^{-1}(V_2)$ are disjoint and open. It follows that either $f^{-1}(V_1)$ or $f^{-1}(V_2)$ is empty, say $f^{-1}(V_1)$ is empty. Finally, therefore, V_1 is empty, since $V_1 \subseteq f(f^{-1}(V_1))$. Q.E.D.

(Note that no properties of "open sets" were needed in this proof.)

The mathematical thinking involved here is somewhat different from what we have seen before; it consists primarily of constructing chains of implications from the hypotheses to the desired conclusions, using a repertoire of facts like "$f^{-1}(A \cap B) = f^{-1}(A) \cap f^{-1}(B)$". This is analogous to constructing chains of computer instructions that transform some input into some desired output, using a repertoire of subroutines, although the topological facts have a more abstract character.

Another type of mathematical thinking is involved here, too, and we should be careful not to forget it: Somebody had to define the concepts of continuity and connectedness in some way that would lead to a rich theory having lots of applications, thereby generalizing many special cases that had been proved before the abstract pattern was perceived.

Book 4: From the 18th Century

Another book on my list was Struik's *Source Book in Mathematics*, which quotes authors of famous papers written during the period 1200–1800 A.D. Page 100 is concerned with Euler's attempt to prove the fundamental theorem of algebra, in the course of which he derived the following auxiliary result: "*Theorem 4. Every quartic polynomial $x^4 + Ax^3 + Bx^2 + Cx + D$ with real coefficients can be factored into two quadratics.*"

Here's how he did it. First he reduced the problem to the case $A = 0$ by setting $x = y - \frac{1}{4}A$. Then he was left with the problem of solving $(x^2 + ux + \alpha)(x^2 - ux + \beta) = x^4 + Bx^2 + Cx + D$ for u, α, and β, so he wanted to solve the equations $B = \alpha + \beta - u^2$, $C = (\beta - \alpha)u$, $D = \alpha\beta$. These equations lead to the relations $2\beta = B + u^2 + C/u$, $2\alpha = B + u^2 - C/u$, and $(B + u^2)^2 - C^2/u^2 = 4D$. But the cubic polynomial $(u^2)^3 + 2B(u^2)^2 + (B^2 - 4D)u^2 - C^2$ goes from $-C^2$ to $+\infty$ as u^2 runs from 0 to ∞, so it has a positive root, and the factorization is complete.

(Euler went on to generalize, arguing that every equation of degree 2^n can be factored into two of degree 2^{n-1}, via an equation of odd degree $\frac{1}{2}\binom{2^n}{2^n-1}$ in u^2 having a negative constant term. But this part of his derivation was not rigorous; Lagrange and Gauss later pointed out a serious flaw.)

When I first looked at this example, it seemed to be more "algorithmic" than the preceding ones, probably because Euler was essentially explaining how to take a quartic polynomial as input and to produce two quadratic polynomials as output. Input/output characteristics are significant aspects of algorithms, although Euler's actual construction is comparatively simple and direct so it doesn't exhibit the complex control structure that algorithms usually have. The types of thinking involved here seem to be (a) to reduce a general problem to a simpler special case (by showing that A can be assumed zero, and by realizing that a sixth-degree equation in u was really a third-degree equation in u^2); (b) formula manipulation to solve simultaneous equations for α, β, and u; (c) generalization by recognizing a pattern for the case of 4th degree equations that apparently would extend to degrees 8, 16, etc.

Book 5: Abstract Algebra

My next choice was another standard textbook, *Commutative Algebra* by Zariski and Samuel [29]. Their page 100 is concerned with the general structure of arbitrary fields. Suppose k and K are fields with $k \subseteq K$; the *transcendence degree of K over k* is defined to be the cardinal number of any "transcendence basis" L of K over k, namely a set L such that all of its finite subsets are algebraically independent over k and such that all elements of K are algebraic over $k(L)$; i.e., they are roots of polynomial equations whose coefficients are in the smallest field containing $k \cup L$. The exposition in the book has just found that this cardinal number is a well-defined invariant of k and K, i.e., that all transcendence bases of K over k have the same cardinality.

Now comes Theorem 26: *If $k \subseteq \mathcal{K} \subseteq K$, the transcendence degree of K over k is the sum of the transcendence degrees of $\mathcal{K}$ over k and of K over $\mathcal{K}$.* To prove the theorem, Zariski and Samuel let L be a transcendence basis of $\mathcal{K}$ over k and $\mathcal{L}$ a transcendence basis of K over $\mathcal{K}$; the idea is to prove that $L \cup \mathcal{L}$ is a transcendence basis of K over k, and the result follows since L and $\mathcal{L}$ are disjoint.

The required proof is not difficult and it is worth studying in detail. Let $\{z_1, \ldots, z_m, X_1, \ldots, X_M\}$ be a finite subset of $L \cup \mathcal{L}$, where the z's are in L and the X's in $\mathcal{L}$, and assume that they satisfy some polynomial equation over k, namely

$$\sum_{\substack{e_1, \ldots, e_m \geq 0 \\ E_1, \ldots, E_M \geq 0}} \alpha(e_1, \ldots, e_m, E_1, \ldots, E_M)\, z_1^{e_1} \ldots z_m^{e_m} X_1^{E_1} \ldots X_M^{E_M} = 0 \qquad (*)$$

where all the $\alpha(e_1, \ldots, e_m, E_1, \ldots, E_M)$ are in k and only finitely many α's are nonzero. This equation can be rewritten as

$$\sum_{E_1, \ldots, E_M \geq 0} \left(\sum_{e_1, \ldots, e_m \geq 0} \alpha(e_1, \ldots, e_m, E_1, \ldots, E_M)\, z_1^{e_1} \ldots z_m^{e_m} \right) X_1^{E_1} \ldots X_M^{E_M} = 0, \qquad (**)$$

a polynomial in the X's with coefficients in $\mathcal{K}$, hence all of these coefficients are zero by the algebraic independence over $\mathcal{L}$ over $\mathcal{K}$. These coefficients in turn are polynomials in the z's with coefficients in k, so all the α's must be zero. In other words, any finite subset of $L \cup \mathcal{L}$ is algebraically independent.

Finally, all elements of $\mathcal{K}$ are algebraic over $k(L)$ and all elements of K are algebraic over $\mathcal{K}(\mathcal{L})$. It follows from the previously developed theory of algebraic extensions that all elements of K are algebraic over $k(L)(\mathcal{L})$, the smallest field containing $k \cup L \cup \mathcal{L}$. Hence $L \cup \mathcal{L}$ satisfies all the criteria of a transcendence basis.

Note that the proof involves somewhat sophisticated "data structures," i.e., representations of complex objects, in this case polynomials in many variables. The key idea is a *pun*, the equivalence between the polynomial over k in $(*)$ and the polynomial over $k(L)$

in (**). In fact, the structure theory of fields being developed in this part of Zariski and Samuel's book is essentially a theory about data structures by which all elements of the field can be manipulated. Theorem 26 is not as important as the construction of transcendence bases that appears in its proof.

Another noteworthy aspect of this example is the way infinite sets are treated. Finite concepts have been generalized to infinite ones by saying that all finite subsets must have the property; this allows algorithmic constructions to be applied to the subsets.

Book 6: Metamathematics

I chose Kleene's *Introduction to Metamathematics* [13] as a representative book on logic. Page 100 talks about "disjunction elimination": Suppose we are given (1) $\vdash A \vee B$ and (2) $A \vdash C$ and (3) $B \vdash C$. Then by a rule that has just been proved, (2) and (3) yield

$$(4) \quad A \vee B \vdash C.$$

From (1) and (4) we may now conclude "(5) $\vdash C$". Kleene points out that this is the familiar idea of reasoning by cases. If either A or B is true, we can consider case 1 that A is true (then C holds); or case 2 that B is true (and again C holds). It follows that statement C holds in any case.

The reasoning in this example is simple formula manipulation, together with an understanding that familiar thought patterns are being generalized and made formal.

I was hoping to hit a more inherently metamathematical argument here, something like "anything that can be proved in system X can also be proved in system Y," since such arguments are often essentially algorithms that convert arbitrary X-proofs into Y-proofs. But page 100 was more elementary, this being an introductory book.

Book 7: Knuth

Is my own work [14] algorithmic? Well, page 100 isn't especially so, since it is part of the introduction to mathematical techniques that appear before I get into the real computer science content. The problem discussed on that page is to get the mean and standard deviation of the number of "heads" in n coin flips, when each independent flip comes up "heads" with probability p and "tails" with probability $q = 1 - p$. I introduce the notation p_{nk} for the probability that k heads occur, and observe that

$$p_{nk} = p \cdot p_{n-1,k-1} + q \cdot p_{n-1,k}.$$

To solve this recurrence, I introduce the generating function

$$G_n(z) = \sum_{k \geq 0} p_{nk} z^k$$

and obtain $G_n(z) = (q + pz)G_{n-1}(z)$, $G_1(z) = q + pz$. Hence $G_n(z) = (q + pz)^n$, and

$$\mathrm{mean}(G_n) = n \, \mathrm{mean}(G_1) = pn; \qquad \mathrm{var}(G_n) = n \, \mathrm{var}(G_1) = pqn.$$

Thus, the recurrence relation is set up by reasoning about probabilities; it is solved by formula manipulation according to patterns that are discussed earlier in the book. I like to think that I was being like al-Khwârizmî here—not using a special trick for this particular problem, rather illustrating a general method.

Book 8: Pólya and Szegő

The good old days of mathematics are represented by Pólya and Szegö's famous *Aufgaben und Lehrsätze*, recently available in an English translation with many new *Aufgaben* [19]. Page 100 contains a real challenge:

$$217. \quad \lim_{n \to \infty} \int_{-\pi}^{\pi} \frac{n! 2^{2n \cos \theta}}{|(2ne^{i\theta} - 1) \ldots (2ne^{i\theta} - n)|} \, d\theta = 2\pi.$$

Fortunately the answer pages provide enough of a clue to reveal the proof that the authors had in mind. We have $|2ne^{i\theta} - k|^2 = 4n^2 + k^2 - 4nk \cos \theta = (2n-k)^2 + 4nk(1 - \cos \theta) = (2n-k)^2 + 8nk \sin^2 \theta/2$. Replacing θ by $x/\sqrt{n}$ allows us to rewrite the integral as

$$\frac{n! \, 2^{2n}}{((2n-1) \ldots n)\sqrt{n}} \int_{-\infty}^{\infty} f_n(x) \, dx,$$

where $f_n(x) = 0$ for $|x| > \pi\sqrt{n}$, and otherwise

$$f_n(x) = 2^{2n(\cos x/\sqrt{n} - 1)} \prod_{1 \le k \le n} \left(1 + \frac{8nk}{(2n-k)^2} \sin^2 \frac{x}{2\sqrt{n}}\right)^{-1/2}$$

$$= \exp\left((2\ln 2)n\left(\cos \frac{x}{\sqrt{n}} - 1\right) - \sum_{1 \le k \le n} \frac{1}{2} \ln\left(1 + \frac{8nk}{(2n-k)^2} \sin^2 \frac{x}{2\sqrt{n}}\right)\right)$$

$$= \exp\left(-x^2 \ln 2 + O\left(\frac{x^4}{n}\right) + \frac{1}{2} \sum_{1 \le k \le n} \left(\frac{-2nk}{(2n-k)^2} \frac{x^2}{n} + O\left(\frac{x^4}{n^2}\right)\right)\right)$$

$$= \exp\left(-x^2 \ln 2 - (1 - \ln 2)x^2 + O\left(\frac{1 + x^4}{n}\right)\right).$$

Thus, $f_n(x)$ converges uniformly to e^{-x^2} in any bounded internal. Furthermore we have $|f_n(x)| \le 2^{2n(\cos x/\sqrt{n} - 1)}$ and

$$\cos \frac{x}{\sqrt{n}} - 1 \le -\frac{x^2}{2n} + \frac{x^4}{24n^2}$$

$$\le -\left(\frac{1}{2} - \frac{\pi^2}{24}\right)\frac{x^2}{n} \quad \text{for } |x| \le \pi/\sqrt{n},$$

since the cosine function is "enveloped" by its Maclaurin series; therefore $|f_n(x)|$ is less than the integrable function e^{-cx^2} for all n, where $c = 1 - \pi^2/12$. From this uniformly bounded convergence we are justified in taking limits past the integral sign,

$$\lim_{n \to \infty} \int_{-\infty}^{\infty} f_n(x) \, dx = \int_{-\infty}^{\infty} e^{-x^2} \, dx = \sqrt{\pi}.$$

Finally, the coefficient in front of $\int_{-\infty}^{\infty} f_n(x) \, dx$ is $2^{2n+1} n!^2/\sqrt{n}(2n)!$, which is equal to $2\sqrt{\pi}(1 + O(1/n))$ by Stirling's approximation, and the result follows.

This derivation gives some idea of how far mathematics had developed between the time of al-Khwârizmî and 1920. It involves formula manipulation and an understanding of the asymptotic limiting behavior of functions, together with the idea of inventing a suitable function f_n that will rigorously permit us to make the interchange $\lim_{n \to \infty} \int_{-\infty}^{\infty} f_n(x) \, dx = \int_{-\infty}^{\infty} (\lim_{n \to \infty} f_n(x)) \, dx$. The definition of $f_n(x)$ requires a clear understanding of how functions like $\exp x$ and $\cos x$ behave.

Book 9: Bishop's Constructive Mathematics

The last book I chose to sample turned out to be most interesting of all from the standpoint of my quest; it was Errett Bishop's *Foundations of Constructive Mathematics* [2], a book that I had heard about but never before read. The interesting thing about this book is that it reads essentially like ordinary mathematics, yet it is entirely algorithmic in nature if you look between the lines.

Page 100 of Bishop's book contains Corollary 3 to the Stone-Weierstrass theorem developed on the preceding pages: *Every uniformly continuous function on a compact set $X \subseteq \mathbf{R}$ can be arbitrarily closely approximated on X by polynomial functions over $\mathbf{R}$.* And here is his proof: "By Lemma 5, the function $x \mapsto |x - x_0|$ can be arbitrarily closely approximated on X by polynomials. The theorem then follows from Corollary 2."

We might call this a compact proof! Before unwrapping it to explain what Lemma 5 and Corollary 2 are, I want to stress that the proof is essentially an algorithm; the algorithm takes any constructively given compact set X and continuous function f and tolerance ϵ as input, and it outputs a polynomial that approximates f to within ϵ on all points of X. Furthermore the algorithm operates on algorithms, since f is given by an algorithm of a certain type, and since real numbers are essentially algorithms themselves.

I will try to put Bishop's implicit algorithms into an explicit ALGOL-like form, even though the capabilities of today's programming languages have to be stretched considerably to reflect his constructions. First let's consider Lemma 5, which states that for each $\epsilon > 0$ there exists a polynomial $p : \mathbf{R} \to \mathbf{R}$ such that $p(0) = 0$ and $\big||x| - p(x)\big| \leq \epsilon$ for all $|x| \leq 1$. Bishop's proof, which makes the lemma an algorithm, is essentially the following.

```
R polynomial procedure Lemma 5(real ε);
begin integer N;  R polynomial g, p;
N := suitable function of ε;
g(t) := 1 − ∑_{1 ≤ n ≤ N} (1/2 choose n)(−1)ⁿtⁿ;
p(t) := g(−t²) − g(1);
return p;
end.
```

Here N is to be computed large enough that $|g(t) - (1 - t)^{1/2}| \leq \frac{1}{2}\epsilon$ for $0 \leq t \leq 1$.

The other missing component of the proof on page 100 is Corollary 2, which states that if X is any compact metric space and if G is the set of all functions $x \mapsto \rho(x, x_0)$, where $x_0 \in X$ and where $\rho(x, y)$ denotes the metric distance from x to y, then "$\mathcal{A}(G)$ is dense in $C(X)$." That is, all uniformly continuous real-valued functions on X can be approximated to arbitrarily high accuracy by functions obtained from the functions G by a finite number of operations of addition, multiplication, and multiplication by real numbers. As stated, Corollary 2 turns out to be false in the case that X contains only one point, since G and $\mathcal{A}(G)$ then consist only of the zero function. I noticed this oversight while trying to formulate his proof in an explicitly algorithmic way, but the defect is easily remedied.

For our purposes it is best to reformulate Corollary 2 in the following way: "*Let X be a compact metric space containing at least two points, and let G be the set of all functions of the form $x \mapsto c\rho(x, x_0)$, where $c > 0$ and $x_0 \in X$. Then G is a separating family over X.*" I'll repeat his definition of separating family in a minute; first I want to mention his Theorem 7, the Stone-Weierstrass theorem whose proof I shall not discuss in detail, namely the fact that $\mathcal{A}(G)$ is dense in $C(X)$ whenever G is a separating family of uniformly continuous functions over a compact metric space X. In view of this theorem, my reformulation of Corollary 2 leads to the corollary as he stated it.

A *separating family* is a collection of real-valued functions G over X, together with a function δ from the positive reals R^+ into R^+, and also together with two selection algorithms σ and τ. Algorithm σ takes elements x, y of X and a positive real number ϵ as input, where $\rho(x,y) \geq \epsilon$, and selects an element g of G such that for all z in X we have

$$\rho(x,z) \leq \delta(\epsilon) \quad \text{implies} \quad |g(z)| \leq \epsilon,$$
$$\rho(y,z) \leq \delta(\epsilon) \quad \text{implies} \quad |g(z) - 1| \leq \epsilon.$$

Algorithm τ takes an element y of X and a positive real number ϵ as input, and selects an element g of G such that the second of the above implications holds, for all z in X.

Thus the reformulated Corollary 2 is an algorithm that takes a nontrivial compact metric space X as input and yields a separating family (δ, σ, τ), where σ and τ select functions of the form $\rho(z, z_0)$. Here is the construction:

X-separating family procedure *Corollary 2*(compact metric space X;

$\qquad\qquad\qquad\qquad\qquad\qquad\qquad\qquad\qquad\qquad$ X-element y_0, y_1);

comment y_0 and y_1 are distinct elements of X;
begin $\mathrm{R}^+ \to \mathrm{R}^+$ function δ;
$X \times X \to \mathrm{R}^+$ function d;
$X \times X \times \mathrm{R}^+ \to C(X)$ function σ;
$X \times \mathrm{R}^+ \to C(X)$ function τ;
$X \times X \to \mathrm{R}$ function d;
$d(x, y) := X.\rho(x, y)$; comment this is the distance function in X;
$\delta(\epsilon) := \min(\epsilon^2, \frac{1}{2}\epsilon d(y_0, y_1))$;
$\sigma(x, y, \epsilon) := (\mathrm{R}$ procedure $g(X$-element $z)$;
$\qquad\qquad\qquad$ return $d(x, z)/d(x, y))$;
$\tau(y, \epsilon) := (\mathrm{R}$ procedure $g(X$-element $z)$;
$\qquad\qquad\qquad$ return$(\text{if } d(y, y_1) \leq \frac{1}{2}d(y_0, y_1)$
$\qquad\qquad\qquad\qquad$ then $d(y, z)/d(y, y_0)$
$\qquad\qquad\qquad\qquad$ else $d(y, z)/d(y, y_1)))$
return (δ, σ, τ);
end.

My notation for the complicated types involved in these algorithms is not the best possible, but I hope it is reasonably comprehensible without further explanation. The selection rule σ determined by this algorithm has the desired property since, for example, $\rho(x, y) \geq \epsilon$ and $\rho(y, z) \leq \delta(\epsilon) \leq \epsilon^2$ implies that $|g(z) - 1| = |\rho(x, z) - \rho(x, y)|/\rho(x, y) \leq \rho(y, z)/\rho(x, y) \leq \epsilon$.

Bishop's proof of Corollary 3 can now be displayed more explicitly as an algorithm in the following way. If X is a compact subset of R, under Bishop's definition, we can compute $M = \text{bound}(X)$ such that X is contained in the closed interval $[-M, M]$. Let us assume that his Theorem 7 is a procedure whose input parameters consist of a compact metric space X, a separating family (δ, σ, τ) over X that selects functions from some set $G \subseteq C(X)$, and a uniformly continuous function $f : X \to \mathrm{R}$, and a positive real number ϵ. The output of this procedure is an element A of $\mathcal{A}(G)$, namely a finite sum of terms of the form $Cg_1(x)\ldots g_m(x)$ where $m \geq 1$ and each $g_i \in G$; this output satisfies $|A(x)-f(x)| \leq \epsilon$ for all x in X.

Here is the fleshed-out form of Corollary 3:

```
    R polynomial procedure Corollary 3(compact real set X;
                                        X-continuous function f;
                                        positive ε);
    begin R polynomial p, q, r;  real M, B;  X-element y₀, y₁;
    A(G)-element A, where G is the set of functions x ↦ c|x − x₀|;
    M := bound(X);
    y₀ := element(X);
    if trivial(X) then r(t) := f(y₀)
    else begin y₁ := element(X \ {y₀});
        A := Theorem 7(X, Corollary 2(X, y₀, y₁), f, ½ε);
        B := suitable function of A, see below;
        p(t) := Lemma 5(ε/B);
        q(t) := 2Mp(t/2M);
        comment ||x − x₀| − q(x − x₀)| ≤ ε/B for all x;
        r(x) := substitute cq(x − x₀) for each factor gᵢ(x) = c|x − x₀|
                of each term of A;
        comment B was chosen so that |q(x − x₀) − |x − x₀|| ≤ ε/B
                    implies that |r(x) − A(x)| ≤ ½ε;
        end;
    return r;
    end.
```

Clearly it would be an extremely interesting project from the standpoint of high-level programming language design to find an elegant notation in which Bishop's constructions are both readable and explicit.

Tentative Conclusions

What insights do we get from these nine randomly selected examples of mathematics? In the first place, they point out something that should have been obvious to me from the start, that there is no such thing as "mathematical thinking" as a single isolated concept; mathematicians use a variety of modes of thought, not just one. My question about computer-science thinking as distinct from math thinking therefore needs to be reformulated. Indeed, when I reflect further about my student days, I realize that I would not only wear my CS hat when programming computers and my math hat when taking courses, I also had other hats representing various modes of thought that I used when I was editing a student magazine or when I was acting as officer of a fraternity, etc. And al-Bîrûnî's biography shows that he had more hats than anybody else.

Thus, it seems better to think of a model in which people have a certain number of different modes of thought, something like genes in DNA. It is probable that computer scientists and mathematicians overlap in the sense that they share several modes of thought, yet there are other modes peculiar to one or the other. Under this model, different areas of science would be characterized by different "personality profiles."

I tried to distill out different kinds of reasoning in the nine examples, and I came up with nine categories that I tentatively would diagram as follows. (Two z's means a strong use of some reasoning mode, while one z indicates a mild connection.)

	Formula manipulation	Representation of reality	Behavior of function values	Reduction to simpler problems	Dealing with infinity	Generalization	Abstract reasoning	Information structures	Algorithms
1 (Thomas)	zz	zz	zz						
2 (Lavrent'ev)	zz		z		zz				
3 (Kelley)	z					zz	zz		
4 (Euler)	zz		zz	z		zz			z
5 (Zariski)	z			z	zz	z	zz	zz	
6 (Kleene)	z					zz	zz		z
7 (Knuth)	zz	z		z					
8 (Pólya)	zz		zz	zz	zz				
9 (Bishop)	zz		zz	zz		z	zz	zz	z
"Algorithmic thinking"	z	zz		zz			zz	zz	zz

These nine categories aren't precisely defined, and they may represent combinations of more fundamental things; for example, both formula manipulation and generalization involve the general idea of pattern recognition, spotting certain kinds of order. Another fundamental distinction might be in the type of "visualization" needed, whether it be geometric or abstract or recursive, etc. Thus, I am not at all certain of the categories, they are simply put forward as a basis for discussion.

I have added a tenth row to the table labeled "algorithmic thinking," trying to make it represent my perception of the most typical thought processes used by a computer scientist. Since computer science is such a young discipline, I don't know what books would be appropriate candidates from which to examine page 100; perhaps some of you can help me round out this study. It seems to me that most of the modes of thought listed in the table are common in computer science as well as in mathematics, with the notable exception of "reasoning about infinity." Infinite-dimensional spaces seem to be of little relevance for computer scientists, although most other branches of mathematics have been extensively applied in many ways.

Computer scientists will notice, I think, that two types of thinking are absent from the examples we have studied, so this may be what separates mathematicians from computer scientists. In the first place, there is almost no notion of "complexity" or economy of operation in what we have discussed. Bishop's mathematics is constructive, but it does not have all the ingredients of an algorithm because it ignores the "cost" of the constructions. If we carry out the details of his Stone-Weierstrass theorem with respect to simple functions, we are likely to wind up with a polynomial approximation of degree 10^6, say, although a suitable polynomial of degree 6 could have been found by a more efficient scheme.

The other missing concept is related to the "assignment operation" $:=$, which changes values of quantities. More precisely, I would say that the missing concept is the dynamic notion of the *state* of a process: "How did I get here? What is true now? What should happen next if I'm going to get to the end?" Changing states of affairs, or snapshots of a computation, seem to be intimately related to algorithms and algorithmic thinking. Many of the concepts of data structures, which are so fundamental in computer science, depend very heavily on an ability to reason about the notion of process states, and we rely on this notion also when studying the interaction of processes that are acting simultaneously.

Our nine examples don't have anything resembling "$n := n + 1$", except for Euler's discussion where he essentially begins by setting $z := z - \frac{1}{4}A$. The assignment operations in Bishop's constructions aren't really assignments, they are simply definitions of quantities, and those definitions won't be changed. This discrepancy between classical mathematics and computer science is well illustrated by the fact that Burks, Goldstine, and von Neumann did not actually have the notion of assignment in their early notes on computer programming; they used a curious in-between concept instead (see [15]).

The closest thing to "$:=$" in classical mathematics is the reduction of a relatively hard problem to a simpler one, since the simpler problem replaces the former one. Al-Khwârizmî did this when he divided both sides of a quadratic equation by the coefficient of x^2; so I shall conclude this lecture by once again paying tribute to al-Khwârizmî, a remarkable pioneer in our discipline.

The preparation of this paper was supported in part by National Science Foundation grant MCS72-03752 A03 and in part by Office of Naval Research contract N0014-76-C-0330. My wife and I wish to thank our Uzbek hosts for their incomparable hospitality. Many people too numerous to name have contributed their insights during informal discussions about the topics discussed here.

References

[1] A. D. Aleksandrov, A. N. Kolmogorov, and M. A. Lavrent'ev, eds., *Mathematics: Its Content, Methods and Meaning* 1 (Cambridge, Mass.: MIT Press, 1963). Translated by S. H. Gould and T. Bartha from *Matematika: Eё Soderzhanie, Metody i Znachenie* (Akad. Nauk SSSR, 1956).

[2] Errett Bishop, *Foundations of Constructive Analysis* (N.Y.: McGraw-Hill, 1967).

[3] Baldassarre Boncompagni, ed., Algoritmi de Numero Indorum. *Trattati D'Aritmetica* 1 (Rome, 1857).

[4] Solomon Gandz, "The Mishnat Ha Middot," *Proc. Amer. Acad. for Jewish Research* 4 (1933), 1-104. Reprinted in S. Gandz, *Studies in Hebrew Astronomy and Mathematics* (New York: Ktav, 1970), 295-400.

[5] Solomon Gandz, "Sources of al-Khowârizmi's Algebra," *Osiris* 1 (1936), 263-277.

[6] Solomon Gandz, "The origin and development of the quadratic equations in Babylonian, Greek, and early Arabic algebra," *Osiris* 3 (1938), 405-557.

[7] Solomon Gandz, "The algebra of inheritance," *Osiris* 5 (1938) [sic], 319-391.

[8] Fred Gruenberger, "The role of education in preparing effective computing personnel," in F. Gruenberger, ed., *Effective vs. Efficient Computing* (Englewood Cliffs, N.J.: Prentice-Hall, 1973), 112-120.

[9] A. P. Ĵushkevich, "Arifmeticheskiĭ traktat Mykhammeda Ben Musa Al-Khorezmi," *Trudy Inst. Istorii Estestvoznaniia i tekhniki* 1 (1954), 85-127.

[10] Louis Charles Karpinski, ed., Robert of Chester's Latin Translation of the *Algebra* of Al-Khowârizmi. Univ. Michigan Humanistic Series 11, part 1 (Ann Arbor, 1915), 164 pp. Reprinted in 1930.

[11] John L. Kelley, *General Topology* (Princeton: D. Van Nostrand, 1955).

[12] E. S. Kennedy, "al-Bīrūnī," *Dictionary of Scientific Biography* 2 (N.Y.: Charles Scribner's Sons, 1970), 147-158.

[13] Stephen Cole Kleene, *Introduction to Metamathematics* (Princeton: D. Van Nostrand, 1952).

[14] Donald E. Knuth, *Fundamental Algorithms* (Reading, Mass.: Addison-Wesley, 1968).

[15] Donald E. Knuth and Luis Trabb Pardo, "The early development of programming languages," *Encyclopedia of Computer Science and Technology* 7 (N.Y.: Marcel Dekker).

[16] Îu. Kh. Kopelevich and B. A. Rosenfel'd, tr., Mukhammad al'-Khorezmi: *Matematicheskie Traktaty* (Tashkent: Akad. Nauk Uzbekskoĭ SSR, 1964). [Includes al-Khwârizmî's arithmetic and algebra, with commentaries by B. A. Rosenfel'd.]

[17] Seyyed Hossein Nasr et al., *Historical Atlas of Iran* (Tehran, 1971).

[18] D. Pingree, review of [28], *Math. Reviews* 30 (July, 1965), No. 5.

[19] G. Pólya and G. Szegö, *Problems and Theorems in Analysis* 1 (Berlin: Springer, 1972).

[20] Ed. Sachau, "Algebraisches über das Schach bei Bîrûnî," *Zeitschrift d. Deutsche Morgenländische Gesellschaft* 29 (1876), 148–156.

[21] C. Edward Sachau, transl. and ed., al-Bîrûnî's *Chronology of Ancient Nations* (London: William H. Allen and Co., 1879).

[22] A. S. Saidan, *The Arithmetic of al-Uqlîdisî* (Dordrecht: D. Reidel, 1975).

[23] S. Kh. Sirazhdinov and G. P. Matvievskaîa, *Abu Raĭkhan Beruni i Ego Matematicheskie Trudy* (Moscow: Prosveshchenie, 1978).

[24] D. J. Struik, ed., *A Source Book in Mathematics, 1200–1800* (Cambridge, Mass.: Harvard University Press, 1969).

[25] George B. Thomas, *Calculus and Analytic Geometry*, 2nd ed. (Cambridge, Mass.: Addison-Wesley, 1956).

[26] G. J. Toomer, "al-Khwârizmî," *Dictionary of Scientific Biography* 7 (N.Y.: Charles Scribner's Sons, 1973), 358–365.

[27] J. F. Traub, *Iterative Methods for the Solution of Equations* (Englewood Cliffs, N.J.: Prentice-Hall, 1964).

[28] Kurt Vogel, ed., Mohammed Ibn Musa Alchwarizmi's *Algorismus*, Das früheste Lehrbuch zum Rechnen mit indischen Ziffern (Aalen/Osnabruck: Otto Zeller Verlagsbuchhandlung, 1963). [This edition contains a facsimile of the manuscript, from which a correct transcription can be deduced.]

[29] Oscar Zariski and Pierre Samuel, *Commutative Algebra* 1 (Princeton: D. Van Nostrand, 1958).

Note on the spelling of Khwârizm: In the first and second editions of my book [14], I spelled Muḥammad ben Mûsâ's name "al-Khowârizmî," following the convention used in most American books up to about 1930 and perpetuated in many other modern texts. Recently I learned that "al-Khuwârizmî" would be a more proper transliteration of the Arabic letters, since the character in question currently has an 'oo' sound; the U.S. Library of Congress uses this convention. The Moorish scholars who brought Arabic works to Spain in medieval times evidently pronounced the letter as they would say a Latin 'o'; and it is not clear to what extent this particular vowel has changed its pronunciation in the East or the West, or both, since those days. At any rate, from about 1935 until the present time, the leading American scholars of oriental mathematics history have almost unanimously agreed on the form "al-Khwârizmî" (or its equivalent, "al-Khwārizmī", which is easier to type on conventional typewriters). They obviously know the subject much better than I do, so I shall happily conform to their practice from now on.

WHAT ARE THE GAINS OF THE THEORY OF ALGORITHMS:

Basic Developments Connected with the Concept of Algorithm and with Its Application in Mathematics

V.A. Uspensky and A.L. Semenov

It is striking to realize how much we can learn from the theory of algorithms. It helps to clarify fundamental concepts such as provability, complexity, and randomness. The discoveries in the theory of algorithms (as, probably, in many other cases) consist not so much in obtaining new results as in introducing new concepts and refining old ones.

The development of the theory of algorithms meets the difficulty provoked by the fact that the algorithms themselves are objects of a very special kind and have a property non-typical for mathematical objects--the semantic property "to have a meaning". In this respect the theory of algorithms is similar to symbolic logic whose terms and formulas also have meanings. The meaning of a term or a formula is indicative: a term indicates a thing, a formula--a fact. The meaning of an algorithm is imperative: an algorithm is to be

This paper contains the expanded text of an address "What does the theory of algorithms give?" presented on September 17, 1979, in Urgench at the Symposium "Algorithm in modern mathematics and its applications". The Symposium was dedicated to al-Khorezmi (the great scientist's name is also spelled as Al Chwarizmi and Al-Khowarizmi). Information about this Symposium can be found in [ErA 80], [ErA Us 80], [Sem Us 80]. The idea of giving an introductory lecture surveying the basic concepts connected with the general notion of algorithm, came from A.P. Ershov--the organizer of the Symposium.

performed. (Besides that there are calculuses and the meaning of a calculus is permissive.) The theory of algorithms can be treated as a linguistics of imperative sentences. Mathematicians have not yet found out how to do properly with the linguistic objects filled with meanings. In order to create an adequate theory of algorithms certain semantics should be drawn in because the pure mathematical approach is essentially incomplete.

It would be more correct to call the theory of algorithms the theory of algorithms and calculuses (the combined use of the terms "algorithms and calculuses", though understood in a different sense, first appeared in Schröder's work "Über Algorithmen und Kalkuln", see [Schrö 1887]).

The theory of algorithms can be divided into two parts. The first is the general theory dealing with the structure of algorithms themselves. The second is the applied theory which deals with problems arising in different fields of mathematics and connected with the concept of algorithm. Accordingly the paper is composed of two Parts: "The general theory of algorithms" and "The applied theory of algorithms". The paper is not intended for giving a full historical survey. In particular, the notes in the article do not necessarily refer to the author who first introduced a given idea: they sometimes serve simply as an indication of a source of further information.

In the text we refer to various books and articles by using an abbreviated form of the author's surname and, if necessary, his initials bracketed together with the year of publication (for the XXth century only two last digits are given). If a page or a theorem reference is mentioned, it is given within the same brackets. Some difficulties arise over the English spelling of Russian names. In our bibliography we have used the AMS system for transliteration of Cyrillic. In the body of the text we have chosen to write Russian names in a traditional way so as to reflect their pronunciation. Thus, Шанин, Яновская are written as Shanin, Yanovskaya in the text and as Šanin, Janovskaja in the bibliography. Some examples of how to change from one system of transliteration to the other are given at the end of the bibliography.

Notation

$\mathbb{N}$ is the set of all natural numbers $\{0, 1, 2, \ldots\}$;

$\mathbb{N}^+$ is the set of all positive integers $\{1, 2, 3, \ldots\}$;

$\mathbb{Q}$ is the set of all rational numbers;

$\mathbf{Q}^+$ is the set of all positive rational numbers;

Ξ is the set of all binary words (i.e. finite sequences over $\{0,1\}$);

Ω is the set of all infinite binary sequences;

$\simeq$ the proposition $A \simeq B$ means that for all values of variables the expressions A and B are both defined or both undefined, and if defined, have the same value (for example: $x - x \simeq y - y$ is true while $\frac{x}{x} \simeq \frac{y}{y}$ is false);

$\lessapprox$ the proposition $A \lessapprox B$ means that there exists a natural number c such that the inequality $A \leqslant B + c$ holds for all values of variables for which A and B are defined;

$\mathcal{F}(X,Y)$ is the set of all functions from X into Y;

$\left.\begin{array}{l} f : X \to Y \\ \quad \text{or} \\ f \text{ is a mapping} \\ (=\text{function}) \\ \text{from } X \text{ into } Y \end{array}\right\}$ implies that the domain of f is a subset of X and the range of f is a subset of Y;

$\left.\begin{array}{l} f \text{ is a mapping} \\ \quad \text{of } X \end{array}\right\}$ implies that the domain of f is X;

$\left.\begin{array}{l} f \text{ is a mapping} \\ \quad \text{onto } Y \end{array}\right\}$ implies that the range of f is Y.

Part I. THE GENERAL THEORY OF ALGORITHMS

In the general theory of algorithms we can distinguish a descriptive component and a metric one. The descriptive component deals with the problem of the existence and nonexistence of certain algorithms and calculuses as well as with the methods of their description; the metric component deals with the evaluation of the complexities of constructive objects as well as with the complexities of processes of computation and generation.

The basic discoveries related to the general notion of algorithm are:

1. The general notion of algorithm as an independent (separate) concept.
2. Representative computational models.
3. The general notion of calculus as an independent (separate) concept.
4. Representative generative models.
5. Interrelations between algorithms and calculuses.
6. Time and space as complexities of computation and generation.
7. Computable functions and generable sets; decidable sets; enumerable sets.
8. The concept of μ-recursive function.
9. Possibility of arithmetical and even Diophantine representation of any enumerable set of natural numbers.
10. Construction of an undecidable generable set.
11. Post's reducibility problem.
12. The concept of relative algorithm, or oracle-algorithm.
13. The concept of computable operation.
14. The concept of program: programs as objects of computation and generation.
15. The concept of numbering and the theory of numberings.
16. First steps of the invariant, or machine-independent, theory of complexity of computation.
17. The theory of complexity and entropy of constructive objects.
18. Time-and-space-saving and proper computational models.

Part I consists of eighteen sections, each section is devoted to a specific discovery and related topics. Now we shall list the basic notions which have not been mentioned in the titles of the sections and indicate the sections these are introduced in. The notion of constructive object and of aggregate (i.e. of space of constructive objects) are introduced in §1, the notion of volume of construc-

tive object, volumed aggregate and bounded-distortion mapping--in
§6, notion of universal algorithm, of main (=Gödel) algorithm and of
"volume-of-program-saving" (=optimal) algorithm--in §14.

In Part I we have tried to give exact and complete formulations
of the definitions and theorems of the theory of algorithms. There
are two reasons for this. First we believe that many achievements of
the theory of algorithms have a general mathematical, and perhaps a
much more general human interest. This is why we have established as
a basic principle that the text could be clearly understood by any
mathematician. The second reason is the state of disorder which exists
in the terminology of this field--sometimes even experts in the field
can hardly recognize which particular variant of a notion is meant in
a paper. The only way to avoid ambiguity is to formulate everything
explicitly. Nevertheless there are two important exceptions to our
principle of formulating everything--the definitions of particular
computational and generative models. We have given a definition of
one computational model, that of Kolmogorov machines; definitions
of Turing machines, Markov algorithms, etc. as well as a definition
of μ-recursive functions can be found in standard text-books (e.g.
about multitape Turing machines see [Aho Hop Ull 74, chap. 1]), as
well as in the original works which we cite in the text. The same is
true of generative models: Post's systems, etc. The term "computational model" which has been used above can be intuitively understood,
but one can also regard it as "collective noun" to denote any of the
known families of similar computational devices. For example, all
Kolmogorov machines constitute the above mentioned family, as well as
all multitape Turing machines and all one-tape Turing machines. All
one-tape Turing machines with a fixed tape alphabet or all Kolmogorov
machines over Kolmogorov complexes labelled by letters of a fixed alphabet can also be regarded as computational models.

§1. The general notion of algorithm as an independent (separate) concept

The most important discovery in the science of algorithms was
undoubtedly the discovery of the general notion of algorithm itself
as a new and separate entity. We emphasize that this discovery should
not be confused with the discovery of representative computational
models (constructed by Turing, Post, Markov, Kolmogorov) which will
be discussed in §2. Sometimes it is wrongly believed that the concept
of algorithm cannot be satisfactorily understood without certain

formal constructions (usually without the models we have just mentioned). But we are of the opinion that these constructions were only introduced in order to provide a formal characterization of the informal concept of algorithm. Thus the concept itself was recognized as existing independently from this formal characterization and as preceding in time. As Gödel indicated in [Göd 58], the question whether Turing's definition of the computability of a function is adequate is meaningless until the notion of a computable function is intelligible a priori. Such a situation is rather typical: the general intuitively understood notion, say, of surface has a sense which is independent of definitions offered in topology and differential geometry. The only difference is that the concept of surface has been known from ancient times (in fact it is mentioned in the first lines of Euclid's "Elements"), while the concept of algorithm has only appeared in the XXth century.

For historians of mathematics it would be instructive to trace the arisal and formation of the concept of algorithm (this process of formation has probably not yet been completed). Euclid and al-Khorezmi gave us the first examples of algorithms which are still used to this day. As for the general notion of algorithm, i.e. of effective computational procedure, the earliest examples of the use of this notion can be found only in the first quarter of the XXth century in the works of Borel (1912) and of Weyl (1921). Borel (see [Bor 12, p. 161]) singles out "les calculs qui peuvent être réellement effectués" and emphasizes: "Je laisse intentionnellement de côté la plus ou moins grande longueur pratique des opérations; l'essentiel est que chacune de ces opérations soit exécutable en un temps fini, par une méthode sûre et sans ambiguïté" (see [Bor 12, p. 162]). Weyl (see [Weyl 21]), while discussing "functio discreta" explicitly singles out the algorithmic mappings from among arbitrary ones. In fact they both arrived at the concept of computable function (and Borel even used the term "fonction calculable" though he had in mind a different algorithmic notion, see below, Part II, §4). In the paper [Church 36] presented in 1935 Church confidently used the term "effectively calculable" function, regarding it as a commonly accepted term preceding any formal characterization. Note that in the early works on the theory of algorithms (see for example [Tu 36], [Tu 37a] and especially [Tu 39, §2]) the term "effectively calculable" referred to an informal notion while the term "computable" referred to the functions computable by a certain computational model. In modern works the term "computable" refers to these both notions while the term "calculable" is not commonly used.

The concept of algorithm like that of set and of natural number is such a fundamental concept that it cannot be explained through other concepts and should be regarded as undefinable one. The statements like "an algorithm is a precise prescription specifying a computational process which starts with some initial datum (chosen from a set fixed for this algorithm) and directed to obtaining a result fully defined by this initial datum" should be regarded only as an explanation and not as a definition. However explanations of this kind are sufficient to establish certain meaningful facts. For example, we can deduce the statement that not every natural-valued function of natural argument can be computed by an algorithm (because the uncountable set of prescriptions is impossible). The more advanced study requires more detailed explanations (see such explanations in [Kol 53], [Kol Us 58] , [Rog 67, §1.1], [Knuth 68, §1.1], [Us 70], [Us 77]). Kolmogorov writes:

"We proceed with the following obvious ideas of algorithms:

1) An algorithm Γ being applied to any "datum" (="initial state") A which belongs to a set $\mathfrak{S}(\Gamma)$ (the domain of the algorithm) gives a "solution" (="final state") B.

2) An algorithmic process is divided into separate steps of limited complexity, each step consisting in "immediate" processing the state S which has been obtained by this moment into the state S* $=\Omega_\Gamma(S)$.

3) The processing of $\overset{0}{A}=A$ into $A^1 =\Omega_\Gamma(A^0)$, A^1 into $A^2 =\Omega_\Gamma(A^1)$, A^2 into $A^3 =\Omega_\Gamma(A^2)$, etc. goes until the unresulted stopping occurs (i.e. if operator Ω_Γ is not defined for the obtained state) or until the signal that the "solution" has been obtained appears. This process can be unlimited in time (if the "solution signal" never appears).

4) Immediate processing of S into S* $=\Omega_\Gamma(S)$ is performed only on the basis of information about the form of the limited "active part" of the state S and affects this active part only" ([Kol 53]).

One of the basic notions in the theory of algorithms is that of constructive object. Only such objects algorithms deal with (see [Šan 62, p. 16], [Mart 70, §1.1], [ErA 77, §2.1], [Nag 79]). The "states" mentioned in Kolmogorov formulation (in particular "datum" and "solution ") are constructive objects.

A word over an alphabet $\mathfrak{b}$ is called a $\mathfrak{b}$-word. Any $\mathfrak{b}$-word for a finite alphabet $\mathfrak{b}$ is a constructive object. Another example:

a finite directed tree with vertices labelled by elements of a finite alphabet Б is a constructive object provided that for each tree vertex a all vertices b such that ⟨a, b⟩ is an edge have different labels. This tree is called Б-tree and if all outdegrees of the vertices are bounded by an integer k then the Б-tree is called (Б, k)-tree.

Kolmogorov in [Kol 53], [Kol Us 58] examined constructive objects of most general type--Kolmogorov complexes. In graph terms Kolmogorov complexes can be defined as follows:

1. A Kolmogorov complex is either a directed graph or an undirected one. Correspondingly it is called a directed Kolmogorov complex or undirected Kolmogorov complex.

2. A Kolmogorov complex is an "initialized" graph, i.e. exactly one of its vertices (initial vertex) is marked out from the others.

3. A Kolmogorov complex is a connected graph, i.e. each of its vertices can be reached via a (directed) path from the initial vertex.

4. Each vertex of a Kolmogorov complex is labelled by a letter of a finite alphabet and for each vertex a all vertices b such that ⟨a, b⟩ is a (directed) edge are labelled by different letters.

If a Kolmogorov complex is labelled by letters of an alphabet Б we call this complex a Kolmogorov complex over Б or a Kolmogorov Б-complex. A directed (respectively, undirected) Kolmogorov Б-complex is called a Kolmogorov (Б, k)-complex if all outdegrees (respectively, degrees) of its vertices are bounded by an integer k. One can wish to work with graphs with labelled edges. In this case it is sufficient to insert a labelled vertex into an edge in order to label it.

Constructive objects are gregarious objects. They naturally flock in special sets, each set consisting of all "similar" objects. Simple examples of such sets are ℕ, Ξ . These special sets such as ℕ, Ξ and so on can be called "herds", "shoals", "flocks" and even "broods". We, however, prefer to call them "aggregates": though this term is rather cumbersome it is more neutral and less zoological.

We do not use here the term "space of constructive objects" as it can easily be confused both with the term "space" of [Shoen 71] which has a slightly different meaning and with the term "space" of complexity theory.

The basic aggregates are: 1) The Б-word aggregate, or the word aggregate over Б , i.e. the set of all Б-words for a finite alphabet Б . 2) The (Б, k)-tree aggregate, i.e. the set of all (Б, k)-trees

for a finite alphabet Б and for an integer k. 3) - 4) The underec-
ted (respectively, directed) (Б, k)-complex aggregate, i.e. the set
of all undirected (respectively, directed) Kolmogorov (Б, k)-comple-
xes for a finite alphabet Б and for an integer k.

   We do not know any other examples of aggregates. It is very likely that the concept of aggregate is in fact more primary than that
of constructive object--no constructive object can be regarded as
existing independently outside an aggregate.

   For any Б the word aggregate over Б can be regarded as the
(Б, 1)-tree aggregate, the root of a tree corresponding to the first
letter of a word. The (Б, k)-tree aggregate is naturally embedded
into the directed (Б, k)-complex aggregate--the root of a tree is
the initial vertex of a complex. If k is not smaller than the cardinality of Б the (Б,k)-complex aggregate consists of all Б-complexes and is called (directed or undirected) Б-complex aggregate.

   As is the case in graph theory, an undirected graph can be regarded as a directed graph of a special kind. So for every Б , k the
undirected (Б, k)-complex aggregate is naturally embedded into the
directed (Б, k)-complex aggregate. It is clear that the Cartesian
product of aggregates can naturally be embedded in another aggregate.
Similarly a set of corteges (=of finite sequences) of elements from
a given aggregate can be embedded in another aggregate. On the contrary, a finite subset of a given aggregate is not immediately a constructive object. So if we wish to work with algorithms over finite
sets, these sets should be represented by corteges provided the results (of computations by our algorithms) do not depend on ordering
of members of corteges. Finally for any two aggregates there exists
one-one correspondence between these aggregates which is given (in
both directions) by two algorithms; such a correspondence is usually
called isomorphism of aggregates.

   Any algorithm implies the existence of two aggregates: "the aggregate X of allowed initial data (or allowed imputs)" and "the aggregate Y of allowed results (or allowed outputs)". The aggregate
X is called input aggregate and the aggregate Y is called   output aggregate. Any algorithm with an input aggregate X and an output aggregate Y is shortly called an X-Y-algorithm. It makes sense
to try to apply an X-Y-algorithm to each element of X and if the
result exists it belongs to Y. The domain of an algorithm is a subset of the input aggregate, this set consists of the inputs for which
the algorithm produces a result. Let A, B be any sets. If the domain
of 𝔄 is a subset of A and each result of 𝔄   belongs to   B

the algorithm $\mathfrak{A}$ is called "algorithm from A into B" (we write:
"$\mathfrak{A}$: A $\longrightarrow$ B".).

§2. Representative computational models.

The discovery discussed in this section is the discovery of well-
outlined and representative classes of algorithms. "Representative"
means that for suitable aggregates X, Y the class contains an algorithm equivalent to (=determining the same function as) any previously given arbitrary X-Y-algorithm.

The problem of the existence of such classes is extremely nontrivial. A priori it is not clear whether a representative class of
algorithms can be described in exact terms and treated as a subject
of study in the set-theoretical mathematics. Historically the first
examples of such classes are the classes of algorithms realized by a
computational model of Turing (see [Tu 36]) and by that of Post (see
[Post 36]).

It is important to understand that representative computational
models are not formalizations of the algorithm concept; they only provide the way to achieve formalization of the notion of computable
(by an algorithm) function. Indeed, if we accept that, the only algorithms are those realized by Turing machines, then Markov algorithms
could not be regarded as algorithms, and we could not measure complexities of computation for Markov algorithms.

Kolmogorov explanation (see §1) gives a general scheme for deterministic and local transformation of constructive objects. All computational models with local transformation of information can easily
be described in Kolmogorov terms. So we call them Kolmogorov-type models. Post and Turing models are examples of these models. On the
other hand the models with non-local steps such as Markov normal algorithms (see [Mark 51], [Mark 54]) or random access machines (see
[Aho Hop Ull 74], [Sli 79]) require a preliminary splitting of each
step into local ones and consequently they are not Kolmogorov-type
models. In order to define a computational model with local transformation of information it is necessary to specify the notions in Kolmogorov formulation (see §1) such as "state", "immediate processing",
"active part", "solution signal". Kolmogorov offered a general scheme
of such a specification in [Kol 53]. This scheme can be regarded as
an adequate formalization of the very notion of algorithm (when dealing with models with non-local transformation of information we agree
to split non-local steps into local ones as mentioned above). We call

the computational model defined by this scheme Kolmogorov
machines.

   Kolmogorov machines can be described as follows (cf. the quotation from [Kol 53] in §1). The states are Kolmogorov complexes from
a ($\mathfrak{b}$, k)-complex aggregate. An active part of a state is a subcomp-
lex constituted by vertices reachable from the initial vertex via
(directed) paths of length not greater than a certain value, fixed
for the machine. Let us denote the set of all vertices of a complex
G by v(G). An operator Ω_Γ is defined by a finite number of inst-
ructions of the form U $\rightarrow$ $\langle W, \gamma, \delta \rangle$ where U, W are complexes, γ
is a mapping from v(U) into v(W) preserving labelling, δ is a
one-one mapping from v(U) into v(W), and for each x $\in$ v(U) the
set of labels of vertices adjacent to $\delta(x)$ is included into the
set of labels adjacent to x. In cases of undirected complexes γ
is to be identical to δ . In order to obtain a new state S* $= \Omega_\Gamma$(S)
we have 1) to find an instruction, say, U $\rightarrow \langle W, \gamma, \delta \rangle$ with the
left side identical to the active part of the state S, then 2) to
extract this active part U and 3) to replace it by the complex W;
mappings γ , δ are used to connect vertices of v(S) $\smallsetminus$ v(U) with
the vertices of v(W) in the following way: for each a $\in$ v(U),
b $\in$ v(S) $\smallsetminus$ v(U) if $\langle$b, a$\rangle$ is an edge of S then $\langle$b, γ(a)$\rangle$ is an
edge of S*, if $\langle$a, b$\rangle$ is an edge of S then $\langle \delta$(a), b$\rangle$ is an
edge of S*; after these connections have been made 4) to eliminate
all vertices of v(S) not reachable from the initial vertex and all
edges incident to them. Thus the new state S* is also a connected
graph. The "solution signal" appears if an active part of a state belongs to a given finite set of complexes.

   For undirected graphs Kolmogorov's approach leads to algorithms
from [Kol Us 58]. A particular form of Kolmogorov machines over directed graphs is examined in [Schön 70], [Schön 79]; actually graphs
from two last papers have labelled edges, but as we have already mentioned in §1 it is not essential.

   Every computational model implies the existence of a certain,
specific for this model, class of formal descriptions of algorithms
which can be realized by this model. For example, for Markov normal
algorithms the role of formal description is played by scheme of a
normal algorithm, for Turing machines by command system, for Kolmogo-
rov machines by set of instructions of the form U $\rightarrow \langle$W, γ, $\delta \rangle$. In
fact to explain a certain model is to give a certain Universal Recipe
which for every formal description and every input permits to obtain
the corresponding output (=result). Provided both formal description

and initial datum has been reasonably coded, the pair $\langle$formal description, initial datum $\rangle$ turns into an element of a suitable aggregate and the Universal Recipe becomes the universal algorithm (see §14 below). Because of the above said the whole theory of algorithms can be treated as a theory of a single universal algorithm constructed on the basis of a certain representative model.

Let's point out those features which distinguish a formal description of algorithm of computation by a given model from an informal notion of algorithm as a prescription, or an order. First, a formal description must be a mathematical object. Then, a formal description describes only the operator of immediate processing, but the starting and concluding procedures (see below) and condition of ending (i.e. description of solution signal) are not included in a formal description. Finally, all orders (=directions) prescribing computations by a given model contain certain general information. For example, in case of Markov normal algorithm such information includes the convention that substitution formula is applied to the first occurrence from the left. For Turing machine the prescription includes the explanation of the notions "tape", "head", "shift to the left", etc. Naturally the general information is not necessarily included in a formal description of a concrete algorithm.

Let X, X', Y, Y' be aggregates. In view of isomorphism of aggregates, every representative class of algorithms from X into Y automatically supplies a representative class of algorithms from X' into Y'. So for the descriptive theory of algorithms (but not for the complexity theory and for the construction of specific algorithms) it is sufficient to study only X-Y-algorithms for arbitrary but fixed X and Y. In particular one can assume that $X = Y$. Then the set of all words over an alphabet can be regarded as X (in case of a one-letter alphabet this set can be treated as the set $\mathbb{N}$ of all natural numbers), cf. [Rog 67, §1.10].

Let a computational model be given and let X and Y be aggregates. Let's agree on a certain <u>starting procedure</u> by which any element $x \in X$ is put into this model in the form of the initial state, and on a certain <u>concluding procedure</u> by which element $y \in Y$ is extracted from the final state. We suppose that these procedures transform an object locally--in "Kolmogorov terms" they are single-step applications of suitable operators of immediate processing. Then any formal description of an algorithm for our model determines the following algorithm from X into Y: an element x is taken as an input, the formal description is applied, the process of application

lasts until the final state appears and "y" is extracted from it.
Thus a certain class of algorithms from X into Y (which, of
course, is well-outlined in view of proposed construction) turns out
to be linked with the computational model. Further on when considering a computational model we shall--for the sake of simplicity--fix
the corresponding aggregates X and Y and omit mentioning the
starting and concluding procedures, regarding them as determined by
the model, input and output aggregates.

So let a computational model, an aggregate X and an aggregate
Y be given. Then if the class of algorithms from X into Y linked to this model (and therefore well-outlined) is representative (in
the sense that for any X-Y-algorithm an equivalent algorithm from
this class can be found) the model is called X-Y-representative. A
model is called representative if it is X-Y-representative for some
X,Y. Turing's and Post's computational models are chronologically
the first examples of representative models. (Post's machine is ℕ-ℕ-
representative and Turing machine is X-Y-representative if X, Y
are word aggregates). Of course, Kolmogorov machines also constitute
a representative model. Moreover, all Kolmogorov machines working in
a suitable (Б,k)-complex aggregate constitute a representative mo-
del--in this case states of a machine are Kolmogorov Б-complexes
over a fixed alphabet Б .

Statement about the representativity of a well-outlined class
of algorithms (i.e. about representativity of the corresponding computational model) forms Church's thesis for this class or for this
model. We understand it in the broad sense (as in [Rog 67, §1.7]).
Church's thesis in the narrow sense states that every computable
natural-valued function of natural argument is partial recursive (see
[Klee 52,§63]). Strictly speaking this formulation should be called
Church - Kleene thesis because the initial Church's formulation relates only to total computable functions and states that they are general recursive (see [Klee 52, §60]). Turing in [Tu 36] and Post in
[Post 36] have asserted that the class of all total functions which can
be computed by certain models coincides with the class of all total
computable functions (for fixed aggregates). Therefore Church's thesis can be called Turing's thesis or Post's thesis or Church - Turing
- Post thesis. Having in mind Kleene's role in the formation of this
thesis--transfer to the partial functions--we can also use the name
Church - Turing - Post - Kleene thesis. In [Post 36] Post called the
statement about the identification of these two classes of functions
"a working hypothesis". He argued: "Actually the work already done

by Church and others carries this identification considerably beyond
the working hypothesis stage. But to mask this identification under
a definition hides the fact that a fundamental discovery in the limitations of the mathematicizing power of Homo Sapiens have been made
and blinds us to the need of its continual verification".

Programming languages can also be regarded as an adequate formalization of the concept of algorithm: indeed, these languages can be
used to define well-outlined and representative class of algorithms.
However, not every meaningful text in a programming language can be
regarded as an algorithm. What is important is that every algorithm
can be expressed in the language. For mathematicians dealing with the
theory of algorithms the languages LISP by McCarthy and ALGOL-68 by
van Wijngaarden are of the main interest. It is possible to construct
abstract programming languages. These abstract languages, in their
turn, can be regarded as formal characterizations of the concept of
algorithm. Among abstract programming languages we single out the language of operator algorithms by A.P. Ershov (see [ErA 62], [ErA 60]).
These algorithms--called then "computational algorithms"--were first
presented in A.P. Ershov's report in February - March 1958 at Novikov
- Yanovskaya Seminar at Moscow University.

§3. <u>The general notion of calculus as an independent (separate)</u>
    <u>concept</u>

The concept of calculus, or deductive system, is as fundamental
as the concept of algorithm and should be regarded separately from
any formal definitions. Roughly speaking a calculus is a system of
permitting rules (also called generation rules, see [Šan 55, §1], or
rules of inference), i.e. the rules which permit to perform certain
operations with constructive objects (unlike an algorithm, which is
a system of prescribing, or directing, rules). Chess rules give us a
typical example of calculus and chess positions serve as constructive objects under operation. Similar to algorithmic processes the
process of **generation**, or the process of **inference**, corresponding to
a calculus can be split into separate steps. At each step a new object is obtained (=deduced) by application of a rule of the calculus
to some objects already obtained (=deduced) which are called premises
of the rule. For each rule the number of premises is fixed. If all
these numbers are not greater than k the calculus is called **k-pre-
mise**. For example, chess can be regarded as one-premise calculus.
For any one-premise calculus $\mathcal{C}$ there exists the inverse one-premise

calculus $\mathcal{C}^{-1}$: calculus $\mathcal{C}^{-1}$ permits immediate transition from a
to b if and only if $\mathcal{C}$ permits immediate transition from b to a.
Any calculus also contains some concluding rules that permit to conclude the process of generation and obtain a <u>generated</u> object from
some deduced objects.

For each algorithm there is a function computed by this algorithm, for each calculus--a set generated by this calculus (in our
example it is the set of positions which can really occur during
chess games). The notion of calculus reflects the intuitive idea of
inductive generation of a set (see [Mas 67], [Eb 70], [Mas 79]). Mathematical roots of the concept of calculus go back to antiquity
(see [Janovs 62]).

Games with strict rules--such as chess or cards--are probably
the earliest examples of calculuses. The differential and integral
calculuses can be regarded as examples of calculuses because they can
be treated as procedures enabling one to generate true equalities of
the form $dF(x) = f(x)dx$ and $\int f(x)dx = F(x)$ starting from initial,
or tabular, equalities and applying rules like the rule of differentiation of composite function or that of integration by parts. Calculuses of mathematical logic, or logistic systems, have played an
important role in the development of the general notion of calculus.
The first logistic systems appeared at the end of the XIXth century
in the work of Frege (see [Frege 1879]).

The general notion of calculus is less popular than the general
notion of algorithm; in particular, the general notion of calculus
with local transformation of information has never been studied at
all. Perhaps the reason for this discrimination can be found in the
general pressure exerted by computational practice.

There is a special class of calculuses which is widely used in
computer science, namely the class of one-premise calculuses. Note
that for any calculus from this class the inverse calculus belong to
the same class. For some reasons calculuses of this class came to be
called "non-deterministic algorithms" which is a terminological mon-
ster (for a calculus is not an algorithm at all and no algorithm can
be non-deterministic). This monstrosity should and could easily be
eliminated. For instance, the central concept connected with so-called nondeterministic algorithms is the concept of set recognizable
by a given nondeterministic algorithm. To define a recognizable set
E for a nondeterministic algorithm $\mathcal{C}$ one must choose an object c,
called "terminal state"; then $e \in E$ if and only if there exists "a
computation" by $\mathcal{C}$ which transforms e to c. Let us put this

definition into calculus terms. Firstly, $e \in E$ if and only if there
is an inference admissible for calculus $\mathcal{C}$ (=an inference in $\mathcal{C}$) of
terminal state c from e. Secondly, c can be deduced from e in
$\mathcal{C}$ if and only if e can be deduced from c by an inference in
the inverse calculus $\mathcal{C}^{-1}$, i.e. e belongs to the set generated by
c in $\mathcal{C}^{-1}$ (so it would be more correct to call c "initial state").
If the state c is fixed one can simply call the set E "recogniz-
able by $\mathcal{C}$ " or, in calculus terms, "generable by $\mathcal{C}^{-1}$". In this way
any nondeterministic algorithm $\mathcal{C}$ can be fully replaced by a suitable one-premise calculus (sometimes by $\mathcal{C}$ itself, sometimes by its
inverse $\mathcal{C}^{-1}$). We shall use this fact below in §7 when discussing
the definition of $\mathcal{NP}$-class, (An example. The card game of patience
can be regarded as a nondeterministic algorithm and the recognizable
set consists of all those orderings of the pack that can be transformed to the correct terminal configuration. This set is also the set
generated by the "inverse patience" which treats the correct configuration as initial, starts with this configuration and proceeds by applying inverse rules.)

It is with the help of the general notion of calculus that some
of the most fundamental results of mathematical logic can be more fully understood. Namely, the famous Gödel completeness theorem states
that the set of all true formulas of the first order predicate logic,
i.e. the set of all laws of elementary predicate logic, can be generated by a calculus; and the famous Gödel incompleteness theorem states that the set of all true formulas of arithmetic (and consequently the set of all formulas valid in the predicate logic of the second
order) can not be generated by a calculus.

§4. Representative generative models.

The discovery is the very possibility of presenting a class of
calculuses which is both well-outlined and representative, i.e. contains an equivalent for any pregiven calculus. (To be more precise
we should not speak about a representative generative model but about
X-representative one. Let X be an aggregate; a generative model is
called X-representative if for any calculus which generates an element of X there exists a calculus for the model which generates
the same element.) The concept of generative model came into existence
in the same way as the concept of computational model did. Post's canonical systems present the earliest example of a representative generative model. However canonical systems (see [Post 43], [Mas 64],

[Mins 67, §12.5 and §13.2], [Mart 70, §2]) are calculuses with non-local transformation of information--in contrast with Post's normal systems (see [Post 43], [Mark 54, chap. VI, §4], [Mas 64], [Mins 67, chap. 13]) which also form a representative generative model. Generative grammars of mathematical linguistics are calculuses with local transformation of information (see [Glad 73], [Glad 77]). The general form of calculuses with local transformation of information (=Kolmogorov-type calculuses) can easily be obtained by constructing natural generative model similar to Kolmogorov machines.

For calculuses as well as for algorithms one can define the notion of formal description. For every generative model there is a "Universal Recipe". For algorithms a "Universal Recipe" is computational while for calculuses it is generative: for a given generative model the Universal Recipe enables one to generate all pairs formed by the formal description of a calculus of this model and by an object generated by this calculus.

§5. Interrelations between algorithms and calculuses.

1) For every algorithm there exists a calculus which generates the domain of this algorithm. Moreover, 2) for every algorithm $\mathfrak{A}$ it is possible to indicate a calculus generating those and only those pairs $\langle x, y \rangle$ for which $\mathfrak{A}(x)=y$. On the other hand, 3) every calculus that generates a single-valued (=functional) set of pairs $\langle x, y \rangle$ can be transformed into an algorithm of transition from x to y. Then, 4) for every algorithm solving the membership problem for any set located in an aggregate there exists a calculus which generates this set. Finally, 5) every calculus can be replaced by an algorithm whose results are just the objects generated by this calculus. Moreover, 6) provided these objects do exist (i.e. the generated set is not empty) it is possible to assume that the domain of the obtained algorithm is the set $\mathbb{N}$ of natural numbers; thus, it turns out that ramified time in which the generating process develops can be replaced by sequential time.

We would like to note that both concepts of algorithm and calculus are understood by the authors in the most general informal sense. Many theorems of algorithm theory--e.g. all theorems of this section --can be formulated and proved only with the use of untuitive understanding without any reference to computational or generative models. This situation is rather typical; of course, a lot of theorems about sets and integers are formulated and even proved without appealing to any formal (e.g. axiomatic) notions.

§6. <u>Time and space as complexities of computation and generation</u>

Realization that every computation has time complexity (time) and space complexity (space) was an important milestone in the development of the concept of algorithm. Study of these concrete complexities began in the middle of the 50's with the works by Trakhtenbrot (see [Trah 56], [Trah 67]) and Tseytin (see [Janovs 59, p. 44]). First of all we shall consider time and space complexities from the general point of view and expose their connection with another fundamental notion of the metric theory of algorithms, namely, the notion of volume of a constructive object.

Intuitively, every computation is performed in the physical Time--so it has some duration, and in the physical Space--so it occupies some room. We want to define abstract notions of duration and room so that the definition should meet our intuitive ideas and be useful in computational practice. These abstract duration and room are integer-valued functions of input of computation. In the theory of algorithms these functions are called "time" and "space".

To formalize our intuitive ideas we have to choose a computational model for which the duration and room will be measured. The choice of a model was irrelevant for the definitions of the notions of computable function and generable set, see §7, as well as for the descriptive theory based on these notions. It is not the case for the definitions of complexity of computation and generation--and for the metric theory. Different models can reflect different aspects of real computations and, of course, lead to different time and space functions. The model widely used in complexity theory is multitape Turing machine. In our opinion the most interesting and convenient from the theoretical and practical complexity point of view is the model of Kolmogorov machines.

Now, let us choose a suitable computational model, fix an algorithm of the computation and take an input. What are the values of time and space functions? Clearly (the value of) <u>space</u> is the maximum volume of memory used in the process of computation. At each step of computation the corresponding state can be regarded as memory used at this step. This interpretation of memory is useful for many purposes. But there is also another approach. Recall that every application of an algorithm begins with the starting procedure which slightly transforms an input, in particular adds something to it. In cer-

tain interesting cases further computation also does not greatly
change an input but only accepts information from it. In other words
in these cases a state of computational process can be divided into
two parts: an immutable input and a mutable memory (well-known example: Turing machine with input tape.) Since space measures only memory volume it does not include volume of input. Of course, for particular computational models the described notions of input and output should be formalized in details.

It is natural to make the second step and distinguish algorithms
with states divided into three parts: 1) input, 2) memory and 3) output. Output is gradually formed and its part already obtained remains
unchanged. Now we see that in every case the definition of space complexity requires the notion of memory volume, i.e. the notion of volume of a constructive object. We shall postpone for a while the discussion of this notion and turn to time complexity.

The first answer to the posed question about time is: (the value
of) time is the number of steps in the process of computation. Is the
number of steps in accordance with the intuitive notion of computational duration? From a certain point of view--no. Really, in practical
computations different steps have different durations. On the other
hand, in theoretical considerations the way of measuring time as the
number of steps also leads to the following undesirable effect: we
can blow up steps of computation by uniting several consecutive
steps into one macro-step and obtain a "new" computation which is as
a matter of fact the old one, but has smaller number of steps. This
effect is utilized by the so-called linear speed-up theorem, see below in
the next section. To sum up: <u>time</u> of computation is the sum of durations of all computational steps. The latter point of view on computational time is not commonly accepted though used in study of computational models with non-local transformation of information--random
access machines (see [Aho Hop Ull 74, chap. 1]). There are different
ways to estimate the duration of a computational step. For Kolmogorov-
type models one way is to measure the duration by the volume of the
changed part of a state, i.e. by the volume of the left (to be definite) side of the instruction to be performed. Of course, there is
another way. One can simply assign the duration equal to one to each
step of computation. It is evidently equivalent to the definition of
time as a number of steps. Speaking about time as the sum of durations
we shall always suppose that duration would be equal to the volume
of the changed part of a state. In this Part of our paper, however,
save for the linear speed-up theorem (see §7), it makes no difference

which understanding of time we use--time as a number of steps or
time as the sum of durations of steps. We shall return to the point
in Part II, §8.

Let us stress now that the sum-of-durations way of measuring
time as well as   measuring space requires the notion of volume of
a constructive object: in case of time we need volume of an active
part of a state while in case of space we need memory volume. There
is one more reason for introducing the notion of volume of a constructive object, namely, the study of complexity of these objects,
see below, §17. This notion, or, to be more exact, the notion of volumed aggregate, is very important for the metric theory of algorithms.

One can try to define the notion of volumed aggregate axiomatically. We do not know if someone has done this, but we think requirements formulated in [Kol 65], [Blum 67a] can be useful in an axiomatic definition.

An <u>aggregate with volume</u>, or a <u>volumed aggregate</u>, is a pair $\langle X,$
$1 \rangle$, where X is an aggregate and 1 is a "volume" function mapping X into ℕ. Basic example: $X= \Xi$, $1(x)$ is the length of a
word $x \in \Xi$. Of course, some other volumes can be introduced on Ξ ,
but we shall not consider them and when writing $\langle \Xi, 1 \rangle$ we shall always presume that 1 is the length.

Let us note that the word "volume" has two different meanings:
1) $volume_1$ is a volume of an object, i.e. $volume_1$ is an integer;
2) $volume_2$ is a mapping which puts into correspondence to each object
   (of a pregiven aggregate) its $volume_1$, i.e. $volume_2$ is a function
   on an aggregate (=volume function). The same is true of the words
   "time", "space", etc.

Theorems of the descriptive theory of algorithms do not depend
on a particular aggregate they use. This important Invariance Property is secured because any two aggregates are isomorphic. If we want
to secure this property for the theorems using (in addition to the
means of the descriptive theory) only volumed aggregates we have to
define properly volume functions and isomorphisms of volumed aggregates. To define isomorphisms of that kind we shall first give the
definition of bounded-distortion mapping. Let two volumed aggregat-
es $\langle X, 1 \rangle$ and $\langle Y, 1 \rangle$ be given; we say a mapping f: $X \rightarrow Y$ is a
<u>bounded-distortion mapping</u> if the condition
$$1(f(x)) \lesssim 1(x)$$
holds for all $x \in X$. If f is given by an algorithm $\mathfrak{D}: X \rightarrow Y$
we call this $\mathfrak{D}$ <u>bounded-distortion algorithm</u>. An <u>isomorphism</u> of volumed aggregates $\langle X, 1 \rangle$ and $\langle Y, 1 \rangle$ is an isomorphism of X

120

and Y given back and forth by bounded-distortion algorithms.

Now we want to define volumes on various aggregates so as to guarantee the isomorphism of volumed aggregates to be obtained.

As a matter of fact in the works on complexity theory we can
find only one type of volume, namely, the length of words. We take
the length of binary words as our main example of volume. Unfortunately we find that the length of words over other alphabets do̶es̶ not satisfy us for volumed aggregates in this case are not isomorphic to
the standard aggregate $\langle \Xi , 1\rangle$. For this reason we take the following (natural, in our opinion) definition of volume on word aggregat-
es. We denote by $\lfloor \alpha \rfloor$ the greatest integer not exceeding a real number α . For $x \in \mathbb{N}$ we define $l(x)$ as $\lfloor \log_2(x+1) \rfloor$. Let an alphabet b consists of n letters and let x be a word over b. If n=1
we put $l(x)=\lfloor \log_2(1+\text{length } x)\rfloor$. If $n \geqslant 2$ we define $l(x)$ as $\lfloor \text{length}$
$x \cdot \log_2 n \rfloor$. So bb has volume equal to 2 as a word over the alpha-
bet $\{a, b\}$ and the volume equal to 4 as a word over $\{a, b, c, d,$
$e, f\}$. Isomorphisms between the defined volumed aggregates are easi-
ly constructed. In particular the aggregate $\langle \mathbb{N}, 1\rangle$ is isomorphic to
the aggregate $\langle \Xi , 1\rangle$ under the following mapping we shall fix in
the sequel: zero $\leftrightarrow$ empty word, one $\leftrightarrow$ O, two $\leftrightarrow$ 1, three $\leftrightarrow$ 00,
four $\leftrightarrow$ 01, ... In fact, this isomorphism does not change volumes
at all. We do not know how volume for other (not word) aggregates
can be defined. Of course, it is easy to define a volume function on
an aggregate to provide isomorphism between the obtained volumed aggregate and the volumed aggregate $\langle \Xi, 1\rangle$. In the sequel we shall
suppose that such volumes and isomorphisms exist. However it is natural to put further conditions on volumed aggregates. For example,
if we consider a b-complex aggregate it is nice to have a volume on
it which is an extension of the volume on the b-word aggregate.
Another requirement is "continuity" of volume. Namely, when we locally (i.e. by application of Kolmogorov's operator of immediate processing) transform a constructive object its volume can change only to
a constant which depends only on an operator but not on an object.
If we want to save Invariance Property for theorems dealing with objects of descriptive theory as well as with volumed aggregates and
space complexity it seems natural to require that all bounded mappings
forming isomorphisms between volumed aggregates must be performed by
algorithms such that their computation space $\leqslant$ volume of input
(and, consequently, $\leqslant$ volume of output).

In most works on complexity theory input aggregates and output
aggregates are realized as word aggregates over certain alphabets.

Usually these alphabets contain more than one letter. Speaking about computational complexity we consider only those alphabets.

If we do not want to include input and output into memory, we must formalize the division of computation state into three parts. For this purpose input and output devices through which connection between memory, input, and output is established are usually introduced. Besides more accurate measuring of space, the introduction of input and output devices has some further advantages. Input data and output results can now belong to aggregates which have no relation to aggregates of memory of a computational model. For example one can consider Turing machine with one-dimensional memory tapes which has access to two-dimensional information array through its input device or--another example --Kolmogorov machines with input being supplied with words over an alphabet which are not allowed to stick to two different letters of the word at the same time. Comparing complexity of computations for various computational models it seems natural to modify each model so that all of them would have the same "standard" input and output devices (in addition to the same aggregates of input and output data). Tape on which an input word is written together with a reading (but not writing) head is considered to be a standard input device; the head can move along the tape in two directions remaining within the written word (sometimes models with one-way move of the reading head or with several reading heads are regarded). It makes sense, however, to consider input data of more general form, for example, labelled trees and corresponding input devices. A "standard" output device is a tape with a writing head which is put to and moves in one direction. Certainly if the objects of more general type than words are regarded as initial data then both results and input devices will be of more general type. Surely the definitions of input and output tapes can easily be formulated in terms of division of state into three parts. For Kolmogorov machines input-memory-output partition can be done in the following manner. Kolmogorov machines with separate input and output are Kolmogorov machines with states of a special type. First we replace states by triples $\langle$ In, Mem, Out $\rangle$ $(= \langle$ Input, Memory, Output $\rangle$) and then define states through triples. For each step of computation In, Mem, and Out are Kolmogorov complexes with mutually disjoint sets of vertices, and initial vertices, say, i_0, m_0, q_0. Then the state S of the computation is the union of In, Mem, Out supplemented with two edges--(m_0, i_0) and (m_0, q_0)-- and the only initial vertex m_0. For each step of computation In equals to the input of the algorithm (but may have a different initial vertex) and Out contains the output of the preceeding step (save for the first step, of course). The containment means here that all old (labelled) vertices and edges remain, some new vertices and edges can be added, and "initial" mark can be moved to a new vertex. Later on speaking about multitape and multidimensional Turing machines and Kolmogorov machines we shall imply the existence of input and output devices and therefore shall not include volumes of inputs and outputs in space of computation. In case of Post and one-tape Turing machines we traditionally don't introduce input and output devices. It follows then that their computational space is not less than the length of input and output. For theoretical and practical reasons it is important to know in what way complexities of computation of a function by different computational models are related. Comparative study of usual computational models shows that every function computable in time T by Post machine can be computed in the same or less time by one-tape Turing machine. Thus Post machines are not faster than one-tape Turing machines. Denoting the relation "not faster" by $\leqslant$ one can write "Post machines" $\leqslant$ "one-tape Turing machines" $\leqslant$ "multi-tape Turing machines" $\leqslant$ "Turing machines with multidimensional tapes" $\leqslant$ "Kolmogorov machines over undirected graphs" $\leqslant$ "Kolmogorov machines over directed graphs". On the other hand it turns out that the difference in time of computation of functions by different computational models is not so serious: if a function $\Psi: \mathbb{N} \longrightarrow \mathbb{N}$ is computable by Kolmogorov machines over directed graphs in time T then it is computable by a suitable Post machine in time $T^{2,5}+c$ for an integer c. If one consider space of computation instead of time the situation turns out to be more simple. For models listed above any function computable on a certain space by one of them is computable on the same space multiplied by some constant by any other of those models (of course for one-tape Turing machines only computations on space not less than the length of input and output are considered).

The study of time and space of computation raises a natural question: Does any relation between these complexities exist? This relation can easily be found: it is clear that no computation short in time can use too large memory and that no accomplished computation on a given space can be too long in time. For example, for every Turing machine there exists a number k such that space S and time T satisfy the inequality $S \leqslant kT$, and if $T(x) < \infty$ —the inequality $T(x) \leqslant k^{S(x)}$. Nontrivial theorem on the relation between

time and space is (see [Hop Paul Valia 77]): every predicate computable by a multitape Turing machine in time T can be computed by
some multitape Turing machine on space $\frac{cT}{\log T}$, where c is a constant.

Concepts of time and space of generation can be defined for calculuses similarly to the corresponding concepts for algorithms (see
[Glad 73, chap. 2 and chap. 7]). In particular if volume of memory
is determined in a suitable way then a generation on space smaller
than the volume of the generated element becomes possible. Additional effects appear because the same objects can be generated in several ways. In this case complexity can be defined as minimum complexity of all the ways of generation. As examples of theorems on the complexity of generation we can cite theorems on "nondeterministic algorithms", in particular, hierarchy theorems for nondeterministic
Turing machines (see [Sei Fi Mey 78]). In view of §3 they can be regarded as theorems about complexity of generation for the corresponding one-premise generative models.

Finally, an important part of the complexity theory is constructing specific efficient algorithms for solving particular problems
and proving that these algorithms have pregiven bounds of complexity
(i.e. that they are really effective). This constitutes an important
field of applied complexity theory (see Part II, §8).

§7. Computable functions and generable sets; decidable sets;
enumerable sets

A computable function is a function which can be computed by an
algorithm. By the words "can be computed" we mean that when applied
to any input, the computing algorithm must produce a result identical
to the function value for this input if the value exists and must
produce no result at all if the function is not defined for this input. Let A be a subset of an aggregate and B be a subset of an
aggregate; by Com (A, B) we denote the class of all informally computable functions from A into B, so Com (A, B) $\subset \mathcal{F}$(A, B). If we
have an X-Y-representative model, X, Y being arbitrary aggregates,
we, of course, can formally define Com (X, Y) as the class of all
functions from $\mathcal{F}$(X, Y) which can be computed by this model.

A generable set is a set generated by a calculus (again in the
sense that all the elements of this set and nothing else are generated). Every aggregate is generable. The concept of generable set has
been introduced and studied by Post (see [Post 44]) though he used

the term "generated set". Let A be a subset of an aggregate. The class of all generable subsets of A is denoted by Gen(A). So Gen(A) ⊂ 2^A, where 2^A is the class of all subsets of A. For any X-representative generative model the class Gen(X) can be formally defined as the class of all subsets of X which can be generated by this model.

A set is called <u>decidable</u>, or recognizable, if it is contained in an aggregate and there is a decision algorithm for this set. An algorithm 𝒰 is called a <u>decision algorithm</u> for a subset A of an aggregate X if the set of allowed inputs for 𝒰 coincides with X and 𝒰 answers all questions: Does x ∈ X belong to A? The problem of finding   such an algorithm is called a decision problem for A (cf. Part II, §1). So a set is decidable if and only if its decision problem is solvable (i.e. has a solution).

The concepts of generable and decidable sets make it possible to clarify many central ideas and results of mathematical logic. Thus, for example, the most important requirement to any reasonable formalization of the idea of proof is that a set of all proofs of a given logistic system has to be decidable. In essence, the completeness and incompleteness Gödel theorems state the generability of one set and non-generability of the other.

Concepts of computable function and of generable set are closely interrelated. One of the main interrelations is the criterion of the decidability of a set: a set A situated in an aggregate W is decidable if and only if A ∈ Gen(W) & (W∖A) ∈ Gen(W). Evidently, the decidability of a set is also equivalent to the computability of its characteristic function. Other relations are immediate consequences of the relations between algorithms and calculuses listed in §5. Thus the domain of any computable function is a generable set. Then, a function is computable if and only if this function regarded as a set of pairs is generable. So the generability can be used in order to define the concept of computable function. It is indeed a remarkable historical fact that both first versions of formal definition of this notion   consisted in identification (proposed by Church, see [Church 36]) of computable function with function generated (as a set of pairs) by a calculus of a special type; namely, by Church - Kleene   λ-conversion calculus in the first case and by Herbrand - Gödel calculus in the second.

Any two infinite generable sets W and W' are isomorphic-- there exists a one-one computable mapping of W onto W'; the computability of this mapping implies the computability of the inverse

mapping. Under any such isomorphism any generable (respectively, decidable) subset of W corresponds to a generable (respectively, decidable) subset of W'. This correspondence induces the obvious one-
one correspondence between Gen(W) and Gen(W'). Now let X be isomorphic to X' and Y be isomorphic to Y'; under these isomorphisms
every computable function from X into Y corresponds to a computable function from X' into Y', so the obvious correspondence between Com(X, Y) and Com (X', Y') arises. Therefore, when studying
generable sets and computable functions, one can fix special generable sets W, X, Y and consider only subsets of W and functions
from X into Y. Often $\mathbb{N}^s$ serves as X and $\mathbb{N}$ serves as Y and
W. Under this approach the subject of the theory of computable func-
tions is the family of computable functions $\mathbb{N}^s \rightarrow \mathbb{N}$ (for all s).
Any function belonging to $\bigcup_{s=0}^{\infty} \mathcal{F}(\mathbb{N}^s, \mathbb{N})$ is called number-theoretic. Study of computability
of number-theoretic functions plays the central role in the general theory of algorithms.

An **enumerable set** is either a range of a total computable function of natural argument or empty. In view of statement 6) from §5,
every non-empty generable set is enumerable. Thus both Gödel theorems
mentioned above can be formulated in terms of enumerability and non-
enumerability of the corresponding sets.

One of the main motives to introduce the concepts of time and
space complexity is the desire to order all computations according
to their complexity. This ordering in its turn enables us to classify computable functions and predicates according to the complexity
of computation. A class of such classification for a given computational model and for a given upper bound of complexity consists of
all functions or predicates such that there exists an algorithm (for
their computation by a given model) with complexity not greater than
a given bound. As a rule, the role of such bounds is played by functions depending only on the length of input. All the theorems formulated below were proved by their authors only for these functions.
We however don't think it reasonable to narrow the class of bounds
beforehand (see also the end of §17). There are functions which are
prominent among all upper bounds; these functions are known as "con-
structible functions" (see [Aho Hop Ull 74]). A function f is called **time-constructible** by a given computational model if there exists
an algorithm with the time of computation equal to f. Similarly by
substituting space for time **space-constructible** functions are defined.

The fundamental opportunity to classify computable functions according to their complexity of computation is provided by the hierarchy theorems. The hierarchy theorem for a given computational model and for a given complexity (of time or of space) indicates what decrease of complexity leads to the narrowing of the class of functions (or predicates) computable with this complexity. In particular for multitape Turing machines and for Komogorov machines there is a following theorem on space-hierarchy (see [Sei 77]). Let S be a space-constructible function, $S(x) \geqslant \log \log l(x)$, and let S_1 be any function satisfying the condition $\lim \frac{S_1(x)}{S(x)} = 0$; then there exists a set of words recognizable on space S and not recognizable on space bounded by S_1. Thus, characteristic function of this set belongs to the class determined by the upper bound S and does not belong to the class determined by the upper bound S_1. In this theorem the condition $S(x) \geqslant \log \log l(x)$ is due to the fact that the initial data are words. Probably, this condition can be weakened if initial data of more general form are allowed. As to words, any set recognizable on space $o(\log \log l(x))$ can be recognized on space zero (see [Hop Ull 69, theorem 10.8]). Theorem on time-hierarchy is different for different computational models. For example, in case of multitape Turing machines it can be formulated as follows. Let T be a time-constructible function, $T(x) \geqslant l(x)$ and let T_1 be any function satisfying the condition

$$\lim_{n \to \infty} \max_{l(x)=n} \frac{T_1(x) \log T_1(x)}{T(x)} = 0.$$ Then there exists a set of words

recognizable in time T but not recognizable in time bounded by T_1 (see [Sei Fi Mey 78]). For many practically interesting functions T, for instance, polynomials and exponents, it is possible to replace $\log T_1(x)$ in the previous theorem by $\log^{\alpha} T_1(x)$ where α is an arbitrary positive number (see ibid.). It is not known if it is possible to do this in the general case. For Kolmogorov algorithms it is possible to strengthen the hierarchy theorem, namely, we can omit the term $\log T_1(x)$ in the previous formulation.

The linear speed-up theorem gives a "limit of exactness" of classification of computable functions by their computational times (see [Hop Ull 69, §10.3]), if we use the definition of time as the number of computational steps (see §6). So, let us use this definition; for Kolmogorov machines and multitape Turing machines theorem of linear speed-up looks as follows. For an arbitrary positive number c any function computable by these models in time bounded by T can be computed in time bounded by $\max \{cT, (1+c)(l(x)+l(f(x)))\}$.

127

It is almost evident that for any Kolmogorov-type algorithm
there exists some constant C for which (number-of-steps time)
(sum-of-durations time) ≤ C·(number-of-steps time). Using this argument everybody can easily verify that each theorem of this section
--save for linear speed-up theorem--is valid for both definitions of
time.

Practical needs have stimulated study of classes of functions
having in a certain sense small complexity of computation and of
classes of sets having small complexity of generation. One can consider all the functions computable in time that linearly depends on
the length of inputs. (Usually they are simply called functions computable in linear time, so in the sequel we shall omit the words
"the length of inputs"). Here however we must specify the model by
which the computation is performed. Indeed, there are predicates computable in linear time by a multitape Turing machine though its computation by a one-tape machine requires quadratic time (see [Bar 65],
[Hop Ull 69, theorem 10.7]). On the other hand, for many practically
interesting functions time of computation by the known algorithms
is bounded by a polynomial but is not bounded by any linear function,
time of computation of superposition of two functions is, certainly,
also bounded by a polynomial, degrees of these polynomials being arbitrary. At the same time as we have already seen in §6, if time of
computing a function is polynomially bounded for a certain computational model it is also polynomially bounded for any other model we
have considered. Thus we arrive at the definition of one of the most
important classes of computable functions, namely class $\mathcal{P}$. Class $\mathcal{P}$
consists of all functions computed by Kolmogorov machines in polynomially bounded (in inputs volume) time; the same notation is used
for the corresponding class of predicates (and sets).

Of course, for every aggregates X, Y we can define X-Y-$\mathcal{P}$
class of functions as the subclass of $\mathcal{P}$ which consists of functions
computed by X-Y-algorithms in polynomial time. Similarly to the situation in the descriptive theory of algorithms we may consider only
fixed X, Y. Indeed, save for word aggregates over one-letter alphabets we can set isomorphisms between different word and Kolmogorov
complex aggregates by Kolmogorov-type algorithms with polynomial working time. For this and other reasons mentioned above we
could fix a suitable computational model (e.g. multitape Turing machines) different from Kolmogorov machines and even fix input-output
aggregates in the definition of $\mathcal{P}$ (e.g. take ⊂ for an input aggregate and for an output aggregate).

The class of sets generated by one-premise Kolmogorov-type calculuses in time bounded by a polynomial in the volume of generated elements is denoted by $\mathcal{NP}$. This class is as important to the theory of calculuses as the class $\mathcal{P}$ of all sets which are decidable in polynomial time is to the theory of algorithms. Traditionally the class $\mathcal{NP}$ is defined as a class of sets recognizable in polynomial time by nondeterministic Turing machine (see [Aho, Hop Ull 74, §10.2]). But in view of §3 and our discussion of X-Y-$\mathcal{P}$ classes above we do not think that this definition is terminologically appropriate one.

From the point of view of "practical" polynomial theory of algorithms and calculuses the classes $\mathcal{P}$ and $\mathcal{NP}$ are similar to those of decidable and of generable sets. The classes $\mathcal{P}$ and $\mathcal{NP}$ are classes of sets recognizable or, respectively, generable in time that depends polynomially on the volume of an element of the set provided that information is locally transformed at each step of application of recognizing algorithm or of generating calculus. Here are the examples of sets from the class $\mathcal{P}$:

1) an arbitrary context-free language (see [Young 67], [Valia 74]):
2) the set of pairs of isomorphic planar graphs (see [Hop Tarj 72], [Hop Wong 74]):
3) the set of all systems of linear inequalities with integer coefficients which are solvable in real (and consequently in rational) numbers (see [Hač 79]).

And here are the examples of sets from the class $\mathcal{NP}$:

1) an arbitrary context language;
2) the set of all pairs of isomorphic graphs;
3) the set of all solvable in integers systems of linear inequalities with integer coefficients.

We would like to note that many of practically important problems belong to $\mathcal{NP}$ (in the sense that the set of objects satisfying the conditions of the problem is a set from the class $\mathcal{NP}$). It is clear that $\mathcal{P} \subset \mathcal{NP}$. The problem if it is true that $\mathcal{P} = \mathcal{NP}$ is an important unsolved problem.

§8. <u>The concept of μ-recursive function.</u>

As said in §7 the important problem is to study the class $\bigcup_S \mathrm{Com}\,(\mathbb{N}^S, \mathbb{N})$. This class is defined as a class of all computable number-theoretic functions. Computability is understood here in an intuitive sense on the basis of the informal mathematical notion of algorithm. The prominent and unexpected fact is that the class $\bigcup_S \mathrm{Com}(\mathbb{N}^S,$

N) can be described in purely functional terms, without any use of a computational or generative model. This discovery is due to Kleene. Namely, Kleene found out that the concept of computable number-theoretic function coincides in extension with the concept of μ-recursive function he introduced (see [Klee 43]). When we use the term "μ-recursive" to denote Kleene's notion we follow, for example, [Her 65, chap. 3] and [Mart 70, §6]. A "μ-recursive" function is defined as a number-theoretic function obtained from the fixed set of simple initial functions by applications of an arbitrary number of fixed simple operators (see [Her 65, chap. 3], [Mal 65, §2], [Us 60, n°2.3, n°2.7, and n°3.5]). These initial functions are zero constant and successor function ($x \longmapsto x+1$); these operators are substitution (in the broad sense of [Us 60, n°2.3]), primitive recursion, and minimization (or μ-operator). The fact that this concept is equivalent to the concept of computable functions makes it possible to study the completely new (from the logical point of view) concept of computability by standard algebraic and functional methods.

Of course a system of functions and operators used to define μ-recursive function is not a unique one. For example from practical programming point of view all operators determined by operator schemes can naturally be taken as a set of operators . These sets of simple functions which make it possible to obtain all computable functions are constructed in [ErA 60]. Now the problem naturally arises --to find conditions sufficient and/or necessary for a given system of functions and operators to generate the whole class of computable functions (and only this class). For the system of operators consisting of all operator schemes (in other words, of all standard program schemes) this problem has been posed in [ErA Lja 67]. The solution of the problem in one particular case can be found in [Nep 72], [Nep 72a].

The method used to define μ-recursive functions later on was applied for constructing numerous hierarchies of computable functions. These hierarchies don't use the concept of complexity of computation. A higher class is defined starting with a lower one and with the use of a set of fixed functions and operators so that every successive class is obtained from the preceding one by addition of a certain function and application--in arbitrary number--of operators. It is remarkable, however, that classes naturally obtained in this way prove to be closely related with those arising in computational complexity theory (see [Muč 70]).

§9. <u>Possibility of arithmetical and even Diophantine representation</u>
<u>of any enumerable set of natural numbers</u>.

An arithmetical, or polynomial, term is an expression obtained
from natural numbers and variables by the operations of addition and
multiplication. In other words, it is a polynomial with natural coefficients. A polynomial equality is an equality of two polynomial terms.
Any polynomial equality in n variables defines a certain n-ary
relation and consequently defines a set of points in N^n. This relation and this set are called <u>polynomial</u>. A relation obtained from polynomial one by quantifiers (and respectively a set obtained from a
polynomial set by projections and complementations) is called <u>arith-</u>
<u>metical</u>.

Any enumerable set of either natural numbers of corteges of fixed length of natural numbers is arithmetical. This fact is a consequence of Gödel's proposition from [Göd 31], namely the proposition
V which states that any primitive recursive relation is arithmetical
(see also [Klee 52, §49]). Now it is clear that the arithmetical representation of enumerable sets implies the incompleteness of arithmetic (because of the existence of an enumerable set of natural numbers such that its complement is not enumerable), see [Da Mat RobJ 76].

If only existential quantifiers (or operations of projection respectively) are used an arithmetical relation (or set) is called
<u>Diophantine</u> (see [Mat 79], [Mat 79a]). As Matijasević has establish-
ed (see [Mat 70], [Mat 71], [Mat 72]) any enumerable set or corteges
of fixed length of natural numbers is Diophantine. Theorem on Diophantine representation of any enumerable set strengthens not only the
result of arithmetical representation of this set but the following
result as well: any enumerable set can be presented as a projection
of a decidable one. (This decidable set can be chosen as a set of dimension of the enumerable set increased by one; in case of polynomial
sets it is sufficient to increase dimension by 9, see [Mat 77], [Mat
77a]).

From Matijasević's theorem on Diophantine representation of enumerable sets another remarkable representation for these sets can be
obtained (see [Da Mat RobJ 76]): every enumerable set can be represented as a set of values of an appropriate polynomial with integer coefficients whose variables range over natural numbers.

The possibility of arithmetical and all the more Diophantine representation of enumerable sets shows the specific role of operations
of addition and multiplications in mathematics (cf. also Tennenbaum's

theorem in Part II, §5 below).

§10. Construction of an undecidable generable set.

An undecidable generable set can be constructed in an arbitrary aggregate X. From the philosophical point of view this fact clarifies the relation between the notions of decidability and generability. Namely there exists a calculus such that there is no algorithm to decide whether or not an arbitrary element of X is generated by this calculus. On the other hand, from the practical point of view it is remarkable that all decision problems naturally arising in mathematical practice (i.e. problems of constructing of decision algorithms) are decision problems for generable sets (of course in the very theory of algorithms and calculuses as well as in mathematical logic there are also decision problems of different, more complicated kind). This phenomenon can be partly explained if one takes into account the following property of sets whose decidability is studied in mathematical practice: x belongs to a set if and only if there exists t related to x by a pregiven computable relation. It is clear that any such set is generable. The existence of an undecidable generable set is equivalent to the existence of a computable function which cannot be extended to a total computable function. This set and this function can be easily constructed by the diagonal method (see, for example, [Kol 54]).

Thus a procedure of generation of a set $P \subset X$ is not necessarily accompanied by a decision procedure. But if there exists a function defined for each element $x \in X$ and limiting the complexity of generation of x for $x \in P$ then a corresponding decision procedure exists. Naturally the question of the relation between the generation complexity and the decision complexity for the same set arises. On the one hand, for each algorithm recognizing a decidable set in some time and on some space on can easily construct a calculus generating the same set and having less or equal time and space complexity. On the other hand, the following theorem holds for most computational and generative models: for an arbitrary space-constructible function S any set generable on a space S is recognizable on the space cS^2 where c is a constant (see [Aho Hop Ull 74, theorem 10.1]). This theorem was proved independently by Savitch (see [Sav 70]) and (in 1970) by Tseytin (see, e.g. [Nep 74]). It is not known whether it is possible to replace S^2 by a lower bound, for example, by S. As to time, all important problems are unsolved. In particular it is not known whether the classes $\mathcal{P}$ and $\mathcal{NP}$ coincide. The problem of coincidence of these two classes is quite important and has the following practical meaning: "Do problems arising in practice (problems from the class $\mathcal{NP}$) belong to the class of really solvable problems (to the class $\mathcal{P}$)?"

Nevertheless there exists a class of algorithms and the corresponding class of calculuses for which naturally defined classes of "generable", "enumerable", and "decidable" sets coincide. This class consists of all algorithms realized by finite automata. However it turned out that the concept of finite-automaton (f.a.) decidability is not equivalent to that of f.a. generability and f.a. enumerability in different quantitative sense (though even in this quantitative sense concepts of f.a. generability and f.a. enumerability coincide in extension). For finite automata it proves to be "practically impossible" to put into correspondence a decision (f.a.) algorithm to any enumerating algorithm: for some enumerating algorithms it requires exponential growth of size (i.e. of the number of states) of a computational device (see [ErY 62], [Kor 63]). The same is true if we try to go from finite-automaton calculuses to finite-automaton algorithms (see [Lup 63]).

§11. Post's reducibility problem.

The very submission for consideration of this problem is a discovery. During the study of decision problems for undecidable generable sets arising in mathematical practice it was noticed that these decision problems (which, of course, have no solution) can, in a sense, be reduced to each other. Namely, the non-existence of solution for any of such problems can be deduced from the non-existence of the solution for any other. Let us underline that we don't mean all imaginable undecidable generable sets but only those of them which historically appeared (including all possible concrete examples of "diagonal" sets). Therefore the unsolvability of decision problem for any such set can be reduced to the unsolvability of a "standard" decision problem for a diagonal set. This very reduction—directly or indirectly—is often being made in mathematical practice. The natural problem arises whether this phenomenon is of universal character, i.e. if it is true that all decision problems for all imaginable undecidable generable sets are reduced to each other. Of course the term "are reduced" needs a formal definition. The problem itself is known as the reducibility problem. Together with the cor-

responding formal definition it was proposed by Post in his address
[Post 44] in 1944. In the same address Post gave examples of undecidable generable sets whose undecidability can be naturally proved without any use of a standard problem (these were the first examples of such unusual proofs of undecidability of sets). Of course it was not a solution of the reducibility problem. Moreover Post and his followers managed to find the traditional proofs of undecidability for his sets based on unsolvability of a standard problem. Post's reducibility problem was fully and negatively solved by Muchnik (see [Muč 56], [Muč 58]) and Friedberg (see [Fried 57]): they constructed undecidable generable sets with non-equivalent decision problems (and consequently--a generable set whose undecidability can be ascertained only by methods different from the diagonal one, about the diagonal method see [Šen' 79]).

The refinement of the concept of reducibility of decision problems (which is a pre-condition for formal stating of Post's problem) was effected, as we have already mentioned, by Post in [Post 44]. For arbitrary problems A and B the reducibility of B to A means something more than the implication "A has a solution $\Rightarrow$ B has a solution" (the implication is trivially true if both problems are solvable or both unsolvable). If A and B are problems then the problem of reducing B to A is a new problem. Kolmogorov was apparently the first who pointed out this circumstance in [Kol 32] (cf. Part II, §2). If A and B are decision problems the following interpretation seems to be natural and this very interpretation was proposed by Post. Let X and Y be aggregates, $P \subset X$, $Q \subset Y$, A and B be the decision problems respectively for P and Q. According to Post, B is reducible to A or, in other words, Q is decision reducible to P if there exists a method to transform the information on the question--whether or not an element from X belongs to P--into the information: whether or not an element from Y belongs to Q. This decision reducibility was then made more concrete and rendered more precise by Post as Turing reducibility (see [Rog 67, §9.4]). The exact definition of Turing reducibility (and therefore of decision reducibility) will be given in the next section. Here we content ourselves with the informal notion of decision reducibility.

Post's problem stimulated two directions, or trends, of the research. The first tries to answer the question: Can Post's problem be solved by Post's original methods (from his address [Post 44])? Namely, can any non-complete enumerable undecidable set be constructed by Post's methods? (A set is called complete if it is enumerable

and any enumerable set can be decision reduced to it; so all "diagonal" sets are complete.) Post's methods can be understood in a specific or in a general sense. Accordingly there are two possible ways
to formulate the question:

1) Is there any non-empty property of enumerable sets as to have a
   small ("almost-finite", see [Rog 67, §12.6]) complement such that
   any set satisfying this property is not complete?
2) Is it possible to formulate (without any use of the concept of
   "Turing reducibility") a non-trivial property of enumerable undecidable sets such that any set satisfying this property is not
   complete?

Post himself considered various concepts like "almost-finiteness"
of complement such as simpleness, hypersimpleness, hyperhypersimple-
ness). Neither of them (and even the stronger concept of maximalness
later introduced by Friedberg) as turned out was able to provide an
affirmative answer to the first question. (The existence of the complete maximal sets is proved in [Yates 65].)

Marchenkov in [Marč 76] answered affirmatively the second question. He proved that no enumerable undecidable set with a certain
property (namely, no set which is semirecursive and α-hypersimple
for a positive equivalence α) can be complete. The existence of
sets with this property was established by Degtev in [Deg 73].

The first direction is closely connected with the study of the
structure of a set situated in a fixed aggregate (for example one
can be interested in density of this set in the aggregate or in the
amount of enumerable subsets of its complement). Depending on the complement structure any enumerable (=generable) set can be referred to
one or an another class (see [Rog 67, §8.7]). An enumerable set can
be decidable (if its complement is enumerable), or simple (if its
complement, though infinite, contains no infinite enumerable subsets),
or creative (if any program, see §14, of any enumerable subset of its
complement can be effectively processed into an element which belongs
to the complement but not to the subset), etc. One of the central results of the first direction is Myhill's theorem (see [My 55]) which
states that any two creative sets situated in an aggregate can be obtained one from the other by computable permutation of the aggregate.

The second direction is related to the degrees of unsolvability.
For the family of all sets situated in a given aggregate (or even in
different aggregates) a quasiorder   can be defined, namely $P \geqslant Q$
if and only if the decision problem for the set Q is reducible to
the decision problem for the set P i.e. Q is decision reducible

to P. Classes of equavalence of this quasiorder are called <u>Turing</u>
<u>degrees of unsolvability</u>, in short, degrees of unsolvability, or Tu-
ring degrees or T-degrees. All decidable sets constitute a Turing
degree denoted by O and named degree zero. A Turing degree is called enumerable if it contains at least one enumerable set. The existence of an undecidable enumerable set implies the existence of a non-
zero enumerable degree. The question whether two non-zero enumerable
degrees do exist is Post's reducibility problem. In fact, the set of
all enumerable degrees is infinite though it is countable (see [Muč
56, theorem 2] and also [Rog 67, §10.2]). Turing degrees can be naturally ordered, with respect to this ordering they form an upper semilattice (of the cardinality of continuum). Numerous literature is
devoted to the study of its properties beginning with the paper of
Post and Kleene [Klee Post 54], see also [Rog 67, chap. 13], [Shoen
71]. Among non-zero degrees the re are minimal ones (see [Rog 67,
§13.5] and [Shoen 71, §11]). On the other hand, there are no minimal
elements in the partially ordered set of non-zero enumerable degrees
(see [Muč 56, theorem 3] and [Rog 67, exercise 10-11]).

§12. <u>The concept of relative algorithm, or oracle-algorithm.</u>

To obtain the definition of oracle-algorithm with an oracle A
it is necessary to modify Kolmogorov's formulation from the above §1
as follows. An oracle A is a set in an aggregate. An <u>oracle-algo-</u>
<u>rithm</u> has a questioning device which is an auxillary algorithm $\mathcal{J}$
defined (i.e. giving a result) on all possible states S. Each step
of the process determined by an oracle-algorithm depends not only on
the state S formed by this step but on the truth value of the sta-
tement $\mathcal{J}(S) \notin A$ as well. Thus operator of immediate processing Ω_Γ,
producing the next state S*, is now a function of two arguments--of
a state S and of the 0-1 truth value of the statement $\mathcal{J}(S) \in A$.
An oracle-algorithm with an oracle A is also called an algorithm
relative to A (see [Rog 67, §9.2]).

The concept of oracle-algorithm is important from the methodological point of view. The point is that the theory of algorithms and
calculuses as well as mathematical logic (understood according to
Church as the theory of formalized languages) provides formalization
of certain aspects of human activity. (Other mathematical disciplines
formalize those things that do not require the necessary presence of
a human being). In particular the theory of algorithms uses the concept of "elementary operation"--the essentially human concept. What

is elementary for human beings may be not elementary for other beings and vice versa. It is possible to assume that during the computational process a man asks an oracle of some questions but these questions (for example, Are these two symbols identical?) are so "elementary" that nobody can notice them. One can imagine computing facilities more powerful than the ones man has. These facilities use a less trivial (from the human point of view) oracle (which in the framework of these facilities cannot be regarded as an external oracle and should be regarded as a proper part of the facilities themselves).

As we shall see in a while our considerations are supported by the following. Analizing the proofs occurred in the theory of computable functions one can notice that the following way of discourse is possible--and used sometimes, e.g. in [Rog 67]. First of all certain basic and intuitively evident properties of the class of computable functions are established and then necessary statements are deduced from them. (The details can be found in [Us 74, §8]). Let us formulate the above mentioned basic properties for the class K of all computable number-theoretic functions:

1) The axiom of functional constants:

The class K contains all computable functions.

This property is used to prove that a certain function belongs to K. It can be replaced by: The class K contained zero constant and successor function.

2) The axiom of operator constants:

The class K is closed under operators of substitution, recursion and minimization.

This property is used to deduce the fact that a function that can be expressed by means of functions of the class K also belongs to the class K. For the first two axioms cf. §8 above.

3) The axiom of protocol:

For any function of the class K there exists:

I. a set E of natural numbers such that its characteristic function belongs to K

and II. functions $a \in K$ and $b \in K$ such that the function value for a number x is equal to y if and only if there is $q \in E$ such that $a(q) = x$ and $b(q) = y$.

This axiom can be interpreted as follows. We assume that for any computation there is a protocol (=record) which is a sequence of consequitive states (see §1). A set E is a set of codes of all protocols. If K is the class of all computable functions then a set of all protocols is decidable and consequently, its characteristic func-

tion belongs to K. Functions a and b distinguish initial datum
and result of computation from protocol's code.

4) The axiom of universal function:

In the class K there is a function U of two variables universal for all functions of one variable for K ("universal" means
that $\forall f \in K \; \exists x \forall y \; f(y) \simeq U(x,y)$).

As a basis for a computable function theory these axioms are much
more evident that Church's thesis is. Indeed, they do not assert that
a certain function is non-computable. In contrast, the most non-evi-
dent part of Church's thesis states that functions not computable by
the model are not computable anyway.

Besides other advantages due to any axiomatic approach--e.g. replacement of a complicated direct construction by short axioms--we
have the following two. The first is that axioms are not only more
evident but also less technical than Church' thesis. The second advantage (and disadvantage as well) is that the axiomatic system can
(and does) have different models. In fact, the four axioms listed
above are valid not only for the class of all computable functions
but also for any class of all functions computable with a given oracle. So all theorems deduced from 1) - 4) are valid for the latter
class. This explains the possibility of "relativization" of many theorems (see [Klee 52, §58, theorem X; §65, theorem XXIV; etc.]). And
vice versa, only those theorems can be relativized that follow from
axioms 1) - 4). It is a consequence of the fact that any class of
functions satisfying these axioms is actually a class of all functions computable with a fixed oracle. (The proof of the latter statement can be found in [Šen' 80].)

So, we see that in the pure theoretical aspect the concept of an
oracle-algorithm enables us to relativize the theory of algorithms
(see [Rog 67, §9.3]). In a more practical aspect it makes it possible
to give a precise definition of the general notion of decision reducibility and, consequently, to give a precise formulation of the fundamental reducibility problem (see §11). Indeed, the following definition can now be given. A set Q is Turing reducible (=decision
reducible) to a set P if and only if there exists a relative algorithm computing the characteristic function of the set Q relative
to the set P, or, in oracle terms, there exists an oracle-algorithm
which computes this characteristic function with the oracle P. The
concept of oracle-algorithm and the term "oracle" itself first appeared in Turing's paper [Tu 39] and because of this Post introduced in
[Post 44] the term "Turing reducibility" to denote the most general

type of reducibility for decision problems.

An important and natural case of Turing reducibility is polynomial-time reducibility. (It can be defined by requiring an oracle-algorithm to work polynomial-of-volume-of-input time.) It is natural to state the following polynomial-time reducibility problem: Can all sets from class $\mathcal{NP} \setminus \mathcal{P}$ be reduced to each other in polynomial time? (Of course, if $\mathcal{NP} = \mathcal{P}$ the problem is trivial). Many representatives of class $\mathcal{NP}$ arising in mathematical practice can be reduced in polynomial time to each other: all sets from $\mathcal{NP}$ are polynomially reducible to any representative of these (see [Aho Hop Ull 74, chap 10]). It is not known whether all sets from $\mathcal{NP}$ can be reduced to the set of all pairs of isomorphic graphs (see §7 above, the second example of sets from $\mathcal{NP}$).

§13. The concept of computable operation

By operation we mean a function whose arguments and values are sets. While a conventional computable function effectively produces one constructive object from another, a computable operation effectively produces one set of constructive objects from another; informally, effectiveness here means that the operation makes it possible to generate the resulting set provided a process of generation of the argument set is given. Because of the above said a computable operation transforms generable sets into generable sets. We can sum up these ideas in the following definition of computable operation (see [Us 55] or   [Rog 67, §9.7] where computable operations are called enumeration operators). Let X and Y be generable sets, X_F be the set of all finite subsets of X (these subsets can be processed as constructive objects in a manner mentioned in §1). Now let R be an arbitrary generable relation between X_F and Y (i.e. a generable subset of the product X_F x Y). Define a mapping Φ of the set 2^X into the set 2^Y by the formula: $\Phi(A) = \{y \mid \exists D(D \subset A \ \& \ \langle D, y \rangle \in R)\}$. Any mapping Φ obtained in this way is called computable operation; evidently, if $A \in \text{Gen}(X)$, then $\Phi(A) \in \text{Gen}(Y)$. According to the informal idea of computable operation the process of transformation of one set into another can be described as follows. We generate simultaneously finite subsets of an argument set A and elements of the relation R. If the first component of a generate element of the relation R turns out to be a generated finite subset of the set A then we put its second component in the set $\Phi(A)$.

Actually we have defined only one-place computable operations.

The notion of multi-place computable operation can be defined in the same way (or be reduced to the notion of one-place computable operation).

In terms of computable operations computable operators can be easily defined as follows (see [Rog 67, §9.8] where these operators are called partial recursive operators; Kleene invented them and called them partial recursive functionals, see [Klee 52, §63 and §64]). By an operator we mean a function which arguments and values are functions. For any operation Φ which maps $2^{U \times V}$ into $2^{X \times Y}$ we define the operator Ψ which determines a mapping from $\mathcal{F}(X, Y)$ into $\mathcal{F}(U, V)$: the operator Ψ is defined for a function $f \in \mathcal{F}(X, Y)$ if and only if $\Phi(f) \in \mathcal{F}(U, V)$ and in this case $\Psi(f) = \Phi(f)$. An operator Ψ obtained in this way for X, Y, U, V generable and Φ computable is called __computable__ or __partial recursive__. Evidently, if $f \in \text{Com}(X, Y)$ then $\Psi(f) \in \text{Com}(U, V)$. The operator is called __recursive__ if it is defined for each function from $\mathcal{F}(X, Y)$.

It is remarkable that the idea of computable operation can be formalized on the basis of the concept of algorithm alone and does not require any new basic notions. This fact confirms "capacity" and "universality" of the concept of algorithm. Another remarkable fact is that computable operations are continuous mappings provided the family of sets $\mathcal{T}$ is regarded as topological space with the topology we shall now define as in [Us 55], [Rog 67, exercise 11-35]. For any finite set D we put $\mathcal{O}_D = \{A \mid D \subset A \in \mathcal{T}\}$ and declare the collection of all such sets $\mathcal{O}_D$ to be a base of topology. By means of computable operations computability of a function relative to another function and Turing reducibility of sets can easily be defined: a function g is __computable relative__ to a function f if there exists a computable operation which transforms f (as a set of pairs) into g (as a set of pairs); a set Q is Turing reducible to a set P if the characteristic function of Q is computable relative to characteristic function of P (or, explicitly, in terms of operations over sets, if there exist computable operations Φ_1 and Φ_2 such that $Q = \Phi_1(P, \bar{P})$, $\bar{Q} = \Phi_2(P, \bar{P})$ where $\bar{P}$ and $\bar{Q}$ are complements of P and Q in the corresponding aggregates). One of the most fundamental facts about computable operations (in particular for partial recursive operators) is established by the __fixed-point theorem__, or the __first recursion theorem__ of Kleene (see [Rog 67, §11.5]). This theorem states that the equation $\Phi(A) = A$ for any computable operation Φ has a minimum solution (the same is true of any monotone function Φ) and this solution is enumerable (if Φ is a recursive operator then this

solution is single-valued and consequently is a computable function).
The first recursion theorem enables one to describe a generable set
(in particular, a computable function) with the help of a computable
operation. The description of a computable operation is regarded as
a finitary description of a set or a function which is a fixed-point
of the operation. This was one of the starting-points for works on
mathematical theory of computations by McCarthy and Scott (see
[Manna 74, chapt. 5]).

The study of special methods of description of computable opera-
tion--namely of program schemes (see [Luck Park Pat 70], [ErA 72])--
proved to be very fruitful. The most important program schemes are:
de Bakker - Scott recursive schemes (see [Kot 78]), Ershov's standard
schemes (see [ErA 73]), Glushkov's structured schemes (see [Gluš 65],
[Sem 78]). The whole theory of program schemes originated from the
study of Yanov schemes, i.e. standard schemes in one variable, see
[Janov 58], [ErA 67]. Glushkov's works on structured program schemes
is a part of his theory of systems of algorithmic algebras (see
[Gluš Ceĭtl Jusč 78]). This theory made it possible to use algebraic
and logical methods for the study of program schemes and was a basis
for intensive development of program logic (see [Valiev 79]).

The computable operations lead not only to the definition of the
reducibility for the sets of constructive objects but also to some
variants of the idea of reducibility for collections of these sets.
Let $\mathcal{A}$, $\mathcal{B}$ be collections of sets, elements of the sets being constructive objects. Then $\mathcal{B}$ is called weakly reducible to $\mathcal{A}$ if for
each $A \in \mathcal{A}$ there is a computable operation Φ such that
$\Phi(A) \in \mathcal{B}$; and $\mathcal{B}$ is called strongly reducible to A if there is a
computable operation Φ such that $\Phi(A) \in \mathcal{B}$ for each $A \in \mathcal{A}$.
When $\mathcal{A}$, $\mathcal{B}$ are collections of total number-theoretic functions,
the concepts of strong reducibility and weak reducibility were respectively proposed by Medvedev in [Med 55], [Med 56] and by Muchnik in
[Muč 63], so the strong reducibility can be called Medvedev reducibility and the weak reducibility can be called Muchnik reducibility;
we shall refer to these reducibilities at the end of §1, Part II.
There are two collections of total functions such that one collection
is weakly but not strongly reducible to the other (see [Muč 63]). A
class of all collections of total functions which are weakly (respectively, strong) reducible to each other is called a weak (resp.
strong) degree of difficulty (see [Med 55], [Med 56], [Muč 63]). Let
A, B be (strong or weak) degrees of difficulty, then $A \leq B$ if a
member of A is reducible to a member of B.

The strong degrees of difficulty partially ordered by the relation of strong reducibility form a lattice which is called the <u>Medvedev lattice</u> (see [Rog 67, §13.7]). It turns out that the upper semilattice of T-degrees (see §11 above) can be naturally embedded into the Medvedev lattice. The weak degrees of difficulty partially ordered by the weak reducibility also form a lattice, which can be called <u>Muchnik lattice</u>. There is an obvious mapping of the Medvedev lattice onto the Muchnik lattice, and this mapping turns to be a homomorphism, see [Muč 63]. For either lattice the least element $\mathbb{O}$ is the (strong or weak) degree of difficulty of any collection containing a computable function, and the greatest element $\mathbb{1}$ is the degree of difficulty of the empty collection. These lattices will be used in Part II, §2.

§14. <u>The concept of program: programs as objects of computation and generation.</u>

An important stage in the development of the theory of algorithms came when it was realized that formal descriptions of algorithms and calculuses (see §2, §4   ) can themselves serve as objects for algorithmic transformations. This discovery was made by Turing in [Tu 36].

Any formal description is a constructive object. However the set of all formal descriptions naturally appearing in study of a fixed computational (generative) model is not necessarilly situated in an aggregate. Consequently all elements of this set can neither serve as initial data for any given algorithm nor be generated by a single calculus. Formal descriptions can serve as inputs or outputs of an algorithm or be generated by a calculus provided they are first coded in such a way that these codes belong to the same aggregate. This preliminary processing is not necessary for real programming languages because in this case descriptions of all algorithms are words over the same alphabet of the programming language. This processing is also not necessary for Kolmogorov machines over directed or undirected Kolmogorov complexes with fixed labelling alphabet: formal descriptions of all these machines can be imagined to lie in the same aggregate. On the other hand, for Turing machines a preprocessing is necessary. Formal description of an algorithm for Turing machine can include symbols of an alphabet (in particular symbols of inner states) which is not bounded beforehand. The simplest way out is to regard these symbols as combinations of other contained in a bounded alphabet. This way is widely used in mathematical papers where the symbol q_{236} may occur to denote a state of Turing machine.

So, we come to the concept of <u>program</u>. Every computational model can be linked with an aggregate P of constructive objects which is called the <u>programming aggregate</u> for the model. Each algorithm of computation by the model has a program in P. This program contains "minimal information" sufficient to distinguish this algorithm from other algorithms of computation by this model. This program can be obtained in a "simple" and "natural" way from the formal description of the algorithm. This way reveals a "fine intracellular" structure in formal descriptions. Because of this structure all formal descriptions can be regarded as embedded into the same aggregate. The programs constitute a decidable subset P_o of the programming aggregate P and, in general, $P_o \neq P$. However we can agree to regard each element from P as a program treating each $p \in P \setminus P_o$ as a program of an algorithm with the empty domain.

Let us take a computable function f. Any program of any algorithm computing f is called a <u>program of the function</u> f.

Now we can formalize the idea of "Universal Recipe" introduced in §2. Let a computational model with a programming aggregate P, an input aggregate X and an output aggregate Y be given. A <u>universal algorithm for</u> this <u>model and</u> the <u>aggregates</u> X, Y is any algorithm $\mathcal{U} : P \times X \rightarrow Y$ which for any input pair $\langle p, x \rangle$ applies algorithm with program p to argument x. (So all universal algorithms—for a given model and aggregates X, Y—are equivalent in the sense that they compute the same function $\langle p, x \rangle \mapsto y$.) Then X-Y-representativity of the model can be expressed by the following condition on any algorithm $\mathcal{U}$ universal for this model and aggregates X, Y:

(UM) for any X-Y-algorithm $\mathcal{U}$ there exists a program $p \in P$ such that $\mathcal{U}(x) \simeq \mathcal{U}(\langle p, x \rangle)$.

The concept of algorithm universal for a given computational model is connected with the concept of algorithm <u>universal</u> (=representative) for a pair X, Y. Let X, Y, E be arbitrary sets of constructive objects, E being called an index set and its elements being called indices. An algorithm $\mathcal{U} : E \times X \rightarrow Y$ is called <u>universal</u>, or <u>representative, for sets</u> X, Y <u>with the index set</u> E if it satisfies the following condition:

(U) for every X-Y-algorithm $\mathcal{U}$ there exists $e \in E$ such that $\mathcal{U}(x) \simeq \mathcal{U}(\langle e, x \rangle)$.

Of course, a model with a programming aggregate P is X-Y-representative if and only if any algorithm universal for this model and for aggregates X, Y is universal for X, Y with the index set P. In this case programs serve as indices. The existence of the

universal algorithm for X, Y with the index set X immediately
leads to such an important result as the existence of generable undecidable sets (see §10).

The property (UM) of algorithms $\mathcal{U}$ does not imply that correspondence between $\mathcal{U}$ and p is effective. Naturally, from the algorithmic point of view it is interesting to "effectivize" this property. In order to obtain this "effectivization" let us consider an ar-
bitrary family of algorithms $\mathcal{U}_i$ parametrically given: $\mathcal{U}_i(x) \simeq$
$\mathcal{U}(\langle i, x \rangle)$, $i \in I$ where $\mathcal{U}$ is an algorithm and I is a generable
set. In particular we can define in such a way the family of all al-
gorithms of computations by a given computational model with the help
of an algorithm universal for this model, programs of this model
playing the role of parameter. The required "effectivization" is that
for any i a program p such that $\mathcal{U}(\langle i, x \rangle) \simeq \mathcal{U}(\langle p, x \rangle)$ can be
effectively found. So we obtain the following property:

   (GM) for every generable I and every algorithm $\mathcal{U}: I \times X \rightarrow$
   Y there exists an algorithm $\mathcal{D}: I \rightarrow P$ with the domain I
   such that $\mathcal{U}(\langle i, x \rangle) \simeq \mathcal{U}(\langle \mathcal{D}(i), x \rangle)$.

Let two computational models CoM_1 and CoM_2, an input aggregate X and an output aggregate Y be given; the property (GM) of
the universal algorithm for CoM_1, X, Y makes it possible to translate programs of CoM_2 into programs of CoM_1, i.e. to make an effective transition from an arbitrary program of computation of a
function by CoM_2 to a program of computation of the same function
by CoM_1.

Of course, the property (GM) seems quite natural. Intuitively,
if P is a programming aggregate containing a program for each X-Y-
-algorithm, then property (GM) is valid. Indeed, it is sufficient to
take for $\mathcal{D}$ an algorithm which being applied to i simply produces
a program of the algorithm: "form a pair $\langle i, x \rangle$ and apply the algorithm $\mathcal{U}$ to it". The underlined statement has logical status similar to
that of Church's thesis, so it also can be called a thesis. Church's
thesis is a statement about the informal notion of algorithm (or, if
one pleases, about the informal notion of computable function). The
thesis we have just formulated is a statement about the informal notion of program. This thesis as well as Church's one cannot be proved in usual mathematical sense, but can be confirmed by scrutinizing
various representative computational models. In fact, for any computational model the property (GM) is equivalent to the Kleene s-m-n
theorem (in fact, s-1-1 theorem) for this model (see [Rog 67, §1.8]).
Originally this famous theorem was not stated for computational mo-

dels but for the class of recursive functions. If we are working in
the computable functions theory we can disregard the difference between aggregates (because all aggregates are isomorphic) as well as
between computational models (in view of coincidence of classes of
functions they define). Then, if we add the notion of program to the
theory we suppose that we should have one specific theory, say, for
Turing computable functions and Turing programs or another specific
theory, say, for Kolmogorov machines, etc., but that is not the case.
The Invariance Property is valid for the theory with the notion of
program as well as with the notion of volume (cf. §6). Indeed theorems
which use the notion of program remain valid when we change from one
computational model to another. The main reason for this is Rogers'
theorem about the isomorphism of Gödel numberings, see the next section. This theorem can be treated as the fact that there is exactly
one programming system i.e. exactly one mapping: a program→the function computable by this program. So if we add any specific notion of
program (for any specific computational model) to the theory of computable functions we shall obtain the theory which, in essence, is
unique (i.e. does not depend on this specific notion).

On the abstract level the property (GM) leads to the concept of
main, or Gödel, universal algorithm. Let X, Y, E be sets. An algorithm $\mathcal{U} : E \times X \rightarrow Y$ us called Gödel, or main, for sets X, Y with
an index set E if it   satisfies the following condition:

> (G) for every generable I and every algorithm $\mathcal{U} : I \times X \rightarrow Y$
> there exists an algorithm $\mathcal{D} : I \rightarrow E$ with the domain I such
> that $\mathcal{U}(\langle i, x \rangle) \simeq \mathcal{U}(\langle \mathcal{D}(i), x \rangle)$.

As we have already mentioned, every algorithm universal for any
known X-Y-representative model is main.

Nevertheless, not every algorithm universal for given X, Y
with a given index set E is the main one. To be more exact, let X,
Y, E be infinite generable sets; then there exists an algorithm
which is universal but not the main one for X, Y with the index set
E.

The property (G) in its turn can be proposed (and actually was
proposed in [Us 56], [Us 56a]) as a formal definition of the notion
of programming system, or of method of programming,--and hence for
the notion of the program itself. Under this definition a programming
system is identified with a Gödel algorithm. The following two facts
justify the exact definition corresponding to the informal notion of
a programming system:
1) any real programming system has the property (GM) and hence the

property (G) (with a programming aggregate serving as E);

2) any two Gödel algorithms $\mathcal{U}_1$ and $\mathcal{U}_2$ are translatable into each other and even "isomorphic" in the sense of Rogers' theorem mentioned above.

Property of universality (UM) can be looked upon from quite a different point of view. Namely, from the point of view of "optimality" of a description of a computable function with the help of a universal algorithm. To be more exact, our question is: "Does the program p contains no or almost no additional information compared to i?" The words "no or almost no" can be understood as inequality $l(p) \lesssim l(i)$, provided P and I are volumed aggregates. By combining this requirement of "optimality" with property "to be main" we come to the following:

(VPS) for every volumed aggregate I and every algorithm

$\mathcal{U}$: I x X ⟶ Y there exists a bounded-distortion algorithm

$\mathcal{D}$: I ⟶ P with the domain I such that
$$\mathcal{U}(\langle i, x \rangle) \simeq \mathcal{U}(\langle \mathcal{D}(i), x \rangle).$$

A universal algorithm (for a model with the programming aggregate P, an input aggregate X and an output aggregate Y) which satisfies the condition (VPS) is called <u>volume-of-program-saving</u>, or <u>optimal</u> (see [Ag 75, §3.2]). It turns out that volume-of-program-saving algorithms do exist. One example is a universal algorithm constructed for Kolmogorov machines (over directed as well as over undirected complexes). The universal algorithm for Turing machines is not volume-of-program-saving (see [Ag 75, p. 45 and exercise 1 on p. 66]). By fixing X, Y (a programming aggregate is not being fixed), any two volume-of-program-saving algorithms are "isomorphic" in the sense of Schnorr's theorem (see the next section). So the theory of computable functions can be regarded as a unique one, the notion of a program volume being added.

In the general, index case we can propose the following definition of a volume-of-index-saving algorithm. Let X, Y be sets, E be a volumed aggregate. An algorithm $\mathcal{U}$: E x X ⟶ Y is called <u>volume-of-index-saving</u> if it has the following property:

(VIS) for every volumed aggregate I and every algorithm

$\mathcal{U}$: I x X ⟶ Y there exists a bounded-distortion algorithm

$\mathcal{D}$: I ⟶ E with the domain I such that $\mathcal{U}(\langle i, x \rangle) \simeq \mathcal{U}(\langle \mathcal{D}(i),$ x$\rangle)$.

Everything we have said about algorithms, their formal descriptions, and programs remains true of calculuses. In particular one can consider generative programs of calculuses and of generated sets meaning records of formal descriptions in certain aggregates (we can also regard non-programs as programs generating the empty set). By fixing an aggregate whose elements are generated by calculuses of a generative model we come to the concepts of calculus universal for a given model and calculus universal for a given set X--the latter "contains", in a certain sense, a calculus for generating every generable subset of X. The first calculus generates pairs $\langle p, x \rangle$ where p is a program and the second generates pairs $\langle e, x \rangle$, where e is an index. Provided that pairs $\langle p, x \rangle$ are coded we come to a broad interpretation of the notion of universal calculus. Namely, a calculus is universal if for a certain coding φ it generates $\varphi(\langle p, x \rangle)$ if and only if the corresponding program p generates x. Many logistic systems (the predicate calculus, formal arithmetic, axiomatic set theory) turn out to be universal calculuses in the broad sense. Those universal calculuses had appeared in mathematics before the general notion of calculus was formed. As the whole theory of calculuses can be treated as a theory of a single universal calculus (cf. §4 where the theory of algorithms was treated as the theory of a single algorithm) one can assume that formalization of the idea of calculus and the general theory of calculuses appeared earlier than the general notion of calculus did. In this historical respect the development of the notion of calculus differs from that of the notion of algorithm.

Similarly, the notions of **main** calculus and of **volume-of-program-saving** (and **volume-of-index-saving**) calculus are introduced. For example, a calculus $\mathcal{U}$, generating a subset of E x X is called main (for X with an index set E) if for any calculus $\mathcal{U}$, generating a subset of I x X (where I is generable), there exists an algorithm $\mathcal{D} : I \rightarrow E$ with the domain I such that $\mathcal{U}$ generates a pair $\langle i, x \rangle$ if and only if $\mathcal{U}$ generates the pair $\langle \mathcal{D}(i), x \rangle$. Calculuses universal for known representative generative models turn out to be main if we take programming aggregates as index sets. However not every calculus universal for a given X with a given index set is main.

Let X-Y-representative computational model CoM be given. Let GeM be an (X x Y)-representative generative model. Then for every computable function from X into Y there exist computational programs in CoM and generative programs in GeM : there latter arise provided that the function is regarded as a (generable) set. The property "to be main" for the algorithm universal for CoM and that of the calculus universal for GeM enables one to translate effectively generative programs into computational ones and vice versa.

As to algorithms over programs, a fundamental theorem--the second recursion theorem--is due to Kleene (see [Rog 67, chap. 11]).
The most intelligible though slightly weakened formulation of this
theorem is: an algorithm which transforms any program of any computable function into a program of the different (from the first) computable function is impossible. The same is true of programs of generable sets. It is natural to ask: What properties of generable sets
(in particular, computable functions) can be recognized by a fixed
algorithm if a program of a set is given? None of them (except
trivial) turned out to be recognizable (see [Rice 53], [Us 55a], [Us
60, §11.2]). It is remarkable that it follows from the fact that both
the system of all generable sets and the system of all computable functions with natural topology defined in §13 are topologically connected. Indeed, the set of all programs of sets (or programs of functions)
satisfying (or not satisfying) a property algorithmically recognizable through these programs is enumerable. On the other hand, any collection of sets or functions such that all their programs constitute
an enumerable set (such a collection is called completely enumerable)
turns out to be open in this topology (see [Us 55a]).

Let us fix a generative model. Every computable operation Φ
evidently leads to an algorithm that transforms any program of generation of any set A into a program of generation of the resulting
set $\Phi(A)$. Similarly, let us fix a computational model. Every computable operator Ψ leads to an algorithm that transforms any program
of any function f from the domain of Ψ into a program of the resulting function $\Psi(f)$. The theorem that a completely enumerable collection of sets or functions is open in the topology of §13 makes it
possible to establish the following fundamental result which is the
converse of the statement cited at the beginning of this paragraph--
each algorithm which transforms any program into another program in
such a way that all programs of one object are transformed into the
programs of one object, corresponds to a computable operation (see
[Us 55a], [My Shep 55]). To be more exact: let X and Y be generable sets, F be a mapping of 2^X into 2^Y such that $A \in \mathrm{Gen}(X)$
implies $F(A) \in \mathrm{Gen}(Y)$; let computable function φ exist so that for
any program P of any $A \in \mathrm{Gen}(X)$ the image $\varphi(p)$ is a program of
$F(A)$;   then there exists a computable operation Φ such that
$F(A) = \Phi(A)$ for each $A \in \mathrm{Gen}(X)$. The same is true of partial mappings
from $\mathcal{F}(X, Y)$ into $\mathcal{F}(U, V)$, as well as of programs of computable
functions and of computable operators. A similar theorem is true of

algorithms, that can be applied to any program of a total function
and that transform all programs of one total function into programs
of one total function; any such algorithm corresponds to a certain
computable operator (see [Ceĭtin 62, theorem 2]).

§15. The concept of numbering and the theory of numberings.

A numbering (or to be more exact, an integer numbering) of a set
M is a mapping α of some set $E \subset \mathbb{N}$ onto M. If $\alpha(e) = m$, then e
is called the (α-) number of m (see [Us 55a], [Us 60, §11], [Mal
61], [Mal 65, chap. IV]).

The set E is called the base of the numbering α (as in [Us
60]) or the number set (as in [Mal 61], [Mal 65]) of the numbering α.
If $E = \mathbb{N}$ the numbering is called "natural" as in [Us 60], or
"simple" as in [Mal 61], [Mal 65, n°9.1]. If each element has only
one number (i.e. α is a one-one correspondence) a numbering is called a numbering without repetition or a one-one numbering (see [Mal
61], [Mal 65, n°9.1]). A numbering is called decidable if there exists
an algorithm which can be applied to any pair of elements from E
and which answers the question whether both elements of the pair are
the numbers of the same element from M (see [Mal 61]).

It is natural to understand the term "numbering" in the broad
sense. Then any subset of any aggregate can serve as a base of numbering. The definition of numberings without repetition and that of decidable numbering can be formulated for this general case in the same
way. In this case the role of natural numberings is played by
a numberings whose base is the whole aggregate. These numberings are
called total. Examples of numberings:

1) The programming system, or the method of programming, for a fixed
   computational or generative model--i.e. the mapping which puts
   into correspondence to any program a computable function or a generable set determined by this program (see [Us 56], [Us 56a]).
2) A system of notation for ordinals (see [Rog 67, §11.7]).
3) A mapping for going from any name of some collection to its denotation (see [Church 56, §01]); it is the main philosophical motivation of the theory of numberings.

A set together with its numbering is called a numbered set (see
[Us 55a], [Us 60], [Mal 61], [Mal 65]). A numbering α of a set M
is called reducible to a numbering β of the same set if and only if
there exists an algorithm reducing α to β ; i.e. giving for the
α-number of any element of M the corresponding β-number of the

same element (see [Us 56], [Mal 61 , n°2.2]). Finally, two numberings
are _equivalent_ if they are reducible to each other.

For a fixed M the relation of reducibility determines a quasi-
ordering on the set of all (integer) numberings of M. This, in turn,
creates a partial ordering on the family of all equivalence classes
of numberings of M. Partially ordered set of these equivalence classes forms an upper semilattice. The same construction can be effected
for total (integer) numberings alone. In this case one also gets upper semilattice which can be isomorphically embedded into the first.

The idea of abstract study of numberings was first suggested by
Kolmogorov in February 1954 in his talk at the Seminar on recursive
arithmetic at Moscow University. This idea was fundamentally developed in the works of Mal' cev (reprinted later in [Mal 76]) and of his
disciple Yu.L. Ershov. Their treatises [Mal 65], [ErJ 77] sum up
these investigations. The theory of numberings can be regarded as an
original branch of mathematics which has arisen out of the theory of
algorithms. The originality of this new branch rests on the existence
of quite a _lot of_ profound theorems. Some of these theorems are almost
evident. For example: a total numbering of an infinite set is decidable if and only if it is equivalent to a total numbering without repetition (of the same set), see [ErJ 77, chap. 1, §3]. We shall use
this theorem in part II, §5. Other results are not   evident and are
even surprising. For example: for any two finite sets (each having
more than one element) the upper semi-lattice of the equivalence classes of total numberings of one set is isomorphic to that of another
set (see [ErJ 77, suppl. II]).

Many notions and results of the theory of numberings are due to
the study of programming systems (which provided the first example of
numberings in this section). Programming systems have the important
properties which are sufficient to prove some propositions on these
systems. As usual in mathematics, one can try to single out and study
these properties alone. As a result of abstract study the important
types of numberings, first of all computable numberings (see [Us 55a],
[Lav 77]) arise. Regarding a programming system as a numbering one
can point out the following specific features of this numbering α:

1)The numbered set is a family of subsets of a fixed generable
   (=enumerable) set.
2)The numbering of this family is _computable_ (that is, its base is enumerable and the set of all pairs $\langle e, w \rangle$ such that $w \in \alpha(e)$ is
   also enumerable); hence each set $\alpha(e)$ is enumerable.

Let us recall that a family of functions is also a family of sets, a function being identified with the corresponding set of pairs. Consequently if α is a numbering of a family of functions from X into Y then the computability of α means the enumerability of the two sets:

1) the base of α ,

2) the set of all triples $\langle e, x, y \rangle$ such that $\langle x, y \rangle \in \alpha(e)$

(it implies that each function $\alpha(e)$ is computable).

The enumerability of the latter set of triples is equivalent to the computability of the function $\langle e, x \rangle \mapsto y$ (which reveals the origin of the term "computable numbering").

So for any computable numbering there is a calculus generating the set of pairs $\langle e, w \rangle$ such that $w \in \alpha(e)$ ("universal set" of the numbering). In the important case of a function family as the numbered set there is an algorithm computing the function $\langle e, x \rangle \mapsto y$ ("universal function" of the numbering). Consequently the study of computable numberings can be reduced to the study of calculuses and algorithms. If the numbered set is the whole Gen(W) or the whole Com(X, Y) (in the sense of §7) these algorithms and calculuses belong to those algorithms and calculuses which were discussed in §14. Any index set from §14 (see properties (U) and (G)) is, in fact, a base of a numbering. Therefore some properties of numberings correlate to those of algorithms and calculuses from §14. Let us list these correlations providing X, Y are generable (=enumerable):

1) Every algorithm $\mathcal{U}$ which is universal for X and Y with a generable index set E determines a computable numbering α from Com(X, Y) with the base E. Namely, for any $e \in E$ let $\alpha(e)$ be a function $f : X \to Y$ such that $f(x) \simeq \mathcal{U}(\langle e, x \rangle)$, or, in other words

$$(*) \quad \alpha(e)(x) \simeq \mathcal{U}(\langle e, x \rangle).$$

Conversely, if α is a computable numbering of Com(X, Y) with a base E then the "universal function" $\langle e, x \rangle \mapsto y$ (see above in this section) is computable and any algorithm $\mathcal{U}$ computing this function is universal for X, Y with the index set E.

2) Now the concept of Gödel, or main, numbering can be introduced. A numbering of a family of sets (in particular, a family of functions) is called Gödel, or main, if it is computable and each computable numbering of the same family is reducible to it (see [Us 55a]; when numbered family is Com(X, Y) this definition is equivalent to the definition of acceptable numbering from [Rog 67, exercise 2-10]). For any algorithm $\mathcal{U}$ which is main for X, Y with a generable index set E, the numbering α of Com (X, Y) induced by (*) is main Conversely, if α is a main numbering of Com(X, Y) with an infi-

nite base E, then any algorithm $\mathcal{U}$ computing the "universal function" of this numbering is the main algorithm for X, Y with the
index set E. Certainly, any programming system is Gödel numbering
of Gen (W) or of Com(X, Y) for some aggregates W, X, Y. On the
other hand, for any enumerable X, Y a Gödel numbering of all computable functions from X to Y is unique up to isomorphisms produced
by a computable one-one mapping of numbering bases (this is <u>Rogers'</u>
<u>theorem</u>, see [Rog 58], [Mal 63, theorem 7.1], [Mal 65, §9, theorem 5]).
The same can be said about numberings of Gen(W) for any enumerable
W. It follows then that many statements true of programming systems
are also true of any Gödel numberings. Let us formulate two of them.
- It is impossible to recognize a non-trivial property of a computable function by its number.
- Any computable operation is equivalent to some computable function
  over numbers.

3) Finally, one can define the concept of Schnorr, or "optimal",
or volume-of-number-saving numbering similar to the concept of volume-of-index-saving algorithm. Let us call any subset of any volumed aggregate "volumed set". So we can consider volumed numbering bases.
Let W, X, Y be enumerable sets, α be a total numbering of the family Gen(W) or Com(X,Y) with a volumed aggregate serving as a numbering base. In these conditions the numbering α is called <u>Schnorr</u>,
or "optimal", or <u>volume-of-number-saving</u>, if it is computable and any
computable numbering of the same family having a volumed numbering
base is reducible to α by a bounded-distortion algorithm. Let E
be a volumed aggregate; if an algorithm $\mathcal{U}$ is volume-of-index-saving
for X, Y with an index set E then the numbering of Com(X, Y)
induced by (*) is a Schnorr numbering; and conversely, if α is a
Schnorr numbering of Com(X, Y) with base E, any algorithm computing the "universal function" of this numbering is volume-of-index-
saving. Evidently, any Schnorr numbering is a Gödel one. For any enumerable W, X, Y the theorem of the existence of a Schnorr numbering
of Gen(W) or of Com(X, Y) is valid. Schnorr numbering is unique
up to an isomorphism of volumed aggregates serving as numbering bases
(this is <u>Schnorr's theorem</u>, see [Schnorr 72], [Schnorr 75]).

§16. <u>First steps of the invariant, or machine-independent,</u> <u>theory of complexity of computation</u>

By the invariant theory of complexity we mean the theory that
can be formulated independently of any computational (or generative)

model. It can be done in three ways.

The first way is to find some complexity bounds which do not depend on the computational model. In §6 we have said that (provided volume of constructive objects is properly chosen) space complexity of computations by some computational model with local transformation of information   considered to within addition of a bounded function does not change if we take any other such model. Similarly we can consider a complexity bound to within given transformations. By this we mean the following: the set of transformations is fixed, a complexity class is not determined by a single bound but by a system of bounds, and for every two bounds α, β of the system there are transformations U, V from a fixed set such that $\alpha \leqslant U \circ \beta$ and $\beta \leqslant V \circ \alpha$ (for example, all non trivial polynomials constitute a system of bounds provided transformations are exponentiations to a positive degree). A function belongs to a complexity class if complexity of its computation is bounded by a bound from a given system. For example, $\mathcal{P}$ can be defined as a class of functions with computational time lineary bounded to within exponentiation to a positive degree.

The second way tries to include certain parameters of a computational model in complexity functions as arguments. Strict and meaningful formalization of those parameters is a difficult task. Up to now only the number of tapes and the cardinality of alphabet of a multitape Turing machine have been regarded as the parameters (see, for example [Sei 77]).

The third way is axiomatic one. Blum in [Blum 67] proposed two axioms satisfied by every reasonable complexity of computation; in these axioms the notion of a complexity of computation is formalized as the notion of a complexity measure.

For a fixed main (for X, Y with an index set E) algorithm $\mathcal{U} : E \times X \longrightarrow Y$ an algorithm $\mathcal{C} : E \times X \longrightarrow N$ satisfying the following two axioms is called <u>complexity measure</u> (see [Blum 67]):
1) $\mathcal{U} (\langle i, x \rangle)$ is defined $\Leftrightarrow$ $\mathcal{C} (\langle i, x \rangle)$ is defined;
2) the set $\{\langle i, x, y \rangle \mid \mathcal{C} (\langle i, x \rangle) = y \}$ is decidable.

The examples of complexity measures are all described above variants of time and space for all computational models. In [Blum 67] Blum proved remarkable theorems on complexity measures. The following invariance theorem from this work shows that there is only one complexity measure if we restrict ourselves in the complexity bounds to within arbitrary total computable transformations.

Recursive Relatedness Theorem. Let $\mathcal{C}_1$, $\mathcal{C}_2$ be two complexity measures. Then there exists an algorithm $\mathcal{D}: X \times \mathbb{N} \to \mathbb{N}$ with the domain $X \times \mathbb{N}$ such that for all $i \in I$ the inequality $\mathcal{D}(\langle x, \mathcal{C}_1(\langle i, x \rangle) \rangle) \geqslant \mathcal{C}_2(\langle i, x \rangle)$ is satisfied for all, but finitely many x for which $\mathcal{U}(\langle i, x \rangle)$ is defined.

So, Blum's theory can be regarded as an extremal case of the first approach to the invariant complexity theory.

Another remarkable consequence of Blum's axioms is the following speed-up theorem.

Blum Speed-up Theorem. Let $\mathcal{C}$ be a complexity measure and let an algorithm $\mathcal{R}: \mathbb{N} \to \mathbb{N}$ be total, i.e. have $\mathbb{N}$ as the domain. Then there exists a decidable subset of the set X such that for each decision algorithm $\mathcal{U}$ for this set and each $i \in E$ such that $\mathcal{U}(x) \simeq$ $\mathcal{U}(\langle i, x \rangle)$ there exists $j \in E$ such that $\mathcal{U}(x) \simeq \mathcal{U}(\langle j, x \rangle)$ and for all but finitely many $x \in X$ holds the inequality $\mathcal{C}(\langle i, x \rangle) \geqslant \mathcal{R}(\mathcal{C}(\langle j, x \rangle))$, (see [Blum 67]).

Blum's theory can be regarded as a "descriptive part" of the metric theory of algorithms. In fact the notions and methods of Blum's approach are very close to the classical theory of the descriptive theory of algorithms.

Of course, the great generality of Blum's axioms implies certain disadvantages. If we want to prove more about our complexity measures in an axiomatic way, we must pose new axioms and restrict the class of complexity measures. It seems natural to use as complexities only such functions whose complexity is not great, e.g., not greater than the value of the complexity function itself. It is possible however (for $Y = \mathbb{N}$) to require this from all complexity functions corresponding to the given complexity measure and include the requirement into the definition of complexity measure; so we add the third axiom to the axiom system of complexity measures;

3) $\forall i \; \exists j (\mathcal{C}(\langle i, x \rangle) \simeq \mathcal{U}(\langle j, x \rangle) \; \& \; \mathcal{U}(\langle j, x \rangle) \geqslant \mathcal{C}(\langle j, x \rangle))$

Complexity measures such as space and time for Turing machines as well as Kolmogorov machines satisfy the third axiom (and even its "effective" variant when j is found for i by an algorithm). In [Hart Hop 71, §4] complexity measure is called proper if it $\vee$ satisfies the "effective" variant of the third axiom.

§ 17. The theory of complexity and entropy of constructive objects

The general approach to complexity of a constructive object as to the minimal volume of the program describing this object is due to Kolmogorov (see [Kol 65]). (Independently though in less explicit form similar ideas were expressed by Solomonoff in [Sol 64]) In the course of the development of this approach it was found out that different intuitive ideas of complexities correspond to different exact definitions of complexity.

At the informal level the distinctions appear because of the following. Any constructive object (for example, a word) can be regarded as a message about the object itself or on the contrary, as a message about all objects in which, in a certain sense, it is conained (for example, about all extensions of the word). It is clear that the second message is less informative than the first one and that in the first case the message about a part of an object may contain more information than the message about the whole object. Therefore, a program describing an object can define the object itself as well as its extension provided the object is regarded as a message of the second type. The same considerations of the "part-whole" relation can be applied to programs, or descriptions, themselves. In particular, if some objects is determined by their parts then, from a certain point of view, those objects cannot "contradict each other", they must be "concordant". So for any aggregate a concordance relation should be given. An example of a concordance relation is the relation "one of two objects is a part of the other". It is natural to assume that a concordance relation is decidable.

Accordingly, in this section by the term "aggregate" we mean an arbitrary aggregate considered together with a given decidable binary relation which is called a <u>concordance relation</u>. The fundamental role will be played by the aggregates $\mathbb{N}$ and Ξ --they will be aggregates of descriptions. Here $\mathbb{N}$ denotes the aggregate of natural numbers with the equality relation as a concordance relation and Ξ denotes the aggregate of all words over the alphabet $\{0,1\}$ with the following concordance relation: two words are concordant if one of them is a prefix, or initial segment, of the other. For these aggregates the volume 1 is given as in §6.

So let X be either the volumed aggregate $\mathbb{N}$ or the volumed aggregate Ξ and let Y be an arbitrary aggregate. Let us consider the following condition on the relation R between elements of X and Y:

x, x' are concordant & $R(x, y)$ & $R(x', y') \Longrightarrow y, y'$ are concordant.

An arbitrary enumerable relation R between aggregates X and Y satisfying this condition is called a <u>mode of description</u> (of elements of Y by elements of X). An object x is called a _description_ of an object y under a mode R if R(x,y) is true.

The minimal volume of a description of an object y is called the _complexity_ $K_R(y)$ of y under a mode R (if no description exists at all then the complexity is equal to ∞). Let, for example, X = $\mathbb{N}$, Y = Ξ and let R consist of all pairs $\langle x,y\rangle$ where x is a program of a Markov normal algorithm $\mathfrak{A}$:$\mathbb{N} \rightarrow \{0,1\}$ and y be an initial segment of the sequence $\mathfrak{A}(0)$, $\mathfrak{A}(1)$, $\mathfrak{A}(2)$, ... , then K_R is the decision complexity introduced by Markov (see [Mark 64], [Mark 67]).

As Kolmogorov established in [Kol 65] among all modes of description for given X and Y (in Kolmogorov's paper X = Y = $\mathbb{N}$) there is an _optimal mode_ R_0, i.e. such a mode that the inequality $K_{R_0} \overset{<}{\sim} K_R$ holds for any mode R. For given aggregates X, Y the complexity of an object under any fixed optimal mode of description is called the _entropy_ K(y) of this object; to indicate explicitly the aggregates X and Y we call this entropy "X-Y-entropy". So X-Y-entropy is a mapping of Y into $\mathbb{N} \cup \{\infty\}$. Of course, for any given X, Y there are many X-Y-entropies. But all these functions are asymptotically equivalent: it means that for any two X-Y-entropies K' and K" the (asymptotic) inequality $|K'(y) - K"(y)| \overset{<}{\sim} 0$ is valid. Up to this equivalence X-Y-entropy is unique. In fact, the very notion of entropy is defined up to this equivalence.

Of course an $\mathbb{N}$-Y-entropy remains the same (up to the equivalence just mentioned) if we replace $\mathbb{N}$ by any volumed aggregate X with the equality as the concordance relation. If both concordance relations on X and on Y are equality relations, the X-Y-entropy is called "simple Kolmogorov entropy".

The main lemma (it is almost evident). For any computable function from $\mathbb{N}$ into $\mathbb{N}$ it is true that ($\mathbb{N}$ - $\mathbb{N}$ entropy of f(n))$\overset{<}{\sim}$ ($\mathbb{N}$ - $\mathbb{N}$ entropy of n). In general, let U, V be arbitrary aggregates, E be a mode of description of elements of V by elements of U the inequality (X - U entropy of u) $\overset{>}{\sim}$ (X - V entropy of v) holds for any u, v such that E(u,v) is true.

The entropies arising when both aggregates X and Y are the aggregates $\mathbb{N}$ or Ξ have been extensively studied. There are four such entropies: $\mathbb{N}$ - $\mathbb{N}$ entropy, or _simple Kolmogorov entropy_ (see [Kol 65]), $\mathbb{N}$ - Ξ entropy, or _decision entropy_ (see [Zvon Le 70, n°2.1]), Ξ - Ξ entropy, or _monotone entropy_ (see [Le 73]) and Ξ -$\mathbb{N}$ entropy, or _prefix entropy_ (see [Le 76]). It is easy to check

that for these entropies the following--presented in a table below--
relations are true. In this table we consider natural numbers to be
identified with their images in Ξ under the isomorphism of §6, so
all entropies turn out to be functions from Ξ into $\mathbb{N}$; the name of
entropy is written in front of K. For any two functions f and g
from the table function f is placed to the left of g if and only
if $f \lesssim g$.

$\mathbb{N} \; \Xi \; K$	$\mathbb{N}\mathbb{N}K$	$\Xi\mathbb{N}K$	$1+1,5 \log_2 l$
	$\Xi\Xi K$	1	

An example of other properties of those entropies is a monotony
of Ξ-Ξ entropy: if a word x is an initial segment of a word y
then $\Xi\Xi K(x) \leq \Xi\Xi K(y)$.

The notion of entropy provides the possibility to characterize
from the entropy point of view such antipodal concepts as computability and randomness. Informally, if a computable sequence is determined by a certain law, then the complexities of its initial segments
are bounded. If this informal complexity is treated as monotone entropy, these considerations lead to the following theorem:

A sequence is computable $\iff$ monotone entropy of its initial
segments is bounded $\iff$ decision entropy of its initial segments is
bounded (see [Zvon Le 70, theorem 2.2]). A random sequence does not
satisfy any law, its entropy is maximal (see Part II, §6).

Along with the entropies mentioned above it is natural to consider the entropies determined by algorithms with bounded complexity of
computation. Kolmogorov suggested to study this entropy in [Kol 65].

Moreover, conditional entropy of one object relative to an
other can be introduced. In order to define any conditional entropy
it is necessary to add one more aggregate namely an aggregate A of
conditions. In fact, a conditional entropy has been studied only for
$X = Y = A = \mathbb{N}$ (see [Kol 65]). In this case a mode of relative description R is defined as an arbitrary enumerable relation on $X \times Y \times$
A for which the implication: $R(x,y,a) \; \& \; R(x,y',a) \implies y = y'$ holds.
If R is a mode of conditional description one can introduce the fol-
lowing notion and notation--the complexity $K_R(y|a)$ of an object y
relative to an object a. By definition $K_R(y|a)$ is the minimal vo-
lume of an object x_o from among the objects x such that $R(x,y,a)$
is true.

Among all modes of relative description there is an optimal one, i.e.
such a mode R_o that the inequality $K_{R_o} \leq K_R$, holds for any mode R.
For example, any mode defined by the relation $R_o(x,y,a) \iff \mathcal{U} (\langle x,a \rangle) =$
$= y$ where $\mathcal{U}$ is an optimal algorithm for aggregates A, Y with an

index set X (see §14) is optimal. The conditional complexity under
an optimal mode of description is called a conditional entropy and
denoted by K(y|a). By fixing an object a in K(y|a) we obtain a
simple Kolmogorov entropy and all simple Kolmogorov entropies can be
obtained in such a way from conditional entropies.   It is in this
way that Kolmogorov introduced his simple entropy in [Kol 65].

With the help of the notion of entropy we can examine the volume-of-program-saving property of universal algorithms (see §14). The
requirement "program p contains no or almost no additional information compared to i" can now be understood in the following way: the
simple Kolmogorov entropy of p cannot exceed the entropy of i except by an additive constant independing of i. The definition of
entropy-of-index-saving algorithm is obvious. It turns out that any
main universal algorithm is entropy-of-index-saving. We obtain the
following property valid for any main algorithm $\mathcal{U}$: E x X → Y:
(EIS) for every generable I and every algorithm $\mathcal{U}$: I x Y → Y there
exists an algorithm D: I → E with the domain I such that $\mathcal{U}(\langle i,$
$x\rangle) \simeq \mathcal{U} (\langle \mathcal{D}(i), x\rangle)$ and $\text{NNK}(\mathcal{D}(i)) \lesssim \text{NNK}(i)$. In particular, for
any known representative computational model every   universal al-
gorithm is entropy-of-program-saving.

Introduction of the concept of entropy of a word enables one to
reexamine the concept of complexity of recognizing of a set. Namely
we can assume that one algorithm works longer than another if for each
value of an argument the time complexity (regarded as a function of
algorithm's argument) of the first algorithm is greater than the time
complexity of the second. However under this approach it may occur
that algorithms intended to recognize two set of words such that
words of one set are obtained by renaming letters of words from the
other set have incomparable complexities. At the same time it is
clear that these algorithms are in fact one and the same algorithm.
In order to extend the relation "to have equal complexities of computation" to these algorithms, words should be grouped in classes according to their length and a new complexity function namely a function of a length instead of a function of word can be constructed.
The value of the new function is a maximum value over all words of a
given length of the complexity function of words. Nevertheless it
does not solve the problem. If, say, we add 100 zeros to each word
from a set of binary words or if we write each letter of the word
twice it may occur that the obtained set could be recognized more
easily than the initial set. However, one can put into one class all
the words of the given entropy determined by algorithms with bounded

complexity of computations (for example, consider computation in real time). In this case the complexity functions for sets of intuitively equal complexity turn out to be proximate.

§18. Time-and-space-saving and proper computational models

All over this Part we have pointed out axiomatic requirements on computational model. We feel that the really, completely representative computational model has to satisfy a rather simple axiomatic system; the system guarantees the possibility of proving the main theorems of the descriptive and metric theory without any use of a specific model. At the same time if we choose a proper model satisfying all axioms then the whole theory can be regarded as the theory of this particular model.

The important axiomatic requirements are those posed on a universal algorithm for a model.

In §14 we distinguished the universal algorithms which were a volume-of-program-saving algorithms (see also §17, entropy-of-program-saving algorithms). However it is also natural to require the universal algorithm to be computational-complexity-saving. Let us imagine universal algorithm as a device simulating work of concrete algorithms according to their programs. Then it is reasonable to require that the universal algorithm should be time-saving, i.e. save time of computation to within multiplication by a function which is bounded and separated from zero and space-saving, i.e. save space of computation to within addition of a bounded function. If for a given model there exists the universal algorithm which is volume-of-program-saving, time-saving and space-saving then we call this model economical, or proper, model. It is not known if the model of multitape Turing machines is economical but we can note that usual universal algorithms for this model are not time-saving. Nevertheless there exists a proper computational model: namely, the model of Kolmogorov machines over undirected complexes as well as the model of Kolmogorov machines over directed complexes.

Part II. THE APPLIED THEORY OF ALGORITHMS

In Part I, §1, we mentioned some of the algorithms invented
long before a general notion of algorithm came into existence. But
only the birth of this general concept can give rise to the <u>theory</u>
of algorithms. Indeed, in order to appreciate this theory one must
comprehend the general concept of algorithm, it is not sufficient to
be able to work with individual patterns of algorithms.

A vast number of theorems requiring the construction of a certain algorithm and obtained in various fields of mathematics do not
require any general notion of algorithm to understand them. Consequently these theorems should not be regarded as belonging to the applications of algorithm theory. The construction of a particular algorithm for the purposes of a specific area of mathematics or of computational practice and with the help of methods of this specific
area comes within the province of the area and not of the theory of
algorithms. (It may occur, of course, that this specific area is algorithm theory itself.) On the contrary, a theorem on non-existence
of an algorithm appeals to the idea of the whole class of algorithms
in its totality, and therefore such a theorem is a theorem of algorithm theory.

Similarly we do not regard complexity evaluations for particular
algorithms as an application of algorithm theory unless they have been
obtained for a representative computational model. So, theorems on
algebraic complexity are not considered in this Part (note that certain statements deduced from them -- e.g. some theorems on Turing
machine complexity -- can belong to the applied theory).

Here we are only interested in mathematical applications of algorithm theory and we shall not consider applications to biology (e.
g. description of reflexes through relative algorithms, interpretation of the genetic code as a program, treating the macroevolution
as a generating process -- about the latter see [Mas 78]), or to psy-
chology (see [Mas 79a]), or to control theory (though the experts in
that field are exhibiting a growing interest in the most abstract aspects of the theory of algorithms -- see [Pet Ula Ul' 79]).

We list below the main mathematical applications of the theory
of algorithms:

1. Investigation of mass problems.

2. Applications to foundations of mathematics: constructive semantics.

3. Applications to mathematical logic: the analysis of formalized languages of logic and arithmetic.

4. Computable analysis.

5. Numbered structures.

6. Applications to probability theory: definitions of a random sequence.

7. Application to information theory: algorithmic approach to the concept of quantity of information.

8. Evaluation of complexity for solving particular problems.

9. Influence of the theory of algorithms on algorithm practice.

Thus Part II consists of nine sections.

However there are other applications. We shall start with the following   example. In Part I, §9 we mentioned the consequence of the general theory: any enumerable set of natural numbers can be presented as the set of all natural values of a suitable polynomial. Particular cases of this statement (for particular enumerable sets) can be regarded as number-theoretical results and some of them were found quite surprising by experts in this area of mathematics. For example, the set of primes is identical with the set of positive values of some polynomial with integer coefficients and variables ranging over natural numbers. Such a polynomial is given in [Da Mat RobJ 76] and it only takes a few lines to write it down. In the same paper it was noticed that many celebrated problems of number theory such as Fermat's conjecture, Goldbach's conjecture, or Riemann's hypothesis can be reduced to the problems of solvability of suitable Diophantine equations. Possibly these facts may change the landscape of number theory.

§1. <u>Investigation of mass problems</u>

<u>An algorithmic problem</u> is a problem of constructing an algorithm which posesses some properties (for instance, an algorithm to enumerate a given set, or an algorithm with a given bound of complexity). Algorithmic mass problems are algorithmic problems of a special kind (the algorithmic problems just mentioned are <u>not</u> of this kind). But sometimes algorithmic mass problems are simply called "algorithmic problems", e.g. in [Adj 77]. The concept of algorithmic mass problem itself arose from the investigation of mass problems. Mass problems constitute the main field of applications of algorithmic theory: moreover the creation of the very notion of algorithm is due to those problems.

<u>A single problem</u> is a request to present an object satisfying a given conditions: this object is called the solution of the problem;

to solve the problem is to find a solution. A <u>mass problem</u> is a series (mostly, infinite) of single problems, to solve a mass problem is to solve all particular problems simultaneously. Of course, the expression "to solve simultaneously" must be explained in exact terms. An example of a single problem: for the equation $x^2-x-1=0$ to find a rational approximation to the negative root of the equation within 10^{-6}. An example of a mass problem: in the same context for every n to find a rational approximation to the root within 10^{-n}.

Another example of a single problem--the <u>decision problem</u> for a set A situated in an aggregate W : to get a decision algorithm for A; the existence of a solution to this problem is of course equivalent to the decidability of A (cf. Part I, §7). One more example (of a single problem)--the <u>decidability problem</u> for a set A: to get an answer ("Yes", "No") to the question: "Is A decidable?" Another example of a mass problem--<u>mass decidability problem</u> for Gen(W) and for a fixed W-representative generative model: to furnish an answer to any question: "Is a subset with a generative program p decidable?" Unfortunately, the terms (and hence the concepts) "decision problem", "decidability problem", "mass decidability problem" are often confused. The same is true of the following triple of terms (and concepts): separation problem, separability problem, mass separability problem. Let us expound them. At first, a preliminary definition. Let A, B be subsets of an aggregate W. A <u>separating (or separation) function</u> for the pair $\langle A,B \rangle$ is a mapping of W into $\{$ "Yes", "No"$\}$ taking the value "Yes" for all elements of A and the value "No" for all elements of B. The <u>separation problem</u> for a pair $\langle A, B \rangle$ is to find an algorithm computing a separating function for the pair. Sets A, B are called <u>separable</u> if such an algorithm does exist. The (single) <u>separability problem</u> for a pair of sets $\langle A, B \rangle$ is the problem to get an answer ("Yes", "No") to the question: "Are A, B separable?" The <u>mass separability problem</u> for Gen(W) and for a fixed generative model is the problem to answer all the questions (for all generative programs): "Are two sets with generative programs p_1 and p_2 separable?"

The idea of mass problem is somewhat vague, and it is natural to try to find a formal equivalent for this idea. The usual way to find such an equivalent is to introduce the concept of <u>algorithmic mass problem</u>. To specify an algorithmic mass problem is to determine
1) a generable set X (the set of questions or single problems),
2) a generable set Y (the set of answers or single solutions),
3) a subset $E \subset X$ (the restriction on questions), 4) a subset

$R \subset X \times Y$ (the question-answer relation). Then the problem is to find an algorithm from X into Y which transforms each $\alpha \in E$ into an answer $\beta \in Y$ with the property $\langle \alpha, \beta \rangle \in R$. In the foregoing example related to the quadratic equation: $X = \mathbb{N}$, $Y = \mathbb{Q}$, $E = X$, $R = \{\langle n, r \rangle \mid |r - x_0| < 10^{-n}$ where x_0 is the desired root. Another example: $X = \mathbb{N}^+ \times \mathbb{N}^3$, $Y = \mathbb{Q}$, $E = \{\langle a, b, c, n \rangle \mid b^2 - 4ac \geqslant 0\}$, $R = \{\langle \langle a, b, c, n \rangle, r \rangle \mid |r - x_0| < 10^{-n}$, where x_0 is the least root of the equation $ax^2 + bx + c = 0\}$.

The replacement of a mass problem by the corresponding algorithmic mass problem not only furnishes a vague notion with a precise definition but also change the mass problem into a single one. Indeed, the algorithmic mass problem is a request to present a single object (=solution), namely an algorithm (cf. decision and separation problems above).

Of course, even if any single problem of a given mass problem has a solution, i.e. if for each $\alpha \in E$ there is such β that $\langle \alpha, \beta \rangle \in R$, the algorithmic mass problem may have not a solution. For instance, if a computational model is fixed for every program of a computable function there is a program of the minimal volume of the same function; but there is no algorithm to find a minimal volume program equivalent to a given program.

Here are three instructive examples from [Mat 74]:

Example 1. (See also [Mat 74a].) As early as 1908 Thue proved, that for every irreducible binary form F with integer coefficients of degree not less than 3 the following statement is true (all variables range over integers): $\forall \alpha \; \exists \beta \; \forall x \; \forall y \; [F(x,y) = \alpha \implies |x| + |y| < \beta]$.

Nevertheless it took 60 years to establish the existence of an algorithm which gives β for any F and α (see [Bak 68]).

Example 2. (See also [Da Mat RobJ 76].) Roth proved (see [Roth 55]) that for algebraic θ, positive rational r and integer p, q, s the statement $\forall \theta \; \forall r \; \exists s \; \forall p \; \forall q \; [q > s \implies |\theta - \frac{p}{q}| > q^{-2-r}]$ is true. At the same time no effective method to find s for any given θ and r is known.

Example 3. Matijacevič in [Mat 74a] constructed a polynomial A with integer coefficients for which

$$\forall \alpha \; \exists \beta \; \forall y \; \forall z_1 \ldots \forall z_n \; [A(\alpha, z_1, \ldots, z_n) = y + 4^y \implies y + z_1 + \ldots + z_n \leq \beta]$$

(here $\alpha, \beta, y, z_1, \ldots, z_n$ range over natural numbers), but no algorithm exists to transform α into β.

Every decision problem is an algorithmic mass problem. Indeed, let W be an aggregate and $A \subset W$. Then the decision problem for A has (as algorithmic mass problem) W as the set of questions and the same W as the restriction on questions; the set of answers is

$\{$"Yes", "No"$\}$ and the question-answer relation is the set

$\{\langle w, \text{ "Yes"}\rangle \mid w \in A\} \cup \{\langle w, \text{ "No"}\rangle \mid w \in W \smallsetminus A\}$.

Many algorithmic problems can be restated as decision problems or can be reduced to such problems (namely to the decision problem for the domain of an appropriate function or to the decision problem for the function as a set).

Let us fix, for example, an aggregate W, a W-representative generative model and its programming aggregate, say P.

Then the <u>algorithmic</u> <u>mass decidability</u> problem for Gen(W) is the decision problem for a subset of P, namely, for the set $\{p \mid p$ is a program of a decidable set$\}$. The algorithmic <u>mass separability</u> problem for Gen(W) is the decision problem for a subset of PxP, namely, for the set $\{\langle p_1, p_2\rangle \mid$ the sets generated by p_1 and p_2 are separable $\}$. The real importance of the decision problems is due to their gnostic   aspect: they are problems of recognizing properties. The central though undoubtedly unsolvable decision problem is: to recognize whether a given mathematical statement is true or not.

As has already been noted in the preamble of this Part, the construction of an algorithm which is a solution of one or another algorithmic mass problem is not an application of the theory of algorithms but belongs to the field of mathematics where that particular problem arose. The whole area of mathematics is full of such algorithms. However if such an algorithm does not exist, the proof of non-existence turns out to be an application of the general theory of algorithms. Many such non-existence theorems are proved for decision problems. Here is an example of a decision problem for which the solvability has neither been proved nor disproved (example is due to Church, see [Church 36]): for a natural number n to recognize, if there exist such natural numbers x,y,z   that $z^n = x^n + y^n$.

The first proofs of unsolvability for algorithmic mass problems were obtained in 1936 by Church and Turing and were published in [Church 36], [Church 36a], [Church 36b] and [Tu 36], [Tu 37]. These unsolvable problems are decision problems concerned with the representative generative model (namely, Church's λ-conversion) and representative computational model (Turing machines); but it was Church who pointed out (and he said it in the title of his publication [Church 36]) that any such unsolvability theorem immediately produces an unsolvable number-theoretic problem.

We should like to give prominence to seven unsolvable decision problems which we consider important because of their philosophical significance or because of the simplicity of their formulation.

1. <u>The problem of recognizing the truths</u> among formulas of elementary arithmetics. Those formulas are constructed using logical operations (logical connectives and quantifiers), equality sign, arithmetic operations, and variables which range over natural numbers. The problem is to find an algorithm which decides whether an arithmetical formula is true in the domain of natural numbers. The impossibility of such an algorithm is the immediate consequence of the existence of an undecidable enumerable set of natural numbers (Part I, §10) and of the fact that this set is arithmetical (Part I, §9).

2. The decision problem for the first order logic (das <u>Entscheidungsproblem</u>)--see below, §3.

3. <u>The Post correspondence problem</u>. Let V be a finite set of pairs of words over a finite alphabet. We call this set "correspondable" if there is a sequence of pairs $\langle A_1, B_1 \rangle$, $\langle A_2, B_2 \rangle, \ldots, \langle A_s, B_s \rangle \in$ $\in V$ such that $A_1 \ldots A_s = B_1 \ldots B_s$. The problem is to decide whether a set V over a given alphabet is correspondable. This problem was posed by Post in [Post 46] where he proved the unsolvability of the problem, provided the alphabet contains more than one letter (in the case of the one-letter alphabet the problem is solvable). For the strengthening of Post's result see [Mark 54, chap. VI, §9].

4. <u>The word problem</u> for a fixed Thue system (= the problem of equality recognition for the corresponding semigroup), see [Nag 77a]. It is commonly accepted that the word problem was formulated by Thue in [Thue 14]. There exist Thue systems with an unsolvable word problem. First examples of such systems were independently constructed by Markov (see [Mark 47], [Mark 47a], [Mark 54, chap. VI]) and Post (see [Post 47]). However, the first examples were rather cumbersome. A comparatively simple example of the Thue system in a 5-letter alphabet for which the word problem is unsolvable was constructed in [Ceĭtin 58]: 1) ac $\leftrightarrow$ ca 2) ad $\leftrightarrow$ da 3) bc $\leftrightarrow$ cb 4) bd $\leftrightarrow$ db 5) eca $\leftrightarrow$ ce 6) edb $\leftrightarrow$ de 7) cca $\leftrightarrow$ ccae. In [Mat 67] a Thue system in a two-letter alphabet with three defining relations is constructed; the longest of the relations consists of a 304-letter word and a 608-letter word. For two-relations systems almost nothing is known. For one-relation systems (or one-relation semigroups) the solving algorithm exists in a wide variety of examples (see [Adj 66], [Adj Og 78]) and it is possible that it exists in all cases.

5. <u>The matrix representability problem</u>. Matrix U is representable through matrixes $U_1, \ldots U_q$, if for some $r_1, \ldots r_t$ the equality $U = \bigcap_{i=1}^{t} U_{r_i}$ holds. Let us consider integer (n x n)-matrixes.

The general problem of representability is to find an algorithm which
for every list of matrixes U, U_1, ..., U_q decides if U is representable through U_1, ... , U_q. As found by Markov (see [Mark 58]),
the general problem of representability has no solution provided
that $n \geqslant 4$ (as it follows from [Pat 70], see below, 4 can be replaced by 3). A special representability problem for fixed U_1 ... U_q
is to find an algorithm which for every matrix U decides if U can
be represented through U_1 ... U_q. In [Mark 58] one can find 27 matrixes of sixth order for which this problem is unsolvable. Another
special representability problem is to find for a fixed matrix U
an algorithm to decide for given U_1 ... U_q if U is representable
through U_1 ... U_q. As proved in [Pat 70], this problem is unsolvable
if U is the zero matrix of the third order.

6. Hilbert's tenth problem. The tenth of 23 Hilbert's problems
formulated as follows: "10. Entscheidung der Lösbarkeit einer diophan-
tischen Gleichung. Eine diophantische Gleichung mit irgendwelchen
Unbekannten und mit ganzen rationalen Zahlkoeffizienten sei vorgelegt:
man soll ein Verfahren angeben, nach welchem sich mittels einer end-
lichen Anzahl von Operationen entscheiden lässt, ob die Gleichung in
ganzen rationalen Zahlen lösbar ist. 11..." ([Hil 35, S. 310]). The
impossibility of solving this problem results from the existence of
an unsolvable enumerable set and from a Matijasevic̆ theorem (see
Part I, §9; see also [Manin 73]). The problem of whether an algorithm
exists to determine if an arbitrary polynomial equation with integer
coefficients has a rational solution, is still open.

7. The problem of identity for elementary real functions. Let T
be a class of terms defined inductively: x, π are terms, if u, v
are terms, then (u + v), (u : v), sin u, |u| -- are also terms. Algo-
rithmic problem of construction of an algorithm to decide if two
terms from T define the same function of real argument x is unsolvable (see [Mat 73]). There are many other unsolvable problems
about the real functions. For example, let a function f(x) be defined by a term, similar to terms from T, but constructed using arbitrary rational constants and without operations of division and ab-
solute-value. Then the problem of whether an equation f(x) = 0 has
a real solution is unsolvable (see [Wang 74]). Another example: Does
a function defined by a term from some class have an integral defined by a term from the same class? This problem in unsolvable for the
variety of term classes (see [Rich 68]). So the ordinary integral
calculus already produced algorithmically unsolvable problems.

Mass problems arise in all areas of mathematics. The most fundamental ones are problems of recognition of true statements in a certain mathematical language (see, for example, the first of the seven problems listed above). Mathematical languages which are in use always admit natural numbers and arithmetical operations (on them) -- and, as a rule, set variables and functional ones -- and consequently the corresponding sets of truths are undecidable. So the question of decidability of a certain formal theory is nontrivial only in the case when means of expression are scarce. In fact, renouncing the use of set and functional variables restricts us to only considering algebraic objects. There is another reason for this, namely, the fact that algebraic objects have natural constructive descriptions (see below, §5): so questions about them can easily be formulated in algorithmic form.

Thus nontrivial results on the undecidability of logical theories mainly concern elementary (i.e. first order) theories of algebraic structures from the dividing-line between the decidable and the undecidable: in fact many important undecidability results help to locate this dividing-line amongst fields (see [RobJ 49], [Mal 60], [ErJ 65], [ErJ 66]). Theories of other structures are usually undecidable. For example, this is true of groups, rings and various classes of these structures (see [Tar Mos Rob 53]). The rare exceptions are abelian groups and ordered sets (see [ErJ 64], [Rab 69]), as well as free algebras (see [Mal 62]). The detailed table summing up the results on undecidability and decidability of elementary theories can be found in [ErJ Lav Taĭm Taĭc 65].

In order to formulate a mass problem for elements of a certain algebra it is necessary to link certain constructive objects to these elements. For example we can suppose that elements of free finitely generated algebra are elements of an aggregate. Of course if a certain (not necessarily free) algebra has a finite signature and a finite number of generators, then each of its elements can be defined by a constructive object--by its expression through generators. But it may happen that two different objects define the same element of algebra. Then the mass problem of recognizing this equality arises, i.e. for a given algebra to construct an algorithm which decides whether two constructive objects define one and the same element of the algebra. As we have already mentioned this problem is unsolvable for certain semigroups. Moreover it is unsolvable for some finitely presented groups (see [Nov 52], [Nov 55]). Of course, one can be interested not only in the recognition of properties of elements of an algebra but in the recognition of   properties of   algebras themselves. To

consider the corresponding mass problems one has to link certain con-
structive objects to   algebras. This can easily be done when an algebra is defined by a generable (in particular, finite) set of   defining relations. The important class of mass problems is given by
problems of recognition of invariant (under isomorphisms) properties
of algebras. Let α be such a property and there are 1) some finitely presented semigroups which have property α and 2) some finitely presented semigroups which are not embeddable in any semigroup
having α . Then the problem of deciding whether a semigroup given
by its presentation has property α is unsolvable (see [Mark 54,
chap. VI]). A similar result was also proved for groups (see [Adj 57],
[Adj 58]). On the subject of other algorithmic problems in algebra
see [Adj 73], [Adj 77].

There is another field in which constructive descriptions of mathematical objects naturally appear. This is the field of combinatorial topology where polyhedrons (in particular, topological manifolds)
are described by their triangulations. As soon as such a description
is introduced the corresponding homeomorphy problem immediately
arises; this is similar to the word problem for group elements or to
the isomorphy problem for groups. The general homeomorphy problem
for polyhedrons (resp. for topological manifolds) is the problem of
finding an algorithm of recognizing whether two polyhedrons (resp.
two topological manifolds) given by their triangulations are homeomorphic or not (see [Mark 58a]). A special homeomorphy problem arises
if we pose some restrictions, for example by fixing the dimension or
by fixing the first element of the pair. Some of these special prob-
lems(the homeomorphy problem for two-dimentional polyhedrons, for
example) were solved long ago. As was proved by Markov there is no
solution for the general homeomorphy problem for topological manifolds
(hence for polyhedrons); moreover he proved that for every $n > 3$ one
can find an n-dimensional topological manifold such that the problem
of homeomorphy to this manifold is unsolvable (see [Mark 58a], [Mark
58c]). In [Mark 58b], [Mark 62], [Boone Hak Po 68], [Hak 73] this
result has been strengthened and generalized. The general homeomorphy
problem for three-dimensional polyhedrons is still open.

Only a little is known about nontrivial algorithmic problems in
other areas of mathematics (sometimes the researchers have a clear
feeling of the effectiveness of some construction in spite of the
fact that the corresponding algorithmic problem happens to be unsolvable or that the algorithmic formulation can not be achieved at all).
Nevertheless we shall mention two examples for differential equations:

the unsolvability of the problem of the existence of the solution
defined in [0,1] segment of the system of differential equations
(see [Adl 69]) and the algorithmic formulation of the stability problem (see [Ar 76]).

We shall mention also two more algorithmic mass problems about
integers. Their description is extremely simple but the question of
existence of a solution is still open. (Let us recall that two examples of this kind, one related to Fermat's conjecture, another connected with Hilbert's 10th problem, have already been mentioned above).

The first problem is posed in [Sa   So 78]: to construct an algorithm, which for a given integer matrix decides if a positive power of this matrix having zero in its rightupper corner exists. Let
us point out that for the similarly formulated problem: "for integer
matrix A and integer vectors x,y to decide if $i \in \mathbb{N}$ for which
$A^{i}x=y$ exists" an algorithm was recently obtained in [Kan   Lip 80].

The second problem is about commutative calculuses, known as
vector addition systems. It was posed by Karp and Miller in 1969
(see [Karp   Mil 69]). We shall give the multiplicative formulation
of the problem; the additive formulation is more natural but longer.
Let a natural number a and a finite set of rationals V be given.
A natural number is called reachable (for given a and V) if it is
equal to a or can be obtained from some reachable b by multiply-
ing by the element from V. The algorithm must decide whether a given number b is reachable. In 1977 Sacerdote and Tenney announced
the solution of reachability problem for any V and a (see [Sac
Ten 77]). However their description of the corresponding algorithm
is contradictory. If one tries to eliminate the contradictions, the
resulting algorithms turn out to work properly only in trivial cases
and we do not know how to rescue the situation. One of the authors
of this paper wrote a letter about those difficulties to Sacerdote
in May 1978 but got no reply. Since then the main achievement has been
the result of [Hop Pan 79].

We'd like to end the listing with the most clear-cut example. It
is the game of "Life", see [Gar 70 - 71]. A position of the game is
an infinite sheet of squared paper. A square can be occupied or empty
(correspondingly alive or dead). There is a finite number of occupied
squares (cells) in every position. Every cell has eight neighbours:

A move in the game consists in simultaneously changing   the
contents of all the squares according to the two following rules:
1) <u>Birth of a new cell</u>: an empty square which has exactly three

occupied neighbours becomes occupied.

2) <u>Death of a cell</u>: an occupied square which has more than three neighbours becomes empty (dies of overcrowding): an occupied square,
which has less than two occupied neighbours becomes empty (dies
of isolation).

For example, empty squares with one occupied neighbour remain
empty while occupied squares with two occupied neighbours remain occupied. So there is a single player in the game (or, if one prefers,
-- no player at all), and the game has no end. However it is natural to consider the game finished if all the squares become empty. Let
us call a position which ends up with all the squares being empty--
a "doomed" position. It is not known if there exists an algorithm,
recognizing whether a position is "doomed" or not.

Our understanding of the term "mass problem" is close to [Mark
54, chap. V, preamble]. Another way was proposed by Medvedev in [Med
55], [Med 56]. According to Medvedev, a <u>mass problem</u> is an arbitrary collection of total functions from $\mathbb{N}$ into $\mathbb{N}$, and a mass problem
is called (algorithmically) solvable if it contains a computable function. So a mass problem $\mathcal{A}$ (in Medvedev's sense) may be regarded
as a problem to find a computable function in the collection $\mathcal{A}$. Of
course one has no need to restrict oneself to function from $\mathbb{N}$ into
$\mathbb{N}$ and may consider total (it is essential) functions from X into Y
for arbitrary aggregates X, Y. Here are two examples of mass problem
in Medvedev's sense (X being an aggregate):

1. The <u>decision problem</u> for a set $A \subset X$ is the collection consisting
of a single function φ such that $\varphi(x)=1$ for $x \in A$ and $\varphi(x)=0$
for $x \in X \setminus A$ (so φ is the characteristic function for A).

2. The <u>separation problem</u> for a pair of sets A,B , where $A \subset X$, $B \subset X$,
is the collection of all separating functions for A, B (a function
φ is called a separating function for A, B if $\varphi(x)=1$ for $x \in A$,
$\varphi(x)=0$ for $x \in B$).

Let $\mathcal{A}$, $\mathcal{B}$ be mass problems in the Medvedev sense. The weak
(hence strong) reducibility (see Part I, §13) of $\mathcal{B}$ to $\mathcal{A}$ implies
that if $\mathcal{A}$ is solvable so is $\mathcal{B}$. Because of this fact weak and
strong reducibilities of Part I, §13, may be interpreted as reducibilities of problems. The theorem 1 from [Muč 65] states that no unsolvable decision problem for a generable set can be strongly reducible
to the separation problem for a pair of generable sets. The proof of
the theorem 2 from [Muč 65] shows that the algorithmic mass decidability problem for Gen($\mathbb{N}$) is reducible to the algorithmic mass separability problem for Gen($\mathbb{N}$); here "reducible" is understood in the

decision reducibility sense of Part I, §11.

§2. Applications to the foundations of mathematics: constructive semantics

The emergence of the concept of algorithm and development of the theory was stimulated not only by practical needs of solving mass problems but also by speculative attempts to comprehend the meaning of the combination of quantifiers $\forall x \exists y$. Both tasks are closely related: on the one hand, if mass problem is solvable then ($\forall$ individual problem) ($\exists$ solution), on the other hand, to prove statement that begins with $\forall x \exists y$ is to find for any x the corresponding y, i.e. to solve a certain mass problem. The understanding mass problem as an algorithmic ones is a base of <u>constructive mathematics</u> (see [Mark 62a], [Šan 62, Introduction and Appendix], [Šan 70], [Kuš 73, Introduction]): constructive mathematics use peculiar "constructive" logic. For example, in this logic to prove the statement $\forall x(A(x) \vee \neg A(x))$ means to construct an algorithm which for every x finds true clause of the disjunction (therefore if A is undecidable then the statement is false). It is presupposed when working with algorithms in the framework of constructive logic to restrict oneself to using a limited logical technique. Markov allows to use (among others) two specific logical principles (see [Mark 62a, p. 11]): 1) If the assumption of non-terminating of the process of application of an algorithm $\mathfrak{A}$ to a word P is refuted, then $\mathfrak{A}$ being applied to P produces a result; 2) if for a property $\mathfrak{B}$ there exists an algorithm recognizing this property for every natural number and the assumption that there is no number with the property $\mathfrak{B}$ is refuted then there exists a natural number n having this property. The second principle was first formulated in [Mark 54a]; in [Mark 56] it is called "the Leningrad principle", and in [Mark 62a] - "the method of constructive glean" (see also [Kuš 79]).

However, one can study constructive logic and use usual "classical" logic as in [Nov 77]. This way was outlined by Kolmogorov in [Kol 32] (Kolmogorov wrote about intuitionistic logic, but the difference between intuitionistic and constructive logics is irrelevant for the discussion). Kolmogorov's approach is to interpret constructive logic as <u>logic of problems</u>; it is important that for every two problems A and B the problem of reduction B to A is a new independent problem (cf. Part I, §11). This general approach makes it possible to interpret propositional formulas as expressions of problems (not of statements, as in traditional logic). Under this interpretation the values of propositional variables are problems and propositional connectives are interpreted correspondingly: $A \wedge B$ means "to solve A and B", $A \vee B$ -- "to solve at least one of the problems A and B", $A \rightarrow B$ -- "to reduce solving B to solving A", $\neg A$ -- "assuming that a solution of A is given to come to a contradiction". Predicate formulas are interpreted in the similar way.

Kolmogorov's approach got its fullest development in the concept of <u>Kleene's realizability</u> (see [Klee 52, § 2], [Nov 77, chap. V, §7]). Kleene's semantics of realizability can be described as the problem semantics in the following way. Each arithmetic formula is interpreted as a problem of constructing some number, called <u>realization</u> of the formula and encoding the information about its constructive validity. A formula is called realizable if it has a realization.

For the formulas without free variables we have: realization of a formula $\forall x\, A$ is a program (coded by some number) of an algorithm which for every value of x gives a realization of the result of substitution of the value of x into the formula A; realization of a formula $A \rightarrow B$ is a program of algorithm, which processes every realization of A into a realization of B. Now the realizability can be extended over predicate (in particular, propositional) formulas. Namely a predicate formula is called (we follow (Pli 78])):
1) <u>irrefutable</u> (in [Nov 77] -- "realizable") if for every substitution of arithmetic formulas for its predicate (in particular, propositional) letters there exists a realization of the resulting arithmetic formula; 2) <u>realizable</u> (in [Nov 77] -- "effectively realizable") if there is an algorithm finding this realization for each substitution. There exist predicate formulas which are irrefutable but are not realizable (see [Pli 76], [Pli 78]); it is unknown if there exists such a formula among propositional formulas. Shanin in [Šan 58], [Šan 58a] criticized Kleene's concept of realizability (Kleene discussed Shanin's critics in [Klee 60]) and proposed his own version of constructive semantics. Shanin's version links constructive problems not with all propositions but with only some of them and is based on an algorithm revealing constructive problems (as well as on algorithms for majorizing arithmetical propositions, see [Šan 73]).

Another application of Kolmogorov's conception is the semantics of propositional formulas introduced in [Med 55], [Med 56]. A similar semantics was introduced in [Muč 63]. The first semantics is based on the strong and the second--on the weak degrees of difficulty.

To regard each semantics as a problem semantics, one must recall
(from Part I, §13, and from Part II, §1) that a strong (resp. weak)
degree of difficulty is a mass problem in Medvedev's sense being
considered up to a strong (resp. weak) reducibility. Let us take the
Medvedev or the Muchnik lattice. For an arbitrary $\mathbb{E}$ from the lattice propositional connectives have the following interpretation on
the initial segment $S_{\mathbb{E}} = \{X | \mathbb{O} \leqslant X \leqslant \mathbb{E}\}$ of the lattice; conjunction $\wedge$
is $\cup$, dijunction $\vee$ is $\cap$, implication $\mathbb{A} \to \mathbb{B}$ is the least ele-
ment (its existence is proved) of the set $\{\mathbb{C} | \mathbb{B} \leqslant \mathbb{A} \cup \mathbb{C}\}$; finally,
$\neg \mathbb{A}$ is $\mathbb{A} \to \mathbb{E}$. Every formula proved in intuitionistic propositional calculus identically equals to $\mathbb{O}$ on every $S_{\mathbb{E}}$. Now for the
Medvedev lattice only: let us take $\mathbb{E} = \mathbb{1}$ and consider only formulas
without negation, then the completeness theorem can be proved (see
[Med 62]); each formula that identically equals to $\mathbb{O}$ on $S_{\mathbb{1}}$ is
provable in intuitionistic calculus; for formulas containing negations the theorem is evidently false (contrary to what is said in
[Rog 67, §13.7]) and to find suitable $\mathbb{E}$ to satisfy the completeness
theorem in the general form (i.e. for all formulas of intuitionistic
propositional calculus) is an open problem. No completeness theorem
for the Muchnik lattice is known.

Speaking on constructive logic we have so far restricted ourselves to propositions only. We discussed the ways to understand them
and the ways of establishing constructive evidence of their validity.
(It should be pointed out that in constructive logic the understanding of meaning and the understanding of proving coincide.) But logic
also deals with notions, constructive interpretation of notions has
to be a subject of constructive logic as well. The origins of contemporary constructive mathematics can be found in intuitionism and there
were some attempts to interpret intuitionistic notions on the basis
of the theory of algorithms: in particular it was done in [Klee 52a]
for the Brouer's concept of set and in [Us 57, §7] for the Weyl's
concept of function.

The specific area of application of the theory of algorithms to
constructivization of notions is the study of definitions from the
point of view of their constructiveness. A definition is conventionally called "constructive" if the defined property implies the existence of some construction: such is the definition of enumerable set.
On the other hand, the definition of non-enumerable set is "non-constructive" in the sense that it consists in the simple negation of
the existence of a construction. But sometimes among all "non-A objects" i.e. the objects which do not have property $\mathbb{A}$ one can

single out objects which do not have property A in some constructive sense --"constructive non-A objects". Namely, "constructive non-
A objects" are such objects that there exists an algorithm to distinguish them from any object having the property A. For example in
[Us 60, §13] the constructivizations of definitions of non-finite
set, non-enumerable set and non-separable pair of sets are considered and in [Us 74, §9] the notion of a set effectively distinguishable
from all sets of a given family in introduced.

Finally it is natural to call a problem effectively (=construc-
tive) unsolvable, if there exists an algorithm finding for every
would-be solution the reason why it actually is not a solution. In
[Med 69] for the parametric problems this general and vague conception is formalized in the exact concept of effectively refutable parametric problem.

§3. __Applications to mathematical logic: formalized languages of__
    __logic and arithmetic__

In [Church 56, §07] mathematical logic or symbolic logic, or logistic, is defined as "the subject of formal logic, when treated by
the method of setting up a formalized language". Among formalized
languages there are purely logical (propositional and predicate) languages, languages of arithmetic and languages of set theory. Predicate languages-- elementary (=of the first order) as well as non-ele-
mentary (of higher orders)-- is used for the axiomatic description
of mathematical and first of all algebraic structures. Languages of
arithmetic describe the natural numbers (which can hardly be described axiomatically, and anyway must be regarded as going before any
axiomatic considerations). A language of set theory has no clear semantics and is intended to formulating various axiomatic theories.

In some cases it is reasonable to define for formulas of a language the notion of truth (for one or another class of structures
served by the language) and to state algorithmic mass problem of recognition of the truth, or semantic decision problem: to construct
an algorithm to recognize whether a formula of a certain language is
true or not. For the languages rich in their means of expression
(namely sufficiently rich to express--in a reasonable sense--an undecidable predicate), the semantic decision problem is unsolvable.
We have mentioned the unsolvability of this problem for a certain
language of arithmetic in §1. Now we should like to add that the unsolvability of the problem, i.e. undecidability of the set of true

arithmetical formulas, is a trivial consequence of the fact that
this set is not arithmetical. The latter fact in its turn is a simple
consequence of Tarski theorem on the impossibility to express truthness in a language by means of the same language. For a language of
arithmetic it is natural to study the truthness on one structure (the
natural numbers), for a predicate languages it is natural to study
the truthness on all conceivable structures under all interpretations;
this kind of truthness is called "validity". For the predicate languages of higher order the understanding of the very concept of validity meets with the fundamental set-theoretical difficulties. For the
first-order predicate language the validity recognition problem has
attracted mathematical logicians since 1915 (see [Church 56, §49]),
this problem called "Entscheidungsproblem" is considered in [Hil
Ack 38, chap. III, §12] as the main problem of mathematical logic.
In virtue of Gödel's completeness theorem the Entscheidungsproblem
is equivalent to the problem of recognizing the provability of elementary predicate formulas provided the concept of "provability" is properly defined. The unsolvability of the Entscheidungsproblem was proved in 1936 independently by Church and Turing (see [Church 36a],
[Church 36b], [Tu 36], [Tu 37]). Similar statements are valid for the
semantics of realizability for predicate formulas (see §2): there is
no algorithm to decide if a formula is realizable and there is no algorithm to decide if a formula is irrefutable. These results follows
from the theorems by Plisko: the set of realizable predicate formulas is not arithmetical (see [Pli 73], [Pli 77]); the set of irrefutable predicate formulas is not arithmetical (see [Pli 76], [Pli 78]).
It is not known if the set of realizable propositional formulas or set of irrefutable propositional formulas is decidable and whether any of those
sets is arithmetical.

Besides the decision problem for truth (which is a problem of
constructing an algorithm) it is natural to ask how these truths can
be generated. This is actually a problem of constructing a calculus,
namely of a calculus generating all true formulas and only them (or,
equivalently, to construct a logistic system where all such formulas
can be proved). Gödel's completeness theorem solves this problem affirmatively for the language of the first order predicate logic while
Gödel's incompleteness theorem provides its negative solution for the
language of elementary arithmetic. In [Glu 79] the incompleteness
theorem is considered from the theoretical programming point of view.

The incompleteness theorem can be regarded as a pure non-existence theorem. But Gödel's proof (and implicitly even Gödel's formu-

lation) reveals an algorithm which for any given calculus (logistic system) can indicate the difference between the set generated by this calculus (=the set of all formulas provable in the logistic system) and the set of all true formulas of arithmetic (see [Göd 31]). Evidently this property of "effective Gödelness" (cf. [Us 74, §10]) is possessed by those and only those languages which have their sets of all true formulas effectively different (see §2) from all enumerable (=generable) subsets of the set of all formulas.

The impossibility to introduce for a given language an adequate (i.e. coinciding in extension with truth)notion of provability is closely related to the notion of inseparability (i.e. non-separability, see §1). Kleene (see [Klee 50], [Klee 52, §61]) and Kolmogorov (see [Us 53] or [Us 53a]) noticed that if two inseparable (=non-separable) sets of formulas from a certain language are given, and all formulas from the first set are true while all formulas from the second set are false (i.e. their negations are true), then for this language no complete consistent logistic system (i.e. no consistent system in which all true formulas are provable) exists.

The latter makes it possible to derive incompleteness theorems without any use of rather complicated set of all true formulas (there are formulas with truthness hard evaluated). Namely, one can construct a set of some "a priori true" formulas and a set of some "a priori false" formulas, the sets being relatively plain, but inseparable. (Various constructive versions of the notion of inseparability see [Us 53a], [Smu 58], [Smu 60], [Us 60, §13], lead to corresponding various versions of effective Gödelness.)

This inseparability technique can also be applied to establish unsolvability of semantic decision problems (see [Trah 53]).

Proof theory can be regarded as a branch of the applied theory of algorithms. The reason is not only that its results are algorithmic but also that its grounds are of this kind. The very notions of formal proof and of provable formula treated in most general form are based on fundamental conceptions of algorithmic character. Here we see two approaches (evidently equivalent) which, correspondingly, give preference to the notion of calculus or to the notion of algorithm.

The first approach is to introduce the notion of provable formula directly, without using the notion of proof: a formula is called provable if it is generated by a given logistic system. Proofs appear later as protocols (=records) of generations. As for the notion of logistic system understood in the sense of [Church 56, §7] and

[Mins 67, §12.2] it can hardly be distinguished from the general notion of calculus. One can say that logistic systems are calculuses
oriented to prove formulas of formalized languages (this orientation
reflected in relevant terminology).

The second approach is to define the notion of proof first and
then--using this notion--to define the notion of provable formula.
The main point here is the existence of an algorithm distinguishing
proofs from non-proofs, in other words the decidability of the set
of proofs; this requirement is defended in [Church 56, §07]. The
approach leads us to the notion of deductics (see [Us 74, §3]). A de-
ductic over the alphabet Б of a language under consideration is an
arbitrary triple $\langle \Delta, D, \delta \rangle$, where Δ is an alphabet (the alphabet
of proofs), D--a decidable set of words over the alphabet Δ (the
set of all proofs) and δ--a computable function (the theorem extracting function) totally defined on D and having words over Б
as its values. The words from the range of δ are called provable in
the given deductics. The notion of deductics can be regarded as a refinement of the most general idea of a formal proof system.

Finally we should like to note, that algorithmic notions are
useful not only for introducing the notion of provability, but also
on the earlier stages of the development of formalized languages, for
instance when defining the notion of (well-formed) formula, see
[Church 56, §07].

§4. Computable analysis

The concepts of computable number and of computable function of
real variable go back to the paper of Borel [Bor 12]; in the same paper some fundamental facts of computable analysis were outlined.
Section II of the paper is called "Nombres calculables" and begins
with the following definition: "Nous dirons qu'un nombre α est calculable lorsque, étant donné un nombre entier quelconque n, on sait
obtenir un nombre rationnel qui diffère de α de moins de $\frac{1}{n}$". The
footnote to this definition talking on "une méthode sûre et sans ambiguïté" of obtaining the result (this footnote was quoted in Part I,
§1) leaves no doubt that Borel means the notion of algorithmic computability in the most general form. Nowadays we say: "a real number α
is computable if there exists an algorithm to process every natural
number n into rational approximation to the number α to within $\frac{1}{n}$".
Borel points out that if two computable numbers are not equal, then
the unequality can be detected sooner or later by taking suitable

rational approximations (though the required accuracy of the approximation cannot be forecast beforehand), but if two computable numbers are equal, then an attempt to detect the equality can meet "difficultés insolubles". The modern formulation: "for every constructive real y the algorithm to point out for every x the valid clause of the disjunction $(x=y) \lor (x \neq y)$ is impossible" [Kuš 73, chap. 4, §1, theorem 3]. Section III of Borel's paper is called "Les fonctions calculables et les fonctions à définition asymptotique". The literal formulation states: "Nous dirons qu'une fonction est calculable, lorsque sa valeur est calculable pour toute valeur calculable de la variable". But in the comments following the formulation Borel requires the existence of an algorithm to find $f(\alpha)$ to within $\frac{1}{n}$ for given α and n; he notices that "donner le nombre calculable α, c'est simplement donner le moyen d'obtenir α avec une approximation arbitraire". The modern definition of computable function of real variable (see below) can be regarded as the refinement of Borel's definition. (More properly, this refinement goes hand in hand with the restriction of the domain of functions: only computable numbers can be arguments of "modern" computable functions.) Borel formulated the following proposition concerning continuity of computable function (proof of that statement was found in 1956 by Tseytin, see below). He writes: "Une fonction ne peut donc être calculable que si elle est continue, au moins pour les valeurs calculables de la variable", and "il faut, de plus, supposer connue la mesure de la continuité de la fonction, c'est-à-dire l'ordre infinitésimal (au sens généralisé) de la variation de la fonction comparée à la variation de la variable". If one understands "la mesure de continuité" as computable continuity adjuster (see below), he can deduce that Borel meant not ordinary but computable continuity.

Systematical development of computable analysis on the basis of exact algorithmic concepts began with the papers of Turing [Tu 36], [Tu 37]. The history of that development is traced in [Kuš 73, Introduction, n°2]. Publications in the field can be divided in two groups. First group can be formed under the name of "computable analysis", the second usually is called "constructive analysis". Objects of the first group have names "computable numbers", "computable functions" etc. Objects of the second are called "constructive numbers", "constructive functions" etc. Unfortunately this difference in terminology is not always strictly observed. The difference between this two trends is following. Among traditional objects-- numbers and functions --the computable analysis singles out computable ones connected with algorithms. The constructive analysis treats computable numbers and functions not as members of some vast collection of ordinary numbers and functions but as themselves. Moreover the concepts of program of a number and of program of a function are primary for it: the constructive analysis uses the names "constructive number" and "constructive function" for the same things for which the computable analysis uses the names "program of a computable number" and "program of a computable function". Then, in the constructive analysis, we must define the relation of equality on constructive numbers and constructive functions; this relation, of course, does not coincide with the identity of corresponding constructive objects, but with the identity of numbers and functions defined by those objects. This approach makes it possible to discuss directly algorithms over constructive numbers and constructive functions. It is clear that notions and results of the computable and constructive analysis can easily be translated back and forth. However it must be pointed out that when talking about "constructive analysis" one usually allows the use of a constructive logic only (see [Kuš 79a]).

The basic notions of the computable analysis are:

1. A <u>computable sequence</u> of rationals; this notion needs no explanation.

2. A <u>computably convergent</u> (or <u>computably fundamental</u>) sequence. It is a sequence which has a computable fundamentality adjuster. A <u>fundamentality adjuster</u> (or a <u>convergence-in-itself</u> adjuster) for a sequence $\{a_n\}$ is a mapping h of the set Q^+ into N such that $|a_p - a_q| < \varepsilon$ for any p and q greater than $h(\varepsilon)$. In [Mark 54a], [Mark 58d] a sequence $\{a_n\}$ is called <u>regularly convergent</u>, if the inequality $|a_n - a_m| < 2^{-m}$ holds for any m and n such that $m < n$. Evidently any computable and computably convergent sequence of rationals has a computable and regularly convergent subsequence.

3. A <u>computable real number</u>. There are several equivalent definitions of this notion:

1) Borel's definition modified to include the notion of algorithm (see above);

2) Turing's definitions from [Tu 36], [Tu 37] --the first definitions making use of a computational model (and the first precise definitions as well);

3) Specker's definition from [Spe 49]: a real number is computable if it is the limit of a computable and computably convergent sequence of rationals;

4) Markov's definition [Mark 54a], [Mark 58d], restated in terms of
the computable analysis: a real number is computable if it is the
limit of a computable regularly convergent sequence of rationals;

5) Dedekind-style definition: α is computable, if each of the sets
$\{r \in \mathbb{Q} \mid r < \alpha\}$ and $\{r \in \mathbb{Q} \mid r > \alpha\}$ is enumerable.

The set of all computable reals is called computable continuum.

4. A program of computable real number. This notion can be easily defined starting from any definition of computable number. For
example, Borel's definition gives: a program of α is a program of
an algorithm which for any $\varepsilon \in \mathbb{Q}^+$ gives the rational ε-appro-
ximation of α. We shall not consider the programming system emerg-
ing from one of Turing's definitions, namely from the definition using infinite decimal expansion and requiring it to be computable;
this system is "bad" and not equivalent to a programming system emer-
ging from any of other definitions. Programming systems corresponding
to all other definitions are equally "good" and a transition from a
program corresponding to one definition to a program corresponding to
any other can be effected algorithmically (in other words the corresponding numberings of computable real numbers by their programms are
equivalent in the sense of Part I, §15). We now give a precise definition of the notion of a program of a computable real number corresponding to Specker's definition of computable reals. Let us fix any
two representative computational models computing functions from $\mathbb{N}$
into $\mathbb{Q}$ and from $\mathbb{Q}$ into $\mathbb{N}$ correspondingly. Then corresponding
programming systems will also be fixed (see Part I, §15). Following
Shanin (see [Šan 56], [Šan 62]) we call a real duplex, or simply a
duplex a pair $\langle p_1, p_2 \rangle$ where p_1 is a program of a sequence of rationals and p_2 is a program of some fundamentality adjuster of this
sequence. Thus any duplex defines a certain computable and computably
convergent sequence of rationals and therefore a certain computable
real which is the limit of this sequence. This duplex is called a
program of this real. It would be wrong to call only the first member
of a duplex a program since it does not include information that makes
it possible to compute the real to within any pregiven accuracy. Indeed, there exists no algorithm which for any program of any computable and computably convergent sequence gives a program of some fundamentality ajuster of this sequence (see [Ceĭtin 62a, §3, corollary
3], [Kuš 73, chap. 4, §2, theorem 2]). A mapping which for any duplex
gives a real defined by this duplex is an example of numbering (under
its general interpretation, see Part I, §15) of the computable continuum. The base of this numbering--the set of all real duplexes-- is called

constructive continuum; it is non-enumerable, and more than that, for any enumerable set of duplexes there is a computable real which has no program in this set (see [Kuš 73, chap. 3, §4], [Us 60, §12, theorem 11]). If we replace one pair of representative models by another then the transition from a program of a computable real number corresponding to the first pair of models to the program of the same number corresponding to another pair of models can be effected algorithmically. This is a consequence of the existence of translation we mentioned in Part I, §14.

5. A <u>computable function of computable real argument</u>. For the sake of simplicity we shall consider the case of one variable only. Our definition (up to some unessential modification) belongs to Markov of [Mark 58d] (who used the term "constructive function of real variable"). First of all we fix some definition of program of a computable number, say, duplex definition. A function from the computable continuum into the computable continuum is called <u>computable</u> if there is an algorithm which 1) for any program of an argument produces a program of the function value and 2) produces no output for any program of a computable real which does not belong to the domain of the function.

The more advanced study deals with the notions of differentiation and integration for computable functions of computable real variable (see [Kuš 73, chap. 6 and 7]).

Among many facts of computable analysis there are two which we think are the most fundamental:

1. <u>Specker's example</u> (see [Spe 49]) of a monotone bounded computable sequence of rationals which does not converge to any computable real. Specker's construction was considerably simplified by Rice (see [Rice 54], [Us 60, §12, n°3], [Mart 70, §16], [Kuš 73, chap. 3, §3]).

2. The <u>Borel - Tseytin theorem</u> (see [Bor 12, sect. III], [Ceĭtin 59], [Ceĭtin 62, chap. V, theorem 3]) about the continuity and even the computable continuity of any computable function of real variable. Now let f be a function of real variable with the domain E and let $x_0 \in E$. A function h mapping $\mathbb{Q}^+$ into $\mathbb{Q}^+$ is called a <u>continuity adjuster</u> of a function f at a point x_0 if $\forall \varepsilon \in \mathbb{Q}^+ \; \forall x \in E$ $|x-x_0| < h(\varepsilon) \Rightarrow |f(x)-f(x_0)| < \varepsilon$. Evidently, the continuity of f at x_0 is equivalent to the existence of a continuity adjuster at x_0; the <u>computable continuity</u> of f at x_0 means by definition the existence of a computable adjuster. Borel - Tseytin theorem states that any computable function of computable real variable is computably continuous at every point where it exists, and, more than that,

for any given f the corresponding program of adjuster can be algorithmically found by the program of a real x_0 (see [Kuš 73, chap.
5, §2, theorem 2]).

As we know, many notions and results of the traditional analysis
can be extended and proved in the general case of any metric space
as well. The same is true of the computable analysis. Thus Borel -
Tseytin theorem is a particular case of the more general Tseytin -
Moschovakis theorem (see [Kuš 73, chap. 9, §2, theorem 11]) about .
the continuity of any computable partial mapping from one effectively metric space into another (subject to some conditions on the first
space, see below).

Effectively metric space (see [Nog 66], [Nog 78, chap. II]) is
a metric space together with a certain numbering of it and satisfying the requirement that the distance between any two points of this
space is a computable real and that there is an algorithm producing
a program of this real for any given numbers of the points. This notion is essentially equivalent to the notion of constructive metric
space introduced by Shanin (see [Šan 62, §9], and [Ceĭtin 59], [Ceĭ-
tin 62]), and to the notion of recursive metric space introduced by
Moschovakis (see [Mosc 64]); two last notions differ only by some
minor technical details. It is for constructive and, correspondingly,
recursive metric spaces that Tseytin - Moschovakis theorem was in
fact proved by its authors. A recursive space of Moschovakis (and a
constructive space of Shanin as well) consists of constructive
objects with an equivalence relation defined on them. It turns into
an effectively metric space if we identify equivalent objects and declare equivalence classes to be points of a new space and each of the
original constructive objects to be a number of the class containing
this object. So the computable continuum with the ordinary distance
and numbering of computable reals by their programs serves as an
example of an effectively metric space; and the constructive continuum serves as an example of constructive metric space. Another example is an effectively metric space of all computable sequences of
natural numbers with Baire distance (correspondingly, constructive
metric space of programs of such sequences).

Let us return briefly to the Tseytin - Moschovakis theorem
which illustrates very well some properties of effectively metric
spaces. The conditions required in this theorem and ensuring the continuity of functions are that a space where partial mapping is defined should be 1) effectively separable and 2) effectively almost complete. Effective separability (called thus in [Nog 78, chap. II];

Moschovakis calls this recursive separability and Shanin, Tseytin
and Kushner--simply separability) means the existence of an enumerable dense subset. Effectively almost completeness (which is called
weakly completeness by Kushner and condition (A) by Moschovakis)
means the existence of an algorithm which for any program of a computable sequence of points from the space and for any program of a
computable fundamentality adjuster of this sequence gives the limit
of this sequence provided that the limit exists.

Both the above mentioned examples of spaces are effectively separable and effectively almost complete.

A further extension is the notion of <u>effectively topological
space</u> introduced and studied by Nogina (see [Nog 66], [Nog 69], [Nog
78, chap. III]). Effectively topological space is a topological space
together with two numberings. The first numbers the space itself and
the second numbers its (topology) base, therefore both the space and
its base are presumed countable. Then there must be an algorithm which
for numbers of any two topology base elements A, B and a number of
a point $x \in A \cap B$ gives a number of such an element C from the topology base that $x \in C \subset A \cap B$. For effectively topological spaces one
can introduce natural analogues of the separation (in Hausdorff's
sense) axioms (see [Nog 78, chap. IV]), each of these analogues requires the existence of an algorithm producing the numbers of separating neighbourhoods. One of the major achievements was formulation
of conditions which are necessary and sufficient for an effectively
topological space to be an <u>effectively metrizable</u> one, i.e. effectively homeomorphic to an effectively metric space (see [Nog 66],
[Nog 78, chap. V]). Tseytin - Moschovakis theorem can be extended to
the general case of effectively topological spaces (see [Vaĭn   Nog
76]).

Besides the computable analysis in this exact sense another --
"<u>partly computable" analysis</u> is possible. We apply these words to algorithmic constructions which describe sets of ordinary real numbers.
Thus among ordinary open sets one can distinguish <u>effectively open</u>
sets: a set is called effectively (constructively, recursively) open
if it is the union of an enumerable system of intervals with rational
ends. Such an "effectivization"can be performed for many types of
sets (for example, for Borel sets--see [Mart 70, §30]).

Now we are interested in "effectivization" of the notion of set
with measure zero. These sets are also called <u>negligible</u> sets. Among
all negligible sets we can single out effectively (constructively,
recursively) negligible sets (=effectively of measure zero sets).

A set is called effectively negligible if one can effectively find containing it effectively open set of arbitrarily small measure. To be more exact, a set is called effectively negligible if there is an algorithm which for any $\varepsilon \in \mathbb{Q}^+$ produces a program of a set of an enumerable system of intervals with rational ends which covers our set and has the sum of interval lengths $< \varepsilon$. Note that the sum itself can be a non-computable number (recall Specker's example). As announced in [Za Ceĭtin 56] and proved in [Za Ceĭtin 62] computable continuum is an effectively negligible set. The main result here is Martin-Löf's theorem (see [Mart 66], [Mart 66a], [Mart 70, §35]): among the sets which are effectively negligible there is the greatest one, i.e. for which any other effectively negligible set is a subset. (The fact that the computable continuum is effectively negligible follows immediately therefrom. Indeed each set consisting of a single computable real number is effectively negligible. Therefore the union of all such sets is contained in the greatest effectively negligible set.) The set of effectively full measure is the complement of the greatest effectively negligible set. It is called in [Mart 66a, chap. IV], [Mart 70, §35] constructive support of measure. Partly computable analysis includes also study of usual functions of one variable having certain algorithmic properties--for example, admitting computable approximation (see [Spe 49], [Kla 61, §7]) or of computable continuity (see [Kla 61, §8]).

Of course, "partly computable analysis" should not be restricted to the real line only. Notions of effectively open, effectively G_δ etc. sets have definite meaning for any topological space with countable topology base. In [Kuz Trah 55] these notions are used in case of Baire's space to study computable (partially recursive) operators (see also [Us 57, §11]). The Martin-Löf theorem and its proof remain true in a more general situation we now proceed to describe.

First, two definitions.

1) Let M be a numbered set with the numbering α and numbering base E. Let μ be a function from M into the computable continuum; μ is called computable if there exists an algorithm which for any $n \in E$ produces a program of the number $\mu(\alpha(n))$ (cf. definition of computable function of computable real variable and the definition of distance in effectively metric space).

2) Let α be a total integer numbering of a system of sets M and let μ be a real-valued function defined on M. A set A is called effectively negligible if there exists an algorithm which for any $\varepsilon \in \mathbb{Q}^+$ gives a program of an enumerable set $K \subset \mathbb{N}$ such that the

family of sets $\{\alpha(k)\,|\,k \in K\}$ covers A and $\sum_{k \in K}\mu(\alpha(k)) < \varepsilon$.

The general formulation of Martin-Löf theorem is: let M be a countable system of sets with total integer numbering and let μ be a computable total function from M into the computable continuum. Then, among all effectively negligible sets there exists the greatest set. (In the most of applications M is a countable semi-ring of sets in the sense of [Kol Fo 76, chap. I, §5] and μ is a measure on this semi-ring.)

§5. Numbered structures

A numbered structure is a mathematical structure (in the broad sense) considered along with a numbering (see Part I, §15) of one of constitutive sets or with numberings of several such sets. An example: a numbered topological space (see §4) has a numbering of the set of its points and a numbering of its topology base. The numbering or the numberings must be immanently related to the structure itself -- e.g. to $\in$-relation for topological spaces.

The interest in numbered structures consists in the desire to give (constructive) names to (non-constructive) objects under consideration. Let us consider ordinals, for example. An ordinal is a non-constructive object, but "small" ordinals have (constructive) names, or notations, such as ω^2, $\omega^{\omega+3} \times 10 + \omega^4 + 1$, and so on. It is natural to pose a question: How far a similar notation system can be extended? So we come to the notion of a system of notation for ordinals. Such a notation (as defined by Kleene, see [Rog 67, §11.7]) is an integer numbering of an initial segment of ordinals which satisfies certain natural conditions connecting the algorithmic properties of the numbering with order properties of the segment. An ordinal is called constructive if there is a system of the notation ν in which this ordinal has a ν-number. A theorem of Kleene shows the existence of the maximal system of notation, that is a system in which every constructive ordinal has a number.

The ordered set of all constructive ordinals was historically the first mathematical structure which appeared in mathematics along with its numbering --to be more accurate, with a family of its numberings. It was the example that impelled Kolmogorov to formulate the general notions of numbering and that of reducibility of numberings.

As we have seen, for the set of constructive ordinals the notion of "admittable" numbering, i.e. of a numbering which conforms to the ordering, is defined in an axiomatic way by listing the desired pro-

perties of this numbering. Of course, there is another and more pre-
vailing way in which numbered structures come into mathematics. This
way is to introduce a structure together with an "easy" numbering,
i.e. with a numbering which corresponds to the essence of that structure. In this way a usual numbering for algebraic reals or a programming system for $Com(X,Y)$ is introduced. These two numberings are
the examples of the two classes of numbered structures--structures
with program-type numberings and structures with decidable total numberings.

   A program-type numbering is a numbering that can be obtained
from a programming system by using the following operations: 1) direct
product of numberings and 2) transition to a hereditary numbering.
Let us recall (see Part I, §15), that a programming system is a numbering of $Gen(X)$ or of $Com(X,Y)$ where X,Y are aggregates; a
representative generative or computational model must be given and
programs of these models be numbers of the numbering. The notions of
direct product of numberings and of hereditary numbering are evident;
here are their formal definitions. Let α and β be numberings of
A and B with bases E and F, then: 1) the __direct product__ of α
and β is the numbering γ of the set $A \times B$ with base $E \times F$
given by the formula: $\gamma(\langle a,b \rangle) = \langle \alpha(a), \beta(b) \rangle$; 2) a numbering β
is __heriditary__ for a numbering α , if $B \subset A$, $F = \alpha^{-1}(B)$ and β is
the restriction of α on F. The typical example of a program type
numbering is the numbering of the computable continuum by duplexes
(see §4).

   It is known that an algorithm to decide if two programs define
one entity is impossible. So, if α is a program-type numbering,
then (save for trivial cases) there is no algorithm to decide for arbitrary m and n from the numbering base if $\alpha(m) = \alpha(n)$. Moreover if in constructing a numbering we use a heredity transfer then
(for non-trivial examples) the base of the numbering turns to be undecidable and most likely--even non-enumerable;
for instance the set of all programs of total computable functions
from X to Y is non-enumerable. The concepts of effectively metric
space and effectively topological space considered in §4 appeared
as generalizations when studying the computable continuum and other
sets with program-type numberings. So it is unreasonable to restrict
the study of those spaces by total numberings only.

   The examples of numberings of other (not program) type is a numbering of algebraic reals using polynomials with integer coefficients.
The most important property of that numbering is the existence of an

algorithm to decide if two numbers define the same algebraic real.
There exists also an algorithm to decide which of two algebraic reals
(given by their numbers) is greater. Finally, the operations of addition and multiplication are computable in the sense that for both of
them there exists an algorithm to compute the number of the result by
numbers of arguments. We do not go into technical details of the numbering of algebraic reals. It is sufficient to realize that such a
numbering is possible, in fact, it is proposed in usual proofs of
countability of the set of algebraic numbers. So we achieve a total
integer numbering ν of algebraic reals for which 1) the set
$\{<m, n> \in \mathbb{N}^2 \mid \nu(m) = \nu(n)\}$ is decidable (this property of a numbering implies the decidability of the numbering and if the numbering
is total this property is equivalent to the decidability), and 2) the
predicate $<$ and the operations $+, \cdot$ are computable.

This example leads us to the concept of numbered and then to the
concept of constructive algebraic system. The numbered algebraic systems theory was founded by Mal'cev and developed by Y.L. Ershov (see
[Mal 61], [ErJ 73], [ErJ 74], [Gon 79]). Algebraic systems are also
called elementary structures, later on in this section we shall call
them simply "_structures_". We give some formal definitions.

Let a signature $6 = \{=, P_1, P_2 \ldots f_1, f_2, \ldots \}$ be given,
where $=, P_1, P_2 \ldots$ are predicate symbols, $f_1, f_2 \ldots$ --functio-
nal symbols. It is natural to study only the signatures for which the
numbers of places for P_i and f_i are computed by i. For such signatures the set of all formulas of a logical language (say, the first-
order language) is naturally placed in a suitable aggregate of all
words over some alphabet and is decidable.

Now, let $\mathcal{M} = <M, 6>$ be a structure. The pair $\langle \mathcal{M}, \nu \rangle$ where
ν is a total integer numbering of M is called _numbered structure_.
Let us denote by $6'$ the signature obtained by adding to 6 constant
symbols $c_0, c_1 \ldots$. We postulate that the value of c_i is $\nu(i)$
for each $i \in \mathbb{N}$. A numbered structure $\langle \mathcal{M}, \nu \rangle$ is called _constructive_
structure (or recursive structure) if the set of all quantifier-free
sentences in the signature $6'$ which are true in $\langle M, 6' \rangle$ is decidable; in that case the numbering ν is called a _constructivization_
of the structure $\mathcal{M}$. A structure is called _constructivizable_ if it
has a constructivization. If we now consider all sentences instead of
quantifier-free sentences in signature $6'$, then we obtain the definition of _strongly constructive structure, of strong constructivization_
and of _strong constructivizability_. It is clear that the strong constructivizability of a structure implies the constructivizability of it.

Evidently every constructivization is a decidable total numbering. It is known (see Part I, §15) that every decidable total numbering is equivalent to some numbering without repetition. So, if a
structure admits a constructivization, then it admits a constructivization without repetition.

The origins of the constructive structures lies mainly in the
study of numbered fields, see [Rab 60]. It is typical for the theory
of fields to consider extensions of a given structure. In case of
constructive structures   the question arises: Can any constructivization be extended onto the extension of the structure? ·In many important cases any constructivization can be extended. For example,
every constructivization of a field can be extended to its algebraic
closure, see [Rab 60], the same is true of real closure of an ordered field--see [ErJ 74, chap. 3, §1, proposition 10; §4, theorem 3].
If we have an arbitrary algebraic extension F' of a field F, then
the condition of constructivization $\vee$: N $\rightarrow$ F to be extendable onto
F' is as follows. Having a numbering $\vee$ we can naturally embed all
systems of algebraic equations with coefficients from F into a suitable space of constructive objects. Now the necessary and sufficient
condition for $\vee$ to be extendable is the enumerability of the set
of all   systems having a solution in F', see [ErJ 74, chap. 3, §4,
theorem 2]. Of course the questioned extendability of a constructivization is of interest not only for fields. For example every constructivization of a torsion-free nilpotent group can be extended to a constructivization of its completion, see [ErJ 74, chap. 3, §3].

In general, let a structure $\mathcal{M}$, its constructivization $\vee$ and
its extension $\mathcal{M}$ be given. Can $\vee$ be extended onto $\mathcal{M}$? In many si-
tuations--in particular, in all above mentioned examples--the answer
can be obtained using Ershov's kernel theorem, see [ErJ 72], [ErJ 74,
chap. 3, §9]. We sketch one of possible schemes to use this theorem
and do not try to give the general definitions. Let us begin with the
notion of kernel. Roughly speaking, structure $\mathcal{M}'$ is called a kernel
if $\mathcal{M}$ is minimal in a certain class of extensions of $\mathcal{M}$. In more
detail, this class of extensions consists of all extensions of $\mathcal{M}$ satisfying a suitable axiom system T. For example, if $\mathcal{M}$ is a torsion-
free group, a class of extensions can be choosen as the class of all
complete torsion-free groups, which contain $\mathcal{M}$; if $\mathcal{M}$ is an ordered field a class of extensions can be constituted by all really clos-
ed extensions of $\mathcal{M}$, etc. To make $\mathcal{M}'$ a kernel we must find (besides T) a family φ of formulas with one variable in the language of
the structure $\mathcal{M}$ in such a way that the following is true. If $\mathcal{M}''$ is

an arbitrary extension of $\mathcal{M}$ from our class, then there is an embedding of $\mathcal{M}'$ into $\mathcal{M}''$ with the image identical to the union of all finite sets which are defined by elements of φ (a set is defined by a formula if it consists of all elements for which the formula is true). The kernel theorem states that if $\mathcal{M}'$ is a kernel for some generable T and φ then ϑ can be extended onto $\mathcal{M}'$.

The central problem of the classical model theory is to study connections between properties of a set S of formulas and properties of a set of all models of S. In a similar way the constructive model theory studies properties of the classes of all constructive and all strongly constructive models of a set S. (Constructive or strongly constructive model of S is a constructive or strongly constructive numbered structure $\langle \mathcal{M}, \vartheta \rangle$ where $\mathcal{M}$ is a model for S in the usual sense.) If S is a theory, i.e. a consistent set of formulas closed relative to consequences, then the necessary and sufficient condition for S to have a strongly constructive model is decidability of S (the necessity is evident, on sufficiency see [ErJ 74, chap. 2, §3, proposition 1]). The requirement on S to be a theory is essential; there exists a consistent decidable set S (even a singleton S), which does not allow strongly constructive and even constructive models. First examples of such singletons S were constructed in [Krei 53] and [Most 53]; moreover there is such an example of formula containing only one predicate symbol which is a binary symbol (see [Rab 58]). Each of the mentioned examples is formed as the conjunction of axioms which form a suitable axiomatic system of set theory, but such examples can be constructed on the arithmetic base too, see [Most 55], [Baur 74], [ErJ 74, chap. 1, §2].

There are theories each countable model of which is strongly constructivizable: as follows from [ErJ 74, chap. 2, §3, proposition 1], it is the case for every decidable $\aleph_0$-categorical theory. It turns out that every decidable theory categorical in some uncountable cardinality also has this property, see [ErJ 74, chap. 3, §1, p. 74,]. In other cases some countable models of a given theory have constructivizations, others have not. In particular for every $n \geqslant 3$ there exists a complete decidable theory having exactly n different countable models, and exactly one of these models is constructivizable (moreover, that model has a strong constructivization), see [Per 73]. As it was noticed by Mostowski in his survey [Most 66, lecture 6] - "It is not quite clear what causes that peculiar behaviour of various axiomatic theories and what prevents some of them from admitting recursive models at all and others from admitting more than one such a model".

The question how many different (i.e. non-isomorphic) constructivizable models of the axiomatic arithmetic exist is one of the most important questions of the whole mathematics. When speaking on the axiomatic arithmetic we mean the usual system of axioms for addition and multiplication including the axiom scheme of induction. There is at least one constructivizable model of this axiomatic theory--the set of all natural numbers. It is known that there are nonstandard (i.e. non-isomorphic to the set of the natural numbers) models of axiomatic arithmetic , and--among them--countable nonstandard models. This fact is usually interpreted as the impossibility to describe the natural numbers by a first order axiomatic system. But if we want to have only constructivizable models the situation radically changes: there is exactly one (up to an isomorphism) constructivizable model of axiomatic arithmetics, that is the usual set of natural numbers. This fact is stated by Tennenbaum's theorem, announced as theorem 4.3 in [Scott 61] (proof see in [Cohen 66, chap. 1, §11]).

Because of its importance we will formulate Tennenbaum's theorem more explicitly.

Tennenbaum's theorem. Let a model of axiomatic arithmetic be given and symbols "+" and "." are interpreted by functions s and p in it (i.e. s, p satisfy axioms of arithmetics for addition and multiplication including the axiom scheme of induction). Let ν be a total integer one-one numbering of model carrier and let functions f and g from $\mathbb{N}^2$ into $\mathbb{N}$ be defined by equalities:

$$\nu(f\ (m,\ n)) = s\ (\nu(m),\ \nu(n)),$$
$$\nu(g\ (m,\ n)) = p\ (\nu(m),\ \nu(n))$$

If f and g are computable, then the model is isomorphic to the set of natural numbers. (More careful analysis shows that an isomorphism exists provided f or g is computable.)

So, we see that the effect of nonstandard models is due to the non-computability of nonstandard arithmetical operations. But if we restrict our considerations to computable "addition" and "multiplication" (and where can one see them to be non-computable?) nonstandard models disappear and--to everybody's delight--the natural numbers are described axiomatically.

§6. Applications to probability theory:
definitions of a random sequence

Let us consider infinite sequences of letters from a finite alphabet--binary sequence, for example. We can intuitively distinguish

random and non-random sequences, while the traditional probability
theory is unable to do this. Probability theory tells us nothing
about any individual sequence, it only deals with ensembles of sequences. In probability theory one can sometimes say "Let us take a random sequence", but   to use Bourbaki's words, it is "abus
de langage"; when something is stated about "a randomly taken sequence", e.g. "the sequence has a property A"--the exact sense of the
statement is "an absolute majority of sequences has the property A".

   In our opinion to give a precise mathematical definition to the
notion of "a random sequence" is an important methodological and practical task. (From the practical point of view we first of all have
in mind the Monte Carlo method.) It is one of the most prominent applications of the theory of algorithms to provide a definition of an
individual random sequence--a definition that should probably be considered as final. We mean Kolmogorov's definition of randomness and
the equivalent definition proposed by Martin-Löf. We shall formulate
both definitions below in this section.

   Formalization of the notion of random sequence can be attempted
in three ways. We shall call them frequency approach, complexity approach and quantitative approach. We intend first to discuss these approaches in general philosophical terms and then to give formal definitions.

   Under frequency approach we require that a random sequence should
have the stable frequency property and that this stability should be
observed for any "admissible" subsequence of the sequence. Thus in
case of a binary sequence in which 0 or 1 appears independently
and with equal probabilities, they should be uniformly distributed
not only in the sequence itself but also in any of its subsequences
chosen by some rule. In that way the frequency approach tries to ensure the absence of any explicit pattern in any random sequence.

   Complexity approach is based on the idea that a random sequence
should be of complex structure in the sense that entropies of its
initial segments should be sufficiently great.

   Finally, quantitative approach makes use of our feeling that random sequences are many while non-random are very few. More precisely
--in terms of conventional probability--a sequence is random with probability 1. Thus we might call this approach probability theoretic
or measure theoretic approach keeping in mind that probability distribution is nothing but a measure on the space of all sequences.

   Before giving three corresponding precise algorithmic definitions
we should like to point out that any notion of randomness depends on

a   probability distribution defined on the set Ω of all binary
sequences (for simplicity we consider binary sequences only). If a
sequence has an evident majority of zeros it cannot be regarded as
random provided probabilities to encounter 0 or 1 are equal but
it may turn out to be random in another case. We consider computable
distribution only: a computable probability distribution on Ω is a
computable measure μ on Ω satisfying the condition $\mu(\Omega)=1$. A
measure μ on Ω is called computable if there exists an algorithm
giving for any binary word $x \in \Xi$ a program of the real $\mu(\Gamma_x)$ where
$\Gamma_x = \{\omega \in \Omega | x$ is an initial segment of $\omega\}$.

A simple class of computable distributions is given by computable
Bernoulli measures. Such a measure corresponds to the case when 0
and 1 are encountered with probabilities p and q respectively.
Then if a word $x \in \Xi$ contains m zeros and n ones then $\mu(\Gamma_x)=$
$=p^m q^n$. In case of the uniform Bernoulli measure $(p=q=\frac{1}{2})$ we have
$\mu(\Gamma_x)=2^{-l(x)}$. If ω is a sequence then by $\omega(i)$ we denote the digit occupying the i-th position in it and by $(\omega)_n$ --its initial
segment of the length n, i.e. the word $\omega(0)$ $\omega(1)$ ... $\omega(n-1)$.

We now return to our main goal: to formalize the expounded three
approaches by means of exact definitions.

Frequency approach. It was formulated by von Mises in [Mis 19],
[Mis 28] and can be applied to Bernoulli measures only. It is not
clear how it can be extended on arbitrary computable distributions.
An infinite binary sequence ω is called random (Mises used the term
"das Kollektiv") if there is such q that for any subsequence χ
taken from ω according to any selection rule the equality

$$\lim_{n \to \infty} \frac{\chi(o)+\chi(1)+ ... +\chi(n-1)}{n} = q$$

holds.Then q is called the probability to encounter 1 and p=1-q
is called the probability to encounter 0. Two words here require
more precise definition --"subsequence" and "selection rule".

To define any subsequence of the sequence ω it is necessary
to specify a function k: $\mathbb{N} \to \mathbb{N}$ giving a subsequence $\chi : \chi(n)=$
$=\omega(k(n))$. Function k is usually required to be monotone: $k(n+1)>$
$> k(n)$. We shall call subsequences corresponding to such functions
strict subsequences. However one can replace monotony by a weaker requirement of injectivity: $i \neq j \Rightarrow k(i) \neq k(j)$. Those subsequences we
shall call generalized. The first matter to agree on then is which
subsequences ("Teilfolgen")--strict or generalized--one should be allowed to consider (von Mises gives no clear instructions).

Now what should be understood by a "selection rule"? The rule

prescribing to choose only zero elements of ω is evidently unlaw-
ful. The choice should be based on the knowledge of elements already
chosen and not of the elements which is to be chosen. It seems natural to refine the notion of "rule" with the help of algorithmic terms.
The first refinement of that kind was proposed by Church in [Church
40] (it is also formulated in [Mart 68]). Church understood subsequence as a strict subsequence. But his definition of randomness (Mises
- Church randomness) turned out to be rather narrow that can be demonstrated by two examples. The first example was constructed by Ville
(see [Mart 68], [Knuth 69, sect. 3.5, exercise 31], [Jac 70]). He
gave an example of a sequence which satisfies Church's definition
and for which the following property is valid: "frequency of zeros of
any initial segment does not exceed 1/2"; this property goes contrary
to our intuition and to laws of probability (the probability of a sequence to have this property equals to zero). The second example constructed by Loveland in [Love 66, §3] is a sequence which also satis-
sfies Church's definition but can be obtained from a non-random
sequence by a computable permutation of its members. This also
contradicts our intuition. Kolmogorov in [Kol 63, Remark 2] suggested a modification of Church's definition. In particular, he proposed to consider generalized subsequences (and this invalidates Loveland's example). The definition of Mises - Kolmogorov randomness later was independently found by Loveland (see [Love 66a, p. 499]). Definitions of randomness according to Mises - Church and Mises - Kolmogorov - Loveland are included in [Knuth 69, n°3.5 C] as definition
R5 and R6 respectively. With regard to definition R6 Knuth
notes that "this definition surely meets all reasonable philosophical
requirements for randomness".

Now we give the exact definition of Mises - Church randomness
and of Mises - Kolmogorov - Loveland randomness.

Let a Bernoulli measure be defined on Ω and let the probabilities of encountering 0 and 1 be equal to p and q respectively.

<u>Definition of randomness according to Mises - Church</u>. A "rule"
is any decidable set $S \subset \Xi$. For any given sequence $\omega \in \Omega$ this
rule gives a strict subsequence ω^S which includes those and only
those $\omega(n)$ for which $(\omega)_n \in S$. A sequence is called <u>Mises -
Church random</u> if for any rule the average frequency of zeros in the
subsequence ω^S equals to p (i.e. the limit of frequencies computed for initial segments of subsequence ω^S does exist and is equal
to p).

<u>Definition of randomness according to Mises - Kolmogorov - Love-</u>

land. A computable function $f: \Xi \to \mathbb{N}$ is called "rule" (of selection of elements from the sequence ω) if a function ω^f defined recurrently $\omega^f(n) \simeq \omega(f(\omega^f(o) \ldots \omega^f(n-1)))$ is a generalized subsequence of the sequence ω. More precisely it means that $\omega^f(n)$ is defined for any $n \in \mathbb{N}$ and all numbers $f(\quad)$, $f(\omega^f(o))$, $f(\omega^f(o) \omega^f(1))$, ... are different. A sequence ω is called <u>Mises - Kolmogorov - Loveland random</u> if for any rule f the corresponding generalized subsequence ω^f is Mises - Church random.

<u>Complexity approach</u>. It was proposed by Kolmogorov in [Kol 63], [Kol 65], [Kol 69] and is connected with what we discussed in Part I, §17. Kolmogorov starts with the idea of random numbers table as a long but finite sequence of digits (binary, for example) which is disorderly in the sense that it admits no simple description; the complexity of any description of the sequence must be sufficiently great and be approximately equal to the length of the sequence. Then randomness of an infinite sequence means that the entropy of an initial segment increases rapidly enough (see [Kol 69, n°2]). As it turns out the simple Kolmogorov entropy is not well suited for this definition but the notion of monotone entropy is quite good for this purpose.

<u>Definition of randomness according to Kolmogorov.</u> First we consider the case of uniform Bernoulli measure. Recall (see Part I, §17) that the inequality $\exists \exists K((\omega)_n) \lessapprox n$ holds for any $\omega \in \Omega$. A sequence ω is called <u>Kolmogorov random</u> if $\exists \exists K((\omega)_n) \gtrapprox n$. In case of an arbitrary computable distribution μ it is possible to prove that the inequality $\exists \exists K((\omega)_n) \lessapprox -\log_2 \mu(\Gamma(\omega)_n)$ holds for any $\omega \in \Omega$ (see [Le 73]). In this general case we call a sequence <u>Kolmogorov random</u> if

$$\exists \exists K((\omega)_n) \gtrapprox -\log_2 \mu(\Gamma(\omega)_n).$$

(Note. For uniform Bernoulli measure $\mu(\Gamma(\omega)_n) = 2^{-n}$. In this special case randomness of ω is equivalent to $\exists \mathbb{N} K((\omega)_n) \gtrapprox n$, see [V'ju 80, corollary 3.2]. But even in this simple case no sequence is possible for which $\mathbb{N} \mathbb{N} K((\omega)_n) \gtrapprox n$, see [Mart 66], [Zvon Le 70, theorem 2.6], [Jac 70, n°2.2]).

<u>Quantitative</u>, or <u>measure theoretic, approach</u>. It was developed by Martin-Löf (see [Mart 66a], [Zvon Le 70, §4], [Jac 70, §4]) who declared a sequence to be random if it passes some series of tests (=trials of randomness). By a test we mean a division of Ω into two parts E and F of measure one and measure zero respectively:

$$E \cup F = \Omega, \quad E \wedge F = \emptyset, \quad \mu(E) = 1, \quad \mu(F) = 0.$$

Elements from E are regarded as having passed the test. Surely there is no use to require a sequence to pass any test -- such sequences simply do not exist. Martin-Löf proposed to consider only effective test, i.e. the tests for which F is effectively of measure zero (=effectively negligible). Let us recall the Martin-Löf theorem which proves the existence for any computable measure μ, of a greatest effectively negligible set (see §4). The theorem shows that there are sequences which pass any effective test. Exactly these sequences constitute the constructive support of the measure.

Definition of randomness according to Martin-Löf. Let a computable distribution of probability on Ω be given. A sequence is called Martin-Löf random if it passes any effective test or, equivalently, if it belongs to the constructive support of measure.

If a sequence is Martin-Löf random under uniform Bernoulli measure, then frequency of zeros in its initial segments tends to 1/2. Indeed, one can find an effective test rejecting all the sequences for which that frequency does not tend to 1/2. Such a test can be extracted out of proofs of probability theorems. In case of Bernoulli measure any sequence Martin-Löf random is also Mises - Church random (see [Ag 75, section 5.1]) and even Mises - Kolmogorov - Loveland random (see [Knuth 69, n°3.5D, theorem M]).

It is very remarkable that both complexity and quantitative approaches give the same final result. Namely, the following theorem is true (see for its formulation [Le 73, theorem 2], [Schnorr 73, theorem 3], [Schnorr 77, theorem 4.2] and for its proof [Schnorr 73], [V'ju 80, theorem 3.2]: for any computable probability distribution a sequence is Martin-Löf random if and only if it is Kolmogorov random.

It is instructive to realize, however, that (for each of the above definitions) if one adds a billion of zeros to the beginning of a random sequence the new sequence will be random. That is why any practical application of the notion of random sequence to the Monte Carlo method should be approached with care.

If the only property required of the sequence is its randomness then there is nothing that can stop it from starting with a billion of zeros. Thus from the practical point of view it is essential to have the notion of a finite random sequence, for which the notion of infinite random sequence is--in a sense--an approximation from the top. Such a notion was outlined by Kolmogorov in [Kol 63] (see also [Knuth 69, n°3.5E]). We cite [Kol 65, §4]: "Roughly speaking the point is the following. If a finite set M with a very large number of elements N can be defined by a program, its length is negligibly small in comparison with $\log_2 N$, then almost all the elements from M have the complexity $K(x)$ close to $\log_2 N$. The elements $x \in M$

having such complexity are regard as "random" elements of the
set M".

Actually Monte Carlo method only makes use of finite sequences.
One can even assume that the practical test for "randomness" of a
given finite sequence should be its success when used in Monte Carlo
computations. Then identification of finite random sequences with
sequences of complex structure (i.e. having the sufficiently great
complexity with respect to some "natural" mode of description) seems
quite reasonable. In fact as can be shown by a rather simple argument
high complexity of a finite sequence can be regarded as a guarantee
of its successful application in Monte Carlo computations.

We should like to conclude this section with the following remark made by Kolmogorov in January 1965 at his public lecture at Moscow University: any attempt to detect a highly developed extra-terre-
strial civilization by trying to intercept a message sent out for the
same or a similar civilization is apparently doomed to failure. A
highly developed civilization probably knows how to code its messages in a very economical way. That means that its messages have great
specific complexity (i.e. complexity divided by the length of the
message) and these messages are therefore practically undistinguish-
able from random sequences of signals (i.e. from noise).

§7. Applications to information theory: algorithmical approach to
   the concept of quantity of information

It is very tempting to be able to answer the question how much
information a particular message has (i.e. to be able to measure the
amount of information). One way is to measure this amount by the
length of the most economical description of the message. From this
standpoint a message from space discussed at the end of preceding
section carries a great amount of information--approaching the maximum possible for messages of a given length. Surely the method of description should also be economical, i.e. it should give for all messages as short descriptions as possible. It should also be possible
to rebuild the message effectively and unequivocally from the description.

We shall consider descriptions to be binary words, i.e. the elements of Ξ. Let us recall the standard isomorphism between Ξ and
$\mathbb{N}$ constructed in Part I, §6; as we know, the length of an element of
Ξ and the volume of the corresponding element of $\mathbb{N}$ are equal. So
we shall identify binary words with the corresponding natural numbers.

Let Y be an aggregate of messages, i.e. some aggregate whose elements we shall call "messages". A mode of <u>description</u> is such an enu-
merable relation $R \subset \mathbb{N} \times Y$ that if $\langle n, y_1 \rangle \in R$ and $\langle n, y_2 \rangle \in R$
then $y_1 = y_2$. In other words a mode of description is understood in
the sense of Part I, §17, provided the concordance relation defined
on each of spaces $\mathbb{N}$ and Y coincides with the relation of equality.
Therefore by Kolmogorov theorem among all modes of descriptions there
are optimal ones. Let us fix such a mode. The length of a shortest
description of an object $y \in Y$ is called a simple Kolmogorov entropy
$\mathbb{N}\,Y\,K(y)$ of the object y (recall that any entropy is regarded only
to addition of a bounded function). Now we shall shortly denote this
entropy by $K(y)$. Thus

the amount of information in the message y can be naturally measured by simple Kolmogorov entropy $K(y)$ of the message.
The integer $K(y)$ is declared to be the quantity of information in
y, and this is the starting point of algorithmic theory of information, see [Bar 77].

Note that the quantity of information in y is defined to within an additive quantity of order $O(1)$. Indeed, for different optimal
modes of descriptions R_1 and R_2 we get entropies K_1 and K_2
respectively. But in virtue of Part I, §17 $|K_1(y) - K_2(y)| \lesssim 0$.

Consider now a one-one computable numbering of the aggregate Y,
i.e. a computable (1-1)-mapping of $\mathbb{N}$ onto Y. Recalling Main Lemma
of §17 of Part I we can conclude that if m is the number of message
y, then $|\mathbb{N}\,\mathbb{N}\,K(m) - \mathbb{N}\,Y\,K(y)| \lesssim 0$. Thus the quantity of information
in a message coincides (up to a quantity of the order $O(1)$) with the
quantity of information in its number. So it remains to recall that
the quantity of information itself is defined up to the similar additional value. The same argument can be used to measure the amount of
information in the pair $\langle y_1, y_2 \rangle \in Y \times Y$. Let W be such an aggregate that $(Y \times Y) \subseteq W$. The quantity of information in $\langle y_1, y_2 \rangle$ can
be defined either as $\mathbb{N}$-W-entropy of the pair itself or, equivalently,
as $\mathbb{N}$-$\mathbb{N}$-entropy of the number of the pair.

The algorithmic theory of information was founded by Kolmogorov
(see [Kol 65]) in an endeavour to ascribe exact meaning to such intuitive notions as "quantity of information" and "entropy" in the case
when these notions are applied to individual objects. In conventional
(based on probability) information theory constructed by Shannon these
notions are applied to random objects, or more precisely to random variables. It would be more correct to call this (historically the
first) theory of information "theory of transfer of information"

(see [Dob Pre 79]) or "mathematical theory of communication" as the famous founding Shannon's article [Shann 48] on the subject was

entitled. Indeed, this theory does not cover all (and first of all semantic) aspects of the notion of information. It is not clear how these various aspects can be described in the framework of algorithmic theory of information. In any case the problem of the theory's relation to semantics has not even been formulated so far. Real achievements of the algorithmic theory of information can be seen in two directions. The first of them includes the attempts to establish which formulas obtained for random variables remain true for individual objects. The second tries to find relations between Kolmogorov's and Shannon's notions of entropy.

According to [Kol 69] the starting point of the theory of information (either probabilistic or algorithmic) is the notion of conditional entropy of an object y subject to another object x. It is denoted $H(y|x)$ and is interpreted as the amount of information necessary to describe the object y provided the object x is already given. Now one defines:

(1) the (unconditional) _entropy_ of an object y; it is denoted by $H(y)$ and defined by the equality $H(y)=H(y|e)$, where e is an "a priori known object";

(2) the _amount of information_, contained in an object x, about an object y; it is denoted $I(x : y)$ and is defined by the equality

$$I(x : y) = H(y) - H(y|x)$$

In the algorithmic theory of information both x and y are constructive objects; in the probabilistic theory they are random variables. In the latter case we shall write ξ and η instead of x and y. For the sake of simplicity we shall assume that both ξ and η have finite range of values. Let ξ take $x_1, \ldots x_m$ with probabilities $p_1, \ldots, p_m$ respectively and η take $y_1, \ldots, y_n$ with probabilities $q_1 \ldots q_n$. Now denote by $r_{i,j}$ the probability that $\xi = x_i$ and $\eta = y_i$ simultaneously. Then by definition

$$H(\eta|\xi) = - \sum_{i,j} r_{i,j} \log_2 \left(\frac{r_{i,j}}{p_i}\right).$$

Now, (Shannon unconditional) entropy $H(\eta) = - \sum_j q_j \log_2 q_j$ can be defined (see (1)) as $H(\eta|\varepsilon)$, where ε takes in a single value. It turns out that $H(\eta)$ is an average number of binary digits necessary to define a single value of η. Finally, $I(\xi : \eta)$ is defined as in (2). From these definitions it follows immediately that

$$H(\eta|\eta)=0 \qquad\qquad (P\ 1)$$
$$I(\xi : \eta) \geqslant 0 \qquad\qquad (P\ 2)$$

$$I(\xi : \eta) = I(\eta : \xi) \qquad\qquad (P\ 3)$$
$$H(\langle \xi, \eta \rangle) = H(\xi) + H(\eta \mid \xi) \qquad (P\ 4)$$

(values of random variable $\langle \xi, \eta \rangle$ are pairs $\langle x_i, y_i \rangle$ with the probabilities $r_{i,j}$).

In the algorithmic theory of information one takes $K(y|x)$ in place of $H(y|x)$. The meaning of $K(y \mid x)$ has been explained in Part I, §17, (substituting $\mathbb{N}$ by an arbitrary Y presents no difficulty). In the same section we have mentioned that any simple Kolmogorov entropy (i.e. entropy $K_R(y)$, derived for an arbitrary optimal R) can be obtained from some conditional entropy $K(y \mid x)$ (i.e. the entropy $K_T(y \mid x)$ corresponding to some optimal T) by a suitable choice of x:

$$K_R(y) = K_T(y \mid e)$$

or, in a more general form,

$$|K(y) - K(y \mid e)| \lesssim 0$$

Thus in the algorithmic theory definition of $H(y)$ $(=K(y))$ beginning with $H(y \mid x)$ $(=K(y \mid x))$ is in accordance with (1). The quantity of information is introduced according to (2) by the equality $I(x : y) = K(y) - K(y \mid x)$.

In the context of the algorithmic theory of information relations of probabilistic theory undergo some modifications both evident and not so evident. Evident modifications are due to the fact that "all propositions of algorithmic theory of information in their general form are true only up to $O(1)$-term" ([Kol 69]). Therefore (P1) and (P2) are replaced by (A1) and (A2):

$$0 \leqslant K(y \mid y) \lesssim 0 \qquad\qquad (A1)$$
$$I(x : y) \gtrsim 0 \qquad\qquad (A2)$$

Not so evident modification is that in the algorithmic version of (P3) and (P4) a logarithmic term appears

$$I(x:y) = I(y:x) + O(\log_2 K(\langle x,\ y \rangle)) \qquad\qquad (A3)$$
$$K(\langle x,\ y \rangle) = H(x) + H(y \mid x) + O(\log_2 K(\langle x,\ y \rangle)) \qquad (A4)$$

Shannon's approach can be applied to an individual word A in the following way: one can consider that A as a value of a random variable ξ and then compute the entropy of ξ. It is natural to take such a ξ that A could be regarded as its "typical" realization. For example, one may assume that letters of the word A are independent and have the probabilities equal to their frequencies in A. Consider a k-letter word over an n-letter alphabet. Then ξ takes n^k values and $H(\xi)$ is k times greater than the entropy of a random variable η whose values are letters of the alphabet with the probabilities equal to the frequencies of corresponding letters in the word A. The entropy $H = H(\eta)$ can naturally be called <u>Shannon</u> <u>specific entropy</u> of the word A.

The meaning of H can be cleared by the following. Consider some method of letter-by-letter encoding   of words over n-letter alphabet by binary words. Suppose that it allows to reconstruct a word by its coding. Now if we replace each letter of A by its code from $\subseteq$, then the whole word A will be replaced by some word from Ξ having the length k'. The ratio $L = \frac{k'}{k}$ is an "elongation coefficient". It is known (see [Pro 73]) that $L \geqslant H$ is always true and that there exists such a method of coding that $L \leqslant H + 1$. Thus the number $k \cdot H$ can be regarded as a "true binary length" of the word A, or its <u>Shannon   complexity</u> (in more precise terms--Shannon 1-complexity; if one encodes pairs of adjacent letters and takes into account frequences of two-letter combinations it leads to Shannon 2-complexity and so on). So the Shannon specific entropy H of a word A shows what part of Shannon complexity corresponds to each letter of the word, and thus it is natural to compare it to Kolmogorov specific entropy of the same word. There is the following basic inequality for a word A (see [Zvon Le 70, theorem 5.1], [Bar 77]):

$$\frac{K(A)}{k} \leqslant H + \frac{c \ \log_2 k}{k}$$

where H is the Shannon specific entropy of the word A, k is the length of the word and c   depends only on the number n of letters in the alphabet and entropy K.

Another theorem on the relation between the Kolmogorov and the Shannon entropies deals with initial segments of random sequences. Consider a random variable ξ with values in a finite alphabet and assume that for any letter the corresponding probability is a computable (e.g., rational) number. Consider the set of all infinite sequences of letters from that alphabet. Then under the assumption that letters appear independently ξ defines a computable measure on that set (for a two-letter alphabet it is Bernoulli measure). Among all the sequences one can distinguish random ones (in the sense of Martin-Löf or Kolmogorov, see the preceding section). The Shannon entropy $H(\xi)$ can then be treated as "the specific Shannon entropy of a random sequence". As it turns out, for any random sequence ω the specific Kolmogorov entropy $\frac{K((\omega)_m)}{m}$ of its initial segments tends to $H(\xi)$, see [Bar 77], [Ag 75, §5.5, p. 134].

§8. Evaluation of complexity for solving particular problems

This field of applications deals with obtaining upper and lower bounds. The problems and methods used to obtain bounds of those two types are extremely different.

The upper bound is constructed as follows. One finds an informal algorithm for computing of a given function f. Then this algorithm is formalized as an algorithm of computation by a suitable computational model. Then the theorem that for all arguments the complexity (time or space) or computation for that algorithm does not exceed a suitable function φ is proved. That function φ is declared to be the upper bound of complexity.

Naturally our wish is to obtain such upper bounds which are useful for computational practice. Reexamining the types of bounds mentioned in Part I, §16, we see, that bounds "up to" (or "to within") are not completely satisfactory from the practical point of view, they are very rough approximations to the real state of affairs. From the same point of view the bounds within the multiplicative term are worse than those within the additive term and so on. On the first glance, "absolute time bounds" are impossible because of the linear speed-up theorem, see Part I, §7. But the point is that when speeding up the computation by the construction of the theorem we increased the complexity of each computational step. If we bound the complexity of one computational step then the speed-up theorem construction is inapplicable. The absolute bounds of computation time when time is understood as the sum of step durations (see Part I, §6) and the absolute time bounds accompanied with bounds on complexity of individual steps are really possible; of course, they are of the greatest practical value.

From the time complexity point of view the functions computed in the number-of-steps time equal to the volume of argument are the simplest ones; if we consider the model with the input tape then every step of computation supposes that the input head moves and reads the input symbol. That kind of computation is called _real-time computation_ (see [Rab 63], [Ros 67]). In the last years it became clear that many pattern-matching problems can be solved in real time (in particular the problem of symmetry recognition, see [Sli 77]). For the most important of the pattern-matching problems the decision algorithm is not Kolmogorov-type one (see [Sli 77a], [Sli 78]). So it is interesting to obtain Kolmogorov algorithms for solving those problems in real time.

The next class of complexity bounds is formed by polynomial upper bounds of time, i.e. bounds of the type $T(x) \leqslant p(l(x))$, where
p is a polynomial. Three examples of sets recognizable in polynomial
time were mentioned when we discussed the $\mathcal{P}$ class in Part I, §7.
As a rule bounds obtained for the functions from $\mathcal{P}$ are "up-to"
bounds, mainly "up to a multiplicative term" bounds. In this respect
titles of relevant publications are characteristic. They contain
such expressions as "linear time algorithm", "less then cubic time",
"polynomial algorithm".

The bounds "up to" sometimes create a paradoxical situation.
The progress in obtaining a "more effective" algorithm for a certain
problem may consist in going from an algorithm with upper bound of
time $c_1 \cdot n^{d_1}$ to an algorithm with upper bound of time $c_2 n^{d_2}$, where
$d_2 < d_1$. But, at the same time, c_2 can be so much greater then c_1
that for all imaginable inputs the new algorithm is worse than the
old one. The situation with the upper bound for matrix multiplication is instructive in this respect. (To simplify the discussion we
shall talk on the number of arithmetical operations, but the picture
for the time of computation by representative Kolmogorov-type models
is similar.) The classical algorithm gives the bound $c_1 n^3$ for nxn
matrixes. Strassen's algorithm gives $c_2 n^{2.81}$ (see [Aho Hop Ull 74,
§6.2]). The study of this algorithm shows that using suitable organization of computations we can surpass the classical algorithm for
matrixes greater than 14 x 14 (see [FiP 74]). In the last years new
algorithm were proposed which lowered the degree from 2.81 to (ap-
proximatly) 2.5, but these "effective" methods give some gain only
for matrixes of astronomical order (much greater then 10^{10}). Of
course, the new methods contain new powerful mathematical ideas which
can lead to a real improvement of the existing algorithms.

As for space of computation, the most important for applications
are also polynomial (in inputs volume) bounds. But this bounds would
be dubious if not accompanied by a polynomial time bound, as a polynomial bound of space automatically gives (see Part I, §6) only an
exponential time bound. Many functions currently in use can be computed with the space bounded by logarithm of the input volume or by
some degree of this logarithm and (in the same computation) with
time bounded polynomially.

Perhaps the upper bounds not majorized by a polynomial (e.g. exponential etc. bounds) are not of practical significance; they only
make it possible (along with corresponding lower bounds) to classify
in theoretical aspect solvable algorithmic problems by their "comple-

xity". On such a classification of group theory algorithmic problems
see [Can Gat 73].

As we have noticed the situation with lower bounds differs from
that with upper ones. To find a lower bound is to prove that no algorithm of computation on a given model for a given function has the
complexity smaller than a certain function φ . The main technique
of obtaining lower bounds is the diagonalization method. Examples of
the use of this method are hierarchy theorems (see Part I, §7). Diagonal constructions were used in proofs of lower complexity bounds
for logical theories, see [Fer   Rack 79]. It can be said that for
the majority of logical theories the exponential lower bounds on time
and space of decision procedures are proved. For the monadic second
order theory of succession the things are much worse: the (time and
space) complexity of any decision procedure is not majorized by any
super-exponent with the fixed number of levels - $2^{2^{\cdot^{\cdot^{\cdot^{2^n}}}}}$, see [Mey

75]. The similar result is true for elementary theory of any non-cyc-
lic free group: though the problem of the decidability of the theory
is open, it is "practically unsolvable": there is no decision algorithm
with the complexity majorized by any super-exponent with fixed number
of levels, see [Sem 80].

In the complexity theory there are lower bounds which were obtained not by the diagonal method. They are quadratic lower bounds
for the pattern-matching problems solved on the one-tape Turing machines (without input tape). For the simmetry recognition problem
such a bound was found in [Bar 65]. Another example is the integers
multiplication problem provided each digit of the result is to be out-
puted fairly soon, see [Pat Fi Mey 74]. For space we mention the lower
bound o $(\log \log l(n))$ for the space of recognition of sets which
are not recognizable with null space. It is interesting to obtain similar bounds for computation of functions (not only of predicates)
and for generation (not only for recognition) of sets provided the
generation space is defined in a proper way. From a certain point of
view all mentioned "non-diagonal" bounds have negative meaning - they
demonstrate that a model under consideration is not universal enough
in the complexity sense.

Finally we note that the comments on "up to" bounds are valid
for lower bounds as well.

§9. Influence of the theory of algorithms on algorithm practice

Nowadays the absolute majority of algorithms explicitly constructed and used by man in his activity consists of computer programs (see [Knuth 74], [Knuth 74a]). The scale of programming activity can be partly realized by examining the management problems of that field, see [Brooks 75]. So programming can be regarded as synonimous to the algorithm practice and theoretical programming to the whole theory of algorithms (for example Gödel's incompleteness theorem can be regarded as a theorem of theoretical programming, cf. [Gluš 79]). However the term "theoretical programming" is commonly used in a different sense, meaning the part of algorithm theory concentrated around the relation between a program as syntactic, uninterpreted object and a meaning, semantics of a program. Naturally it is typical for theoretical programming to be interested in practice motivated themes, which are not considered by the classical theory of algorithms, such a parallel programming (see [Kot 74]) or data structures (see [Scott 71]). Nevertheless the "common part" of theoretical programming and the theory of algorithms is rather great, and the classical theory of algorithms no doubt influenced the programming. This influence however was of ideological nature, any theorems can hardly be used for practical purposes. Here we will try to trace the influence by mentioning related results of algorithm theory.

The general notion of algorithm and the possibility to formalize it. It was important for computational practice to realize that every computer (if ignoring material supply problems) can compute every theoretically computable function and no computational device can compute an uncomputable function. The statement that every problem solvable by man can be solved by a suitable computer also plays an important but sometimes controversial role.

The existence of unsolvable mathematical problems and the unsolvability of many naturally arising problems. It became clear that for many problems attempts to find complete and exact solution are doomed to failure. So it is necessary to work out some realistic approach renouncing completeness, absolute validity or something else. Of course, dividing problems into two classes -- solvable and unsolvable ones -- also had a negative effect. The temptation appears; to consider every solvable problem as practically solvable (almost solved) if not today then tomorrow.

Complexities of computation and generation. The possibility to define exactly and abstractly what is in fact complexity of computation stimulated development of effective algorithms and gave an oportunity to compare them (see [Sli 79]). The definition of $\mathcal{NP}$ class and proofs of polynomial time equivalence of the many combinatorial problems was of great practical importance. This along with proofs of exponential lower bounds helped to resist the above mentioned temptation; it became clear that algorithmic solvability is not enough for practical purposes. Because of that importance of non-traditional (heuristic, approximate etc.) approaches greatly increased (see [Rab 74]). On the other hand theoretically constructed algorithms, for which "good" polynomial upper bounds of complexity were proved get their application in practice.

Non-algorithmical description of computable functions (μ-recursive functions, Herbrand - Gödel calculus, calculus of λ-conversion, fixed points of computable operators, etc.). Non-algorithmical (non-procedural) description of computable functions turned out to be a powerfull tool for programming. Starting with LISP language similar constructions were introduced in many programming languages. Besides that non-algorithmic descriptions form the basis for many formal definitions of program semantics.

Computational and generative models. The major part in programming is not played by representative computational and generative models themselves but by their (yet non-representative) modifications and restrictions. The typical examples of such restrictions are pushdown automata and context-free grammars. Context-free grammars are widely used to describe syntax of programming languages, starting with ALGOL-60. The problem of the description of ALGOL-68 required calculuses of a more general type — van Wijngaarden grammars. The fact that models are restricted and non-representative allows one to use them in effective algorithms (first of all translation algorithms) design. The variety of different models appeared to be superfluous from the point of view of general theory of algorithms; but in practice that variety is very meaningful when the problem of convenience to write down programs becomes vital. The increase of the number of programming languages of the end of 60s - beginning of 70s (one can count hundreds and even thousands of them, see [Sem Sem 74]) started the talk on "Tower of Babel" in programming.

Treating programs as objects of computation. It was von Neumann who implemented this fundamental discovery of the theory of algorithms into algorithmic practice (see [Neu 63]). The principle of a stored and modified program became one of the foundations of the system

programming. The inevitable parts of every computer are compilers and
other components of operating system oriented to modify and execute
user's program. A machine with a running interpreter is exactly a
universal algorithm in the sense of algorithm theory.

<u>Treating programs as objects of generation</u> as well as developments on logical calculuses stimulated the creation of systems for proving statements on programs, see [Hoare 69], [Nep 79]. An important
class of such statements consists of statements about program correctness, i.e. statements that "program does what I want."

<u>Programming techniques</u>, i.e. methods of program constructing
and proving their correctness appeared inside the theory of algorithms.
The most instructive example is that of a structured programming. The
main operators of structured programs constructing (composition, conditional operator, iteration) were introduced at the beginning of the
50s for Markov normal algorithms (see [Mark 54, chap. III], [Nag 77]).
At the same time non-trivial examples of inductive proofs of correctness of programs constructed by those operators (including programs
of universal algorithms--i.e. interpreter programs) were given. In
abstract algebraic form operations of structured programming were
developed in the systems of algorithmic algebras by Glushkov; at the
same time practically meaningful examples of program transformations
and proofs of their correctness were given in [Gluš 65]. In the 70s
structured programming became one of the tools of practical programmers.

*   *   *

BIBLIOGRAPHY

Abbreviations

АиЛ – Алгебра и логика/ Институт математики Сибирского отделения Академии наук СССР.- Новосибирск

БСЭ – Большая советская энциклопедия

ВИНИТИ – Всесоюзный институт научной и технической информации

ВКМЛ-3 – Третья Всесоюзная конференция по математической логике (23 – 27 июня 1974 г.): Тезисы докладов/ Институт математики Сибирского отделения Академии наук СССР. – Новосибирск, 1974. – 237 с.

ДАН – Доклады Академии наук СССР

ИАН – Известия Академии наук СССР. Серия математическая

ИКММЛ – Исследования по конструктивной математике и математической логике

МИАН – Математический институт им. В.А.Стеклова Академии наук СССР

ММО – Московское математическое общество

МЭ – Математическая энциклопедия

НГУ – Новосибирский государственный университет

НС ЛОМИ – Научные семинары Ленинградского отделения МИАН

ПК – Проблемы кибернетики. М.: Физматгиз (till вып. 9) and Наука (from вып.15)

ПКНМ – Проблемы конструктивного направления в математике

ТПММЛ – Теоретические применения методов математической логики

ТТВМС – Труды Третьего Всесоюзного математического съезда

УМН – Успехи математических наук

ACM – the Association for Computing Machinery

AW – Reading, Mass., etc.: Addison-Wesley Publishing Company

JCSS – Journal of computer and system sciences

JSL – the Journal of symbolic logic

LMS – the London Mathematical Society

LN – Lecture notes

NH – Amsterdam: North-Holland Publishing Company

SIAM – the Society for Industrial and Applied Mathematics

Springer – Berlin, etc.: Springer-Verlag

ZmLGM – Zeitschrift für mathematische Logik und Grundlagen der Mathematik

Adjan S.I. (Адян С.И.)

[Adj 57] Адян С.И. Конечно-определенные группы и алгоритмы. -
ДАН, 1957, т. 117, № 1, с. 9 - 12.

[Adj 57a] Адян С.И. Неразрешимость некоторых алгоритмических
проблем теории групп. - Труды ММО, М.: Физматгиз,
1957, т. 6, с. 231 - 298.

[Adj 57b] Адян С.И. Проблема алгоритма. - Наука и жизнь, 1957,
№ 8, с. 13 - 14.

[Adj 58] Адян С.И. Об алгоритмических проблемах в эффективно-
полных классах групп. - ДАН, 1958, т. 123, № 1, с.
13 - 16.

[Adj 66] Адян С.И. Определяющие соотношения и алгоритмические
проблемы для групп и полугрупп. М.: Наука, 1966.
123 с. (Труды МИАН, т. 85).

[Adj 73] Адян С.И. О работах П.С.Новикова и его учеников по
алгоритмическим вопросам алгебры. - В кн.: Математическая логика, теория алгоритмов и теория множеств. М.:
Наука, 1973 (Труды МИАН, т. 133), с. 23 - 32.

[Adj 77] Адян С.И. Алгоритмическая проблема. - В кн.: МЭ. Т.
I. 1977, с. 214 - 218.

Adjan S.I., Oganesjan G.U. (Адян С.И., Оганесян Г.У.)

[Adj Og 78] Адян С.И., Оганесян Г.У. К проблемам равенства и
делимости в полугруппах с одним определяющим соотноше-
нием. - ИАН, 1978, т. 42, № 2, с. 219 - 225.

Adler A.

[Adl 69] Adler A. Some recursively unsolvable problems in
analysis. - Proceedings of AMS, 1969, v. 22, N 2,
p. 523 - 526.

Agafonov V.N. (Агафонов В.Н.)

[Ag 75] Агафонов В.Н. Сложность алгоритмов и вычислений:
Спецкурс для студентов НГУ, часть 2. Новосибирск:
Изд-во НГУ, 1975. 146 с.

Aho A.V., Hopcroft J.E., Ullman J.D.

[Aho Hop Ull 74] Aho A.V., Hopcroft J.E., Ullman J.D. The
design and analysis of computer algorithms. AW,
1974. X + 470 p.

Arnol'd V.I. (Арнольд В.И.)

[Ar 76] Arnol'd V.I. Dynamic systems and differential equations
(B). - In: [Brow 76], p. 59.

Baker A.

[Bak 68] Baker A. Contributions to the theory of Diophantine
equations. I : On the representation of integers by
binary forms. - Philosophical transactions of the
Royal Society of London, ser. A, 1968, v. 263,
N 1139, p. 173 - 191.

Barzdin' Ja.M. (Барздинь Я.М.)

[Bar 65] Барздинь Я.М. Сложность распознавания симметрии на машинах Тьюринга. - ПК, 1965, вып. 15, с. 245 - 248.

[Bar 77] Барздинь Я.М. Алгоритмическая теория информации. -
В кн.: МЭ. Т. I. 1977, с. 219 - 222.

Baur W.

[Baur 74] Baur W. Uber rekursive Strukturen. - Inventiones
mathematicae, 1974, v. 23, N 2, p. 89 - 95.

Blum M.

[Blum 67] Blum M. A machine-independent theory of the complexity of recursive functions. - Journal of ACM, 1967,
v. 14, N 2, p. 322 - 336.

[Blum 67a] Blum M. On the size of machines. - Information and
control, 1967, v. 11, N 3, p. 257 - 265.

Boone W.W., Cannonito F.B., Lyndon R.C.

[Boone Can Lyn 73] Boone W.W., Cannonito F.B., Lyndon R.C.
(Eds.) Word problems: Decision problems and the
Burnside problem in group theory. NH, 1973,
XII + 646 p.

Boone W.W., Haken W., Poénaru V.

[Boone Hak Poé 68] Boone W.W., Haken W., Poénaru V. On recursively unsolvable problems in topology and their
classification. - In: Contributions to mathematical
logic. / Schmidt H.A. et al., eds. NH, 1968, p. 37 -
74.

Borel E.

[Bor 12] Borel E. Le calcul des intégrales définies. - Journal
de Mathematiques pures et appliquées. Sér. 6, 1912,
v. 8, N 2, p. 159 - 210. (Reprinted in revised form
under the title "La théorie de la mésure et la théorie de l'intégration" in Borel E. Leçons sur la
théorie des fonctions. 2-e éd., augmentée. Paris:
Gauthier-Villars, 1914, p. 217 - 256.

Brooks F.P., Jr.

[Brooks 75] Brooks F.P. The mythical man-month. AW, 1975.

Browder F.E.

[Brow 76] Browder F.E. (Ed.) Mathematical developments arising from the Hilbert problems. Providence: AMS, 1976.
(Proceedings of symposia in pure mathematics, v. 28.)
628 p.

Butts R.E., Hintikka J.

[Butts Hin 77] Butts R.E., Hintikka J. (Eds.) Logic, foundations of mathematics, and computability theory. (Proceedings of the fifth International congress of logic,
methodology and philosophy of science. Part I.)
Dordrecht, Holland: D.Reidel, 1977. X + 406 p.

Cannonito F.B., Gatterdam R.W.

[Can Gat 73] Cannonito F.B., Gatterdam R.W. The computability
of group constructions. I. - In: [Boone Can Lyn 73],
p. 365 - 400.

Ceitin G.S. (Цейтин Г.С.)

[Ceĭtin 58] Цейтин Г.С. Ассоциативное исчисление с неразреши-
мой проблемой эквивалентности. - В кн.: ПКНМ. I. М.;
Л.; Изд-во АН СССР, 1958 (Труды МИАН, т. 52),
с. I72 - I89.

[Ceĭtin 59] Цейтин Г.С. Алгоритмические операторы в конструктивных полных сепарабельных метрических пространствах. - ДАН, 1959, т. I28, № I, с. 49 - 52.

[Ceĭtin 62] Цейтин Г.С. Алгоритмические операторы в конструктивных метрических пространствах. - В кн.: ПКНМ. 2.
М.; Л.: Изд-во АН СССР, 1962 (Труды МИАН, т. 67),
с. 295 - 361.

[Ceĭtin 62a] Цейтин Г.С. Теоремы о среднем значении в конструктивном анализе. - В кн.: ПКНМ. 2. М.; Л.: Изд-во
АН СССР, 1962 (Труды МИАН, т. 67), с. 362 -
384.

Church A.

[Church 36] Church A. An unsolvable problem of elementary
number theory. - American journal of mathematics,
1936, v. 58, N 2, p. 345 - 363.

[Church 36a] Church A. A note on the Entscheidungsproblem. -
JSL, 1936, v. 1, N 1, p. 40 - 41.

[Church 36b] Church A. Correction to a note on the Entscheidungsproblem. - JSL, 1936, v. 1, N 3, p. 101 -
102.

[Church 40] Church A. On the concept of a random sequence. -
Bulletin of AMS, 1940, v. 46, N 2, p. 130 - 135.

[Church 41] Church A. The calculi of lambda-conversion.
Princeton, N.J.: Princeton University Press, 1941.
77 p. (Annals of mathematical studies, N 6).

[Church 56] Church A. Introduction to mathematical logic.
V. 1. Princeton, N.J.: Princeton University Press,
1956. IX + 376 p.

Cohen P.J.

[Coh 66] Cohen P.J. Set theory and the continuum hypothesis.
New York; Amsterdam: W.A.Benjamin, 1966. 144 p.

Davis M., Matijasevič Ju., Robinson J.

[Da Mat RobJ 76] Davis M., Matijasevic Ju., Robinson J.
Hilbert's tenth problem. Diophantine equations:
positive aspects of a negative solution. - In:
[Brow 76], p. 323 - 378.

Degtev A.N. (Дегтев А.Н.)

[Deg 73] Дегтев А.Н. О tt- и m-степенях. - АиЛ, 1973,
т. 12, № 2, с. 143 - 161.

Dobrušin R.L., Prelov V.V. (Добрушин Р.Л., Прелов В.В.)

[Dob Pre 79] Добрушин Р.Л., Прелов В.В. Информации теория. -
В кн.: МЭ. Т. 2. 1979, с. 653 - 655.

Ebbinghaus H.-D.

[Eb 70] Ebbinghaus H.-D. Aufzählbarkeit. - In: [Jac 70a],
p. 64 - 113.

Eršov A.P. (Ершов А.П.)

[ErA 60] Ершов А.П. Операторные алгорифмы. I. (Основные понятия). - ПК, 1960, вып. 3, с. 5 - 48.

[ErA 62] Ершов А.П. Операторные алгорифмы. II. (Описание ос-
новных конструкций программирования). - ПК, 1962,
вып. 8, с. 211 - 233.

[ErA 67] Ершов А.П. Об операторных схемах Янова. - ПК,
1967, вып. 20, с. 181 - 200.

[ErA 72] Ershov A.P. Theory of program schemata. - In:
[Frei Grif Rosenf 72], V. 1, p. 28 - 45.

[ErA 73] Ершов А.П. Современное состояние теории схем программ. - ПК, 1973, вып. 27, с. 87 - 110.

[ErA 77] Ершов А.П. Введение в теоретическое программирование (беседы о методе). М.: Наука, 1977. 288 с.

[ErA 80] Ершов А.П. Международный симпозиум "Алгоритм в современной математике и ее приложениях". - Кибернетика, 1980, № 2, с. 145 - 147.

Eršov A.P., Ljapunov A.A. (Ершов А.П., Ляпунов А.А.)

[ErA Lja 67] Ершов А.П., Ляпунов А.А. О формализации понятия программы. - Кибернетика, 1967, № 5, с. 40 - 57.

Eršov A.P., Uspenskiǐ V.A. (Ершов А.П., Успенский В.А.)

[ErA Us 80] Ершов А.П., Успенский В.А. Алгоритмы на родине аль-Хорезми. - Научно-техническая информация. Серия 2. Информационные процессы и системы, 1980, № 1, с. 28 - 30.

Eršov Ju.L. (Ершов Ю.Л.)

[ErJ 62] Ершов Ю.Л. О гипотезе В.А.Успенского. - АиЛ, 1962, т. 1, вып. 4, с. 45 - 48.

[ErJ 64] Ершов Ю.Л. Разрешимость элементарной теории дистрибутивных структур с относительными дополнениями и теории фильтров. - АиЛ, 1964, т. 3, вып. 3, с. 17 - 38.

[ErJ 65] Ершов Ю.Л. Неразрешимость некоторых полей. - ДАН, 1965, т. 161, № 1, с. 27 - 29.

[ErJ 66] Ершов Ю.Л. Новые примеры неразрешимых теорий. АиЛ, 1966, т. 5, вып. 5, с. 37 - 47.

[ErJ 72] Ершов Ю.Л. Существование конструктивизаций. - ДАН, 1972, т. 204, № 5, с. 1041 - 1044.

[ErJ 73] Ершов Ю.Л. Конструктивные модели. - В кн.: Избранные вопросы алгебры и логики. Новосибирск: Наука, 1973, с. 111 - 130.

[ErJ 74] Ершов Ю.Л. Теория нумераций. Часть 3. Конструктивные модели. Новосибирск, 1974. 139 с. (Библиотека кафедры алгебры и математической логики Новосибирского университета, вып. 13.)

[ErJ 77] Ершов Ю.Л. Теория нумераций. М.: Наука, 1977. 416 с.

Eršov Ju.L., Lavrov I.A., Taǐmanov A.D., Taǐclin M.A. (Ершов Ю.Л., Лавров И.А., Тайманов А.Д., Тайцлин М.А.)

[ErJ Lav Taǐm Taǐc 65] Ершов Ю.Л., Лавров И.А., Тайманов А.Д., Тайцлин М.А. Элементарные теории. - УМН, 1965, т. 20, вып. 4 (I24), с. 37 - I08.

Ferrante J., Rackoff C.W.

[Fer Rac 79] Ferrante J., Rackoff C.W. The Computational
complexity of logical theories. Springer, 1979. 243
p. (LN in mathematics, v. 718).

Fischer P.C.

[Fiᵖ74] Fischer P.C. Further schemes for combining matrix
algorithms. - In: Automata, languages and programming. 2nd colloquium (Saarbrücken, July 29 - August 2,
1974). Springer, 1974 (LN in computer science, v. 14),
p. 428 - 436.

Frege G.

[Frege 1879] Frege G. Begriffsschrift, eine der arithmeti-
schen nachgebildete Formelsprache des reinen Denkens.
Halle, 1879. X + 88 S. (English translation: Frege G.
Begriffsschrift, a formula language, modeled upon
that of arithmetic, for pure thought. - In [Hei 67],
p. 1 - 82.)

Freiman C.V., Griffith J.E., Rosenfeld J.L.

[Frei Grif Rosenf 72] Freiman C.V., Griffith J.E., Rosenfeld
J.L. (Eds.) Information processing 71. Proceedings of
IFIP congress 71 (Lubljana, August 23 - 28, 1971).
1622 p. (in two volumes).

Friedberg R.M.

[Fried 57] Friedberg R.M. Two recursively enumerable sets of
incomparable degrees of unsolvability (solution of
Post's problem 1944). - Proceedings of the National
Academy of Sciences, v. 43, N 2, p. 236 - 238.

Gardner M.

[Gard 70 - 71] Gardner M. Mathematical games. - Scientific
American, 1970, v. 223, N 4, p. 120 - 123; 1971,
v. 224, N 2, p. 112 - 117.

Gladkiĭ A.V. (Гладкий А.B.)

[Glad 73] Гладкий А.В. Формальные грамматики и языки. М.:
Наука, 1973. 368 с.

[Glad 77] Гладкий А.В. Грамматика порождающая. - В кн.: МЭ.
Т. I. 1977, с. I092 - I093.

Gluškov V.M. (Глушков В.М.)

[Gluš 65] Глушков В.М. Теория автоматов и формальные преобразо-
вания микропрограмм. - Кибернетика, 1965, №5, с. I - 9.

[Gluš 79] Глушков В.М. Теорема о неполноте формальных теорий с
позиции программиста. - Кибернетика, 1979, №2, с. I - 5.

Gluškov V.M., Ceĭtlin G.E., Juščenko E.L. (Глушков В.М., Цейтлин
Г.Е., Ющенко Е.Л.)

[Gluš Ceĭtl Jušč 78] Глушков В.М., Цейтлин Г.Е., Ющенко Е.Л.
Алгебра, языки, программирование. 2-е изд. Киев:
Наукова думка, 1978. 318 с.

Gödel K.

[Göd 31] Gödel K. Über formal unentscheidbare Sätze der Principia Mathmatica und verwandter Systeme I. - Monatshefte
für Mathematik und Physik, 1931, Bd. 38, H. 1, S. 173 -
198. (English translation: On formally undecidable propositions of Principia Mathematica and related systems
I. - In [Hei 67], p. 596 - 616.)

[Göd 58] Gödel K. Über eine bisher noch nicht benützte Erweiterung des finiten Standpunktes. - Dialectica, 1958, v.
12, N 3/4, p. 280 - 287.

Gončarov S.S. (Гончаров С.С.)

[Gon 79] Гончаров С.С. Конструктивных моделей теория. - В кн.:
МЭ. т. 2. 1979, с. I058 - I060.

Hačijan L.G. (Хачиян Л.Г.)

[Hač 79] Хачиян Л.Г. Полиномиальный алгоритм в линейном программировании. - ДАН, 1979, т. 244, №5, с. I093 - I096.

Haken W.

[Hak 73] Haken W. Connections between topological and group
theoretical decision problems. - In [Boone Can Lyn 73],
p. 427 - 441.

Hartmanis J., Hopcroft J.E.

[Hart Hop 71] Hartmanis J., Hopcroft J.E. An overview of the
theory of computational complexity. - Journal of
ACM, 1971, v. 18, N 3, p. 444 - 475.

van Heijenoort J.

[Hei 67] van Heijenoort J. From Frege to Gödel. A source
book in mathematical logic, 1879 - 1931. Cambridge,

Mass.: Harvard University Press, 1967. XII + 660 p.

Hermes H.

[Her 65] Hermes H. Enumerability. Decidability. Computability. An introduction to the theory of recursive functions. Springer, 1965. IX + 245 p.

Hilbert D.

[Hil 35] Hilbert D. Mathematische Probleme. - In: Hilbert D. Gesammelte Abhandlungen. Bd. 3. Berlin: Springer-Verlag, 1935, S. 290 - 329.

Hilbert D., Ackermann W.

[Hil Ack 38] Hilbert D., Ackermann W. Grundzuge der theoretischen Logik. 2-te Aufl. Berlin: Springer, 1938. VIII + 133 S. (Reprinted: New York: Dover Publications, 1946, VIII + 155 p.)

Hoare C.A.R.

[Hoare 69] Hoare C.A.R. An axiomatic basis for computer programming. - Communications of ACM, 1969, v. 12, N 10, p. 576 - 580, 583.

Hopcroft J., Pansiot J.-J.

[Hop Pan 79] Hopcroft J., Pansiot J.-J. On the reachability problem for 5-dimensional vector addition systems. - Theoretical computer science, 1979, v. 8, N 2, p. 135 - 159.

Hopcroft J.E., Paul W.J., Valiant L.G.

[Hop Paul Valia 77] Hopcroft J.E., Paul W.J., Valiant L.G. On time versus space. - Journal of ACM, 1977, v. 24, N 2, p. 332 - 337.

Hopcroft J.E., Tarjan R.E.

[Hop Tarj 72] Hopcroft J.E., Tarjan R.E. Isomorphism of planar graphs. - In: Complexity of computer computations (Proceedings of the symposium, IBM Thomas J. Watson Research Center, Yorktown Heights, N. Y., 1972), New York: Plenum, 1972, p. 131 - 152.

Hopcroft J.E., Ullman J.D.

[Hop Ull 69] Hopcroft J.E., Ullman J.D. Formal languages and their relation to automata. AW, 1969. X + 242 p.

Hopcroft J.E., Wong J.K.

[Hop Wong 74] Hopcroft J.E., Wong J.K. A linear time algorithm

for isomorphism of planar graphs: Preliminary report.
- In: Sixth Annual ACM symposium on theory of computing (Seattle, Wash., April 30 - May 2, 1974). N.Y.:
ACM, 1974, p. 172 - 184.

Jacobs K.

[Jac 70] Jacobs K. Turing-Maschinen und zufällige 0-1-Folgen.
- In: [Jac 70a], p. 141 - 167.

[Jac 70a] Jacobs K. (Ed.) Selecta mathematica. II. Springer,
1970.

Janov Ju.I. (Янов Ю.И.)

[Janov 58] Янов Ю.И. О логических схемах алгоритмов. - ПК,
1958, вып. I, с. 75 - 127.

Janovskaja S.A. (Яновская С.А.)

[Janovs 59] Яновская С.А. Математическая логика и основания
математики. - В кн.: Математика в СССР за сорок лет.
/ Курош А.Г. и др., ред. Т. I. М.: Физматгиз, 1959,
с. I3 - I20.

[Janovs 62] Яновская С.А. Исчисление. - В кн.: Философская
энциклопедия. Т. 2. 1962, с. 387 - 390.

Kannan R., Lipton R.J.

[Kan Lip 80] Kannan R., Lipton R.J. Orbit problem is decidable. - In: Twelfth Annual ACM Symposium on the
theory of computing (Los Angeles, California, April
28 - 30, 1980). N.Y.: ACM, 1980, p. 252 - 268.

Karp R.M., Miller R.E.

[Karp Mil 69] Karp R.M., Miller R.E. Parallel program schemata. - JCSS, 1969, v. 3, N 2, p. 147 - 195.

Klaua D.

[Kla 61] Klaua D. Konstruktive Analysis. Berlin: VEB
Deutscher Verlag der Wissenschaften, 1961. VIII + 160
S. (Mathematische Forschungsberichte, Bd. 11).

Kleene S.C.

[Klee 36] Kleene S.C. General recursive functions of natural
numbers. - Mathematische Annalen, 1936, Bd. 112,
H. 5, S. 727 - 742. (In [Klee 52 , Bibliography]
the author writes: "For an erratum and a simplification cf. JSL v. 2, p. 38 and v. 4, top p. IV at
end".)

[Klee 43] Kleene S.C. Recursive predicates and quantifiers.
- Transactions of AMS, 1943, v. 53, N 1, p. 41 - 73.
(In [Klee 52, Bibliography] the author recommends
to omit 15.)

[Klee 50] Kleene S.C. A symmetric form of Gödel's theorem. -
Koninklijke Nederlandsche Akademie van Wetenschappen,
Proceedings of the Section of sciences, ser. A, 1950,
v. 53, N 5 - 6, p. 800 - 802. (The same in: Indaga-
tiones mathematicae, 1950, v. 12, N 3, p. 244 - 246.)

[Klee 52] Kleene S.C. Introduction to metamathematics. N.Y.;
Toronto: D. Van Nostrand Company, 1952. 516 p.

[Klee 52a] Kleene S.C. Recursive functions and intuitionistic
mathematics. - In: Proceedings of the International
congress of mathematicians. (Cambridge, Massachu-
setts, USA, August 30 - September 6 1950). V. 1.
Providence: AMS, 1952, p. 679 - 685.

[Klee 60] Kleene S.C. Realizability and Shanin's algorithm
for the constructive deciphering of mathematical
sentences. - Logique et analyse. Nouvelle série,
1960, t. 3, N 11 - 12, p. 154 - 165.

Kleene S.C., Post E.L.

[Klee Post 54] Kleene S.C., Post E.L. The upper semi-lattice
of degrees of recursive unsolvability. - Annals of
mathematics, ser. 2, v. 59, N 3, p. 379 - 407.

Knuth D.E.

[Knuth 68] Knuth D.E. The art of computer programming. V. 1.
Fundamental algorithms. - AW, 1968. XXI + 634 p.

[Knuth 69] Knuth D.E. The art of computer programming. V. 2.
Seminumerical algorithms. - AW, 1969.

[Knuth 74] Knuth D.E. Computer science and its relation to
mathematics. - American mathematical monthly, 1974,
v. 81, N 4, p. 323 - 343.

[Knuth 74a] Knuth D.E. Computer programming as an art. -
Communications of ACM, 1974, v. 17, N 12, p. 667 -
673.

Kolmogorov A.N. (Колмогоров А.Н.)

[Kol 32] Kolmogoroff A. Zur Deutung der intuitionistischen
Logik. - Mathematische Zeitschrift, 1932, Bd. 35,
H. 1, S. 58 - 65.

[Kol 50] Колмогоров А.Н. Алгоритм. - БСЭ, 2-е изд. Т. 2.

1950, с. 65.

[Kol 53] Колмогоров А.Н. О понятии алгоритма. - УМН, 1953, т. 8, вып. 4 (56), с. 175 - 176.

[Kol 54] Колмогоров А.Н. Предисловие редактора перевода. - В кн.: Петер Р. Рекурсивные функции. Перевод с немецкого. М.: ИЛ, 1954, с. 3 - 10.

[Kol 63] Kolmogorov A.N. On tables of random numbers. - Sankhya. The Indian journal of statistics. Ser. A, 1963, v. 25, part 4, p. 369 - 376.

[Kol 65] Колмогоров А.Н. Три подхода к определению понятия "количества информации". - Проблемы передачи информации, 1965, т. I, вып. I, с. 3 - II.

[Kol 69] Колмогоров А.Н. К логическим основам теории информации и теории вероятностей. - Проблемы передачи информации, 1969, т. 5, вып. 3, с. 3 - 7.

Kolmogorov A.N., Fomin S.V. (Колмогоров А.Н., Фомин С.В.)

[Kol Fo 76] Колмогоров А.Н., Фомин С.В. Элементы теории функций и функционального анализа. 4-е изд. М.: Наука, 1976. 543 с.

Kolmogorov A.N., Uspenskiĭ V.A. (Колмогоров А.Н., Успенский В.А.)

[Kol Us 58] Колмогоров А.Н., Успенский В.А. К определению алгоритма. - УМН, 1958, т. I3, вып. 4 (82), с. 3 - 28.

Korpelevič G.M. (Корпелевич Г.М.)

[Kor 63] Корпелевич Г.М. О соотношении понятий разрешимости и перечислимости для конечных автоматов. - ДАН, 1963, т. I49, № 5, с. I023 - I025.

Kotov V.E. (Котов В.Е.)

[Kot 74] Котов В.Е. Теория параллельного программирования: прикладные аспекты. - Кибернетика, 1974, № I, с. I - 16; № 2, с. I - 18.

[Kot 78] Котов В.Е. Введение в теорию схем программ. Новосибирск: Наука, 1978. 257 с.

Kreisel G.

[Krei 53] Kreisel G. Note on arithmetic models for consistent formulae of the predicate calculus. II. - In: Proceedings of the XIth International congress of philosophy (Bruxelles, August 20 - 26, 1953), v. 14, Amsterdam; Louvain, 1953, p. 39 - 49.

Kušner B.A. (Кушнер Б.А.)

[Kuš 73] Кушнер Б.А. Лекции по конструктивному математиче-
скому анализу. М.: Наука, 1973, 1973. 448 с.

[Kuš 79] Кушнер Б.А. Конструктивного подбора принцип. - В
кн.: МЭ. Т. 2. 1979, с. I049 - I050.

[Kuš 79a] Кушнер Б.А. Конструктивный анализ. - В кн.: МЭ.
Т. 2. 1979, с. I054 - I057.

Kuznecov A.V., Trahtenbrot B.A. (Кузнецов А.В., Трахтенброт Б.А.)
[Kuz Trah 55] Кузнецов А.В., Трахтенброт Б.А. Исследование
частично-рекурсивных операторов средствами теории
бэровского пространства. ДАН, 1955, т. I05, № 5,
с. 897 - 900.

Lavrov I.A. (Лавров И.А.)

[Lav 77] Lavrov I.A. Computable numberings. - In:
[Butts Hin 77], p. 195 - 206.

Levin L.A. (Левин Л.А.)
[Le 73] Левин Л.А. О понятии случайной последовательности. -
ДАН, 1973, т. 2I2, № 3, с. 548 - 550.

[Le 76] Левин Л.А. О различных мерах сложности конечных объектов. - ДАН, 1976, т. 227, № 4, с. 804 - 807.

Loveland D.

[Love 66] Loveland D. A new interpretation of the von Mises'
concept of random sequence. ZmLGM, 1966, Bd. 12,
H. 4, S. 279 - 294.

[Love 66a] Loveland D. The Kleene hierarchy classification
of recursively random sequences. - Transactions of
AMS, 1966, v. 125, N 3, p. 497 - 510.

Luckham D.C., Park D.M.R., Paterson M.S.
[Luck Park Pat 70] Luckham D.C., Park D.M.R., Paterson M.S.
On formalized computer programs. - JCSS, 1970,
v. 4, N 3, p. 220 - 249.

Lupanov O.B. (Лупанов О.Б.)
[Lup 63] Лупанов О.Б. О сравнении двух типов конечных ис-
точников. - ПК, 1963, вып. 9, с. 32I - 326.

Mal'cev A.I. (Мальцев А.И.)
[Mal 60] Мальцев А.И. О неразрешимости элементарных теорий
некоторых полей. - Сибирский математический журнал,
1960, т. I, № I, с. 7I - 77. (Перепечатано в

[Mal 76], с. II3 - II9.)

[Mal 61] Мальцев А.И. Конструктивные алгебры, I. - УМН, I96I, т. I6, вып. 3 (99), с. 3 - 60. (Перепечатано в [Mal 76], с. I32 - I85.)

[Mal 62] Мальцев А.И. Аксиоматизируемые классы локально свободных алгебр некоторых типов. - Сибирский математический журнал, 1962, т. 3, № 5, с. 729 - 743. (Перепечатано в [Mal 76], с. 216 - 229.)

[Mal 63] Мальцев А.И. Полно нумерованные множества. - АиЛ, 1963, т. 2, вып. 2, с. 4 - 30. (Перепечатано в [Mal 76], с. 275 - 293.)

[Mal 65] Мальцев А.И. Алгоритмы и рекурсивные функции. М.: Наука, 1965. 392 с.

[Mal 76] Мальцев А.И. Избранные труды. Т. 2. Математическая логика и общая теория алгебраических систем. М.: Наука, 1976. 388 с.

Manin Ju.I. (Манин Ю.И.)

[Manin 73] Манин Ю.И. Десятая проблема Гильберта. - Современные проблемы математики. М.: ВИНИТИ, 1973, т. I (Итоги науки и техники), с. 5 - 37.

Manna Z.

[Manna 74] Manna Z. Mathematical theory of computation. N.Y.: McGraw-Hill, 1974. 448 p.

Marčenkov S.S. (Марченков С.С.)

[Marč 76] Марченков С.С. Об одном классе неполных множеств. - Математические заметки, 1976, т. 20, № 4, с. 473 - 478.

Marčenkov S.S., Matrosov V.L. (Марченков С.С., Матросов В.Л.)

[Marč Matr 79] Марченков С.С., Матросов В.Л. Сложность алгоритмов и вычислений. - Теория вероятностей. Математическая статистика. Теоретическая кибернетика. М.: ВИНИТИ, 1979, т. I6 (Итоги науки и техники), с. I03 - I49.

Markov A.A. (Марков А.А.)

[Mark 47] Марков А.А. Невозможность некоторых алгорифмов в теории ассоциативных систем. ДАН, 1947, т. 55, № 7, с. 587 - 590.

[Mark 47a] Марков А.А. Невозможность некоторых алгорифмов в теории ассоциативных систем. П. - ДАН, 1947, т. 58, № 3, с. 353 - 356.

[Mark 51] Марков А.А. Теория алгорифмов. - Труды МИАН, 1951, т. 38, с. 176 - 189.

[Mark 54] Марков А.А. Теория алгорифмов. М.; Л.: Изд-во АН СССР, 1954. 375 с. (Труды МИАН, т. 42).

[Mark 54a] Марков А.А. О непрерывности конструктивных функций. - УМН, 1954, т. 9, вып. 3 (61), с. 226 - 230.

[Mark 56] Марков А.А. Об одном принципе конструктивной математической логики. - В кн.: ТТВМС. Т. 2. М.: Изд-во АН СССР, 1956, с. 146 - 147.

[Mark 58] Марков А.А. К проблеме представимости матриц. - ZmLGM, 1958, Bd. 4, H. 2, S. 157 - 168.

[Mark 58a] Марков А.А. Неразрешимость проблемы гомеоморфии. - ДАН, 1958, т. 121, № 2, с. 218 - 220.

[Mark 58b] Марков А.А. О неразрешимости некоторых проблем топологии. - ДАН, 1958, т. 123, № 6, с. 978 - 980.

[Mark 58c] Марков А.А. Неразрешимость проблемы гомеоморфии. - УМН, 1958, т. 13, вып. 4 (82), с. 213 - 216.

[Mark 58d] Марков А.А. О конструктивных функциях. - В кн.: ПКНМ. 1. М.; Л.: Изд-во АН СССР, 1958 (Труды МИАН, т. 52), с. 315 - 348.

[Mark 62] Марков А.А. О вычислимых инвариантах. - ДАН, 1962, т. 146, № 5, с. 1017 - 1020.

[Mark 62a] Марков А.А. О конструктивной математике. - В кн.: ПКНМ. 2. М.; Л.: Изд-во АН СССР, 1962 (Труды МИАН, т. 67), с. 8 - 14.

[Mark 64] Марков А.А. О нормальных алгорифмах, вычисляющих булевы функции. - ДАН, 1964, т. 157, № 2, с. 262 - 264.

[Mark 67] Марков А.А. О нормальных алгорифмах,связанных с вычислением булевых функций. - ИАН, 1967, т. 31, № 1, с. 161 - 208.

Martin-Löf P. (Мартин-Леф П.)

[Mart 66] Мартин-Леф П. О понятии случайной последовательности. - Теория вероятностей и ее применения, 1966, т. 11, № 1, с. 198 - 200.

[Mart 66a] Martin-Löf P. The definition of random sequences. - Information and control, 1966, v. 9, N 6, p. 602 - 619.

[Mart 68] Martin-Löf P. On the notion of randomness. - In: Intuitionism and proof theory / Kino A. et al., eds. N.Y., 1968, p. 73 - 78.

221

[Mart 70] Martin-Löf P. Notes on constructive mathematics.
Stockholm: Almqvist, Wiksell, 1970. 109 p.

Maslov S.Ju. (Маслов С.Ю.)
[Mas 64] Маслов С.Ю. Некоторые свойства аппарата канониче-
ских исчислений Э.Л.Поста. - В кн.: ПКНМ. 3. М.; Л.:
Наука, 1964 (Труды МИАН, т. 72), с. 5 - 56.

[Mas 67] Маслов С.Ю. Понятие строгой представимости в общей
теории исчислений. - В кн.: ПКНМ. 4. Л.: Наука, 1967
(Труды МИАН, т. 93), с. 3 - 42.

[Mas 78] Maslov S.Yu. Macroevolution as deduction process. -
Synthese, 1978, v. 39, p. 417 - 434.

[Mas 79] Маслов С.Ю. Исчисление. - В кн.: МЭ. Т. 2. 1979,
с. 685 - 686.

[Mas 79a] Маслов С.Ю. Теория поиска вывода и вопросы психо-
логии творчества. - Семиотика и информатика. М.:
ВИНИТИ, 1979, вып. 13, с. 17 - 46.

Matijasevič Ju.V. (Матиясевич Ю.В.)
[Mat 67] Матиясевич Ю.В. Простые примеры неразрешимых ассоциативных исчислений. - ДАН, 1967, т. 173, № 6,
с. 1264 - 1266.

[Mat 70] Матиясевич Ю.В. Диофантовость перечислимых множеств. - ДАН, 1970, т. 191, № 2, с. 279 - 282.

[Mat 71] Матиясевич Ю.В. Диофантово представление перечислимых предикатов. - ИАН, 1971, т. 35, № 1, с. 3 - 30.

[Mat 72] Матиясевич Ю.В. Диофантовы множества. - УМН, 1972,
т. 27, вып. 5 (167), с. 185 - 222.

[Mat 73] Matijasevič Ju.V. On recursive unsolvability of
Hilbert's tenth problem. - In: Logic, Methodology
and Science IV. / Suppes P. et al., eds. NH, 1973,
p. 89 - 110.

[Mat 74] Матиясевич Ю.В. Эффективные и неэффективные методы
в теории чисел. - В кн.: ВКМЛ-3, с. 141 - 142.

[Mat 74a] Матиясевич Ю.В. Существование неэффективизируемых
оценок в теории экспоненциально диофантовых уравне-
ний. - В кн.: ИКМЛ. УI. Л.: Наука, 1974 (Записки НС
ЛОМИ, т. 40), с. 77 - 93.

[Mat 77] Matijasevič Yu.V. Some purely mathematical results
inspired by mathematical logic. - In: [Butts Hin 77],
p. 121 - 127.

[Mat 77a] Матиясевич Ю.В. Простые числа перечисляются полиномом от 10 переменных. - В кн.: ТПММЛ. П. Л.: Наука, 1977 (Записки НС ЛОМИ, т. 68), с. 62 - 82.

[Mat 79] Матиясевич Ю.В. Диофантов предикат. - В кн.: МЭ. Т. 2. 1979, с. 157.

[Mat 79a] Матиясевич Ю.В. Диофантово множество. - В кн.: МЭ. Т. 2. 1979, с. 161 - 162.

Medvedev Ju.T. (Медведев Ю.Т.)

[Med 55] Медведев Ю.Т. Степени трудности массовых проблем. - ДАН, 1955, т. 104, № 4, с. 501- 504.

[Med 56] Медведев Ю.Т. О понятии массовой проблемы. - УМН, 1956, т. 11, вып. 5 (71), с. 231 - 232.

[Med 62] Медведев Ю.Т. Финитные задачи. - ДАН, 1962, т. 142, № 5, с. 1015 - 1018.

[Med 69] Медведев Ю.Т. Об одном способе доказательства неразрешимости алгоритмических проблем. - ДАН, 1969, т. 185, № 6, с. 1232 - 1235.

Meyer A.R.

[Mey 75] Meyer A.R. Weak monadic second order theory of successor is not elementary-recursive. - In: Logic colloquium (Boston, 1972 - 1973) / Parikh R., ed. Springer, 1975 (LN in mathematics, v. 453), p. 132 - 153.

Minsky M.L.

[Mins 67] Minsky M.L. Computation: finite and infinite machines. Englewood Cliffs, N.J.: Prentice-Hall, 1967. 317 p.

von Mises R.

[Mis 19] von Mises R. Grundlagen der Wahrscheinlichkeitsrechnung. - Matematische Zeitschrift, 1919, Bd. 5, S. 52 - 99.

[Mis 28] von Mises R. Wahrscheinlichkeitsrechnung, Statistik und Wahrheit. Wien: J.Springer, 1928.

Moschovakis Y.N.

[Mosc 64] Moschovakis Y.N. Recursive metric spaces. - Fundamenta mathematicae, 1964, v. 55, N 3, p. 215 - 238.

Mostowski A.

[Most 53] Mostowski A. On a system of axioms which has no

recursively enumerable model. - Fundamenta mathematicae, 1953, v. 40, N 1, p. 56 - 61.

[Most 55] Mostowski A. A formula with no recursively enumerable model. - Fundamenta mathematicae, 1955, v. 42,
N 1, p. 125 - 140.

[Most 66] Mostowski A. Thirty years of foundational studies.
Oxford: Basil Blackwell, 1966. 180 p. (Acta philosophica fennica, fasc. 17).

Mučnik A.A. (Мучник А.А.)

[Muč 56] Мучник А.А. Неразрешимость проблемы сводимости
теории алгоритмов. - ДАН, 1956, т. 108, № 2,
с. 194 - 197.

[Muč 58] Мучник А.А. Решение проблемы сводимости Поста и
некоторых других проблем теории алгоритмов. I. -
Труды ММО. М.: Физматгиз, 1958, т. 7, с. 391 - 405.

[Muč 63] Мучник А.А. О сильной и слабой сводимости алгоритмических проблем. - Сибирский математический журнал,
1963, т. 4, № 6, с. 1328 - 1341.

[Muč 65] Мучник А.А. О сводимости проблем разрешения перечислимых множеств к проблемам отделимости. - ИАН,
1965, т. 29, вып. 3, с. 717 - 724.

[Muč 70] Мучник А.А. О двух подходах к классификации рекур-
сивных функций. - В кн.: Козмидиади В.А., Мучник
А.А. (Ред.) Проблемы математической логики. Сложность алгоритмов и классы вычислимых функций. Сбор-
ник переводов. М.: Мир, 1970, с. 123 - 138.

Myhill J.

[My 55] Myhill J. Creative sets. - ZmLGM, 1955, Bd. 1,
H. 2, S. 97 - 108.

Myhill J., Shepherdson J.C.

[My Shep 55] Myhill J., Shepherdson J.C. Effective operations on partial recursive functions. - ZmLGM,
1955, Bd. 1, H. 4, S. 310 - 317.

Nagornyĭ N.M. (Нагорный Н.М.)

[Nag 77] Нагорный Н.М. Алгоритмов сочетание. - В кн.: МЭ.
Т. I. 1977, с. 225 - 226.

[Nag 77a] Нагорный Н.М. Ассоциативное исчисление. - В кн.:
МЭ. Т. I. 1977, с. 338 - 340.

[Nag 79] Нагорный Н.М. Конструктивный объект. - В кн.: МЭ.
Т. 2. 1979, с. 1057 - 1058.

Nepomnjaščiĭ V.A. (Непомнящий В.А.)

[Nep 72] Nepomnjaščii V.A. Conditions for the algorithmic
completeness of systems of operations. - In:
[Frei Grif Rosenf 72]. V. 1, p. 52 - 55.

[Nep 72a] Непомнящий В.А. Критерий алгоритмической полноты
систем операций. - В кн.: Теория программирования:
Труды симпозиума (Новосибирск, 7 - II августа
1972 г.) Ч. I / Непомнящий В.А., ред. 279 с. Новосибирск: Вычислительный центр Сибирского отделения
АН СССР, 1972, с. 267 - 279.

[Nep 74] Непомнящий В.А. О емкостной сложности распознавания
рудиментарных предикатов и формальных языков. - В
кн.: ВКМЛ-3, с. 153 - 155.

[Nep 79] Непомнящий В.А. Практические методы проверки пра-
вильности программ. - Семиотика и информатика. М.:
ВИНИТИ, 1979, вып. 12, с. 86 - 87.

von Neumann J.

[Neu 63] von Neumann J. The computer and the brain, New
Haven, Yale Univ. press, 1963. XIII + 82.

Nogina E.Ju. (Ногина Е.Ю.)

[Nog 66] Ногина Е.Ю. Об эффективно топологических пространствах. - ДАН, 1966, т. 169, № I, с. 28 - 31.

[Nog 69] Ногина Е.Ю. Соотношения между некоторыми классами
эффективно топологических пространств. - Математические заметки, 1969, т. 5, № 4, с. 483 - 495.

[Nog 78] Ногина Е.Ю. Нумерованные топологические пространства. - ZmLGM, 1978, Bd. 24, H. 2, S. 141 - 176.

Novikov P.S. (Новиков П.С.)

[Nov 52] Новиков П.С. Об алгоритмической неразрешимости
проблемы тождества. - ДАН, 1952, т. 85, № 4, с.
709 - 712. (Перепечатано в [Nov 79], с. 205 - 209.)

[Nov 55] Новиков П.С. Об алгоритмической неразрешимости
проблемы тождества слов в теории групп. М.: Изд-во
АН СССР, 1955. 143 с. (Труды МИАН, т. 44). (Перепечатано в [Nov 79], с. 210 - 323.)

[Nov 77] Новиков П.С. Конструктивная математическая логика
с точки зрения классической. М.: Наука, 1977. 328 с.

[Nov 79] Новиков П.С. Избранные труды. Теория множеств и
функций. Математическая логика и алгебра. М.: Наука,
1979. 396 с.

Paterson M.S.

[Pat 70] Paterson M.S. Unsolvability in 3 x 3 matrices. -
Studies in applied mathematics, 1970, v. 49, N. 1,
p. 105 - 107.

Paterson M.S., Fischer M.J., Meyer A.R.

[Pat Fi Mey 74] Paterson M.S., Fischer M.J., Meyer A.R.
An improved overlap argument for online multiplication. - In: Complexity of computation.
Providence: AMS, 1974 (SIAM - AMS proceedings,
v. 7), p. 97 - 111.

Peretjat'kin M.G. (Перетятькин М.Г.)

[Per 73] Перетятькин М.Г. О полных теориях с конечным числом
счетных моделей. - АиЛ, 1973, т. 12, № 5, с. 550 -
576.

Petrov B.N., Ulanov G.M., Ul'janov S.V. (Петров Б.Н., Уланов Г.М.,
Ульянов С.В.)

[Pet Ula Ul' 79] Петров Б.Н., Уланов Г.М., Ульянов С.В.
Сложность конечных объектов и информационная теория
управления. - Техническая кибернетика. М.: ВИНИТИ,
1979, т. 11 (Итоги науки и техники), с. 77 - 147.

Plisko V.E. (Плиско В.Е.)

[Plis 73] Плиско В.Е. О реализуемых предикатных формулах. -
ДАН, 1973, т. 212, № 3, с. 553 - 556.

[Plis 76] Плиско В.Е. Некоторые варианты понятия реализуе-
мости для предикатных формул. - ДАН, 1976,
т. 226, № 1, с. 61 - 64.

[Plis 77] Плиско В.Е. Неарифметичность класса реализуемых
предикатных формул. - ИАН, 1977, т. 41, № 3,
с. 483 - 502.

[Plis 78] Плиско В.Е. Некоторые варианты понятия реализуе-
мости для предикатных формул. - ИАН, 1978,
т. 42, № 3, с. 636 - 653.

Post E.L.

[Post 36] Post E.L. Finite combinatory processes - formulation 1. - JSL, 1936, v. 1, N 3, p. 103 - 105.

[Post 43] Post E.L. Formal reductions of the general combinatorial decision problem. - American journal of mathematics, 1943, v. 65, N 2, p. 197 - 215.

[Post 44] Post E.L. Recursively enumerable sets of positive integers and their decision problems. - Bulletin of AMS, 1944, v. 50, N 5, p. 284 - 316.

[Post 46] Post E.L. A variant of a recursively unsolvable problem. - Bulletin of AMS, 1946, v. 52, N 4, p. 264 - 268.

[Post 47] Post E.L. Recursive unsolvability of a problem of Thue. - JSL, 1947, v. 12, N 1, p. 1 - 11.

Prohorov Ju.V. (Прохоров Ю.В.)

[Pro 73] Прохоров Ю.В. Кодирование. - В кн.: БСЭ, 3-е изд. Т. 12. 1973, с. 373 - 374.

Rabin M.O.

[Rab 58] Rabin M.O. On recursively enumerable and arithmetic models of set theory. - JSL, 1958, v. 23, N 4, p. 408 - 416.

[Rab 60] Rabin M.O. Computable algebra, general theory and theory of computable fields. - Transactions of AMS, 1960, v. 95, N 2, p. 341 - 360.

[Rab 63] Rabin M. Real time computation. - Israel journal of mathematics, 1963, v. 1, N 4, p. 203 - 211.

[Rab 69] Rabin M.O. Decidability of second-order theories and automata on infinite trees. - Transactions of AMS, 1969, v. 141, N 7, p. 1 - 35.

[Rab 74] Rabin M.O. Theoretical impediments to artificial intelligence. - In: Information processing 74. Proceedings of IFIP Congress 1974 (Stockholm, August 3 - 10, 1974)./ Rosenfeld J.L., ed. NH, 1974, p. 615 - 619.

Rice H.G.

[Rice 53] Rice H.G. Classes of recursively enumerable sets and their decision problems. - Transactions of AMS, 1953, v. 74, N 2, p. 358 - 366.

[Rice 54] Rice H.G. Recursive real numbers. - Proceedings of AMS, 1954, v. 5, N 5, p. 784 - 791.

Richardson D.

[Rich 68] Richardson D. Some undecidable problems involving elementary functions of a real variable. - JSL,
1968, v. 33, N 4, p. 514 - 520.

Robinson J.

[RobJ 49] Robinson J. Definability and decision problems in
arithmetic. - JSL, 1949, v. 14, N 2, p. 98 - 114.

Rogers H., Jr.

[Rog 58] Rogers H., Jr. Gödel numberings of partial recursive functions. - JSL, 1958, v. 23, N 3,
p. 331 - 341.

[Rog 67] Rogers H., Jr. Theory of recursive functions and
effective computability. New York et al.: McGraw-
Hill Book Company, 1967. XIX + 482 p.

Rosenberg A.L.

[Rosenb 67] Rosenberg A.L. Real-time definable languages. -
Journal of ACM, 1967, v. 14, N 4, p. 645 - 662.

Roth K.F.

[Roth 55] Roth K.F. Rational approximations to algebraic
numbers. - Mathematika, 1955, v. 2, N 3, p. 1 -
20 (corrigendum p. 168).

Sacerdote G.S., Tenney R.L.

[Sac Ten 77] Sacerdote G.S., Tenney R.L. The decidability
of the reachability problem for vector addition
systems. - In: Conference record of the ninth
annual ACM symposium on theory of computing. Papers
presented at the symposium held in Boulder, Colo.,
May 2 - 4, 1977. N.Y.: ACM, 1977, p. 61 - 76.

Salomaa A., Soittola M.

[Sal Soi 78] Salomaa A., Soittola M. Automata-theoretic
aspects of formal power series. Springer, 1978.
X + 171 p.

Šanin N.A. (Шанин Н.А.)

[Šan 55] Шанин Н.А. О некоторых логических проблемах ариф-
метики. М.: Изд-во АН СССР, 1955. 112 с. (Труды
МИАН, т. 43.)

[Šan 56] Шанин Н.А. Некоторые вопросы математического
анализа в свете конструктивной логики. -

ZmLGM, 1956, Bd. 2, H. 1, S. 27 - 36.

[Šan 58] Шанин Н.А. О конструктивном понимании математиче - ских суждений. - В кн.: ПКНМ. I. М.; Л.: Изд-во АН СССР, 1958 (Труды МИАН, т. 52), с. 226 - 311.

[Šan 58a] Шанин Н.А. Об алгоритме конструктивной расшифровки математических суждений. - ZmLGM, 1958, Bd. 4, H. 4, S. 293 - 303.

[Šan 62] Шанин Н.А. Конструктивные вещественные числа и кон- структивные функциональные пространства. - В кн.: ПКНМ. 2. М.; Л.: Изд-во АН СССР (Труды МИАН, т. 67), с. 15 - 294.

[Šan 70] Шанин Н.А. О рекурсивном математическом анализе и исчислении арифметических равенств Р.Л.Гудстейна. - В кн.: Гудстейн Р.Л. Рекурсивный математический ана- лиз. Пер. с англ. М.: Наука, 1970, с. 7 - 76.

[Šan 73] Шанин Н.А. Об иерархии способов понимания суждений в конструктивной математике. - В кн.: ПКНМ. 6. Л.: Наука, 1973 (Труды МИАН, т. 129), с. 203 - 266.

Savitch W.J.

[Sav 70] Savitch W.J. Relationships between non-determinis- tic and deterministic tape complexities. - JCSS, 1970, v. 4, N 2, p. 177 - 192.

Schnorr C.P.

[Schnorr 72] Schnorr C.P. Optimal Gödel numberings. In: [Frei Grif Rosenf 72]. V. 1, p. 56 - 58.

[Schnorr 73] Schnorr C.P. Process complexity and effective random tests. - JCSS, 1973, v. 7, N 4, p. 376 - 388.

[Schnorr 75] Schnorr C.P. Optimal enumerations and optimal Gödel numberings. - Mathematical systems theory, 1975, v. 8, N 2, p. 182 - 191.

[Schnorr 77] Schnorr C.P. A survey of the theory of random sequences. - In: [Butts Hin 77], p. 193 - 211.

Schönhage A.

[Schön 70] Schönhage A. Universelle Turing Speicherung. - In: Automatentheorie und formale Sprachen./ Dörr J., Hotz G., eds. Mannheim, 1970, S. 369 - 383.

[Schön 79] Schönhage A. Storage modifications machines. University of Tubingen, 1979 (Preprint), 43p.

Schröder E.

    [Schrö 1887] Schröder E. Über Algorithmen und Kalkuln. -
        Archiv für Mathematik und Physik, 1887, 2. Reihe,
        Teil 5.

Scott D.

    [Scott 61] Scott D. On constructing models for arithmetic. -
        In: Infinitistic methods. Proceedings of the Sympo-
        sium on foundations of mathematics (Warsaw, 2 - 9
        Sept. 1959). Warszawa etc., 1961, p. 235 - 255.

    [Scott 71] Scott D. Outline of a mathematical theory of
        computation. - In: Proceedings of the fourth con-
        ference on information sciences and systems, 1971,
        p. 169 - 176.

Seiferas J.I.

    [Sei 77] Seiferas J.I. Relating refined space complexity
        classes. - JCSS, 1977, v. 14, N 1, p. 100 - 129.

Seiferas J.I., Fischer M.J., Meyer A.R.

    [Sei Fi Mey 78] Seiferas J.I., Fischer M.J., Meyer A.R.
        Separaring nondeterministic time complexity classes.
        - Journal of ACM, 1978, v. 25, N 1, p. 146 - 167.

Semenov A.L. (Семенов А.Л.)

    [Sem 78] Семенов А.Л. Некоторые алгоритмические проблемы
        для систем алгоритмических алгебр. - ДАН, 1978,
        т. 239, № 5, с. 1063 - 1066.

    [Sem 80] Семенов А.Л. Интерпретация свободных алгебр в сво-
        бодных группах. - ДАН, 1980, т. 252, № 6, с. 1326 -
        1332.

Semenov A.L., Semenova E.T. (Семенов А.Л., Семенова Е.Т.)

    [Sem Sem 74] Семенов А.Л., Семенова Е.Т. Программирование и
        математическое обеспечение. - В кн.: Радиоэлектроника
        в 1973 г. Обзор по материалам иностранной печати.
        Вып. 6. Вычислительная техника. Программирование.
        М.: НИИЭИР, 1974, с. 76 - 91.

Semenov A.L., Uspenskiĭ V.A. (Семенов А.Л., Успенский В.А.)

    [Sem Us 80] Семенов А.Л., Успенский В.А. Международная
        встреча ученых в Хорезме. - Международный форум по
        информации и документации, 1980, т. 5, № 1, с. 36 -
        37. (English translation: Semenov A.L., Uspensky

V.A. International meeting of scientists at Khoresm.
- International forum on information and documentation, 1980, v. 5, N 1, p. 37 - 38.)

Šen' A.H. (Шень A.X.)

[Šen' 79] Шень А.X. Метод приоритета и проблемы отделения.
- ДАН, 1979. т. 248, № 6, с. 1309 - 1313.

[Šen' 80] Шень А.X. Аксиоматический подход к теории алгоритмов и относительная вычислимость. - Вестник
Московского университета. Сер. I, Математика, ме-
ханика, 1980, № 2, с. 27 - 29.

Shannon C.

[Shann 48] Shannon C. A mathematical theory of communication. - Bell system technical journal, 1948, v. 27,
N 3, p. 379 - 423; N 4, p. 623 - 656.

Shoenfield J.R.

[Shoen 71] Snoenfield J.R. Degrees of unsolvability. NH,
1971. VIII + 111 p.

Slisenko A.O. (Слисенко А.О.)

[Sli 77] Слисенко А.О. Упрощенное доказательство распозна-
ваемости симметричности слов в реальное время на
машинах Тьюринга. - В кн.: ТПММЛ. П. Л.: Наука,
1977 (Записки НС ЛОМИ, т. 68), с. 123 - 139.

[Sli 77а] Слисенко А.О. Распознавание предиката вхождения в
реальное время. Л. 1977. 24 с. (Препринт / Ленин-
градское отделение МИАН: Р 7 - 77.)

[Sli 78] Slisenko A.O. String-matching in real time: some
properties of the data structure. - In: Mathematical
foundations of computer science 1978. / Winkowski J.,
ed. Springer, 1978 (LN in Computer Science, v. 64),
p. 493 - 496.

[Sli 79] Слисенко А.О. Сложностные задачи теории вычислений:
Предварительная публикация. М.: Научный совет по
комплексной проблеме Кибернетика, АН СССР, 1979.
32 с.

Smullyan R.M.

[Smu 58] Smullyan R.M. Theories with effectively inseparable
nuclei. - JSL, 1958, v. 23, N 4, p. 458.

[Smu 60] Smullyan R.M. Theories with effectively inseparable
nuclei. - ZmLGM, 1960, Bd. 6, H. 3 - 4, S. 219 - 224.

Solomonoff R.J.
[Sol 64] Solomonoff R.J. A formal theory of inductive
inference I. - Information and control, 1964,
v. 7, N 1, p. 1 - 22.

Specker E.
[Spe 49] Specker E. Nicht Konstruktiv beweisbare Sätze der
Analysis. - JSL, 1949, v. 14, N 3, p. 145 - 158.

Tarski A., Mostowski A., Robinson R.M.
[Tars Most RobR 53] Tarski A., Mostowski A., Robinson R.M.
Undecidable theories. NH, 1953. XI + 98 p.

Thue A.
[Thue 14] Thue A. Probleme über Veränderungen von Zeichen-
reihen nach gegebenen Regeln. - Skrifter utgit av
Videnskapsselskapet i Kristiania, I. Matematisk -
naturvidenskabelig klasse, 1914, N 10. 34 p.

Trahtenbrot B.A. (Трахтенброт Б.А.)
[Trah 53] Трахтенброт Б.А. О рекурсивной отделимости. -
ДАН, 1953, т. 88, № 6, с. 953 - 956.
[Trah 56] Трахтенброт Б.А. Сигнализирующие функции и таб-
личные операторы. - Ученые записки Пензенского го-
сударственного педагогического института им. В.Г.
Белинского. Пенза, 1956, т. 4, с. 75 - 87.
[Trah 67] Трахтенброт Б.А. Сложность алгоритмов и вычисле-
ний: Спецкурс для студентов НГУ. Новосибирск:
Изд-во НГУ, 1967. 258 с.

Turing A.M.
[Tu 36] Turing A.M. On computable numbers, with an applica-
tion to the Entscheidungsproblem. - Proceedings of
LMS. Ser. 2, 1936, v. 42, N 3, 4, p. 230 - 265.
[Tu 37] Turing A.M. On computable numbers, with an applica-
tion to the Entscheidungsproblem. A correction. Pro-
ceedings of LMS. Ser. 2, 1937, v. 43, N 7, p. 544 -
546.
[Tu 37a] Turing A.M. Computability and λ-definability. -
JSL, 1937, v. 2, N 4, p. 153 - 163.

[Tu 39] Turing A.M. Systems of logic based on ordinals. - Proceedings of LMS. Ser. 2, 1939, v. 45, N 3, p. 161 - 228.

Uspenskiĭ V.A. (Успенский В.А.)

[Us 53] Успенский В.А. Теорема Геделя и теория алгоритмов. - УМН, 1953, т. 8, № 4 (56), с. 176 - 178.

[Us 53a] Успенский В.А. Теорема Геделя и теория алгоритмов. - ДАН, 1953, т. 91, № 4, с. 737 - 740.

[Us 55] Успенский В.А. О вычислимых операциях. - ДАН, 1955, т. 103, № 5, с. 773 - 776.

[Us 55a] Успенский В.А. Системы перечислимых множеств и их нумерации. - ДАН, 1955, т. 105, № 6, с. 1155 - 1158.

[Us 56] Успенский В.А. Вычислимые операции и понятие программы. - УМН, 1956, т. 11, вып. 4 (70), с. 172 - 176.

[Us 56a] Успенский В.А. Понятие программы и вычислимые операторы. - В кн.: ТТВМС. Т. 1, с. 186.

[Us 57] Успенский В.А. К теореме о равномерной непрерывности. - УМН, 1957, т. 12, вып. 1 (73), с. 99 - 142.

[Us 60] Успенский В.А. Лекции о вычислимых функциях. М.: Физматгиз, 1960. 492 с. (French translation: Ouspenski V.A. Leçons sur les fonctions calculables. Paris: Hermann, 1966. 412 p.)

[Us 70] Успенский В.А. Алгоритм. - В кн.: БСЭ. 3-е изд. Т. 1. 1970, с. 400 - 401.

[Us 74] Успенский В.А. Теорема Геделя о неполноте в элементарном изложении. - УМН, 1974, т. 29, вып. 1 (175), с. 3 - 47.

[Us 77] Успенский В.А. Алгоритм. - В кн.: МЭ. Т. 1. 1977, с. 202 - 206.

[Us 79] Успенский В.А. Машина Поста. М.: Наука, 1979. 95 с.

Vaĭnberg Ju.R., Nogina E.Ju. (Вайнберг Ю.Р., Ногина Е.Ю.)

[Vaĭn Nog 76] Вайнберг Ю.Р., Ногина Е.Ю. О двух типах непрерывности вычислимых отображений нумерованных топологических пространств. - Исследования по теории алгорифмов и математической логике. / Марков А.А., Кушнер Б.А., ред. М.: Вычислительный центр АН СССР, 1976, т. 2, с. 84 - 99.

Valiant L.G.

    [Valia 75] Valiant L.G. General context-free recognition in
           less than cubic time. - JCSS, 1975, v. 10, N 2,
           p. 308 - 315.

Valiev M.K.

    [Valiev 79] Valiev M.K. On axiomatization of deterministic
           propositional dynamic logic. - In: Mathematical
           foundations of computer science 1979. / Becvar J.,
           ed. Springer, 1979 (LN in computer science, v. 74),
           p. 482 - 491.

V'jugin V.V. (Вьюгин В.В.)

    [V'ju 80] Вьюгин В.В. Алгоритмическая энтропия (сложность)
           конечных объектов и ее применение к определению
           случайности и количества информации. - Семиотика и
           информатика. М.: ВИНИТИ, 1980, вып. 16, с. 14 - 43.

Wang P.

    [Wang 74] Wang P. The undecidability of the existence of
           zeros of real elementary functions. - Journal of
           ACM, 1974, v. 21, N 4, p. 586 - 589.

Weyl H.

    [Weyl 21] Weyl H. Uber die neue Grundlagenkrise der Mathe-
           matik. - Mathematische Zeitschrift, 1921, Bd. 10,
           S. 39 - 79.

Yates C.E.M.

    [Yates 65] Yates C.E.M. Three theorems on the degrees of
           recursively enumerable sets. - Duke mathematical
           journal, 1965, v. 32, N 3, p. 461 - 468.

Younger D.H.

    [Young 67] Younger D.H. Recognition and parsing of context-
           free languages in time n^3. - Information and
           control, 1967, v. 10, N 2, p. 189 - 208.

Zaslavskii I.D., Ceĭtin G.S. (Заславский И.Д., Цейтин Г.С.)

    [Za Ceĭtin 56] Заславский И.Д., Цейтин Г.С. О соотношении
           между основными свойствами конструктивных функций.
           - В кн.: ТТВМС. Т. I. М.: Изд-во АН СССР, 1956,
           с. 180 - 181.

[Za Ceĭtin 62] Заславский И.Д., Цейтин Г.С. О сингулярных
покрытиях и связанных с ними свойствах конструктивных функций. - В кн.: ПКНМ. 2. М.; Л.: Изд-во АН
СССР, 1962 (Труды МИАН, т. 67), с. 458 - 502.

Zvonkin A.K., Levin L.A.   (Звонкин А.К., Левин Л.А.)
[Zvon Le 70] Звонкин А.К., Левин Л.А. Сложность конечных
объектов и обоснование понятий информации и случай-
ности с помощью теории алгоритмов. - УМН, 1970,
т. 25, вып. 6 (156), с. 85 - 127.

Transliterations

Russian	AMS	In the text
й	ĭ	y,j
х	h	kh
ц	c	ts
ч	č	ch
ш	š	sh
ю	ju	yu
я	ja	ya

ON INDUCTIVE SYNTHESIS OF PROGRAMS

J.M.Barzdin
Computing Center of the Latvian State University
Riga, USSR

1. INTRODUCTION

When somebody explains an algorithm, it is often done by the description how the algorithm performs an initial fragment of a computation. E.g., the Euclidean algorithm for the greatest common divisor of two natural numbers X and Y, where $X \geqslant Y$, is usually described in the following way.

Let A_1 denote X, and A_2 denote Y.

1) We divide A_1 by A_2, find the remainder A_3 and check whether $A_3 = 0$ or not. If $A_3 = 0$, then the process terminates, and A_2 is the result. If $A_3 > 0$, then

2) we divide A_2 by A_3, find the remainder A_4. If $A_4 = 0$, then the process terminates, and A_3 is the result. If $A_4 > 0$, then

3) we divide A_3 by A_4, etc.

Descriptions of such a kind will be called inductive descriptions. Of course, an inductive description differs essentially from a complete description in traditional programming languages. A given inductive description can be sufficient for one person to understand the algorithm, and at the same time be insufficient for another person. Nevertheless it seems to us that the person explaining an algorithm usually feels whether the inductive description produced by him is sufficiently complete, i.e. whether it is possible to synthesize a complete description of the algorithm in some traditional programming language. Obviously, the inductive description of the Euclidean algorithm given above is complete. It would be extremely interesting to understand the logical foundations of this completeness.

To our mind, in many cases inductive descriptions are more "human" than "machine" descriptions of the algorithms in the traditional programming languages.

In this paper the formal synthesis of complete descriptions of algorithms (programs) from their inductive descriptions is studied and some instrumental facilities for this purpose are presented.

Theoretical aspects of the inductive synthesis are in fact considered in many papers on the theory of inductive inference [1]. Nevertheless our research is more related to papers by A.Biermann [2,3], M.Bauer [4] et al. on the synthesis of programs from example computations. An inductive description of an algorithm can be thought of as a symbolic description of a certain initial fragment of the computations performed by the algorithm.

2. EXAMPLES OF INDUCTIVE DESCRIPTIONS OF ALGORITHMS

We begin with description of a simple language for presentation of the inductive descriptions of the algorithms. We do not claim that this language is general enough for practical applications. Our only aim is to present the main ideas.

The inductive description of the algorithm consists of two components - INPUT and DESCRIPTION (in §5 there will be introduced also the third component - EXAMPLE):

    INPUT: description-of-input-variables
    DESCRIPTION:
            description-of-an-initial-fragment-of-the-computations

The description-of-input-variables is a finite sequence
$$\alpha_1, \alpha_2, \ldots, \alpha_n$$
where α_i is an elementary variable, e.g., A, A1, X3, or an array, e.g., A[N], B[N,M], N,M - bounds of arrays.

The values of elementary variables as well as the values of elements of arrays are fixed-point numbers, the values of bounds of arrays are integers. A[N] is a 1-dimensional array (a vector), B[N,M] is a 2-dimensional array (a matrix). The elements of arrays are A(I), A(7), B(2,3) etc. The B(I,) is the I-th column of the matrix B[N,M].

If, for example, there is given
    INPUT: S,B[N,M]
then S,B,M,N as well as the elements of array B are called external variables.

The description-of-an-initial-fragment-of-the-computations can consist of the following instructions:

1. Assignment instructions of the form

    variable ← expression

Expressions can contain usual operations: +,-,* ,/. The first
occurrence of some variable in an assignment instruction is considered as a declaration of this variable. E.g., the occurrence of
the variable X in the instruction X(2) ← 7.5 means that X is a
1-dimensional array; the length of this array will be determined
stepwise according to its filling. Variable RES has special meaning - it is used to denote the result of the algorithm. (In the
example mentioned below the assignment RES ← 'NO' has a special
meaning - "system has no solution".) The following abbreviation
will also be used: instead of, e.g., X ← X+Y we shall write
shortly X+Y. The instruction X ↔ Y means the exchange of the
values of X and Y.

2. Logical instructions (predicates). They can contain comparison operators: =,≠, < , >, ≤, ≥. Every logical instruction has
two exits: if the value of the predicate is true then the exit "+"
is used, otherwise - the exit "-". The logical instructions are
used for conditional constructions IF...THEN...ELSE.

3. END instruction. It indicates the end of the performance
of the algorithm.

The inductive description of the algorithm or, more precisely,
the description-of-an-initial-fragment-of-the-computations consists
of separate steps constructed from above-mentioned instructions.
The steps must be enumerated, e.g., 1),2),3),... or A1),A2),A3),...
(the number of the final step can be replaced by dots as well, e.g.,
A...)

Now the inductive description of the above-mentioned Euclidean
algorithm can be represented in our language in the following way
(MOD(a b) is the remainder from the division a/b):

    INPUT: X,Y

    DESCRIPTION:

        A(1) ← X

        A(2) ← Y

      1) A(3) ← MOD(A(1),A(2))

         A(3) = 0 ——+——┐

            -│   ↓

                    RES ← A(2)

           │   END

           ↓

2) $A(4) \leftarrow MOD(A(2),A(3))$

$A(4) = 0 \xrightarrow{\ +\ }$

$\quad RES \leftarrow A(3)$

$\quad END$

3) $A(5) \leftarrow MOD(A(3),A(4))$

.....

Fig.1 shows us an inductive description of an algorithm for solving a system of linear equations. Here the system of linear equations is given by the matrix $A[N,M]$. E.g., the matrix

$$\begin{pmatrix} 8 & -3 & 1 \\ 2 & 1 & 9 \end{pmatrix} \text{ corresponds to system } \begin{cases} 8X_1 - 3X_2 = 1 \\ 2X_1 + X_2 = 9 \end{cases}$$

The solution of this system is a vector $X=(2,5)$.

It is clear that an algorithm has many different inductive descriptions. One inductive description can differ from the other by the length of example computations replaced by the dots.

The other versions of inductive descriptions will be considered in §5.

3. GRAPHICAL DO-STATEMENT AND AN ASSOCIATED PROGRAMMING LANGUAGE

To synthesize an algorithm from its inductive description means in fact to understand how the given inductive description can be generalized to longer computations. Humans usually perform such synthesis in a purely syntactic way. The synthesizing person finds out which parts of the inductive description are similar, recognizes simple regularities (e.g. fragments of arithmetical progressions) and makes generalization of these regularities. This means that the human uses a certain graphical programming language in the mentioned process of synthesis. More precisely, he uses a certain graphical language for generalization, and the semantics of the involved objects has practically no role in this generalization. We will describe one such language. The central notion in this language is so-called graphical DO-statement.

The graphical DO-statement is used for a short description of strings of elements of the same type (e.g., strings of statements). We will distinguish between vertical and horizontal graphical DO-statement.

239

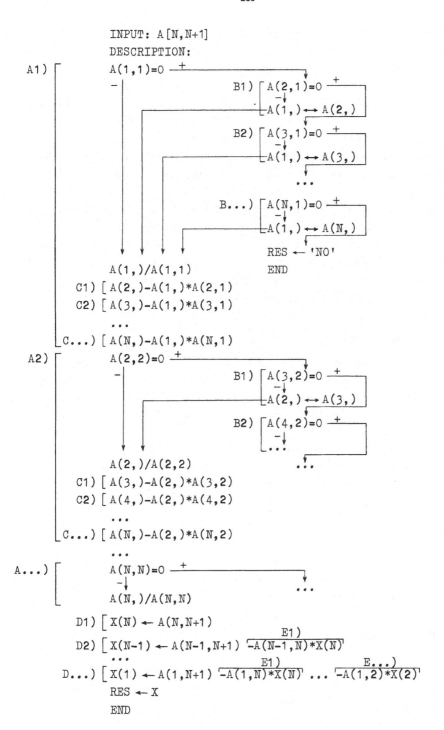

Fig. 1

Fig.2 schematically represents an example of the vertical
graphical DO-statement (the verticality of the statement is indicated by a vertical arrow in the graphical representation). The
symbol I here is the loop variable. It takes values from 1 to 7
by step 2. ⌐⌐⌐ denotes the body of the loop. The pointed areas
are meant to contain I or I±C. This DO-statement is used to denote
the vertical concatenation, as shown in Fig.3.

Fig.4 represents an example of the horizontal graphical DO-
statement. It is used to denote the horizontal concatenation, as
shown in Fig.5.

In general case the vertical graphical DO-statement can contain arrows going out of the body of the statement. These arrows
we shall call horizontal arrows. Fig.6 represents an example of
the graphical DO-statement with the horizontal arrows. It is used
to denote the vertical concatenation, as shown in Fig.7.

The heading of the graphical DO-statement, as shown in previous figures, can be in the form:

$$\text{loop-variable: } \alpha \text{ TO } \beta \text{ [BY } \gamma \text{]}$$

The bounds α and β can be constant (fixed integers), elementary
external variables ± constants, loop-variables of the enclosing
DO-statements ± constants, or ∞ (only one of the two bounds can
be ∞). The step γ can be only a constant (the default value of
γ is 1).

Fig.8 and 9 demonstrate how to use graphical DO-statements.
Fig.8 shows a program for the Euclidean algorithm. Fig.9 shows a
program for solving a system of linear equations corresponding to
the inductive description given in Fig.1.

4. THE ALGORITHM OF SYNTHESIS

We begin with a more precise definition of the inductive description of an algorithm. We use a "reverse method" for this.
Assume that we already have the program to be synthesized, e.g.
the program in Fig.9. (Speaking about programs, we mean only programs with the graphical DO-statement as their principal tool.)
We associate an identifier to every DO-statement in this program.
(In Fig.9 all the identifiers are already associated, namely, A,B,
C,D,E.) After this we expand all the DO-statements according to
their definitions. These expansions are in fact concatenations of
the bodies of DO-statements, the variables of which are substituted

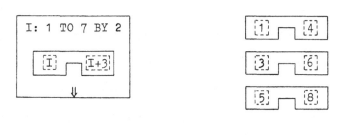

Fig. 2

Fig. 3

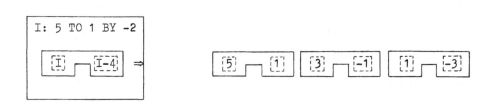

Fig. 4

Fig. 5

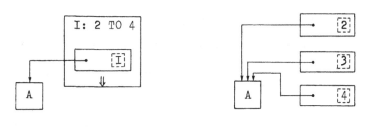

Fig. 6

Fig. 7

242

```
INPUT: X,Y
PROGRAM:
A(1) ← X
A(2) ← Y
```

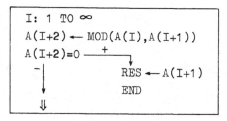

```
I: 1 TO ∞
A(I+2) ← MOD(A(I),A(I+1))
A(I+2)=0 ──── +
  _                      RES ← A(I+1)
                         END

  ⇓
```

Fig. 8

```
INPUT: A[N,N+1]
PROGRAM:
```

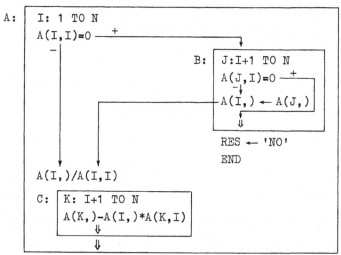

A:
```
I: 1 TO N
A(I,I)=0 ──── +

  _
```
B:
```
J:I+1 TO N
A(J,I)=0 ──── +
  _
A(I,) ← A(J,)
  ⇓
```
```
RES ← 'NO'
END
```
```
A(I,)/A(I,I)
```
C:
```
K: I+1 TO N
A(K,)-A(I,)*A(K,I)
  ⇓
```
```
  ⇓
```

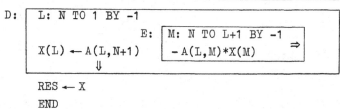

D:
```
L: N TO 1 BY -1
```
E:
```
M: N TO L+1 BY -1
 -A(L,M)*X(M)     ⇒
```
```
X(L) ← A(L,N+1)
  ⇓
```
```
RES ← X
END
```

Fig. 9

by their values. These bodies will be called the steps of the
inductive description and will be denoted by A1),A2),A3),... ,
where A is the identifier of the DO-statement considered. A part
of the steps can be replaced by dots. If a bound of the DO-statement A is variable, there is no other possibility than to write
A1),A2),... or A1),A2),...,A...), where A...) denotes the last
step. Dots can be used within the steps as well. Every fragment
of a step can be replaced by dot. The result of such expansions
and replacements is called an inductive description of the given
program (or algorithm). Fig.1 shows an example of an inductive
description of an algorithm, corresponding to the program shown in
Fig.9. Of course, in practice we construct the inductive description of the algorithm first (from our intuitive feeling what the
algorithm should do), and then we use this description to write
the program itself. (This is exactly what was done to produce the
examples in Fig.1 and 9.) Two inductive descriptions of the same
program can differ by the length of the fragments of the expansions
of the DO-statements replased by dots.

Let J and J' be two inductive descriptions of the same program. We say that $J \geqslant J'$ if all the fragments of expansions
replaced by dots in J are replaced by dots in J' as well.

Now let us consider the algorithm of synthesis. We explain
our algorithm only by an example.

Consider the inductive description shown in Fig.1. To synthesize a program from a given description means in fact to synthesize
a DO-statement from its expansions. Expansions of DO-statements
which do not contain any expansions of another DO-statement within
it, are called expansions of rank 0. Expansions which contain
expansions of rank 0 are called expansions of rank 1, and so on.

We begin the process of synthesis with the expansions of rank
0. In case of Fig.1 there are

B1),B2),...,B...) from the step A1,	(1)
B1),B2),... from the step A2,	(2)
C1),C2),...,C...) from the step A1,	(3)
C1),C2),...,C...) from the step A2,	(4)
E1) from the step D2,	(5)
E1),E2),...,E...) from the step D...	(6)

Every expansion corresponds to a certain DO-statement. We can find
these statements. Thus we obtain:

$$
\text{B:} \quad
\begin{array}{|l|}
\hline
\text{J: 2 TO N BY 1} \\
\text{A(J,2)=0} \\
\text{A(1,)} \leftrightarrow \text{A(J,)} \\
\hline
\end{array}
\qquad (7)
$$

from the expansion (1),

$$
\text{B:} \quad
\begin{array}{|l|}
\hline
\text{J: 3 TO ...BY 1} \\
\text{A(J,3)=0} \\
\text{A(2,)} \leftrightarrow \text{A(J,)} \\
\hline
\end{array}
\qquad (8')
$$

from the expansion (2) using expansion (1) to determine the position of loop-variable J in the body of the loop,

$$
\text{C:} \quad
\begin{array}{|l|}
\hline
\text{K: 2 TO N BY 1} \\
\text{A(K,)-A(1,)*A(K,1)} \\
\hline
\end{array}
\qquad (9)
$$

from the expansion (3),

$$
\text{C:} \quad
\begin{array}{|l|}
\hline
\text{K: 3 TO N BY 1} \\
\text{A(K,)-A(2,)*A(K,2)} \\
\hline
\end{array}
\qquad (10)
$$

from the expansion (4),

$$
\text{E:} \quad
\begin{array}{|l|}
\hline
\text{M: N TO 2 BY -1} \\
\text{-A(1,M)*X(M)} \\
\hline
\end{array}
\qquad (11)
$$

from the expansion (6),

$$
\text{E:} \quad
\begin{array}{|l|}
\hline
\text{M: N TO N BY -1} \\
\text{-A(N-1,M)*X(M)} \\
\hline
\end{array}
\qquad (12)
$$

from the expansion (5) using expansion (6) to determine the position of loop-variable M in the body of the loop.

All these statements are completely constructed except (8'). The statement (8') does not contain the upper bound. In this case we consider the other statements with the same identifier (in this case it is (7)) and try to fill in the empty parts. Thus we obtain:

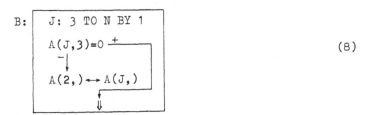

(8)

Now we substitute the obtained DO-statements in place of the corresponding expansions. As a result we obtain Fig.10.

Further we consider the expansions of rank 1:

$$A1),A2),...,A...)$$ (13)

$$D1),D2),...,D...)$$ (14)

These expansions contain the DO-statements constructed above. We treat these DO-statements like any other instructions. At first, we construct the body and the step γ of the statement A from the steps A1 and A2 of the expansion (13). Then we obtain the bounds α and β of the statement A from the steps A1 and A... . Analogously we construct the statement D. As a result we obtain the program shown in Fig.9.

It is interesting that the program shown in Fig.9 can be synthesized from an essentially shorter inductive description (see Fig.11) if we introduce some natural defaults, e.g., if the step γ of the loop α TO β is not indicated, then its default value is 1 if $\alpha < \beta$, and -1 if $\alpha > \beta$.

We denote the algorithm of synthesis considered above by Σ . The precise definition of it is omitted here but we hope the considered example describes it clearly enough. This example also shows that the running time of the algorithm is rather small.

There is another important feature of algorithms of synthesis, namely, completeness. Algorithm σ is called complete if for every program P in the considered programming language there is an inductive description J such that for every $J' \geqslant J$ the algorithm σ synthesizes from J' a program equivalent to P.

THEOREM. The algorithm Σ is complete.

246

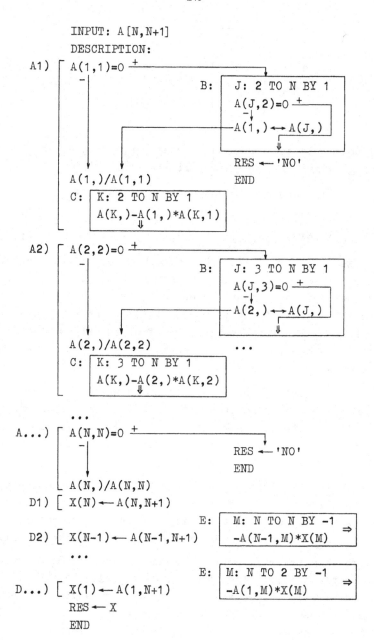

Fig. 10

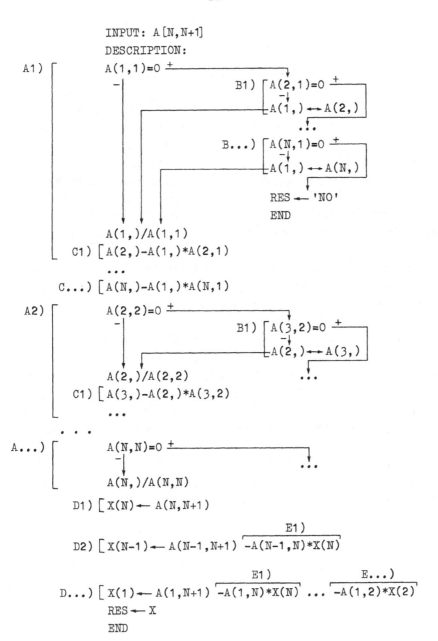

Fig. 11

5. ANOTHER VERSIONS OF INDUCTIVE DESCRIPTIONS

We will call the inductive descriptions considered above segmented inductive descriptions because steps corresponding to the body of the DO-statement under consideration are clearly indicated in the inductive description itself. For a programmer there are no serious difficulties to produce such a segmentation. Nevertheless there is some interest to develop methods of synthesis from unsegmented inductive descriptions. It turns out to be possible construct a sufficiently effective heuristic algorithm also for this case. This algorithm performs the segmentation and the synthesis simultaneously beginning with the objects of rank 0, i.e. with the innermost DO-statements. If the segmentation (i.e. separation into steps) has been performed incorrectly, then, as a rule, the construction of the DO-statement cannot be completed (e.g. the value of the loop variable in these steps do not form an arithmetical progression, as it is demanded in the expansions of DO-statements).

One more version of inductive descriptions is possible, namely, a version when the inductive description is given for fixed values of some input variables. For example, in the case of algorithm for solving a system of linear equations we can take A[3,4] instead of A[N,N+1] and demonstrate the performance of the algorithm for A[3,4] (see Fig.12). Such inductive descriptions also can be segmented and unsegmented. In the case of segmented inductive descriptions notations of the type A(3=N) (see Fig.12) are allowed. Additional information of such a kind can be easily produced by the person constructing the inductive description but it helps the synthesis very much. This additional information allows a sufficiently effective heuristic algorithm of synthesis. In the case of unsegmented descriptions the construction of effective heuristic algorithms is more difficult. It becomes equivalent to the well-known problem of the synthesis of programs from example computations investigated in papers by A.W.Biermann [2,3], M.A.Bauer [4], etc.

6. THE SYNTHESIS OF ASSERTIONS

The above-mentioned method of inductive synthesis can be used also for the synthesis of assertions about programs. This method of synthesis can sometimes yield a wrong result. But it seems to

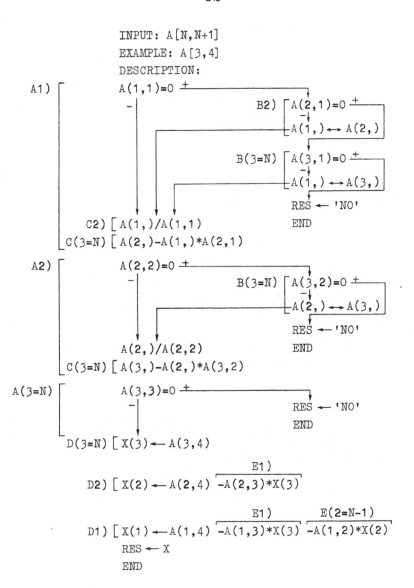

INPUT: A[N,N+1]
EXAMPLE: A[3,4]
DESCRIPTION:

Fig. 12

INPUT: A[N]
DESCRIPTION:

A1) ⌈ B1) ⌈ A(1) ⩽ A(2) ──────────┐
   │   │   ↓
   │   │   +│   A(1) ↔ A(2)
   │   │   └──────┘
   │   └ ⟨A(1) ⩽ A(2)⟩

   │   B2) ⌈ A(2) ⩽ A(3) ──────────┐
   │   │   +│   A(2) ↔ A(3)
   │   │   └──────┘
   │   └ ⟨A(2) ⩽ A(3)⟩

   │   ....

   │   B...) ⌈ A(N-1) ⩽ A(N) ──────┐
   │   │   +│   A(N-1) ↔ A(N)
   │   │   └──────┘
   └   └ ⟨A(N-1) ⩽ A(N)⟩

A2) ⌈ B1) ⌈ A(1) ⩽ A(2) ──────────┐
   │   │   +│   A(1) ↔ A(2)
   │   │   └──────┘
   │   └ ⟨A(1) ⩽ A(2) & A(N-1) ⩽ A(N)⟩

   │   B2) ⌈ A(2) ⩽ A(3) ──────────┐
   │   │   +│   A(2) ↔ A(3)
   │   │   └──────┘
   │   └ ⟨A(2) ⩽ A(3) & A(N-1) ⩽ A(N)⟩

   │   ...

   │   B...) ⌈ A(N-2) ⩽ A(N-1) ──────┐
   │   │   +│   A(N-2) ↔ A(N-1)
   │   │   └──────┘
   └   └ ⟨A(N-2) ⩽ A(N-1) & A(N-1) ⩽ A(N)⟩

A3) ⌈ B1) ⌈ A(1) ⩽ A(2) ──────────┐
   │   │   +│   A(1) ↔ A(2)
   │   │   └──────┘
   │   └ ⟨A(1) ⩽ A(2) & A(N-2) ⩽ A(N-1) & A(N-1) ⩽ A(N)⟩

   │   ...

   │   B...) ⌈ A(N-3) ⩽ A(N-2) ──────┐
   │   │   +│   A(N-3) ↔ A(N-2)
   │   │   └──────┘
   └   └ ⟨...⟩

          ...

A...) ⌈ B1) ⌈ A(1) ⩽ A(2) ──────────┐
     │   │   +│   A(1) ↔ A(2)
     │   │   └──────┘
     │   └ ⟨...⟩
     │   RES ← A
          END

Fig. 13

us that such cases will appear rarely. We shall not treat this
subject in details. We shall consider here only some examples.
Fig.13 shows an inductive description of the buble-sort algorithm.
The initial steps in this description are given together with the
assertions ⟨••••⟩ that hold after these steps. The assertions are
given by the human simultaneously with the inductive description.
Usually it is not hard to supply these assertions for initial steps.
But in general it is the final assertion of the program that makes
of interest for us. Let us consider some method for the synthesis
of this assertion. The method as in the case of program synthesis
will be completely syntactic, without considering the semantics of
objects to deal with. Because of this it can fail sometimes.

Let us go back to the Fig.13. At first, as usually, we synthesize the innermost DO-statements. The assertions ⟨••••⟩ are
treated like any other statements in the process. The result so
obtained is shown in Fig.14. Then we proceed to the synthesis of
the outer DO-statement. However, the bodies of DO-statement B
corresponding to the steps A1, A2, A3 are not similar because the
corresponding assertions are not similar (assertions are treated
simply as sequences of symbols here). Let us try to make these
assertions similar by using the horizontal DO-statement. Let us
begin with the assertion from A3)B:

A3)B ┌───┐
      │ • │
      │ ⟨ A(I)⩽A(I+1) & A(N-2)⩽A(N-1) & A(N-1)⩽A(N)⟩ │
      └───┘

It is possible to write it down by the following DO-statement:

A3)B ┌──┐
      │ • • • • • • • • • • • • • • • • • •   │
      │ ⟨ A(I)⩽A(I+1) ┌─K: N-2 TO N-1─┐ ⟩   │
      │   │ & A(K)⩽A(K+1) ⇒│   │
      │   └───────────────┘   │
      └──┘

Now we apply the obtained form of the assertion to the other bodies
of statement B and get the following:

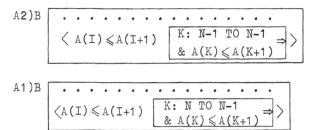

A2)B ┌──┐
      │ • • • • • • • • • • • • • • • •   │
      │ ⟨ A(I)⩽A(I+1) ┌─K: N-1 TO N-1─┐ ⟩   │
      │   │ & A(K)⩽A(K+1) ⇒│   │
      │   └───────────────┘   │
      └──┘

A1)B ┌──┐
      │ • • • • • • • • • • • • • • • •   │
      │ ⟨A(I)⩽A(I+1) ┌─K: N TO N-1─┐ ⟩   │
      │   │ & A(K)⩽A(K+1) ⇒│   │
      │   └──────────────┘   │
      └──┘

```
INPUT: A(N)
DESCRIPTION:
```

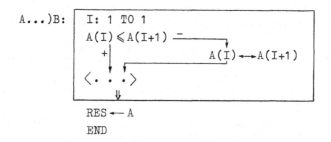

```
A1)B: ┌─────────────────────────────────────────┐
      │ I: 1 TO N-1                             │
      │ A(I)⩽A(I+1) ─────────────┐              │
      │    +│              A(I)←──→A(I+1)        │
      │     │     ┌────┘                        │
      │ ⟨A(I)⩽A(I+1)⟩                           │
      │     ⇓                                   │
      └─────────────────────────────────────────┘

A2)B: ┌─────────────────────────────────────────┐
      │ I: 1 TO N-2                             │
      │ A(I)⩽A(I+1) ─────────────┐              │
      │    +│              A(I)←──→A(I+1)        │
      │     │     ┌────┘                        │
      │ ⟨A(I)⩽A(I+1) & A(N-1)⩽A(N)⟩            │
      │     ⇓                                   │
      └─────────────────────────────────────────┘

A3)B: ┌─────────────────────────────────────────────────────────┐
      │ I: 1 TO N-3                                             │
      │ A(I)⩽A(I+1) ─────────────┐                              │
      │    +│              A(I)←──→A(I+1)                        │
      │     │     ┌────┘                                        │
      │ ⟨A(I)⩽A(I+1) & A(N-2)⩽A(N-1) & A(N-1)⩽A(N)⟩           │
      │     ⇓                                                   │
      └─────────────────────────────────────────────────────────┘

                    . . .

A...)B: ┌─────────────────────────────────────────┐
        │ I: 1 TO 1                               │
        │ A(I)⩽A(I+1) ─────────────┐              │
        │    +│              A(I)←──→A(I+1)        │
        │     │     ┌────┘                        │
        │ ⟨. . . .⟩                               │
        │     ⇓                                   │
        └─────────────────────────────────────────┘
        RES ←── A
        END
```

Fig. 14

INPUT: A[N]
PROGRAM:

```
A:  J: N-1 TO 1 BY -1
      B:  I: 1 TO J
          A(I) ≤ A(I+1) ─────────┐
             +│                   A(I) ←→ A(I+1)
                                ┌──────────────────────────┐
              │    │            │ K: J+1 TO N-1          ⇒ │
          ⟨A(I) ≤ A(I+1)        │ & A(K) ≤ A(K+1)          │ ⟩
                                └──────────────────────────┘
                   ⇓
                ⇓

RES ── A
END
```

Fig. 15

INPUT: A[N]
PROGRAM:

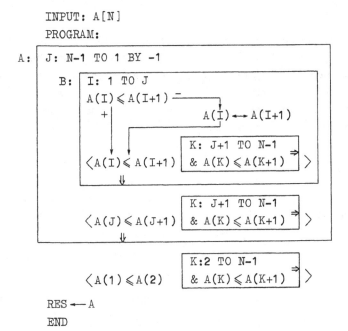

```
A:  J: N-1 TO 1 BY -1
      B:  I: 1 TO J
          A(I) ≤ A(I+1) ─────────┐
             +│                   A(I) ←→ A(I+1)
                                ┌──────────────────────────┐
              │    │            │ K: J+1 TO N-1          ⇒ │
          ⟨A(I) ≤ A(I+1)        │ & A(K) ≤ A(K+1)          │ ⟩
                   ⇓            └──────────────────────────┘

                                ┌──────────────────────────┐
                                │ K: J+1 TO N-1          ⇒ │
          ⟨A(J) ≤ A(J+1)        │ & A(K) ≤ A(K+1)          │ ⟩
                   ⇓            └──────────────────────────┘

                                ┌──────────────────────────┐
                                │ K:2 TO N-1             ⇒ │
          ⟨A(1) ≤ A(2)          │ & A(K) ≤ A(K+1)          │ ⟩
                                └──────────────────────────┘
RES ←─ A
END
```

Fig. 16

As a result all the bodies of the statement B are similar. Now we synthesize the statement A. So we obtain the Fig.15. It contains the program to be found together with assertions. We are interested in the final assertion, i.e. the assertion after statement A. We introduce the following rule of inference:

$$
C \quad \boxed{\begin{array}{l} \text{I: } \alpha \text{ TO } \beta \\ \cdots\cdots\cdots \\ \langle \alpha (\text{I}) \rangle \end{array}} \quad \Longrightarrow \quad C \quad \boxed{\begin{array}{l} \text{I: } \alpha \text{ TO } \beta \\ \cdots\cdots\cdots \\ \langle \alpha (\text{I}) \rangle \end{array}} \\ \langle \alpha (\beta) \rangle
$$

It means that if each step I of a statement C is followed by assertion $\langle \alpha (\text{I}) \rangle$ then we can add the assertion $\langle \alpha (\beta) \rangle$ after the statement C. So we obtain Fig.15. Here the statement A is followed by assertion

$$
\langle A(1) \leqslant A(2) \quad \boxed{\begin{array}{l} \text{K: 2 TO N-1} \\ \text{\& } A(K) \leqslant A(K+1) \end{array}} \Rightarrow \; \rangle
$$

i.e., $\langle A(1) \leqslant A(2) \ \& \ A(2) \leqslant A(3) \ \& \ \ldots \ \& \ A(N-1) \leqslant A(N) \rangle$.

In this case the obtained assertion evidently is true.

It is clear that the method of inference described above can be formalized. This method of inference sometimes fails, but for real situations it gives as a rule correct results. It is plausible that a human uses some similar method during the intuitive verification of his program.

REFERENCES

[1] J.M.Barzdin. Inductive inference of automata, functions and programs. Proceedings of the International Congress of Mathematicians, Canada, 1974, vol.2, p. 455-460.

[2] A.W.Biermann. Approaches to automatic programming. -In: Advances in Computers, vol.15, N.Y. Academic, 1976, p. 1-63.

[3] A.W.Biermann. Constructing programs from example computations. IEEE Trans. of Software Engineering, vol. SE-2, no.3 (1976), p. 141-153.

[4] M.A.Bauer. Programming by examples. Artificial Intelligence, vol.12 (1979), p. 1-21.

EXPANDING CONSTRUCTIVE UNIVERSES

Yu.I.Manin
V.A.Steklov Mathematical Institute
Vavilova Str., 42, Moscow V-333
USSR

1. Applications of mathematics are conventionally divided into
two large fields. Mathematics can help us to act more efficiently
in the World or to comprehend more profoundly the World. Geo-metry
started as land-measuring. It developed into abstract mathematics
turing into measuring-of-nothing and then reverted to applications
as measuring-of-anything, e.g. of "quantum tunneling amplitude between vacua with different topological charges".

Efficient algorithms are devised precisely to help us to act
efficiently in control, technology, navigation etc. According to
common-place wisdom, abstract computability theory only sets down
reference points and outlines the far-away frontiers of possible in
this domain. But isn't this attitude too narrow? Good mathematics
always gives more than is asked from it. We would be deprived of
vast layers of scientific culture including quantum mechanics if we
decided that $\sqrt{-1}$ is only introduced to make our formalisms more
tangible and that wave equation describes only those waves it was
originally devised to describe.

I believe that computability theory is now sufficiently mature
to justify systematic attempts to find broader interpretations of
its ideas. The deep work of A.N.Kolmogorov and his coworkers may
serve as a pattern. In this work the notion of chance was analyzed
as an embodiment of everything that cannot be revealed in the
course of algorithmic interaction between the researcher and the
object of his research. A complementary aspect of this problem is
less well understood. I have in mind the idea that a general notion
of an abstract computation process can serve as a model of determinism. In the post-Newtonian physics the idea of determinism is
manifested principally in the generally accepted principle that the
evolution of a system can be described by differential equations

("laws of Nature") and initial (boundary) conditions. The idea of
an abstract computation process is largely similar. The structure
of Turing machine, say, defines the "law" and the program corresponds to the initial conditions. The decomposition of the computation into elemntary steps only too easily brings to the mind the
idea of infinitesimal calculus. But in the classical mathematics
of the real continuum there is nothing even remotely reminiscent of
the Church thesis which could garantee that our understanding of
the idea of determinism is complete enough. On the other hand,
computability theory conspicuously lacks its own versions of such
fundamental ideas as the principle of extremal action or the notion
of conjugate variables. (Everybody knows that memory can be saved at
at the expense of the computer time and vice versa but how to
express this in exact terms?)

2. One difficulty hindering a comparison between models of
"algorithmic" and "classical" mathematics is the lack of a techni-
cally elaborated notion of "expanding the constructive universe".

To speak concretely I start by recalling two high-level
abstractions of computability theory which are readily translated
into set-theoretic language. These are the notion of a constructive universe U and of a class R_U of partial functions U→U which
are algorithmically (semi)computable. The standard example is:
U=N (the natural numbers), $R_U=R$ (the partial recursive functions).

A couple consisting of a set and a class of its partial maps
to itself is a structure in the Bourbaki sense. Two such structures are isomorphic if there is a bijection between the two sets
inducing a bijection between set of listinguished maps.

The Church thesis (in broad sense) asserts that each constructive universe (U,R_U) is constructively isomorphic to the universe
(N,R). The notion of constructive isomorphism in this statement is
not subject to formalization, just as Church's thesis itself is not
subject to proof.

Various Gödel numberings making it possible to code texts,
graphs, Turing machines, descriptions of recursive functions, etc.
by integers are of course working versions of Church's thesis.

Nevertheless there are compelling reasons not to consider
(N,R) (or any fixed couple (U,R_U)) as the Universe. The principal objection to a decision of this sort is that a process of

computation is also always a linguistic[*])$_1$ act. The inherently
linguistic$_1$ nature of a calculation makes it necessary to have the
means at any given moment to add to the initial universe a new description of an object of this universe (or of a process, or of
attribute, etc.)

Take for example a function f:U→U introduced by means of a
non-constructive definition as is usual in classical mathematics.
How are we to look at it from a constructive point of view? It is
suggested to introduce a description of f, say "f" as an element
of an expanded constructive universe V. If it is revealed later
that f∈R_U we will interpret this result as discovery of a function in R_V taking the value f(u) at the point ⟨"f",u⟩∈V. But
we may be interested not in values of f but, say, in the value of
its integral from 0 to 1, or in the number of its zeroes on the
unit circle, or else in its homotopy class. This means that one
should always consider a constructive object replacing the classical notion of a function as a potential argument of a new computable function in a new constructive universe and not just a symbol
of the initial function. For this reason traditional constructive
versions of theorems of classical calculus too literally interpreting their meaning seem to me inadequate.

The spirit of computability theory is largely determined by
this dialectics of expanding constructive universes, each level in
the hierarchy being isomorphic to any other.

This hierarchy in many respects is similar to a system of
neighbourhoods of a point in a topological space: e.g. each constructive universe can be considered as "a constructive neighbourhood
of empty set". It is natural to interpret the notion of "oracle"
in the same spirit. A constructive neighbourhood of, say, an element x∈$\mathscr{P}$(N) whose characteristic function is told by an oracle
is the set of subsets of N recursive relative to x. A structure
consisting of a set covered by constructive naighbourhood of its
elements might have been an interesting model in the borderline
between classical and algorithmic mathematics.

---

*) "The English adjective linguistic is ambiguous between 'pertain-
ing to language (s)' (Ger. sprachlich) and 'pertaining to linguistics' (Ger. sprachwissenschaftlich). Since in this paper the
distinction is crucial, we will use the following: linguistic$_1$
denotes the first sense, linguistic$_2$ the second". (I.A.Mel'cak,
in: Proc. VIIth Ann. Meeting of the Berkeley Linguistics Society,
1979, Berkeley).

3. The linguistic$_1$ flavour of the principal notions of computability theory was clear since its origin and led to a search for truly linguistic$_2$ applications. Work on automatic translation resulted in the crystallization of a major modern linguistic$_2$ conception: the model "Meaning $\longleftrightarrow$ Text". According to this model the subject of linguistics is a correspondence between two potentially infinite sets, "texts" and "meanings". The first set consists of texts of a natural language, the second set of texts composed in an artificial semantic language. Linguistics is conceived of as a theory of two-way algorithmic translation passing through a series of intermediate stages called "representation levels" of a natural language. Neither the language of meanings nor the algorithms of translations are given beforehand. They are to be synthesized. It is suggested that all the results of traditional linguistics as well as conceptions of various modern trends would find their natural plase in the realization of this vast program.

The elaboration of a detailed model seems such an immense undertaking that this idea leads me to search for a simpler "model$_2$ of the model$_1$ Meaning $\longleftrightarrow$ Text" which would help one to recognize some essential features of this project in vitro and to guess which class of recursive functions might be relevant to linguistic translation problems. It is natural to choose first a restricted set of meanings having a simple semantic representation given beforehand. The "phenomenon of business oration" suggested by A.P.Ershov looks like an interesting candidate.

But a mathematician is tempted to step away of the natural language and to consider as a set of meanings simply the positive integers S with the semantic representation by finite sequences |,||,||| ,... Then a system of denomination of integers will be a model of a natural language. But it is hardly reasonable to borrow this denomination system from a natural language. In fact even a superficial analysis shows that the numerals (with the exception of the first few) are usually not the names of numbers but of their decimal representations. If we wish to get rid of the definitely non-linguistic$_1$ influence of the decimal system we should go one step further and model the natural language also by a mathematical object. Let us consider a "translation map" $f:N \rightarrow S$ where N denotes the second universe of natural numbers i.e. names. I wish to draw attention to the fact that if we take for f an "asymptotically optimal numbering" due to Kolmogorov we get a situation which is unexpectedly linguistic$_1$ one. Recall that f, by definition, is a surjective partial recursive mapping which makes it possible to "call" a number f(n) by its shortest possible "name" n (up to an unavoidable indeterminacy in a bounded amount of bits). An optimal numbering exists and has the following properties.

a) Every number has an infinity of names.

b) Not every number is a name. In fact the domain of f has an infinite complement.

c) To construct the number starting from its name i.e. to calculate f is a difficult task. Actually optimal numberings are constructed using universal recursive functions, hence they are in a way as complex as possible.

d) The problem of finding the shortest name of a number (relative to a given f) is algorithmically unsolvable.

This list of properties of an optimal numbering can be compared with the following characteristics of a natural language.

A) The abundance of synonymy. Every meaning can be expressed by a great number of texts.

B) The openness of a natural language which is expressed in the possibility to form perfectly grammatical but "meaningless" texts. (In the model "Meaning $\longleftrightarrow$ Text" this property usually is relegated to the semantic level where the problem of "meaning of a meaning" is not discussed if this latter meaning is syntactically correct).

C) The translation Text $\longrightarrow$ Meaning involves a many-stage implementation of a system of complex algorithms making evident the great structural complexity of linguistic constructions.

D) The translation Meaning $\longrightarrow$ Text is far more difficult and was never realized even in theory.

If we adopt the idea that optimal numbering reflects essential properties of the enigmatic way in which language conveys meaning we can draw an unexpected conclusion: characteristics A)-D) of a natural language at least partially are due to its optimality i.e. the capacity for expressing a complicated meaning briefly if this is possible at all. The abundance of synonymous and of meaningless texts which superficially seems to contradict this assumption actually becomes its corollary. Our model$_2$ also gives an intuitive explanation of the "openness" of a natural language using the concept of expanding the universe. One can prove that the restriction of an optimal numbering of a universe to a smaller universe is still optimal. Under this restriction an infinity of names used to denote the thrown out objects become "meaningless". Although it is not strictly correct to invert this reasoning this seems to be a nice formalization of the notion that meaningless statements are potentially meaningful in an expanded "discursive universe". Poets and linguists are so well acquainted with this that only mathematicians couls ask for more explanations.

4. These impressionistic notes are a tribute to the informal style of our meeting. I borrowed the title from physicists. It is intended not only to serve as a metaphor of a principal notion but also to recall that we are living in the epoch after the Big Bang of computer technique.

I wish to acknowledge my indebtness to A.P.Ershov who in long discussions helped me to formulate my thoughts on the subject; to D.Knuth for his inspiring observations on algorithmic thinking-style; to Yu.D.Apresyan and V.A.Uspensky who stimulated me to try to collect in a coherent picture the first vague analogies.

THE LOGICAL APPROACH TO PROGRAMMING

N.N.Nepeivoda

Izhevsk, USSR

1. GENERAL CHARACTERISTICS OF THE APPROACH

One of the fundamental questions in programming is "Where are programs taken from?" Previously, programs were given ad initio as an algorithm and the subject of study was their functioning or functionally equivalent transformation. Later syntactic studies and problems of translation from one algorithmic language into another one had emerged. Now we study correctness problems. As a result, process of systematic construction of a correct program comes to the stage.

The enormous growth of software and proliferation of computers have made program reliability and programmers' productivity the most critical issues in programming. Programming has accumulated a great empirical material that sometimes contradicts to the established theoretical tradition and has to be thought of. In particular, interesting examples of such contradictions may be found in G.S.Tseitin's essay [1].

On the other hand, modern mathematics again is getting some features of an experimental science but a kind of God's play. Our programs are new and sometime mad worlds. We are both their creators and explorers. It is worth to note that the most abstract disciplines of mathematics such as mathematical logic (proof and model theories) general algebra (cathegory theory and universal algebra), set theory and others are broadly used and possess a rich variety of practically important structures.

The author is convinced that the wall between theoretical and practical knowledge is the main obstacle on the way to the solution to many problems. This wall happens to be hardly penetratable even inside a man who perfectly masters any of these knowledges separately. We have heard about the existence of this wall here, at the

Symposium, from G.S.Tseitin [30] and D.Knuth [31] who assuringly spoke on difficulties encountered when trashing this internal barrier.

There are many reasons for that wall to be so solid. Perhaps, the main one is an artificially distilled from life tradition of the treatment of mathematical notions. It prevents from understanding many intuitively transparent and well applicable ideas presented in an artificially complicated form. No less distractable is the custom of many applied mathematicians to work only with "one axe" using only traditional methods not trying to analyze pecularities of an initial problem; the "sportistic" spirit of theoretical mathematicians where an only long ago stated problem is worth to solve; narrow-minded style of practitioners who (sometimes pushed by customers) trade quality for speed; another "love" of theoreticians of polishing again and again traditional concepts useful somewhen but obsolete now; the non-critical repetition by practitioners of ones found decisions.

It were the works [1-5] that helped to the author to have his internal wall broken and understood how interesting are the theoretical problems which are put forward by contemporary practice, how carefully the theory should be prepared to be usable in applications. In a sense, this paper is an antythesis to Tseitin's paper from this volume [30]. The author has experienced an opposite transition in his practical work, i.e., from proceduralism to logicism. It is interesting to note that in frequent personal discussions with G.S.Tseitin both sides based on the same facts but with different conclusions.

The logical approach to programming is characterized by the following features:

- In all cases reasoning is primary and algorithm writing is secondary.

- The logic used, both formal and informal, varies depending on the problem tackled or even on the stage of work.

- Algorithm and logical derivation must be merged in one entity. It requires a reconsideration of both notions with an emphasis to their naturalness and mutual consistency.

- Formal theories are considered as "metaprograms" for a problem class.

- Program development starts with finding a constructive proof of reachability of the goal and then its cleaning from non-algorithmic details.

- Main attention is paid to concepts of weak computability.

From the logic side our approach is a direct extension of the structured proof theory; from the programming side it emerges from structured programming.

2. RELATION TO OTHER APPROACHES

We shall compare our approach with three other programming styles which we identify as Manna's pragmatical approach [12-14], Ershov's transformational approach [2, 17-19], and Barzdyn's inductive approach [20]. There is nothing with respect to priority considerations we just mention names in whose works the corresponding approach was most clearly outlined.

Analyzing [12-14], we may identify the following <u>Manna's cycle</u> of program development:

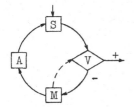

S - synthesis
A - analysis
M - modification
V - verification

We start having synthesized by any method a piece of program. Then we check whether we have obtained accidentally a complete solution. If not, we modify the fragment (perhaps, returning to verification) trying to achieve the subgoal under consideration. Then we analyze the situation, identify a new goal and try to synthesize the corresponding piece of program. This process of program development does not depend essentially on the algorithmic languages used and logic formalism adopted. This is, in fact, a bottom up process. It is appropriate when the problem is poorly stated and must be corrected during the programming process.

In its current form, this approach is helpless in designing conditional clauses but this can be resolved if to overcome a purely traditional preference of the classical logic formalism. But there is another fundamental and unavoidable deficiency of this method though not much felt so far. This method can't advance programming practice and give recommendation of its improvement, for it is inherently based on the existing methods of programming.

The transformational, inductive and logical approaches also give raise to the corresponding development cycles.

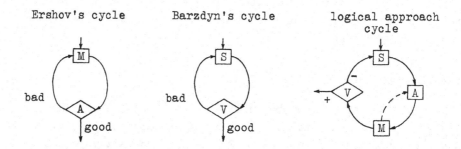

The transformational approach works when the problem statement alone gives us an algorithm "in principle" perhaps expressed in a very high level language. For example, for sorting problem it could be a set-theoretic definition of a sorted array [17]. Then this impractical algorithm is modified in order to improve its performance. Each new modification is then evaluated with respect to its efficiency. The synthesis is terminated when desired efficiency and detailness are achieved.

This approach requires a continuous spectrum of well balanced languages from a very high level to a low one. Its main assumption is that algorithms came from algorithms. If it works at all it works perfectly. It provides a transition from theoretical computability to practical computations (see [29]).

The inductive approach is based on an initial collection of examples of computation. Looking at them we try to guess the logical structure of a program that could fit these examples. The current version is then tested against new examples. If the test fails we must modify or even redesign the program. Here verification resembles practical debugging. By the way, such an understanding of verification is appropriate for Manna's cycle, too. This approach provides a reverse transition from computation to computability.

The logical approach is applicable when we have a precise formulation of the problem and a good description of the computation environment. On the other hand, we do not assume that we have in advance a precise computability proof (in fact we are interested in computability in a restricted class of computable functionals not necessary coinciding with the class of all recursive functionals). Program synthesis generates a correct text by virtue. It is possible,

however, that the program synthesized does not fit the Prokrustian
bed of the computation environment. If the analysis discovers such
an unfitting, new specifications are introduced and some modifications are tried to meet these specifications. If it fails then
synthesis is repeated.

We may conclude that the transformational approach relates to
the logic one as Barzdyn's approach does to the pragmatic Manna's
approach.

3. BASIC PROBLEMS AND MODELS

It is known (see, for example, [6]) that in the general problem
of the purposeful behaviour formation the following extreme subcases
can be singled out.

1. Pure programming. Output data satisfying given conditions
must be found for any input data from some set. All input and intermediate data are equally available without any restrictions their
volume and duration of their storing. As it was shown several times
(see, for example, [3]) the intuitionistic logic is a natural logic
for this problem. Moreover, the corresponding instrument prepared
for practice had been developed yet in 30s and 40s (intuitionistic
calculus of natural deduction and Kleene's realizability concept
[7]). However, both, practitioners and theoreticians, ignored it.
In particular, some unjustified conclusions about non-usability of
intuitionistic logic as a practical instrument can be found in [15,
16].

The practical problem to which we orient our discussion will
be assembling of a program from a collection of correct subroutines
forming an application package. For that problem the pure programming approach is studied best of all and we shall deal essentially
with it.

2. Programming with restriction. The general problem is the
same but resource restrictions are essential. For that problem
there were no appropriate natural constructive logic. First attempts
to develope such logic can be found in [21,22]. The corresponding
constructive logic is still based on the intuitionistic logic but
modifies the latter considerably.

3. Simplest planning. It assumes a passive world and an active
robot which actions change the world. The problem is to develop a
plan of actions which provide a transition from the state satisfying

a given precondition to a state satisfying a given postcondition. The volume of intermediate data can be restricted as well as the capacity of the channel through which the robot communicates with the world. This framework suits programming in machine instructions and in conventional algorithmic languages with assignments. Constructive logics for simplest planning belong to the class of relevant logics but they have no direct accentor among traditional relevant logics. We shall show an elementary fragment of such a logic that could be most naturally considered as a logic style arrangement of the production grammar concept and of the methods used in GPS (see, e.g. [6]).

Let us consider the simplest model of the planning problem. It consists of a universum U (the set of world states) and a collection of subsets from U, put in correspondence to each propositional letter (predicate). Each elementary action is a function $U \rightarrow U^U$ (nondeterministic function). For this model a propositional logic can be constructed in which proof finding corresponds finding a branched composition of elementary actions that provides reaching the goal (see [23]).

The central concepts in this logic is that of programming triad: action, premise, promise. There are two kinds of connectives for action description: <u>constructive</u> connectives which require actions and <u>descriptive</u> connectives which are similar to those of Boolean logic.

We shall exemplify the use of programming triads by prescribing how to open and close a door. A triad is written as $f(r) A \Rightarrow B$ where f is an elementary action, A is its premise (applicability condition), and B is its promise. This notation is read as "f is applicable under A and promises B" or "f implement the transition from A to B". Notations <u>and</u>, <u>or</u>, <u>not</u>, $\Rightarrow$ and &, $\vee$, $\neg$, $\Rightarrow$ will be used for descriptive and constructive connectives, respectively.

<u>Example 1</u>. Let our universum be the set of states of the key and the door. Let us have the following predicates: KP (the key is in the pocket), KD (the key is in the door), DO (the door is open), DC (the door is closed) and elementary actions: tkp (take the key out of the pocket), ik (insert the key), tkd (take the key out of the door), pk (put the key into the pocket), tuk (turn the key).

Our model can be described by the following axioms (most of them are triades).

A1. tkp ⓡ KP ⇒ <u>not</u> KP <u>and</u> <u>not</u> KD
A2. ik ⓡ <u>not</u> KP <u>and</u> <u>not</u> KD ⇒ KD
A3. tkd ⓡ KD ⇒ <u>not</u> KP <u>and</u> <u>not</u> KD
A4. pk ⓡ <u>not</u> KD <u>and</u> <u>not</u> KP ⇒ KP
A5. tuk ⓡ (DC <u>and</u> KD ⇒ DO <u>and</u> KD) <u>and</u>
          (DO <u>and</u> KD ⇒ DC <u>and</u> KD)
A6. KP ⇒ <u>not</u> KD
A7. DC ⇒ <u>not</u> DO

Here we suppose the predicates divided into two semantic classes: {KP,KD} and {DO,DC}. The descriptive axioms A6,A7 contain
predicates from one and the same class only. This is a general
condition on descriptive axioms. Each of them relates predicates
from one semantic class. By default, a constructive axiom does not
change predicates belonging a semantic class not represented in the
axiom.

Example 2. A proof and a program for the Example 1. Let us
consider the goal KP <u>and</u> DC ⇒ KP <u>and</u> DO (i.e., having the key in
the pocket and the door opened, to open the door and put the key back
into the pocket). The realizability proof will be written in a
notation adopted for the functional system of inference rules [9].
The sign] means "let us assume that ...", the bar | means an auxi-
liary derivation under the corresponding assumption; statements
appearing in one line are claimed to be valid together.

```
]KP;DC
|not KP, not KD;
|not KP,KD;
|      KD,DO;
|not KP, not KD;
|KP;
KP and DC ⇒ KP and DO
Program: begin tkp; ik; tuk; tkd; pk end.
```

Note, that the construction of the derivation does not requires
actions realizing constructive axioms. However, some characteristics of realizing actions may help greatly to the derivation search.
It is appropriate to add these characteristics to the axioms as
constructive <u>modalities</u> that inform resource consumption when performing the action (see, e.g. [21,22]).

4. _Observations_. They deal with an active external world and various probers. They supply us with an information that is insufficient by quality and quantity to reconstruct a precise world model. Auxiliary information can degradate as the time goes on or just be available only a limited time. The problem is to recognize some world states. The logic for such problems is the so called temporal constructive logic and its development is at only a very initial stage.

5. _General problems_ of purposeful behaviour are naturally subdivided into subproblems of these three kinds. For example, manipulator control is subdivided into planning and computation, production control consists of computation and observation, etc.

6. _Antilogic direction_. The wave of the first enthusiasm about logic methods in artificial intelligence have caused some negative reaction. The most strong arguments against the logic approach were pronounced by G.S.Tseitin [30]. However, the drawbacks of logic that were criticized as obstacles of its application were, even in

stronger terms, criticized by G.Kreisel [4] as obstacles of its development. Kreisel's paper was more positive because, besides the critique, accumulated but poorly used treasures were shown and some ways to overcome obstacles were suggested.

Summing up the antilogic arguments it can be said that all of them blame the traditional logic in its traditional form. The critics equalize logic with the classical logic, moreover, with one of its traditional form, formalization with its traditional methodology, or - in general - science with its tradition (here = prejudice).

Some scholars offer attributes and frames as substitutes for logic methods. However, attribute is just one of the three faces of predicates in programs and frame is one the forms of the constructive implication. The author believes that, in principle, there is no such a thing as algorithmic thinking; on the other hand, logic has much more forms than we accustomed to distinguish.

The departure for frames and attributes has the same disadvantage as Manna's approach has. It is quite worthwhile to generalize an accumulated practical experience but a collection of techniques is not yet a generalization. Genuine theory forms practice and goes in advance of it. Behind a collection of practical observations very few rather abstract notions and principles generating these observations must be found. There is no way to such generalizations other than through logic.

However, it must be remembered that almost nothing from the contemporary logic in its traditional form can be applicable. If the contents should maximally be taken from the theory then the form should be brought from the good practice.

Let us note one of the most difficult problems of the new constructive logic. This is the problem of interaction of several theories, sometimes based on different logics. For example, when working with action planning, we deal with a variety of descriptive theories even if the constructive theory is fixed.

4. PRELIMINARIES TO THE LOGICAL PROGRAMMING LANGUAGE

In the sequel we shall deal with the pure programming problem only.

The logical approach to this problem evolved in three stages. First, among the variety of formalisms for logical derivation and program presentation two models were chosen as fitting each other best of all. These are the Fitch form of natural deduction and the ALGOL 68 programming language. The close analysis has showed that the level of the deduction system was a little below that of the algorithmic language; as a consequence, the logical formalism has been modified. As a result we have obtained a complete natural derivation system consisting of three rules: procedure declaration, procedure application and definition by case. Each of them has an obvious programming interpretation, and the actual development of a formal derivation in this system proceeds in a more natural way than in the traditional system. The system is described in [9,11] and we shall not repeat its presentation here.

The very first analysis of ALGOL 68 from the constructive point of view has showed the most attractive concepts of the language as well as its weaker points. So the problem of their improvement arised that gradually lead to a new, logical programming language. Here we show the process of transition from constructive logic rules to algorithmic language.

First, we explicitate the basic analogies that support the algorithm of extraction of a program from a proof [8-11]. The proof looks as a chained collection (net) of formulas and subordinate derivations. Each initial formula in these chains is an axiom and each remaining formula is labelled by inference rules used in obtaining the formula. Subordinate derivation has a similar structure except that initial formulas may be assumptions. Any information contained in a subordinate derivation can be forwarded only to a formula which is a direct conclusion of the derivation. Formulas of a subordinate derivation which transmit an outside information are called results. A subordinate derivation can be used only once as a premise of an inference rule.

Inference rules are divided into describing (among logical rules, only the procedure declaration rule is describing) and constructing rules. Each constructing rule may create one or several new object denoted by auxiliary constant symbols c_i.

The program extraction process consists of two phases: classification of the derivation objects into acting and non-acting and assembling the program from acting objects.

Few words on two special features of the used logical language. First, we use a language of the many-sorted first order predicate calculus without equality. Variable sorts (= basic data types in the algorithmic language) are partially ordered by the inclusion relation $\subseteq$; an object of type $\underline{m} \subseteq \underline{n}$ automatically coerced to the type $\underline{n}$ when necessary; types may be empty. Second, not all used predicates must be computable. So called theoretical predicates are allowed which do not require the characteristic function to be computable. The first feature is widely used in practical formalizations; we shall use, however, only one type $\underline{ob}$ in our examples. The second feature is inherent. Moreover, according to the author's technique, the number of computable predicates should be minimised, especially, in applied occurrences. However, all members of the initial disjunctions must be computable, perhaps, except one.

Example 3. Let a computational environment [10] be characterized by the following axiom system (each constructive axiom is preceded by a notation of its realisation):

A1. $\forall x(A(x) \Rightarrow B(x) \lor C(x) \lor D(x) \lor E(x) \lor F(x))$
A2. $f(r) \ \forall x(B(x) \Rightarrow \exists y K(x,y))$
A3. $g(r) \ \forall x,y(A(x)\&K(x,y) \Rightarrow \exists z L(x,z))$
A4. $h(r) \ \forall x(C(x) \Rightarrow \exists y M(x,y))$
A5. $j(r) \ \forall x(D(x) \Rightarrow \exists y K1(x,y))$
A6. $j1(r) \ \forall x(A(x) \Rightarrow \exists y K2(x,y))$
A7. $j2(r) \ \forall x,y,z(K1(x,y)\&K2(x,z) \Rightarrow \exists u L(x,u))$
A8. $k(r) \ \forall x(E(x) \Rightarrow \exists y H1(x,y))$
A9. $k1(r) \ \forall x,y(H1(x,y) \Rightarrow \exists z(M(x,z)\&P(x,z)))$

A10. k2 (r) $\forall x(F(x) \Rightarrow \exists yQ(x,y))$
A11. k3 (r) $\forall x,y(Q(x,y) \Rightarrow \exists zQ1(x,y,z))$
A12. $\forall x,y,z(Q1(x,y,z) \Rightarrow \neg A2(x))$
A13. l1 (r) $\forall x,y(L(x,y) \& A1(x) \Rightarrow \exists zR(x,z))$
A14. l2 (r) $\forall x,y(M(x,y) \& A2(x) \Rightarrow \exists zR1(x,z))$
A15. l3 (r) $\forall x,y(R1(x,y) \Rightarrow \exists zH1(x,z))$
A16. l4 (r) $\forall x,y(P(x,y) \Rightarrow \exists zR(x,z))$

Let the predicates B,C,D,E,F be computable and the remaining ones be theoretical. We prove the theorem (= program goal):

$$x(A(x) \& A1(x) \& A2(x) \Rightarrow \exists yR(x,y)).$$

We shall give two variants of the proof of the goal: in the Fitch form and in the structured net form.

The Fitch form:

1.	$]A(x),A1(x),A2(x)$	x is arbitrary
2.	$B(x) \lor C(x) \lor D(x) \lor E(x) \lor F(x)$	by A1
3.	$]B(x)$	1st case
4.	$K(x,c1)$	by A2
5.	$L(x,c2)$	by A3
6.	$]C(x)$	2nd case
7.	$M(x,c3)$	by A4
8.	$]D(x)$	3rd case
9.	$K2(x,c4)$	by A6
10.	$K1(x,c5)$	by A5
11.	$L(x,c6)$	by A7
12.	$]E(x)$	4th case
13.	$H1(x,c7)$	by A8
14.	$M(x,c8),P(x,c8)$	by A9
15.	$]F(x)$	5th case
16.	$Q(x,c9)$	by A10
17.	$Q1(x,c9,c10)$	by A11
18.	$\neg A2(x)$	by A12
19.	$\curlywedge$	contradiction
20.	$L(x,c11) \lor M(x,c11)$	intermediate construction
21.	$]L(x,c11)$	1st alternative
22.	$R(x,c12)$	by A13
23.	$]M(x,c11)$	2nd alternative
24.	$R1(x,c13)$	by A14
25.	$H1(x,c14)$	by A15
26.	$M(x,c15),P(x,c15)$	by A9
27.	$R(x,c16)$	by A16

```
28. |R(x,c17)                          QED
29. ∀x(A(x)&A1(x)&A2(x) ⇒ ∃yR(x,y))    goal
```

The same derivation in the structured net form:

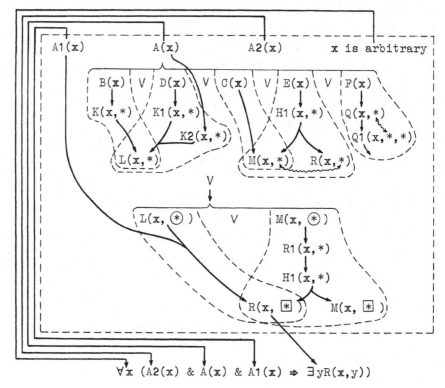

$$\forall x \ (A2(x) \ \& \ A(x) \ \& \ A1(x) \ \Rightarrow \ \exists yR(x,y))$$

The asterisk * denotes auxiliary constants, arrows denote logical
dependencies, wavy lines denote identity of objects. The two most
important constants are singled out: ⊛ and ⊡ for c_{11} and c_{17},
respectively. The analysis of the information connections suggests
that the program must construct c_{11} and then yield c_{17}. Besides
the value of c_{11} we must remember which of the cases, L or M, actually took place, since the direct check of these predicates is impossible. This is a particular instance of the general situation when
we have to obtain a non-computable information from indirect computable objects.

Yu.M.Smetanin (private communication) noticed a direct analogy
between such derivations and finite automata.

5. ESSENTIALS OF THE LOGICAL PROGRAMMING LANGUAGE

Many previous attempts to represent proofs as programs have failed. The most frequent reasons for such failures are: ignorance of the predominance of non-computable theoretical objects in proofs or too straightforward use of the existing techniques in logic and languages in programming. We can provide a _natural_ correspondence between proofs and programs only if we require a direct link between inference rules in the logical theory and statements of the algorithmic language. Each construct of the algorithmic language must be an image of a construct in the logical derivation. Neither ambiguous constructs nor alternative realizations of one elementary step are permissible.

Here are the main features of a logical programming language influenced by the analysis of constructive proofs.

1. There are no variables and assignments in the language. Intermediate results are remembered as constant declarations. Memory economy in provided by the block structure. Since one rule may yield several constants, simultaneous constant declarations are intoduced, for example:

   real a,b = sqrt(x↑2+y↑2),x+y; or _real_ a, _bool_ b = a1,b1 _of_ f(x,y)

2. _Each_ statement yields a value.

3. The block structure of the proof is mapped into the block structure of the program.

4. The data type hierarchy corresponds to the formula hierarchy in the proof. Auxiliary constants correspond to basic data type values. Formulas with bound acting variables or with non-computable acting disjunctions correspond to composite types (the last corresponds to marked unions).

5. Acting inference rules are one-to-one mapped inro program statements.

6. A statement of the programming language appears when we reach the top of a detour. Remember, that a detour appears in the proof when we apply a formula already proved by a describing rule.

7. Non-acting objects are mapped into "ghost" values which are useful for verification.

8. The information and control structures of the program are intimately connected.

Let us now describe some language constructs. They look as an ALGOL 68 stylization of acting objects of the proof. The language is adjustable to a specific computational environment, so the basic data types and operations are not determined except bool, void and logical operations. The basic data types correspond to the variable sorts in the logical theory and, similarly to them, are ordered by the relation $\subseteq$.

The composite types resemble the corresponding ALGOL 68 mode declarations. Fields in a structure are not ordered; in a union each member is marked by a so called case identifier (accordingly, all restrictions on the union of mutually coercible modes ceases to exist).

Example 4. The program extracted from Example 3.

```
proc aim =(ob x)ob:
    (union(ob p,q)c11= if B(x) then p:g(x,f(x)) □
                          C(x) then q:h(x) □
                          D(x) then p:j2(x,j(x),j1(x)) □
                          E(x) then q:k1(x,k(x)) □
                          F(x) then error
                       fi;
    new case c11 in p:l1(x,c11) □
                       q:l4(x,k1(x,l3(x,l2(x,c11))))
        esac
    );
```

Note, that the new symbol marks the value yielded by the block.

Program elaboration in defined by the transformational semantics approach [2]. For example, constant declaration elaboration consists of elaboration of the phrase which yields the constant value and then of substitution of all occurrences of that constant by the yielded values.

In particular, the value of a procedure identifier is the procedure body denotation with substituted names of global values. A procedure value can be yielded as a result of block elaboration. Such an approach is equivalent to the generation of new procedures by means of partial parametrization. Conditional expressions are used in the Dijkstra form. We allow, however, an else-part corresponding to a non-computable disjunction member. Dijkstra's objections against such a default rule are completely destroyed by his own use of this method in such a central place as the loop termination criterium.

Now we explain a new concept of <u>surprise</u> which did not appear previously in programming languages. It is a generalization of exceptions and loop terminators in the ADA language and many similar concepts of the structured <u>goto</u>.

When constructing a proof, we, as a rule, start with some assumptions of a subordinate derivation and try to define the logical structure of its results (perhaps, with some empty places for values to become known later on). However, it happens that, in an internal subordinate derivation, we encounter a conclusion which can serve as the result of an embracing derivation. In a program, it is appropriate to stopthe dirty work with which we are busy and to terminate the outermost block whose result can be satisfied by the value we possess. The value has to be properly transmitted. This is a <u>good</u> <u>surprise</u>.

Another reason for a surprise is when, during program elaboration, we meet a situation which was excluded in the proof as a contradiction. This is a <u>bad</u> <u>surprise</u> showing either incorrect data or computer failure. When encountered, a bad surprise has to be localized and then an appropriate error handling routine has to be invoked after receiving necessary data.

Let us consider program realization of surprises. A straightforward approach suggests to write surprise processors like procedure bodies and envoke a surprise like a procedure call. This approach, however, looses the idea of surprise itself, since we look for not a situation which is identical to the given one but a situation which handles predicates satisfied at the given situation. Different goals can use different predicates and same predicates can be satisfied in different contexts.

It means that a surprise is best of all identified by listing the predicates that have been surprisingly satisfied. Their arguments should be considered as data that have to be transmitted to the handling routine. The predicates appear here as data attributes:

$$\left(\begin{array}{c} \underline{good} \\ \underline{bad} \end{array} \right) \quad \underline{surprise} \quad P_1(\overline{t}_1), \ldots, P_n(\overline{t}_n);$$

where P_i is a predicate identifier and $\overline{t}_i$ is a term vector.

Respectively, in order to "catch" a surprise, the list of predicates to be satisfied must be given. The predicates may contain either expressions whose values are a priori known when excountering the surprise or free variables to which corresponding values are assigned when catching the surprise:

$$\underline{when}\ \left(\begin{array}{c}\underline{good}\\ \underline{bad}\end{array}\right)\ P_1(\overline{r}_1),\ldots,P_k(\overline{r}_k)\ \underline{with}\ \underline{m1}\ x1,\ldots,\underline{ml}\ xl\ \underline{give}\ S\ \underline{evig}$$

where $\overline{r}_i$ are either terms or variables from the list $x1,\ldots,x$; S is
the yielded result.

The <u>when</u> statement may appear in a regular block only after
<u>new</u> and the normally yielded value; in an <u>if</u> statement as one of
alternatives.

When processing a good surprise, an outermost <u>when</u> statement
is sought whose predicate list is a sublist of the surprise predicate list. If there is no such a <u>when</u> statement, then the surprise
is ignored.

When processing a bad surprise, an innermost <u>when</u> statement is
sought. If an appropriate <u>when</u> statement is not found then the
program execution aborts.

Even this basic subset of the logical language has constructs
which have no adequate constructive interpretation. In particular,
existing rules which introduce recursive procedures are not yet
satisfactory [9,11].

6. LOOPS AND ARRAYS

Loops appear from mathematical induction rules. In particular,
by a direct application of the induction by regular formulas, i.e.,
in the form $\exists \overline{x}\ \mathcal{Ot}(\overline{x})$ where $\mathcal{Ot}$ is normal, we obtain the following
arithmetical progression for statement:

$$\underline{for}\ i,\ \underline{m1}\ x1,\ldots,\underline{mn}\ xn\ \underline{from}\ i0,y1,\ldots,yn\ \underline{by}\ step\ \underline{to}\ lim$$
$$\underline{give}\ t\ \underline{evig}\ \{W\}\ \underline{do}\ S\ \underline{rof}.$$

Here (int) i is the control variable of the loop, step is the incre-
ment, lim is the upper bound, x_j are the iterated variables, m_j are
their modes, i0, yj are the initial values, t is the yielded value,
$\{W\}$ are optional surprise processors, S is the statement yielding
new values of the iterated variables.

<u>Example 5</u>. Fibonacci numbers.
<u>proc</u> fibonacci = (<u>nat</u> n) <u>nat</u>:
<u>for</u> i,<u>nat</u> x,y <u>from</u> 1,0,1 <u>by</u> 1 <u>to</u> n <u>give</u> y <u>evig</u> <u>do</u> x:y,y:x+y <u>rof</u>.

Loop elaboration starts from evaluating initial values, lim
and step; then the upper bound is checked and if the heading is
not exhausted then an instance of S is taken with i, xj replaced by
their initial values, this instance is elaborated and its results

are assigned to yj and i0 is incremented by step. Thus, the loop
is ready to be repeated. If i > lim then the loop normally terminates and the for statement is replaced by the value of t. Similarly,
if a surprise happens inside the loop and is catched by one of its
processors then the loop value is yielded by the corresponding with
statement and the loop is terminated surprisingly. Surprise processors make traditional while conditions obsolete. At the first time
this technique was systematically used in the YARMO language [24].

The deeper constructive analysis shows, however, that the logical conditions which lead to while loops have other expression than
the surprise method has. Namely, they appear due to the following
induction principle reducible to the conventional one but more convenient:

$$\frac{A(0,\overline{t0}) \; B_1 V \ldots VB_k \quad \left| \begin{array}{c}]A(n,\overline{x}), \; n,\overline{x} \text{ arbitrary} \\ \vdots \\ A(n+1,\overline{t}) \lor B_1 V \ldots VB_k \end{array} \right.}{A(m,c) \lor B_1 V \ldots VB_k}$$

Here all $B_1,\ldots,B_k$ are computable. It is natural to place the check
of B_is at the position of surprise processors but in a simpler form:
when B_i give r_i evig.

The first natural generalization of the loop is to take for
the control variable an arbitrary given well-ordered set as its
domain. In such a case the control variable may just disappear,
for it can be treated as an iterated variable controlled by surprises and explicit loop conditions. Here we encounter a programmistic
interpretation of the Markov principle [25]: the loop must be synthesized constructively but its termination can be proved classically.

Example 6. McCarthy 91-function.
proc f91 = (nat x) nat:
   for nat n,z from 1,x when n=0 give z evig do
      if z>100 then n-1,z-10 else n+1,z+11 fi rof.

Now we shall consider the cases when the domain of the control
variable is not linear. Such cases generate loops of various kinds;
one of them, Brouwer loop, will be considered in more details.

This loop implements the Brouwer bar-induction principle (see,
e.g., [26]). Let X be a net (loopless or-graph) with finite chains,
Y be the set of initial elements, Z be the set of terminal elements,
← be the direct predecessor relation. Then

$$\forall x \in YA(x) \ \& \ \forall x \in X(\forall y \in X(y \leftarrow x \Rightarrow A(y)) \Rightarrow A(x)) \Rightarrow \forall x \in ZA(x).$$

New composite data types may be needed to implemente such loops and other logically natural constructs. It could be, for example, sets of a type m(set m type), partially ordered sets poset m, nets net m, etc.

These data types induce some natural operations. In particular, we shall use a restriction of a set

$$\text{set } \underline{\text{union}}(b1 \ \underline{m1},\ldots,bk \ \underline{mk})x$$

by a fixed attribute bi denoted by x⌐bi, relations $\subseteq, =, \in, \leqslant$ (for posets), ← (for nets).

Now we may present the general form of the Brouwer loop, or data flow loop:

bar for $x \in X$,m1 x1,...,mk xk from Y give t evig {W} do S rof. Here, Y is the set of initial values, X is the net of control variable values, S yields new values of iterated variables, W are surprise processors, t is the normally yielded value.

Now we shall describe the loop elaboration. The phrase Y yields an array whose components are structures of values of xi subscripted by initial elements of the net X. The value of Y may be followed by an explicit subscripts check by comparing their range with a prescribed set XO:

compare XO bad surprise ... ,

this bad surprise activating an appropriate error handling.

Having initialized and checked Y we choose some x which is the least element outside of the range of subscripts of Y. If x is terminal then the loop is terminated by elaborating t, otherwise S is elaborated. All xi's are referred to as array components subscripted by y←x. All new elements are added to Y with the subscript x, while elements whose subscript has x as its only outside direct successor are deleted from Y.

Example 7. Evaluation of an arithmetical expression in the net form

```
mode acx = net union(string var,struct(ref a,b)plus,minus,mult,div);
proc compute = (acx a,[set string] int environ) int:
    (set string avar = a⌐var;
    new
    bar for x∈a, int i from environ {avar}
```

```
      compare avar bad surprise q (avar, range environ)
      give i evig do
      case x in plus: i[a of x]+i[b of x] □
               minus: i[a of x]-i[b of x] □
                mult: i[a of x]×i[b of x] □
                 div: i[a of x]÷i[b of x]
         esac
   rof
   when bad q(x1,x2) with set string x1,x2 give
         signal ("no data",x1-x2); skip evig
   );
```

Here, range a is the set of subscripts of the array a, a{z} is a subarray selected by the restriction of the subscripts by the set {z}.

This example gives some hints how to work with arrays. As a rule, arrays appear as operands of special statements and operations. However, according to the orthogonality principle, arrays enjoy full right of values and can be used in standard statements as well as initialized.

Usually, array is formalized as a function which yields a value for given subscripts. To this end, conventional descriptive formalizations hide distinctions between arrays and procedures. From the constructive viewpoint, procedure corresponds to the formula $\forall \overline{x}(A \Rightarrow \exists \overline{y} B)$. The well-known comprehension rule allows to obtain the formula

$$\exists \overline{f} \, \forall \overline{x}(A(\overline{x}) \Rightarrow !\overline{f}(\overline{x}) \ \& \ B(\overline{x}, \overline{f}(\overline{x}))$$

where the access function is written explicitly. We shall see, however, in the Section 8 some deficiencies of explicit functions in comparison with implicit ones. These deficiencies are unimportant only if function evaluation costs almost nothing, that is, if it is precalculated and its table is arranged as an array. Naturally, it is possible only if $A(\overline{x}) \equiv \overline{x} \in A_1$ where A_1 is finite.

The examples given make feasible the following hypothesis. Each reasonable logic rule has a simple and natural programmistic interpretation, and vice versa, every general programming technique can be deduced from a constructive logic rule. The search of such analogies, however, may require an unsusal viewpoint.

7. ON THE DECIDABILITY OF CONSTRUCTIVE THEORIES

The derivation search problem for constructive theories is quite for from to be explored. As the next section will show, variations on the theme of the resolution method are absolutely fruitless. Before to seek for a derivation, it is necessary to get a clear understanding what to seek, why to seek, and where to seek. It means that the derivation search problem is tightly connected with the search for a good formalization methodology. We shall present in this section some formula classification which allows to specify theories in a "standardized" form and to find decidable subclasses. Note, that the classification, though based on semantic considerations, is purely syntactical.

Let $\mathcal{A}, \mathcal{B}, \mathcal{L}$ be conjunctions of elementary formulas. $\mathcal{A}(\bar{\bar{x}})$ denotes that every predicate in $\mathcal{A}$ contains all variables from the vector $\bar{x}$ and $\mathcal{A}(\tilde{x})$ denotes that every predicate in $\mathcal{A}$ contains at least one variable from $\bar{\bar{x}}$.

Let us consider the following classes of formulas.

1. Facts, or elementary closed formulas and their negations.
2. Connections, or $\forall \bar{x}(\mathcal{A}(\bar{x}) \Rightarrow \mathcal{B}(\bar{\bar{x}}))$.
3. Classifications, or $\forall \bar{x}(\mathcal{A}(\bar{x}) \Rightarrow \mathcal{B}_1(\bar{\bar{x}}) \vee \ldots \vee \mathcal{B}_k(\bar{\bar{x}}))$, where $\mathcal{B}_1, \ldots, \mathcal{B}_k$ are computable, except no more then one.
4. Refutations, or $\forall \bar{x} \neg \mathcal{A}(\bar{\bar{x}})$.
5. Constructions, or $\forall \bar{x}(\mathcal{A}(\bar{x}) \Rightarrow \exists \bar{y} \mathcal{B}(\bar{x}, \tilde{y}))$.
5a. Composite constructions, or $\forall \bar{x}(\mathcal{A}(\bar{x}) \& \vartheta \Rightarrow \exists \bar{y} \mathcal{B}(\bar{x}, \bar{y}))$, where ϑ is a conjunction of composite constructions (may be empty).
6. First kind criteria, or $\forall \bar{x}\bar{y}(\mathcal{A}(\bar{x}, \bar{y}) \Rightarrow \mathcal{B}(\bar{\bar{x}}))$.
7. Second kind criteria, or $\forall \bar{x}(\forall \bar{y} \mathcal{A}(\bar{x}, \bar{y}) \Rightarrow \mathcal{B}(\bar{\bar{x}}))$.
8. Third kind criteria, or $\forall \bar{x}((\mathcal{A}(\bar{x}) \Rightarrow \mathcal{B}(\bar{x})) \Rightarrow \mathcal{L}(\bar{\bar{x}}))$.

A theory is <u>standardized</u> if each of its axioms belongs to one of these nine classes. We shall mention several statements (proofs are omitted).

LEMMA 1. If a derivation consists of standardized formulas only then the program extracted from it satisfies the following conditions:
- connections are completely ignored;
- negated facts and refutations exclude some alternatives in conditional statements;
- constructions generate terms and constant declarations;
- classifications generate conditional statements;

- criteria generate ghosts, that is, non-acting constructs which do not penetrate into the program.

LEMMA 2. For each constructive theory T, there exists its standardized conservative extension T' such that:
- T' contains no composite constructions;
- there exists a correspondence C:d ↔ d' between derivations in T and T' such that, for every derivation d in T of the length $\Delta(d)$, $\Delta(d')/\Delta(d) \leqslant 3$.

Comment. The correspondence C, however, does not preserve extracted programs. Preservation can be provided only with an additional, rather natural, condition on T: all constructive axioms are seminormal, that is, they have the form $\forall \overline{x}(\mathcal{OL}(\overline{x}) \Rightarrow \exists \overline{y} \mathscr{b}(\overline{x},\overline{y}))$ where $\mathscr{b}$ is normal [9]. Informally, this means that all basic functions yield structures of basic type elements as their values.

LEMMA 3. If all axioms of T are normal or seminormal, then there exist a standardized conservative extension T' of T and a correspondence C:d ↔ d' between derivations in T and T' such that
- $\Delta(d')/\Delta(d) \leqslant 3$;
- p(d')=p(d) where p(d) is the program extracted from d.

Note, that we do not compare the sets of provable formulas of two different theories; rather, we compare restrictions of the sets corresponding to derivations of bounded complexity. Equivalence in principle has no value for us: a simple transformation is what we need (see Kreisel's comments [4]).

A construction is noncontractable if any predicate in $\mathscr{b}$ has no less different variables than in the prefix $\forall \overline{x}$. A composite construction is noncontractable if all construction premises of constructions from ϑ are noncontractable and if any predicate in $\mathscr{b}$ has no less different variables than in the prefix $\forall \overline{x}$ plus number of results of all constructions from ϑ.

THEOREM. If T is a finite standardized theory without first kind criteria and such that all its constructions (including composite ones) are noncontractable then the deducibility problem for constructions in T is decidable.

COROLLARY. The deducibility problem for composite constructions with noncontractable construction premises is decidable.

Theories that do not contain criteria appear naturally in formalization of application program packages and are the first candidates to have a derivation search algorithm.

8. WHAT IS NOT TO BE DONE

This section is devoted to discussion. However, we shall try to argue by exact theorems, even where previous discussions appealed to common sense, phylosophical considerations, or occasional experiments.

We shall discuss, as promised, the resolution method from the viewpoint of its appropriatness to program synthesis. We shall point out five serious obstacles on the way of its nontrivial application in this field.

The first obstacle. Noncomputable Skolem functions.

It is well known that an application of the resolution method is preceded by a formula preprocessing: quantifiers are removed and "replaced" by Skolem function (skolemization) and the formula is transformed into a conjunction of disjuncts. This preprocessing alone can completely destroy computability of the result.

Example 8. Let a formula $\forall x(\exists y B(x,y) \Rightarrow \exists z A(x,z))$ be given. Its prenex form in $\forall x \exists z \forall y(B(x,y) \Rightarrow A(x,z))$. Skolemizing its negation and splitting it into disjuncts we obtain: $B(c,f(z))$, $\neg A(c,z)$. Synthesizing the program by the resolution method, we must trace a unifying substitution for z when deriving the empty disjunct. We can, however, encounter f in this substitution while f is neither given nor known how to compute.

In this particular case the obstacle is overcome by applying another order of quantifiers in the prefix: $\forall x \forall y \exists z(B(x,y) \Rightarrow A(x,z))$ but it will be helpless in the next example.

Example 9. Let a formula $\forall x \exists y \forall z A(x,y,z)$ be given. After preprocessing, it has the form $\neg A(c,y,f(y))$. Here, f is inherently noncomputable, unavoidable but it can appear in the solution.

In order to overcome this obstacle one has to restrict the class of unifying substitutions for the results of the constructed procedure and to codify strictly the order of quantifiers during the skolemization.

The second obstacle. Nonadequacy of computable Skolem functions.
Example 10. For the formula
$$\forall x(\forall y \exists z A(x,y,z) \,\&\, \forall y' \exists z' B(x,y',z') \Rightarrow \exists u C(x,u))$$
we have three essentially different variants of its prenex form:
$$\forall x \exists y \forall z \exists y' \forall z' \exists u(A(x,y,z) \,\&\, B(x,y',z') \Rightarrow C(x,u))$$
and two others with the prefixes $\forall x \exists y,y' \forall z z' \exists u$ and $\forall x \exists y' \forall z' \exists y \forall z \exists u$. After preprocessing we obtain either $A(c,y,f(y)),B(c,y',g(y,y'))$,

¬C(c,u) or A'c,y,f(y,y')),B(c,y',g(y,y')), ¬C(c,u), or A(c,y,f(y,y')),
B(c,y',g(y)), ¬C(c,u). At least one of the Skolem functions contains
an unnecessary argument.

Example 11. The meaning of the formula

$$\forall x((\forall y \exists z A(x,y,z) \Rightarrow \exists u B(x,u)) \Rightarrow \exists v C(x,v)$$

is such that v must be constructed as a result of a procedure whose
parameter is a procedure that constructs u whose parameter, in turn,
is a procedure that compute z by y for a given x. Concequently, the
correct constructive skolemization must be

$$\exists \Psi \forall x, \varphi (\forall f(\forall y A(x,y,f(y)) \Rightarrow B(x, \varphi(f)(x))) \Rightarrow C(x, \Psi(x, \varphi))).$$

The classical prenex form has the prefix $\forall x,y \exists z \forall u \exists v$, and preprocessing results in disjuncts $\neg C(c_1,v), \neg A(c_1,c_2,z) \lor B(c_1,f(z))$. On
the other hand, it has been shown that f must be applied not to z
directly but to a procedure that yields z (perhaps, for various
values of y).

This obstacle is hard to overcome. However, the following
theorem shows that it is possible, at least in principle.

THEOREM (on constructive skolemization).

a) There exists a natural (that is, recursively defined by the
formula structure) algorithm $\mathscr{P}$ that transforms any formula A to
the form $\exists \alpha_A \exists \beta_A \forall \gamma_A SA(\alpha_A, \beta_A, \gamma_A)$ where SA is a quantifier-free
formula in the language described in [28] and $\alpha_A, \beta_A, \gamma_A$ are variable
functions (possibly, of a higher type);

b) The formula A is intuitionistically derivable in a theory T
iff there exist:

- axioms $B_1,\ldots,B_n \in T$;
- terms $t_i^1,\ldots,t_i^{k_i}$ fitting the type of γ_B ;
- a term r fitting the type of α_A and depending on x_i^j only;
- a term s fitting the type of β_A and not depending on c

such that SA(r,s,c) is derivable from $SB_1(x_1,y_1,t_1^1),\ldots,SB_1(x_1,y_1,t_1^{k_1});\ldots$
$\ldots;SB_n(x_n,y_n,t_n^1),\ldots,SB_n(x_n,y_n,t_n^{k_n})$ in the classical propositional
calculus with term conversion rules.

This theorem has been published in [27]. In order to grasp its
meaning it is sufficient to know that the term calculus from [28]
is similar to the typed λ-conversion calculus including direct sum
and product types and conditional terms.

Example 12. The constructive skolemization of the formula from
Example 11 yields

$$\exists\,\Psi\,\exists\,v_5 v_1 v_4 \forall x, \varphi, v_2, v_3$$
$$((A'(x, v_3(v_5(x,\varphi)), v_5(x,\varphi)(v_3(v_5(x,\varphi))), v_1(x_1,\varphi)(v_3(v_5(x,\varphi)))) \Rightarrow$$
$$B'(x, \varphi(v_5(x,\varphi))(x), v_2(v_5(x,\varphi))(v_1(x,\varphi)))) \Rightarrow$$
$$C'(x, \Psi(x,\varphi), v_4(x,\varphi)(v_2,v_3))).$$

Here, all new variables introduced in predicates are of the type <u>ghost</u> not present in the source language.

Thus, the price of the wish to work in the constructive environment by conventional methods can be very high: we must manipulate with arbitrary λ-terms.

<u>The third obstacle</u>. Partial functions.

Sometimes, Skolem functions are realized by procedures defined only for some argument values. The check of a function for applicability can be no easier than the application itself (for example, singularity check of linear equations). In such cases a disjunct $\neg A(x) \vee B(x,f(x))$ can appear where $f(x)$ is applicable (or $!f(x)$) only if $A(x)$.

<u>Example 13</u>. Let us consider a derivation ($E(z)$ is the goal, z is the variable in question):

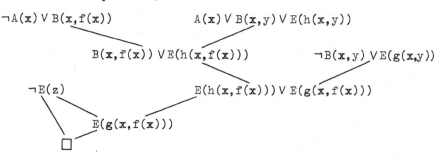

The synthesized program is <u>if</u> $B(x,f(x))$ <u>then</u> $g(x,f(x))$ <u>else</u> $h(x,f(x))$ <u>fi</u>. The condition check is, however, impossible because $f(x)$ may be undefined.

<u>The fourth obstacle</u>. Theoretical predicates.

<u>Example 14</u>. Let Q be a theoretical predicate and z be a variable in question. Let us consider a derivation

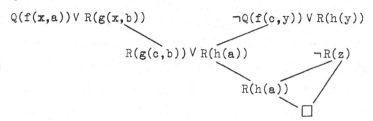

The synthesized program for z is <u>if</u> $Q(f(c,a))$ <u>then</u> $h(a)$
<u>else</u> $g(c,b)$ <u>fi</u> but Q cannot be evaluated.

Both last obtacles are not so fundamental as the previous two
ones but they cause much more troubles on the derivation search
phase. They require all unifying substitutions to be carefully
checked.

The fifth obstacle. Non-structured proof.

The resolution method induces no inherent structure into a
derivation. It makes the program both, "flat" (no auxiliary procedures) and non-structured.

Example 15. Let a derivation be given

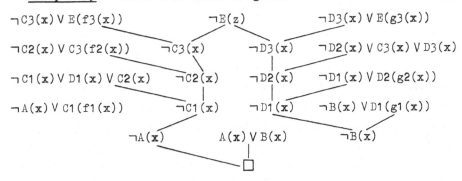

The program is extracted in the following form:

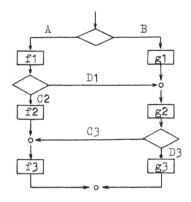

We can overcome this obstacle by an appropriate tactics of the
derivation search.

Having closed with more or less expences these gaps we may
obtain a typical program synthesis procedure by the resolution
method. Many examples can be demonstrated but, frankly speaking,

most of them are so depressing that we shall give no references. Naturally, besides restrictions explicitely imposed by the programmer, it will contain many restrictions which he is absolutely unaware about (it usually happens when an approbated but not very suitable method is applied). Moreover, one more problem still remains. Preprocessing in the resolution method transforms all functions used in the theory and in the proved assertion in an explicit form. In functional systems, however, implicit forms are preferable. We compare these two representations from the viewpoint of their influence on the length and quality of the extracted program.

Using a constructive deciphering algorithm similar to Kleene's approach (see, e.g., [11]) we may reduce any formula A to the form $\exists \alpha_A KA(\alpha_A)$ where KA is a normal formula. The corresponding α_A, without any modification, appears in the algorithm $\mathcal{P}$ by the constructive skolemization theorem. Let us now replace all axioms $B \in T$ by $KB(\xi_B)$ where ξ_B are constants of the same type as α_B are. The corresponding theory will be denoted by KT.

THEOREM (on the explicit form). The proof of the formula $\exists \alpha_A KA(\alpha_A)$ in the theory KT is rearrangable, with loosing neither length no complexity, into a proof of the formula A in the theory T. The program extracted from the second proof is the program extracted from the first proof and optimized by the precalculation of common terms.

So the implicit form turns out to be better.

Similarly, it can be shown that, logically, it is easier to synthesize a maximally parallel program than a sequential one. It means, that the desequention problem discredits itself being laid out at the Procrustean bed of the strictly sequential language.

Finally, few words about the fashionable now verification problem. If A expresses the program synthesis problem then KA(t) expresses the problem of verification of the program t.

Thus, the explisit form theorem implies, in particular, that the verification problem is <u>no easier</u> then the synthesis problem and, moreover, the only way to achieve a <u>complete</u> verification is to synthesize it anew! Now we may say openly that the complete verification problem is meaningless. However, the partial verification problem naturally arises in the cycle of program synthesis as mentioned in Section 2.

9. CONCLUSION

This paper is the first attempt to expose the logical approach as a unifying concept of the programming theory. It is well seen now that potential benefits are great but a radical reconstruction of the way of mathematical and programmistic thinking is required. In principle, programming has to be merged with mathematics. The author sees this merging accomplished on the basis of the reborn and reconstructed constructive approach that could be called empirical constructivism.

The author is grateful for the support and valuable discussions to many scholars, and especially, A.P.Ershov, V.A.Nepomnyashchy, G.S.Tseitin, and E.Engeler.

REFERENCES

I. Цейтин Г.С. Нематематическое мышление в программировании. "Перспективы системного и теоретического программирования", Новосибирск, 1979, стр. I28-I32.

2. Ershov A.P. On the essense of compilation. Formal description of programming concepts. Amsterdam, North-Holland, 1977, p.391-420.

3. Марков А.А. О конструктивной математике. Тр. МИАН СССР, вып.67, 1962, стр. 8-I4.

4. Kreisel G. Some uses of proof theory for finding computer programs. Colloq. Intern. Log., Clermont-Ferrant, 1975, p. 151.

5. Dahl O.-J., Dijkstra E.W., Hoare C.A.P. Structured programming. London & New York, Academic Press, 1972.

6. Попов Э.В., Фирдман Г.Р. Алгоритмические основы интеллектуальных роботов и искусственного интеллекта. "Наука", М., 1976.

7. Kleene S.K. Introduction to metamathematics. New York, Van Nostrand, 1952.

8. Непейвода Н.Н. Соотношение между правилами естественного вывода и операторами алгоритмических языков высокого уровня. ДАН СССР, т. 239, 1978, № 3, стр. 526-529.

9. Непейвода Н.Н. О построении правильных программ. "Вопросы кибернетики", вып. 46, 1978, стр. 88-I22.

IO. Непейвода Н.Н. Об одном методе построения правильной программы из правильных подпрограмм. "Программирование", 1979, № I, стр. II-2I.

II. Непейвода Н.Н. Применение теории доказательств к задаче построения правильных программ. "Кибернетика", 1979, № 2, стр. 43-48.

I2. Manna Z., Waldinger R. The logic of computer programming.
IEEE Trans. on Software Engineering, vol. SE-4, no.5 (1978).

I3. Manna Z., Waldinger R. The synthesis of structure-changing
programs. Proc. of the 3-d Intern. Conf. on Software Engineering,
May 1978.

I4. Manna Z., Waldinger R. A deductive approach to program synthesis.
Proc. 6-th Intern. Conf. on AI, Tokyo, 1979, p. 542.

I5. Rasiowa H., Sikorski R. The mathematics of metamathematics.
Warszawa: PWH, 1963.

I6. Тыугу Э.Х. Система программирования с автоматическим синтезом
алгоритмов. "Тр. Всес. симп. по методам реализации новых алгоритмических языков", вып. 2, Новосибирск, 1975, стр. 94-I08.

I7. Darlington J. A synthesis of several sorting algorithms.
Acta Informatica, 1979, vol.12, no.1, p.1.

I8. Ершов А.П. Смешанные вычисления: потенциальные применения и
проблемы исследования. "Методы математической логики в проблемах искусственного интеллекта и систематическое программирование", ч.2, Вильнюс, 1980, стр. 26-55

I9. Burstall R.M., Darlington J. A transformation system for developing recursive programs. J. of ACM, vol.24, no.1 (1977), p.44.

20. Barzdyn J.M. On inductive synthesis of programs (this volume).

2I. Непейвода Н.Н. Конструктивные логики ограниченных построений.
"Релевантные логики и теория следования", М., 1979, стр.76-80.

22. Бельтюков А.П. Формальная теория для порождения правильных
программ заданной вычислительной сложности. "Методы математической логики в проблемах искусственного интеллекта и систематическое программирование", ч.I, Вильнюс, 1980, стр. 64-66.

23. Непейвода Н.Н. Логическое программирование. М., Научн. совет
по кибернетике АН СССР, I980, I6 с.

24. Гололобов В.И., Чеблаков Б.Г., Чинин Г.Д. Описание языка ЯРМО.
Препринт 247, ВЦ СО АН СССР, Новосибирск, 1980.

25. Марков А.А. Об одном принципе конструктивной математической
логики. "Тр. 3-го Всес. математ. съезда", т.2. АН СССР, I956,
стр. I46-I47.

26. Heiting A. Intuitionism. Amsterdam, North-Holland, 1972
(3rd ed.).

27. Nepeivoda N.N. The connections between the proof theory and
computer programming. 6th Intern. Congr. of Logic, Methodology
and Philosophy of Science, Hannover, 1979, vol.1, p. 7-11.

28. Nepeivoda N.N. A proof theoretical comparizon of program synthesis and program verification. 6th Intern. Congr. of Logic,
Methodology and Philosophy of Science, Hannover, 1979, vol.1,
p. 47-51.

29. Bauer F.L. et al. Report on a mide spectrum language for prog-
    ram specification and development. TUM-I 8104. München, TUM
    Institut für Informtik, May 1981, 236 p.

30. Tseytin G.S. From logicism to proceduralism (this volume).

31. Knuth D.E. Algorithms in modern mathematics and computer
    science (this volume).

THE STRUCTURAL SYNTHESIS OF PROGRAMS

E.H. Tyugu

Institute of Cybernetics

10 Lenin Ave, Tallinn 200104, U.S.S.R.

A method for proving the existence of a solution of a problem is represented for a class of computational problems. The derivation of programs from the existence proofs is described, which enables to synthesize large programs practically. The search at the proving of the existence theorems is reduced to the practically acceptable level in the following ways:
1) a special theory is built for every problem by substituting constants for free variables in axioms; 2) only structural properties of computations are proved and the correctness of primitive functions is assumed to be guaranteed in some other way.

1. Introduction

At least four different approaches exist to the synthesis of programs:
1) stepwise refinement of programs;
2) synthesis from given examples of input-output pairs or example computations;
3) synthesis from data descriptions;
4) synthesis by proving a theorem which states that the asked output exists.

The last of the four approaches is considered here and a technique is described for practical synthesis of programs from the descriptions of problems, given in some nonprocedural specification language - problem oriented language (POL).

We shall consider the synthesis of programs for solving problems which can be presented as follows: "for given x which satisfies $P(x)$ compute such y which satisfies $R(x,y)$". Here x and y are finite sets of variables, called input and output variables of the program.
$Q = (P(x), R(x,y))$ represents problem conditions which must contain enough information for synthesizing the proper program. The form of the problem conditions can vary, and it depends on the synthesis technique.

To any solvable problem (x,y,Q) corresponds an existence theorem "for any x which satisfies input conditions P(x) exists y, satisfying output conditions R(x,y)" which states the existence of a solution of the problem.

The way from a problem to a program which solves it can be represented by the following schema: problem → theorem → proof → program. There are three general steps:
1) obtaining a formal description of the problem in the form of the existence theorem;
2) proving the theorem;
3) deriving a program from the proof.

When these steps are performed automatically, then the user can be sure that he has got a program which correctly satisfies its specifications. But the correctness of the specifications is up to him, and instead of debugging a program he has to debug a problem description. It is easier to do, because it can be done at the conceptual level where no details of an implementation are involved.

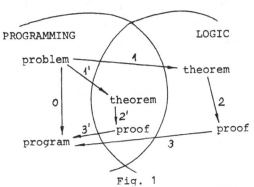

Fig. 1
Ways from a problem to a program

The general situation in program synthesis by theorem proving is illustrated in Fig. 1. This field belongs partially to programming and partially to logic. The know-how of programming which has been obtained during several decades, makes the way (O) from a problem to a program considerably shorter than it was in early days of automatic computing. Going from the problem to the program through theorem proving makes the way longer again. The step (1) from a problem to an existence theorem leads from programming to logic. The process of theorem proving (2) belongs to logic, and the derivation of the program

(3) brings us back to programming. The way can be shortened again
using special theories for representing existence theorems and proving
these theorems. The aim is 1) to shift theorems and proofs from logic
logic closer to programming; 2) to simplify the most complicated step-
-proving the existence theorems. Thereby the difference between a problem description and an existence theorem may even increase and the
first step (1') in Fig. 1 may become longer. Well developed translation
techniques allow to get existence theorems from problem descriptions
without any difficulty and to make a long step (1') in proper direction.

The following two general ideas lay behind the structural synthesis
of programs:
1) A special theory is built for every particular problem. The theory
is needed for proving only one existence theorem, so it can be taylor-
ed to facilitate the proof and to fit the problem. In particular constants are substituted for variables in the axioms when the particular
theory is being built.
2) Only structural properties of computations are used almost every-
where in the proof. The correctness of primitive steps of computations
is not proved at all. It is assumed that if something can be computed,
then it is computed correctly.

This can be justified by the consideration that to describe the correctness conditions for primitive steps of computations is not more
reliable than to describe the steps of computations themselves. Actually a "primitive step" of computations can be described by a program
of any lenth as soon as the correctness of the program has been determined.

2. Computational model of a problem

We are going now to consider a universe which will contain all the objects needed for solving a problem as well as functional relations
between these objects. Having the model we shall try to build a program
which contains functions only from this model and operates only on
the objects from the model. A computational model of a problem is a
pair of sets: a set X of all objects, which may be built during the
computations, and a set F of functional relations between the objects, which are used in one or another solving process. Elements of

X correspond to different states of variables of the program, which must be built. For instance, if there is a loop in the program, then a sequence of objects appears in X , and it may be infinite. Only if every variable in a program is evaluated at most once, then for one run of the program there exists one to one correspondence between the variables of the program and objects of X . If, in addition to this, the program does not contain conditional branching and recursion, then the computational model of the problem itself can be obviously considered as a program in which computations are completely controlled by information flow.

Usually it is much easier to derive a program from a computational model of a problem than to prove an existence theorem in some intuitionistic theory.

From the other side, the computational model can be in many cases derived directly from a problem description in POL. The semantics of POL statements may be represented by semantic models, which are building blocks for computational models. This approach was already described in /1/ and has been used in compiler for UTOPIST language which is an extendible language for generating POL-s as its extensions. In addition to the computational model some control information is needed, at least the lists of the objects, which are given, and of those, which must be calculated, i.e. input x and output y of the problem.

The notion of computational model can be defined otherwise as a set of axioms of a special form, which contain constant symbols for the objects of X, and functional symbols for the relations of F.

Axioms of a theory, describing a class of problems, may contain variables. These variables are eliminated, when a particular problem description is considered. This is actually the way, how a POL sentence is translated into a set of axioms i.e. a part of the computational model of a problem.

3. Computability statements

Let us denote $a \underset{f}{\vdash} b$ a statement, that b is computable from a, a and b being objects or finite sets of objects. More precisely, for any given values of objects from a, the values of objects from b can be computed using functions of the tuple $f = \langle f_1, \ldots, f_n \rangle$ so, that $b_i = f_i(a)$ for any element of b. In particular, if x, y are variables, then $x \vdash_{\overline{f}} b \rightleftharpoons (\forall x \ \exists y \ (y = f(x)$ and f is a realizable function). We shall call expressions $a \vdash_{\overline{f}} b$ <u>computability relations</u>.

Computability of objects may depend on some consditions expressed by a formula Γ . <u>Computability statement</u> is any expression $\Gamma \Rightarrow a \vdash_{\overline{f}} b$, where is a formula in some theory. Γ expresses <u>computability conditions</u>.

Computability statements are useful in the following ways:
1) Any computational model can be represented more formally as a set of computability relations (i.e. a set of computability statements, where computability conditions are identically true).
2) The existence theorem can be expressed by the formula
$$\exists f (x \vdash_{\overline{f}} y)$$
3) Any set of computability statements can be regarded as a set of axioms of some theory, in which a proof of the existence theorem can be searched. Depending on the complexity of computability conditions of the axioms different search strategies can be used for constructing the proofs.

The existence theorem is a formula of a theory of higher order. But using the inference rule

$$O^o \qquad \frac{x \vdash_{\overline{f_o}} y}{\exists f (x \vdash_{\overline{f}} y)}$$

the proof of the theorem can be obtained as soon as $x \_f y$ is proved for particular f_o. So we shall consider the derivation of $x \vdash_{\overline{f_o}} y$ from the set of axioms given in the form of computability statements.

4. Structural synthesis technique

4.1. Synthesis of programs, determined by information flow

Computability relations can be regarded as computability statements of the form <u>true</u> $\Rightarrow x \vdash_{\overline{f}} y$. They enable to represent any information flow for a finite set of objects. As soon as no object must be computed more than once, such an ordering can be found on any set of computability relations for any set of given objects, which guarantees that computations are possible when functions are applied in this order. The idea is that, if we have a $_{f_1}$ b and a $_{f_2}$ c then serial application of f_1 and f_2 yields c from a, i.e. a new computability relation a $_{f_1;f_2}$ c can be derived.

Let x,y,... be finite sets of objects (constants or variables). Then computability is expressed by the following three inference rules

1°

$$\frac{y \stackrel{\subseteq}{} x}{x \xmapsto{\quad s_{xy} \quad} y}$$

where s_{xy} denotes a selector function, selecting values of elements of x from the given values of the elements of y

2°

$$\frac{x \xmapsto{\ f_1\ } y, \quad x \xmapsto{\ f_2\ } z, \quad w = y \cup z}{x \xmapsto{\ (f_1,f_2)\ } w}$$

where (f_1,f_2) denotes parallel application of the functions f_1 and f_2.

3°

$$\frac{x \xmapsto{\ f_1\ } y, \quad y \xmapsto{\ f_2\ } z}{x \xmapsto{\ (f_1;f_2)\ } z}$$

where $(f_1;f_2)$ denotes sequential application of the functions f_1 and f_2.

If a formula x $_f$ y can be derived in a theory with the set Q of axioms in the form of computability relations, and with the inference rules 1°, 2°, 3° then the problem (x,y,Q) is solvable and the program for solving it is the description of the function f built by means of the same rules 1°, 2°, 3°.

Assuming that the computed values of objects do not depend on the order in which the computability relations are used in the proof of f(x $_f$ y), the second inference rule can be changed:

$2'$

$$\frac{x \xmapsto{\ f_1\ } y, \quad x \xmapsto{\ f_2\ } z, \quad w = y \cup z}{x \xmapsto{\ (f_1;f_2)\ } w}$$

This certainly implies an arbitrary restriction on the results of program synthesis but enables us to perform all computations sequentially.

In fact this restriction can be motivated by the assumption mentioned earlier, that if something can be computed, it is computed correctly. Further on we shall consider only sequential programs. Some results on parallel synthesis of programs are presented in /3/.

The algorithm for proving the solvability of problems (and for deriving a program for a solvable problem) is actually an algorithm for finding a transitive closure on a graph. Objects and functions from Q are the vertices of the graph. This algorithm makes less than $k \cdot n$ steps for deriving a program, which contains k functions, when the number of computability relations in Q is n.

Derivation of programs using information flow analysis has been known long ago. Programmers in different application areas discover it again, because it is really a simple way for composing a number of preprogrammed subroutines in a sequential program.

4.2. Handling sequences of objects

Let $x_1, x_2, \ldots$ be a sequence of objects where computation relations $x_i \xrightarrow{f} x_{i+1}$ are given for any $i = 1, 2, \ldots$ and $u \xrightarrow{f} x_1$ is given for the first element of the sequence. Applying the inference rule 3° n times gives, that the n-th element of the sequence can be computed by $f_0; \underbrace{f; \ldots; f}_{n-1 \text{ times}}$. This can be done by a program with a loop $f_0; \underline{\text{for}}\ i\ \underline{\text{to}}$ $n-1\ \underline{\text{do}}\ \varphi\ \underline{\text{od}}$ where φ_0, φ are operators, computing functions f_0 and f.

The problems is a little different, if the result of computation must be the element x_i for which $P(x_i)$ and $P(x_j)$ if $j < i$. Then the program will be

$$f_0; \underline{\text{while}}\ P(x)\ \underline{\text{do}}\ \varphi\ \underline{\text{od}},$$

where x is the variable, to which the computed value of x_i is assigned at every step.

The synthesis of loops for handling of sequences was described already in 1958 /4/. More general results were presented in /5/. There a set of objects $x_{s,j}$, $s = 1, 2, \ldots, n$, $j = 1, 2, \ldots$, is considered. It is assumed that for some given $m_1^0, \ldots, m_n^0$, $m_1, \ldots, m_n$ the objects $x_{s,i}$, $i < m_s^0$ have given values. The values of x_{s,m_s} are asked. Computational relations are

$$\{x_1, \; i - \Delta(s,1), \ldots, x_n, \; i - \Delta(s,n)\} \vdash_{f_s} x_{s,i}$$

where $\Delta(s,j)$ are nonnegative integers, $\Delta(s,j) \leq m_j^o$. It was shown that for a solvable problem there exists a sequence of functions f_s, which computes one new element $x_{s,i}$ for every sequence $x_{s,1}, x_{s,2} \cdots$ The program φ for this sequence of functions can be taken as the body of a loop, which solves the problem.

4.3. Synthesis of branching programs

Let formulas Γ in the left parts of computability statements be computable predicates $P_1, P_2, \ldots$, and let $p_1, p_2, \ldots$ respectively be programs for computing the values of the predicates. An inference rule

$$4^o \quad \frac{P_1(w) \vee \ldots \vee P_k(w), P_1(w) \Rightarrow x \vdash_{f_1} y, \ldots, P_k(w) \Rightarrow x \vdash_{f_k} y}{x \cup w \vdash_f y}$$

enables to derive a branching program for computing y from x:

$f = \underline{if} \; p_1(w) \; \underline{then} \; f_1 \; \underline{elif} \; p_2(w) \; \underline{then} \; \ldots \; \underline{else} \; f_k \; \underline{fi}$

Applying the rule 4° together with the rules 1°, 2°, 3° gives programs, which are combined from branching and linear parts. If $p_1(w) \vee \ldots \vee p_k(w)$ must not be proved (for instance, if it can be assumed to be true on the basis of some general considerations), then a very simple search strategy can be used. First of all, unconditional computability relations are checked and used whenever it is possible, then all computability statements $p_i(w) \Rightarrow x \vdash_{f_i} y$ with evaluated w and x are checked and a conditional statement $\underline{if} \ldots \underline{fi}$ is generated. For every branch of the statement the same strategy is recursively applied.

In a more general case the formulas $P_i(w)$ may be normal formulas, as defined in /6/. Even then the form of the derived program will be the same. Though in this case the search of the proof becomes more complicated because of the subproofs of these formulas. The demonstration of the truth of the formula $p_1(w) \vee \ldots \vee p_k(w)$ may be put on a user. But in some simple cases it can be done automatically, as it is done, for instance, in translators for decision tables.

If partial programs are accepted as results of the synthesis, then there is no need at all to prove the truth of the formulas like

$P_1(w) \; v \ldots v P_k(w)$. Let us denote by $a \vdash_f \to b$ that a partial function exists for computing b from a. Then instead of rule 4° a more simple rule is applicable:

4'
$$\frac{P_1(w) => x \vdash_{f_1} \to y, \ldots, P_k(w) => x \vdash_{f_k} \to y}{x \; \cup \; w \vdash_f \to y}$$

where

$f = \underline{if} \; P_1(w) \; \underline{then} \; f_1 \; \underline{elif} \; \ldots \; \ldots \; \underline{elif} \; P_k(w)$
$\qquad \underline{then} \; f_k \; \underline{else \; failure} \; fi.$

<u>failure</u> is a procedure signalling that the function f can not be used for the particular input data, because $P_1(w) \; v \ldots v \; P_k(w)$ is not true.

4.4. Synthesis of procedures

It is practically very useful to specify as much subproblems as possible, before a solution of a problem is planned. In this case the problem is divided into smaller, and presumably simpler parts, and the existence proof can be devided as well. This can be done, when axioms are being specified. Particulary, subproblems can be specified, which must be proved to be solvable, before a computational relation can be applied. For instance, in order to calculate a value of an integral $z = h(x) = \int_a^x y \, du$ one must solve a problem "how to calculate a value of y for a given value of u?" This can be expressed by the following formula

$$\forall f \, (u \vdash_f \to y \; => \; x \vdash_{H(f)} \to z)$$

where $H(f_0)$ is realized by a numerical integration program. A proof that the solution of the subproblem exists, yields a procedure specification for f_0. The procedure is called from the program H which realizes the function h in the computability statement.

The formula here contains a quantified functional variable f, consequently, no first order theory can be used for proving in this case. Nevertheless, an efficient search strategy can be used for constructing existence proofs, if it is known, that no computability relation must be applied more than once in any proof for one and the same subproblem. Only finite search is needed than for any subproblem, analogically to the search, used for constructing a transitive closure

on a graph, described in p. 4.1. Though a search on an and-or tree of
subproblems is needed for proving the solvability of the whole problem.

Let us point out, that a body of a loop can be derived from a proof
of a subproblem. In particular, control structures for loops, corresponding to different induction schemas, can be programmed, and represented axiomatically as computability statements with subproblems.
This is how loops and recursive programs are synthesized in the programming system PRIZ /7/.

5. Application examples

5.1. Synthesis of programs for data handling

Tree-structures. Tree-structures appear, when objects are bound by
structural relations like "x is a structure of $x_1, \ldots, x_k$". Any component x_i may in its turn be a compound object. Two computability relations, describing applicability of selector and constructor functions, can be defined for any structural relation:

$$x \longmapsto \underset{\text{select}}{\longrightarrow} \{x_1, \ldots, x_k\}$$

$$\{x_1, \ldots, x_k\} \longmapsto \underset{\text{constr}}{\longrightarrow} x$$

These computability relations describe completely all computations,
which result from the data structure.

Using only inference rules 1°, 2°, 3° and the most primitive synthesis
method from p. 4, it is possible to get programs for computing values
of components of the tree structure from values of other components,
the values of which are determined on the tree structure.

Program synthesis on semantic networks. A set of computability relations can be built as a semantic network of a text which describes a
data structure as well as a number of relations expressed more explicitly, - equations, for instance. Again, the inference rules 1°, 2°, 3°
are sufficient for program synthesis. Here is an example of a text in
UTOPIST language /2/ the compiler of which uses program synthesis:

```
let triangle (a,b,C, alpha, beta, gamma; real;
              eqn alpha + beta + gamma = 180;
              eqn a/sin alpha = b/sin beta:

              ⋮

              );
```

```
    T1: triangle alpha = 60;
    T2: triangle alpha = T1. beta, a = T1.b;
```

The text represents problem conditions for problems like the following:

    compute T2.b from T1.a, T1. beta, T2.beta.

What has been said about the synthesis on semantic networks is true
also for data base schemas. A program for answering a query to a
data base can be synthesized just in the same way as it is done for
a computational problem on a semantic network. In the data base management system DABU the structural synthesis method is directly
used both for handling queries and for data manipulations /8/.

Sequential data processing. A sequential file can be presented as a
sequence of its records u_1, u_2,... or as a sequence of its states
x_o, x_1, x_2,... . Computational relations exist for getting records
from states:

$$x_i \overset{}{\underset{get}{\longmapsto}} u_i \; , \quad i = 1,2,\ldots;$$

for getting a new state from the previous state

$$x_{i-1} \overset{}{\underset{next}{\longmapsto}} x_i \; , \quad i = 1,2,\ldots;$$

as well as for getting new states from a previous state and a new
record:

$$\{x_{i-1} \, , \, u_i\} \overset{}{\underset{put}{\longmapsto}} x_i \; .$$

(The usual GET statement in programming languages is a combination
of the functions 'get' and 'next').

Now it is quite simple to present processing of sequential files as
a problem described in p. 4.3 for sequences. For instance, let us
have an input file u_{11}, u_{12}, ... and an output file u_{21}, u_{22},... ,
Obviously there must be computational relations for computing any
objects of the output file. Let them be

$$u_{1i} \xmapsto{\quad f \quad} u_{2i} \; , \; i = 1,2,\ldots ;$$

These relations together with the relations for the 'next', 'get'
and 'put' operations

$$\left.\begin{array}{l} x_{1;i-1} \xmapsto{\text{ next }} x_{i,i} \\[2mm] x_{1,i} \xmapsto{\text{ get }} u_{1i} \\[2mm] \{x_{2,i-1} \, , \, u_{2i}\} \xmapsto{\text{ put }} x_{2i} \end{array}\right\} \quad i = 1,2,\ldots$$

give us a computational model on which a loop can be synthesized as
described in p. 4.3.

The function f in computational relations for records of output
file can itself be synthesized. Particularly, if elements of the
files are tree-structured records, the results of p. 5.1 are applicable.

A teqhnique for synthesis of programs (not automatically) for sequential data processing is thoroughly discussed in /9/. This approach
actually is a basis for building report program generators, which are
quite popular software packages.

5.2. Synthesis of semantic evaluators

An interesting example of practical usage of program synthesis is its
application in a compiler for specification languages [2].This approach
can be generalized and the semantic part of a compiler can be built
from a formal description of the semantics of a language.

Let G be an attribute grammar /10/ with a set P of production
rules and a set X of attributes. A set $(x \xmapsto{\; f \;} y, \ldots, \; v \xmapsto{\; g \;} w)$ of
computability relations on occurences of attributes is attached to
every rule $p \in P$. These relations express the computability of attributes from X, and together with preprogrammed functions f,...,g,...
represent the semantics of the language described by G. Let us
assume that G represents correctly a programming language L and <u>prog</u>
is an attribute, the value of which is an executable code for a
text in L. It is shown in /11/ how to build a computational model for
a derivation tree of any text in L, so that the problem $\exists\, f(\emptyset \xmapsto{\; f \;} \underline{\text{prog}})$

will be solvable on the model. The model will contain just those computability relations which are attached to the production rules of the derivation tree. Experiments were described in /11/ where programs were synthesized automatically from derivation trees and a description of an attribute grammar written in UTOPIST language. The UTOPIST compiler which contains program synthesizer was actually used as a dynamical semantic evaluator for another language. It merits investigation if, applying a technique similar to the technique of visits for evaluating of attributes and using UTOPIST compiler, it would be possible to synthesize a complete semantic part of a compiler from a description of an attribute grammar.

References

1. E.H. Tyugu, Data base and problem solver for computer aided design, "Information Processing 71", North Holland Publ. Co., Amsterdam, 1972, pp.

2. M.A. Männisalu et al., UTOPIST language. Data processing algorithms and management, "Statistika", Moscow, 1977, pp. 80-118 (Russian).

3. T.P. Plaks, Synthesis of parallel programs on computational models, "System programming and computer software", No. 4, 1977, pp. 55-63.

4. E.Z. Ljubimskij, Automatic programming and method of programming procedures. Dr. Phil. Thesis, Institute of Mathematics of the Acad. Sc. of the USSR, Moscow, 1958 (Russian).

5. I.B. Zadyhailo, Constructing loops from parametric specifications "Journal of computational mathematics and mathematical physics", v. 3, No. 2, 1963, pp.

6. N.N. Nepeivoda, Constructing correct programs, Problems of Cybernetics, vol. 46, Acad. of Sc. of the USSR, Moscow, 1978, pp. 88-122 (Russian).

7. E.H. Tyugu, A programming system with automatic program synthesis, Lecture Notes in Computer Science, v. 47, Methods of Algor. Lang. Implementation, Springer-Verlag, Berlin, 1977, pp. 251-267.

8. A.P.Kalja, M.B. Matskin, Intelligent dialogue with data bases, Proc. Soviet-Finnish Symposium on Interactive Systems, Part Tbilisi, 1979, pp. 124-136.

9. M.A. Jackson, Principles of program design, Acad. Press, London,
   N.Y., San Francisco, 1975.
10. D. Knuth, Semantics of context-free languages, Math. Syst. Theory,
    v. 2, No. 1, 1968, pp. 127-144.
11. J. Penjam, A method for automatic realization of semantics in
    compilers, Cybernetics,   No. 2, 1980, pp. 36 - 41

ON FINDING INVARIANT RELATIONS OF PROGRAM

A.A. Letichevsky
Institute of Cybernetics
Ukrainian Academy of Sciences
252207 Kiev 207, USSR

The algorithm as a mathematical object is a discrete dynamical system
that generates processes of computations. In simple dynamical models
of sequential computations this system consists of two components:
the control component and the information environment. The modern
technology of designing the algorithms is reduced to the solution
of a set of problems concerned with mathematical models of the system
that has to realize these algorithms [1]. These problems may be
often formulated as mathematical problems and mathematical methods
of their solution can be developed.

The sequential conversion of a formal mathematical specification
of a problem or a method into a program, the proving of correctness
and other properties, formal transformations, optimization of programs are examples of such problems.

In this paper the problem of finding the invariant relations of a
program is considered. Generally this problem may be formulated as
follows. What can we say about the state of information environment
in the instant when the control component is in the given state?
It is well known that this question is the main question when we
try to prove the correctness of the program using, for instance,
the Floyd method. In [2] it has been shown that many optimizing
procedures are reduced to the problem of finding invariants.

The answer to the problem under consideration depends on a language
that is used to express properties of the information environment.
If this language is a language of the first order predicate calculus
then we can easily describe all invariants using methods of algorithmic logic. But it is very difficult to do with this description
because it may, for instance, use the Gedel numbering of all passes
in the program. So it is natural to consider the problem for simple
restricted languages. Important examples of such languages are the

language of equalities and the language of atomary conditions. These languages are considered here. Some special cases were considered previously in [3] .

Definitions. As a standard model of program we use here the notion of interpreted $V - Y$ scheme of program or V -Y -program. Let D be the data domain on which the operations denoted by symbols of the signature Ω and the predicates denoted by means of the signature Π are defined. So D is a universal Ω-algebra and Ω-Π- algebraic system. Consider the set R of variables and the set $B= D^R$ of memory states. The propositional function of atomary conditions $\pi(t_1,..,t_n)$, where $\pi \in \Pi, t_1,..,t_n$ are terms constructed of variables by means of operations from Ω , is called the elementary condition. The assignment is an expression of the type $(r_1:=t_1,..., r_n:=t_n)$, where $r_1,..,r_n \in R, t_1,..,t_n$ are Ω -terms over R . On a given memory state the terms assume values in D and elementary conditions in $\{0,1\}$. Each assignment $y= (r_1:=t_1,...,r_n:=t_n)$ defines transformation of the set B . If $b \in B$, then $y(b)$ is a memory state after the simultaneous assigning of values $t_1,...,t_n$ computed on b to all of the variables $r_1,...,r_n$. In other words the state $b'= y(b)$ is defined by the following relations: $b'(r_i)= =b(t_i)$, $b'(s) = b(s)$ if $s \in R$ and $s \neq r_i$, i=1,...,n.

Let V be some set of elementary conditions and Y the set of assignments. V-Y -program A is a set of states with the set of transitions. Each transition is 4-touple (a,u,y,a') where $a,a' \in A$ are states of the program, $u \in V$, $y \in Y$. The set A_0 of initial states and the set A of terminal states are picked out in A . If (a,u,y,a') is a transition of A , then we write $a \xrightarrow[A]{u/y} a$ or $a \xrightarrow{u/y} a'$, if A is fixed. The process of computations of V-Y -program A with the given initial state $b \in B$ of information environment is a finite or infinite sequence of pairs$(a_0,b)(a_1,b_1)...$ such that for each pair (a_i,a_{i+1}) there is a transition $a_i \longrightarrow a_{i+1}$ and $u(b_i)=1$, $b_{i+1}=y(b)$, i=0,1,... . The process is called the initial process, if $a_0 \in A_0$ and terminal, if it is a finite initial process with the last pair (a_m,b_m) such that $a_m \in A^*$. The program is not assumed to be determinate so the next step of the process of computations generally speaking is not defined unicly. The program computes the relation $f_A \subset B^2$ that is defined as follows:$(b,b') \in f_A \Longleftrightarrow$ there exists the terminal process $p=(a_0,b)...(a^*,b')$.

Suppose that each statement of the language L used to express
the properties of information environment may be expressed by the
formula $p(r_1,..,r_n)$ of the first order predicate calculus in which
only $r_1,..,r_n \in R$ are free variables and which is interpreted on
the domain D . The signatures of functional and predicate symbols
of this calculus contain the signature Ω and Π , respectively.
Sentences of the language L will be called the conditions or L
-conditions.

The conditon $p(r_1,..,r_n)$ is called the invariant of a state $a \in A$,
if it is true every time when the program is going through this
state, that is, $p(b(r_1),..,b(r_n))=1$ for each initial process of
computations ...(a,b).... If the initial conditions $u_a(r_1,...,r_n)$
are given for each initial state $a \in A_0$, then $p(r_1,..,r_n)$ is called
the invariant (or the relative invariant for the given initial conditions), if $p(b(r_1),..,b(r_n))=1$ for any initial process $(a_0,b_0)...(a,b)...$
such that u_a $(b_0(r_1),..., b_0(r_n)) = 1$.

Language of Equalities of Data Algebra

Let $R =\{r_1,..,r_n\}$ and the sentences of L be the equalities
$g(r)=h(r)$ where $r=(r_1,..,r_n)$, $g(r)$ and $h(r)$ are Ω -terms over R .
Let $M \subset L$ be a system of equalities. Denote by $D(M)$ the set of
all n -tuples $z \in D^n$ that satisfy all the equalities of M , that
is, such z that for any equality $g(r)=h(r) \in M$ the equality
$g(z)=h(z)$ is true in the algebra D . So $D(M)$ is a set of all solutions of M considered as a system of equations in D .

Let $a_i \xrightarrow{u_i/y_i} a$, $i=1,...,k$ be all transitions that lead to the state
a of the given program A . Let $M_i \subset L$ be the set of invariants
of the state $a_i, i=1,...,k$. If $y_i=(r:=t_i(r)=(r_1:=t_{i1}(r),...,r_n:=t_{in}(r))$,
then all equalities of the set $M=M_1' \cap ... \cap M_k'$, where $g(r)=h(r) \in M_i \Leftrightarrow$
$g(t_i(z))=h(t_i(z))$ for all $z \in D(M)$ are invariants of the state $a \notin A_0$.
If $a \in A_0$, then M has to be intersected with the set of all
equalities that are consequences of the initial conditions for this
state. At that time if every transition to a is possible and at
the beginning of the transition $a_i \xrightarrow{u_i/y_i} a$ the information environment
may be in any of the states $b \in B$ such that $b(r) \in D(M_i)$, then
the condition that M_i is the set of all the invariants of a_i implies
that M is a set of all the invariants of a . Let $I(M,Y)$ denote

for the given set of equalities M and assignment $y=(r:=t(r))$ the
set M such that $g(r)=h(r) \in M' \Leftrightarrow g(t(z))=h(t(z))$ for all $z \in D(M)$.
The construction described above may be used for generating in each
state a sequence of sets $M_a^{(0)} \subset M_a^{(1)} \subset \ldots$ of equalities that are invariants
of the state a . Here $M_a^{(0)} = M_0$ is a set of all identities of the
algebra D , $M_a^{(i+1)} = N_a \cap \bigcap_{j=1}^{k} I(M_{a_j}^{(i)}, y_j)$ where $N_a = M_0$, if $a \notin A_0$ and
is a set of all equalities that are true for the initial state of
B , if $a \in A_0$. The set $M_a = \bigcup_{i=0}^{\infty} M_a^{(i)}$ is a maximal set of invariants
that may be obtained without using the information about the elemen-
tary conditions.

If all equalities from M are invariants for a , then the equalities $g(r) = h(r)$ such that $g(z)=h(z)$ for all $z \in D(M)$ are also
invariants for a . Let $C_D(M)$ denote the set of all such equalities
and be called the D -closure of M . The set M is called to be
D -closed , if it is the same as its D-closure. The subset $N \subset M$
of the D -closed set M is called the D -basis of M, if $C_D(N)=M$.

The sets $M_a^{(i)}$ are D-closed. If they should have finite D-bases,
these bases might be used for the constructive representation of the
sets M_a . Then everything is reduced to the solution of the
following two main problems.

1) The relation problem: The D -basis of the D-closed set M
being given, find the D-basis of the set $I(M,Y)$.
2) The intersection problem: The D-bases of the sets M_1 and M_2
being given, find the D-basis of the set $M_1 \cap M_2$

Being able to solve these problems we may begin to construct the
sequence M_a . For some programs and algebras this process will
stop after some number of steps and we shall obtain the complete
description of all invariant relations. In other cases we can stop
the process after obtaining sufficiently many invariants.

The constructions given below are useful for the solution of the
mentioned problems. Let $T_D(R)$ denote the set of Ω -terms, considered up to the identities of data algebra D . In other words
two terms $g(r)$ and $h(r)$ are regarded as equal, if $g(r)=h(r)$ is an
identity, that is, $g(z)=h(z)$ for any $z \in D^n$. The set $T_D(R)$ is
Ω -algebra that is free in the least variety that includes D .
We define this variety as basic. Each equality may be considered

as a pair and the set M as a binary relation defined on the set $T(R)$ of all Ω -terms over R . Let us define the operation of algebraic closure $C(M)$ of the system of relations M with respect to the basic variety. The set $C(M)$ is the least set of equalities that contains the reflexive, symmetric and transitive closure of M, all identities of the basic variety and for any m -ary operation ω the equality $\omega(g_1(r),..,g_m(r))=\omega(h_1(r),...,h_m(r))$ together with equalities $g_1(r)=h(r),...,g(r)=h(r)$. The set M is called to be (algebraically) closed, if $C(M)=M$. The subset $N \subset M$ of the closed set is called its (algebraic) basis, if $C(N)=M$. It is obvious that the D -closed set is also algebraically closed and the D -basis of closed set is its D -basis, too. The reverse statements generally speaking are not true.

The set M , being considered as a relation on $T(R)$, is algebraically closed iff it is the congruence of the absolutely free algebra $T(R)$ that contains all identities of basic variety. Therefore M also induces the congruence on $T_D(R)$. The corresponding factor-algebra will be denoted by $T_D(R)/M$, its elements by $t(\text{mod } M)$, $t \in T_D(R)$ and equalities by $t=t'(\text{mod } M)$. The homomorphism $\gamma_{y,M}: T_D(R) \to T_D(R)/C_D(M)$ is defined for each assignment $y=(r:=t(r))$ and the set M of equalities by $\gamma_{y,M}(r_i)=t_i(\text{mod } C_D(M))$.

<u>Theorem 1</u>. The set $I(M,Y)$ is a kernel of the homomorphism $\gamma_{y,M}$, that is, $g=h \in I(M,y) \Leftrightarrow \gamma_{y,M}(g)= \gamma_{y,M}(h)$. This theorem follows immidiately after definitions.

<u>Corollary 1</u>. The algebra $T_D(R)/I(M,Y)$ is isomorphic to the sub-algebra $F[t_1,...,t_n]$ of the algebra $F=T_D(R)/C_D(M)$ generated by the elements $t_1,...,t_n$.

let us consider in more detail the structure of relations that generate the set $M= I(M,Y)$ assuming that M is D-closed, that is, $M= C_D(M)$. Let $v_1,.., v_m$ be an unreduced system of generators of the algebra $F[t_1,...,t_n]$ .There may be dependencies between the elements $t_1,...,t_n$, in F so m may be less then n. Let us express t_i by $v=(v_1,...,v_m)$:

$$t_i=u_i(v) \quad (\text{mod } M), \quad i=1,...,n .$$

We have also

$$v_i=f_i(t) \quad (\text{mod } M), \quad i=1,...,m,$$

because t_i generate the algebra under consideration. All of the relations $r_i = u_i(f(r))$, $i = 1,..,n$ are included in M , because $\gamma_{y,M}(r_i) = t_i = u_i(v) = u_i(f(t)) = \gamma_{y,M}(u_i(f(r)))$ (mod M). Denote the set of these relations by M_0' . If $g(v) = h(v)$ (mod M) then $g(f(t)) = h(f(t))$ (mod M) , so $g(f(r)) = h(f(r)) \in M'$. Denote by M the set of all relations $g(f(r)) = h(f(r))$ such that $g(v) = h(v)$ (mod M) and $g(x) = h(x)$ is not the identity $(x = (x_1, \ldots, x_m))$.

Theorem 2. The set $I(M,Y)$ is generated by $M_0' \cup M_1'$. To prove it let $g(r) = h(r) \in M'$. Therefore $g(t) = h(t)$ (mod M) $g(u(f(t))) = h(u(f(t)))$ (mod M) and if the last equality is not the special case of identity, then $g(u(f(r))) = h(u(f(r))) \in M'$. So $g(r)$ may be transformed to $g(u(f(r)))$ by means of relations from M_0 and then to $h(u(f(r)))$ by means of relations from M_1 and, finally, to $h(r)$ by means of M_0.

The system $a_1,..,a_m$ of the algebra A is called to be algebraically independent, if any relation $g(a) = h(a)$ that is constructed by these elements is a consequence of the identity $g(x) = h(x)$.

Corollary 2. If the system $v_1,..,v_m$ is algebraically independent in $T_D(R)/M$, then $I(M,Y)$ is generated by the set M_0 , the algebra $T_D(R)/I(M,Y)$ is free and $f_1(r),\ldots,f_m(r)$ are its free generators.

The sequence $F_a^{(0)} = T_D(R)/M_a^{(0)}$, $F_a^{(1)} = T_D(R)/M_a^{(1)}, \ldots$ corresponds to the sequence $M_a^{(0)} \subset M_a^{(1)} \subset \ldots$ of equality sets. The mapping $\gamma_i : F_a^{(i)} \to F_a^{(i+1)}$ defined by the equality $\gamma_i(t(\text{mod } M_a^{(i)}) = t(\text{mod } M_a^{(i+1)})$ is a homomorphism of $F_a^{(i)}$ onto $F_a^{(i+1)}$, and if γ_i is an isomorphism, then $M_a^{(i)} = M_a^{(i+1)}$ that is, the construction of M_a needs only finite number of iterations.

There are some interesting classes of algebras that allow effective construction of M_a . Let us consider them.

Inheritably free algebras. The algebra that is free in some variety is called the inheritably free algebra, if each subalgebra of this algebra is free in the same variety. We consider the inheritably free algebras A that satisfy additional condition:

(α) If M_1 and M_2 are congruences such that A/M_1 and A/M_2 are free then $A/M_1 \cap M_2$ is also free.

Let algebra $T_D(R)$ be inheritably free and satisfy condition (α). Then every algebra $F^{(i)}$ is free in the basic variety. It is true because $M_a^{(i+1)} = M_1' \cap \ldots \cap M_k'$ where $M_j = I(M_a^{(i)}, \mathbf{y}_j)$, and if $F_a^{(i)}$ is free in the basic variety, then $T_D(R)/M_j$ is also free bacause the inheritance and corollary 2. But then $F_a^{(i+1)}$ is also free because of the condition (α).

The rank of algebra is a minimal number of elements in the set of generators. All $F_a^{(i+1)}$ being free, $F_a^{(i+1)}$ is isomorphic to $F_a^{(i)}$ or has the rank strongly less then the rank of $F_a^{(i)}$. Therefore the sequence $M_a^{(o)} \subset M_a^{(l)} \ldots$ becomes stable after the finite number of steps. This results is also true for any inheritably free algebras because every $M_a^{(k)}$ may be represented as finite intersections of the sets $N_j^{(k)}$ such that $A/N_j^{(k)}$ are free and $N_j^{(k)} \subset N_{j'}^{(k+1)}$. Thus to find M_a for inheritably free algebras we must be able to solve such problems:

1. Find the free basis of subalgebra $F[t_1,\ldots,t_n]$ of the free algebra $F=T_D(R)/M$, where M is generated by equalities of the type $r_i = \varphi_i(r)$, $i=1,\ldots,n$.

2. Find the basis or D-basis of the intersection $M_1 \cap M_2$ where M_1 and M_2 are D-closed and generated by equalities of the type $r_i = \varphi_i(r)$ and such that $T_D(R)/M_1$ and $T_D(R)/M_2$ are free. Absolutely free algebras, free Abelian groups and linear spaces are examples of the inheritably free algebras with condition (α). The algorithms that solve two main problems mentioned above may be derived from the well known algorithms for these kinds of algebras. Free groups do not satisfy condition (α) but there is an algorithm for solving the first problem (Nilson's method, for instance) and the sets M_a may be obtained as intersections of finitely generated subgroups of $T_D(R)$. So the following theorem may be proved.

Theorem 3. There exist the algorithms for finding M_a, if $T_D(R)$ is absolutely free, or is a free group, free Abelian group or linear space.

The mentioned kinds of algebras may be met very often in practice. Absolutely free algebras, for instance, are used in formula or data structures manipulations. String manipulations are connected with free semigroups that are not inheritably free. But every free semigroup may be immersed into the free group and the question of finding the invariants for semigroups is reduced to the same question for the groups. Let D be the set of rational numbers. If we use only addition and subtraction, then $T_D(R)$ is a free Abelian group, generated by R . The introduction of constants (every program uses only a finite number of them) increases the rank of this group. If multiplication by constants is used, then $T_D(R)$ is the linear space and theorem 3 works. But if the multiplication of any two elements of D is allowed, then $T_D(R)$ is the ring of polinomials with integer coefficients. This algebra is not inheritable but some classical results of the commutative algebra may be used. Each equality in the algebra of polinomials may be represented as $t = 0$ and therefore may be identified with the element of $T_D(R)$. Every algebraically closed set of equalities M is an ideal of the ring $T_D(R)$. Hence by the theorem of Hilbert each ideal $M_a^{(i)}$ has the finite basis and the sequence $M_a^{(o)} \subset M_a^{(1)} \ldots$ becomes stable after a finite number of steps. If D is an algebraically closed field (if not, we may extend it), then the D-closure of M is its radical and the problem of intersection may be solved by means of the D-bases. Really, the radical of intersection $M_1 \cap M_2$ is equal to the radical of the product $M_1 \cdot M_2$ and the basis of the last is a set of all products gh , where g is an element of the basis of M_1 , and h is the element of the basis of M_2 . The relation problem seems to be difficult, and the author does not know its constructive solution. It may be noticed that every set $M_a^{(i)}$ is solvable but the problem is to find out whether $M_a^{(i)} = M_a^{(i+1)}$

Atomary conditions language. The language L may be extended by adding to the equalities atomary conditions, that is, expressions of the type $\pi(t_1, \ldots, t_m)$ where $t_1, \ldots, t_m \in T(R), R = \{r_1, \ldots, r_n\}$. It may be assumed that the sign of equality belongs to $\prod$ and the equalities are also atomary conditions. Let $M \subset L$ be the set of atomary conditions. Denote by $D(M)$ the set of all $z \in D^n$ that satisfy all conditions from M . Let u be the atomary condition and $y = (r := t)$. Denote by $I(M, u, y)$ the set M', that consists of all conditions of the type $\pi(v(r))$ such that $\pi(v(t(z))) = 1$ for all $z \in D(M \cup \{u\})$.

Let us consider all transitions $a_i \xrightarrow{u_i/y_i} a$, $i = 1, \ldots k$ to the state a of a given program and let M_i be the sets of invariants of the state $a_i (i = 1, \ldots, k)$. If $y_i = (r := t_i(r))$ and $u_i = \pi(s_{i1}, \ldots, s_{imi}) = \pi(s_i)$ then the set $M = M_1' \ldots M_k'$ where $M_i' = I(M, u_i, y_i)$ is a set of invariants of noninitial state. If a is initial, then M must be intersected by the set of all atomary conditions valid on the initial state of information environment. The sequence $M_a^{(0)} \subset M_a^{(1)} \subset$ may be constructed in the same way as for the language of equalities using $I(M, \textbf{u}, \textbf{y})$ instead of $I(M, \textbf{y})$ and $M_a = \bigcup_{i=0}^{\infty} M_a^{(i)}$ is a good approximation to the set of all atomary invariant conditions of a .

The notions of D-closure and D-basis are introduced in the same way as for the equalities. Two main problems may be formulated also using atomary conditions instead of equalities. The data domain D is now considered as an algebraic system [4] . The algebra $T_D(R)$ is an algebraic system $\pi(t_1, \ldots, t_m)$ being considered valid, if it is identically true, that is, $(t_1(z), \ldots, t_m(z)) = 1$ for all $z \in D^n$. The system $T_D(R)$ is free in the basic variety which is now the least variety of algebraic systems that contains D . The notion of algebraic closure needs adding the following rule: if $\pi(t_1, \ldots, t_m) \in C(M)$ and $t_1 = t_1', \ldots, t_m = t_m' \in C(M)$, then $\pi(t_1', \ldots, t_m') \in C(M)$. If M is closed, then the set of equalities from M is a congruence of $T_D(R)$ and and the factor-system $T_D(R)/M$ may be defined.

Let $\gamma_{u,y,M}: T_D(R) \rightarrow T_D(R)/C_D(M \cup \{u\})$, and $\gamma_{u,y,M}(r_i) = t_i(\text{mod } C_D(M \cup \{u\}))$. Then the following theorem and corollary are true.

<u>Theorem 1'</u>. $I(M, \textbf{u}, \textbf{y})$ is the kernel of homomorphism $\gamma_{u,y,M}$.

<u>Corollary 1'</u>. System $T_D(R)/I(M, \textbf{u}, \textbf{y})$ is isomorphic to the subsystem $F[t_1, \ldots, t_n]$ of the system $F = T_D(R)/C_D(M \cup \{u\})$ generated by $t_1, \ldots, t_n$.
The theorem and corollary similar to the theorem and corollary 2 may be also proved for equalities of $I(M, \textbf{u}, \textbf{y})$.

It is useful sometimes to shorten the signature of predicates throwing off the predicates that may be expressed by others. Let the equivalence $\pi(g_1, \ldots, g_m) \leftrightarrow \pi'(h_1(g), \ldots, h_k(g))$ be the identity of basic variety. Then every D-clased set has the D-basis that does not contain conditions of the type $\pi(\ldots)$. Let us denote the set of all conditions of the type $\pi(\ldots)$ from $I(M, \textbf{u}, \textbf{y})$ by $I_\pi(M, \textbf{u}, \textbf{y})$ and the set of such conditions from $C_D(M)$ by $C_D^\pi(M)$. Having in mind dependencies between conditions of the main variety one can compute not the entire set $I(M, \textbf{u}, \textbf{y})$ but only $I_\pi(M, \textbf{u}, \textbf{y})$ for such π that may be used to express others. If π is unary, then computation of I^π is especially easy. Let $\gamma = \gamma_{u,y,M}$, $N^\pi = \{ g \mid \pi(g) \in C_D(M \cup \{u\}) \}$, $K = \{ g \mid \pi(g) \in I^\pi(M, u, y) \}$. Then the following statement may be proved as a corollary of theorem $1'$.

<u>Corollary $2'$</u>. $K^\pi = \gamma^{-1}(N^\pi)$.

<u>Linear inequalities</u>. This case was considered in $[3]$. The results described above give another more powerfull way for computing linear invariants. Let D be the numerical field that is considered as an algebraic system with operations of addition, subtraction, multiplication by constants and with the predicate of inequality. Then $T_D(R)$ is n-dimensional vector D-space generated by R with the inequality $t_1 \leq t_2$ that is true only when $t_1 = t_2$. Every inequality is equivalent to the unary inequality $t \leq 0$, and it is naturally to consider only inequalities of this type and equalities of the type $t = 0$.

Let M be the D-closed set of atomary conditions. Denote by $E(M)$ the set of left parts of equalities and by $E'(M)$ the set of left parts of inequalities from M . It is obvious that $E(M) \subset E'(M)$ The set $E(M)$ is a subspace of $T_D(R)$ and has a finite basis. The set $E'(M)$ is closed under addition and multiplication by non-negative scalars, so it is a linear convex cone. If $E'(M)$ has a finite algebraically generating set $h_1, \ldots, h_k$ then it is the set of all non-negative linear combinations $\sum_{i=1}^{k} \mu_i h_i$ $(\mu_i \geq 0)$ of the vectors $h_1, \ldots, h_k$. Taking off the vectors from $E(M)$ and then vectors that may be represented as non-negative linear combinations of others a non-reduced generating set for $E'(M) \setminus E(M)$ may be obtained. Adding to this set the elements $g_1, \ldots, g_m$ of the basis for $E(M)$ and vectors inverse of them the D-basis of $E(M)$ may be obtained. It may be noticed that $h_1, \ldots, h_k$ are defined uniquely up to the non-negative constant factor, and $E'(M)$ consists of all linear combinations of the type $\sum_{i=1}^{m} \lambda_i g_i + \sum_{i=1}^{k} \mu_i h_i$, where λ_i are arbitrary numbers and $\mu_i \geq 0$.

If γ is a linear transformation and M is a closed set with the finite basis, then $\gamma^{-1}(M)$ also has the finite basis. Really, the generating set for $\gamma^{-1}(M)$ may be obtained by taking one element from each set $\gamma^{-1}(t)$, where t are taken from the basis of $E(M)$, and adding to the resulting set the basis of subspace

$\gamma^{-1}(E(M))$.

The problem of intersection may be easily solved as a simple geometrical problem of the intersection of subspaces and convex linear cones. So the sequence $M_a^{(o)} \subset M_a^{(1)}$ ... is defined effectively. But it may be infinite, because of addition of the condition u every time when $I(M,\mathbf{u},\mathbf{y})$ and M are computed.

The considered method may be easily extended to the case of affine equality and inequality, that is, for the data algebra that permits the operation of addition of constants. One of the ways consists in follows. Let the constants $a_1,\ldots,a_k$ be used in the program. Then we introduce new variables $r_1,\ldots,r_k,r_{k+1}$ and relations $r_1 = a_1 r_{k+1},\ldots,$ $r_k = a_k r_{k+1}$ as initial conditions. Then the linear problem may be considered for the extended set of variables.

REFERENCES

1. Glushkov V.M., Kapitonova Yu.V., Letichevsky A.A., Theoretical foundations of discrete systems design, Kibernetika, No.6, 1977 (in Russian).
2. Letichevsky A.A., Equivalence and optimization of programs, International Symposium on Theoretical Programming, Lecture Notes in Computer Science, No.5, 1974.
3. Cuasot P., Halbwachs N., Automatic discovery of linear restrictions among variables of program, Conference Record of the 5-th Annual ACM Symposium on Principles of Programming Languages, Jan. 23-25, 1978, USA.
4. Mal'tsev A.I., Algebraic systems, Nauka, Moscow, 1970 (in Russian).

WHAT CAN WE DO WITH PROBLEMS OF EXHAUSTIVE SEARCH?

G.M.Adel'son-Vel'skii
Krzhizhanovskogo 14-2
VNIISI, Moscow
USSR

A.O.Slisenko
Fontanka 27
LOMI, Leningrad
USSR

1. INTRODUCTION

We treat a computational problem, i.e. a problem of evaluating some function, to be hard, if we do not know whether it can be actually solved on real computers. From the point of view of classical theory of algorithms or set-theoretic mathematics (but hardly from the point of view of Al-Khwarizmi) such a problem may be solvable: there is a trivial way of solving it, which consists (for a given argument) in more or less exhaustive search in a finite set of candidates for a solution of the problem and in rather a simple test for any such candidate whether it is a solution. (By Kleene normal form theorem [1], §1.10, every computable function can be evaluated in such a way in its domain.) However, one could hardly implement such a method: the sun will die out and computer still will be at the beginning of the computation by the program defining it.

We define the time complexity of a program Π as a function mapping an argument, i.e. input datum, into the number of computer operations done by the program for this argument. The value of this function for X will be denoted by $t_\Pi^*(X)$. It is not simple to get a detailed description of the behaviour of t_Π^*, and the information, we obtain from it, often does not justify expenses. It is more convenient and enough informative to get upper bounds on $t_\Pi^*(X)$ for a given class of arguments. This way we come to the notion of the worst-case complexity: the worst-case time complexity is a function mapping a natural number n into the maximum of $t_\Pi^*(X)$ for X with the length not greater than n. The worst-case time complexity will be denoted by $t_\Pi(n)$ and referred to as complexity.

Besides the time of processing we have other complexity characteristics of computation which are worth being estimated - they are the size of the memory (space complexity), the length of registers, etc. However, without estimation of time, estimations of other complexity characteristics are of little value, as a rule. On the other hand, if we reasonably choose our computational model, e.g.

see [2], then upper bound on the time may give rather a nontrivial, sometimes even good, bounds on the other complexity characteristics.

The complexity of a problem is defined by 2 bounds: upper and lower. Unary function φ is an upper bound on the complexity of a given problem f if one can construct a program Π solving this problem (i.e. evaluating f) and such that $t_\Pi(n) \geqslant \varphi(n)$ for all n. Binary function ψ is a lower bound on the complexity of f if for every Π, evaluating f, we have $t_\Pi(n) \geqslant \psi(|\Pi|,n)$ for all n, where $|\Pi|$ is the length of Π. These definitions show that we can speak about coincidence of upper and lower bounds within some type of proximity. "Ideal" proximity of these bounds is given by the equality $\psi(k,n)= \psi_1(k)\,\varphi(n)$ with some ψ_1, decreasing "enough slowly". But such a proximity can not be always achieved even in theory.

We can prove some problems to have no practically effective algorithms for all inputs. We shall call them genuinely hard. And if we cannot prove such a property, and do not know an effective algorithm solving the problem, then we shall call it non-effectivized or vaguely hard.

Problems of evaluating functions with large values are genuinely hard, e.g. problem of enumerating elements of a finite set with very large number of elements. Once computer designers begged the first author to develop a program enumerating all the directed circuits of a digraph. Its number may be not large but it can reach $\sum_{k=1}^n k!$, where n is the number of vertices of the graph. We are not aware of what would do the designers if the amount of circuits had been only 10^6 times less than this value, when $n \geqslant 90$.

One can get genuinely hard problems using various diagonal constructions. In particular, for a given bound φ one can construct a two-value function (i.e. a set recognition problem) which has both complexity bounds very close to φ (we assume φ being computable enough simply, e.g. φ being a polynomial, exponential function and so on). Though examples of genuinely hard problems, built by this method, are artificial, they can be sometimes rather simply reduced to natural problems, and so a high lower bound on the complexity of the latter problems can be gained. This way of reasoning is rather a faithful copy of proofs of algorithmic unsolvability of concrete problems. Results of this kind are of negative flavour; as a rule, they mean the problem under consideration to be practically unsolvable, and we are to modify its formulation. A proof of genuine hardness of a concrete problem may be of a definite

positive significance for seeking for more a realistic formulation
of the corresponding "physical" problem. These considerations can
be elucidated by the solvability problem for Tarski algebra. We
start from polynomial inequalities of the form $P(x_1,...,x_n) \geqslant 0$,
where P is a polynomial with rational coefficients and $x_1,...,x_n$
are variables for reals. Sentences are formed of such inequalities
with the help of usual logical connectives. As a simpliest sentence
we can take a sentence asserting solvability of a system of concrete
polynomial inequalities with one variable over the field of reals.
The solvability problem for Tarski algebra consists in finding an
algorithm detecting the validity of an arbitrary sentence of the
above type. Such an algorithm exists and is known well, however the
complexity of this problem is not less than exponent (e.g. see [3);
this lower bound is enough convincing to consider the problem to be
genuinely hard. Even a passing glance at the proof reveals that
formulas (of Tarski algebra) solvable with high complexity have very
long, in total unbounded chains of embedded quantifiers:
$\forall x_1... \forall x_2... \forall x_3...$. And usually we are interested in formulas
with relatively small number of quantifiers, e.g. whether a system
of polynomial inequalities of a given type has a solution for any
evaluation of parameters. We can continue such an analysis of proof
of genuine hardness of problem, and extract from it various restrictions which would permit us to make the problem under consideration
more pliable for effectivization and which still preserve its "physical" meaning. But usually this analysis of such a proof does not
lead us to such a restricted class of inputs which gives a practically efficient algorithm, - the problem remains vaguely hard.

In general, vaguely hard problems form a scantily explored area.
During recent years some success was achieved in classifying then in
some sense, and this clarified its relative complexity and expedi-
ency of its mutual reductions.

A lot of interesting vaguely hard problems, including many
problems of discrete optimization, are in the class of NP-complete
problems [4]. We shall remind a definition of this class.

Firstly, we introduce the class P - that is the class of recognition problems (i.e. of 2-valued functions), any of which can be
solved with polynomial complexity. E.g. recognizing the property
a list of edges y is a Hamiltonian circuit in a graph x is in P,
if, of course, x and y are coded in a usual manner (see [5], ch.10).
In other words, there is an algorithm α and a polynomial p, such

that α recognizes the above property and $t_{\alpha}^{*}(x,y) \leqslant t_{\alpha}(|x|+|y|) \leqslant$ $\leqslant p(|x|+|y|)$; here $|z|$ is the length of z, when we consider z as a word (we mean the used alphabets to contain at least 2 symbols). Now let us consider conditions of the form

$$|y| \leqslant q(|x|) \text{ \& } Q(x,y) \tag{1}$$

where q is a polynomial and $Q \in P$. Let us treat x as variable for codes of inputs and y as a parameter of search which runs in a set containing a desired solution (e.g. y is a variable for lists of distinct edges of graph x). The inequality $|y| \leqslant q(|x|)$ defines the domain of search, the number of elements in this domain is $c^{q(|x|)} \geqslant 2^{|x|}$.

The class of search recognition problems (the class NP) is the class of all the problems of the form «there exists y, such that (1)», where q,Q are fixed for a given problem. E.g. the problem of existence of a Hamiltonian circuit in a graph is in NP - its search domain is defined by the inequality $|y| \leqslant |x|$.

The class of search minimization problems (the class NP_{min}) is the class of all the problems of the form

$$f(x)=\min \{ \nu (y):(1)\}, \tag{2}$$

where ν is a rational-value function, computable in polynomial time. E.g. if x is a graph with integer weights on its edges and $\nu(y)$, where y is a list of edges, is the sum of weights on these edges, then the formula (2) gives the traveling salesman problem, if $Q(x,y)$ stands for «a list y is a Hamiltonian circuit in x» and $q(|x|)=|x|$.

In the classification of search problems below the class P is treated as a class of "simple" problems, and the whole reasoning is "module transformations with polynomial complexity". Surely, we do not mean practical effectiveness of computations with polynomial complexity, we mean only that all the known algorithms for vaguely hard problems under consideration stand very far from computations with polynomial complexity - the known upper bounds on the complexity of these problem are not less than exponential function. And we put a question about rough estimation of complexity: polynomial or not; or whether it is possible to diminish exhaustive, exponential search down to polynomial search.

The class NP contains many known problems, namely, recognition of primality, of graph isomorphism and others. The most interesting problems of this type have not been yet proved about whether they are in P or not. However, for a lot of such natural problems we have a proof of the following universality property:

《if a given problem is in P then P=NP》.
Those problems in NP which have this property are called NP-complete.
Similarly one can define NP-completeness for problems in NP_{min} -
one need to replace NP by NP_{min} and P by the class of functions computable in polynomial time.

A large number of known for a long time problems of discrete
optimization and recognition problems, corresponding to them, has
proved to be NP-complete - see [5], ch.10. In particular, the mentioned above problems about traveling salesman and Hamiltonian circuit (even in plane graphs [6]) are of this type.

NP-complete problems are usually hard to solve. But not in
every case, i.e. not for every input. There are various methods of
reducing of search, e.g., the branch and bound method [7]. However,
for no "serious" problem one has managed to prove the latter method
to guarantee solving the whole problem in polynomial time, but many
particular cases of many mass problems were solved by this method.
(On speaking about solving a problem for a concrete argument, we use
such words as 《solving a concretization of a problem》, 《solving
a particular case》 etc.)

2. DO ONE NEED TO SOLVE HARD PROBLEMS?

The known genuinely hard problems are at most interesting,
perhaps, by the only fact of its hardness, and those its particular
cases which are really solved on computers, take no so much time.
It is difficult to prove and, apparently, even more difficult to
disprove the assertion that it has to be so. This maybe partly sus-
tained by the following reasoning. For a computable nontrivial
lower bound of complexity ψ , especially of the "good" type mentioned above, we are not able to construct even an artificial recognition problem which would have its complexity not less than ψ on
rather dense sets of inputs. And to gain this for all the arguments
is provably impossible (as the equality $\psi(|\Pi|,x)=0$ may take place
for small x's, actually we speak about all the arguments standing
after some place, computable from ψ and Π). Unfortunately, density considerations in this topic are too vulnerable and unconvinc-
ing.

It is worth to note that widely used considerations that
actually we are interested in a small finite set of cases of a
given problem and so, in principle, there exists an algorithm solving them fast - these considerations are groundless. We simply

forget that computational complexity can be "pumped over" to the complexity of proof of correctness of algorithm; if this latter complexity characteristic is taken into consideration then in finite (even small) domains we shall have similar algorithmic unsolvabilities, high lower bounds on complexity etc. as in infinite domains [8].

2.1. One has fewer arguments to say that vaguely hard problems are not interesting, as compared with genuinely hard problems. Many naturally formulated problems of discrete mathematics, operations research, econometrics, pattern recognition and artificial intelligence are NP-complete, or, at any rate, vaguely hard. Above we gave 2 examples of NP-complete problems - the Hamiltonian circuit problem and the traveling salesman problem. One can easily see that the latter can be reduced (by dichotomy) to several problems about Hamiltonian circuit of a given weight, and the number of these problems is not greater than the size (the length of code) of the traveling salesman problem. Among NP-complete problems one can find problems of technological or economical optimization, e.g. the Johnson's problem for the line of 3 or more machines, or optimization of technological models that needs solving integer or partially integer problems of linear programming, or minimization of deadline in scheduling of jobs under the resource constraints, and so on. We shall give some formulation of the latter problem. The structure of its inputs may seem to be complicated, but many details in this structure and lucid physical meaning of every parameter give us an opportunity to see those substantial considerations which could help us to solve it. The problem given below is NP-complete [5].

A particular input for the scheduling problem we discuss consists of: a set of resources $\{R_1,...,R_r\}$, together with a bound B_i for each R_i, B_i is the whole amount of the resource of ith type; a set of tasks $\{T_1,...,T_m\}$ with a partial order $\prec$ on it, and for each T_j, a corresponding task time τ_j and resource requirements $R_i(T_j)$ of every type. Let D be a natural number (deadline). A function $f:\{T_j\} \to \{0,1,...,D-1\}$ is a schedule, if

a) $f(T_i)+\tau_i \leqslant D$;

b) $T_i \prec T_j \Rightarrow f(T_i)+\tau_i \leqslant f(T_j)$;

c) $\displaystyle\sum_{\{T_i:f(T_i)\leqslant t<f(T_i)+\tau_i\}} R_j(T_i) \leqslant B_j$ for $0 \leqslant t < D$.

The problem is to minimize D which has s schedule, and for the minimal D to find a corresponding schedule.

We conclude our list of NP-complete problems with the problem which is a starting point in founding NP-completeness of concrete problems, and which, in a sense, saliently shows difficulties of solving these problems in general case - we mean the propositional satisfiability problem. Inputs of this problem are tables of height 3 and of arbitrary length l, each cell of the table contains a variable or a negation of a variable:

$$
\begin{array}{|c|c|c|c|}
\hline
x_{1,1} & x_{2,1} & \cdots & x_{1,1} \\
\hline
x_{1,2} & x_{2,2} & \cdots & x_{1,2} \\
\hline
x_{1,3} & x_{2,3} & \cdots & x_{1,3} \\
\hline
\end{array}
\qquad (\phi)
$$

We may consider x_{ij} to be either binary natural numbers (proper variables) or expressions of the form $\daleth x$, where x is a natural number, and $\daleth$ is the negation sign. A path in a table ϕ is a list of the form $x_{1,i_1}, x_{2,i_2}, \ldots, x_{1,i_1}$. A path is closed if it contains a contrary pair, i.e. a variable and its negation; a path is open if it in not closed. The problem of propositional satisfiability: given a table, to get to know whether it has an open path.

2.2. Many problems of artificial intelligence are actually hard. E.g. the problem of choosing the best, or at least a good, move in a given chess position. One is hardly able to prove P-completeness of this problem now - even if to put aside formal consideration about finiteness of the problem, the difficulty of testing a move to be winning is almost the same as to find such a move. But the problem is clearly hard - try to develop a good chess-playing program.

As a rule, problems of theorem proving in various formal systems are genuinely hard. Even the simplest problem of this class - the detecting of satisfiability in classical propositional calculus is NP-complete; and this is only a model problem. Just as we go to the problem of theorem proving in more reach formal systems, we stumble upon exponential lower bounds [3],[9], or upon algorithmic unsolvability. Nevertheless, interest in automatic theorem proving does not weaken. Now the main efforts are concentrated on proving theorems from narrow areas of mathematics, intensively using specific modes of reasoning in these areas. Even if to put aside such an outstanding achievement as the solution of the four colour problem, one can find areas in mathematics where some bright results in computer theorem proving were achieved - see [10],[11].

2.3. In spite of the considerations, exposed above, which show
the importance of solving hard problems, some people think these
problems are not worth spending time on their investigation. To
sustain such a viewpoint, various arguments are used, beginning with
"lofty" phylosophic and aesthetic principles and ending with very
pragmatic speculations. Among the arguments of the first type one
can find reasoning that genuine science is developed by "bare brains",
and thus scientific discoveries obtained with the help of computer
(e.g. the solution of the four colour problem) cannot be understood
by man, and that is why they are of no theoretical significance.
From this point of view many problems of artificial intelligence
seem to be some kind of whim. And the true harmony of the world
must be simple, and complications (which are surely generated by the
devil) only lead us away from perceiving it.

The other extreme viewpoint looks as follows. Mathematical
formulation of a practical problem, e.g. a problem of production
optimization, is always got as a result of some simplifying assumptions. We accept them because we believe in "the honest word of the
Crown prince", i.e. of the man who investigated the problem not from
the mathematical point of view but in essence. Then let us speak
with him, and we will be able to make the problem quite simple, with
almost evident solution.

We see little sense in arguing with these viewpoint appealing
to general considerations only. The results having been obtained,
permit us to share more optimistic views on the value of investigations of hard problems. Our viewpoint can be expressed as follows.

1) Classification of mathematical problems by the complexity of
solving them, including relative complexity, is of principal theoretical significance. Yet more important are estimations of particular algorithms, and, especially, of the complexity of the problems -
the estimations which do not depend on specific methods of solving
the problems. Without answers to the questions, arising in investigating the complexity of the problems, our world picture is incomplete. In particular, it is very important to find out whether P
and NP coincide or not. Any solution of this problem would be a
firm ground for solvers of NP-complete problems. The alternative
P=NP would stimulate seeking for better methods of solving for
concrete classes of problems with polynomial complexity. The opposite
alternative would draw our attention to questions of the very formu-

lation of problem.

2) Besides the methods of developing simple models, based on
"substantial" investigation of situations, there are general mathematical methods which deserve to be used. (Our survey concerns the
latter methods, however we do not mean to give an exhaustive account
on the topic.) This is a place to note that algorithmics investiga-
tes a world, which is in essential part created by man and, in this
sense, an artificial world, and algorithmics affects on formation
of this world of algorithms it creates. Thus, an algorithm, effective in some situation, which did not exist, can bring this situation
into being.

3) Mathematical formulation of a problem may prove to be more
or less correct even when there exist sound objections to some
assumptions. This means that solutions of problems, having been formulated under some dubious assumptions, may prove to be not bad in
practice.

4) Problems of artificial intelligence are urgent even now, and
their urgency will only grow up. Though we cannot say about very
large success, but there are definite achievements in programming of
games, in automatic theorem proving, in pattern recognition. On investigating these problems there have been achieved some results of
theoretical significance.

... Once two magicians - F.S.Kivrin and C.Junta - got into argument.

"My dears", said Fiodor Simeonovich puzzled, after having examined the handwritings. "Don't you see it to be the Ben Bezahlel's
problem. Kaliostro has yet proved it to have no solution".

"We know ourselves that it has no solution", Junta said, immediately bristling up. "We want to know how to solve it".

"You are reasoning somehow queery, Cristo... How can one seek
for solution, if it is absent. Somewhat nonsense..."

"Pardon, Theodor, but this is you who reason queery. It is
nonsense to seek for solution when it exists by itself. We speak
how to deal with a problem which has no solution. This is deeply a
principal question..." ([12], p.385).

It is to be clear from the above section that we share the viewpoint of Cristobahl Junta.

How to solve problems of the search type

3. One has to solve problems of the search type and does it
successfully for their concrete cases. Sometimes a problem, which

seems to be hard, proves to be simple in some aspects, and this simplicity gives a clue to its effective solution. There are too many particular modes, working in small classes of problems, to try to survey them. We shall take into account only some general principles, which may lead to effectivization of some search problems.

All the surveyed below approaches to solving hard problems offering, in fact, some modification of the initial formulation of a problem. Surely, these modifications try to preserve the "physical" essence of the problem. Various considerations show that such approaches to dealing with hard problems are now, and apparently in the nearest future, the most useful for practice and the most fruitful for theory. Roughly speaking, these approaches are diveded into 2 types. Within approaches of the first type we narrow the input domain, and within approaches of the second type we sacrifice the accuracy of solution.

The first type approach is represented by methods of describing subclasses with polynomial complexity. This describing means that we restrict ourselves with some subset of initial data which peculiarities give us an opportunity to develop an algorithm, solving our given problem for the arguments from this subset, and doing it with small (polynomial) complexity. In some sense, heuristic algorithms belong to the same approach. The second type approach gives us approximate and probabilistic solutions.

We do not know general principles of singling out substantial subclasses with polynomial complexity, and, apparently, to develop such principles is a serious problem. At first glance one may think the problem of describing "simply" solvable subclasses of a given hard problem is not mathematical and only demand some analysis of substantial origin of considered problems. However, actual attempts to single out polynomial subclasses show that complexity, algorithmic considerations play more active part in this process. This can be illustrated by the graph isomorphism problem. Trying to develop effective algorithms for recognition of graph isomorphism, it was found that natural local considerations are non-effective only for strongly regular graphs. Thus, graphs without nontrivial strongly regular subgraphs form a class of graphs whose isomorphism problem can be solved by an algorithm with low complexity [13]. But in practice, e.g. for classifying structural chemical formulas, we deal just with such graphs which stand very far from strongly regular ones. Supposedly, this method of describing of sufficiently sub-

stantial and simply solvable subclasses of hard problems, namely,
the method of banning "very symmetric" substructures in structures
under consideration is rather universal. The difficulties in applying it lay in our unsufficient understanding what kind of "symmetry"
in the structure of inputs prevents us from effectivization of algorithms. Note that for some simple problems [14], which are not
genuinely of the search type in our sense, all the "symmetries",
which hamper effectivization of natural algorithms, can be classi-
fied and used as a basis for developing very fast algorithms.

The above mentioned graph property (not to have strongly regular subgraphs) is neither palpable nor easily recognizable, though
we may claim it due to physical considerations and even to prove
it for some class of problems on the basis of these considerations.
Properties of the same kind are often used for developing various
heuristic modes of solving problems. Properties with more lucid
syntactic structure are more attractive from mathematical viewpoint.
Surely, one can get easily solvable problem, having restricted the
dimension of inputs or some other parameters, characterizing the
number of "degrees of freedom". But this way rarely lead to genuinely interesting problems, such as the marriage, one-product flow
problem etc. [15],[16].

One can expect to aggregate generality, syntactic simplicity
and physical substantiality, if he would use some sufficiently simple
calculus, e.g. context-free grammar (or something like grammar with
"weak" context sensivity), for describing the domain of a problem.
We shall elucidate this idea (which was pointed out in [2]) not very
strictly - though, it seems to deserve more careful developing.

Let us consider the Hamiltonian circuit problem. As a physical
ground we shall keep in mind the classical traveling salesman problem, and let us try to describe a class of networks of roads, which
evolve in some simple way. We shall try to describe this evolution
by a context-free graph grammar (surely, we do not mean that any
production, i.e. inference rule, corresponds to a step of the evolution). Nodes and edges of graphs can be labeled with some auxiliary
characters, in particular, some nodes can be marked as terminal
(and which cannot be transformed further) and nonterminal. The axiom
and productions are of the form:

  axiom: .S
(a node with ascribed nonterminal character);

productions:

     can be transformed into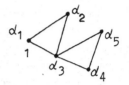

(a node is appended with a concrete graph, the correspondence is marked by the numeral 1);

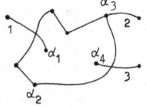   can be transformed into

(a node is replaced by a graph; some nodes, coming out of the graph – their number is equal to the degree of the replaced node – are attached to those nodes which were incident to the corresponding nodes of the replaced node); in this description S,A are nonterminal characters; $\alpha_1, \alpha_2, \ldots$ are arbitrary characters (e.g., empty).

While generating a graph by the rules of the described type, we can easily maintain the knowledge of a property which generalizes the following one: for any given pair of edges, incident to a given node, the current graph has a Hamiltonian circuit which goes along the edges from the pair. Thus, the Hamiltonian circuit problem for a graph is reduced to the problem of finding an inference (i.e. a way of generating) of the graph in our grammar. As at natural assumptions the latter problem is solvable in polynomial time, the initial problem is also solvable in this time.

So, for a set of graphs, generated by a sufficiently simple grammar, the Hamiltonian circuit problem is solvable in polynomial time.

3. SEARCHING WITH PRUNING

We are almost helpless in front of a purely discrete problem in general formulation. Let us recall the general linear programming problem:

$$\sum_{j=1}^{n} c_j x_j \rightarrow \min,$$

$$\sum_{j=1}^{n} a_{ij} x_j = A_i X \leqslant b_i, \quad i=1,2,\ldots,m \tag{3}$$

where a_{ij}, b_i, c_j are integers. The question whether (3) has a solution, when $x_j \in \{0,1\}$, is a NP-complete problem. The same for its solvability in integers. Its solvability in rationals may seem to be not much easier, though in this case the problem becomes non-discrete in the obvious sense. However, experiments showed long ago that in practice this non-discrete problem is easily solvable. Recently Hačijan [17] showed, using an elegant construction, that the non-discrete linear programming problem is in P. So, continuity in some general consideration crucially decreasing the search. We shall give the main ideas of Hačijan's construction. For simplicity we assume all the inequalities in (3) to be strict, and consider only the problem of consistency (solvability) of (3).

Let L be the bitwise length of an input. To some degree, this problem, as any other computational problem, is discrete. If (3) is consistent, then in the sphere E_0 with zero center and radius 2^L there is a sphere with radius 2^{-Ln} which is wholly contained in the polyhedron (3). By induction we build the following sequence of ellipsoids. Let $E_0, E_1, ..., E_k$ be built and their centers be $X_0, X_1, ..., X_k$ correspondingly. We check whether X_k obeys (3). If yes then the process is ended. If not then $A_i X_k > b_i$ for some $1 \leqslant i \leqslant m$. Then we build E_{k+1} (see fig. below) which, firstly,

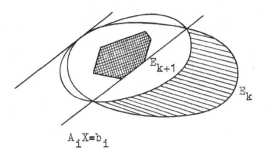

$$A_i X = b_i$$

contains the intersection of E_k and the hyperplane $A_i X = b_i$, secondly, touches E_k at the point, where E_k is touched by the hyperplane, which is parallel to $A_i X = b_i$ and lies in semispace $A_i X < b_i$, and, thirdly, has minimal volume among such ellipsoids. The volume of E_{k+1} is C times, where C is a constant greater than 1, less than that of E_k, and, besides that, E_{k+1} contains the intersection of E_0 and the polyhedron (3). It is clear that within time, polynomially depending on n+L, the volume of E_l becomes smaller than the volume of sphere of radius 2^{-Ln}. If during this time no center X_k, $k \leqslant l$, was in the polyhedron (3), then the latter is empty.

3.1. The algorithm described above uses some type of pruning, which makes searching for solution (or looking through candidates for solution) rather purposeful. Various considerations, concerning structurizing the search, are widely used in practical algorithms. Unfortunately, mathematical ideas, which lie at the basis of such algorithms, are not often deep and usually do not lead to good theoretical estimations of the complexity. Hačijan's algorithm (if to treat it from this viewpoint) is rather a rare exception. However in general, the main ideas of structurized search may feed serious investigation.

Within the framework of structurized search a finite (and, as a rule, very large) set of elements, which are looked through is partitioned into subsets or, more generally, is covered by subsets of smaller size. These subsets are analysed, a part of them is excluded from further processing as free from solutions, and the remaining part is again reduced to smaller ones and so on. If the number of exclusions (i.e. prunings) is small, then we have almost exhaustive search. In the best case, when all the subsets, except one, are pruned, we have deterministic (some people say directed) search (e.g. as in Hačijan's algorithm), and gain a polynomial upper bound on the complexity.

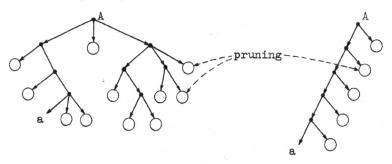

Search with pruning   Deterministic search

If we treat Hačijan's algorithm as an algorithm of deterministic search, then as its specific feature we observe different non-monotony: E_{k+1} is not contained in E_k (i.e. covering, but not partitioning of E_k takes place), the proximity value $\max_i(b_i - A_i X_k)$ changes non-monotonically, when moving from E_k to E_{k+1}.

3.2. A structurized search can often be represented as an application of branch and bound method [7], though this is not always natural. General framework of this method looks as follows. Let f be a rational-value function defined on a finite set A, we are to find an element $a_0 \in A$, such that $f(a_0) = \min\{f(a):a \in A\}$, and $f(a_0)$ itself. Let $\{B_\alpha\}$ be a family of subsets of A, which structurized the search, and we can define a function μ (lower bound) with the property

$$\mu(B_\alpha) \leqslant \min\{f(a):a \in B_\alpha\}.$$

The method analizes the current B and produces some elements $a_1,...,a_m \in A$. If $f(a_i) < \mu(B_\alpha)$ for some i, $1 \leqslant i \leqslant m$, then B is to be pruned off. Sometimes one can introduce an upper bound M, such that $\min\{f(a):a \in B_\alpha\} \leqslant M(B_\alpha)$. Then $\mu(B_\alpha) > M(B_\beta)$ also leads to pruning B_α.

A lot of algorithms is described due to the branch and bound framework. Though the number of publications, concerning particular cases of the method, diminished during recent time, the branch and bound method is as often used in practice as before. Unfortunately, theoretical investigation of effectiveness of the method leaves much to be desired. Meanwhile, it deserves serious theoretical studying. The following 2 questions are of the importance first of all.

1) There are more or less general considerations about ways of choosing the subsets B_α and defining bounds μ and M. But they are not systemized and not given sufficiently complete comparative analysis. In particular, the behaviour of the branch and bound method is not clear when applyed to "canonical" NP-complete problem of propositional satisfiability, as compared with known methods of theorem proving - the latter methods are better investigated theoretically than methods of solving other NP-complete problems.

2) A comparative complexity analysis of the branch and bound method has not been done. There is a pessimistic conjecture that in the worst case it gives algorithms with the exponential complexity for NP-complete programs.

3.3. We are not always able to drive our ideas of reducing the search up to strict formulations, such as a description of bounds. Then, on implementing in our algorithm some ideas of "commomn sense", we cannot found its correctness or satisfactory estimate the quality of the algorithm - this concerns both the time of its processing and the accuracy of the obtained solution. Algorithms of this kind are often called heuristic.

E.g., in the above mentioned problem of job scheduling with resource constraints heuristic considerations can be formulated as ascribing priorities to tasks in conflicting situations. While designing a schedule, i.e. while assigning starting time of tasks,

conflicting situations arise: there is lack of resources to start
all tasks, which are permitted due to the partial order. Then we
calculate the priorities of these tasks, i.e. express by numbers
our considerations about tasks, mostly impeding the whole process.
On having got the priorities we resolve the conflicts, giving preference to tasks with greater priorities [18].

It is easier to treat heuristic algorithms as standing out of
mathematics. However, investigation of heuristics is, besides all
of other, a source of new mathematical questions and, probably, new
ideas. The time for mathematical study of nonstrict conclusions
from "substantial" considerations has come, and such studies are
done. In the final part of our survey we shall give an example of
such a study - an estimation of the quality of choosing a move in a
two person game with complete information, using Shannon's game
model.

And now we stay on some general ideas, concerning description
of heuristic algorithms and their properties.

4. THE STRATEGY OF INCREASING OF THE FREEDOM OF CHOICE

S.Yu.Maslov [19] proposed as a model for investigating heuristic algorithm to use a representation of such an algorithm as an
algorithm of inference search in some calculus. This calculus is
built due to a given problem and tries to incorporate our considerations about modes of solving it. The calculus consists of a finite or infinite number of inference rules. Surely, only sufficiently
simple rules are of interest, e.g. inference rules of logical calculuses. In the latter case we have a finite number of inference rule
schemata, and the number of its concretizations, i.e. of inference
rules themselves, is infinite. An inference (or derivation) in such
a calculus F starts with a concrete input of the given problem, in
other words, we deal with solving a particular case of our problem.
At every step of inference we can apply one of the finite number of
inference rules of F, until we get an axiom. We assume the rules
to be one-premise, as it does not diminish generality. Roughly
speaking, any inference rule reduces our problem (more precisely, a
concrete case of our problem) to another problem which is, probably,
of some different type - the latter is essential, as for preserving
one-premiseness of our calculus we write down, say, a reduction to
several problems of one type as a reduction to a list of problems.
Thus, a concrete argument of the problem has in correspondence a

a tree of possible inferences of this argument in F. Properties of
this tree may be an indicator of influence of various heuristic
ideas on inference search - see [19]. The branching is an important characteristic of the tree, especially, if we assume all the
inference rules to be equal or close due to the force of heuristic
ideas, incorporated in them. Under these assumptions some reasons
show that the maximal chances to succeed belong to the strategy of
moving to a direction of the biggest branching, i.e. to a direction,
mostly preserving freedom of choice.

In [19] these ideas are formalized as follows. Into correspondence to the calculus F we put an algorithm α, which ascribes
to any word X with one-step consequences $Y_1, \ldots, Y_1$

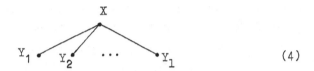

$$(4)$$

probabilities $p_1, \ldots, p_1$ (here p_i is a probability of moving from X
to Y_i, $p = 1 - \sum_i p_i \geq 0$, p is interpreted as some "special" probability
stopping short, i.e. the probability that the searching for inference stops at X). The algorithm α defines a probabilistic measure
on the set of all inferences; for any Q there is defined the probability p_Q of stopping the search at the word Q. Then the pair F,α
has in correspondence the information

$$\textit{И}(X) = \textit{}_{F,\alpha}(X) = \sum_{\substack{Q \text{ is derivable} \\ \text{from X in F}}} p_Q \cdot |\log_2 p_Q|,$$

which is a meassure of uncertainty on the set of derivable words.

Proper probabilistic considerations may play a small part here.
In this connection, further we deal with the "uniform probability"
algorithm α_p, i.e. such that $p_1 = \ldots = p_1$ and p is the same for all X.
By this, $\textit{И}(X)$ becomes a function $\textit{И}_p(X)$ of p only. An essential
characteristic is given by the asymptic of $\textit{И}_p(X)$ when p→0. (For
example [19], for finite calculuses this function is bounded, for
deterministic ones it behaves as $\log\frac{1}{p}$, for ones with uniformly
bounded branching - as $\frac{1}{p}$, for arbitrary canonic Post calculuses -
as $\frac{1}{p^2}$ and so on.)

The strategy of increasing freedom of choice consists in the
demand that in the branching (4) one is to move along the path,

where $\max\{И(Y_i):1\leqslant i\leqslant l\}$ is achieved. This strategy is natural for many maze problems and position games with complete information. Pure theoretically, these problems can be solved by this strategy in the sense that for sufficiently small p the search becomes deterministic. Surely, in nontrivial cases p must be so small that to compute $И$ becomes unfeasible in practice. Thus, to implement this strategy one needs enough good and simply computable approximations to $И$. Partly, this idea is used, say, in chess programs by including in estimator function such a parameter as the number of possible moves.

Let us take as an example the propositional satisfiability problem, which we describe in the section 2.1 above. Let ϕ be a table where we are to detect an open path. One of the simpliest approximations is based on the analysis of one variable. Let x be chosen. Then ϕ can be represented in the form

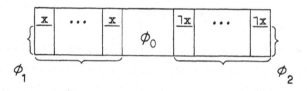

where ϕ_0 is free of x and $\neg$x. The strategy, determined by the corresponding approximation to $И$, prescribes appending to the open path under construction the variable x, if ϕ_1 is larger then ϕ_2 (this is one of the simpliest approximations to the measure of freedom of choice, as the part $\phi_0\phi_2$ contains an open path with more probability than the part $\phi_0\phi_1$). Otherwise we chose $\neg$x as an extension of the constructed path. More precisely, every time we choose such an x (or $\neg$x), where maximal overfall in the length of the corresponding ϕ_1 and ϕ_2 takes place.

An experiment was accomplished with this strategy of recognizing satisfiability, when random (uniformly distributed) formulas were tested - almost always an open path was found by the first attempt (the program by Yu.N.Kur'erov).

Now we stay upon approaches, which sacrifice accuracy of solution.

5. APPROXIMATE SOLUTIONS

Instead of seeking for a precise solution of minimization problems of the form

$$f(\mathbf{x})=\min \{ \nu(y):|y|\leqslant q(|\mathbf{x}|) \ \& \ Q(\mathbf{x},y)\},$$

one may put a question about finding approximate values of $f(\mathbf{x})$ (maybe, "approximate" in various sense), or about finding approximate values of y_0, such that $f(\mathbf{x})=\nu(y_0)$ and so on. We shall pay the main attention to the problem of searching for approximate value of $f(\mathbf{x})$. We begin with approximations, described in the term of relative error.

We say z is an ε-approximation to $f(\mathbf{x})$, if

$$|z-f(\mathbf{x})| \leqslant \varepsilon \cdot z.$$

The complexity of finding such z, naturally, is to be estimated as function of $|\mathbf{x}|$ and $1/\varepsilon$.

It was discovered [20] that NP-complete problems behave themselves differently with respect to finding ε-approximations - some of them remain NP-complete, other become members of P. Among the most interesting problems one can find the traveling salesman problem and the knapsack problem [5]. To find ε-approximation to the solution of the first problem is again NP-complete [20]. On the other hand, there is such an algorithm for finding an ε-approximate solution for the knapsack problem, which has an upper bound on the complexity, polynomially depending of the input length and $1/\varepsilon$ [21].

The following fact is of interest. Additional restrictions on input graph in the traveling salesman problem make the problem more pliable to fast finding of approximate solutions. E.g. [22], if the edge weights obey triangle inequality, then $\frac{1}{2}$-approximate solutions can be found in polynomial time.

The whole situation does not change, if we shall consider the absolute (not ratio) error, when speaking about approximate solution. As an example of problem which preserves the complexity in this situation, one can take, apparently, again the traveling salesman problem. We point out one more interesting example, concerning, however, the problem which NP-completeness is unknown, namely, the problem of finding minimal disjunctive normal form is polynomially reducible to the problem of finding such a form, minimal within the additive error h, where $h \geqslant 1$ is an arbitrary constant [23].

As an example of problem, when even "small" absolute error gives an opportunity to construct an algorithm solving it with polynomial complexity, we take the banknote problem [24]:

$$\sum_{i=1}^{n} x_i \to \min;$$

$$\sum_{i=1}^{n} a_{ji}x_i \geqslant A_j, \quad j=1,2,\ldots,m;$$

$$x_i \in \{0,1\}, \quad i=1,2,\ldots,n,$$

and $a_{ji} \geqslant 0$. We restrict ourselves to the case m=2. Then this problem may have the following interpretations.

(a) There are n banknotes of double value, the ith banknote costs a_i dollars and b_i francs. One is to choose the smallest number of banknotes so that its total cost in dollars in not less than A and in francs - not less than B (this original formulation of the problem is due to A.S.Kronrod).

(b) One is to find two persons by telephone, and he knows the probabilities a_i and b_i of finding them by every (ith) of n telephone numbers ($\sum a_i = \sum b_i = 1$). What is the smallest list of telephone numbers, which guarantees the probability $1-\varepsilon_1$ of finding the first person and $1-\varepsilon_2$ of finding the second one?

The problem under discussion is NP-complete. But if to allow the error (nonoptimality), equal to 1, the a corresponding approximate solution can be found within the time $O(n^2)$. The case of arbitrary m is also studied in [24].

Other kinds of approximations are also reasonable, but they are little investigated now (recently, M.Sh.Levin studied the problem of distributing blocks of a program in outward memory, dealing with approximations to optimal value (as usual) and to constraints, and developed an algorithm with polynomial complexity for this problem).

6. PROBABILISTIC SOLUTIONS

"Probability" in solving computational problems may have different origins. We may deal with some probability distribution on inputs, and estimate algorithm from the viewpoint of the probability of obtaining precise solution or the probability of finding a solution within some definite amount of time. And we may use probabilistic algorithm, i.e. algorithm choosing some of its steps after query to a random number generator (i.e. some kind of Monte-Carlo algorithm). Surely, one may take various combinations of these approaches, and the very principles of using probabilistic approaches are not exhausted by the two ideas, mentioned above. It would

be interesting to elucidate connections between various approaches
- cf. [25].

Among distributions on inputs, the uniform distribution was
mainly studied (the normal distribution was considered in [26]).
Under this distribution rather simple (sometimes trivial) algorithms
were shown to solve, with low complexity (something like n^2 or
smaller) and large probability, the traveling salesman problem, the
graph colouring problem etc. - see [27],[28]. The triviality of
the used algorithms alone immediately forces us to put a question
about the adequacy of the considered distribution and the physical
distribution of inputs. The traveling salesman problem shows that
graph, we meet in practice, stand very far from expected graph of
the uniform distribution. One can better see inadequacy of this
distribution when taking as inputs some artificially created control
circuits, such as combinational circuits.

The question of constructing an adequate distribution is, apparently, rather complicated; it is similar to the question of describing practical subclasses of the polynomial complexity. A possible approach to solving this problem is to analyse ways of
generating input data being met in practice; here one may try to
use the same considerations we spoke about, when discussing subclasses of polynomial complexity.

The second approach, namely, the one based on algorithms with
random number generator, is more attractive, at least, from the
viewpoint of algorithmic constructions involved. The most familiar
results within this approach are fast algorithms for primality testing with the probability, arbitrary close to 1; the algorithm due
to [29] makes $6m \cdot |x|$ steps to check the primality of x with the
probability $1-2^{-m}$. And the algorithm uses the simpliest Bernoulli
random number generator (plainly speaking, for testing the primality
of x it randomly takes numbers from the segment [1,x-1] and compute
some simple functions on them).

While analysing this approach we stumble upon the question of
implementing random number generator. The possibility of using
pseudorandom generator for such algorithms is obscure, and the
question about the existence of appropriate physical generators is
still open and, moreover, the possibility of solving it positively
is under some doubt. In connection with the latter remark, there
is some sense to mention the unfinished experiments due to the late
M.M.Bongard, which concern algorithmic predicting the behaviour

of a nuclear radiation counter. He developed a simple program that
on having got an initial sequence of data of the counter, either
refused to "play" with it (i.e. to predict its behaviour) or "played"
with it. On the whole, the algorithm gained a small win. Bongard
was going to check whether this win could be explained by the fatigue
of the sensory device. He did not do it. Such questions are apparently very interesting and deserve further studying. Physical
generators with high density of inputs (i.e. the number of bits per
second, e.g. 10^4) are of special interest.

Probability ideas are attractive as a tool for analysis of
heuristic algorithms. This possibility was mentioned in the section 4 above, but they played an auxiliary part there. We shall
describe an approach due to G.M.Adel'son-Vel'skii and V.L.Arlazarov
[30], where probability ideas are used in essence.

7. USAGE OF THE PROBABILISTIC ORACLE

The approach due to [30], which is named the usage of the probabilistic oracle, is applied to analysis of algorithms (first of
all, chess players), which not always output right answers. In
situations, unlike considered above, the probability of right answer
is estimated and shown in some cases to be able to be done rather
high.

Let us imagine a computation, using an oracle (i.e. the possibility to get in one step a solution of some problem for an argument
worked out by this computation), but an oracle, which not always
give a right answer, say, give a right answer with some probability.
The problem of estimating the correctness and complexity of such an
algorithm is formulated with respect to a given probability to
receive a right answer by the oracle. The oracle in [30] gives
answers for inputs of a mass problem, but for a given input it
always gives the same answer, and the probabilities are defined on
all the inputs we are interested in.

We consider a game with complete information, e.g. the chess.
As Zermelo [31] showed, every position of the game has the true
evaluation, i.e. the result of constinuation of the game from this
position if both players play the best way. Let us consider the
final tree of the game from this position

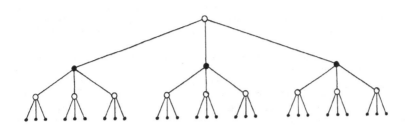

Then the evaluations of the final positions are known (each is equal
to the result of the finished game), and the evaluations of the rest
positions are recurrently defined by Zermelo's formula, which in
the case we are interested in (we mean that the considered game, as
the chess, has the sum, equal to 1, and players make their moves in
turn):

$$Z(A) = \max_{(A,B)} (1-Z(B)),$$

where Z(A) is the winnings of the player who is to move at the position A, (A,B) is a move from the position A to the position B, and
max is taken over all such moves.

However, when the tree of the game is enormously large (and we
keep in mind just such a game - the chess), it is practically impossible to calculate the evaluations by Zermelo's formula. Shannon
[32],[33] proposed to examine not the whole tree, but a part of it,
which spreads from the root down to the depth n, and to consider the
positions at the depth n to be final, and to calculate their evaluations, having formalized general chess theory principles about strong
and weak sides of positions. So, for every position there is defined
the value of some function f(A), which will be called estimator
function, and the considered part of the tree of the initial game
and the values of the estimator function on the positions of the
depth n - all this defines a model game, and the evaluations of its
positions can be computed.

Why do everybody, beginning from Shannon, believe the model
evaluations of positions, calculated in this way, to be proximate
to its true evaluations, and the proximaty to increase with increasing n, i.e. depth of the search?

In [30] this hypothetical relation is studied under the assumption that f and Z are connected in a probabilistic manner. An idea-
lized game is treated, for which all the necessary probabilities are
computed easily, and the qualitative results are shown to preserve
themselves within more realistic assumptions.

Let G be a game of 2 persons, which positions obey the following conditions:

1) the possible outcomes of the game are the winnings ($Z(A)=1$) or the loss ($Z(A)=0$) only;

2) from every non-final position one can make the same number of moves m, and all the final positions have the same large enough depth N;

3) the players make their moves in turn;

4) every winning position A (i.e. such that $Z(A)=1$) has exactly s winning moves (A,B), where $Z(B)=0$; the rest m-s moves are losing (in a losing position all the moves are losing);

5) the estimator function $f(A)$ is random, and its values are independent for different positions, besides that for all the winning positions the probabilities

$$P(f(A)=1 \mid Z(A)=1) = p$$

are the same, and for all the losing positions

$$P(f(A)=1 \mid Z(A)=0) = q.$$

Thus, the values of f are answers of the oracle, which are true with some probabilities. One can put to the oracle a question about the evaluation of a given position; but we cannot increase the probability of the validity of the evaluation by repeated querying the oracle: repeated query about the evaluation of the same position gives the same answer.

Let $S_n(A)$ be the evaluation of position A, which is the root of the Shannon's model of our game, where n is the depth of the model and n is much less than n. Define the probabilities

$$P_n = P(S_n(A)=1 \mid Z(A)=1),$$
$$Q_n = P(S_n(A)=1 \mid Z(A)=0).$$

They are computed due to the recurrent formulas

$$P_0=p, \quad Q_0=q,$$
$$P_{n+1}=1-P_n^{m-s}Q_n^s,$$
$$Q_{n+1}=1-P_n^m.$$

Depending on the values p and q, either $P_n \to 1$ and $Q_n \to 0$ (i.e. the probability of achieving the right evaluation grows when the depth grows) or the both probabilities alternatively come nearer end nearer to 1 and 0, that means uselessness of increasing the depth of the search. At the figure below the "good" area of

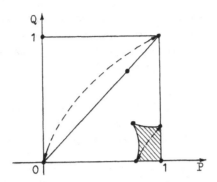

the values is hatched - for these values we can derive benefit by
increasing the depth (stationary points and pairs of points are also
marked on the picture).

The accomplished investigations show that

1) for the problem under consideration the use of the probabilistic oracle, described above, gives us an opportunity to develop
an algorithm, which produces a right answer with the probability not
less than $1-e^{-\theta t}$, where t is the time of computation and θ is a
positive constant;

2) for implementation of such an algorithm the oracle is to be
good enough, i.e. the probabilities of its correct answers must be
greater than some threshold values, besides that, the winnings in
the game have to be gained not in the only way (i.e. the number of
winning moves is to be greater than one);

3) the calculation of the model evaluations due to Zermelo's
formula can be replaced by calculations due to more complicated
formulas, reflecting probabilistic assumptions about the game, and
the values of thresholds can be improved (these results are due to
N.E.Kosach'ova).

The qualitative character of the results remains unchanged for
models, more like to the real games. Namely,

1) one can abandon the independence of values of the estimator
functions and to accept more a realistic assumption about the positive correlation of the values of the estimator function before and
after the move;

2) the assumption about the uniform character of the game (the
same number of moves in every position etc.) can be replaced by the
assumption that there is given the probability of the number of
moves and so on;

3) one can treat the case, when f and Z have as the values not

only 0 and 1, but also all the intermediate reals;

4) one can add substantial characteristics such as the sharpness of position, being of the end-game type and so on, which the considered probabilities will depend on.

Acknowledgements. We thank A.P.Ershov, who stimulated this paper to be written by having invited us to Urgench symposium dedicated to Al-Khwarizmi. We are also thankful to S.Yu.Maslov for useful discussions.

REFERENCES

1. Rogers H. Theory of recursive functions and effective computability. - McGraw Hill Co., 1967.

2. Слисенко А.О. Сложностные задачи теории вычислений. - М. 1979 (Препринт/Научн. совет по компл. проблеме "Кибернетика" АН СССР).

3. Fischer M.J., Rabin M.O. Super-exponential complexity of Presburger arithmetic. -In: Complexity Comput.: SIAM-AMS Proc., v.7, Providence, 1974, p. 27-41.

4. Cook S.A. The complexity of theorem-proving procedures. -In: Conf. Rec. 3d Annu. ACM Symp. Theory Comput., Shaker Heights, 1971, p. 151-158.

5. Aho A.V., Hopcroft J.E., Ullman J.D. The design and analysis of computer algorithms. - London a.o.: Addison Wesley, 1974.

6. Garey M.R., Johnson D.S., Tarjan R.E. The planar Hamiltonian circuit problem is NP-complete. - SIAM J. Comput., 1976, v.5, no.4, p. 704-714.

7. Land A.H., Doig A.G. An automatic method of solving discrete programming problems. - Econometrica, 1960, v.28, no.3, p. 497-520.

8. Слисенко А.О. Финитный подход к задаче оптимизации алгорифмов установления выводимости. - Записки научн. семинаров Ленингр. отд. Матем. ин-та АН СССР, 1975, т.49, с. 123-130.

9. Lewis H.R. Complexity of solvable cases of decision problem for the predicate calculus. -In: IEEE 19th Annu. Symp. Found. Comput. Sci., Ann Arbor, 1978, p. 35-47.

10. Матросов В.М., Васильев С.Н., Каратуев В.Г., Новиков М.А., Суменков Е.А., Ядыкин С.А. Машинный вывод теорем о динамических свойствах с вектор-функциями Ляпунова. - Кибернетика, 1979, №2, с. 27-36.

11. Калужнин Л.А., Стогний А.А. Теория и практика применения ЭВМ в алгебраических исследованиях. - В кн.: Вычисления в алгебре и комбинаторике, Киев, 1978, с. 3-40.

12. Стругацкий А.Н., Стругацкий Б.Н. Понедельник начинается в субботу. - В кн.: Библиотека современной фантастики, т.7, М., 1966.

13. Corneil D.G., Gotlieb C.C. An efficient algorithm for graph isomorphism. - J. Assoc. Comput. Mach., 1970, v.17, no.1, p. 51-64.

14. Slisenko A.O. Computational complexity of string and graph identification. -In: Lect. Notes Comput. Sci., 1979, v.74, p. 182-190.

15. Адельсон-Вельский Г.М., Диниц Е.А., Карзанов А.В. Потоковые алгоритмы. - М.: Наука, 1975.

16. Galil Z., Naamad A. Network flow and generalized path compression. -In: Proc. 11th Annu. ACM Symp. Theory Comput., Atlanta, 1979, p. 13-26.

17. Hačijan L.G. A polynomial algorithm in linear programming. - Soviet Math. Dokl., 1979, v.20, no.1, p. 191-194.

18. Келлен Дж. Календарное планирование. - В кн.: Экономические модели в управлении. М., 1967.

19. Маслов С.Ю. Информация в исчислении и рационализация переборов. - Кибернетика, 1979, №2, с. 20-26.

20. Sahni S., Gonzales T. P-complete problems and approximate solutions. -In: IEEE 15th Annu. Symp. Switch. and Automata Theory, New Orleans, 1974, p. 28-31.

21. Ibarra O.H., Kim C.E. Fast approximation algorithm for the knapsack and sum of subset problems. - J. Assoc. Comput. Mach., 1975, v.22, no.4, p. 463-468.

22. Christofides N. Worst-case analysis of a new heuristic for the traveling salesman problem. -In: Algorithms and complexity: New directions and recent results, ed. J.Traub. New York a.o., Academic Press, 1976, p. 441.

23. Нигматуллин Р.Г. Сложность приближенного решения комбинаторных задач. - Докл. АН СССР, 1975, т.224, №2, с. 289-292.

24. Диниц Е.А., Карзанов А.В. Булева задача оптимизации при ограничениях одного знака. М., 1978, - 42 с. (Препринт/ВНИИ системных исследований).

25. Yao A.C.-C. Probabilistic computations: toward a unified measure of complexity. -In: IEEE 18th Annu. Symp. Found. Comput. Sci., Providence, 1977, p. 222-227.

26. Lueker G.S. Maximization problems on graphs with edge weights chosen from a normal distribution. -In: Proc. 10th Annu. ACM Symp. Theory Comput., San Diego, 1978, p. 13-19.

27. Гимади Э.Х., Глебов Н.И., Перепелица В.А. Алгоритмы с оценками для задач дискретной оптимизации. - В кн.: Проблемы кибернетики, М., 1976, вып.31, с. 35-42.

28. Angluin D., Valiant L.G.   Fast probabilistic algorithms for
    Hamiltonian circuits and matching. - Edinburgh, 1977, - 59 p.
    (Univ. of Edinburgh, Dept. Comput. Sci., CSR-17-77).

29. Solovay R., Strassen V.   A fast Monte-Carlo test for primality.
    - SIAM J. Comput., 1977, v.6, no.1, p. 84-85.

30. Адельсон-Вельский Г.М., Арлазаров В.Л., Донской М.В. Программи-
    рование игр. - М.: Наука, 1978.

31. Zermelo E.   Uber eine Anwendung der Mengenlehre auf die Theorie
    des Schachspiel. -In: 5th Intern. Congress Mathem., Cambridge,
    v.2, 1912, p. 501.

32. Shannon C.   Chess playing machine. - The world of math., 1956,
    no.4, p. 2124-2134.

33. Shannon C.   Game playing machines. - J. Franklin Inst., 1955,
    v.260, no.6, p. 447-453.

The Algorithmic Complexity of Linear Algebras

Dedicated to Al-Khowarizmi

by A. Alder and V. Strassen, University of Zürich

Abstract: The complexity $L(A)$ of a finite dimensional associative algebra A is the number of non-scalar multiplications/divisions of an optimal algorithm to compute the product of two elements of the algebra. We show

$$L(A) \geq 2 \cdot \dim A - t,$$

where t is the number of maximal two-sided ideals of A.

1. Introduction

Let k be a field. To avoid complications with the model of computation, we assume k to be infinite. Let $x_1, \ldots, x_n$ be indeterminates over k. Following Ostrowski (1954) we have:

Definition 1: A sequence of rational functions $g_1, \ldots, g_r \in k(x_1, \ldots, x_n)$ is called a computation sequence, if for any $\rho \leq r$ there are $u_\rho, v_\rho \in k + kx_1 + \ldots + kx_n + kg_1 + \ldots + kg_{\rho-1}$, such that

$$g_\rho = u_\rho \cdot v_\rho \quad \text{or} \quad g_\rho = u_\rho / v_\rho .$$

(In the latter case $v_\rho \neq 0$ is assumed.)

Definition 2: Let $f_1, \ldots, f_q \in k(x_1, \ldots, x_n)$. The complexity $L(f_1, \ldots, f_q)$ of $f_1, \ldots, f_q$ is the smallest number r with the following property: There exists a computation sequence $g_1, \ldots, g_r$, such that for all $i \leq q$

$$f_i \in k + kx_1 + \ldots + kx_n + kg_1 + \ldots + kg_r .$$

The idea of this model is to allow linaer operations, such as additions, subtractions and scalar multiplications at no cost and to minimize the number of multiplications/divisions. The indeterminates $x_1, \ldots, x_n$ represent the inputs. (For details see Borodin-Munro (1975).)

In this paper we mean by an algebra A always a finite dimensional associative algebra with 1. Let $e_1, \ldots, e_n$ be a basis of the vectorspace A,

$$e_i \cdot e_j = \sum_{\ell=1}^{n} \tau_{ij\ell} \, e_\ell$$

with $\tau_{ij\ell} \in k$. Then we have

$$(\sum_{i=1}^{n} \xi_i e_i) \cdot (\sum_{j=1}^{n} \eta_j e_j) = \sum_{\ell=1}^{n} (\sum_{i,j=1}^{n} \tau_{ij\ell} \xi_i \eta_j) e_\ell .$$

Definition 3: The complexity of A is

$$L(A) = L(\{\sum_{i,j=1}^{n} \tau_{ij\ell} x_i y_j : 1 \leq \ell \leq n\}),$$

where $\sum\limits_{i,j=1}^{n} \tau_{ij\ell} x_i y_j \in k(x_1,\ldots,x_n,y_1,\ldots,y_n)$.

It can be seen immediately that L(A) does not depend on the chosen basis and that it is invariant under isomorphisms. Moreover the complexity does not increase when one replaces an algebra by a subalgebra or a homomorphic image and one always has

$$L(A \times B) \le L(A) + L(B).$$

If dimA = n then

$$L(A) \ge n$$

with equality if $A \cong k^n$. (Strassen (1973); actually these facts are stated and proved there for rank, not for complexity.)

The study of the interplay between algebraic and algorithmic aspects of algebras, as represented by structure theory and complexity theory, seems to be a suitable theme to honour Al-Khowarizmi with whom the words algebra and algorithm originated.

Several authors noted L($\mathbb{C}$) = 3, where $\mathbb{C}$ is considered as algebra over the reals. Fiduccia-Zalcstein (1977) proved that for a division algebra A

(1) $$L(A) \ge 2 \cdot \text{dimA} - 1.$$

They also showed that one has equality whenever A is a simple field extension. One does not always have equality, however. Dobkin (1973), de Groote (1975), Lafon-Howell (1975) and Stoss (1979) proved

(2) $$L \text{ (real quaternions)} = 8.$$

A subject of great importance is the study of the complexity of the full matrix algebra M_n or equivalent the complexity of matrix multiplication. An older result

$$L(M_{2q}) \le 7^q, \quad L(M_n) = O(n^{2.81})$$

by Strassen (1969) has recently been improved by Pan (1978, 1980), Bini-Capovani-Lotti-Romani (1979), Bini (1979), Schönhage (1979, 1980), Pan (1979, 1980) to

$$L(M_n) = O(n^{2.52}).$$

As to lower bounds, Hopcroft-Kerr (1971) and Winograd (1971) show

$$L(M_2) = 7$$

and Brockett-Dobkin (1978) and Lafon-Winograd (1980) give the general lower bound

(3) $$L(M_n) \geq 2n^2-1.$$

There is also some knowledge about non-semisimple algebras. Let the nullalgebra have basis $1, e_2, \ldots, e_n$ where $e_i \cdot e_j = 0$ for all i, j. Then

(4) $$L \text{ (nullalgebra)} = 2n-1.$$

A beautiful result by Fiduccia-Zalcstein (1977) and Winograd (1977) gives the complexity of an algebra that is generated by a single element: Let $f \in k[t]$ be a non-zero polynomial of degree n with m different prime-factors. Then

(5) $$L(k[t]/(f)) = 2n-m.$$

Although the proofs of the lower bounds quoted above differ greatly from each other they all use the so-called substitution method (Pan 1966) as a basic ingredient. This suggests that one should try to unify them by a single result. The following theorem, proved in section 2, almost achieves this goal.

Theorem: Let A be any algebra. Then $L(A) \geq 2 \cdot \dim A$ - number of maximal two-sided ideals of A.

Since division algebras and full matrix algebras as well as the nullalgebra have only one maximal two-sided ideal, we get (1), (3) and (4). Since the number of maximal ideals of $k[t]/(f)$ equals the number of different primefactors of f we get the lower bound of (5). (The upper bound follows easily from the chinese remainder theorem.) Only the result on quaternions (2) is not a consequence. On the other hand there are of course numerous new applications of which we give just one example:

Let $k = \mathbb{C}$. If G is a finite abelian group of order g, $\mathbb{C}[G]$ its group algebra, then obviously

$$L(\mathbb{C}[G]) = L(\mathbb{C}^g) = g$$

Let D_{2n} be the dihedral group of order $2n$. Then our theorem implies

$$L(\mathbb{C}[D_{2n}]) = \begin{cases} (7n-3)/2 & n \text{ odd} \\ (7n-6)/2 & n \text{ even} \end{cases}$$

For if n is odd we have (using character theory)

$$\mathbb{C}[D_{2n}] \simeq \mathbb{C}^2 \times M_2(\mathbb{C})^{(n-1)/2},$$

if n is even we have

$$\mathbb{C}[D_{2n}] \cong \mathbb{C}^4 \times M_2(\mathbb{C})^{n/2-1}.$$

2. Proofs

Multiplication in an algebra A is a bilinear map $A \times A \to A$. We will have to consider the computational complexity of slightly more general maps, namely homogeneous quadratic maps.

<u>Definition 4</u>: Let E, W be finite dimensional k-vectorspaces with bases $e_1, \ldots, e_n$ resp. $\hat{e}_1, \ldots, \hat{e}_q$. A map

$$f: E \to W$$

is called quadratic, if there are quadratic forms $f_1, \ldots, f_q$ in $k[x_1, \ldots, x_n]$ such that for all $\xi_1, \ldots, \xi_n \in k$

$$f(\sum_{j=1}^{n} \xi_i e_i) = \sum_{\ell=1}^{q} f_\ell(\xi_1, \ldots, \xi_n) \hat{e}_\ell.$$

We call

$$L(f) = L(f_1, \ldots, f_q)$$

the complexity of f. ($f_1, \ldots, f_q$ are considered here as elements of $k(x_1, \ldots, x_n)$.)

The notion of a quadratic map and the complexity of f does not depend on the chosen bases. If $\varphi: E' \to E$, $\psi: W \to W'$ are linear maps then $\psi \circ f \circ \varphi$ is again quadratic and

(6) $$L(f) \geq L(\psi \circ f \circ \varphi).$$

<u>Proposition</u>: Let

$$f: E \to W$$

be a quadratic map. Then $L(f) \leq r$ iff there are u_ρ, $v_\rho \in E^*$, $w_\rho \in W(\rho=1,\ldots,r)$ such that for all $x \in E$

$$f(x) = \sum_{\rho=1}^{r} u_\rho(x) \cdot v_\rho(x) \cdot w_\rho,$$

where E^* denotes the dual of E.

The proof of this proposition is well known and follows from the fact that sets of quadratic forms can optimally be computed without division. (See Strassen 1973 .)

The next Lemma collects a few facts about algebras, which will be needed later. They are all immediate consequences of the classical structure theory of Wedderburn. If A is an algebra we denote by radA the radical of A.

Lemma 1:

(7) A and A/radA have the same number of maximal two-sided ideals.

(8) A/radA is semisimple.

(9) Any left ideal of a semisimple algebra has a complement which is a left ideal. Similarly for right ideals.

(10) Any semisimple algebra is a finite direct product of simple algebras.

(11) If A is simple, L resp. R are minimal left resp. right ideals, then

$$\dim L = \dim R.$$

(12) If A is simple, $x \in A$ and R a non-zero right ideal such that $ax = 0$ for all $a \in R$, then $x = 0$. Similarly, if L is a non-zero left ideal such that $xa = 0$ for all $a \in L$, then $x = 0$.

We divide the major part of the proof of the theorem into two lemmas.

Lemma 2: Let A, B be algebras. Then

$$L(A \times B) \geq L((A/radA) \times B) + 2 \cdot \dim(radA)$$

Proof: We will show

$$L(A) \geq L(A/radA) + 2 \cdot \dim(radA).$$

(Taking into account B is then trivial.)

Let $L(A) = r$. Then there are u_ρ, $v_\rho \in (A \times A)^*$, $w_\rho \in A$ such that for all $a, b \in A$

(13) $\qquad a \cdot b = \sum_{\rho=1}^{r} u_\rho(a,b) \cdot v_\rho(a,b) \cdot w_\rho.$

Let $q = \dim(radA)$. It suffices to find a representation (13) with the additional property that

(14) $u_1, \ldots, u_{2q}$ are linearly independent on $radA \times radA$. (In particular $2q \leq r$.)

For assume (14) and let

$$E = \{u_1 = \ldots = u_{2q} = 0\} \subset A \times A$$

and

$$f: E \to A$$

be the restriction of the multiplication. f is a quadratic map with

(15) $\qquad\qquad L(f) \leq r - 2q.$

(For $f(a,b) = \sum_{\rho=2q+1}^{r} u_\rho(a,b) \cdot v_\rho(a,b) \cdot w_\rho$ on E.)

Let μ resp. μ' be the multiplication on A resp. A/radA. The commutative diagram

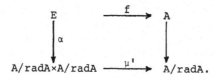

yields (by restriction) a commutative diagram

$$
\begin{array}{ccc}
E & \xrightarrow{\ f\ } & A \\
\downarrow{\alpha} & & \downarrow \\
A/radA \times A/radA & \xrightarrow{\ \mu'\ } & A/radA.
\end{array}
$$

Since E∩(radA×radA) = 0 α is an isomorphism. Then

$$
\begin{array}{ccc}
E & \xrightarrow{\ f\ } & A \\
\uparrow{\alpha^{-1}} & & \downarrow \\
A/radA \times A/radA & \xrightarrow{\ \mu'\ } & A/radA
\end{array}
$$

commutes. By (6) and (15) we therefore have

$$L(A/radA) = L(\mu') \leq L(f) \leq r-2q = L(A)-2\cdot\dim(radA).$$

This shows that it is sufficient to have (13) with the property (14).

We claim that this can be achieved by permuting the terms of the sum (13) and by interchanging some u_ρ with v_ρ.
Otherwise there exists p<2q, p≤r such that w.l.o.g.

(16) $u_1,\ldots,u_p$ are linearly independent on radA×radA,
$u_{p+1},\ldots,u_r,\ v_{p+1},\ldots,v_r$ are linearly dependent on
$u_1,\ldots,u_p$ as linear forms on radA×radA.

Since p<2q there are x,y ∈ radA, not both equal to 0, such that $u_1(x,y) =\ldots= u_p(x,y) = 0$, and therefore by (16)

$$u_1(x,y) =\ldots= u_r(x,y) = v_{p+1}(x,y) =\ldots= v_r(x,y) = 0.$$

We fix such a pair (x,y) for the following discussion.
If a,b ∈ A, $u_1(a,b) =\ldots= u_p(a,b) = 0$ we have

(17)
$$(a+x)(b+y) = \sum_{\rho=1}^{r} u_\rho(a+x,b+y)\cdot v_\rho(a+x,b+y)\cdot w_\rho$$

$$= \sum_{\rho=1}^{r} (u_\rho(a,b)+u_\rho(x,y))\cdot(v_\rho(a,b)+v_\rho(x,y))\cdot w_\rho$$

$$= \sum_{\rho=p+1}^{r} u_\rho(a,b)\cdot v_\rho(a,b)\cdot w_\rho$$

$$= a\cdot b$$

If $a,b \in A$ are arbitrary we use the linear independence of $u_1,\ldots,u_p$ on $\mathrm{rad}A \times \mathrm{rad}A$ to find $s,t \in \mathrm{rad}A$ such that

$$\forall i \le p \quad u_i(s,t) = -u_i(a,b).$$

Then

$$u_1(a+s,b+t) = \ldots = u_p(a+s,b+t) = 0.$$

Together with (17) we get the following.

(18)   If $a,b \in A$ then there are $s,t \in \mathrm{rad}A$ such that
$$(a+s)(b+t) = (a+s+x)(b+t+y).$$

For some $i \ge 1$ we have

$$x,y \in (\mathrm{rad}A)^i \text{ and } x \notin (\mathrm{rad}A)^{i+1} \quad (\text{say}).$$

Taking $a=0$, $b=1$ in (18) we get

$$s(1+t) = (s+x)(1+t+y),$$

therefore

$$x = -x(t+y)-sy \in (\mathrm{rad}A)^{i+1},$$

a contradiction.

<u>Lemma 3</u>: Let A,B be algebras, A simple. Then

$$L(A \times B) \ge 2 \cdot \mathrm{dim}A - 1 + L(B).$$

<u>Proof</u>: As in the preceding lemma we content ourselves with showing

$$L(A) \ge 2 \, \mathrm{dim}A - 1.$$

Let

$$\mathrm{dim}A = n$$
$$L(A) = r.$$

Then there are u_ρ, $v_\rho \in (A \times A)^*$, $w_\rho \in A$ such that

(19) $\forall a,b \in A \quad a \cdot b = \sum\limits_{\rho=1}^{r} u_\rho(a,b) \cdot v_\rho(a,b) \cdot w_\rho.$

Let

$$A = R_1 \oplus R_2,$$

where R_1, R_2 are right ideals, R_1 minimal.
Put

$$\mathrm{dim} \, R_1 = m,$$

thus

$$\mathrm{dim} \, R_2 = n-m.$$

(i) It is clear that $w_1, \ldots, w_r$ generate A. Therefore $r \geq n$ and w.l.o.g. we can assume that $w_1, \ldots, w_{m-1}$ are linearly independent and that, taking

$$W = kw_1 + \ldots + kw_{m-1}$$

we have

(20) $$W \cap R_2 = 0.$$

$(w_1, \ldots, w_{m-1}$ are to chosen such that $w_1 + R_2, \ldots, w_{m-1} + R_2$ are linearly independent in A/R_2.)

Let

$$\pi : A \rightarrow R_1$$

be the projection along R_2.

$$(\pi(W) : R_1) = \{a : R_1 a \subset \pi(W)\}$$

is a left ideal $\neq A$ and therefore it is contained in a maximal left ideal L_2. Let L_1 be a complementary left ideal. Then

$$A = L_1 \oplus L_2$$

and by lemma 1

$$\dim L_1 = m$$
$$\dim L_2 = n-m.$$

If $n = m$ omit the next two steps of the proof.

(ii) We claim that w.l.o.g. $u_m, \ldots, u_{n-1}$ are linearly independent on $0 \times L_2$:

We proceed as in the proof of lemma 2 and try to achieve the stated linear independence by permuting the terms $\rho = m, \ldots, r$ of the sum (19) and by interchanging some u_ρ with v_ρ for $\rho \geq m$. Failure would yield a p such that $m - 1 \leq p < n - 1$ and w.l.o.g.

(21)
$$u_m, \ldots, u_p \text{ are linearly independent on } 0 \times L_2.$$
$$u_{p+1}, \ldots, u_r, v_{p+1}, \ldots, v_r \text{ are linearly dependent on}$$
$$u_m, \ldots, u_p \text{ as linear forms on } 0 \times L_2.$$

Since $p-m+1 < n-m = \dim L_2$ we can choose

(22) $$y \in L_2, \ y \neq 0$$

such that $u_m(0,y) = \ldots = u_p(0,y) = 0$, and therefore by (21)

$$u_m(0,y) = \ldots = u_r(0,y) = v_{p+1}(0,y) = \ldots = v_r(0,y) = 0.$$

If $a,b \in A$, $u_m(a,b) = \ldots = u_p(a,b) = 0$ we have

$$a(b+y) = \sum_{\rho=1}^{r} (u_\rho(a,b) + u_\rho(0,y))(v_\rho(a,b) + v_\rho(0,y)) \cdot w_\rho$$

$$= \sum_{\rho=1}^{r} u_\rho(a,b) \cdot v_\rho(a,b) \cdot w_\rho + \tilde{w} = a \cdot b + \tilde{w},$$

where $\tilde{w} \in k \cdot w_1 + \ldots + k \cdot w_{m-1} = W$, i.e.

(23) $\qquad\qquad ab - a(b+y) \in W.$

We do not simplify the term on the left side of (23) since our present discussion will serve as a model for cases (iii) and (iv).

If $a,b \in A$ are arbitrary we use the linear independence of $u_m, \ldots, u_p$ on $O \times L_2$ to find $t \in L_2$ such that

$$u_m(a,b+t) = \ldots = u_p(a,b+t) = 0.$$

Together with (23) we get

(24) $\qquad \forall a,b \in A \; \exists \; t \in L_2 \qquad a(b+t) - a(b+t+y) \in W.$

Using (20) this implies

$$\forall a \in R_2 \qquad a \cdot y \in W \cap R_2 = 0,$$

which is impossible by lemma 1 and (22).

(iii) W.l.o.g. $u_m, \ldots, u_{2n-m-1}$ are linearly independent on $R_2 \times L_2$ (in particular $r \geq 2n-m-1$):

Otherwise we proceed as in (ii), leaving the first $n-1$ terms of the sum (19) fixed. We get

$$x \in R_2, \; y \in L_2, \; x \neq 0$$

such that

$$\forall a,b \in A \; \exists \; s \in R_2, \; t \in L_2 \qquad (a+s)(b+t)-(a+s+x)(b+t+y) \in W.$$

(Compare (24). The case $x = 0$, $y \neq 0$ is not possible since $u_m(0,y) = \ldots = u_{n-1}(0,y) = 0$ implies $y = 0$ by (ii).) We choose $a = 0$, $b \in L_1$. Then

$$x(b+t+y) + sy \in W.$$

Since $x,s \in R_2$ using (20) we have

$$xb + x(t+y) + sy = 0$$

and because of $t,y \in L_2$, $b \in L_1$ we get

$$xb \in L_1 \cap L_2 = 0.$$

Since $b \in L_1$ is arbitrary we get $x = 0$ by lemma 1, a contradiction.

(iv) W.l.o.g. $u_m, \ldots, u_{2n-1}$ are linearly independent on $R_2 \times A$ (In particular $r \geq 2n-1$, which is the assertion of the lemma.): Otherwise there exist

$$x \in R_2, \; y \in A, \; y \notin L_2$$

such that

$$\forall a,b \in A \quad \exists s \in R_2, \ t \in A$$

$$(a+s)(b+t) - (a+s+x)(b+t+y) \in W.$$

This time, the first $2n-m-1$ terms of (19) are to be held fixed. We choose $a \in R_1$, $b = 0$. Then

$$(a+s)y + x(t+y) \in W,$$

therefore

$$\pi((a+s)y + x(t+y)) = ay \in \pi(W).$$

Since $a \in R_1$ is arbitrary we get

$$y \in (\pi(W): R_1) \subset L_2,$$

a contradiction.

Proof of the theorem:

Let

$$A/\mathrm{rad}A \cong A_1 \times \ldots \times A_t$$

where $A_1, \ldots, A_t$ are simple algebras. Then

$$L(A) \geq L(A_1 \times \ldots \times A_t) + 2 \cdot \dim(\mathrm{rad}A)$$

(by lemma 2)

$$\geq \sum_{i=1}^{t} (2 \dim A_i - 1) + 2 \cdot \dim(\mathrm{rad}A)$$

(by lemma 3 using induction)

$$= 2 \cdot \dim A - t$$
$$= 2 \cdot \dim A - \text{number of maximal two-sided ideals of } A/\mathrm{rad}A$$
$$= 2 \cdot \dim A - \text{number of maximal two-sided ideals of } A.$$

Our proof of the theorem actually shows the following more general result:

If A, B are algebras, then

$$L(A \times B) \geq L(B) + 2 \cdot \dim A - \text{number of maximal ideals of } A.$$

This even holds if B is replaced by an arbitrary quadratic map.

Acknowledgment: Walter Baur contributed to the proof of lemma 2 and we kindly thank him for this.

References

D. Bini, M. Capovani, G. Lotti and F. Romani 1979, $O(n^{2.7799})$ complexity
for matrix multiplication. Information Proc. Letters 8, pp. 234-235.

D. Bini 1979, Relations between EC-algorithms and APA-algorithms,
applications.
Nota interna B79/8 (March 1979) I.E.I. Pisa.

A. Borodin and I. Munro 1975, The Computational Complexity of Algebraic
and Numeric Problems. American Elsevier.

R.W. Brockett and D. Dobkin 1978, On the optimal evaluation of a set
of bilinear forms.
Linear Algebra and its Applications 19, pp. 207-235.

D. Dobkin 1973, On the arithmetic complexity of a class of arithmetic
computations. Thesis, Harvard University.

C.M. Fiduccia and I. Zalcstein 1977, Algebras having linear multiplicative complexity. Journal of the ACM 24, pp. 311-331.

H.F. de Groote 1978, On varieties of optimal algorithms for the computation of bilinear mappings II. Optimal algorithms for 2×2-matrix
multiplication.
Theoretical Computer Science 7, pp. 127-148.

J. Hopcroft and L. Kerr 1971, On minimizing the number of multiplications
necessary for matrix multiplication.
SIAM J. Applied Math. 20. pp. 30-36.

T.D. Howell and J.C. Lafon 1975, The complexity of the quaternion
product. Cornell University TR 75-245.

J.C. Lafon and S. Winograd 1980, to appear.

A.M. Ostrowski 1954, On two problems in abstract algebra connected with
Horner's rule. Studies presented to R. von Mises, Academic Press,
New York, pp. 40-48.

V. Ya. Pan 1978, Strassen's algorithm is not optimal. Proc. 19th Ann.
Symp. on Foundations of Computer Science, pp. 166-176.

V. Ya. Pan 1980, New Fast Algorithms for Matrix Operations. SIAM J. on
Computing, 9/2, pp. 321-342.

V. Ya. Pan 1979, Field Extension and Trilinear Aggregating, Uniting
and Cancelling for the Acceleration of Matrix Multiplication, Proc.
20th Ann. Symp. on Foundations of Computer Science, pp. 28-38.

V.Ya. Pan 1980, New Combination of Methods for the Acceleration of Matrix Multiplication. Preprint, State University of New York at Albany.

A. Schönhage 1979, Partial and Total Matrix Multiplication. TR, Mathematisches Institut der Universität Tübingen, June 1979.

A. Schönhage 1980, Partial and Total Matrix Multiplication. TR, Math. Inst. Univ. Tübingen (January 1980). To appear.

H.J. Stoss 1979, Private communication.

V. Strassen 1969, Gaussian Elimination is not Optimal. Numer. Math. 13, pp. 354-356.

V. Strassen 1973, Vermeidung von Divisionen. J. für reine und angew. Mathematik 264, pp. 184-202.

S. Winograd 1971, On multiplication of 2×2 matrices. Linear Algebra Appl. 4, pp. 381-388.

S. Winograd 1977, Some bilinear forms whose multiplicative complexity depends on the field of constants. Math. Systems Theory 10, pp. 169-180.

Algorithms in Various Contexts

Stephen C. Kleene
The University of Wisconsin
Madison, Wis., U.S.A.

This paper responds to some of the "more specific remarks" by potential participants quoted in a circular letter from Andrei Ershov[*].

1. Uspenski asked whether the concept of algorithm can "be defined in terms of other standard (say, set-theoretic) mathematical notions" or "is essentially independent and primary".

In any context in which a version of Church's thesis is accepted, the thesis gives an equivalent of each algorithm. These equivalents are defined in standard mathematics. This seems worth remarking, although it does not directly answer Uspenski's query.

2. Skordev asked, "Is it possible to formulate an appropriate generalization of the Church thesis which would embrace ... computability with probabilistic and nondeterministic devices?"

To limit my response, I will confine it to algorithms for a function of a natural number variable $\underline{a}$ with natural numbers as its values.

The simplest case is that the nondeterministic device operates exactly once in each computation, giving to the computation a natural-number input which is independent of the computational situation. Then the computation simply gives a function $\phi_{\underline{t}}(\underline{a}) = \phi(\underline{a}, \theta(\underline{t}))$, where $\phi(\underline{a}, \underline{b})$ is a computable function of two number variables, $\underline{t}$ is a variable ranging over the various "runs" or "trials" of the computation, and $\theta(\underline{t})$ is the natural number which the device feeds into the computation in the trial $\underline{t}$. With a given such algorithm, as embodied in the function $\phi(\underline{a}, \underline{b})$, one could study the distribution as $\underline{t}$ varies of the outputs $\phi_{\underline{t}}(\underline{a})$ as it depends, for a given $\underline{a}$, on the distribution function θ of the device.

A more complicated situation is that the device may give inputs to a computation zero, one or more (but, of course, only finitely many) times, the interventions of the device being triggered by computational situations, but the device being oblivious of them in its input. We can represent this by a modification of a Turing oracle-machine (about which I will say more presently, in responding to Tseitin), which has

[*]See editors' foreword - Eds.

among its configurations (scanned-square conditions paired with machine states) one or more in which the act is to ask the device, "What natural number is your whim at this moment?" At the next moment $m+1$, the device's whim-of-the-moment-m w_t shall be represented on the tape by w_t+1 tallies preceded and followed by blank squares, these w_t+3 squares being immediately to the right of the square that was scanned at the moment m, with the rightmost of the w_t+1 tallies scanned, and with all printing that existed at the moment m to the right of the square scanned then displaced w_t+3 squares to the right. I think of t as having some range, so $w_t = \theta(t)$ with θ the distribution function for the device. I am adapting the treatment on the middle of p. 362 of my book "Introduction to Metamathematics", 1952 (hereafter "IM"). I shall not pursue the analysis of this. At least, I think we have an acceptable formulation.

Similarly (differently adapting IM p. 362), we can formulate computation wherein the machine in zero or more situations queries the device with natural numbers $b_1,\ldots,b_n$, and the device responds with $\alpha_t(b_1,\ldots,b_n)$ where the function α_t varies nondeterministically with the run of the computation and the moment of the query.

3.   Tseitin expressed interest in "relative computability".

Turing (Proc. London Math. Soc., 2, 45, 1939, 161-228, especially 172-173) introduced the idea of a machine which operates with access to an "oracle" who, requested with a b, supplies the answer to a question "$Q(b)$?". Turing dealt with a special class of questions $Q(b)$, called by him "number-theoretic problems". But the idea can be adapted to define when any number-theoretic predicate $P(a)$ is computable relative to any number-theoretic predicate $Q(b)$. More generally (since predicates are representable by functions taking only 0 and 1 as values), we can use number-theoretic functions $\phi(a)$, $\psi(b)$ instead of predicates $P(a)$, $Q(b)$. So we have a definition of the computability of one function ϕ relative to another ψ (IM p. 362). There is an equivalent in terms of general recursiveness (IM p. 266).

I am confining myself here to the number-theoretic context, and to total functions ψ. (This excludes partial functions $\psi(b)$ which are undefined for values of b.) In conjunction with the uniformization to be explained next (responding to Neveipoda), the theory has been developed very much beyond this (e.g. see p. 10 of Kleene, Trans. Amer. Math. Soc., 91, 1959, 1-52).

Neveipoda asked, "What are algorithms on real numbers?"

In Proc. Internat. Congress Math. 1950, 1, 1952, 679-685, I considered (an equivalent of) the computability of $\phi(\underline{a})$ relative to $\psi(\underline{b})$ allowing ψ to vary but with the Turing-machine table fixed. In brief, I took $\phi(a)$ to be computable "uniformly" in $\psi(\underline{b})$ for ψ a variable function, which I then chose to write instead as "α". Thus I defined the computability of a function $\phi(\underline{a},\alpha)$ of one number variable $\underline{a}$ and one one-placed total function variable α. Similarly, for functions $\phi(\underline{a}_1,\ldots,\underline{a}_{n_0}, \alpha_1,\ldots,\alpha_{n_1})$ with any $\underline{n}_0$, $\underline{n}_1$. In particular with $\underline{n}_0 = 0$, $\underline{n}_1 = 1$, we have the definition of a computable function $\phi(\alpha)$ of one function variable. (Actually, I wrote my 1950 Congress paper using the equivalent formulation in terms of general recursiveness.)

A real number $\underline{x}$ can be represented by the function α which gives the sequence of the digits (0's and 1's) in its dual expansion, if $0 \leq x \leq 1$ as we shall assume. (Our discussion is easily extended to the general case, not assuming $0 \leq \underline{x} \leq 1$.) So an algorithm on a real number producing a natural number as value is represented by a computable (or recursive) function $\phi(\alpha)$.

If we want our algorithm to produce a real number, the value is $\lambda\underline{a}\ \phi(a,\alpha)$ where ϕ is a computable function taking only 0 and 1 as values. Similarly, for algorithms on $\underline{n}_1$ real numbers, represented by their dual expansions $\alpha_1,\ldots,\alpha_{\underline{n}}$.

5. Skordev also asked, "Is it possible to formulate an appropriate generalization of the Church thesis which would embrace computability in arbitrary object domains...?"

"Arbitrary object domains" is pretty general. But perhaps an attempt to formulate the theory over sets will go some distance in the desired direction, as mathematicians often take the sets to be an all-embracing domain.

I begin be recalling to you that a very simple formulation of algorithms on the natural numbers is included in the revisitation of my 1959 and 1963 theory (Trans. Amer. Math. Soc., 91, 1-52 and 108, 106-142) which I presented at the 1977 Oslo Symposium, Generalized Recursion Theory II, North-Holland Pub. Co., 1978, 185-222.

I take the variables $\underline{a}$, $\underline{b}$, $\underline{c}$, $\ldots$ to range over the natural numbers, and for the moment $\alpha, \mathscr{b}, \mathscr{c}, \ldots$ to be strings of only such variables (possibly empty). Let θ be a list of assumed partial functions $\theta_1,\ldots,\theta_{\underline{\ell}}$, possibly empty ($\underline{\ell} = 0$), with (for the moment) only natural number variables. A function $\lambda\,\alpha\phi(\theta;\alpha)$ is partial recursive in θ iff it can be computed (in a manner that was explained in my Oslo paper)

with the use of a finite list of equations describing successively
$\phi_1, \ldots, \phi_\ell$ (where $\phi_\ell = \phi$), these equations being chosen from a list of schemata.

The schemata come to mind as follows. First, we need the schemata which give us the constant function 0 and the identity function.

S2.0 $\qquad\qquad \phi(\theta; \alpha) \simeq 0.$

S3 $\qquad\qquad\quad \phi(\theta; \underline{a}, \mathcal{b}) \simeq \underline{a}.$

Then, to find our way around in the natural number sequence, we need schemata for the successor and predecessor functions, as well as to make a choice ("cases") according to whether we are at the begining or not.

S1.0 $\qquad\qquad \phi(\theta; \underline{a}, \mathcal{b}) \simeq \underline{a}' = \underline{a}+1.$

S1.1 $\qquad\qquad \phi(\theta; \underline{a}, \mathcal{b}) \simeq pd(\underline{a}) = \underline{a}-1 = \begin{cases} 0 \text{ if } \underline{a} = 0, \\ \underline{a}-1 \text{ if } \underline{a} > 0. \end{cases}$

S5.1 $\qquad\qquad \phi(\theta; \underline{a}, \underline{b}, \underline{c}, \mathcal{b}) \simeq cs(\underline{a}, \underline{b}, \underline{c}) = \begin{cases} \underline{b} \text{ if } \underline{a} = 0, \\ \underline{c} \text{ if } \underline{a} > 0. \end{cases}$

Thirdly, we need to be able to compose computations, taking the result of one computation as an argument or beginning point for another.

S4.0 $\qquad\qquad \phi(\theta; \alpha) \simeq \psi(\theta; \chi(\theta; \alpha), \alpha).$

In the foregoing schemata, when particular variables had a distinguished role, I took them from the beginning of the list α of all variables. To get by with this, I provide a schema, repeated use of which will enable us to effect any permutation of the variables.

S6.0 $\qquad\qquad \phi(\theta; \alpha) \simeq \psi(\theta; \alpha_1)$

where α results from α_1 by bringing the $\underline{k}$+1-st (number) variable to the front. If the list θ is not empty ($\underline{\ell} > 0$), the functions $\theta_{\underline{t}}$ for $\underline{t} = 1, \ldots, \underline{\ell}$ need to be introduced.

S0 $\qquad\qquad \phi(\theta; \mathcal{b}, \mathcal{L}) \simeq \theta_{\underline{t}}(\mathcal{b}).$

Lastly, I provide what in IM p. 348 I called "the first recursion theorem".

S11 $\qquad\qquad \phi(\theta; \alpha) \simeq \psi(\lambda \, \alpha \phi(\theta; \alpha), \theta; \alpha)$
$\qquad\qquad\qquad\quad [\simeq \psi(\phi, \theta; \alpha) \text{ briefly}].$

This schema gives an absolutely general form of recursion, wherein, for given θ and α, the value $\phi(\theta; \alpha)$ is expressed in terms of θ, α and the function ϕ itself, by means of a previously defined functional $\phi(\eta, \theta; \alpha)$.

Let me digress for a moment. During the Symposium at Urgench,
A. Ershov asked me whether each partial recursive function $\lambda\,\mathcal{O}\!\ell\,\phi(\mathcal{O}\!\ell)$ with
natural number variables $\mathcal{O}\!\ell$ can be obtained by an application of the
first recursion theorem with a suitable primitive recursive functional
$\psi(\eta;\mathcal{O}\!\ell)$ (or in the notation of IM, $F(\zeta;\mathcal{O}\!\ell)$). An affirmative answer to
this question is contained in results of my 1977 Oslo Symposium paper,
if we allow, after the application of the first recursion theorem, the
substitution of a constant for a variable. More generally, any function
$\lambda\,\mathcal{O}\!\ell\,\phi(\Theta;\mathcal{O}\!\ell)$ partial recursive in total functions Θ is obtainable by the
first recursion theorem with a suitable primitive recursive $\psi(\eta,\Theta;\mathcal{O}\!\ell)$
followed by the substitution of a constant for a number variable. For
defining primitive recursive functionals in the Oslo formulation, I
omit the first recursion theorem as a schema S11, and add the schema
of primitive recursion

S5
$$\begin{cases} \phi(\Theta;0,\mathcal{b}) = \psi(\Theta;\mathcal{b}), \\ \phi(\Theta;\underline{a}',\mathcal{b}) = \chi(\Theta;\underline{a},\phi(\Theta;\underline{a},\mathcal{b}),\mathcal{b}), \end{cases}$$

which is redundant (i.e. derivable) in the presence of S11 (Oslo (XII)).
As remarked Oslo top p. 213, this is equivalent to the older definition,
and (I) - (XI) of the Oslo paper hold for primitive recursiveness. By
the enumeration theorem (Oslo (XVI)) and its proof, for any list $\mathcal{O}\!\ell$
of variables (for us, number variables) and any fixed list of total
functions Θ (possibly empty), there is a function $\lambda\underline{z}\,\mathcal{O}\!\ell\{\underline{z}\}^{\Theta}(\mathcal{O}\!\ell)$ which
has the following property and which is defined by an application of
the first recursion theorem with a primitive recursive ψ: for each
partial recursive $\phi(\Theta;\mathcal{O}\!\ell)$, there is a number $\underline{z}$ such that, for all $\mathcal{O}\!\ell$,
$\phi(\Theta;\mathcal{O}\!\ell) = \{\underline{z}\}^{\Theta}(\mathcal{O}\!\ell)$. Substituting (as a constant) $\underline{z}$ for the variable $\underline{z}$
in the function $\lambda\underline{z}\,\mathcal{O}\!\ell\{\underline{z}\}^{\Theta}(\mathcal{O}\!\ell)$ defined by our application of the first recursion theorem, we have the desired result, provided the functions
partial recursive in Θ as characterized in my Oslo paper include (for
total functions Θ and number variables $\mathcal{O}\!\ell$) all which are such under the
usual formulation (e.g. IM § 63). They do, using my normal form theorem
(IM p. 330), since the Oslo theory gives primitive recursion (as (XII))
and the least-number operator (as (XIII)). (Conversely, all functions
of number variables partial recursive in total functions Θ Oslo are
such usually, by the present result using the first recursion theorem
as a theorem of IM.)

Continuing from before the digression, if we add variables of
types 1, 2, 3, ..., where type $\underline{j}+1$ is the one-place total functions
from type $\underline{j}$ to the natural numbers, we add the following schemata for
$\underline{j} = 1, 2, 3, \ldots$.

S4.$\underline{j}$ $\qquad\qquad \phi(\theta;\alpha) \simeq \psi(\theta;\lambda\beta^{\underline{j}-1} \chi(\theta;\beta^{\underline{j}-1},\alpha),\alpha)$.

S6.$\underline{j}$ $\qquad\qquad$ Like S6.0 but advancing a type-$\underline{j}$ variable.

S7.$\underline{j}$ $\qquad\qquad \phi(\theta;\alpha^{\underline{j}},\alpha^{\underline{j}-1},\mathcal{L}) \simeq \alpha^{\underline{j}}(\alpha^{\underline{j}-1})$.

Now the possibility appears of using untyped set variables ρ, σ, τ, ... instead of the type-$\underline{j}$ function variables $\alpha^{\underline{j}}$, $\beta^{\underline{j}}$, $\gamma^{\underline{j}}$, ... for $\underline{j} = 1$, 2, 3, ... I propose then to replace the schemata just given by the following.

S4.s $\qquad\qquad \phi(\theta;\alpha) \simeq \psi(\theta;\lambda\sigma \chi(\theta;\sigma,\alpha),\alpha)$.

S6.s $\qquad\qquad$ Like S6.0 but advancing a set variable.

S7.s $\qquad\qquad \phi(\theta;\sigma,\tau,\mathcal{L}) \simeq |\sigma \, \epsilon \, \tau| = \begin{cases} 0 \text{ if } \sigma \, \epsilon \, \tau, \\ 1 \text{ if } \sigma \, \notin \, \tau. \end{cases}$

For S4.s, ψ is a functional $\psi(\theta;\rho,\alpha)$ with ρ a set variable. In the computations, we assign as values to the set variables members of a fixed non-empty transitive class $\underline{U}$, the "universe" in question. When, for given θ and α , $\lambda\sigma \chi(\theta;\sigma,\alpha)$ is total, I interpret it by the set $\{\sigma \mid \chi(\theta;\sigma,\alpha)=0\}$. This interpretation motivates computation steps by S7.s subsequent to applications of S4.s. The details are analogous to those of the Oslo paper.

I propose the consideration of functions with $\{\emptyset\}$ as an extra argument, i.e. substituted for an extra variable, where $\{\emptyset\}$ is the unit set whose member is the empty set $\emptyset$.

I propose to investigate how many of the previously considered notions of computability (in various domains) can be embraced under this formulation, for various choices of the universe $\underline{U}$.

ROLE OF A NOTION OF ALGORITHM IN THE ARITHMETIC LANGUAGE SEMANTICS

N.A.Shanin

Leningrad Branch Steklov Institute of Mathematics
Fontanka 27,Leningrad 191011,USSR

§ 1. Mathematical activity, even if restricted to a framework of axiomatic (formal-deductive) theories, is usually developed on the basis of some notion of meaning (in other words - semantics) of mathematical sentences formulated by means of a language used in a given particular situation. We shall restrict our attention to situations where one uses first order logico-mathematical languages having individual, function and predicate constants but only one type of variables, namely the individual ones. In mathematical theories with a finite set of possible values for variables (i.e.with a finite individual domain) the intuitive ideas of the meaning of mathematical sentences are made precise in a familiar way using the interpretation of logical connectives $\neg$, $\&$, $\vee$, $\longrightarrow$, $\longleftrightarrow$ as Boolean functions and that of quantifiers $\forall$, $\exists$ as symbols for denoting of finite conjunctions and disjunctions of special forms. When one passes to mathematical theories with infinite individual domains (for example, to arithmetic which has the set of natural numbers as its individual domain) making precise the intuitive ideas of the meaning of sentences is well known to turn into a "hard" question for some reasons of principle. Straightforward extrapolation of the meaning of the quantifiers $\forall$, $\exists$ which is assumed in set-theoretic (called also classical) mathematics and consists essentially in interpreting them as symbols for denoting of "infinite conjunctions" and "infinite disjunctions" of special types, uses the abstraction of actual infinity. The latter is an idealization which was subjected to criticism during the whole history of mathematics, from antiquity up to the present time, as an excessive arbitrariness of human imagination.

Below we discuss only arithmetic languages and only approaches to interpretation of arithmetic sentences keeping the "flight of imagination" in the framework of a more cautious idealization, namely the abstraction of potential realizability (potential infinity). In these approaches the notion of an algorithm plays a fundamental role.

§ 2. In the exposition below we deal mainly with two arithmetic languages: the language $\mathcal{L}^{cl}$ of classical arithmetic and the language $\mathcal{L}^{con}$ of constructive arithmetic. Atomic formulas of both languages are expressions of the form $(\mathcal{U}=\mathcal{V})$, where $\mathcal{U},\mathcal{V}$ are primitive recursive terms obtained in the traditional way from numerals 0, 0I, 0II, 0III,... (to be definite we shall deal with numerals of the unary number system), individual variables and symbols for primitive recursive functions. The language $\mathcal{L}^{cl}$ has $\neg$, &, $\longrightarrow$, $\forall$ as logical connectives. As derived logical connectives one adds classical disjunction $\vee$, classical existence quantifier $\exists$ and equivalence $\longleftrightarrow$:

$$(P\vee Q) \leftharpoondown \neg(\neg P \& \neg Q), \qquad \exists x R \leftharpoondown \neg\forall x \neg R,$$

$$(P\leftrightarrow Q) \leftharpoondown ((P\rightarrow Q)\&(Q\rightarrow P))$$

(the sign $\leftharpoondown$ stands for words « is introduced as a notation for »).

The language $\mathcal{L}^{con}$ is obtained from $\mathcal{L}^{cl}$ by adding the Brouwer's existence quantifier (the quantifier of potential realizability) $\exists$ and adding Brouwer's disjunction $\vee$ as a derived connective: $(P\vee Q) \leftharpoondown \exists x(((x=0)\rightarrow P)\&(\neg(x=0)\rightarrow Q))$ [here x is not free in P,Q] . According to L.E.J.Brouwer the interpretation of a sentence[*) of the form $\exists x R$ is reduced to the interpretation of the condition R via the following stipulation: $\exists x R$ asserts potential realizability of a natural number satisfying the condition R . Production of a "ready-made" natural number N and a demonstration of the sentence $\llcorner R\,{}^{\rho}_{\!N}{}^{x}\lrcorner$ does, of course, constitute a demonstration of the sentence $\exists x R$. (The expression $\llcorner F\,{}^{\rho}_{\!\mathcal{U}}{}^{\alpha}\lrcorner$ for a formula F , an individual variable α and a term $\mathcal{U}$ denotes the result of substituting $\mathcal{U}$ for all free occurrences of α in F). However, in mathematical theories which use the abstraction of potential realizability it is natural to admit also a more abstract kind of a demonstration consisting of (i)a specification (for example in the form of a particular 0-ary recursive function) of a way of developing some constructive process

---

[*) A formula F of a logico-mathematical language is called a sentence if there are no free occurences of variables in F .

and (ii) a demonstration that this process terminates, its result is a natural number and this (potentially realizable) result satisfies the condition R.

A.A.Markov (cf.[1],[2]) paid attention to the following circumstances: if R is an algorithmically decidable condition, then it is not necessary (in principle) to invent a special process of the kind mentioned above to demonstrate the sentence $\exists x R$, because one can always use the process of search for minimal number satisfying the condition R which consists of testing R successively for the numbers $0, 0|, 0||, \ldots$ and which terminates after the first step where the result is affirmative. So if R is an algorithmically decidable condition, then the sentence $\exists x R$ is equivalent to the sentence: the process of search for the minimal root of R terminates.

"Visualisable" meaning of the assertion about termination of some algorithmic process (the process of applying some algorithm to a particular datum) suggests immediately an "absolutely convincing" way of demonstrating such a sentence by actual continuation of the process until the termination step is reached. This way is, however, actually feasible only in the case of a short algoritmic process and, besides, it does not allow extrapolation to sentences asserting completeness (in other words totality) of some algorithm, that is the termination of <u>all</u> algorithmic processes corresponding to data acceptable to a given algorithm. In the mathematical theory of algorithms it is evidently necessary to appeal to criteria having the form of a <u>theoretical prediction</u> concerning termination of an algorithmic process, given some information about the process considered. A.A.Markov formulated the following <u>logical criterion</u>: <u>an algorithmic process terminates if it is not infinitely procee</u>-<u>ding</u> (i.e. if the assumption that the process under consideration proceeds infinitely can be reduced to a contradiction by means of a convincing argument).

If R is an algorithmically testable condition, then the formula $\forall x \neg R$ asserts that the minimal root search process for R goes on arbitrary long. A combination of this remark and the logical criterion formulated above led A.A.Markov to <u>the construc</u>-<u>tive selection principle</u> which can be formulated as follows: <u>given</u> <u>any algorithmically testable condition</u> R, <u>any (convincing) demon</u>-<u>stration of the sentence</u> $\neg \forall x \neg R$ <u>is also a demonstration of</u> $\exists x R$; <u>consequently, the equivalence</u> $(\exists x R \leftrightarrow \exists x R)$

is semantically acceptable.

We single out a class $\mathcal{L}^0$ of "immediately intelligible" formulas of the language $\mathcal{L}^{con}$ consisting of formulas having the form $\exists x \forall y \exists z A$ with A being quantifier-free. It is under-stood that some or all of the quantifiers $\exists x, \forall y, \exists z$ can be absent. In particular any quantifier-free formula belongs to $\mathcal{L}^0$. We consider formulas from $\mathcal{L}^0$ to be immediately intelligible (un-der the abstraction of potential realizability) for the following reasons. Propositional logical connectives in quantifier-free for-mulas are naturally understood as Boolean functions. According to this understanding quantifier-free formulas containing variables turn out to be descriptions of algorithmically testable conditions. This fact and the considerations above enable one to interpret a formula $\exists z A$ in the second of the modes described above, i.e. as a proposition (or a propositional form, if free occurrences of variables are present) of the form «such and such algorithmic pro-cess terminates». Addition of the quantifier $\forall y$ leads to a for-mulation of a generalizing prediction (possibly with occurrences of free variables) concerning the termination of any one of the algo-rithmic processes corresponding to any particular value of the va-riable y . The interpretation of the formula $\exists x \forall y \exists z A$ is reduced to the interpretation of the formula $\forall y \exists z A$ according to the original agreement concerning semantics of $\exists$ (the second mode of the interpretation above is not generally applicable becau-se the latter formula may turn out to express a condition which is not algorithmically testable). The above considerations give us some grounds to consider "situations" described by formulas from the class $\mathcal{L}^0$ as being characterized in a "relatively visualisable way".

The language $\mathcal{L}^{con}$ has in fact great expressive power, des-pite the fact that its set of initial functions is rather "meager" compared to the set of all recursive(here and below recursive means partial recursive) functions and the fact that function variables are absent. One can, for example, model in this language its exten-sion $\mathcal{L}^{con+}$ where symbols for all recursive functions are allo-wed and in which for any natural number n there are function va-riables ranging over all n-ary recursive functions; atomic formu-las of the form $!\Phi$ and $(\Phi \simeq \Psi)$, where Φ and Ψ are re-cursive (in other words partial recursive) terms, are also allowed. Such formulas are read respectively as «the process of computing the value of Φ terminates» and «the value of Φ is conditionally equal to that of Ψ ». Function variables of $\mathcal{L}^{con+}$ can be replaced by individual variables with the help of an algorithmic method for coding (Gödel enumeration) of all words in the alphabet of configurations which are used for representing particular recursive functions. One uses $\{k\}_n$ as symbol for an n-ary recursive function with the Gödel number k (if k is not a Gödel number of any recursive function, then $\{k\}_n$ is considered to represent the totally undefined n-ary recursive function, i.e. the one with nonterminating computation process for any input). Expressions of the form $\{u\}_n$, u being a recursive term, are employed in the language $\mathcal{L}^{con+}$ as functor terms (i.e. ones potentially having as values symbols for particular recursive functions). Details of the translation of $\mathcal{L}^{con+}$ into $\mathcal{L}^{con}$ are "suggested" by S.C.Kleene's normal form theorem for recursive functions (cf.[3], § 63) asserting existence of primitive recursive functions τ_n and ν such that for all values of individual variables $w, t_1, ..., t_n$ we have conditional equality

$$(\{w\}_n (t_1, ..., t_n) \simeq \nu (\mu_s T_n (w, t_1, ..., t_n, s)));$$

here $T_n(w, t_1, ..., t_n, s) \rightleftharpoons (\tau_n(w, t_1, ..., t_n, s) = 0)$ and μ_s stands for the operation of the search for the minimal natural number among the values of the variable s satisfying the condition written to the right of μ_s. In addition, for τ_n we have

$$(T_n(w, t_1, ..., t_n, u) \& T_n(w, t_1, ..., t_n, v)) \rightarrow (u = v)$$

for all the values of the variables.

This theorem, due to S.C.Kleene, "suggests" (together with the constructive selection principle) for example that the translations into the language $\mathcal{L}^{con}$ (and even into the more limited language $\mathcal{L}^{cl}$) of atomic formulas

$$!\{w\} (t_1, ..., t_n) \qquad \text{and} \qquad (\{a\}_1 (t) \simeq \{b\}_1 (t))$$

of $\mathcal{L}^{con+}$ can be defined as

$$\exists u \, T_n (w, t_1, ..., t_n, u)$$

and

$$\left(\exists u\, T_1(a,t,u) \leftrightarrow \exists v\, T_1(b,t,v)\right) \,\&\, \forall u \forall v \left((T_1(a,t,u)\,\&\,T_1(b,t,v)) \rightarrow (v(u)=v(v))\right)$$

respectively.

§ 3. A customary mathematicians "mode of understanding" (mentioned in §1) for sentences formulated in some language of classical arithmetic (say, in $\mathcal{L}^{cl}$) is based on the appeal to the "world of actually infinite sets". It is exactly this mode of understanding that one has in mind when speaking of semantical acceptability of those deductive apparati of classical arithmetic which are actually used. The most commonly used of these deductive apparati (for the cases where the language $\mathcal{L}^{cl}$ is used) consists of the quantifier-free primitive recursive equation calculus (see for example [6]) together with postulated (i.e. axioms and inference rules) of the first order predicate calculus with reference to $\mathcal{L}^{cl}$ for the logical connectives $\urcorner, \&, \rightarrow, \forall$ as well as with some postulate (in the form of an axiom or inference rule) expressing the principle of mathematical induction. This deductive apparatus we shall call the calculus $\mathcal{C}^{cl}$. Semantical acceptability of the calculus $\mathcal{C}^{cl}$ is motivated by an argument appealing to the "world" mentioned above as a source of "intuitive evidence" and leading to the conclusion of the validity of any sentence derivable by means of the deductive apparatus considered.

But "the mode of understanding" of arithmetic sentences based on the abstraction of actual infinity does not satisfy those mathematicians who consider the use of this idealization to be excessive arbitrariness of human imagination. Constructive direction in mathematics (constructive mathematics) which was induced by this critical point of view is putting forward the requirement to restrict the "flight of imagination" to the abstraction of potential realizability as one of the fundamental principles of the theoretical investigation of natural numbers and constructively defined (i.e. given individually by some combinations of signs) objects of other particular types. This restriction is motivated by the wish to pass to the level of notions which are more "realistic" than ones dealt with in Cantor's set theory from the standpoint of knowledge (obtained from the experience) of material sources for the formation of the natural number notion (as well as other constructive mathematical notions). It is natural to ask: what alternatives can constructive direction in mathematics propose to the traditional "mode of understanding" of arithmetic sentences?

In connection with this question let us note first of all that
the term «natural number» is used in the mathematical literature with several meanings. A "signicist" version of understanding
this term is characteristic for the constructive direction in mathematics. Here (as different from set-theoretic version) this term
does not refer to some "abstract objects" to which simultaneous existence in some "world" is ascribed, but rather to potentially realizable combinations of signs of particular type, that is the very
sign combinations which in a more abstract (set-theoretic) version
are called notations for or representations of natural numbers in
some fixed number system (for example unary, decimal etc.). Passing
from one number system to another one leads to a mathematical theory which is equivalent to the original one in all respects except
ones concerning essential specific features of the number systems
used (and in "usual" presentations of arithmetic these features are
dealt with in a section devoted to the properties of representations of natural numbers in specific number systems). So by choosing
a "signicist" version and fixing some particular number system (unary, for example) we are not risking to "impoverish" arithmetic.

A mathematician who "descends" from the level of abstraction
of actual infinity to the level of abstraction of potential realizability faces the problem of "reinterpreting" the language $\mathcal{L}^{cl}$.
When discussing this problem one has to have in mind that the traditional mathematical education develops an impression of "naturalness" and "legitimacy" concerning the widely used deductive apparatus of classical arithmetic. It is advisable therefore to state the
problem of "reinterpreting" of $\mathcal{L}^{cl}$ as one of formulating such a
semantics for this language that would not use the abstraction of
actual infinity and would at the same time be compatible with the
usual deductive apparatus of classical arithmetic (in particular
with $\mathcal{C}^{cl}$), i.e. satisfy the condition: any derivable sentence is
true in the sense of this semantics. But the theorem due to A.Tar-
ski(see for example [4],[5]) concerning the nonarithmetizability of
the notion of true arithmetic sentence[×] warns one that there are obstacles of principle. It says that even such a seemingly moderate
requirement for the semantics (in particular for the mode of expla-
ning it) as the possibility of "singling out" Gödel numbers of true

---

[×] From a correspondence between K.Gödel and E.Zermelo published recently (see [39]) one can see that non-arithmetizability of
the notion of a true arithmetic sentence was known to K.Gödel as
early as 1931.

sentences by means of a condition expressible in $\mathcal{L}^{cl}$ (or even in $\mathcal{L}^{con}$) leads one nowhere: any candidate for the role of the notion «true arithmetic sentence» satisfying some conditions natural for this notion will necessarily turn out to be "bad" from the standpoint of this requirement.

Certain approaches to the "reinterpreting" problem mentioned above began to come into view with the formation process of ideas of intuitionistic mathematics. These ideas are incompatible with the understanding of logical connectives $\longrightarrow$ and $\rceil$ (implication and negation) as Boolean functions. The understanding of implication which came into general use in the intuitionistic mathematics during the initial stages of its formation, was "induced" by the mode of introduction and elimination of this logical connective in the processes of natural deduction (which include, in general, introduction and elimination of assumptions). This understanding of implication can be roughly explained as follous: a sentence of the form $(P \longrightarrow Q)$ is understood as asserting the possibility of demonstrating (in some constructive sense) the sentence Q when P is introduced as an "input datum". The explanation of $\rceil P$ is taken to be the implication $(P \longrightarrow (0 = 0 \, |))$. In this "spirit" the sentences of these two forms were understood by L.E.J.Brouwer as well as by A.N.Kolmogorov in [7] [*] and A.Heyting in [9], [10]. In his paper [11] Kolmogorov proposed a version of partial sharpening of this understanding using the language of problems. The question of a sense for the term «demonstration» suitable for the case considered remained for a long time without clear answer (the discussion of this question can be found for example in [12], § 11). However searches in this direction which were undertaken, in particular some notions and ideas proposed by P.Lorenzen in [13], turned out to be fruitful. (An example is the idea that every occurrence of the sign $\longrightarrow$ or $\rceil$ in a given formula $\vdash$ can be considered as a symbol belonging to a certain "level" of the implication hierarchy, and moreover the understanding of implication changes successively with the growth of the "level").

---

[*] It is in this paper that a certain formalized fragment of the deductive apparatus of intuitionistic (and constructive) logic was proposed for the first time and discussed from a semantical standpoint. This fragment anticipated a number of essential features of wider deductive apparati of constructive logic which were set up later (see [8]).

Realization of the "vague" idea above, of intuitionistic understanding of implication, into a systematically built theory was made
by A.A.Markov (see [14], [15-20]; A.A.Markov considered a language of
a type close to one of $\mathcal{L}^{cl}$ but differing from it in certain features)[*]. Markov's semantical theory can be called (according to
its type) a stepwise semantical theory with deductive understanding
of implication and negation. In agreement with the theorem of Tarski mentioned above, this semantics is characterized with the help
of relatively complicated notions. Its description uses both the
usual inductive definitions and generalized ones, both formal systems and semiformal ones (i.e. employing Carnap's rule). Generalized inductive definitions are usually "deciphered" by means of some
explanation appealing essentially to intuitionistic notions of "free
choice sequences" of suitable constructive objects. Such explanations are out of the framework of constructive mathematics and so the
use of generalized inductive definitions in A.A.Markov's semantic
theory makes one feel that this theory is "not completely constructive". However from the standpoint of the activity which is actually carried out in specific areas of mathematics developed on the basis of informal considerations, it is not necessary to accept this
theory in its full generality: to interpret and substantiate semantically the theorems of suitable type from the "basic stock" of mathematics it is sufficient to use only fragments of the semantical
theory considered which involve generalized inductive definitions
of some special types, namely definitions by transfinite recursion
on some "initial" scales of constructive ordinal numbers. (The scale of ordinal numbers less than $\omega^{\omega^{\omega}}$ is often sufficient and
only in "exotic" cases it is necessary to go outside the ordinal
number ε_o).

In Markov's stepwise semantical theory the negation is defined
in terms of implication. The usual deductive apparatus of classical
arithmetic (noted above to be recognized as an "inspector" for admissibility of semantical definitions) admits also a version where
negation is considered as a primitive connective and implication is
introduced as a derived connective by means of the definition:
$(P \to Q) \leftrightharpoons \neg(P \,\&\, \neg Q)$. While accepting this version we accept
the reductive understanding of implication which is in some res-
pects more close (compared to stepwise semantics with deductive im-

---

[*] A version of semantics of a relatively simple form for the
formulas containing only implications and negations of the first
two "levels", was proposed in [21] .

plication) to understanding "in the spirit" of Boolean function theory, that is to understanding used in the mathematical theories with finite individual domains (cf.§1) and in quantifier-free arithmetic formulas (cf.§2). Using a number of equivalences derivable by means of the deductive apparatus mentioned above (and employing a two-place primitive recursive pairing function x together with its inverses x_1, x_2 for "contracting" the chains of the form $\forall z_1 \forall z_2 ... \forall z_n$ into a single quantifier complex $\forall z$) one can construct for every formula F of the language $\mathcal{L}^{cl}$ a formula F^* of the form

$$\forall y \, \exists u_1 \forall v_1 ... \exists u_k \forall v_k \exists w (f(y, u_1, v_1, ..., u_k, v_k, w, z_1, ..., z_m) = 0) \qquad (\Delta)$$

(with $K \geqslant 0$, $m \geqslant 0$, f primitive recursive and quantifier complexes $\forall y$, $\exists w$ may be absent) such that the equivalence $(F \leftrightarrow F^*)$ is derivable in $\mathcal{C}^{cl}$ [this is a version of the prenex form theorem]. After reducing formula F in this way we are confronted with the problem of interpreting the corresponding formula of the form (Δ).

A theorem due to A.Tarski mentioned above ruined a hope for the possibility of a "relatively simple" and at the same time "precise" semantics for sentences of the form (Δ) ,[*) although it does not rule out a possibility to construct a hierarchy of "very simple" (expressible for example in the language $\mathcal{L}^0$) but approximate interpretations for sentences of the form (Δ) , each stage of the hierarchy being open for refinements.

Below we shall discuss one such hierarchy proposed in [22].In the construction of this hierarchy we bypass the framework of the language $\mathcal{L}^{cl}$,because at certain steps the potential realizability quantifier $\exists$ and formulas of the language $\mathcal{L}^{con}$ appear in a natural way. In view of this it is convenient to consider languages $\mathcal{L}^{cl}$ and $\mathcal{L}^{con}$ together.

§ 4. The starting point for the formation of semantical ideas

---

[*) G.Kreisel [23] proposed an interpretation of arithmetical sentences of the form (Δ) radically different by its idea from the stepwise semantics with deductive implication, but appealing to a set-theoretic notion of number-theoretic function or, after some modification of details, to the intuitionistic notion of a free choice sequence of natural numbers. It is called the no-counterexample interpretation.

concerning the language $\mathcal{L}^{con}$ of constructive arithmetic was the reduction due to L.E.J.Brouwer of interpretation of the sentences having the form $\exists x R$ to the interpretation of the condition R and a corresponding reduction for sentences of the form $(P \vee Q)$ (cf. §2). However the question of interpreting sentences containing formulas of the form $\exists x R$ or $(P \vee Q)$ as proper subformulas (that is ones with depth greater than zero in the whole formula) turned out to be difficult (the main reason being, as became clear later, the absence at that time of necessary "support" in the form of the precise notion of an algorithm). The clarification of this question was achieved as a result of "successive approximations" and took a relatively long time.

Let us note that in the history of mathematical logic the formation of logical deduction apparati (or separate parts of such apparati) was in many cases based only on very "vague" ideas of se - mantical character and preceded making these ideas precise. In addition it often happened that in the process of the search for refinements of original semantical ideas, such "ready-made" and recognized (on intuitive grounds) deductive apparati appeared in the role of some landmarks as well as "inspectors" of acceptability for different refinement versions. In general one can repeat for development of semantics for mathematical languages the sentence M.Born uttered once about the ways of the theoretical physics:
《We ... find our way by trials and errors building our road behind ourselves... 》 .

For example, the interpretation of propositional connectives as Boolean functions appeared in a distinct form when the relatively "rich" logical deduction apparatus of classical mathematics (including in fact the means of logical deduction later made pre - cise and systematized in the form of the classical propositional calculus) had already been formed spontaneously (in outline) and mastered by mathematicians in practice. The following event occured in the history of constructive mathematics, shortly after the basic step due to Brouwer (mentioned above). The intuitive ideas of some "reductive" meaning of the logical connectives $\rightarrow$, $\neg$ (see §3) "suggested" by the deductive apparatus of the classical mathematical logic as well as some notions of the meaning of logical connectives $\&$, $\forall$ which were traditional in the classical mathematics were corrected (again on the level of intuitive ideas) taking into account the presence of logical connectives $\exists$ and $\vee$ (explicitly connected with constructive problems) in some formulas of the employed language. (For example a rule allowing the passage form a formula of the form $\neg\neg P$ to P which is present in the classical propositional calculus, was rejected). On the base of such corrected (but in fact still "vague") understanding of logical connectives some logical and logico-arithmetic calculi were constructed (see [7], [9], [10]) which in their author's opinion were in accordance with corresponding intuitive ideas. A refining semantical idea was contained in the interpretation due to A.N.Kolmogorov [11] of logical formulas as descriptions of certain types of problems.

In the same paper any formula provable in the intuitionistic propositional calculus (the calculus gained some recognition at that time) was shown to describe a type of decidable problems and so this calculus is acceptable from the viewpoint of the proposed semantics.

After the mathematics was enriched by the precise notion of an algorithm there appeared a real possibility to refine previous semantical ideas concerning arithmetic languages in an essential way. One of the principal results of this new stage is constituted by two semantical principles of S.C.Kleene which express constructive understanding of certain combinations of the quantifier $\exists$ with some other logical connectives. These principles can be described in the language $\mathcal{L}^{con}$ as follows:

$$\forall x\exists y\,P \leftrightarrow \exists z\,\forall x(\exists u\,T_1(z,x,u) \,\&\, \forall u(T_1(z,x,y)\rightarrow {}_{\llcorner}P\,{}^{y}_{\nu(u)\lrcorner})), \tag{K_1}$$

$$(Q\rightarrow\exists y\,P)\leftrightarrow\exists z(Q\rightarrow(\exists u\,T_1(z,0,u)\,\&\,\forall u(T_1(z,0,u)\rightarrow {}_{\llcorner}P\,{}^{y}_{\nu(u)\lrcorner}))); \tag{K_2}$$

here P and Q are any formulas of the language $\mathcal{L}^{cl}$ and z, u are variables foreign to P and Q. To explain (K_1) and (K_2) we note[*] first that the formula $\exists u\,T_1(z,x,u)$ means that « the process of computing a value of the recursive function $\{z\}_1$ at the point x terminates » and second, that if z,x,u are such that $T_1(z,x,u)$ then the number $\nu(u)$ is the value of the function $\{z\}_1$ at the point x. Using the principle of constructive selection (see §2) we can replace quantifier complex $\exists u$ in (K_1) and (K_2) by $\underline{\exists}u$ and as the result we shall come to versions of

_____

[*] The expression $T_1(z,0,u)$ in (K_2) can be replaced by $T_0(z,u)$.

S.K.Kleene's semantic principles having the form

$$\forall x \exists y P \leftrightarrow \exists z R_1 , \qquad\qquad (K_1^o)$$

$$(Q \rightarrow \exists y P) \leftrightarrow \exists z R_2 , \qquad\qquad (K_2^o)$$

where R_1 and R_2 are formulas of the language $\mathcal{L}^{cl}$ (and this fact is very important!).

The principle (K_1) was, for the first time, formulated by S.C.Kleene in his paper [24] as Thesis III. The principle (K_2) appears in disguise in the constructive interpretation due to S.C.Kleene of arithmetic sentences based on the relation ≪ natural number e realizes arithmetic formula F ≫ also due to Kleene. An interpretation of the sentence F is taken to be the sentence ≪ F is realizable ≫ (in more detail: ≪ a number e is potentially realizable such that e realizes F ≫). This semantics of $\mathcal{L}^{con}$ is such that the sentence proposed as a clarification of a given arithmetic sentence F is also an arithmetic sentence which is always more complicated than F (and at any rate no simpler than F in its logical structure) under the definition of the relation ≪ e realizes F ≫ which was in fact proposed in [25] (see §5 and refinements in §12) and repeated in §82 of the book [3] (see also [26], p. 158). For the corresponding critical analysis see [27], [28]. This situation arises as a result of postulating a certain point of view asserting that every arithmetic sentence (even an atomic one!) should be considered as a statement of solvability of some constructive problem.

The author of this survey has proposed (see [27] or [28]) changing the original point of view to the following one: constructive problems are assigned (in the same sense as in the realizability theory) only to some arithmetic sentences. Under the new point of view constructive problems are not assigned to formulas of the language $\mathcal{L}^{cl}$ and to those formulas of the language $\mathcal{L}^{con}$ which, while containing sign $\exists$ or sign $\vee$, still can be reduced to formulas of the language $\mathcal{L}^{cl}$ by means of some admissible equivalences (see below). Under this point of view the introduction of the relation ≪ e realizes F ≫ is no longer necessary. Instead of this in [27] and [28] there was proposed the algorithm for explication of constructive problems*). The steps of applying this algo-

---

*) This algorithm was formulated in [27] and [28] with respect to languages differing from $\mathcal{L}^{con}$ by some details of technical

rithm to a given formula $\vdash$ of the language $\mathcal{L}^{con}$ are replacements of certain subformulas by equivalent ones (from the viewpoint
of some intuitive ideas) so that occurrences of the logical connective $\exists$ are progressively "pulled out" or "cancelled" (here the
logical connective $\lor$ is expressed in terms of $\exists$ according to the
definition). Some of the equivalences used are "suggested" by that
part of the deductive apparatus of constructive arithmetic which
was formed and recognized (on the base of considerations of intuitive character) for a long time. We have in mind a logico-arithmetic calculus consisting of the primitive recursive equation calculus (sometimes called primitive recursive arithmetic, see [6]), all
the postulates of the traditional constructive (called also intuitionistic) predicate calculus (see for example [30]) written for the
formulas of the language $\mathcal{L}^{con}$ and the postulate expressing the
principle of complete induction. The following equivalences can serve as examples:

$$(\exists x P \& Q) \leftrightarrow \exists x (P \& Q), \qquad (Q \& \exists x P) \leftrightarrow \exists x (Q \& P),$$

$$(\exists x P \rightarrow Q) \leftrightarrow \forall x (P \rightarrow Q), \qquad \neg \exists x P \leftrightarrow \forall x \neg P,$$

$$\exists x P \leftrightarrow \exists z \llcorner P \S^{x}_{z} \lrcorner, \qquad \exists x \exists y P \leftrightarrow \exists z \llcorner P \S^{x, y}_{x_1(z), x_2(z)} \lrcorner ;$$

here x and y stand for different variables and it is assumed that
x is not free in Q and that z does not occur in P .

It was the two semantical principles of S.K.Kleene mentioned
above [they are used in the algorithm for the explication of constructive problems in versions (K_1^0) and (K_2^0)] *) as well as
A.A.Markov's constructive selection principle (see §2) which introduced in constructive mathematics essentially new equivalences. Ad-

character. So the explanations below also differ from the content
of [27] and [28] in some details of technical character, although
they are in complete agreement with the content of the paper [22]
where one can find complete description of the algorithm for explication of constructive problems for the language $\mathcal{L}^{con}$.

*) The second semantical principle of S.C.Kleene was explicity
singled out from the realizability theory during the definition of
the algorithm for the explication of constructive problems (see the
precedent footnote). However in [27] the formulation of this principle was not in the form of a formula scheme describing equivalences
with a certain structure of left and right hand sides, but as a description of an admissible step of the algorithm. As a description of

ding these equivalences to the "old" logical deduction apparatus of constructive arithmetic mentioned above we obtain a deductive apparatus (call it the calculus $\mathcal{C}^{con}$)[*]) posessing the following very essential property: any formula F of the language $\mathcal{L}^{con}$ can be transformed by successively replacing subformulas by equivalent formulas (using only some equivalences derivable in the calculus $\mathcal{C}^{con}$) into a formula G which either is a formula of the language $\mathcal{L}^{cl}$ [even has the form (Δ)] or is of the form $\exists x P$, P being a formula of the language $\mathcal{L}^{cl}$ [even has the form (Δ)] .

Let us present an example of such a transformation for a formula of the language $\mathcal{L}^{con}$. Let F be a formula of the form

$$(\exists x_0(\exists x_1 P_1(x_0,x_1) \& \neg \exists x_2 P_2(x_0,x_2)) \to \forall x_3 (P_3(x_3) \vee \neg P_3(x_3))),$$

$P_1(x_0,x_1)$, $P_2(x_0,x_2)$ and $P_3(x_3)$ being formulas of the language $\mathcal{L}^{cl}$ (variables listed in brackets are free in the corresponding formula). Expressing the logical connective $\vee$ in terms of the original logical connectives of $\mathcal{L}^{con}$ and using suitable equivalences (picked up among equivalences of the forms listed above) we obtain successively the following formulas:[**])

$$(\exists x_0 \exists x_1 Q_1(x_0,x_1) \to \forall x_3 \exists y R_1(y,x_3)) ,$$

$$(\exists z Q_2(z) \to \exists u R_2(u)) , \qquad \forall z (Q_2(z) \to \exists u R_2(u)) ,$$

$$\forall z \exists v R_3(z,v) , \qquad \exists w R_4(w) ,$$

where the following notation is used:

$$Q_1(x_0,x_1) \rightleftharpoons (P_1(x_0,x_1) \& \forall x_2 \neg P_2(x_0,x_2)),$$

$$R_1(y,x_3) \rightleftharpoons (((y=0) \to P_3(x_3)) \& (\neg(y=0) \to \neg P_3(x_3))) ,$$

a type of equivalences (provable under semantics defined on the basis of the algorithm mentioned) this principle (or more precisely, some generalization of it) appears in the proposition 2.4.2 of [29].

[*]) $\mathcal{C}^{con}$ is a conservative extension of the calculus $\mathcal{C}^{cl}$ (see §2).

[**]) The variables for the construction of these formulas are supposed to be chosen so that collisions are avoided.

$$Q_2(z) \rightleftharpoons Q_1(x_1(z), x_2(z)),$$

$$R_2(u) \rightleftharpoons \forall x_3(\exists \iota\, T_1(u, x_3, \iota)\ \&\ \forall \iota(T_1(u, x_3, \iota) \rightarrow R_1(\nu(\iota), x_3))),$$

$$R_3(z, v) \rightleftharpoons (Q_2(z) \rightarrow (\exists \delta\, T_0(v, \delta)\ \&\ \forall \delta(T_0(v, \delta) \rightarrow R_2(\nu(\delta))))),$$

$$R_4(w) \rightleftharpoons \forall z(\exists t\, T_1(w, z, t)\ \&\ \forall t(T_1(w, z, t) \rightarrow R_3(z, \nu(t)))).$$

$R_4(w)$ is obviously a formula of the language $\mathcal{L}^{cl}$. Using suitable equivalences derivable in $\mathcal{C}^{cl}$ one can transform this formula in one of the form (Δ).

Let $\mathcal{O}$ be an algorithm transforming formulas of $\mathcal{L}^{con}$ into formulas of the same language. We say that $\mathcal{O}$ is an algorithm for the explication of constructive problems (or an algorithm for constructive deciphering of arithmetic formulas) if the formula $\mathcal{O}_\llcorner F_\lrcorner$ for any formula F of $\mathcal{L}^{con}$ is of the form $\exists x\, P$, P being a formula of $\mathcal{L}^{cl}$ (the quantifier complex $\exists x$ may be absent) and the formula $(F \leftrightarrow \mathcal{O}_\llcorner F_\lrcorner)$ is derivable in $\mathcal{C}^{con}$.

Let us fix some algorithm for the explication of constructive problems choosing it so that any result of its application is either a formula of the form (Δ) or one of the form $\exists x\, P$, P being of the form (Δ), and denote the algorithm chosen by π. A detailed description of a particular algorithm suitable for this role is given in [22], §4.

One can see from the considerations above that the calculus $\mathcal{C}^{con}$ which was formed, generally speaking, on the base of "vague" (but constructive in their leading ideas) intuitive notions of semantic character, can serve as a landmark for some refinement of these notions (or using M.Born's words, for « building the road behind ourselves »). This landmark suggests the following point if view: algorithm π is considered to be a combined reductive clarification for the logical connectives of the language $\mathcal{L}^{con}$ by means of formulas of the form (Δ) using if necessary as initial step the basic semantical reduction due to L.E.J.Brouwer concerning sentences of the form $\exists x\, R$.

If F is a closed formula (sentence) of the language $\mathcal{L}^{con}$ and $\pi_\llcorner F_\lrcorner$ is of the form $\exists x\, P$, then it is natural to consider F to be a statement about potential decidability of certain constructive problem "ciphered" in the formula F , namely the problem of constructing some constructive object whose arithmetic code satisfies the condition P . In every case when the algorithm π "sees" that a constructive problem is "ciphered" in the sentence considered, it gives a formulation of the requirement on the desired constructive object.

In various areas of constructive mathematics one uses systematically languages with subordinate variables, so it is appropriate to say something about definition of the algorithm for the explication of constructive problems for the formulas of such languages and about the possibility of gross mistakes when a "direct" extrapolation of the algorithm π is attempted. Let $\mathcal{L}^{con,\sigma}$ be an extension of the language $\mathcal{L}^{con}$ obtained by adding subordinate variables of some type σ (we restrict ourselves to the case when only one type of subordinate variables is introduced) which is characterized by a given formula S of the language $\mathcal{L}^{con}$. The type σ is characterized by the formula S in the sense that the admis - sible values of any subordinate variable of the type σ are consi- dered to be natural numbers satisfying condition S (it is assumed that only one variable is free in S). Let $\mathcal{U}$ be a closed formu- la of the language $\mathcal{L}^{con,\sigma}$. According to the definition (see [27], §8) the process of applying the algorithm for the explication of constructive problems to $\mathcal{U}$ begins with the complete elimination of all subordinate variables from $\mathcal{U}$ carried out by the method which is common to the mathematical logic in general. Then algo - rithm π is applied to the formula of the language $\mathcal{L}^{con}$ obtai- ned in this way. If the initial stage mentioned above "cancelled" (that is if π is applied "directly" to $\mathcal{U}$ so that subordinate va- riables are not distinguished from "ordinary" ones) one can obtain a formula which is not equivalent to the correct result (various examples can be found in [31]). This can happen however only in the case when some constructive problem is actually ciphered in S .[*]

If F is a closed formula of the language $\mathcal{L}^{con}$ derivable in the calculus $\mathcal{C}^{con}$, then for any derivation of this formula in $\mathcal{C}^{con}$ one can construct a derivation of the formula $\pi_{\llcorner}F_{\lrcorner}$ in the calculus $\mathcal{C}^{cl}$, if $\pi_{\llcorner}F_{\lrcorner}$ is a formula of the language $\mathcal{L}^{cl}$, and one can construct a natural number N and a derivation of the

_____

[*] The both ways lead to equivalent results if $\pi_{\llcorner}S_{\lrcorner}$ is a formula of the language $\mathcal{L}^{cl}$ (see [27], §8).

formula $_{\llcorner}P\,{}^x_{\,N}\,{}_{\lrcorner}$ _in the calculus_ $\mathcal{C}^{cl}$ _if_ $\pi_{\llcorner}F_{\lrcorner}$ _is of the form_ $\exists x\,P$. (This proposition is a version of a theorem due to A.V. Idelson from [32] corresponding to languages and calculi considered in this survey)[*]. Below we shall discuss some "approximate" semantics of the language $\mathcal{L}^{cl}$ such that the calculus $\mathcal{C}^{cl}$ is acceptable. Considering the transition from any formula F of the language $\mathcal{L}^{con}$ to the formula $\pi_{\llcorner}F_{\lrcorner}$ as a semantic reduction (clarification of understanding) we shall be able on the basis of last theorem, to conclude that the calculus $\mathcal{C}^{con}$ is admissible relative to superposition of the "intermediate" semantics characterized by the algorithm π and any one of the "approximate" semantics mentioned above.

Clarification of the sentences of the language $\mathcal{L}^{con}$ by means of ones having the form (Δ) [possibly using the basic semantic reduction due to Brouwer] is considered as an "exact" clarification in the semantical theory presented here. However it does not generally advance us sufficiently because the intuition restricted by the abstraction of potential realizability refuses of course to admit closed formulas of the form (Δ) for $k \geqslant 1$ to be "immediately intelligible" sentences. In view of this there arises a problem of formulating some "reasonable" clarification for the sentences of the form (Δ) . Because sentences of this form are in the language $\mathcal{L}^{cl}$, one can appeal to the stepwise semantics with deductive implication stipulating the expression of negation in terms of implication (the merits of this semantics as well as its defects and the possibilities of "alleviating" them were discussed in §3). But this way seems to be an artificial one if we accept the point of view treating (intuitively) negation as a "simpler" logical connective than implication, and so consider a transformation of some formula of the language $\mathcal{L}^{cl}$ into a formula of the form (Δ) to be a clarifying act. It is this point of view that underlies the

---

[*] A theorem due to D.Nelson from [33] (see also [3], §82) stating that any formula in the language of constructive (intuitionistic) arithmetic derivable by means of traditional logical deduction apparatus for this arithmetic is realizable, can be thought of as a predecessor of this theorem due to A.V.Idelson with respect to the character of a question it answers. However the realizability theory which was a base of D.Nelson's considerations, does not provide for reduction of the formulas from the language of constructive arithmetic to ones of the form $\exists x\,P$, P being a formula in the language of classical arithmetic, and neither formulation of D.Nelson's result nor its demonstration contains any mention of formulas or deductive apparatus of the classical arithmetic in a context similar to the A.V.Idelson's theorem.

presentation below.

§ 5. The search for "exact" clarification for the sentences of the form (Λ) by means of "immediately intelligible" sentences is generally speaking doomed to failure by the theorem due to A. Tarski mentioned above. If we require the clarification to be "immediately intelligible" then any realistic approach to the problem considered should stipulate renouncing the requirement for an "exact" clarification and be content with constructing some hierarchies of approximate clarifications. Below we shall discuss the hierarchies proposed in [22][*].

It is natural to require that in any hierarchy proposed with this aim (i) the definition of any particular stage consists in the presentation of some algorithm constructing for any sentence P of the type considered a sentence (let us denote it by Q) which is to be considered the approximate clarification (at a given stage of the hierarchy) of the sentence P , and (ii) Q should majorize P under (partial) ordering of formulas "defined" by implication, that is an "intuitively acceptable" justification of the sentence $(Q \rightarrow P)$ should be possible. In fact we shall have in mind derivability of the formula $(Q \rightarrow P)$ by means of some logical deduction apparatus recognized to be acceptable on the base of intuitive ideas of semantical character (for example by means of the calculus $\mathcal{C}^{con}$).

Let $\mathcal{M}$ be an algorithm defining some stage in such a hierarchy and P be some sentence of the form (Λ) . If the second requirement above is satisfied, then sentence $\mathcal{M}_{\llcorner} P_{\lrcorner}$ (sentence $\mathcal{M}_{\llcorner} \neg P_{\lrcorner}$) can be considered on the intuitive level as a formulation of some sufficient condition for "truth" (respectively, some sufficient condition for "falsity") of the sentence P (these conditions being generalli open for refinements), and this circumstance shows that algorithms satisfying the second requirement[**] are preferable from the semantical point of view.

---

[*] Essential corrections which should be made in [22] are presented in the bibliography to this survey.

[**] The algorithm proposed by Gödel in [34] for interpreting formulas in the language of constructive arithmetic by "immediately intelligible" formulas of a certain language containing in its signature symbols for all primitive recursive functionals of finite types is sometimes thought of as an algorithm for constructing approximate clarification, and some authors even proposed it as an algorithm for constructing "exact" clarifications. (This algorithm ge-

We shall discuss below "approximate clarifications" for senten-
ces of the form (Δ) by means of formulas from the language $\mathcal{L}^0$.
Reasons for considering these formulas to be "immediately intelligible" were given in §2. In fact it is possible to restrict ourselves to obtaining "approximate clarifications" having the form

$$\exists x_1 \forall y_1 \ldots \exists x_K \forall y_K \exists z\, M \qquad (M \text{ being quantifier-free}) \qquad (\Diamond)$$

since using the equivalence (K_1^0) and some other equivalences derivable in $\mathcal{C}^{con}$, one can easily prove:

(A) If W is a formula of the form $(\Diamond)$ then $\pi_{\llcorner} W_{\lrcorner}$ is a
formula of the form $\exists u \forall v\, \dot{\exists} w\, \widetilde{M}$, $\widetilde{M}$ being quantifier-free
(i.e. $\pi_{\llcorner} W_{\lrcorner}$ is a formula of the language $\mathcal{L}^0$).

The "leading considerations" in the process of search for for-
mulas of the form $(\Diamond)$ majorizing a given formula of the form (Δ)
are some equivalences and implications derivable in the calculus
$\mathcal{C}^{con}$. A "key" role is played by the following proposition:

(B) If P, Q, R are formulas in the language $\mathcal{L}^{cl}$ then the
formula

$$(Q \vee (\dot{\exists} u \forall v\, P \dot{\vee} R)) \leftrightarrow \dot{\exists} u' \forall v'((Q \vee \dot{\exists} u \forall v\, P) \dot{\vee} (_{\llcorner} P\,\S^{u,v}_{u',v'\lrcorner} \dot{\vee} R)) \qquad (\square)$$

is derivable in the calculus $\mathcal{C}^{con}$; here u' and v' are distinct
variables foreign to the lefthand side of the equivalence $(\square)$ [for-
mulas Q and R may be absent].[*]

In fact the formula $\dot{\exists} u \forall v\, P \leftrightarrow (\dot{\exists} u \forall v\, P \dot{\vee} {}_{\llcorner} \forall v\, P\,\S^{u}_{u'\lrcorner})$ is derivable in the calculus $\mathcal{C}^{cl}$ (hence in the calculus $\mathcal{C}^{con}$) and

___

nerally "acts" passing over the language of classical arithmetic but
is applicable in particular to the latter language). But the transformations used in this algorithm are such that majorizing discussed above cannot be guaranteed if one has in mind all possible sentences of the form (Δ) (and hence for all formulas of the language
$\mathcal{L}^{con}$). K.Gödel makes the following comments concerning the interpretation he proposed: ≪ ... the definitions 1 – 6 are not claimed to reproduce the meaning of logical connectives introduced by
Brouwer and Heyting≫ . The aim of his algorithm explicitly stated
by K.Gödel is a new consistency proof for traditional deductive apparati of classical and constructive arithmetic and this aim has metamathematical, not semantical, character.

[*] In applications of the equivalence $(\square)$ it is very essential
that the variable u' be bound there by a potential realizability
quantifier $\dot{\exists}$ but not by a classical existential quantifier $\exists$. The
formula obtained from $(\square)$ by replacing the sign $\dot{\exists}$ by the sign
$\underset{\cdot}{\exists}$ is also derivable but of no use for our aims.

this formula implies in $\mathcal{C}^{cl}$

$$(Q\dot{\lor}(\exists u\,\forall v\,P\dot{\lor}R)) \leftrightarrow \forall v'((Q\dot{\lor}\exists u\,\forall v\,P)\lor(\llcorner P\,{}^{u,v}_{u',v'}\lrcorner\lor R)).$$

Since the variable u' is not free in the lefthand side of the latter equivalence, the passage to ($\square$) is admissible in the calculus $\mathcal{C}^{con}$.

The method of using the sentence ($\underline{B}$) to constructing majorants of formulas having the form (Δ) is explained below for a formula H of the form

$$\exists u_1\,\forall v_1\,\exists u_2\,\forall v_2\,\exists w\,(f(u_1,v_1,u_2,v_2,w)=0),$$

f being a primitive recursive function. To simplify notation we introduce abbreviations:

$$G(u_1,v_1,u_2,v_2,w) \leftrightharpoons (f(u_1,v_1,u_2,v_2,w)=0),$$

$$H'(u_1,v_1) \leftrightharpoons \exists u_2\,\forall v_2\,\exists w\,G(u_1,v_1,u_2,v_2,w).$$

Applying proposition ($\underline{B}$) twice we obtain the following equivalences derivable in $\mathcal{C}^{con}$:

$$H \leftrightarrow \exists u_1'\,\forall v_1'(H\dot{\lor}H'(u_1',v_1')),$$

$$H \leftrightarrow \exists u_1'\,\forall v_1'\,\exists u_2'\,\forall v_2'((H\dot{\lor}H'(u_1',v_1'))\lor\exists w\,G(u_1',v_1',u_2',v_2',w)).$$

The righthand side of the latter equivalence we call a_rank 0 quasiclarification of the formula H . This quasiclarification [*] is more complicated than H (in its structure), but after we "delet" from it the subformula $(H\dot{\lor}H'(u_1',v_1'))$, we obtain the formula

$$\exists u_1'\,\forall v_1'\,\exists u_2'\,\forall v_2'\,\exists w\,G(u_1',v_1',u_2',v_2',w)$$

having the form ($\Diamond$) and majorizing H . This formula will be called a rank 0 majorant (trivial majorant) of the formula H and

---

[*] The term « quasiclarification » is used here in a different meaning compared to [22] (there this term means the equivalence as a whole and not only its righthand side).

will be denoted by $\mathcal{M}_{\llcorner}^0 H_{\lrcorner}$.

To construct a rank 1 quasiclarification of the formula H we use first the derivability in $\mathcal{C}^{con}$ of the equivalences ha - ving forms

$$(\underset{\cdot}{\exists} u \forall v \, P \underset{\cdot}{\vee} R) \leftrightarrow \underset{\cdot}{\exists} u \forall v (P \underset{\cdot}{\vee} R) \qquad [u \text{ and } v \text{ are not free in } R] \, ,$$

$$(\underset{\cdot}{\exists} u \forall v \, P \underset{\cdot}{\vee} \underset{\cdot}{\exists} u \forall v \, Q) \leftrightarrow \underset{\cdot}{\exists} u \forall v (\llcorner P_{\vphantom{|}^v_{\mathscr{x}_1(v)}} \lrcorner \underset{\cdot}{\vee} \llcorner Q_{\vphantom{|}^v_{\mathscr{x}_2(v)}} \lrcorner)$$

and transform the formula $(H \underset{\cdot}{\vee} H'(u_1', v_1'))$ occurring in the rank 0 quasiclarification, into the formula

$$\underset{\cdot}{\exists} u_1 \forall v_1 \underset{\cdot}{\exists} u_2 \forall v_2 \underset{\cdot}{\exists} w \, (G(u_1, v_1, u_2, \mathscr{x}_1(v_2), w) \underset{\cdot}{\vee} G(u_1', v_1', u_2, \mathscr{x}_2(v_2), w))$$

having the form (Δ) . We shall denote the latter formula by $H_1(u_1', v_1')$ and introduce further notation:

$$G_1(u_1', v_1', u_1, v_1, u_2, v_2, w) \rightleftharpoons (G(u_1, v_1, u_2, \mathscr{x}_1(v_2), w) \underset{\cdot}{\vee} G(u_1', v_1', u_2, \mathscr{x}_2(v_2), w)),$$

$$H_1'(u_1', v_1', u_1, v_1) \rightleftharpoons \underset{\cdot}{\exists} u_2 \forall v_2 \underset{\cdot}{\exists} w \, G_1(u_1', v_1', u_1, v_1, u_2, v_2, w) \, .$$

It follows from the considerations above that the equivalence

$$H \leftrightarrow \underset{\cdot}{\exists} u_1' \forall v_1' \underset{\cdot}{\exists} u_2' \forall v_2' (H_1(u_1', v_1') \underset{\cdot}{\vee} \underset{\cdot}{\exists} w \, G(u_1', v_1', u_2', v_2', w))$$

is derivable in $\mathcal{C}^{con}$. Applying $(\underline{B})$ twice we shall obtain equi-valence

$$H \leftrightarrow \underset{\cdot}{\exists} u_1' \forall v_1' \underset{\cdot}{\exists} u_2' \forall v_2' \underset{\cdot}{\exists} u_1'' \forall v_1'' \underset{\cdot}{\exists} u_2'' \forall v_2''((H_1(u_1', v_1') \underset{\cdot}{\vee} H_1'(u_1', v_1', u_1'', v_1'')) \underset{\cdot}{\vee}$$

$$\underset{\cdot}{\vee} (\underset{\cdot}{\exists} w \, G_1(u_1', v_1', u_1'', v_1'', u_2'', v_2'', w) \underset{\cdot}{\vee} \underset{\cdot}{\exists} w \, G(u_1', v_1', u_2', v_2', w)))$$

derivable in the same calculus. The righthand side of the latter equivalence we shall call <u>a rank 1 quasiclarification of the formu-la</u> H . After "deleting" from it subformula

$$(H_1(u_1', v_1') \underset{\cdot}{\vee} H_1'(u_1', v_1', u_1'', v_1''))$$

we shall obtain (after moving the quantifier complex $\underset{\cdot}{\exists} w$ forward) formula

$$\exists u_1' \forall v_1' \exists u_2' \forall v_2' \exists u_1'' \forall v_1'' \exists u_2'' \forall v_2'' \exists w \, (\, G_1(u_1'v_1', u_1'', v_1'', u_2'', v_2'', w) \, \vee$$

$$\vee \, G(u_1', v_1', u_2', v_2', w)) \qquad \text{which has the form} \quad (\Diamond) \quad , \text{ majorizes}$$

the formula H and is majorized by the formula $\mathcal{M}_L^o H_\lrcorner$. We shall
call formula thus obtained <u>a rank 1 majorant of the formula</u> H and
denote it by $\mathcal{M}_L^1 H_\lrcorner$.

For any natural number n we can construct <u>a rank</u> n <u>quasicla-</u>
<u>rification</u> and a <u>rank</u> n <u>majorant of the formula</u> H if we carry
the process on according to the pattern shown above.[*] We shall de-
note rank n majorant of H by $\mathcal{M}_L^n H_\lrcorner$ and use $\mathcal{M}^n$ as a notation for an algorithm constructing rank n majorants. Implications

$$\mathcal{M}_L^n H_\lrcorner \rightarrow H, \qquad \mathcal{M}_L^n H_\lrcorner \rightarrow \mathcal{M}_L^{n+1} H_\lrcorner$$

are derivable in the calculus $\mathcal{C}^{con}$. With the help of equivalence (K_1^o) one can transform the method of construction quasiclarifications and majorants into a form suitable for its extension to
the first infinite ordinal ω and to further constructive ordinals. Rank n quasiclarification can be transformed into a formula
of the form

$$\exists u \forall v ((\exists u_1 \forall v_1 \exists u_2 \forall v_2 \exists w \, (\mathcal{A}^n[f](u,v,u_1,v_1,u_2,v_2,w)=0) \, \vee$$

$$\vee \exists w \, (\mathcal{B}^n[f](u,v,w)=0)) \, \& \, \exists w \, (\varphi^n(u,v,w)=0)),$$

$\mathcal{A}^n$ and $\mathcal{B}^n$ being some recursive operators and φ^n being some
primitive recursive function. The latter formula can be transformed

---

[*] There is a certain analogy between this method of successive construction of quasiclarifications and majorants of formulas
on the one side, and some ideas of J.Herbrand conserning classical
predicate calculus with function constants on the other side. We
have in mind not those ideas very familiar from the mathematical literature which lead to famous Herbrand theorem on the criterion for
the provability of a formula in the classical predicate calculus,
rather than ideas that can be found in [36], sect.3, and in [35],
chapter 5, sect.2.2 and 2.3. In particular one can consider the equivalence (□) as an analog in constructive arithmetics (adjusted
to our aims and based on certain possibilities given by the calculus $\mathcal{C}^{con}$) of an equivalence occupying key position among J.Her-
brand's ideas. More detailed explanations see in [22], section 5.2,
remark 2.

in a formula of the form

$$\exists u \,\forall v ((\exists u_1 \forall v_1 \,\exists u_2 \forall v_2 \,\exists w (\tilde{\mathcal{A}}[f](n,u,v,u_1,v_1,u_2,v_2,w)=0)\vee$$

$$\vee \exists w(\tilde{\mathcal{B}}[f](n,u,v,w)=0))\,\&\,\exists w(\tilde{\varphi}(n,u,v,w)=0)),$$

$\tilde{\mathcal{A}}$ and $\tilde{\mathcal{B}}$ being some recursive operators and $\tilde{\varphi}$ being some primitive recursive function. Since such a formula for any n is equivalent to the formula H , it is admissible to pass to equivalence

$$H \longleftrightarrow \exists z \,\exists u \,\forall v ((\exists u_1 \forall v_1 \,\exists u_2 \forall v_2 \,\exists w (\tilde{\mathcal{A}}[f](z,u,v,u_1,v_1,u_2,v_2,w)=0)\vee$$

$$\vee \exists w(\tilde{\mathcal{B}}[f](z,u,v,w)=0))\,\&\,\exists w(\tilde{\varphi}(z,u,v,w)=0)).$$

Finally after "contracting" the chain $\exists z \,\exists u$ into one quantifier complex $\exists u$ we come to equivalence

$$H \longleftrightarrow \exists u \,\forall v ((\exists u_1 \forall v_1 \,\exists u_2 \forall v_2 \,\exists w (\tilde{\mathcal{A}}[f](x_1(u),x_2(u),v,u_1,v_1,u_2,v_2,w)=0)\vee$$

$$\vee \exists w(\tilde{\mathcal{B}}[f](x_1(u),x_2(u),v,w)=0))\,\&\,\exists w(\tilde{\varphi}(x_1(u),x_2(u),v,w)=0)).$$

The righthand side of this equivalence we shall call <u>a rank</u> ω <u>quasiclarification of the formula</u> H , and a formula

$$\exists u \,\forall v \,\exists w ((\tilde{\mathcal{B}}[f](x_1(u),x_2(u),v,x_1(w))=0)\&(\tilde{\varphi}(x_1(u),x_2(u),v,x_2(w))=0))$$

we shall call <u>a rank</u> ω <u>majorant of the formula</u> H and denote by $\mathcal{M}\lfloor^\omega H\rfloor$.

Methods of defining algorithm by means of ordinal recursion familiar from the literature allows us to extrapolate the approach presented above to particular "intelligibly defined" scales of constructive ordinals and to define <u>rank</u> α <u>quasiclarification</u> and <u>rank</u> α <u>majorant</u> for any ordinal α from the chosen scale and any formula F of the form $\exists u_1 \forall v_1 \ldots \exists u_k \forall v_k \,\exists w M$, M being quantifier-free. (For details see [22] after paying attention to corrections in the bibliography to the present survey). Let us denote by $\mathcal{M}^\alpha$ the algorithm constructing rank α majorants.Ma-

jorants of a formula F which can be represented in the form
$M^\alpha_\llcorner F_\lrcorner$, α being an ordinal from the chosen scale, form
some hierarchy of approximate clarifications of formula F , and
any stage of this hierarchy is "refined" by any following one.

The algorithm M^α is extended to all formulas of the langu-
age $\mathcal{L}^{con}$ (in particular to all formulas of the language $\mathcal{L}^{cl}$)
in the following way. Let F be any formula of the language $\mathcal{L}^{con}$.
First the algorithm π for the explication of constructive prob-
lems is applied to F . Formula $\pi_\llcorner F_\lrcorner$ is of the form $\exists x \forall y\, G$,
G being of the form $\exists u_1 \forall v_1 ... \exists u_\kappa \forall v_\kappa \exists w\, M$ (here
$\kappa \geqslant 0$, M is quantifier-free and quantifier complexes $\exists x$, $\forall y$,
$\exists w$ may be absent). If $\kappa = 0$ then $M^\alpha_\llcorner F_\lrcorner$ is $\pi_\llcorner F_\lrcorner$ by
definition; if $\kappa \geqslant 1$ then by definition $M^\alpha_\llcorner F_\lrcorner$ is a formula
$\pi_\llcorner \exists x \forall y\, G^\alpha_\lrcorner$ where $G^\alpha \leftharpoondown M^\alpha_\llcorner G_\lrcorner$. In all cases
$M^\alpha_\llcorner F_\lrcorner$ is a formula of the language $\mathcal{L}^o$.[*)]

For a formula $\exists x \forall y \exists w (f(x,y,w) = 0)$ of the language $\mathcal{L}^o$
one can construct a further hierarchy of majorants having the form
$\exists x \exists z \forall y (f(x,y,\varphi(z,y)) = 0)$, φ being a total two-place
recursive function, treated as a universal one for certain enume -
rable class of total one-place recursive functions (the choice of
the function φ selects a certain stage in every such hierarchy).
Finally for sentences of the form $\forall y (\psi(y) = 0)$, ψ being a
function from some class of total recursive functions (in particular any sentence of the form $\forall y (f(m,y,\varphi(n,y)) = 0)$, m and n
being natural numbers, can be transformed into the form above) one
can construct hierarchies of sufficient conditions for validity,
where each stage is presented as a particular quantifier-free calculus satisfying a semantic admissibility condition: it should be
possible to give an informal argument "showing convincingly" that
any quantifier-free formula derivable in the calculus considered
is true for all values of its variables. Combining the construct-
ons mentioned above one can form majorants for sentences of the
language $\mathcal{L}^{con}$ which are introduced by definitions of syntactic
character.

It is desirable from the intuitive point of view for the hie-

---

[*)] While considering this definition one has to have in mind
that the algorithm π does not affect formulas of the form (Δ)
as well as ones of the form $\exists x\, P$ with P of the form (Δ) ;
in particular $\pi_\llcorner \pi_\llcorner F_\lrcorner \lrcorner \stackrel{o}{=} \pi_\llcorner F_\lrcorner$ for any formula F of the language $\mathcal{L}^{con}$.

rarchy of approximate clarifications to satisfy one further condition, namely it should provide a possibility for "arbitrary close" approximations to any sentence of the form (Δ) . One can ask whether this requirement is realistic. Leaving aside the question of the choice of the "measure of difference" for arithmetic sentences, let us note that when considering this question one apparently cannot avoid turning to the "whole scale" of constructive ordinals as a characterisation of the order type of the hierarchy one is loo - king for. But the general notion of a constructive ordinal is in - troduced by a generalized inductive definition and "deciphering" this definition one uses in essential way intuitionistic ideas about free choice sequences of constructive objects. Because of this the aim formulated above appears to be unrealistic from the view point of such a perception of the foundations of mathematics which qualifies the notion of a free choice sequence to be an abstract idea which does not possess sufficient tractability to be admissible as an object of mathematical considerations.

Refusing to use in this situation (as well as in other similar situations, see $[37]$ in particular) a generalized inductive definition which "suggests itself" we deprive ourselves of the possibility of achieving the "perfect closure" of the theory considered and so may injure the aesthetic feeling of a mathematician. However this refusal (made for the sake of maintaining the "level of clear intelligibility" of the definitions employed) does not deprive us of the possibility of constructing the main chapters of construc - tive mathematics on a clear sementical basis, since approximate cla- rifications of sentences defined on the basis of some "initial sca- les" of constructive ordinals are "practically sufficient" for the attainment of this goal.

The author of this survey was led to this point of view by analysis of some theorems from various areas of recursive function theory and constructive mathematical analysis. For the theorems considered the author succeeded in the construction of true majo - rants having the desired form. The point of view presented above is essentially reinforced by the following assertion which is a combination of a theorem due to G.E.Minc $[38]$ and the theorem of A.V.Idelson mentioned above. For every derivation of a sentence F in the calculus $\mathcal{C}^{con}$ it is possible to construct a constructive ordinal β less than ε_0 , such that $\mathcal{M}^{\beta}_{\ulcorner} F_{\urcorner}$ is true; if moreover complete induction rule was not used in the derivation, then β with this property may be chosen to be finite (i.e. a natural number). If we turn to such chapters of constructive mathematics as the general theory of algorithms and calculi, constructive mathematical analysis, constructive topology etc., then we see that the means of logical deduction used there usually do not exceed (essentially) the framework of the calculus $\mathcal{C}^{con}$, and so the special_semantics defined by the majorizing algorithm $\mathcal{M}^{\varepsilon_0}$ turns out to be "practically sufficient", and in many cases already semantics defined by "a more coarse" majorizing algorithm $\mathcal{M}^{\omega_3}$ (where $\omega_3 \rightleftharpoons \omega^{\omega^{\omega}}$) or even by $\mathcal{M}^{\omega}$ is sufficient.

Bibliography

1. М а р к о в   А.А. О непрерывности конструктивных функций. Успехи матем.наук, 1954, 9, №3 (61), 226-230.

2. М а р к о в   А.А. О конструктивной математике. Труды Матем.инст. АН СССР, 1962, 67, 8-14. (English transl.: Amer.Math.Soc.Transl.(2), 1971, 98, 1-10).

3. K l e e n e   S.C. Introduction to metamathematics. New York-Toronto, 1952.

4. T a r s k i   A. Der Wahrheitsbegriff in den formalisierten Sprachen. Studia Philosophica, 1935, 1, 261-405.

5. S m u l l y a n   R.M. Theory of formal systems. Princeton, N.J., 1963.

6. G o o d s t e i n   R.L. Recursive number theory. Amsterdam, 1957.

7. К о л м о г о р о в   А.Н. О принципе tertium non datur .Матем. сб., 1925, 32, №4, 646-667. (English transl.in[40], 414-437).

8. W a n g   H. Introductory notes to the English translation of[7] in [40], 414-416.

9. H e y t i n g   A. Sur la logique intuitionniste. Bull.Acad.Sci. Belgique, 1930, 16, 957-963.

10. H e y t i n g   A. Die formalen Regeln der intuitionistischen Logik. Sitzungsber.Preuss.Acad.Wiss., phis.-math.Kl., 1930, 42-56. - Die formalen Regeln der intuitionistischen Mathematik.Ibid., 1930, 57-71, 158-169.

11. K o l m o g o r o f f   A. Zur Deutung der intuitionistischen Logik. Math.Zeitschr., 1932, 35, №1, 58-65.

12. G e n t z e n   G. Die Widerspruchsfreiheit der reinen Zahlen - theorie.Math.Ann., 1936, 112, №4, 493-565.

13. L o r e n z e n   P. Einführung in die operative Logik und Mathematik. Berlin, Springer-Verlag, 1955.

14. M a r k o v   A.A. Essai de construction d'une logique de la mathématique constructive. Revue Internat.Philos.,Bruxelles, 1971,$\underline{98}$,4,477-507.

15. М а р к о в   А.А. О языке $Я_0$. Докл.АН СССР,1974,$\underline{214}$,№I,40-43.(English transl.: Soviet Math.Dokl.,$\underline{15}$,38-40).

16. М а р к о в   А.А. О языке $Я_1$. Докл.АН СССР,1974,$\underline{214}$№2, 279-282.(English transl.: ibid.,125-129).

17. М а р к о в   А.А. О языке $Я_2$. Докл.АН СССР,1974,$\underline{214}$№3, 5I3-5I6. (English transl.: ibid.,184-189).

18. М а р к о в   А.А. О языке $Я_3$. Докл.АН СССР,1974,$\underline{214}$№4, 765-768.(English transl.: ibid.,242-247).

19. М а р к о в   А.А. О языках $Я_4,Я_5$,... Докл.АН СССР,1974,$\underline{214}$, №5,I031-I034.(English transl.: ibid.,313-318).

20. М а р к о в   А.А. О языке $Я_\omega$. Докл.АН СССР,1974,214,№6, I262-I264.(English transl.: ibid.,356-360).

21. Ш а н и н   Н.А. К вопросу о конструктивном понимании опорных формул. Труды Матем.инст.АН СССР,1964,$\underline{72}$,348-379. (English transl.: Amer.Math.Soc.Transl. (2),1972,$\underline{99}$,233-275).

22. Ш а н и н   Н.А. Об иерархии способов понимания суждений в конструктивной математике. Труды Матем.инст.АН СССР,1973,$\underline{129}$,203-266.(English transl.: Proc.Steklov Inst.Math.,1973,$\underline{129}$,209-271).

23. K r e i s e l   G. On the interpretation of non-finitist proofs. I.Journ.Symb.Logic,1951,$\underline{16}$,241-267.

24. K l e e n e   S.C. Recursive predicates and quantifiers.Trans. Amer.Math.Soc.,1943,$\underline{53}$,41-73.

25. K l e e n e   S.C. On the interpretation of intuitionistic number theory. Journ.Symb.Logic.,1945,$\underline{10}$,№4,109-123.

26. K l e e n e   S.C. Realizability and Shanin's algorithm for the constructive deciphering of mathematical sentences. Logique et analyse,1960,№11-12,154-165.

27. Ш а н и н   Н.А. О конструктивном понимании математических суждений. Труды Матем.инст.АН СССР,1958,$\underline{52}$,226-3II. (English transl.: Amer.Math.Soc.Transl.(2),1963,$\underline{23}$,109-189).

28. Ш а н и н   Н.А. Об алгорифме конструктивной расшифровки математических суждений.(Zeitschr.math.Logik Grundl.Math.,1958,$\underline{4}$, 293-303.

29. Ш а н и н   Н.А. Конструктивные вещественные числа и конструктивные функциональные пространства. Труды Матем.инст.АН СССР, 1962,$\underline{67}$,I5-294.(English transl.: Transl.Math.Monographs,Amer. Mathem.Soc.,Providence,R.I.,1968,vol.21).

30. G e n t z e n   G. Untersuchungen über das logische Schliessen. Mathem.Zeitschr.,1934,$\underline{39}$,176-210,405-431.

31. М и н ц   Г.Е. О предикатных и операторных вариантах построения теорий конструктивной математики. Труды Матем.инст.АН СССР, 1964,$\underline{72}$,383-436. (English transl.:Amer.Math.Soc.Transl.,1972, $\underline{100}$,1-68).

32. И д е л ь с о н   А.В. Исчисления конструктивной логики с подчиненными переменными. Труды Матем.инст.АН СССР,1964,$\underline{72}$,228-343. (English transl.: Amer.Math.Soc.Transl.,1972,$\underline{99}$).- Замечания об исчислениях конструктивной логики с подчиненными переменными и аксиомой полной индукции. Труды Матем.инст.АН СССР,1967, $\underline{93}$,106-112.(English transl.: Proc.Steklov Inst.Math.,1967,$\underline{93}$).

33. N e l s o n   D. Recursive functions and intuitionistic number theory. Trans.Amer.Math.Soc.,1947,$\underline{61}$,№2,307-368.

34. G ö d e l   K. Über eine bisher noch nicht benutzte Erweiterung des finiten Standpuktes. Dialectica,1958,$\underline{12}$,№3/4,280-287.

35. H e r b r a n d   J. Recherches sur la théorie de la demonstration. Travaux Soc.Sci.et Let.Varsovie,Cl.$\overline{\text{III}}$,1930,$\underline{33}$.

36. H e r b r a n d   J. Sur le probléme fondamental de la logique mathématique. Comp.Rend.Soc.Sci.Varsovie,Cl.$\overline{\text{III}}$,1931,$\underline{24}$,12-56.

37. Ш а н и н   Н.А. Об иерархии конструктивных функционалов Брауэра. Зап.научн.семинаров Ленингр.отд.Матем.инст.АН СССР,1974, $\underline{40}$,142-147.(English transl.:Journ.Soviet Mathem.,1977,$\underline{8}$).

38. М и н ц   Г.Е. Трансфинитные развертки арифметических формул. Зап.научн.семинаров Ленингр.отд.Матем.инст.АН СССР,1975,$\underline{49}$,51-66.(English transl.:Journ.Soviet Mathem.,1978,$\underline{10}$,533-547).

39. G r a t t a n - G u i n n e s s   I. In memoriam Kurt Gödel: His 1931 correspondence with Zermelo on his incompletability theorem. Historia Mathematica,1979,$\underline{6}$,294-304.

40. V a n   H e i j e n o o r t   J. (editor). From Frege to Gödel. Harvard univ.press,1967.

Remark to [22]. The following essential corrections should be made in [22] (and in the English translation of [22]).

Page 252, line 4 (in the English transl. page 256,line 26):

replace $(\mathcal{P}^{\circ}_{m+2,n} \circ \mathcal{P}^{\omega}_{a,i})$ by $(\mathcal{P}^{\omega}_{m+2,n,i} \circ \mathcal{P}^{\circ}_{a})$.

Page 256, line 16 (in the English transl.page 260,line 37):

replace $(\mathcal{P}^{\circ}_{m+2,n} \circ \mathcal{P}_{a,\beta})$ by $(\mathcal{P}_{m+2,n,\beta} \circ \mathcal{P}^{\circ}_{a})$.

Similar changes should be made in the corresponding definitions from the section 6.3.

From Logicism to Proceduralism
(An Autobiographical Account)

G. S. TSEYTIN
Leningrad State University, Leningrad, USSR

THIS IS A STORY of how I changed my views from the belief that good knowledge must always be represented as a set of logical statements, within a suitable mathematical model of reality, to my present opinion that knowledge is basically algorithmic.

I have to explain why I have chosen to go into details of my past rather than to give a systematic exposition of the proceduralist viewpoint. The first reason is that at present I am simply unable to give such an exposition except for a few general notions—a real presentation would be to show how it works. Thus I had to find some reference point with which to compare my views, and the easiest choice was to criticize my own errors. (All references to my papers in this text are intended to illustrate my fallacies, not my present viewpoint.) The second reason is that my present beliefs are based on my personal experience and my own assessment of it; it need not be convincing for everyone and all I can do is to show how it convinced me.

I started (in the early 50s) as a pure mathematician with a subconscious belief that mathematical entities are something that actually exist and can be investigated by means of reasoning; that any meaningful question about them has an "objective" answer that can be eventually discovered; that despite the incompleteness theorems the missing information can be obtained from "the reality" in some yet unclear way. (Of course I knew that mathematical notions are abstractions derived from the physical world, but this didn't affect my style of thinking.) I knew how to write algorithms—originally in the form of Markov normal algorithms—but regarded them as one more type of mathematical object whose properties should be proved by means of standard mathematical reasoning (in the style of [1]), even if they were immediately obvious. I was aware of A. A. Markov's criticisms of the classical set theory and took part in his programme of developing constructive mathematics; but I didn't accept his philosophy and I regarded my work in constructivism as a sort of exercise in self-limitation.

This Platonic attitude was further demonstrated in my approach to automatic language translation. I treated this area much like any conventional application area of mathematics. The ultimate result of such applied research is usually a computational procedure (in my case, a parsing algorithm) but empirical procedures are usually not regarded as a good form of representation of knowledge. It is thought that a "mathematical model" must be developed, i.e., an ideal construct (made up of mathematical entities) that exhibits properties approximately resembling those of the real object, and then all practical procedures should be derived mathematically from the model. In natural language parsing the empirical approach to construction of parsing algorithms very soon proved fruitless—at least, as I would add now, with our programming techniques of 1960, when we had very little experience in modularity and severe hardware limitations. So our research group developed a system for logical description of syntax (dependency grammar), and published a paper [2] in support of non-algorithmic representation of linguistic knowledge.

Indeed, the advantages of non-algorithmic knowledge are obvious. A single equation like Ohm's law, $U = IR$, does the job of several procedures, viz., $U := I*R$, $I := U/R$, and $R := U/I$. What is more, it can combine with a number of other equations to form a description of a complex circuit, whereupon well-known mathematical methods can be used to solve a number of other problems.

Thus, starting from the early 60s, I found myself combatting algorithmic representation of knowledge in various areas of my work. In the theory of algorithms and constructive analysis I developed a technique of replacing direct construction of algorithms (used in existence proofs) by manipulations of enumerable sets [3,4] which proved to be shorter and closer to the usual mathematical style. In computer programming I realized that even a high-level language (which we called "automatic programming") does not relieve the programmer of some routine job of "algorithmizing". A really automatic programming system, I thought, should be able to construct a program—or at least, obvious parts of it—from some other form of task specification, *probably* a logical description. This led me to what is called now program verification [5,6] which I regarded as a preliminary step to automatic algorithmizing.

And even in as concrete a work as the programming of a business information system, I thought of a logical approach. I proposed [7] a set of axioms for a first order theory including a general pattern for new axioms called the completeness principle: it said that any change in the system within the given period of time was due to one of explicitly listed events.

My logicist approach to applications was implicitly based on a presupposition that deserves special discussion. It was the presupposition that the predicate logic is a universal representation of any regular reasoning, i.e., that any regular reasoning can be translated into the predicate logic by a suitable change of notation. Some people may argue that this is an extreme simplification, that they always recognized such things as heuristics, plausible reasoning, fuzzy statements, intuition, insight (and even clairvoyance). Things of this sort are often referred to as a testimony to the limitations of the standard logical approach and sometimes are used as a basis for attempts to overcome these limitations. But I emphasize that my presupposition didn't apply to this type of thinking but rather to what we normally perceive as regular, deterministic, logical thinking. (That was why I believed that thinking involved in programming was also based on logical derivation, which led me to the concept of programming from logical specifications.)

At present I can give a very simple example to show the fallacy. Let Peter have 2 pencils and let Ann give him another 3; how many pencils has Peter got now? The answer is 5, and this is a very exact and logical conclusion. Now I add that Peter has lost one pencil; this makes the answer different. Can a conclusion obtained by means of derivation in some system of predicate logic be invalidated by adding an extra premise? Or should my previous answer be "5, provided that nothing else happened to Peter and/or his pencils"?

Of course, this is a rather crude argument which I wouldn't accept 15 years ago. Under the logicist approach, the problem can be circumvented by means of the completeness principle or by John McCarthy's "minimal entailment". There is a subtler limitation of the predicate logic connected with its way of using names (or variables).

A name is regarded as a separate object bound permanently or temporarily (if it is a variable) to some entity, and the only function of the name is to represent that entity. It is not allowed to consider the external appearance of a name or its composition; terms and expressions can be regarded as composite names, but their structure indicates operations on the denotata rather than on the names. Binding of a particular name to a particular entity is purely accidental. If two names defined in different scopes happen to look alike it is a thing a well-bred logician should avoid or at least ignore.

Most of the current programming languages (but not LISP) take the same attitude; the Algol 68 Report quotes from Shakespeare: "What's in a name? that which we call a rose by any other name would smell as sweet." The Algol identification rule for an identifier not declared in the procedure where it is used mimics the substitution rule of the predicate logic: substituting $f(x)$ for y in $\exists x\, P(x, y)$ yields $\exists z\, P(z, f(x))$. Only at the meta-language level may a name be treated as an object in its own right, which partly accounts for the strict distinction between meta-language and language (in programming: compilation time and run time). We shall see a little later why this attitude is too restrictive.

The change in my views was gradual and several sources had contributed to it: the internal weakness of the concept of "mathematical world" that gradually came to light; the slow progress in automatic theorem proving, automatic programming and representation of natural language semantics based on a strictly logical approach compared with more successful empirical work in the same directions; my experience in developing problem oriented application languages. There were no direct objections to declarative representation of knowledge itself. Formerly I had to stick to it because it was the only form of knowledge supported by the logicist approach. Now I can view it as just one special type of knowledge; and it cannot operate alone, without the aid of procedural knowledge. No equation, however general and elegant, can be used without an algorithm for its solution. (It can be said, in parallel to the well-known principle of Wirchow concerning living cells, that algorithms can be obtained only from algorithms.) Thus the change to proceduralism was in three steps: lifting the restrictions imposed by logicism; extending the techniques of procedural representation of knowledge; understanding the universal role of procedural knowledge.

My faith in the mathematical world was seriously undermined by the difficulties in the foundations of mathematics, by the fact that a number of questions that looked meaningful (because syntactically correct) could not be meaningfully answered. The explanations like "the set of all ordinals doesn't exist while the set of all real numbers does" could be accepted half-heartedly, but P. Cohen's proof of independency of the continuum hypothesis showed that things were much worse. Observe the escalation of incompleteness in mathematics: N. I. Lobachevsky, J. Bolyai—the absolute geometry lacks information to decide which of *two* geometries is true; K. Gödel—the set of theorems provable in any theory is recursively enumerable and hence cannot contain all facts about elements of a non-enumerable set; P. Cohen—no *denumerable* set of statements can approach a description of a far non-denumerable set of entities. It occurred to me that mathematical questions might be no more meaningful than questions about characters in some novel. What, then, was the subject of mathematics? The constructive mathematics didn't present for me a way out: by introducing more subtle differences between statements it increased the number of apparently meaningful questions but gave fewer means for answering them. Once I gave a talk on the foundations of mathematics to an audience of physicists, and I succeeded in communicating to them my perplexity over the subject of mathematics. They reacted with sympathy: that meant, they told me, that mathematics was approaching the level of physics.

Applications of mathematical logic to common thinking were another area where my expectations were not realized. My work on natural languages was guided by the belief that a language can be regarded as a complex calculus with a syntax defined by means of a generative grammar and semantics giving the meaning of every generated object in terms of the meanings of its constituents. There was an uncertainty as to what objects could be used to represent the meanings. Ultimately the meaning should be represented in terms of behavior, but this being a very remote prospect the idea was to use some logic-like language for which the behavior (theorem proving) had a formal definition. Thus I had to build predicate-logic counterparts for sentences as well as for their constituents (see [8]).

This plan started to fail from the very beginning but it took me more than ten years to recognize it. First of all, I had to restrict myself to mathematical texts because of examples like "He knows that ..." where substituting equivalent propositions in place of the dots may result in non-equivalent statements (thus what "he" knows is a *text* rather than proposition; R. Carnap's theory of intensions based on modality was never convincing for me). Then, even the dullest mathematical texts I considered contained only a small fraction of statements for which a perfect translation into predicate logic was possible. A considerable part of each text contained, explicitly or implicitly, information on the structure of the proof, etc.—things that can be regarded as one type of procedural information.

For nouns the natural logical counterpart seemed to be individual variables (with ranges depending on particular nouns). I went further in this direction and, in order to represent the meaning of complex nominal groups, invented a special sort of subordinate variables whose ranges depended on the current *values* of other variables [9]. It looked awkward. Some years later an easier and more general solution was found where special *meaningless* quantifier-like symbols were used in representation of constituents other than complete sentences. And at the same time a group of linguists not interested in predicate logic succeeded [10] in finding a formal description of a number of semantic equivalences which, I had thought, had to be derived from some yet unknown logical representation. There were more examples of successful semantic processing of natural language fragments as in COBOL or in communication with data bases; but a logician would discard them scornfully [11] because they were only particular cases showing no way to a general solution. (I think now that no "general" solution for the natural language is possible, because it is a collection of a great number of relatively independent systems sharing common low-level mechanisms, rather than a single pre-planned system.)

As for logical verification of programs, writing specifications in predicate logic proved to be no easier than simply writing the programs themselves. Once I thought that what was needed was a more convenient specification language with more "syntactic sugar" [6], but I couldn't go far enough in this direction either. On the other hand, E. Tyugu and others, not mathematicians at all, found a very useful approach [12] to automatic programming based on combining pre-stored procedural "computational models". I was disappointed on seeing this idea because it made new programs out of other programs.

No efficient general method had been found in automatic theorem proving, and emphasis was shifted to machine-aided theorem proving in order to make it possible for the human user to supply some mysterious ingredient ("the intuition") that the automatic systems lacked. (Now I believe that the missing ingredient is procedurality rather than clairvoyance.) There were some more successful works in theorem proving for restricted areas (e.g., formula manipulation) or with systems based immediately on natural language representation of mathematical statements (with a restricted set of inference rules and direct indications of their use; such rules can be found in natural language text, but they are lost in the logical representation).

In computer programming my work usually took the form of inventing and implementing various problem-oriented languages. Thus I had an opportunity to create programming constructs that were closer to the way of thinking (and speaking) in the application area than to conventional programming constructs. Some parts of the work, e.g., an elaborate pattern matching system, parallelled some developments in artificial intelligence languages of which I became aware much later. This work showed me a deep affinity between natural languages and programming languages and led me to using programming constructs, along with those from logic, as representations of the meaning of natural language constructs. Very early I had an idea of representing the meaning of a sentence in terms of a boolean procedure with side effects, because this mechanism could account for the use of pronouns; but the attempt failed. It was in this area that I encountered (about 1973) an example that has played a decisive role in my abandonment of logicism.

I had to develop a simulation language for a class of ecological systems involving several populations of fish (of several age groups each) with their growth, propagation, nutrition, preying, etc. Each age group of each population had several numerical characterisitcs for which storage locations had to be assigned. These were the only objects meaningful from the computer side but not from the user side. The user might even be unaware of some intermediate quantity used in simulation; the meaningful things for the user were the fish population and some explicitly or implicitly specified "laws" like "the number of babies equals population times fertility" or "the fertility of some fish is such-and-such a function of its weight", etc. It is important that a law specifies relationships between some characteristics of a population with no reference to what other characteristics the population may possess. The only conventional way to represent laws was to introduce a universal structure for all populations with the full set of characteristics regardless of the fact that only a small number of them might be needed for a particular population and age group. But I was reluctant to do this because I wanted to keep the system open for new laws and characteristics. After a year's hesitation I arrived at a solution that was extremely unusual for me.

The representation of a population was simply a name (a sequence of characters) that could be combined with the *name* of a characteristic and the number of the age group to form a designation of a storage location for the corresponding quantity. A law was explicitly applied to a specific population name but the names of the characteristics involved were intrinsic to the law. A new cell in run-time storage was allocated whenever a new designation of a quantity was synthesized, and the fact that applications of different laws referred to the same quantity was known from the coincidence of the designations, *not vice versa*.

I was astounded by the fact that in order to obtain a meaningful result I had, rather than to stick to the meanings of the names, to treat them as meaningless sequences of characters; and that I had derived the "behavioral" result right from the language, without any "semantic" representation in between. I had a picture that on the way from text to behavior a linguistic sign, after remaining intact during some syntactic transformations, suddenly vanished but at the last moment it showed itself for a short while as a physical object. I could find more instances of this kind (e.g., to find the sum of two decimal numbers one has to work with their digits). I compared it also with the analysis of meaning of natural language adjectives (a *regular* pyramid is not necessarily a *regular* polyhedron; a *good* mathematician need not be a *good* lecturer); here the meaning of the adjective depends on the *word* rather than the *object* it qualifies. Also some other examples from my previous linguistic research could be seen now in new light. And all of this meant that I reached the point where usual mathematical abstraction was losing its power, where it was no longer useful to speak of an abstract entity as if it were an actual object and instead its mental symbolic representation had to be considered.

I came to regard an object (or, to be precise, its mental representation) as a set of named attributes whose values can be selected or altered by specifying the name, much like data sets and catalogued procedures in IBM's OS/360. This representation also makes it possible to define and override defaults. Of course, all of this is contrary to the style of logic: if the attributes of a rectangle are its base and height, why not allow the diagonal or the area? And if allowed, how could they be altered?

I think now that the function of a name (noun) in language is not to specify a fixed object or class of objects but rather to serve as a selector used in different contexts or situations to pick out a thing having the specified function (in some vague sense). And when so used the name can define a further structure of names and attributes. I regard this as an alternative to R. Carnap's theory of extensions and intensions.

In the simulation system for fish the laws were not procedures. They were static schemes (similar to macros) used to generate the list of "orders" which were then ordered and executed in a fixed sequence. But later I began to build procedural systems where selection by name could be done in procedures and moreover the value selected could be a further procedure. I could appreciate the freedom and flexibility of this approach; this experience is probably familiar to LISP users. For some practical purposes procedures could be regarded as direct representations of meanings.

I learned more about the power of procedural representation of knowledge from the work in artificial intelligence, especially by C. Hewitt, T. Winograd and, of course, from M. Minsky's theory of frames. And this completed my transition to proceduralism (about 1976).

A question remains to be answered, why algorithms were not accepted earlier as an appropriate form of knowledge. The answer is that the mathematical notion of algorithm is too crude for the purpose of representing knowledge. What we often know is an informal method rather than a mathematical algorithm. What is the essential difference between them, and what should be added to our programming techniques to cope with the difference? One obvious suggestion is nondeterminism, and this is a very easy extension of the notion of algorithm.

Another popular suggestion is that an informal method may refer to subgoals for which it doesn't define a way to achieve them. But the mathematical notion of algorithm refers to undefined subgoals as well: try to add a letter A to the word if your pen has run out of ink, etc. And if the reference to subgoals were the principal difference between formal and informal methods, we could easily use the notion of relative recursivity and define an informal method as a reduction scheme of a goal to subgoals.

I suggest a different interpretation of this distinction. An algorithm in the mathematical sense is completely self-contained and as soon as the data have been specified it needs no further information. In contrast to this, a realistic procedure (and, to some extent, a modern computer program) can draw information from the environment in a way that *need not be specified in* advance. When we say that a procedure defines a subgoal it means that it tries to extract a method of achieving the subgoal from an unspecified source, i.e., from its own storage or from the environment where it is called. The extraction can take the form of selection by name (I am intentionally not speaking here of pattern-directed invocation). In other words this organization of procedures can be described as *modularity*: only one module at a time needs to be defined or changed, the rest are part of the environment.

There seems to be a third distinction between informal methods and algorithms. It is in the use of some kind of pattern recognition (possibly frame identification, but not the classical pattern matching) in order to identify the situation and then to select the action. It is probably here that usual declarative knowledge can enter the general scheme.

In this picture of procedural organization of knowledge, declarative knowledge doesn't lose its value. But one should remember that it is built on the top of a complex procedural system and that it is rather a happy chance when we can obtain knowledge in such a general and powerful form. Sometimes I even wonder how one could arrive at it.

References

[1] A. A. Markov, *Teoriĭa Algorifmov*, Trudy Matem. inst. im. V. A. Steklova 42 (1954).

[2] B. M. Leĭkina, T. N. Nikitina, M. I. Otkupshchikova, S. Ĭa. Fitialov, G. S. Tseĭtin, "Sistema avtomaticheskogo perevoda, razrabatyvaemaĭa v gruppe matematicheskoĭ lingvistiki VTs LGU," *Nauchno-tekhnicheskaĭa Informatsiĭa* (1966), No. 1, pp. 40–50; No. 4, p. 31.

[3] G. S. Tseĭtin, "Odin sposob izlozheniĭa teorii algorifmov i perechislimykh mnozhestv," *Trudy Matem. inst. im. V. A. Steklova* 72 (1964), 69–98.

[4] G. S. Tseĭtin, "O verkhnikh granitsakh perechislimykh mnozhestv konstruktivnykh veshchestvennykh chisel," *Trudy Matem. inst. im. V. A. Steklova* 113 (1970), 102–172.

[5] G. S. Tseĭtin, "O logicheskom podkhode k avtomatizatsii programmirovaniĭa," *Vse-soĭuzhaĭa konferentsiĭa po problemam teoreticheskoĭ kibernetiki 9–13 Iĭunĭa 1969 g.*, Tezisy dokladov (Novosibirsk, 1969), 5–6.

[6] G. S. Tseĭtin, "Nekotorye cherty ĭazyka dlĭa sistemy programmirovaniĭa, prover-ĭaĭushcheĭ dokazatel'stva," *Teoriĭa Programmirovaniĭa*, Chast' 2, Trudy simpoziuma (Novosibirsk, 1972), 234–249. English translation: G. S. Tseytin, "Some features of a language for a proof-checking programming system," Internation Symposium on Theoretical Programming, *Lecture Notes in Computer Science* 5 (Berlin: Springer, 1974), 394–407.

[7] G. S. Tseĭtin, "Logiko-matematicheskiĭ podkhod k postroeniĭu ékonomiko-informatsi-onnoĭ sistemy," *Metody vychisleniĭ*, vyp. 6 (Izd. Leningradskogo un-ta, 1970), 107–127.

[8] G. S. Tseĭtin, "Ĭazyk matematicheskoĭ logiki kak sredstvo issledovaniĭa semantiki estestvennogo ĭazyka," *Problemy Prikladnoĭ lingvistiki*, Tezisy mezhvuzovskoĭ kon-ferentsii 16–19 dekabrĭa 1969 g., Chast' 2 (MGPIIĬA, Moskva, 1969), 326–335.

[9] G. S. Tseĭtin, "O promezhutochnom étape pri perevode s estestvennogo ĭasyka na ĭazyk ischisleniĭa predikatov," *Tezisy dokladov na konferentsii po obrabotke informatsii, mashinnomy perevodu i avtomaticheskomu chteniĭu teksta* (VINITI, Moskva, 1961), 107–111.

[10] A. K. Zholkovskiĭ, I. A. Mel'chuk, "O semanticheskom sinteze," *Problemy Kibernetiki* 19 (1967), 177–238.

[11] G. S. Tseytin, "Features of natural languages in programming languages," *Proc. Fourth International Congress for Logic, Methodology and Philosophy of Science, Bucharest, 1971*, P. Suppes, L. Henkin, Gr. C. Moisil, A. Joja, eds., *Studies in Logic* 74 (Amsterdam: North-Holland, 1973), 215–222. Russian translation: G. S. Tseĭtin, "Cherty estestvennykh ĭazykov v ĭazykakh programmirovaniĭa," *Mashinnyĭ Perevod i Prikladnaĭa Lingvistika* 17 (MGPIIĬA, Moskva, 1974), 134–143.

[12] K. A. Tinn, É. Kh. Tyugu, M. I. Unt, "Sistema modul'nogo programmirovaniĭa dlĭa TsVM Minsk-22," VKP-2, *Trudy Vsesoĭuzhoĭ Konferentsii po Programmirovaniĭu*, Zasedanie G. (Novosibirsk, 1970), 23–39.

Abstract Computability on Algebraic Structures

A. P. ERSHOV

Computing Center, Siberian Branch, USSR Academy of Sciences, Novosibirsk 630090

THIS PAPER deals with abstract computability—the general theory of computable functions in which an object domain and certain elementary computation steps are taken as formal parameters possessing axiomatically prescribed properties. Although I have been aware of such theories for twenty-five years, it is not simply the inherent interest of this subject that encourages me to discuss such a fundamental problem, which traditionally belongs to the scope of logicians' competence. My main motivation is that these twenty-five years have seen the emergence of computer science—also called informatics, computer mathematics, or simply programming—a science that needs its own viewpoint on fundamental concepts of the theory of computation. A dialog between logicians and computer scientists, which is so characteristic of our symposium, should help computer scientists to develop a more educated view of the foundations of their field, at the same time properly reflecting its own characteristic features and viewpoints.

I shall begin with a brief summary of the reasons I began to study the concepts of abstract computation, since these considerations probably are representative of many other people involved with computers. Then I shall propose an approach to the definition of abstract computability. Since this paper was written after the symposium actually took place, I also have a chance to record the initial reactions of several logicians (on the whole encouraging) and to give a survey of approaches to abstract and generalized computability that have already appeared in the literature. Comparing these approaches with mine, I shall conclude by mentioning several alternative directions in which the indicated problems might be resolved in the future.

Motives

It must be admitted that a rigorous and generally accepted abstract theory of computation does not exist. Extremely well known definitions of effective procedures and effectively computable functions—recursive functions, Turing machines, Markov algorithms, and two or three others—have appeared, but each with its own existence and its own literature. It is reassuring to know that the mutual equivalence of these definitions has been proved, but only when our concern is with the totality of the set of computable functions; the equivalence conceals important practical and conceptual details and tends to confuse complexity specialists, since the complexity of the coding function remains outside of the theory. On the top level a so-called invariant theory has emerged, but the language of this theory happens to be a kind of semiformal jargon. When proving theorems that provide an "entrance point" to the invariant theory, the gap between simple conceptual contents and cumbersome programming rules looks awkward*. A definition of algorithms based on the concept of mechanical computation looks mathematically circular, for it is based on a so-called universal algorithm, which is inherently an informal description of machines' work. The programmability of the universal algorithm in the language of the same machine does not improve the situation.

All basic facts of the general theory of computability are extracted from recursive function theory. And even though a reasonable part of that theory allows invariant formulation, its overly intimate ties with the structure $(\omega, 0, +1, =)$ are obvious. Nobody will dispute the special role that natural numbers play in mathematics; in any axiomatics, natural numbers will perhaps represent the simplest class of constructive objects. However, this simplicity itself causes the concrete theory of arithmetical computable functions to conceal essentials, thus making it difficult to observe important distinctions (see Kreisel, 1969; p. 142).

That, in brief, is a programmer's view of classical computability theory.

On the other hand, computer mathematics constantly stimulates those who work with it to take a more and more abstract view of programming. Recent studies show clearly that it is valuable to deal with a computable function before a corresponding program has been written, and to reason independently of the program in all its details. That is why constructive existence theorems and characterizations of computable functions as fixed points are so important for programmers.

Looking for an algorithm that will solve some problem, a programmer would like to stay as long as feasible in the framework of the subject domain that is natural for the problem statement. This facilitates his or her search for informative relations and properties that will prove to be useful during the subsequent systematic development of the program. A programmer must often carry out the reverse process: starting with a language of data and primitive operations given *a priori*, to find out to what extent and in what manner they could be used to solve some problem. In both cases we program with respect to a given algebraic structure (data, operations, relations). That is why a programmer instinctively feels that the primary notion of computational theory should be one of relative computability rather than a generalization of 'absolute' computability.

A vast area of computer science deals with the manipulations of programs that have already been written. Methods of program transformation are really general only if they are schematic, i.e., if they consider program constants, variables, and operations as formal symbols. Thus, programming essentially needs a theory of computation in arbitrary algebraic structures.

When programs are being manipulated, some invariants should of course be maintained in order to guarantee the correctness of the program performance in all its instances. Such an invariant should also be schematic, and it should be abstract enough to serve various models of computation. Usually, such invariants are of special importance when

---

*See Glushkov, 1979, as an example of a reaction to this situation.

they provide the decidability of the corresponding equivalence problem. That is why programming needs so many schematic characterizations of computable functions that possess both a great generality and a simple structure.

An Approach

In order to clarify the main idea, we shall speak for simplicity about functions of a single variable. Let us start with two generally known basic "definitions":

- A function $f: D \to D$ is computable if there exists an algorithm that produces its values.

- An algorithm is a general effective method of obtaining a desired result in a finite number of elementary steps starting from a given argument.

Any rigorous theory of algorithms begins with a language by means of which constants of the object domain D are represented as data, and also—what is most important— by means of which operations on the objects are represented as programs. A single superalgorithm, which is uniformly applied to every program, defines how the result is obtained from a given argument.

Effectiveness is provided by four "finitenesses": The information about the superalgorithm is finite, evidently comprehensible and the same for any program from the class. The information contained in a program is finite, effectively recognizable by the superalgorithm and the same for any argument of the computable function. The information contained in *given* arguments is finite, effectively retrievable by the algorithm and the same during any realization of the computational process. The fourth "finiteness" is the finiteness of the number of elementary steps performed on the way to the result.

Let us now reformulate our initial thesis: A function may be considered computable if for every point (x, y) of its graph we can 'produce' a 'system' of 'steps' (a protocol) 'directly leading' from x to y, a system 'derived' 'regularly' from a single 'source' of information. The collection of all protocols, corresponding to all points of the graph of f, must completely characterize the function f.

There must be at most a finite number of 'essentially different' steps. However, each step whose execution is recognized to be elementary may be applied to an infinite variety of data instances, so each step is a function. We shall use the notation $\Phi = \{\phi_1, \ldots, \phi_m\}$ to stand for the set of functions used as basic operations in individual steps; these functions need not be unary.

Let us analyze how a 'source' of information produces a 'system' of steps. At each moment we are allowed to perform only one step, so that we obtain chains. It is reasonable also to allow arbitrary choices from a finite number of steps; thus we obtain trees as well as simple chains. In other words, one of the ways to represent a system of steps for obtaining y from x (a protocol) is a functional term (or ϕ-term) in the signature Φ, depending ultimately on the argument x and some constants from D. We consider it straightforward to compute

val $\tau(x)$, the value of such a term $\tau(x)$, and this execution (so called direct computation) is not further formalized.

It is clear that a choice between several steps is not always done arbitrarily but on the basis of a certain decision. We postulate that all of these decisions must be reflected in the 'system of steps' that we produce as the evidence of computability of the result. Thus, a signature of predicate symbols $\Pi = \{\pi_1, \dots, \pi_n\}$ appears by means of which predicate terms (or π-terms) are constructed in the usual way. Evaluation of a π-term is also considered to be direct computation and is not further formalized. If some direct computation τ is conditional on the truth or falsity of a predicate term π, then we will represent this information in the form of a 'conditioned' term $(\pi : \tau)$ or $(\neg\pi : \tau)$, respectively. When a conditioned term is freely constructed its value is defined by the following rule:

$$\mathbf{val}(\pi : \tau) = \begin{cases} \mathbf{val}(\tau), & \text{if } \mathbf{val}(\pi) = \mathbf{true}; \\ \text{undefined}, & \text{if } \mathbf{val}(\pi) = \mathbf{false}. \end{cases}$$

$$\mathbf{val}(\neg\pi : \tau) = \begin{cases} \text{undefined}, & \text{if } \mathbf{val}(\pi) = \mathbf{true}; \\ \mathbf{val}(\tau), & \text{if } \mathbf{val}(\pi) = \mathbf{false}. \end{cases}$$

Evaluation of a conditioned term is also considered to be direct computation and is not further formalized. The result of an operation is undefined if any of its arguments is undefined. Note that a contractictory term (in which both π and $\neg\pi$ occur) is never defined.

Allowing the substitution of conditioned terms into the argument positions of symbols from signatures Φ and Π, we obtain a space T of *computing terms* that will be the source of protocols for evaluation of computable functions.

We shall now present a scheme for defining a computable function. Let us consider an algebraic structure $A = \langle D, C, \Phi, \Pi, R \rangle$ where R is a function from $\Phi \cup \Pi$ to the set ω of natural numbers; here R is the type of the structure, specifying the number of arguments of the functional and predicate symbols in the disjoint sets Φ and Π, respectively; D is a carrier (the object domain); and the finite set $C \subseteq D$ represents constants of the carrier. Let T_A be the space of computing terms with arguments from the alphabet $C \cup \{x\}$.

Scheme of definition. A function $f : D \to D$ is said to be computable on A if there exists a set $\mathrm{Det}_f \subseteq T_A$ (a *determinant* of the function f) such that

(1) $\forall(x, y) \in f \, \exists \tau(x) \in \mathrm{Det}_f : \mathbf{val}\,\tau(x) = y$;

(2) $\forall x \, \forall \tau(x) \in \mathrm{Det}_f : \mathbf{val}\,\tau(x) = y \Rightarrow (x, y) \in f$.

Before going into the substance of the matter, two points may be noted. Firstly, the definition does not preclude multivalued functions. To provide singlevaluedness it would be necessary for all protocols that are defined for a specific x to yield one and the same y. Secondly, the classical definitions of computability can be expressed by this scheme. The notion of protocol, with minor variations, is well known in the theory of algorithms and in programming. Condition (2) can also be provided if protocols are made sufficiently detailed.

Naturally, a determinant must be an effectively generable set. In any existing formalism it happens to be an enumerable set, for it may be generated by a simple extension of the universal algorithm. Moreover, in a finitely generated structure with equality the determinant trivially becomes isomorphic to the function graph by means of the following construction

$$\text{Det}_f = \{(x = c_x : c_y) \mid (x, y) \in f\}$$

where c_x is a constant or a bound term with the value x.

However, it seems to us uninteresting to define a determinant flatly requiring its enumerability, for we are seeking a computability definition that is not based on equivalent notions. Though it is known that enumerable sets may be enumerated by very simple subrecursive functions it seems highly desirable to find an ultimately narrow class of determinant generation methods, say by some simple automata.

The principal approach is to allow the determinant to include non-valued terms, i.e., terms generatable by a generating process but non-realizable by any model of the algebraic structure. Nothing precludes us from putting such protocols into the determinant if only the property (2) of the definition holds.

We may note further that our definition corresponds to the intuitive notion of effective computability. Indeed, we may compute values of a function by its determinant according to the following algorithm: Generate determinant elements one by one and try to evaluate them for a given x. Take the first value as the value of the function.

Replacing the notion of program by the notion of determinant we have abstracted from many things, in particular, from the concrete program syntax and the details of the universal algorithm.

The next very important level of abstraction will be achieved if we succeed in describing and generating determinants without depending on a concrete realization of the basic algebraic structure. Naturally, if we would require that each determinant must fit the function graph exactly, it would be in principle an unachievable goal. However, if we allow the generation of undefined and even contradictory components of the determinant this would allow us, at least in principle, to describe the determinacy counting on only the type of the algebraic structure and using its signature as an alphabet of formal symbols. Certainly, to prove theorems from computability theory we will need some properties of the domain and elementary function-oracles, but we may hope to express these properties axiomatically.

Analysis of related works

Not pretending for completeness, I would like to comment on the papers known to me that contain material that might contribute to the development of abstract computability theory on the basis of the determinant concept. We shall make an attempt to analyze from a single viewpoint a number of works in the theory of programming as well as works that belong to mathematical logic. Although I feel competent in the first field, in the second one I can pretend to be no more than a dutiful reader.

The pioneering works in recursion theory and effective computability certainly contain many premises of the abstract theory. However, their explication requires a special historic study. So I shall confine myself to citing the well-known monograph by Kleene, 1952, remarking only that though the concept of relative recursiveness in the classical theory is based upon the concrete structure $\langle \omega, 0, +1, = \rangle$, it became for many points of departure in the search for abstract computability.

We shall deliberately merge together references to both logic and programming, sorting them on the time axis. Papers presented at a conference will be timed here by the conference date. Some works were unavailable to the author, so only secondhand information is given. Throughout $\langle D, \Phi, \Pi \rangle$ denotes an (algebraic) structure with the carrier D, functional ϕ-symbols $\Phi = \{\phi_1, \ldots, \phi_m\}$ and predicate π-symbols $\Pi = \{\pi_1, \ldots, \pi_n\}$. The functional part may be absent; usually this is compensated for by postulating equality in the structure. Constants may be treated as separate symbols and as operations with no arguments. The symbol ω denotes the natural numbers (with zero). A structure without an interpretation of the signature symbols will sometimes be called an abstract structure. A concrete structure that is obtained by an interpretation of the signature symbols will be called a realization or interpretation of the abstract structure. An algebraic structure on which programs, their schemata, and computable functions are considered will be called a base structure.

Yanov, 1957, extending A. A. Lyapunov's ideas, studied algorithms on systems $\langle D, \Phi, \Pi \rangle$ with unary functions and predicates. Programs were represented as control-flow schemata where conditions were arbitrary Boolean functions on π-symbols and action statements were single ϕ-symbols operating on one memory location. Yanov was apparently the first author to introduce the concept of determinant, taken as a set of configurations generated from the program representation. Let $\Delta = \pi_1^{\sigma_1}, \ldots, \pi_n^{\sigma_n}$ be an arbitrary n-tuple of π-symbol values, where π^σ is either π (val π = true) or $\neg \pi$ (val π = false). A configuration K (empty at the beginning) is generated in the following way: Approach the entry-point of the schema with an arbitrary tuple of π-symbol values. Now suppose that we are walking on the scheme with a tuple Δ. The walk will be defined uniquely while we are walking along logical conditions. There are three alternatives: (1) we reach a ϕ-vertex; (2) we reach an exit (the generation stops); (3) we enter into a loop of conditions (again the generation stops). In the first case the current value of K is concatenated with the pair $(\Delta\,\phi)$, i.e., K becomes $K(\Delta\,\phi)$; an arbitrary new value Δ' of π-symbols is selected and we approach the successor of the ϕ-vertex. The configuration K may be either finite or infinite. Two schemata on one and the same signature are formally equivalent if their determinants are the same. Yanov established that this equivalence is decidable and developed a complete calculus that provides a transformability of a schema into any equivalent one.

It is strange that until now nobody has investigated the class of all Φ and Π such that Yanov schemata on the structure $\langle \omega, \Phi, \Pi \rangle$ will compute all recursive functions.

Ershov, 1958, considered the representation of algorithms as control-flow schemata on arbitrary structures $\langle D, \Phi, \Pi \rangle$ without restrictions on the signature type and number of variables. Action statements were sequences of assignments $(x := \tau)$ where x is a variable and r is an arbitrary ϕ-term. Logical conditions are π-terms or their Boolean compositions. This paper described a universal procedure of the execution of such programs and defined their equivalence as identity of computed functions. A concept of *termal* value (or S-representation) of a variable was introduced, which meant the ϕ-term composed of the operations used to obtain that value. Some so-called algorithmically complete sets of operations and relations on a constructive domain D were studied; such sets compute all computable functions on D.

This computational model, originating in the flowcharts of von Neumann and Goldstine (and introduced independently by many others) gradually became quite widespread. We shall call the program representation in this model a flow-program with memory.

Krinitsky, 1959 (see also Krinitsky, 1970) considered flow schemata with memory on abstract structures $\langle D, \Phi, \Pi \rangle$ in his dissertation. He introduced the notion of functional equivalence of flow schemata as computation of identical functions for any interpretation of the base structure. Krinitsky proved the decidability of functional equivalence for schemata without loops and found for this class a complete transformation system. Flow schemata with memory are often called standard schemata in the literature.

Fraissé, 1959 (according to Moschovakis, 1969b and Lacombe, 1969), connected abstract recursivity (F-recursivity) of a predicate P in a structure $\langle D, \Pi \rangle$ with the notion of derivativity in the ordinary predicate calculus with equality. For this purpose the language L of the predicate calculus is extended with predicate symbols $\pi_1, \ldots, \pi_n$, the defined predicate symbol P, and individual constants c_z for each $z \in D$. With each r-place predicate symbol π_i^r we associate a countable set $\Delta(\pi_i^r)$ of formulas having the form $\pi_i(c_{z_1}, \ldots, c_{z_r})$ if $\pi_i(z_1, \ldots, z_r)$ is true, or $\neg \pi_i(c_{z_1}, \ldots, c_{z_r})$ if $\pi_i(z_1, \ldots, z_r)$ is false. Let $\Delta(\Pi) = \Delta(\pi_1) \cup \cdots \cup \Delta(\pi_n)$ and let $\Phi(P)$ be a formula in the language L. We say that a predicate $P(z_1, \ldots, z_n)$ is F-recursive in the structure $\langle D, \Pi \rangle$ if it is defined by the following rule

$$P(z_1, \ldots, z_n) \leftrightarrow \Delta(\Pi) \cup \{\Phi(P)\} \vdash P(c_{z_1}, \ldots, c_{z_n})$$

and

$$\neg P(z_1, \ldots, z_n) \leftrightarrow \Delta(\Pi) \cup \{\Phi(P)\} \vdash P(c_{z_1}, \ldots, c_{z_n}).$$

Due to the completeness of the predicate calculus this "schematic definition" is equivalent to the model-theoretic definition of the predicate $P(z_1, \ldots, z_n)$ by the formula $\Phi(P)$. Let $\Phi(P)$ be a formula of the predicate calculus, and let $C_\Phi(D, \Pi)$ be the class of all models of Φ obtained by arbitrary extensions of the structure $\langle D, \Pi \rangle$ with one and the same carrier. Then a predicate $P(z_1, \ldots, z_n)$ that preserves its values on every extension from $C_\Phi(D, \Pi)$ is just the F-recursive predicate defined with $\Phi(P)$

If we take ω as the carrier then F-recursivity in $\langle \omega, \Pi \rangle$ becomes equivalent to ordinary relative recursiveness.

McCarthy, 1961, introduced a new model of computation on arbitrary structures $\langle D, \Phi, \Pi \rangle$ in the form of recursive programs or—in the abstract form—recursive schemata. His main construct is a conditional term $(\pi \rightarrow \phi, \psi)$ where π is a predicate term and ϕ

and ψ are functional or conditional terms. A conditional term corresponds to definition by case. Equivalent notations are 'if π then ϕ else ψ' or 'if π then ϕ else ψ fi' or '$(\pi \mid \phi \mid \psi)$'. Conditional and functional terms are united under the name of operational terms. The alphabet of the operational terms is supplemented by symbols of defined functions $F = \{f_1, \ldots, f_k\}$, input variables $X = \{x_1, \ldots, x_s\}$, and formal variables $U = \{u_1, \ldots, u_t\}$. A recursive program has the form

$$H(X, F, \Phi, \Pi)$$
$$f_1(U_1) = \tau_1(U_1, F, \Phi, \Pi)$$
$$\ldots$$
$$f_k(U_k) = \tau_k(U_k, F, \Phi, \Pi).$$

A main program H is an operational term and $f(U_i) = \tau_i(U_i, F, \Phi, \Pi)$ is a recursive equation in which τ is an operational term and U_i is a tuple of formal variables.

McCarthy showed that any flow-schema with memory in a structure $\langle D, \Phi, \Pi \rangle$ is translatable into a recursive schema *in the same* structure. He showed also that recursive programs on the structure $\langle \omega, 0, +1, = \rangle$ compute every arithmetical recursive function.

This model became broadly used in the theory of progamming, for least fixed points of recursive equations happened to be a good semantic representation of functions computed by recursive programs.

Maltsev, 1961, proposed to study recursivity in arbitrary algebraic structures (algebraic systems in his terminology) using a mapping α of natural numbers onto the carrier, so that an operation $f(u_1, \ldots, u_r)$ in the structure is associated with an arithmetical function $F(x_1, \ldots, x_r)$ by the following relation

$$f(\alpha x_1, \ldots, \alpha x_r) = \alpha F(x_1, \ldots, x_r).$$

Though recursion theory proper was not elaborated in detail in Maltsev's paper, his idea not only reflected but considerably stimulated a tendency to study abstract structures by looking at their arithmetical counterparts and the numerations themselves.

Wagner, 1963 (according to Wagner, 1969), offered an approach to abstract computability based on what might be called a high-level axiomatics that characterizes the class of computable functions as a whole. He postulated a priori that elements of the base set U are programs (indices) of functions on that set and that there exists an a priori given operation of taking a function by its index u and applying it to an argument x (denoted as $[u](x)$). The s-m-n-theorem (Kleene, 1952, ch. XII, theorem XXIII) is also postulated and, properly speaking, is used as the definition of a many-place function: by definition $[u](x, y) = [[u](x)](y)$. As a result, it is sufficient for the development of an informative theory to postulate the existence in U of an undefined element $*$ with the axiom

$$[u](*) = * = [*](u); \qquad (I)$$

a so-called 'blending function' with the axiom generalizing the substitution rule:

$$[\alpha](f, g) \neq *$$
$$[[\alpha](f, g)](x) = [f](x, [f](x, [g](x)]; \qquad (II)$$

and the function ψ of definition by cases with the axiom

$$[[\psi](c, b, a)](x) = \begin{cases} a, & \text{if } x = c; \\ b, & \text{if } x \neq c. \end{cases} \qquad (III)$$

Sets that satisfy these axioms are called Uniformly Reflexive Structures (URS) by Wagner. These axioms provide many 'standard' computable functions (constants, identity, projections), powerful closure theorems, and some other properties usually addressed to computable functions and their classes. The existence of recursive constructions in ω that validate URS axioms on ω was also shown. The corresponding functions are exactly the partial recursive functions.

On the other hand the lack of axiomatically formulated properties of constructive objects does not allow us to define, without additional assumptions, a class of functions that would intuitively satisfy the concept of effective computability and, in particular, enumerability.

In order to define such a class, Wagner used the fact that any URS contains a unary function and a constant, which may play the role of successor and zero, respectively. As a result, the natural numbers are mapped into the URS forming a so-called splinter. Further, it is postulated that the splinter is computable in the sense that its characteristic function exists in the URS. This makes it possible to simulate composition (in any URS), primitive recursion (in any URS), and the μ-operator (for a URS with computable splinter), thus obtaining the whole class of partial recursive functions.

It seems that Wagner's work played an important role in stimulating further research on abstract computability.

Kreisel, 1963 (according to Moschovakis, 1969b, and Lacombe, 1969), introduced a rather general notion of invariant definability of a predicate by a formula α in the language of the predicate calculus with equality. Invariantness means satisfiability of predicate symbols on the considered domain. Exploiting the fact that invariant definability and recursivity coincide for arithmetical predicates, Kreisel emphasized the usefulness of this notion for studying generalized and abstract recursion. A combination of this viewpoint may be found also in the literature on programming theory where invariant constructions sometimes happen to coincide with schematic constructions. Cf., e.g., Yanov, 1957; Rutledge, 1964; and Fraissé, 1959.

Rutledge, 1964, showed that Yanov schemata determinants form a language that is accepted by a finite automaton. He introduced the notion of the functional equivalence of Yanov schemata (the computation of equal functions in any interpretation of the base structure) and showed that it coincides with formal equivalence (equality of determinants).

Glushkov, 1965, introduced the notion of a discrete transformer as an abstract model of computation. A discrete transformer operates on some 'information set' S and is constituted by a pair of two automata: a control automaton with an input alphabet X and output alphabet Y and an operational automaton with the input alphabet Y and output alphabet X. Roughly speaking, X is related to the predicate signature, Y is related to the function signature, and the information set is related to the carrier of the base structure.

Taking an input symbol $x \in X$, the control automaton yields an output symbol $y \in Y$ and sends it to the operational automaton, which performs a corresponding operation $f_y :$ $S \rightarrow S$ and yields an output symbol from X defined by the operation. As a result, the distinction between 'logical' and 'computation' features of algorithms became explicit.

Paterson, 1968, introduced independently the model of flow schemata with memory and proved undecidability of the functional equivalence. This negative result greatly influenced the search for formal equivalence relations on program schemata using various notions of determinant (see Itkin, 1972).

Strong, 1968, studied Wagner's concepts (see Wagner, 1963) algebraically and analyzed his postulates and axioms in more detail. Separating the functional space $F = \{f\}$, $f :$ $D^n \rightarrow D$ $(n = 0, 1, \ldots)$, from the domain D, he listed two variants of axioms sufficient to establish that F is a URS. The first variant forms the so-called basic recursive function theory (BRFT).

(1) F contains constant functions for each element of D and projection functions of any number of arguments.

(2) F contains the characteristic function of the predicate $x = c$ where c is constant.

(3) F is closed with respect to substitution.

(4) F contains a universal function for all m-ary functions, for each $m > 0$.

(5) F contains a total function satisfying the s-m-n-theorem for each $m, n > 0$. (Programmers would call this a universal partial evaluator.)

Another variant is destined for the space F_1 of unary functions:

(1) F_1 contains constant functions for any element of D; it also contains the function and both functional inverses of some externally given pairing function.

(2) F_1 contains a function that, taken together with the pairing function, defines the characteristic function of the equality to a constant.

(3) F_1 contains a function that, taken together with the pairing function, defines a universal function for functions from F_1.

(4) F_1 contains a function, that, taken together with the pairing function defines a function satisfying the s-1-1-theorem.

Friedman, 1969a, improved Strong's axiomatics (see Strong 1960, the second variant) showing that the BRFT may be described for the set F of functions on D by the following axioms:

(1) D contains at least two elements.

(2) F contains functions of at most two arguments on D.

(3) F is closed with respect to substitution.

(4) F contains the identity function, the pairing function, and both inverses of the pairing function.

(5) F contains all unary constant functions.

(6) F contains the characteristic function of equality.

(7) F contains a universal function for unary functions.

The improvement is due to the fact that the s-m-n-function is not postulated. Its absence is compensated by subtle distinctions in the other axioms.

Lacombe, 1969, considered computability in relational structures with equality $\langle D, \Pi, = \rangle$ where D is a numerated carrier. As in Maltsev, 1961, the recursiveness of implanted functions on ω is transferred to original functions on D. A predicate $P(x_1, \ldots, x_r)$ is abstractly recursive in Π if it is recursive for any enumeration of D. Abstractly recursive predicates are characterized by primitively recursive sets of Boolean formulas on the alphabet that contains Π, P, their variables $x_1, \ldots, x_t$, and a finite set of constants $a_1, \ldots, a_k$. These sets of Boolean formulas are close to our notion of determinant. The correctness of Lacombe's concept of abstract recursivity is confirmed by the fact that in the structure $\langle \omega, 0, +1, = \rangle$ his computability coincides with relative recursivity. Moreover, Lacombe computability coincides with Fraissé computability (see Fraissé, 1959).

Moschovakis, 1969a (apparently independent of Wagner, 1963, and Strong, 1968), defined a class of recursive functions on an arbitrary set D. Extending D with a 'zero' element 0, he postulated a pairing function $z = (x, y)$, $z: D^* \times D^* \to D^*$ (D^* is the closure of $D \cup \{0\}$ under (x, y)). Then he mapped the natural numbers into D^* where $0, 1, 2, \ldots$ correspond to 0, $(0,0)$, $((0,0),0)$ and so on, with the successor $n + 1$ corresponding to $(n, 0)$. Using this model of natural numbers Moschovakis described a class of 'primitive recursive' functions on D^* relative to a list $\Phi = \{\phi_1, \ldots, \phi_m\}$ of arbitrary functions on D^*. The characteristic feature of the theory is that Φ may contain multi-valued functions, and the definition of the class of pr-functions is controlled by an inductive construction of function indices that, being sequences of natural numbers packed in objects from D^*, contain information about the function definition. Moschovakis showed that pr-functions, thus defined, relativized to the empty Φ model arithmetical pr-functions.

The expansion of the pr-functions onto the partial recursive functions was achieved by postulating computability of the universal (enumeration) function on D^*. This function happens to be defined only if the first argument is a valid index. The necessity to analyze the objects that 'pretend' to be indices (programmers would say to parse source programs) requires operations analogous to the μ-operator in the ordinary recursion theory. Moschovakis considered two variants of such an operator, treating them as search in a set which may be well-ordered or not. In these cases so-called prime and search computabilities are defined, respectively.

For prime and search computabilities Moschovakis developed an elementary theory that includes normal form theorems, closure properties, recursion theorems, and so on.

Moschovakis, 1969b, integrated some of the preceding works. He showed that the F-recursivity by Fraissé, 1959, is implied by the invariant definability by Kreisel, 1963. His main result showed that the invariant definability of a predicate P in a structure $\langle D^*, \Pi \rangle$

implies the search computability of P in the structure $\langle D^*, \Pi, =\rangle$. The subsequent proof of the reducibility of the F-recursivity to the search computability, taken together with the equivalence to the computability of Lacombe, 1969, establishes a solid basis for the understanding of the nature of abstract computability.

Kreisel, 1969, in a very interesting and provocative review, summed up the works of the 60s aimed at the generalization of recursion theory. He gave a detailed analysis of goals and possible approaches to the further development of the theory, identifying many yet unclarified subtleties in its foundations, and formulating interesting problem statements, some of which accord well with the goals of our study. In particular, his analysis permits the clarification of an essential distinction between abstract and generalized recursion theories. The latter, when expanding the usual recursion onto more general structures, essentially uses the classical theory either using enumerations or taking the concept of enumerable set for granted, or transferring schemes of recursive definitions 'literally' onto abstract functional spaces. On the other hand, an abstract computability theory, in our opinion, should be developed as a formal theory with no references to the theory of computable arithmetical functions. We would like to see abstract computability as a logical theory with respect to which the ordinary recursion theory looks like a model or realization.

Friedman, 1969b, had actually anticipated our approach to abstract computability. He attracted attention to cases of the hidden use of ordinary recursion in the study of computability on arbitrary structures. Considering an arbitrary algebraic structure $A = \langle D, C, \Phi, \Pi\rangle$ with constants $C = c_0, \ldots, c_k$, Friedman described two models of computation in A: a P-model, which is practically identical to the flow schemata of Ershov, 1958, Krinitsky, 1959, and Paterson, 1968; and a T-model, which generalizes the concept of Turing machine (allowing squares on the tape to contain either an element from D or an intermediate symbol). Finally, he introduced a model of effective definitions, or D-model, which practically coincides with our notion of determinant. Friedman uses 'clauses' $(C \to t)$ where C is either empty or a non-contradictory conjunction of π-terms or their negations and t is a ϕ-term. Friedman's clause is analogous to our protocol. Naturally, a clause denotes the computation of the ϕ-term t under the assumption that condition C is satisfied. The empty condition C is true by definition. The role of determinant is played by a set of clauses that must be recursively enumerable in the sense of the ordinary recursion theory and such that the conjunction of the conditions of two different clauses from the set is always contradictory. Friedman showed that every computation in the P- and T-models yields a protocol, the set of which forms a determinant in the D-model. The proof $D \to T$ appeals to Church's Thesis (applied to the T-model) and to the enumerability of the determinant. The proof $T \to P$ is more complicated, for P-programs may use only a finite number of memory locations, bounded uniformly for any computation. Friedman uses P-machines with counters that compute by Gödel numbers of determinant clauses; secondly, he postulates existence of equality as a basic predicate.

Friedman used the name T-recursive functions for any function computed by T-machines in algebraic structures $\langle D, \Phi, \Pi\rangle$ using any (finite) number of constants from D.

He listed 13 basic theorems of elementary recursion theory and then, breaking them into six groups (with intersections), he showed which combinations of additional properties of the base structure would provide the validity of theorems from one or another group. There are three such additional properties.

(1) T-recursivity of the equality predicate.

(2) T-recursivity of the pairing function.

(3) The finite generability of D from a finite number of constants and a total T-recursive function. (It happens, further, that (1) & (3) $\rightarrow$ (2)).

This rather interesting analysis is, however, undermined by an unseparable use of the ordinary recursion theory (the enumerability of determinants).

Friedman pointed out that programmers had suggested that he compare his P-model with the flow-schemata by Paterson, 1958. He expressed a hope that his analysis of the P-model would facilitate a mathematical expression of the basic distinctions of various computational models known to programmers.

Moschovakis, 1969c, suggested a new approach to the axiomatization of computability on abstract sets, using a *computation* concept. He required the object domain D to be a 'computation domain', i.e., D must contain a set C of function programs (or indices) that, in turn, must contain a map N of the natural numbers. A pairing function must be defined on C as well. Then Moschovakis introduced the central notion of a computation as a tuple of elements from D, $(e, x_1, \ldots, x_n, y)$ where $e \in C$; the tuple declares that program e computes y by $x_1, \ldots, x_n$. If a set Θ of tuples is given then a function $f(x_1, \ldots, x_n)$ is Θ-precomputable if there exists an $e \in C$ such that for any point $x_1, \ldots, x_n, y$ of the graph of f the tuple $(e, x_1, \ldots, x_n, y)$ belongs to Θ. Due to the reflexivity properties, total functionals and operators on D can be reduced to functions that enable us to define Θ-precomputability of functionals and operators.

Moschovakis calls a set of computations Θ a precomputation theory if the following functions, functionals and operators happen to be Θ-precomputable:

1. Constants, the identity function, and the successor function.

2. The characteristic function of the sets N and C.

3. The pairing function and its two inverses.

4. Substitution and the primitive recursion operators.

5. The universal functions: evaluator, partial evaluator (s-m-n-function) and evaluator with permutation of arguments.

In order to characterize the class of computable functions Moschovakis postulated that every computation must possess a length, i.e., an ordinal (finite or infinite). On the stage of the transition from a precomputation theory to a computation one a distinction emerges between computable functions and computable functionals. A precomputable function is always computable but a precomputable functional F is declared to be computable only if the length of a computation of F is, crudely speaking, no less than the length of the computation of the function indices that are used as arguments of the computation of the functional. Moreover, it is required that the length of a computation of the evaluator (universal function) must be (as a programmer would say) less than the length of the computation by the partial evaluator and of the subsequent computation by the residual program (cf. Ershov, 1980).

Moschovakis showed that Turing machine computation forms a computation theory. He proved the validity of the first recursion theorem in computation theories, and demonstrated that prime and search computabilities (Moschovakis, 1969a) may be represented as computation theories.

This work seems to be very interesting and it is believed that its potential is not yet completely discharged.

Paterson and Hewitt, 1970, gave an example of a recursive scheme by McCarthy for which there exists no equivalent flow-schema with memory on the same abstract structure of operations and relations.

Itkin, 1972, obtained the important result that flow-schemata with memory have a decidable determinant. Formal protocols are constructed in the following way: An arbitrary path is navigated in the flow scheme from the entry point to the exit. The sequence of predicate symbols passed is listed, the π-symbols being negated or not depending on whether the else-arc or then-arc was chosen when passing the predicate. Each argument position in the π-symbol is replaced by the termal value of that argument (see Ershov, 1958) which is defined uniquely by the path chosen. Such a protocol is called a logic termal (lt-) history. The set of all finite lt-histories is called an lt-determinant. Two flow schemata with memory are called lt-equivalent if they have identical lt-determinants. Functions computed by flow programs are completely characterized by lt-determinants, for the lt-equivalence implies the functional equivalence.

Uspensky, 1974, made an interesting observation about the role of protocols in the refinement of the concept of relative computability (or computations with oracles). He realized that in recursion theory a class K of functions computable with an oracle needs to satisfy just four properties in order to imply all statements of recursion theory relativizable to any oracle:

(1) K contains all (ordinary) computable functions.

(2) K is recursively closed (i.e., relative to substitution, recursion and minimization).

(3)   (Protocol Axiom.) For each f from K there exist a pair of functions a and b from K and a set of codes such that for any (x, y) from the graph of f there exists an element q from the set of codes such that $a(q) = x$ and $b(q) = y$.

(4) K contains a universal function (evaluator) of all one-place functions from K.

Buda and Itkin, 1974, showed that the lt-determinant of any flow schema with memory (Itkin, 1972) forms a language accepted by a two-tape automaton.

Nepomniashchy, 1974, studied arithmetical functions computed by flow programs with memory on systems $\langle \omega, \Phi, \Pi \rangle$. He looked for a property of Φ and Π such that the set of functions computed would give all partial recursive functions. Such a property was naturally called algorithmic completeness. He obtained a reduction theorem that reduces the completeness of a system $\langle \omega, \{\phi(y)\}, \{p(y_1, \ldots, y_m)\} \rangle$ to the completeness of the system $\langle \omega, \{y+1\}, \{\pi(y_1, \ldots, y_m)\} \rangle$. For systems $\langle \omega, \{y+1\}, \{\pi(y)\} \rangle$ a criterion of completeness was given in terms of sets acceptable by generalized finite automata; for the system $\langle \omega, \{\phi(y)\}, \{\pi(y)\} \rangle$ a simple sufficient condition of completeness was given. For functions one of these properties is to exhaust all the natural numbers by ϕ-terms of the basic structure; for predicates one such property is the existence of a scheme that allows an automaton to test whether a number equals a given constant.

Grilliot, 1974, also undertook a logical analysis of dissections of abstract recursion depending on initial assumptions on the base algebraic structure. He started his analysis with several warnings that are rather interesting for us:

"... to say that F is recursive in $G_1, \ldots, G_n$ means that F is computable or can be combinatorially generated from the structure $\langle \omega; 0, +1, =, G_1, \ldots, G_n \rangle$. ... It is natural to replace the structure $\langle \omega; 0, +1, =, G_1, \ldots, G_n \rangle$ by an arbitrary structure $\langle A; G_1, \ldots, G_n \rangle$ where A is a set and $G_1, \ldots, G_n$ are functions or predicates on A. This is precisely what our investigation is all about: to find out what recursiveness on an arbitrary structure means. Unfortunately, the matter is not so easy in that the structure of the natural numbers is fairly unique with respect to other structures. Consequently the abstract study of recursiveness and hyperarithmeticalness may tend to be prejudiced by preconceptions based on usual recursiveness and hyperarithmeticalness on the natural numbers."

Grilliot formulated three main assumptions characterizing the structures for which he considered recursive closure.

C-scheme: each constant function must be recursive.

E-scheme: the equality relation must be recursive.

S-scheme: ordered search (in a set) must be recursive. (Equivalently, semicomputable predicates must be closed relative to $\exists$-quantification.)

Grilliot analyzed various definitions of recursive closure. He considered schematic definition of deducibility in the predicate calculus language by Fraïssé, 1959, as a basic definition. He called it syntactic and observed that, due to the completeness of the predicate calculus, the schematic definition is equivalent to the semantic one (i.e., using models that interpret the basic signature) according to the invariant definability by Fraïssé, 1969; Kreisel, 1963; and Moschovakis, 1969a and 1969b. He took the invariance of recursivity with respect to arbitrary enumerations of the carrier (Lacombe, 1969) as a criterion of the completeness of recursive closure.

Grilliot remarked that, in his opinion, the model-theoretic (semantic) definition of recursivity gives a feeling of completeness that is absent in purely combinatorial definitions and becomes an important informal confirmation of the Church Thesis.

Fenstad, 1974, developed a variant of the theory by Moschovakis, 1969c, replacing the explicit definition of the length of a computation by a transitive relation "to be a subcomputation". Thus, $(e\,\sigma\,y) < (e'\,\sigma'\,y')$ means that the computation of y from σ by the program e is a part of the computation of y' from σ' by the program e'. The set Θ of computations together with this relation $<$ is called a computation structure $\langle \Theta, < \rangle$, if for any computation the set of all its subcomputations is finite. A computation structure is declared to be a computation theory if it satisfies Moschovakis's 1969c axioms; however, instead of postulating some inequalities for computation lengths, corresponding relations 'to be a subcomputation' are postulated.

Rosen, 1975, considered a determinant for recursive schemata that is practically identical to our notion of determinant. He showed that two schemata with identical determinants compute identical functions under any interpretation of the basic structure. He showed also that the determinants of recursive programs form a context-free language. However, this cannot be considered as a final result, since the equivalence of CF-grammars is undecidable in the general case, while this is an open problem for recursive schema determinants, with some hopes for a positive solution.

Skordev, 1976, developing the ideas of Platek, 1966, and Moschovakis, 1969a, studied recursion in abstract functional spaces that contain the identity function, are closed under composition, and are partially ordered: $f \leq g \leftrightarrow$ graph of $f \subseteq$ graph of g. A functional space $\mathcal{F}$ is called a combinatorial iterative space if it satisfies the following conditions.

1) $\mathcal{F}$ contains constant functions that constitute a set C containing two elements **true** and false.

2) A pairing function is defined on $\mathcal{F}$ and its inverse operations belong to $\mathcal{F}$.

3) C is closed under the pairing function.

4) A definition-by-case function is defined on $\mathcal{F}$.

5) A fixed-point operation is defined on $\mathcal{F}$ that yields the fixed point of the equation $\psi = $ if χ then I else $\psi\phi$ where I is the identity function.

If Φ is a finite set of elements from $\mathcal{F}$ then any element of $\mathcal{F}$ that is obtained from $\Phi \cup \{$identity function, depairing functions, **true**, false$\}$ by application of a finite number of operations defined on $\mathcal{F}$ is called a function recursive in $\mathcal{F}$.

Skordev showed that such recursive functions contain (modulo a natural isomorphism) all ordinary recursive functions; and they satisfy analogs of the normal form theorem, the first and second recursion theorems and the enumeration theorem. The recursivity of some concretization of combinatorial iterative spaces coincides with the prime recursivity of Moschovakis, 1969a.

Sabelfeld, 1976, constructed for flow programs with memory a complete system of transformations that preserve the lt-equivalence introduced by Itkin, 1972.

Fenstad, 1978, referring to Platek's 1966 dissertation, described an approach to the description of a recursive closure $R_\omega(\Phi)$, where Φ is a set of functions, as a minimal set closed under substitution and fixed-point operators, containing a definition-by-cases function and so-called 'combinators' $I(f) = f$, $K(f,g) = f$ and $S(f,g,h) = f(h)(g(h))$. He showed, in particular, that $R_\omega(\Phi)$ can be represented as a computation theory as described by Moschovakis, 1969c. Recursive closures of that kind may be described as fixed points of some inductive operator that is one of the main concepts of the theory of inductive definitions—a newly formed branch of mathematical logic (see, e.g., Moschovakis, 1973).

Shen, 1980, having extended Uspensky's 1974 observations, showed that a class of arithmetical functions may be partial-recursive relative to some set if and only if it satisfies Uspensky's axioms.

Variants for further study

The author must admit being greatly impressed by just seeing the accumulated material from theoretical programming placed side by side with that of abstract computability theory. It is really surprising that logic and programming seem to be so well prepared for a closer interaction. Trying to avoid over-generalization, I shall say only that, in the context of our study, programming can give a goal to abstract recursion taking a method from it. If the aims and initial assumptions in the works on abstract recursion seem somehow arbitrary, then the mathematical methods used in works on theoretical programming look sometimes equally arbitrary or not elaborated enough. It would be highly desirable if the tendency to reduce the distance between mathematics and computer science, that is so obviously demonstrated at our symposium, will be deeper and more lasting than the brief marriage of logic and programming that occurred in this country in the middle of the 60s, when a common academic specialty 'mathematical logic and programming' was established; this specially regretfully ceased to exist when the VAK was reformed in 1971.*

It is natural to ask whether the works on abstract recursion already contain a solution of the problem that interests us. I believe that this is the case if we think only of the power, or capacity, of the concept of abstractly computable functions. Many equivalence theorems (Moschovakis, 1969b; Lacombe, 1969; Grilliot, 1974) give us the necessary assurances. However, the question: what are *minimal* requirements for the control of algorithm execution—still seems unclear. We do have normal form theorems where the search operator is triggered only at a very last stage of computation while the 'main part' consists of only recursive or even subrecursive computations. But it seems to me that further progress is possible. The requirement for the determinant to be enumerable (Lacombe, 1969; Friedman, 1969b) or for the coding scheme on indices to be computable (Moschovakis, 1969c) seems to be excessive. This feeling is strongly supported by the result

---

*VAK is the Higher Qualification Committee in the USSR responsible for giving academic degrees. In particular, the committee maintains the list of specialties in which degrees are given.

on the structure of schematic determinants in various computational models: context free languages (not the final result) in Rosen, 1975; two-tape finite automata for flow programs with memory (not the final result) in Buda and Itkin, 1974; finite automata(!) for Yanov schemata in Rutledge, 1964.

There is in programming a simple but unique normal form theorem (Harel, 1980) showing that any flow program with memory may have the form of a while-loop the body of which contains only direct computation. It seems that this theorem must be considered further.

Another testimony for having a resource in the control structure used in computation is the equivalence of syntactic and semantic definitions of computability (Fraissé, 1959; Grilliot, 1974). Two facts form the basis for this equivalence: one is general—the completeness of the predicate calculus—and the other is specific. Namely, when we take as premises statements on the values of base predicates (diagrams by Lacombe, 1969, and Moschovakis, 1969b), requiring an ultimate knowledge of the base system, we imitate the computational process in the process of derivation and, having somehow decomposed the initial formula-program, we obtain some statements on the value of the computed predicate.

Let us try now to deduce formal statements on the truth values of protocols instead of predicates. Moreover, let us not only allow the deduction of invariant protocols (i.e., realizable in any model) but something more. In other words, one more approach to the study of the control structure of computation is, instead of the standard predicate calculus, to find a weaker deduction system that deduces protocols still characterizing a computable function.

There is another reason it may be useful to distinguish syntactic and semantic definitions of computability. The determinant of a flow program with memory is said to be strict if, for each protocol of the determinant, there exists an interpretation of the base structure in which the protocol can be evaluated. Itkin and Zwinogrodski, 1972, showed that any equivalence relation for flow programs with memory based on a strict determinant will be undecidable. On the other hand, there exists a schematic (syntactic) determinant with the decidable equivalence (Itkin, 1972).

One more controversy in studies on abstract recursion may be observed. Recursion theory, heavily relying on various 'finitenesses', cannot be built up without a specific combinatorial system that realizes these 'finitenesses'. That is why ordinary recursion theory so victoriously penetrates in practically any abstract theory via enumerations in Maltsev, 1961, and Lacombe, 1969; splinters in Strong, 1968; B^*-sets in Moschovakis, 1969a; or, directly, via enumerability of determinants in Friedman, 1969b. Sometimes, authors avoid unnecessarily specific combinatorics, postulating computability of high-level universal functions: pairing functions, s-m-n-functions, enumeration functions, recursion schemes. All this is meaningful and useful but gives only partial answers on the nature of computation.

One of the approaches that takes account of combinatorics could consist of a general axiomatization of constructive objects. Many think about the general nature of constructive objects but very few write about the subject. Oversimplifying, two approaches may be distinguished: one, which could be called 'inductive', generalizes Peano axiomatics; another, which could be called 'set-theoretic', sees a constructive object as a set with a relation defined on its elements. The first approach is exemplified by the so-called generalized arithmetics in Kleene, 1952, §50 and in the additions made by the translator of the Russian edition (Kleene, 1957). The second approach is related to the concept of algorithms as developed by Kolmogorov, 1953, and Kolmogorov and Uspensky, 1958.

Whatever general axioms for constructive objects might be discovered, they would in any case contain some inherent system of operations and relations on the constructive set. This inherent structure will be sufficient to define computable functions, for example in McCarthy's 1961 formalism, which defines a function as a fixed point of a recursive equation in some standard form.

Such an 'absolute' theory will not, however, solve all problems of abstract computability. In mathematics and computer science a new concept is maturing that might be called the computable (constructive, recursive) closure of arbitrary, not necessarily constructive functions and sets. This concept generalizes the practice of computation in general mathematics as well as concept of computation with an oracle and of relative computability in logic. One of the possible approaches is to single out in an arbitrary carrier D a constructive subset (something similar to ϵ-net) and to build upon this set a recursion theory in the spirit of the previous paragraphs. Some hints about such an approach can be found in Engeler, 1973.

Another possible approach to introducing a concrete combinatorics into abstract recursion is as follows. Let $\langle D, \Phi, \Pi \rangle$ be a base algebraic structure. Let us introduce somehow into the theory a calculus (generative, definitive or computational system) in which Φ and Π are used as elementary symbols (an alphabet) that constitutes constructive objects in the calculus. This calculus can be used then as the combinatorial means of the theory.

Again, two variants might be sketched out. One of them is the definition of a standard interpretation à la Herbrand, which represents D as a set $T(\Phi, \Pi)$ of terms in the alphabet $\Phi \cup \Pi$, and the operations Φ and Π prescribe how to construct and analyze terms from $T(\Phi, \Pi)$. Concrete properties of the standard interpretation will express abstract properties of computability that would remain invariant to any interpretation of the base system. Some confirmation of such an approach can be traced in theoretical programming works. Still unclear, at least for me, is how to define a standard interpretation of predicates.

The second approach could be called grammatical. Since we characterize a computable function by a determinant, i.e., a set of words in the alphabet $\Phi \cup \Pi$, we may consider that the function is described by a grammar of its determinant. Let all determinant grammars belong to a class $\mathcal{G}$. If we succeed in some natural coding of a determinant grammar in the alphabet $\Phi \cup \Pi$ then we may speak of a 'universal grammar' U that accepts a set of words (over the alphabet $\Phi \cup \Pi$) in the form $g * s$ iff g is the code of a determinant grammar and s is a string accepted by that grammar. If we, further, succeed in showing that U belongs to $\mathcal{G}$ then we provide the necessary reflection of programs into the object domain.

Universal grammar problems are well known in the theory of formal languages, but there is a definite variety in problem statements, which even for one and the same class leads either to solvable or unsolvable or open problems. It is not yet clear which problem statements are most adequate to our goals (Kasai, 1975; Rosenberg, 1977).

It seems to us that the logical, or calculative, approach based on inductive and invariant definability should be carefully investigated (Fraissé, 1969; Kreisel, 1963; Grilliot, 1974). One of the most fashionable current problems in programming is how to extract a program systematically from the constructive proof of the existence of a solution of a problem (see e.g. Kreisel, 1975; Nepeivoda, 1981). Such a problem statement alone makes predicate calculus formulas and programs to be comparable objects, so to say, of one and the same order. Further, it becomes evident that extracting an effective program from the existence theorem requires that we append to the calculus some nontrivial premises constituting a special theory of the problem. Moreover, it happens that many kinds of program manipulations met in practice are adequately described by some basic transformations of the program text, and these transformations resemble logical deduction in the formula calculus of Lacombe, 1969 and Grilliot, 1974.

One of the important manipulations is adapting a program to specific information contained in concrete values of its arguments. The principal possibility of such adaptation established by the s-m-n-theorem is getting considerable use in theoretical and systems programming (Ershov, 1977, 1980). It is natural that specific information about an argument may not be necessarily only in the form $x = a$; it may be represented by any predicate $P(x)$ and, as such, be used not only in the program but also in some reasoning about the program or the function it computes. Quite recently Goad, 1980, did a study about how to adapt constructive proofs when given additional information on a problem or its data. Indeed, logic and programming seek a way to embrace each other!

The author is grateful to A. A. Letichevsky, Yu. I. Manin, V. A. Nepomniashchy, and V. A. Uspensky for stimulating discussions that can be easily traced in the paper; to S. Dvornikov who attracted the author's attention to generalized recursion theory; to G. Kreisel, who kindly sent several very useful papers, especially Kreisel, 1969, and Goad, 1980; and to D. Skordev, for constructive suggestions.

Bibliography

If a paper has appeared both in Russian and in some other language, both references are given here when known.

Buda and Itkin

1974   A. O. Buda and V. É. Itkin, "Svodimost' ékvivalentnosti skhem programm k termal'noĭ ekvivalentnosti," in *Trudy 3-go Vsesoĭuznogo sympoziuma "Sistemnoe i teoreticheskoe programmirovanie"*, vol. 1, Kishinev, KGU (1974), 293–324.

Engeler

1980   E. Engeler, "On the structure of algorithmic problems," in K.-H. Böhling and K. Indermark, eds., 1. Fachtagung über Automatentheorie und Formale Sprachen,

Lecture Notes in Computer Science **2** (1973), 2–15.

Ershov

1958   A. P. Ershov, "Ob operatornykh algoritmakh," *Doklady AN SSSR* **122**,6 (1958), 967–970.

1977   A. P. Ershov, "O sushchnosti transliatsii," *Programmirovanie* (1977, No.5), 21–39. Also A. P. Ershov, "On the essence of compilation," in E. J. Neuhold, ed., *Formal Description of Programming Concepts*, Amsterdam, North-Holland (1977), 391–420.

1980   A. P. Ershov, "Smeshannye vychisleniia: potentsial'nye primeneniia i problemy issledovaniia," in *Vsesoiuznaia konf. "Metody matem. logiki v problemakh isk. intell. i sist. programmirovanie,"* part 1, Palanga, 3–5 Sept. 1980, Vil'nius, Inst. matem. i kib. AN LatSSR, 1980, pp. 26–55. Also A. P. Ershov, "Mixed computation: Potential applications and problems for study," *Theoretical Computer Science*, to appear.

Fenstad

1974   J. E. Fenstad, "On axiomatizing recursion theory," in J. E. Fenstad and P. G. Hinman, eds., *Generalized Recursion Theory*, Amsterdam, North-Holland (1974), 385–404.

1978   J. E. Fenstad, "On the foundation of general recursion theory: Computation versus inductive definability," in J. E. Fenstad et al., eds., *Generalized Recursion Theory II*, Amsterdam, North-Holland (1978), 99–110.

Fraissé

1959   R. Fraissé, "Une notion de récursivitè relative," in *Infinitistic Methods,"* *Proc. Symp. Foundations of Math.*, Warsaw 1959, Oxford, Pergamon (1961), 323–328.

Friedman

1969a   H. Friedman, "Axiomatic recursive function theory," in R. O. Gandy and C. M. E. Yates, eds., *Logic Colloquium '69*, Amsterdam, North-Holland (1971), 113–138.

1969b   H. Friedman, "Algorithmic procedures, generalised Turing algorithms and elementary recursion theories," in R. O. Gandy and C. M. E. Yates, eds., *Logic Colloquium '69*, Amsterdam, North-Holland (1971), 361–390.

Glushkov

1965   V. M. Glushkov, "Teoriia avtomatov i voprosy proektirovaniia struktur vychislitel'nykh mashin," *Kibernetika* (1965, No.1), 3–11.

1979   V. M. Glushkov, "Teorema o nepolnote formal'nykh teoriĭ c pozitsiĭ programmista," *Kibernetika* (1979, No.2), 1–5.

Goad

1980   C. A. Goad, "Proofs as descriptions of computation," preprint, Dept. of Computer Science, Stanford Univ. (1980), 14pp.

Grilliot

1974   T. J. Grilliot, "Dissecting abstract recursion," in J. E. Fenstad and P. G. Hinman, eds., *Generalized Recursion Theory*, Amsterdam, North-Holland (1974), 405–420.

Harel

1980   D. Harel, "On folk theorems," *CACM* **23** (1980), 379–389.

Itkin

1972   V. É. Itkin, "Logiko-termal'naîa ékvivalentnost' skhem program," *Kibernitika* (1972, No.1), 5–27.

Itkin and Zwinogrodski

1972   V. E. Itkin and Z. Zwinogrodski, "On program schemata equivalence," *J. Comp. Syst. Sci.* **6** (1972), 88–101.

Kasai

1975   T. Kasai, "A universal context-free grammar," *Information and Control* **28** (1975), 30–34.

Kleene

1952   S. C. Kleene, *Introduction to Metamathematics*, New York, Van Nostrand, 1952.

1957   S. K. Klini, *Vvedenie v metamatematiku*, M. Izd. IL (1957), 526 pp.

Kolmogorov

1953   A. N. Kolmogorov, "O ponîatii algoritma," *Uspekhi Mat. Nauk* **8**,4 (1953), 175–176.

Kolmogorov and Uspensky

1958   A. N. Kolmogorov and V. A. Uspenskiĭ, "K ponîatiiu algoritma," *Uspekhi Mat. Nauk* **13**,4 (1958), 3–28.

Kreisel

1963   G. Kreisel, "Model theoretic invariants: Application to recursive and hyper-arithmetic operations," in *The Theory of Models*, Proc. 1963 international symposium at Berkeley, Calif., Amsterdam, North-Holland (1965), 190–205.

1969   G. Kreisel, "Some reasons for generalizing recursion theory," in R. O. Gandy and C. E. M. Yates, eds., *Logic Colloquium '69*, Amsterdam, North-Holland (1971), 139–198.

1975   G. Kreisel, "Some uses of proof theory for finding computer programs," in *Colloque International de Logique*, Clermont-Ferrand, Colloques Internationaux du CNRS, No.249 (1975), 123–124.

Krinitisky

1959   N. A. Krinitskiĭ, "Ravnosil'nye preobrazovaniîa logicheskikh skhem," avtoreferat dissertatsii, Moscow State Univ. (1959).

1970   N. A. Krinitskiĭ, *Ravnosil'nye preobrazovaniîa algoritmov i programmirovanie*, Moscow, Sovetskoe Radio (1970).

Lacombe

1969 D. Lacombe, "Recursion theoretic structures for relational systems," in R. O. Gandy and C. E. M. Yates, eds., *Logic Colloquium '69*, Amsterdam, North-Holland (1971), 3–17.

McCarthy

1961 J. McCarthy, "Towards a mathematical theory of computation," in *Proc. IFIP Congress 1961*, Amsterdam, North-Holland (1962), 21–28.

Maltsev

1961 A. I. Mal'tsev, "Konstruktivnye algebry, I," *Uspekhi Mat. Nauk* 16,3 (1961), 3–60.

Moschovakis

1969a Y. N. Moschovakis, "Abstract first order computability, I," *Trans. Amer. Math. Soc.* 138 (1969), 427–464.

1969b Y. N. Moschovakis, "Abstract computability and invariant definability," *J. Symb. Logic* 34 (1969), 605–633.

1969c Y. N. Moschovakis, "Axioms for computation theories," in R. O. Gandy and C. E. M. Yates, eds., *Logic Colloquium '69*, Amsterdam, North-Holland (1971), 199–256.

1973 Y. N. Moschovakis, *Elementary Induction on Abstract Structures*, Amsterdam, North-Holland, 1973.

Nepeivoda

1981 N. N. Nepeivoda, "The logical approach to programming," in this volume.

Nepomniashchy

1974 V. A. Nepomniashchiĭ, "Kriterii algoritmicheskoĭ polnoty sistem operatsiĭ," in *Teoriía programmirovaniía*, Novosibirsk, Vych. Tsentr SO AN SSSR (1974), vol. 1, pp. 267–279. Also V. A. Nepomniashchy, "Criteria for the algorithmic completeness of the system of operations," in A. P. Ershov and V. A. Nepomniashchy, eds., Proc. International Symposium on Theoretical Programming, Novosibirsk, 1972, *Lecture Notes in Computer Science* 5 (1974), 172–186.

Paterson

1968 M. S. Paterson, "Program schemata," *Machine Intelligence* 3 (1968), 19–31.

Paterson and Hewitt

1970 M. S. Paterson and C. E. Hewitt, "Comparative Schematology," in Records of Project MAC Conf. on Concurrent Systems and Parallel Computation, ACM (1970), 119–128.

Platek

1966 Richard A. Platek, *Foundations of recursion theory*, Ph.D. dissertation, Stanford University, January 1966.

Rosen

1975   B. K. Rosen, "Program equivalence and context-free grammars," *J. Comp. Syst. Sci.* 11 (1975), 358–374.

Rosenberg

1977   G. Rosenberg, "A note on universal grammars," *Information and Control* 34 (1977), 172–175.

Rutledge

1964   J. D. Rutledge, "On Ianov's program schemata," *JACM* 11 (1964), 1–9.

Sabelfeld

1976   V. K. Sabel'fel'd, "Ékviyalentnye preobrazovaniıa standartnykh skhem," in *Problemy programmirovaniıa*, Novosibirsk, Vych. Tsentr SO AN SSSR (1976), 94–121. Also V. K. Sabelfeld, "Äquivalente Transformationen für Flußdiagramme," *Acta Informatica* 10 (1978), 127–156.

Shen

1980   A. Shen', "Aksiomaticheskiĭ podkhod k teorii algoritmov i otnositel'naıa vychislimost'," *Vestn. Mosk. un-ta*, Ser. 1, Matem. mekhan. (1980, No.2), 27–29.

Skordev

1976   D. Skordev, "Recursion theory on iterative combinatory spaces," *Bull. Acad. Polon. Sci.*, Ser. Math. Astr. Phys. 24 (1976), 23–31.

Strong

1968   H. R. Strong, "Algebraically generalized recursive function theory," *IBM J. Res. Devel.* 12 (1968), 465–475.

Uspensky

1974   V. A. Uspenskiĭ, "Teorema Gedelıa o nepolnote v elementarnom izlozhenii," *Uspekhi Mat. Nauk* 29,1 (1974), 3–47.

Wagner

1963   E. G. Wagner, "Uniformly reflexive structures: Towards an abstract theory of computability," Doctoral dissertation, Columbia Univ. (1963).

1969   E. G. Wagner, "Uniformly reflexive structures: An axiomatic approach to computability," *Information Sciences* 1 (1969), 343–362.

Yanov

1957   Iu. I. Ianov, "O ravnosil'nosti i preobrazovaniıakh skhem programm," *Doklady AN SSSR* 113 (1957), 39–42.

Algorithms and Algebra

By F.L. Bauer

Dedicated to the memory of Al-Khowarizmi

A recent trend in Theoretical Informatics brings essentially algebraic methods into
the foreground. We mention only two instances: the use of lattice theory in the
semantics of programs (SCOTT 1970) and the use of universal algebra in the semantics
of abstract data types (GUTTAG 1975). The purpose of this note is to base algorithms
themselves functionally on algebraic concepts, thus honoring at the Urgench Symposium
in a double sense Al-Khowarizmi.

Informal introduction

Let $.o.$ be a binary operation on a set M of objects - say the semigroup of the
natural numbers under addition or under multiplication. Consider the totality
$W_{(M, .o.)}$ of expressions or terms formed with the help of this operation. It com-
prises, e.g.,

> the terms (with the free variable a)
>
> $((((((a \circ a) \circ a) \circ a) \circ a) \circ a) \circ a) \circ a$
> $(((a \circ a) \circ (a \circ a)) \circ (a \circ a)) \circ (a \circ a)$
> $((a \circ a) \circ (a \circ a)) \circ ((a \circ a) \circ (a \circ a))$
>
> and the terms (with the free variables x, y)
>
> $x \circ y$
> $y \circ x$

Clearly every term defines a computational course of actions: A replacement of free
variables $x_1, \ldots, x_n$ in a term t by elements $e_1, \ldots, e_n$ from M is called
an <u>instantiation</u>, the resulting term is called an <u>instantiated term</u>. If the instantiated term does not contain further free variables, then we speak of a <u>complete</u>,
otherwise of a <u>partial instantiation</u>. Terms without free variables ("closed" terms)
are also called <u>computational terms</u>, their (stepwise) evaluation is commonly called
a <u>computation</u>.

If certain laws hold, certain terms are functionally equivalent, i.e. they define,
although leading to different computations, the same mapping. Under the associative
law, the first three terms above are functionally equivalent, under the commutative
law the last two terms are. Thus, if laws hold, classes of functionally equivalent
terms and computations within $W_{(M, .o.)}$ are obtained.

Writing down a term explicitly can be very cumbersome, even practically prohibitive. Thus mechanisms are needed which allow to give a short description of certain large computational terms. Following common mathematical language we speak of "generating" a term. Using the infamous three dots in

$$\text{pow (a, m)} = \overbrace{(a \circ (a \circ (a \circ \ldots (a \circ a) \ldots)))}^{m}$$

may nowadays no longer be considered decent, but defining

pow (a, m) for $m \in \mathbb{N} \setminus \{o\}$ by

$$\text{pow (a, m)} = \begin{cases} a & \text{if } m = 1 \\ a \circ \text{pow (a, m - 1)} & \text{if } m > 1 \end{cases}$$

is quite standard. Algorithms in the widest sense give such descriptions, they can be understood to generate computational terms and thus computations.

Signatures and terms

We can now proceed to a general definition of algorithm. In doing so, we follow the definition of abstract data types.

Def.   A signature $\Sigma = (M_1, M_2, \ldots, M_m, O_1, O_2, \ldots, O_n)$ is a (finite) family of carriers M_μ together with a (finite) family of operations O_ν, where each carrier M_μ is a symbol for a set[1] and each operation O_ν is a symbol for a mapping of some fixed arity

$$O_\nu : M_{\mu_1} \times M_{\mu_2} \times \ldots M_{\mu_r} \rightarrow M_{\mu_0}$$

Ex. 1 $\Sigma = (M, .o., n, e)$.
        where $.o. : M \times M \rightarrow M, n : \rightarrow M, e : \rightarrow M$.

Def.   A term t over a signature Σ is a well-formed expression in free variables and operation symbols from Σ. If the operation belonging to the ultimate operation symbol of a term is a mapping into the carrier M_μ we say the term leads into M_μ .

$W_\Sigma(X)$ denotes the set of all terms over a signature Σ with free variables from a family $X = (X_1, X_2, \ldots, X_m)$ that can be instantiated by elements from $(M_1, M_2, \ldots, M_m)$ respectively. W_Σ is short for $W_\Sigma(\emptyset, \emptyset, \ldots, \emptyset)$.

---

[1] It is assumed throughout that carriers are small sets (cf. Mac Lane 1971)

Every heterogeneous algebra has a signature. Usually there are many algebras of a particular signature. For the signature of Ex. 1, an algebra M_1 is given by

$M = \{\Lambda\}$, $\Lambda \circ \Lambda = \Lambda$, $n = \Lambda$, $e = \Lambda$ (the _trivial algebra_) ;

algebras of different cardinality are

M_2 : $M = \{n, e\}$, $n \circ n = n$
$\qquad\qquad\qquad n \circ e = e$
$\qquad\qquad\qquad e \circ n = e$
$\qquad\qquad\qquad e \circ e = n$
$M_{\aleph_0}$: $M = \mathbb{N}$, $a \circ b = a + b$, $n = 0$, $e = 1$
$M_{\aleph}$: $M = \mathbb{R}$, $a \circ b = a + b$, $n = 0$, $e = 1$.

Not all algebras are of interest to us. In many cases we consider hierarchical signatures, where a certain subset C_{prim} of carriers and operations is designated as being _primitive_ and the remaining carriers are called _defined carriers_. We call an algebra of a hierarchical signature Σ _generated by a certain set of primitive carriers_ C_{prim} if all the elements of the other, the defined carriers C_{def} can be obtained from the terms over C_{prim} by instantiation. It is called _completely generated_ if C_{prim} is empty and thus all the elements are obtained by operations (including nullary operations to start with). The algebras M_1, M_2 and $M_{\aleph_0}$ are completely generated, $M_{\aleph}$ cannot be: The enumerable set of terms cannot generate $\mathbb{R}$.

We have called this restriction to generated algebras the _generation principle_, and we will assume it throughout this paper. We also assume that primitive carriers are defined carriers in some other, more basic signature or (finally) are completely generated.

A particular algebra of a signature Σ is the _term algebra_ over C_{prim} : elements of the defined carriers C_{def} in this model are the terms in free variables and operations that lead into the defined carriers, operations with these terms being carried out formally. Trivially, the term algebra over C_{prim} can be generated (by C_{prim}). This indicates already why terms play such a prominent role.

Algebraic Definition of Algorithms

We now define:

Def.   A _computational term_ in an arbitrary signature Σ is a term from $W_\Sigma = W_\Sigma(\emptyset)$ (it may originate from a term $t \in W_\Sigma(X)$ instantiated by elements from primitive and/or defined carriers).

Def.   An _algorithm_ over an algebra of signature Σ is a rule (written in a finite way) for generating a set of computational terms, when the free variables occurring in the rule are instantiated with _arguments_. The set of all instantiations which are envisaged is the _domain_ of the algorithm.

Particularly simple algorithms are described by (uninstantiated) terms, like

$$a \circ (a \circ (a \circ (a \circ a))) .$$

We may call them straightforward algorithms; for every envisaged instantiation immediately a computational term results.

Other algorithms may lead to straightforward algorithms after *partial* instantiation[1], e.g. the algorithm

pow(a, 4) is expressed by the term $a \circ (a \circ (a \circ a))$

and all computational terms of the algorithm pow(a, m) can be described by first instantiating m in pow(a, m) and then instantiating a in the resulting terms which are already straightforward algorithms. Parameters such as a in pow are called fixed parameters ("fixed" with respect to recursion).

In general, however, the set of computational terms an algorithm generates will not be described simply by first generating a set of terms and then instantiating them; the generating rule can be quite complex. Note that "computation" so far has not been defined.

Common particular definitions of algorithms fall under this definition; Markov algorithms and Turing machines of course, and also recursive functions where the computational terms are generated by the Herbrand-Kleene text replacement mechanism. The definition is, however, much wider and only additional conditions will bring us into the classical realm.

First of all, the terms we are talking about are not necessarily finite; we may consider certain terms with an infinite number of occurrences of operation symbols and free variables (NIVAT 1975). Whereas until recently such terms have not found much interest in theoretical informatics, since their instantiation leads to a non-finite computation, they have now become important (BAUER 1978) since they describe certain "infinite objects" which so far have been treated by machine-close pointer implementations, in conjunction with the observation (HENDERSON, MORRIS 1976) that "lazy evaluation" (FRIEDMAN, WISE 1976) may produce finite terms even when in a proper environment non-finite objects are used.

Def.   An algorithm is terminating, if it generates finite computational terms only.

For simplicity only, we will restrict our attention in the sequel to terminating algorithms.

---

[1] related to "mixed computation" in the sense of ERSHOV 1977.

Second, we have left open how many computational terms, i.e. instantiated terms belong to one particular instantiation.

Def. If for some instantiation no computational term exists, we say the algorithm is _undefined_ for this instantiation.

By restricting the domain of an algorithm properly it can always be made a _totally defined_ algorithm. Although working formally with << undefined >> has some advantages (MANNA 1974) we will only discuss totally defined algorithms in the following.

There may, however, for the same instantiation several computational terms be generated by the algorithm.

Def. An algorithm is called _deterministic_ if for every instantiation at most one computational term, and _regular_, if for every instantiation at least one computational term is generated.

Classical algorithms are deterministic and regular.

Non-determinism and types

Non-deterministic algorithms, first envisaged by McCARTHY 1962, are of paramount importance. To show this, we recall that so far algorithms have been defined over a signature only, i.e. no particular properties of the algebras of such a signature have been used. Indeed, we have rather _algorithm schemes_ which are first to be _interpreted_ by presenting some algebra, before an instantiation is made.

Properties of a particular algebra may have the consequence that the same instantiation of two different terms leads to the same result, i.e. that different computations are functionally equivalent, resulting in "equal values". It may even happen that two different terms lead for a class of interpretations to equivalent results; we then say that the terms are functionally equivalent (with respect to this class) and write an equation between terms, like

$$a \circ (a \circ (a \circ a)) = (a \circ a) \circ (a \circ a)$$

which holds for any interpretation of $\Sigma = (M, .\circ.)$ for which the associative law holds. In general, however, term equations are too narrow to describe sufficiently the properties of certain algebras, and at least propositions involving term equations must be taken into account (propositions that are assumed to hold for any instantiation of its free variables)[1].

---

[1] For example we may in Ex. 1 require (without free variables) $\neg (n = e)$ which excludes the trivial algebra M_1 .

Ex. 2 :

The following algorithm, described recursively over $\Sigma = (M, .o., \mathbb{N})$ with the help of non-exclusive case guards[2], is non-deterministic:

$$
pow\ (a,\ m) = \begin{cases} a & \underline{if}\ m = 1 \\ pow\ (a,\ u) \circ pow\ (a,\ v) & \underline{if}\ \ u,\ v \in \mathbb{N} \setminus \{0\} : m = u + v \\ pow\ (pow\ (a,\ p),\ q) & \underline{if}\ \ p,\ q \in \mathbb{N} \setminus \{0,\ 1\} : m = p \times q \end{cases}
$$

pow (a, 4) generates by simple partial instantiation the terms

   a ∘ (a ∘ (a ∘ a)), (a ∘ a) ∘ (a ∘ a), ((a ∘ a) ∘ a) ∘ a

The importance of this non-deterministic algorithm lies in the fact that it generates for each instantiation the set of *all* computational terms which are equivalent under the associative law in (M, .o.) mentioned above.

Now we consider apart from a signature also laws to hold.

Def.   A <u>type</u> (Σ, E) is a signature Σ together with a set E of <u>properties</u> of the terms t over Σ ; these are propositions involving equations between terms, assumed to hold for any instantiation of their free variables.

Def.   An <u>algebra</u> of type (Σ, E) is an algebra of signature Σ which fulfills all the properties of E .

Def.   A <u>computational structure</u> of type (Σ, E) is an algebra of type (Σ, E) which can be generated (by a certain set of primitive carriers C_{prim}) .

W_Σ , the set of all terms from a signature Σ , is a particular algebra of the type $(\Sigma, \emptyset)$ of signature Σ with an empty set of properties. $(\Sigma, \emptyset)$ is also called an <u>absolutely free type</u>. W_Σ is an algebra of this type.

Def.   A <u>Σ-homomorphism</u> between two algebras of signature Σ is a mapping which is compatible with the operations of Σ .

Def.   An <u>interpretation</u> of W_Σ in an algebra M of type (Σ, E) is the mapping which attaches to every term from W_Σ the element from M which is obtained by "calculating" the term within the algebra M , i.e. by some stepwise evaluation of the operations.

---

[2] Such case guards have been introduced in connection with statements ("guarded commands") by DIJKSTRA 1975.

Any interpretation is a Σ-homomorphism from W_Σ into M. Computational structures are those algebras for which the interpretation is surjective.

Theorem: Every computational structure of type (Σ, E) is a Σ-epimorphic image of W_Σ. The set of properties E induces an equivalence relation among the computations over Σ which is compatible with the operations of Σ (a congruence relation). Every computational structure of type (Σ, E) is isomorphic to the residual classes of W_Σ modulo E.

Def.   An algorithm over Σ is determinate with respect to a type (Σ, E) if every instantiation of the algorithm generates computational terms which are under E equivalent.

A deterministic algorithm is determinate, of course.

Ex.   The algorithm pow above, although being non-deterministic, is determinate over any type (Σ, E) which includes a binary operation .o. and the

associative law : $(a \circ b) \circ c = a \circ (b \circ c)$

Non-deterministic algorithms allow to derive descendants (McCARTHY 1962), algorithms were the choice of recursion is narrower or even uniquely determined. Narrowing the second line in the example above to the choice $u = 1$, $v = m - 1$ in the case $m > 1$, and dropping the third line, yields the classical recursion given in the introduction. Other, more efficient deterministic algorithms can also be derived immediately.

There can be non-isomorphic computational structures of a given type. A type is said to be monomorphic if no non-isomorphic computational structures of this type exist.

Since for the algorithm itself only the signature Σ matters, and the properties E determine only whether the algorithm is determinate or not, we may have the same algorithm not only for a number of non-isomorphic algebras of a given type, but also for different types (Σ, E_1) and (Σ, E_2) with the same signature, provided the properties E_1, E_2 are each strong enough to make the algorithm determinate.

Computation

A computation of an algorithm for a given instantiation is now defined to be the generation and evaluation of some or all of the computational terms (if any) the algorithm allows to generate for this instantiation.

The *execution* of such a computation is still left open. There is considerable freedom in defining suitable <u>machines</u>,including quite abstract ones which use various
computation rules as described, e.g., in MANNA 1974; in particular, parallel execution is possible (BROY 1980).

Conclusion

The algebraic definition of an algorithm given above is wider than the classical one.
It is an abstract definition based on a signature only, and allows interpretation
by any computational structure of this signature. Even introducing a set of properties does not necessarily determine the interpretation completely. This freedom is
an advantage, it allows to treat a number of related algorithms under one single
roof. Moreover, even for a given monomorphic type algorithms can be non-deterministic.
This freedom allows to go to special descendants which show increased efficiency,
including deterministic ones.

Both degrees of freedom can be used in a program development process in order to
delay design decisions.

In particular, such an abstract algebraic definition of algorithms (in conjunction
with the abstract definition of types and of congruence relations in the term
algebra giving representants of the computational structures of such a type) is a
step to become liberated from the notational pressure that has darkened so much
the genuine issues of programming.

Acknowledgement

The ideas outlined in this paper have been stimulated by discussions with
H. WÖSSNER in 1977, when we were preparing our book "Algorithmic Language and
Program Development" (to be published by Springer). Thanks are also due to
M. BROY, B. MÜLLER, and M. WIRSING for critical remarks.

References

BAUER 1978

>   Bauer, F. L., Detailization and Lazy Evaluation, Infinite Objects and Pointer
>   Representation. In: Program Construction, Lecture Notes in Computer Science <u>69</u>,
>   Springer, Berlin 1979.

BROY   1980

>   Broy, M., Transformation parallel ablaufender Programme. Dissertation, Tech-
>   nische Universität München 1980.

DIJKSTRA 1975

Dijkstra, E.W., Guarded Commands, Nondeterminacy and Formal Derivation of Programs. Comm. ACM 18, p. 453-457 (1975).

ERSHOV 1977

Ershov, A. P., On the Essence of Compilation, Proc. IFIP Working Conf. on the Formal Description of Programming Concepts, North-Holland, Amsterdam 1978.

FRIEDMAN, WISE 1976

Friedman, D. P., Wise, D. S., CONS Should not Evaluate its Arguments. In: Automata, Languages and Programming, Proceedings 1976. Edinburgh University Press 1976 , p. 257-284.

GUTTAG 1975

Guttag, J. V., The Specification and Application to Programming of Abstract Data Types, TR CSRG-59, September 1975, University of Toronto.

HENDERSON, MORRIS 1976

Henderson, P., and Morris, J. H., A Lazy Evaluator. Proc. 3rd ACM Symp. on Principles of Programming Languages (January 1976), Atlanta, p. 95-103.

MAC LANE 1971

Mac Lane, S., Categories for the Working Mathematician, Springer, New York 1971.

MANNA 1974

Manna, Z., Mathematical Theory of Computation. McGraw-Hill, New York 1974.

McCARTHY 1962

McCarthy, J., Towards a Mathematical Science of Computation. In: Information Processing 1962, North-Holland, Amsterdam 1963, p. 21-28.

NIVAT 1975

Nivat, M., On the Interpretation of Recursive Program Schemes, Symposia Mathematica, Vol. XV, Istituto Nationale di Alta Matematica, 1975.

SCOTT 1970

Scott, D., Outline of a Mathematical Theory of Computation. Proc. 4th Princeton Conference on Information Sciences and Systems, 1970.

ON FORMAL TRANSFORMATIONS OF ALGORITHMS

V.M. Glushkov
Institute of Cybernetics
Ukrainian Academy of Sciences
252207 Kiev 207,   USSR

The modern ways of representing the algorithms as the programs in
programming languages may be considered as a natural development
of the formula apparatus of classical mathematics which is used for
constructive representation of mathematical objects. This provides
us with an idea to develop the methods of algorithms transformations
considering them as algebraic expressions. For this purpose some
kind of algebra, lately called algorithmic algebra, was introduced
by the author in 1965 [1] and the analysis theorem that showed the
possibility to represent any program as an expression of this algebra
was proved. In the paper [1] there was given an example of how to
construct the efficient algorithm using the transformations of its
initial description by means of the relations of the algorithmic
algebra. Later, the algorithmic algebra relations were further
studied. This algebra was used in creating some systems for automatized computer hardware and software design.

In [2] the algorithmic algebra formulas that may be used for speeding
up iterations of monotonous operators were worked out. These formulas
generalize the method used in [1] for speeding up the multiplication
algorithm and make it possible to use this method for speeding up
the other algorithms. Let us consider this generalization.

Suppose that the algorithmic algebra under consideration is generated
by elementary operators and conditions defined on the information
set B . As it is known, the algorithmic algebra is two-based and
consists of the two components: the algebra of operators and the
algebra of conditions. The elements of the first algebra are operators,
i.e., the partial transformations of the set B , the elements of
the second algebra are conditions, i.e., the partial functions
defined on B and assuming the values 0 and 1. The operations of
the algebra of operators are a product, α -disjunction ($(P \vee Q) = \underline{if}$
$\alpha \underline{then}$ P $\underline{else}$ Q) and α -iteration ($\{P\}_{\alpha} = \underline{while} \neg \alpha \underline{do}$ P).

In the algebra of conditions the Boolean operations and the multiplication of operator by condition are defined. We shall denote the
latter operation as α^P (α <u>after</u> P).

The operator y is called to be monotonous relative to the condition
α if α (b)=1 implies (α(y (b)))=1 . Suppose that the set B of
the information environment states consists of two components C and
C', that is $B = C \times C'$. The operators P and Q are called C -
equivalent, if they have the same domains of definition and for each
state b = (c,c') the condition $P(C,C')=(C_1,C_1')$ and $Q(C,C')=(C_2,C_2')$
implies $C_1=C_2$. In other words, C -equivalence means the same
actions on the component B . We say that the operator y (condition
α) acts on the component C , if there exists the partial function
φ from C to C (from C to $\{0,1\}$), such that for any $c \in C$,
$c' \in C'$ the condition $y(c,c') = (\varphi(c),c')$ $(\alpha(c,c') = \varphi(c))$ is true.

The main result of the paper [2] may be summarized as such. Let the
operator y and the condition α act on the component C , operators
z_0 and u act on the component C' of the information environment
$B = C \times C'$, and the relations given below hold in the semigroup of
operators of the algorithmic algebra that acts on B :

$$z_0 z = z_0 y;$$
$$z_0 u^{m+1} = z_0 u^m z^2 u, \quad m = 0,1,\ldots$$
$$u z_0 = z_0.$$

Then, if the operator y is monotonous relative to the condition α ,
then the following operators are C -equivalent:

1. $\left\{ y \atop \alpha \right\}$;

2. $\left\{ z_0 \atop \alpha \right. \left\{ u \atop \alpha^{z^2} \right\} z \}$;

3. $z_0 \left\{ \atop \alpha \right. \left\{ u \atop \beta \right\} z \}$, where $\beta = \overline{\alpha}^{\left\{ z^2 \right\}}_{\alpha^z}$;

4. $z_0 \left\{ \atop \alpha \right. (\varepsilon \vee z) u \atop \overline{\beta} \}$, β is the same as in 3.

In addition, if there is an operator u^{-1} in the semi-group of operators which acts on the component C and satisfies the relations

432

$$z_0 u^{m+1} u^{-1} = z_0 u^m, \quad m = 0, 1, \ldots,$$

and also the operator y^{-1} that acts on C and such that $yy^{-1} = \varepsilon$, then the operators 1 - 4 are C-equivalent to the operator

5. $z_0 \left\{ \underset{\alpha^z}{u} \right\} \left\{ \underset{\alpha}{\left\{ \underset{z^{zy^{-1}}}{u^{-1}} \right\}} z \right\}$.

The application of iteration speed-up method usually deals with iteration which is defined for algorithmic algebra that acts on the information environment C . To construct the efficient program one has to extend C up to the set $C \times C'$, where C' is to be chosen so that the operators z_0, u, z and also, if it is possible, the operators u^{-1} and y^{-1} might be defined. After this, one of the programs 2 - 5 is chosen and is realized by means of the algorithmic language which is used. To obtain the usual program it is sufficient to realize the tests of conditions. If simple iteration is repeated on a state of information environment n times, then the program constructed by means of formula 2 is performed in time proportional to $(\log n)^2$; and the programs 3 - 5 are performed in time proportional to log n.

The methods of formal transformations of algorithms are widely used in the design technology that is developed at the Institute of Cybernetics of the Ukrainian Academy of Sciences. This technology is known as a method of formalized specifications [3,4] . Let us consider some examples of formal transformations of algorithms during their design with a method of formalized specifications. These examples are taken from the recent publications. The first example is from [5] . Let us consider the problem of counting the number of connected components of non-directed graph $\Gamma = (G, \rho)$ that is defined by the set of edges G and by symmetric contiguity relation $\rho \subset G^2$. The reflexive and transitive closure of the relation ρ provides the accessibility relation $\hat{\rho}$: g and g' are accessible if $g=g'$ or there exists the sequence $g=g_1, g_2, \ldots, g_m=g' (m \geqslant 2)$ such that g_i and g_{i+1} are adjacent for $i=1, \ldots, m-1$. The accessibility relation is the equivalence. The classes of this relation are called the connected components. The connected component which contains the edge g will be denoted by $\hat{\rho}(g)$.

The following program describes simple algorithm of solving the
problem mentioned above by means of the set-theoretic notions.

```
BEGIN
    k : = 0.
    FOR ALL g ∈ G   DO  φ(g): = 0.
LOOP BEGIN
    FIND g ∈ G   SUCH THAT   φ(g) = 0.
    IF NOT THEN GO OUT.
    k : = k + 1.
    FOR ALL h ∈ ρ̂(g) DO  φ(h) : = k.
END LOOP
END.
```

The correctness of this program may be proved with ordinary methods.
Representing the program in the form

```
BEGIN
    k : = 0
    P.
LOOP BEGIN
    Q.
    k : = k + 1.
    R.
END LOOP.
END.
```

and making the sequential refinement for the operators P, Q,R, we
shall obtain the program in ALGOL. To construct this program we
choose the following way of presenting the graph. Let G be the
integer array having the size $[1 : n, 1 : m]$, where n is the number
of edges of the graph , m is not less than the maximal number of
edges adjacent to any given edge of the graph Γ . The array G
represents the graph Γ if $G[i,j] \neq 0$ iff the edges g_i and $g_{G[i,j]}$
are adjacent, i=1,...,n, j=1,...,m, $G=\{g_1, ..., g_n\}$. The function φ
may be realized by means of an integer array FI $[1 : n]$ if $\varphi(g_i)=FI[i]$
for i=1,...,n   . The program in ALGOL has the form:

```
    PROCEDURE  COMP (G,M,N,K); INTEGER ARRAY  G;
INTEGER N,M,K ; VALUE M,N;
BEGIN INTEGER ARRAY FI [1 : N] ; INTEGER I,J,S; BOOLEAN CHANGE;
```

```
k := 0 ;
FOR  I :=1 STEP 1 UNTIL N DO  FI [I] :=0;
L: FOR I :=1 STEP 1 UNTIL N  DO  IF FI [I] ≠0 THEN
    BEGIN S :=I;  GO TO FOUND  END; GO TO FINE;
FOUND:  K := K+1 ; FI [S] : = K;
REPEAT : CHANGE : FALSE;
   FOR I :=1 STEP 1 UNTIL N DO IF FI [I] = K THEN
   FOR J :=1 STEP 1 UNTIL M DO IF G [I, J] = 0 THEN
      IF FI [G [ I,J]] ≠ K  THEN BEGIN FI [G [ I,J]] := K;
      CHANGE : =TRUE END; IF CHANGE THEN GO TO REPEAT ;
      GO TO L ;
FINE : END.
```

The first program may be considered as a formalized specification
which is realized by the second program. This program is not satisfactory because it is performed in time proportional to mn^2. To
shorten this time let us return to the set-theoretic level, preserving the data representation.

```
BEGIN.
   k :=0
FOR ALL  i = 1,...n DO FI [i] :=0
LOOP BEGIN.
   FIND s SUCH THAT  FI [s] =0.
   IF NOT THEN GO OUT.
   k : = k+1.
FI[s]:=k
DO UNTIL  ¬ CHANGE. BEGIN CHANGE : = FALSE.
   FOR ALL i =1,...,n  SUCH THAT FI [i] =k DO
   FOR ALL j =1,...,m  SUCH THAT G [i,j]  =0
      AND FI [G [i,j]] =k DO
   (FI [G [ i,j]] :=k.   CHANGE : = TRUE).
END UNTIL.
END LOOP.
END.
```

Let us introduce new data structures - the set $V_0 \subset \{1,...,n\}$ and
the set $W \subset \{1,...,n\}$. Add to the program under consideration the
computations on these sets so that during every pass of the external
loop the condition $V_0 = \{1 \leqslant i \leqslant n | FI[i]=0\}$ is true and during every
pass of the internal loop the condition "FI[i]=k and there exists

$1 \leqslant j \leqslant m$, such that $G[i,j]=0$ and $FI[G[i,j]]=k$ implies $i \in W$ " is true. Then the operator Q may be replaced by

IF $V_0=0$ THEN GO OUT ELSE GET s FROM V_0

and the head of the loop of i by the head

FOR ALL $i \in W$ DO.

The execution of the operator GET X FROM A entails the deleting of X from the set A , and the operator FOR ALL $i \in W$ DO T is equivalent to the program

```
WHILE W ≠ ∅ DO
BEGIN
    GET i FROM W.
    T.
END.
```

It is sufficient to add the index of every new edge to the set W in the operator T when this edge is marked for the first time be the number k to make the condition for W to be true before executing T . When the necessary transformations are done it is clear that during the second pass of internal loop the set W is empty and the loop brackets may be dropped. The variable CHANGE then may be also omitted. The transformed program is:

```
BEGIN.
    k : =0.
    FOR ALL  i=1,...,n  DO  FI [i] :=0.
    V₀ : =  1,...,n  .
WHILE V₀≠∅   DO BEGIN.
    GET  s  FROM V₀ .
    k : = k+1.  FI [s] :=k. ⟨ W : ={s} ⟩.
    FOR ALL  i ∈ W  DO
    FOR ALL  j=1,...,m SUCH THAT G [i,j] =0 AND FI [G [ i,j]] =k DO
    (FI [G [i,j]] :=k.⟨DELETE  G [i,j] FROM V₀ . INCLUDE  G [i,j] IN W⟩)
END WHILE.
END.
```

Here the oprators inserted into the program as described above are

taken in the brackets ⟨ ⟩ . The obtained program is performed in
a linear time if including and deleting of the elements of the sets
V_0 and W need time bounded by some constant not depending on the
power of these sets. Similarly, the efficient algorithm might be
obtained for counting the number of the connected components for
the directed graphs with linear time estimation as in Tarjan paper
[8] . The same method was used in [5] to construct the Hopcroft
algorithm [6] of automata minimization in time proportional to
n log n instead of classical minimization that needs n^2.

The following example is also related to the set-theoretic programming and is connected with realization of recursive definitions.

Let Q be n -ary relation defined by the following recursive definition:

1. $P(x_1, \ldots, x_n) \Rightarrow Q(x_1, \ldots, x_n)$;

2. $Q(x_1, \ldots, x_n)$ and $R(z_1, \ldots, z_m) \Rightarrow Q(y_1, \ldots, y_n)$;

3. Q is the least relation satisfying the previous two conditions
for all $x_1, \ldots, x_n$ and $u_1, \ldots, u_k$ such that $S(u_1, \ldots, u_k)$,
where P,R and S are given relations, $z_1, \ldots, z_m$, $y_1, \ldots, y_n$ are
algebraic expressions depending upon the variables $x_1, \ldots, x_n$,
$u_1, \ldots, u_k$.
This definition may be easily converted into the set-theoretic
program that constructs the relation Q if all other relations
mentioned in the definition are finite. The program looks as follows:

```
BEGIN.  Q := ∅ .  Q_0 := P.
   LOOP BEGIN.  Q_1 := ∅ .
      FOR ALL (x_1,...,x_n) ∈ Q_0  DO
      FOR ALL (u_1,...,u_k) ∈ S  SUCH THAT R(z_1,...,z_m)     DO
        IF (y_1,...,y_n) ∉ Q ∪ Q_0 ∪ Q_1  THEN INCLUDE (y_1,...,y_n) IN Q_1 .
        Q à = Q ∪ Q_0
        IF Q_1 = ∅  THEN GO OUT.
         Q_0 : = Q_1 .
END LOOP.
END.
```

Usually such a program works inefficiently because it looks over
the elements of P and S many times. So it should be optimized

using special properties of the sets P, R and S.

Let us consider the well known problem of finding all of the essential variables in the states of the program scheme. This problem is one of the main problems of data flow analysis for programs. Consider the necessary definitions. The program scheme on the memory R is the set A of the states with the set T of transitions that are 4-couples (a, u, y, a') where a is a state of the program, u is the condition of the transition, y is an operator executed during the transition and a' is a state of the program after the transition. If (a, u, y, a') is a transition, then we write $a \xrightarrow{u/y} a'$. For each of the operators two sets are given: the set of used and the set of produced variables from R for this operator, and for each condition the set of variables used by this condition is given. The pass in scheme is the sequence of the transitions $p = t_1 \ldots t_n$ such that $t_i = (a_i, u_i, y_i, a_i')$, $a_1 = a$, $a_n = a'$, $a_{i+1} = a_i'$, $i = 1, \ldots, n$.

If p is the pass from a to a', then we write $a \xrightarrow{p} a'$. If the transition $t = (a, u, y, a')$ is such that u and y use r, then r is said to be used by the state a and the transition t. The main definition is formulated as follows: the variable r is essential in the state a iff a uses r or there exists the pass p and the state a' such that $a \xrightarrow{p} a'$, a uses r and no one of the transitions of the pass p produces r. To obtain the constructive definition of the notion of the essential variable let us consider the relation $Q \subset A \times R$, which is defined as the least relation such that:

1. a uses $r \Rightarrow (a, r) \in Q$;
2. $(a, r) \in Q$ and $a' \xrightarrow{p} a$ for some transition p that does not produce $r \Rightarrow (a', r) \in Q$.

It is easy to prove such a sentence: the variable r is essential for $a \Leftrightarrow (a, r) \in Q$.

Using the previous construction it is easy to obtain the following program that generates the set Q.

```
BEGIN . Q := ∅ . Q_0 := { (a,r) | a USES r}
   LOOP BEGIN . Q_1 := ∅ .
     FOR ALL (a,r) ∈ Q_0 DO
     FOR ALL   a' ∈ A SUCH THAT FOR SOME p ∈ T
```

```
                ( a'─P→a  AND  p   DOES NOT PRODUCE  r  ) DO
             IF(a',r) ∉ Q₀∪Q₁ ∪ Q      THEN INCLUDE  (a',r)     IN Q₁.
        Q : = Q∪Q₀.
        IF Q₁ = ∅        THEN GO OUT.
        Q₀ : = Q₁.
END LOOP.
END.
```

The efficiency of realization of this algorithm may be estimated
now and the methods of representing the sets Q, Q_0, Q_1 may be developed
taking into account the representation of the program schemes.
Suppose that the set A of the program scheme states is represented by the list and the set T of transitions by means of the function T that is defined on A and assumes its values in T so
that $p \in T_1(a) \Leftrightarrow p \in T$ and $a \xrightarrow{P} a'$ for some $a' \in A$. Let us
estimate the time of program performance as a function of the number
of states of A .In doing so we assume that the number of variables
and the number of transitions from each state is bounded, that is,
small relative to n which may be arbitrary large. Then, if Q, Q_0
and Q_1 are represented by usual lists, the time is proportional
to n^3 . The shortening of this time may be achieved by speeding
up the test of the condition $(a,r) \in Q \cup Q_0 \cup Q_1$ and restricting the
set of values of the loop parameter. The first may be done by representing the sets Q, Q_0 and Q_1 by means of the functions F, F_0
and F_1 defined on A   and assuming their values in 2^R , so
that $(a,r) \in Q \Leftrightarrow r \in F(a)$ and similar conditions hold for F_0 and F_1 .
To speed up the generating of the elements of Q_0 and Q_1 it is
convenient to use the auxiliary sets B_0 and B_1 such that
$a \in B_0 \Leftrightarrow F_0(a) \neq \emptyset$, $a \in B_1 \Leftrightarrow F_1(a) \neq \emptyset$. To restrict the set of values
of the parameter a' it is convenient to construct the function G ,
defined on A and assuming the values in 2^A .We assume that
$a' \in G(a) \Leftrightarrow$ there exists $p \in T$ such that $a \xrightarrow{P} a'$. Then the
loop with the parameter a' may be executed taking only the elements
of G(a) but not all of the elements of A   as the values of a' .
After all the necessary formal transformations and substitutions
are done we shall obtain the program:

```
BEGIN . B₀: = ∅.
   FOR ALL  a ∈ A   DO
       BEGIN . F ( a ) : = ∅.
          FOR ALL  r ∈ R    DO
```

IF a USES r THEN INCLUDE r IN F_0 (a).

IF F_0(a) $\neq \emptyset$ THEN INCLUDE a IN B_0 .

END.

LOOP BEGIN.

FOR ALL a $\in B_0$ DO

FOR ALL r $\in F_0$(a) DO

FOR ALL a' $\in G$ (a) DO

IF FOR SOME p $\in T_1$(a') (a' $\xrightarrow{P}$ a AND p DOES NOT

GENERATE r) THEN IF r $\in F$(a) OR F_0(a) OR F_1(a)

THEN INCLUDE r IN F_1(a'), a' IN B_1.

FOR ALL a $\in B_0$ DO F (a) : = F (a) $\cup$ F_0(a).

IF $B_1 = \emptyset$ THEN GO OUT.

FOR ALL a $\in B_0 \cup B_1$ DO

IF a $\in B_0 \setminus B_1$ THEN F_0 (a) : = $\emptyset$ ELSE

IF a $\in B_1$ THEN F_0 (a) : = F_1 (a).

FOR ALL a $\in B_1$ DO F_1 (a) : = $\emptyset$.

END LOOP.

END.

In all the examples considered, the same method was used. We call it the method of inserting and deleting the redundant computations. This method includes the following. New data structures are introduced and computations with these structures are inserted into the algorithm. The inserted computations do not change the result of the algorithm and are redundant at first, however they cause the new useful relations between the data. These relations are used for optimizing transformations of the algorithm. Transformations being finished some of the operators in the algorithm become redundant and may be deleted as usual. Formally, the method of inserting and deleting the redundant computations may be represented as a sequence of formal transformations that can be exactly described.

The methods of formal transformations illustrated here by some simple examples are also used for large programs. For instance , recently the program in PL/I which consists of 2000 operators was developed by means of the method of formalized specifications and optimized by means of the method described above. The application of this method enabled us to speed up this program almost 10 times as much.

The application of the methods of the formal transformations for

the large programs is connected with much routine work to analyze
the program texts and to implement the transformations exactly .
This work can be done easier with the use of the man-machine interactive transformations in the automatized design systems. Such
tools were realized in the system PROEKT for the automatized computer
hardware and software design. This system was developed at the Institute of Cybernetics of the Ukrainian Academy of Sciences. Similar
tools are under development now in the system of the set-theoretic
programming oriented to the problems of artificial intelligence [7] .

REFERENCES

1. Glushkov V.M., Automata theory and formal transformations of
   microprograms, Kibernetika, No.5, 1965 (in Russian).
2. Letichevsky A.A., On a speeding up the iterations of monotonous
   operators, Kibernetika, No.4, 1976 (in Russian).
3. Glushkov V.M., Kapitonova Yu.V., Letichevsky A.A., Theoretical
   foundations of discrete systems design, Kibernetika, No.6, 1977
   (in Russian).
4. Glushkov V.M., Kapitonova Yu.V., Letichevsky A.A., On application
   of formalized specification method to the design of data structures manipulation problems, Programmirovanie, No.6, 1978 (in Russian)
5. Letichevsky A.A., Godlevsky, Optimization of algorithms during
   their design by formalized specification method, Avtomatizacija
   proektirovanija EVM i ikh komponentov, IC Ukr.Acad of Sci.,Kiev,
   1977 (in Russian).
6. Hopcroft J.E., An n log n algorithm for minimizing states in a
   finite automata, in Kohavi Z., Paz A. (edrs) Theory of machines
   and computations, Acad.Press, N.-Y, 1971.
7. Glushkov V.M., Kapitonova Yu.V., Letichevsky A.A., Instrumental
   tools for the design of programs for processing mathematical
   texts, Kibernetika, No.2, 1979 (in Russian).
8. Tarjan R.E., Depth first search and linear graph algorithms, SIAM
   J.Comput., v.1, No.2, 1972.

WHAT SHOULD WE DO HAVING PROVED A DECISION PROBLEM TO BE UNSOLVABLE?

Yuri Matijasevič

Leningrad Branch
Steklov Inst.of Mathematics
27 Fontanka,Leningrad 191011 USSR

Our meeting gives us rather a rare possibility to speak not only mathematics proper but to speak, so to say, around mathematics as well. I am going to take this opportunity to contribute to the topic which has been already touched upon here, namely, what should we do with algorithmically unsolvable problems. I will consider only one particular decision problem but it can serve as a sample for the situation with decision problems in general.

We know from very informative lectures by Prof.H.Zemanek that al-Khuwarizmi was not acquainted with any work of Diophantus. The latter considered in his papers a great number of particular equations of the type which is nowadays named after him.

Imagine for a moment that al-Khwarizmi was aware of Diophantus results which required for different equations ad hoc methods. It would be very much in the spirit of al-Khuwarizmi to look for a uniform method applicable to every Diophantine equation. (In fact,this problem was posed ten centuries later by David Hilbert in his famous "Mathematische Probleme".) But now we know that al-Khuwarizmi would fail to find such a uniform method. We can prove that there exists no algorithm for deciding whether an arbitrary Diophantine equation has a solution. The question arises: what have we gained by such a proof?

One of the possible answers to this question is as follows. Finding an algorithm saves, at least theoretically, the working time of qualified mathematicians since corresponding problem can now be tackled by less qualified ones or by computers. A proof of non-existence of algorithm for a particular problem also saves working time of mathematicians since now they are not to spend their time and efforts for inevitably fruitless attempts to find an algorithm for the problem considered. In a sense, such a proof of non-exi-stence (and only it!) gives mathematicians "moral right" to put a problem aside.

But would al-Khuwarizmi be satisfied with our proof of non-exi-stence of decision procedure for Diophantine equations? Probably, not. Remember that the original problem was not the decision problem for all Diophantine equations but the problem of solving particular and rather simple equations considered by Diophantus. So one can argue that the original problem was "overgeneralized". Intuitively speaking, the impossibility of a general decision procedure for Diophantine equations is due to the presence of some very involved equations. I would like to give you an impression of such equations known today.

Consider the following system of Diophantine equations (which could be easily combined into a single equation):

$$elg^2 + \alpha = (b - xy)q^2, \quad q = b^{5^{60}}, \quad \lambda + q^4 = 1 + \lambda b^5,$$

$$\theta + 2z = b^5, \quad l = u + t\theta, \quad e = y + m\theta, \quad n = q^{16},$$

$$r = [g + eq^3 + lq^5 + (2(e - z\lambda)(1 + xb^5 + g)^4 + \lambda b^5 +$$

$$\lambda b^5 q^4) q^4][n^2 - n] + [q^3 - bl + l + \theta\lambda q^3 + (b^5 - 2) \times$$

$$q^5][n^2 - 1], \quad p = 2ws^2 r^2 n^2, \quad p^2 k^2 - k^2 + 1 = \tau^2,$$

$$4(c - ksn^2)^2 + \eta = k^2, \quad k = r + 1 + hp - h,$$

$$\alpha = (wn^2 + 1) rsn^2, \quad c = 2r + 1 + \varphi, \quad d = bw + ca -$$

$$2c + 4a\gamma - 5\gamma, \quad d = (a^2 - 1)c^2 + 1, \quad f^2 = (a^2 - 1) \times$$

$$i^2 c^4 + 1, \quad (d + of)^2 = ((a + f^2(d^2 - a^2))^2 - 1) \times$$

$$(2r + 1 + jc)^2 + 1.$$

This system was constructed by J.P.Jones who proved that there is no algorithm for deciding for arbitrarily given value of the parameters u, x, y, z whether or not the system has a solution in natural numbers. This system is one of the simplest known today algorithmically undecidable parametric systems, still clearly it is much more complicated than any individual system of Diophantine equations ever considered by number-theorists.

Now one can pose a more modest problem of existence of decision procedure for some proper subclass of the class of all Diophantine equations. In fact a progress in this direction was achieved by K.L.Siegel in 1972 (the unsolvability of the general case was known since 1970). Namely, he considered equations of degree 2 and found for them an appropriate algorithm. Now one is encouraged to look for algorithms for equations of degree 3,4 and so on. Clearly this is an occupation for number-theorists. But as soon as they meet an unsurmountable obstacles, computer-scientists could try to show the difficulties to be principal by proving algorithmical unsolvability of corresponding decsion problem. In our example it is known that there is no decision procedure for Diophantine equations of degree 4. Thus now the only open case is the class of equations of degree 3 which is a challenge for both number-theorists and computer-scientists.

Suppose now that we have got the answer for the case of degree 3, what then? Evidently, we can introduce more subtle classification, for example, by limiting both degree and the number of nuknowns (in fact, the choice of such a classification can turn to be crucial esspecially for finding decision procedures). Having got a more subtle classification we have again a field of activity for both number-theorists and computer-scientists.

Summing up, one can say that a proof of the algorithmical unsolvability of a decision problem is never the final point of our investigations, it always is a starting point for tackling more subtle problems. Figuratively speaking, we can be more or less satisfied with algorithms we have found but we can never be fully satisfied with our theorems about non-existence of algorithms. Al-Khuwarizmi would not approve it.

ON THE EXPERIENCE OF RIDING TWO HORSES IN PROGRAMMING

A. Buda
Institute of Mathematics
Bulgarian Academy of Sciences
1000 Sofia, Bulgaria

Continuing with the "religious" trend of our symposium, I would also like to talk about my faith, but not about my knowledge.

First of all, it is my faith that, staying in his transcendental paradise and having released himself from mundane vanity, our God, Al-Khowarizmi, has attained knowledge of the nature of algorithms far more than others. And we might address to him - to Al-Khowarizmi - our question, "What is to be done after proving a mass problem to be unsolvable?" But apropos of this I would like to remind of an old anecdote.

A certain man was very poor. For a long time he prayed God to help him to win a lot of money in a lottery. At last God responded to his prayers and said, "Well, I shall help you, pray harder." This made the man very happy, he began to offer more prayers and look for the prize. However, several drawings passed without a prize falling to him. Then the man called on God again and asked why he did not keep his promise. "Believe me, I do my utmost to try," answered God meekly, "but you ought to help me a little, too - buy at least one lottery ticket --"

So now a very strange thing is noticeable. Several decades ago, when the first examples of unsolvable mass problems were discovered, the phenomenon of unsolvability seemed to be so exeptional that mathematicians hardly believed in them. Nevertheless, today it may seem to anyone, who found himself in the stormy stream of the papers on theoretical programming, that a decision problem, arising (as authors use to note in their papers) from programming practice is much more inclined to be unsolvable than solvable. But are those problems really evoked by programming practice? It is my opinion that this is not true in many cases. We are prone to consider inherent problems of mathematics reflecting a history of

the development of computable functions theory, but not of computer
work.

Ten years ago I began to take part in the implementation of a
large automatic programming system (150K instructions, 50 man-years).
And hearly at the same time, being a postgraduate student, I began
to work at my PhD thesis on decision problems for program schemas.
In both cases it was professor A.Ershov who was my leader in science. He told me that I would be riding on two horses of the same
science called computer programming. The horse of theoretical programming would help the horse of systems programming and vice versa.
Therefore, I would be riding at double speed. However, only a year
or two later I felt that I was most probably falling between two
stools which were constantly moving away from each other. We have
implemented the programming system, I have defended my thesis, but
all the time I could not get rid of the feeling that I was simultaneously dealing with two unconnected things. Today it costs me
more and more efforts to keep my horses in one team - they are graz-
ing in quite different meadows. But, nevertheless, it seems to me
that the experience of riding two horses in programming has helped
me to sense more precisely the distance between the theory and the
practice of programming and to work out an idea for myself (rather
intuitive than strict) of a practical computing model, i.e. of such
an abstract model which is a proper mathematical framework for putting and solving various problems of systems programming.

A computing model, as I understand it here, is a mathematical
device for which the following concepts are strictly defined:

 (i) data structure - structure of processed information,
 (ii) statement - atomic operation of data processing,
 (iii) control structure - "predecessor-successor" relations on
     a set of statements,
 (iv) computation and its result - accepted sequence of state-
     ments and its "value".

For instance, Turing machines, program schemas, push-down automata
are considered to be computing models, while equations defining
recursive functions and context-free grammars are considered not to
be.

It is my thesis that the following four requirements are the
necessary conditions on a computing model for it to be of practical
use.

Requirement 1. DEVICES HAVE TO BE ABLE TO PROCESS TREES, NOT
STRINGS ONLY. The devices dealing with strings only seem to be
badly adapted to proper representation of practical computations,
which are usually executed over structured storage. In such a case
the most natural approach is to present the final and intermediate
results of computations by means of functional terms (trees). Moreover, the notion of the tree in Computer Science seems to be as
fundamental as the notion of the real number in numerical analysis.
The transition from strings processing to trees processing in programming corresponds to the transition from free semigroups to
universal algebras in algebra. To my mind, another generalization
of programming theory connected with due regard for data structure
by means of defining relations (the transition from free semigroups
to semigroups with relations in algebra) will hardly have more
widespread practical use.

I am surely not the first to note the significance of the
notion of the tree in theoretical programming. There is a considerable number of papers describing various data processing devices
dealing not only with trees, but with more complicated structures,
too. The problem is to construct and investigate (deeply and carefully) a range of trees processing devices satisfying the other
requirements to practical computing models.

Requirement 2. DEVICES HAVE TO BE FREE ENOUGH. Intuitively,
a finite automaton and a program schema might be treated as examples
of absolutely free and severely non-free devices respectively. The
conviction in the necessity of such an informal requirement has
occured to me after some unsuccessful attempts to understand the
reasons of unsolvability in some proper subclasses of program
schemas. Firstly, in many cases the structure of sets of accepted
computations turned out so complicated that they could hardly be
described with the aid of traditional techniques. Secondly, it is
my observation that there are very few results on solvability in
the theory of program schemas, which have no direct analogues in
more pure well-known structures of algebra and logic. Thirdly, in
many cases the subclasses of program schemas, allowing interesting
statements of decision problems, look very artificial from the
standpoint of practice. In order to find the frontier between solvability and unsolvability, it seems more natural to transfer from
more to less free models restricting the "freedom" step by step in
controlled way.

The requirement for devices to be free in programming may be compared with the requirement for functions to be smooth in numerical analysis. The study of functions which are not smooth demands more complicated techniques, in particular, it is the method of approximations by smooth functions which is used. It is quite possible that such an approach will appear in programming, too, but since nowadays we do not possess the knowledge on "smooth functions" of theoretical programming to a sufficient extent, their study should be among the primary tasks.

Requirement 3. THE EQUIVALENCE OF DEVICES HAS TO TAKE ACCOUNT OF THEIR CONTROL STRUCTURES. To put it in another way, the equivalence test has to compare not only the final results of computations, but some "running histories" of devices leading up to these results. A theoretical motivation of this requirement is given by the following unfortunate result: while devices are treated as "black boxes", the functional equivalence problem is proved to be unsolvable in many instances of interesting computing models (devices are said to be functionally equivalent if, for any pair of equal inputs, they compute equal final results). I have repeatedly satisfied myself that in developing a certain program, a programmer follows blindfold his initial idea about its "logical scheme" and changes a control structure considerably less willingly then a data one. He is prone to restrict the functional equivalence class of a given program and to consider only such programs of this class the control structures of which are "alike". This observation might be regarded as a practical motivation of Requirement 3.

A similar requirement for program schemas was first suggested by A.P.Ershov who introduced the concepts of computation history and formal equivalence of program schemas. In the case when the equivalence relation takes account of control structure, it seems to be more natural, firstly, to present histories of computations by means of trees the nodes of which are named by predicate terms and, secondly, to define a denotational semantic in terms of algebraic systems, but not of universal algebras.

Requirement 4. THE EQUIVALENCE OF DEVICES HAS TO BE DECIDED IN POLYNOMIAL TIME. This severe requirement seems to be the necessary condition for the existence of a broad range of fast algorithms for deep equivalent transformations of devices, founding various methods of program parsing, compiling and global optimization.

Today, if a certain algorithm is to be of practical use, it is necessary for its running time (in the worst case) to be of the order of n^3 or, sometimes, n^4. It is hardly to be expected that the order figures will increase more than 2 times during the next 2-3 decades. Therefore, an algorithm deciding equivalence of devices in time $O(n^k)$, where $k > 8$, n is the maximal size of compared devices, can hardly be regarded to be of practical use even in the beginning of the next century.

I do not believe that there may be constructed an universal computing model which could serve as a mathematical framework for an algebra of programming (i.e. for an universal mathematical foundation of numerous methods of program transformations applied in practice). However, I believe that there exists a broad range of practical computing models which could be a ground for such an algebra in toto.

I regard my talk as one more call to investigate more practical computing models. I think the time is proper: today the practice of computer programming has begun directly, not methodologically only, to affect the basic mathematical concepts and structures. To my mind, the scientific program of our symposium is striking evidence of this trend.

All of us, sitting in this hall, admire the same God. And knowing his scientific outlook thanks to the wonderful lectures of professor H. Zemanek, one can guess that right now, fidgeting impatiently about his two stools at once, he is trying to tell us: "Keep close to practice, colleagues! Do help me just a bit!"

CHURCH-ROSSER TRANSFORMERS AND DECIDABLE

PROPERTIS OF TREE PROCESSSING

A.V. Anisimov, Department of Cybernetics, Kiev State University

252 017, Kiev-17, U.S.S.R.

During numerous discussions which took place at this symposium
it has been mentioned many times how usefull to bring algebraic
methods in studying of algorithms. It has been also stressed many
times the benefit of the approach when algorithms are studied
together with data structures to be processed. On this occasion
let me remind only the tytle of the wellknown Wirth's book "Algorithms + Data Structures = Programs". In this report we present
an example of the research confirming strongly these two thesises.

The studying objects are transformers running through data
structures similar to trees. Transformers can chage information
stored in nodes and can make transitions on a tree both from
"father to son" and from "son to father". Transformers can act
nondeterministicly. Such transformers are models of the LISP
garbage collection program (nonrecursive variant), of programs
processing a data base and of many algorithms used in artificial
intelligence systems. Since transitions in two directions→bottom-up
and top-down are allowed in sequential runs on a tree then it is
convinient to consider trees as more general structures - free
groups. In such generalization the algebraic structure of a tree
turns out to be general enough to make possible simulation by considered transformers of many problems connected with trees. Using

450

the general theorem on solvability of the Church-Rosser property for locally-finite marking transformers over a free group we obtain in a discipline way solvability of many tree processing problems that usually were considered separately with a special proof technique.

Let $\mathcal{B}$ be an arbitrary informational domain, $X = \langle x_I, \ldots x_m \rangle$ - a finite alphabet, $\mu : \mathcal{B} \rightarrow X$ - a marking function, $Y = \langle y_I, \ldots, y_n \rangle$ - an alphabet of basic transformations on $\mathcal{B}$, $y_i : \mathcal{B} \rightarrow \mathcal{B}$. A nondeterministic marking descrete transformer over $\mathcal{B}$ is a system $A = (\mathcal{O}, a_o, X, Y, Z, R, F)$ where $\mathcal{O}$ is a finite set of states, $a_o \in \mathcal{O}$ - is a starting state, $Z = \langle z_I, \ldots, z_q \rangle$ - is an alphabet of additional marks, R is a finite set of rules of the type $a x z \rightarrow a' y z'$; $a, a' \in \mathcal{O}$; $x \in X$; $y \in Y$; $z, z' \in Z$. A symbol ε denotes an empty word; $F \subseteq \mathcal{O}$ is a set of final states. The interpretation of a rule $a x z \rightarrow a' y z'$ from R consists in the following.

If a transformer A is in a state a and processes an element b with a mark x and additional mark z, then A can make an action: to change in b the additional mark z on z', to switch the control state from a to a' and to start processing the new element by from $\mathcal{B}$. We assume that at the beginning any element of $\mathcal{B}$ contains the empty additional mark ε.

Thus marking transformers have an ability to memorize in elements of a processed area some information that could have an impact on a transformer's behaviour in repeated visits of marked elements.

A transformer is called reading only if the possibility of making additional marks is not used.

Herein in this paper under a transformer we mean a nondeterministic marking descrete transformer.

Let A be a marking transformer over $\mathcal{B}$. Since A is a nondeterministic then there exists a variety of processes which could be generated by A. We consider a process generated by A to be finished if A comes to a state a, views an element from $\mathcal{B}$ with a mark (x, z) and there is no corresponding right side in R for the triple $a\,x\,z$.

A result of applying a transformer A to an element with a marking function μ is the set $A_\mu(b)$ consisting of all elements c from $\mathcal{B}$ such that A starting the processing of b could come to an element c and stops in one of final states from F.

If there exists a nonterminating process which begins with application of A to b then we assume that a special element ∞ belongs to $A_\mu(b)$.

A transformer A is called locally finite if under any of its realization a number of visits of an arbitrary element in $\mathcal{B}$ is bounded with a constant not depending of a choice of μ.

A transformer is called a Church - Rosser transformer if for all μ and b the set $A_\mu(b)$ consists of one element.

Church - Rosser transformers generalize the notion of Church - Rosser systems [7] which recently attract attention in connection with optimizing program transformations. The theory of Church - Rosser transformers is considered in the paper [3]

A marking transformer over a free group generalizes a Turing
machine since the two - directed tape is a particular case of an
infinite cyclic group. In the theory of Turing computations the
well known Trakhtenbrot - Hennie theorem states that computations
with finite protocols could be fulfilled by one - directed finite
automata and since the equivalence problem for such computations
is decidable. In computations on structures similar to trees   the
situation is more complicated. In 1968 A.A. Letichevsky proved
that for reading only transformers over almost free groups the
equivalence problem is solvable [4]. The class of almost free
groups (β - groups) contains finite and free groups and closed
under the free product and some other operations. It is proved [5]
that the class of so called context-free groups studied in [1]
coinsides with the class of all almost free group.

Slightly modifying the technique developed by A.A. Letichevsky one can prove the analogous result for marking transformers.
This result can be considered as a generalization of the Trakhtenbrot - Hennie result.

Theorem I   For locally - finite marking transformers over
almost free groups the testing of the Church - Rosser property
is effectively solvable.

The proof of this theorem could be concluded similarly to the
Letichevsky's proof for the decidability of the equivalence of
two deterministic transformers over almost free groups. Instead
of comparison of two trasformers it is necessary to compare two

arbitrary processes generated by a transformer. The local finiteness of traces in any point makes possible to use an analogy of
the substitution and nesting lemma. Permission of additional marks
does not break the possibility of nesting and substitution within
every process. Thus the testing of the Church - Rosser property
is reduced to the verification of this property for such interpretations when all generated processes run within some bounded area.

Let us start with consequences of the theorem I.

<u>Corollary I</u>.   The equivalence problem for deterministic mar-
king locally-finite transformers over almost free groups is decidable.

It is plain that for two given deterministic transformers A_1
and A_2 one can construct the nondeterministic transformer A
which at the initial state nondeterministicly transfers control to
A_1 or A_2 and then acts accoding to the chosen processor. The
transformer A possesses the Church - Rosser property iff A_1
and A_2 are functionally equivalent.

Let us consider transformers over an almost free group augmented with right nulls.

Let G be an almost free group, Y is an alphabet of basic transformations on G , (G, ω) is the group G augmented
with a right null ω , i.e. $t\omega = \omega$ for all $t \in G \cup \langle \omega \rangle$. Let w
be a new symbol not belonging to the alphabet of generators of G
$\{w\}$ - is the cyclic group , A is a deterministic reading only
transformer over (G, ω) . Using the possibility of storing labels
of performing y - transitions in elements of $G * \{w\}$ it is easy

to simulate acting of ω on an element t by backtracking ffom t to W . Thus the transformer A can be simulated by the deterministic marking transformer A_ω over $G * \{w\}$. Since A is a deterministic reading only transformer then it cannot passwithout cycling any element from $G \cup \langle\omega\rangle$ more than k times where k is the number of states in A . Thus A_ω is locally - - finite. This implies the following result.

<u>Corollary 2</u>   The equivalence problem for deterministic reading only transformers over almost free groups augmented with a finite number of nulls is solvable.

<u>Corollary 3</u> [6] The equivalence problem for deterministic reading only transformers over a free semigroup with a right null is decidable.

It is plain that any free semigroup can be easily embedded into a corresponding free group. It remains to apply the corollary 2.

In paper [10] the decidability of equivalence problem in the class of $\mathcal{JP}$ - schemes - Ianov schemes augmented with a pushdown stack was proved. The acting of any $\mathcal{JP}$ - scheme can be represented as a run of a stack automation over a tree generated by terms of one argument functional operators. A stack is necessary for providing returns to some vertices which have been passed earlier. Embedding a tree into a free group and using the possibility to put additional marks into elements of a free group make possible a simulation of a work of an $\mathcal{JP}$ - scheme by a deterministic marking transformer over a free group. Local finiteness follows from the easy recognition of cycling in any element.

Corollary 4 [10] In the class of $\mathcal{JP}$ - schemes the equivalence problem is solvable.

Let us now consider the theory of finite automata on finite trees [8, 9, 12]

In considering automata on trees the recognition of trees is formulated by means of parallel runs of a nondeterministic automata over marked tree. A parallel run of an automaton over a tree can be simulated by a tree traverse of a depth-first search type. Information of choices for further path continuation is putted into nodes. Backtracking because of unsuccessful choices for a run is performed by embeddinginto a free group. The depth-first search properties imply the local finiteness of the constructed simulating marking transformer. Thus the following result holds true.

Corollary 5 [8,9] The equivalence of finite automata over finite trees is solvable.

In the same way it is easy to prove the decidability of structured equivalence for context-free grammars proved in [11] and some other similar results

The detailed proof of the corollary 5 is given in [2].

R E F E R E N C E S

I. Anisimov A.V. On Group Languages, "Cybernetics", n.4, Kiev, I97I (in Russian).

2. Anisimov A.V. Backtracking Descrete Transformers, "Cybernetics",

n.6, Kiev, 1979 (in Russian).

3. Glushkov V.M., Anisimov A.V. Church - Rosser Transformers,
   "Cybernetics", n.5, Kiev, 1979 (in Russian)

4. Letichevsky A.A. Equivalence of automata over semigroups, Pro-
   ceedence "Theoretical Cybernetics", v.6, Institute of Cybernetics, Kiev, 1970 (in Russian)

5. Letichevsky A.A., Smikun L.B. On Classes of Groups with Solvable
   Equivalence Problem for Automata, Soviet Math. Dokl., n.I,
   Moscow, 1976

6. Letichevsky A.A. Equivalence of Automata with Final States Over
   Free Semigroups with Right Nulls, Soviet Math. Dokl., n.5,
   Moscow, 1968

7. Aho A.V., Sethi R, Ullman J.D. Code Optimization and Finite
   Church - Rosser Systems, in the book "Design and Optimization of
   Compilers", Prentice Hall, USA, 1972

8. Donner J.E. Decidability of the Weak Second-Order Theory of Two
   Successors, Abstract 65T-468 "Notes of the American Mathematical
   Society", v.12, 1965

9. Thatcher J.W., Wright J.B. Generalised Finite Automata Theory
   with an Application to a Decision of Second Order Logic, Mathematical Systems Theory, v.2, n.I, 1968

10. Tokura N., Kasami T., Furuta S. Ianov Schemes Augmented by a
    Pushdown Memory, IEEE 15th Annual Symposium on Switching and
    Automata Theory, New Orleans, USA, 1974

11. Paul M.C., Unger S.H. Structural Equivalence of Context-Free
    Grammars, "Journal of Computer and System Sciences", v.2, n.4,

I968

I2 Rabin M.O. Decidability of Second-Order Theories and Automata
on Infinite Trees, Transactions of American Mathematical Society,
v.I4I, n.7, I969

SUPPLEMENT 1

SUMMARIES OF ORAL PRESENTATIONS

The texts of these talks were unavailable when the proceedings have been compiled. The summaries are reprinted from Prof. M.S. Paterson's report on the Urgench Symposium published in the Bulletine of the European Association on Theoretical Computer Science, No. 10, January 1980, p. 63-80 with the kind permission of the Editor.

(A. van Wijngaarden
A. Kreczmar
A. Mazurkiewicz
B.A. Trakhtenbrot
J.V. Kapitonova
Yu.L. Ershov
M.S. Paterson
N.M. Nagorny
S.Kh. Sirazhdinov
G.N. Salikhov)

SUMMARIES OF ORAL PRESENTATIONS

Languageless Programming

A. van Wijngaarden

In ordinary programming, e.g. in ALGOL 68, four levels of language construction are involved:

Level 1 defines **the** defining formalism, e.g. a
  two-level grammer (by AVW):
  $VWG := (V_m, V_o, V_t, R_m, R_h, W)$,
  and so on.

Level 2 defines a specific VWG, e.g. that of
  ALGOL 68 (by WG2.1):
  program: strong void new closed clause,
  and so on.

Level 3 defines the representation of some specific terminal production
  of that VWG (by the programmer), e.g.
  <u>begin</u> <u>int</u> n; read (n); print (n 3-691) <u>end</u>.

Level 4 defines the output of this program resulting from its elaboration (by a computer), e.g.
  -391.

We shall now send the working group WG2.1 with its language home, throw the computer out of the window and promote the programmer to programmarer by replacing Levels 2, 3 and 4 by:

Level 2' defines a specific VWG (by the programmarer), e.g.
  pO:pKpiiip42pOp691p41p2.

Level 3' defines a terminal production of the VWG, e.g.
  -391.

We shall define the "and so on" in Level 2' in such a way that the processes with and without the language are equivalent. Moreover, it will be shown that the abolition of the language greatly simplifies and clarifies the whole process. Thereby, the programmarer can not only profit from all high-level means of expression as in, say, ALGOL68, but can also create new possibilities not present in the language - and machine - independent way.

Some Historical Remarks on Algorithmic Logic

A. Kreczmar

Programming logic (theory of schemata, algorithmic logic, dynamic logic) deals with programs, program properties and data structures in a formal, mathematical way. One of the reasons of the coming into existence of this branch of computer science was the natural tendency of programmers to find an algorithm (a method or a semi-algorithm) which can help them to prove (or disprove) the correctness of programs (c.f. Floyd-Hoare's system). But next the scientist began to develop this theory, making it as usual completely useless from the point of view of practice, investigations and observations.

The chronology was as follows:

First, the theory of schemata in the form of Yanov and the others appeared. Next, the systems like that of Ygarashi have tried to describe some properties of programs, as for instance strong equivalence. The paper by Luckham, Park, Peterson proved that these properties are not axiomatizable in a normal sense, because they are not recursively enumerable.

The first notice that the logic of programs is infinitistic, was Engeler (1968). He showed how to express the halting property in the language $L_{\omega,\omega}$ with the use of infinite disjunction. The Polish group started in 1969-70 to develop Algorithmic Logic on the base of this observation. In AL one can express not only the halting property but also many others like, for instance, partial and strong correctness, weak and strong equivalence, looping etc. Salwicki showed how to simplify Engeler's reasoning, next he proposed the axiomatic system with ω-rules. The correctness of this system was proved. Moreover we showed that this system is essentially infinitistic: ω-rules are necessary. Lately, a system called Dynamic Logic was proposed by Harel, Meyer and Pratt. Their logic deals with nondeterministic programs as well, but the properties of both systems are similar.

Concurrent Algorithms Schemata

A. Mazurkiewicz

Let V be a set of symbols representing elementary actions; then a sequential compositions of such actions can be represented by strings over V. Such strings can be used for describing total actions of sequential algorithms. In the case of concurrent algorithms some actions can be executed independently of each other (non-sequentially); therefore we need another mathematical concept which would play a similar part to strings in the theory of concurrent algorithms. For this purpose the notion of a _trace_ is defined as follows.

Let I be a symmetric, irreflexive binary relation over V. Two symbols in I relation are considered as representing _independent_ actions. Now, the trace [w] generated by a string w over V is defined as the equivalence class containing w of the least equivalence ≡ in the set of all strings over V satisfying the condition:

for all strings w', w'', and symbols a, b

$(a,b) \in I \rightarrow w'abw'' \equiv w'baw''$.

Any trace [w] can be thought of also as a partially ordered set of symbol occurrences such that representatives of [w] are exactly all extensions of this partial ordering to linear orderings. An algebra of traces and trace languages can be easily established by defining the concatenation [v]·[w] as [vw].

The crucial point in this construction is the independency relation; this relation can be easily deduced from the description of the concurrent algorithm under consideration. It turns out that the set of all actions of a concurrent algorithm can be expressed by a trace language being the least solution of a set of fixed-point equations following from the structure of the algorithm.

This approach turned out to be useful for investigating properties of concurrent program schemata.

Some Reflections on the Connection between Computer Science and the Theory of Algorithms

B.A. Trakhtenbrot

Reflection 1: on the theoretical significance of recursively invariant notions and notions not having this property.

Reflection 2: on the significance of combinatorial and algorithm-theoretic methods in the theory of complexity.

Reflection 3: on various approaches to algorithmically unsolvable or extremely hard problems.

Reflection 4: how do mathematicians react to languages invented by
programmers.

Reflection 5: on the attractiveness of algorithmic logic and its
practicability.

On Design and Implementation of Algorithms

J.V. Kapitonova

The combined design of a set of algorithms is considered.

Effective realization depends on the impact of the instrumentary
and language tools for designing this set. Descriptive and technology
implementation tools are discussed.

This discussion is based on experience gained in the development
of the hardware and software design system (PROJEKT) and the system
for automating proof search in mathematics (SAD).

How Does Algebra Help to Solve Problems from
the Theory of Algorithms (an Example)

Yu.L. Ershov

Let $<L_m, <>$ be the upper semilattice of many-one degrees; L_m is a
rather natural object for various considerations in the theory of
algorithms. A problem is how to "understand" or "grasp the meaning"
of this semilattice.

The "algorithmic" approach was not very fruitful, for the elementary theory $Th(L_m)$ is undecidable.

The "algebraic" approach happens to be quite successful, for a
clear algebraic characterization of L_m has been obtained (expressed
in notions of the modern algebra) which implies many interesting
"nonelementary" properties of L_m.

Two examples

1) For any $a < L_m$ the subsemilattice
$\check{a} = \{b | b \in L_m, a \leq b\}$ of L_m is isomorphic to L_m.

2) For any $a, b \in L_m$ there is an automorphism f of L_m such that
$f(a) = b$ iff the subsemilattice $\check{a} = \{c | c \in L_m, c \leq a\}$ and
$\hat{b} = \{c | c \in L, c \leq b\}$ are isomorphic.

The semilattice L_m is isomorphic to the semilattice $L(F)$ of all equivalence classes of numberings of F for any finite set F containing more than one element.

The Linear Postman: A Message-Forwarding Algorithm Using Sequential Storage

M.S. Paterson

A basic information-handling problem which we find in several diverse applications can be described in the following way. A row of houses has consecutive addresses from 1 to n and a postman visits each house in turn. At each house he delivers any letters addressed to the house and waits to collect new letters, maybe written as a consequence of those delivered. Any letters written at house i must have addresses greater than i. The volume of mail and processing ability of the postman are such that only very basic storage media, such as sacks or stacks, and simple sorting operations are appropriate.

The applications considered are hereditary screening in a medical file, computing the transitive closure of a symmetric matrix, evaluating an acyclic circuit and topological-sorting a chain. In each case the algorithm described, using sequential storage, requires a factor of logn more time than any algorithm with random access storage.

A paper on this work, jointly authored by M. Fischer, N.Pippenger and M. Paterson, is in (slow) preparation.

Algorithm as a Basis for Formulating Constructive Mathematical Notions

N.M. Nagorny

1. Mathematics as a model; models of mathematics.
2. What constructive mathematical analysis does give for computer science is:
    (a) revealing initial data necessary for actual computation of desired values,
    (b) finding correct formulations of computational problems. Examples.

ON EULER NUMBERS AND EULER POLYNOMIAL ROOTS

S.Kh.Sirazhdinov [*)]

Euler numbers $E_{n,k}$ ($\langle {n \atop k} \rangle$ in D.Knuth's notation) play an important role in combinatorial analysis. They happen to be very useful in studying sorting algorithms.

Theorem 1. Let $k = x\sqrt{(n+1)/12} + (n+1)/2$. Then, for all $1 \leqslant k \leqslant n$, we have

$$(*) \quad \frac{E_{n,k}}{n!} - \sqrt{\frac{6}{\pi(n+1)}} \, e^{-\frac{x^2}{2}} = -\frac{x^4 - 6x^2 + 3}{20(n+1)^{3/2}} \sqrt{\frac{6}{\pi}} \, e^{-\frac{x^2}{2}} + \frac{\theta_{nk}(x)}{n^{5/2}}$$

where $|\theta_{nk}(x)| \leqslant c \leqslant 57.2$.

It improves the other known estimate which offers only $O(n^{-3/4})$ for the right side of $(*)$.

Let $\lambda_{n,k}$ are roots of an Euler polynomial $E_n(x) = \sum_{k=1}^{n} E_{n,k} x^k$.

Theorem 2. For $-M \leqslant \lambda_{nk} \leqslant -M^{-1}$ ($M > 1$) we have

$$\lambda_{n,k} = -\exp\left[\pi \operatorname{tg}(\pi \frac{n-2k+1}{2n+4} + \frac{\varepsilon_{nk}}{n+2})\right] \quad \text{where}$$

$$|\varepsilon_{nk}| < 0.4 \left[\frac{1+(\ln M)^2}{9+(\ln M)^2}\right]^{n/2} \left(\frac{\pi}{6} + \sqrt{1+(\ln M)^2}\right)$$

that improves a related result by S.L.Sobolev.

Let $N = N(\lambda_{nk} < x)$ is the number of roots of $E_n(x)$ which are less than x and $F_n(x) = N/n$.

Theorem 3. For all $x \in (-\infty, 0)$.

$$F_n(x) = \frac{1}{2} - \frac{1}{\pi} \operatorname{arctg} \frac{\ln(-x)}{\pi} + \left(\frac{\ln n}{n}\right)^{1/2} \cdot \theta_r(x)$$

where $|\theta_r(x)| < c$ is an absolute constant.

[*)] Author's resume - Eds

ON AN ALGORITHM FOR FINDING WEIGHTS AND NODES
OF CUBIC FORMULAE

G.N.Salikhov *)

The problem of numerical integration over multidimensional regions consists of finding weights and nodes of for various cubic formulae.

We arge that if such formulae are invariant under some transformation group then it, first, makes easier to construct the algorithm of node evaluation and, second, the corresponding formulae turn out to be optimal or near to optimal in the sense of the algebraic degree of accuracy.

We describe an algorithm that constructs cubic formulae for approximate integration over sphere which are invariant under transformations of the sphere onto itself and present several ready-to-use cubic formulae for integrating over three- and fourdimensional spheres.

---

*) Author's resume - Eds

SUPPLEMENT 2

Technical program

The titles of talks are given as they were announced by the speakers at the symposium. Some titles of the written contributions have been changed.

Monday, September 17, morning session

Corresponding Member of the Academy of Sciences of the USSR, A.P.Ershov, Chairman.

H.Zemanek (Vienna). Q ala Al-Khorezmi (Al-Khorezmi has said). Part I. The background and the personality of Al-Khorezmi (1 h. 20 min).

S.Kh.Sirazhdinov (Tashkent). On Euler numbers and Euler polynomial roots (40 min).

D.E.Knuth (Stanford). Algorithm in modern mathematics and computer science (1 h. 30 min).

Monday, September 17, afternoon session

Member of the National Academy of Sciences of the USA, D.E.Knuth, Chairman.

V.A.Uspensky and A.L.Semenov (Moscow). What does the theory of algorithms give? (Major discoveries in the theory of algorithms for the last half of a century) - (1 h. 30 min).

J.M.Barzdin (Riga). On inductive synthesis of algorithms (1 h.).

Tuesday, September 18, morning session

Member of the National Academy of Sciences of the USA, S.C.Kleene, Chairman.

H.Zemanek (Vienna). Q ala Al-Khorezmi (Al-Khorezmi has said). Part II. The works and the influence of Al-Khorezmi (1 h.).

Yu.I.Manin (Moscow). Algorithm as a mathematical model (1 h.).

A. van Wijngaarden (Amsterdam). Languageless programming (1 h. 30 min).

Tuesday, September 18, afternoon session

Corresponding Member of the Academy of Sciences of the USSR, S.S.Lavrov, Chairman.

N.N.Nepeivoda (Izhevsk). An outline of the mathematical theory of program synthesis (45 min).

E.H.Tyugu (Tallinn). The structured synthesis of programs
(45 min).

A.Kreczmar (Warsaw). From schemata theory to algorithmic and
dynamic logic (30 min).

A.A.Letichevsky (Kiev). On the search for invariant relations
in programs (30 min).

A.Mazurkiewicz (Warsaw). On concurrent algorithms (30 min).

A general discussion on "How to write a program of a million
instructions" took place during the break between morning and after-
noon sessions on September 18.

Friday, September 21, morning session

Professor M.S.Paterson, Chairman.

B.A.Trakhtenbrot (Novosibirsk). Some reflections on the connection between computer science and the theory of algorithms (1 h.).

G.M.Adelson-Velsky (Moscow) and A.O.Slisenko (Leningrad).
What can be done with problems in exhaustive searches?

Yu.V.Kapitonova (Kiev). On goodness and badness of putting
combinatorial processes on a computer (45 min).

V.Strassen (Zurich). Algorithms for algebras (45 min).

Friday, September 21, afternoon session

Professor V.A.Uspensky, Chairman.

S.C.Kleene (Madison). Algorithms in various contexts (45 min).

N.A.Shanin (Leningrad). The role of algorithm in the semantics
of arithmetical languages (45 min).

Yu.L.Ershov (Novosibirsk). How algebra helps to solve problems
in the theory of algorithms (45 min).

G.S.Tseytin (Leningrad). From logicism to proceduralism (an
autobiographical account) - (45 min).

Saturday, September 22, morning session

Member of the Academy of Sciences of the Uzbek SSR,
S.Kh.Sirazhdinov, Chairman.

F.L.Bauer (Munich). Algorithms and algebra (presented by
D.E.Knuth) - (1 h.).

M.S.Paterson (Coventry). The linear postman: message-forwarding algorithms using sequential storage (1 h.).

A.P.Ershov (Novosibirsk). A definition of computable functions (computable functions over algebraic systems) - (45 min).

V.M.Glushkov (Kiev). On formal transformation of algorithms (presented by A.A.Letichevsky) - (45 min).

Saturday, September 22, afternoon open session

Professor H.Zemanek, Chairman.

Brief (1/4 hour) communications.

Y.V.Matijasevič (Leningrad). What should we do having proved a decision problem to be unsolvable?

N.M.Nagorny (Moscow). Algorithm as a basis for formulating constructive mathematical notions.

G.N.Salikhov (Tashkent). On an algorithm for finding weights and nodes of cubic formulae.

A.V.Kabulov (Tashkent).[*] Automation of solving some problems in discrete mathematics.

A.O.Buda (Sofia). Four lessons of riding two horses of theoretical and system programming.

S.S.Lavrov (Leningrad). Our theories are not mad enough.

A.V.Anisimov (Kiev). Backtracking transformers.

A.L.Semenov (Moscow). Choosing complexity functions properly.

A.P.Ershov (Novosibirsk). Concluding remarks.

D.Knuth (Stanford). Mathematics also uses low-level languages (concluding remarks).

Saturday, September 22, evening "Algorithm party"

Honorary Speaker S.C.Kleene (Madison) "The origin of the idea of recursive function (personal reminiscences)" (1 h. 30 min).

---

[*] The presented material has been published in the serial "Algorithms", no.36, Tashkent, Institute of Cybernetics, 1978 and "Kibernetika" (Kiev), no.3, 1979, p. 14-18.

SUPPLEMENT 3

Publications on the symposium

SCIENTIFIC REPORTS

I. Ершов А.П., Успенский В.А. Алгоритмы на родине аль-Хорезми. -
Научно-техническая информация. Серия 2. № I, 1980. М.: ВИНИТИ,
с. 28-30.

2. Семенов А.Л., Успенский В.А. Международная встреча ученых в
Хорезме. - Международный форум по информации и документации,
т. 5, № I, 1980. М.: ВИНИТИ, с. 36-37.

3. Semenov A.L., Uspensky V.A. International meeting of scientists
at Khorezm. - International Forum on Information and Documentation, vol.5, no.1, 1980, Moscow, VINITI, p. 37-38.

4. Paterson M. International symposium on algorithms in modern
mathematics and computer science. - Bulletin of the European
Association for Theoretical Computer Science, no.10, January
1980, p. 63-80, 1p., photo.

5. Оперативно-информационный материал. Ургенчский симпозиум
"Алгоритм в современной математике и ее приложениях". - Новосибирск, Вычислительный центр СО АН СССР, 1980, 37 с.

6. Ершов А.П. Международный симпозиум "Алгоритм в современной математике и ее приложениях". Кибернетика, № 2, 1980, с. 145-147.

MASS MEDIA COVERAGE

I. Форум математиков на родине аль-Хорезми. Беседа с заместителем
председателя Хорезмского облисполкома Ш.Джаббаровым. "Хорезмская
правда", 15.9.1979, p.I.

2. Симпозиум "Алгоритм в современной математике и ее приложениях".
Посвящается Аль-Хорезми. Khorezm television,   17.9.1979,
19^{10} - 19^{30}.

3. Наука - на службе мира и прогресса. Открытие международного симпозиума математиков (information and photo). "Хорезмская правда", 18.9.1979, p.I.

4. А.П.Ершов. Он обессмертил имя и дела свои (interview and photo).
"Хорезмская правда", 18.9.1979, p.2.

5. А.Ванвейнгаарден. Я впервые в Узбекистане... (interview and
photo). "Хорезмская правда", 18.9.1979, p.2.

6. Солаев Н. Шодиёна. Уранчда Халкаро симпозиум иш бошлади

(reportage and photo). "Хоразм Хакикати", 18.9.1979, p. I
(Uzbek).

7. Аль-Хорезми - великий ученый. Khorezm television , 18.9.1979,
21^{05} - 21^{20}.

8. На международном симпозиуме математиков (information). "Хорезмская правда", 19.9.1979, p.I.

9. Х.Земанек. Провозвестник кибернетики (interview and photo).
"Хорезмская правда", 19.9.1979, p.I.

10. Симпозиум "Алгоритм в современной математике и ее приложениях".
Посвящается Аль-Хорезми. Khorezm television , 19.9.1979,
21^{00} - 21^{15}.

11. На международном симпозиуме математиков. В центре внимания -
алгоритмы (information). "Хорезмская правда", 20.9.1979, p.I.

12. С.С.Лавров. Цель - обмен мнениями (interview and photo).
"Хорезмская правда", 20.9.1979, p.I.

13. Сермазмун утмокда. Математикларнинг Халкаро симпозиуми давом
этяпти (information and photo). "Хоразм хакикати", 20.9.1979,
p.4 (Uzbek).

14. Фаннинг максади инсон бахти эъзоз. Халкаро симпозиум давом
этяпти (information). "Хоразм хакикати", 21.9.1979, p.4 (Uzbek).

15. Д.Кнут. Тарихнинг буюк йули (interview and photo). "Хоразм
хакикати", 21.9.1979, p.4 (Uzbek).

16. Ф.Штрассен. Мамнунмиз (interview and photo). "Хоразм хакикати",
21.9.1979, p.4 (Uzbek).

17. М.Патерсон. Ташаккур (interview and photo). "Хоразм хакикати",
21.9.1979, p.4 (Uzbek).

18. Э.Шпеккер. Хамкорлик (interview and photo). "Хоразм хакикати",
21.9.1979, p.4 (Uzbek).

19. Симпозиум "Алгоритм в современной математике и ее приложениях".
Посвящается Аль-Хорезми. Khorezm television, 21.9.1979,
19^{30} - 19^{50}.

20. Ф.Енгулатов, А.Юсупов. Незабываемый день (photoreportage).
"Хорезмская правда", 22.9.1979, p.3.

21. Сафар шодликлари. Математикларнинг Халкаро симпозиуми давом
этяпти (information and photo). "Хоразм хакикати", 22.9.1979,
p.4 (Uzbek).

22. Алгоритм в современной математике и ее приложениях (information). "Правда", 23.9.1979.

23. А.Кречмар. Восхитительно! (interview and photo). "Хорезмская правда", 25.9.1979, p.4.

24. А.Мазуркевич. За сотрудничество! (interview and photo). "Хорезмская правда", 25.9.1979, p.4.

25. Д.Кнут. В поиске (interview and photo). "Хорезмская правда", 25.9.1979, p.4.

26. Ф.Енгулатов. Форум науки и сотрудничества (reportage). "Хорезмская правда", 25.9.1979, p.4.

27. Symposium on the algorithm. "Moscow News information", 74(118), Sep. 22-24, 1979, p.5.

28. (Information about the opening of the symposium) "Pravda vostoka" (Tashkent), 18.9.1979.

29. (Information about the results of the symposium) "Pravda vostoka", 25.9.1979.

LIST OF PARTICIPANTS

From abroad

Prof. Dr. F.L. Bauer, Institut für Informatik, Techn. Univ. München,
    Arcisstraße 21, 8 München 2, Germany

Dr. A. Buda, Institute of Mathematics, Bulgarian Acad. of Sciences,
    Sofia, P.O. Box 373, Bulgaria

Dr. H. Kaufmann, Eichenstraße 18, D-8134 Pöcking, Germany

Prof. S.C. Kleene, Dept. of Mathematics, Univ. of Wisconsin, Madison,
    Wis. 53706, USA

Prof. D.E. Knuth, Dept. of Computer Science, Stanford Univ., Stanford,
    Cal. 94305, USA

Dr. A. Kreczmar, Universitet Warszawski, Institut Informatiki, 00-901
    Warszawa PKiN, Poland

Dr. A. Mazurkiewicz, Institute of Computer Science, Polish Acad. of
    Sciences, P.O. Box 22, 00-901 Warszawa PKiN, Poland

Prof. M.S. Paterson, Dept. of Computer Science, Univ. of Warwick,
    Coventry, CV4 7AL, England

Prof. Z. Pawlak, Institute of Computer Science, Polish Acad. of Sciences,
    P.O. Box 22, 00-901 Warszawa PKiN, Poland

Prof. Dr. E. Specker, ETH-Zentrum, CH-8P92 Zürich, Switzerland

Prof. Dr. V. Strassen, Seminar für Angew. Mathematik der Universität
    Zürich, Freiestraße 36, CH-8032 Zürich, Switzerland

Prof. Dr. A. van Wijngaarden, Mathematisches Zentrum, 2e Boerhaavestraat
    49, 1091 AL Amsterdam, Netherlands

Prof. Dr. H. Zemanek, Postfach 251, A-1011 Wien, Austria

From the Soviet Union

Dr. Sci. Georgii Maksimovich Adel'son-Vel'skii, VNIISI, ul. Ryleeva, 29,
    119034 Moscow G34

Prof. Ian Martynovich Barzdin', Computing Center, LatSSR Acad. Sci.,
    bul. Rainisa, 29, 226050 Riga GSP

Acad.-corr. Andrei Petrovich Ershov, Computing Center, Siberian Branch
    USSR Acad. Sci., 630090 Novosibirsk

Acad.-corr. Iurii Leonidovich Ershov, Institute of Mathematics, Siberian
    Branch USSR Acad. Sci., 630090 Novosibirsk

Acad. Viktor Mikhailovich Glushkov, Institute of Cybernetics, UkSSR
    Acad. Sci., pr. 40 let Oktiabria, 142/144, 252127 Kiev GSP

Dr. Anvar Vasilovich Kabulov, Institute of Cybernetics, UzSSR Acad.
    Sci., ul. Faizully Khodzhaeva, 34, 700125 Tashkent

Acad. Vasil Kabulovich Kabulov, Institute of Cybernetics, UzSSR Acad. Sci., ul. Faizully Khodzhaeva, 34, 700125 Tashkent

Prof. Iuliia Vladimirovna, Institute of Cybernetics, UkSSR Acad. Sci., pr. 40 let Oktiabria, 142/144, 252127 Kiev GSP

Dr. Vladimir Mikhailovich Kurochkin, Computing Center, USSR Acad. Sci., ul. Vavilova, 40, 117333 Moscow V-333

Acad.-corr. Sviatoslav Sergeevich Lavrov, Institute of Theoretical Astronomy, USSR Acad. Sci., nab. Kutuzova, 10, 192187 Leningrad D-187

Prof. Aleksandr Adol'fovich Letichevskii, Institute of Cybernetics, UkSSR Acad. Sci., pr. 40 let Oktiabria, 142/144, 252127 Kiev GSP

Prof. Iurii Ivanovich Manin, Institute of Mathematics, USSR Acad. Sci., ul. Vavilova, 42, 117333 Moscow V-333

Dr. Sci. Iurii Vladimirovich Matiiasevich, Institute of Mathematics, Leningrad Branch, USSR Acad. Sci., nab. Fontanki, 27, 191011 Leningrad

Dr. Nikolai Makarievich Nagorny, Computing Center, USSR Acad. Sci., ul. Vavilova, 40, 117333 Moscow V-333

Dr. Nikolai Nikolaevich Nepeivoda, Dept. of Algebra, Faculty of Mathematics, Udmurt State University, Izhevsk

Prof. Oleg Sergeevich Ryzhov, Computing Center, USSR Acad. Sci., ul. Vavilova, 40, 117333 Moscow V-333

Dr. Sci. Gaibulla Nazrullaevich Salikhov, Faculty of Computational Math. and Cybernetics, Vuzgorodok, Tashkent State University, Tashkent GSP [† December 10, 1979]

Dr. Aleksei L'vovich Semenov, Dept. of Mathematical Logic, Faculty of Mech.-Math., Moscow State University, Leninskie gory, 117234 Moscow V-234

Dr. Valentin Petrovich Semik, INÉUM, ul. Vavilova, 24, 117133 Moscow V-234

Prof. Nikolai Aleksandrovich Shanin, Institute of Mathematics, Leningrad Branch, USSR Acad. Sci., nab. Fontanki, 27, 111011 Leningrad

Acad. Sagdy Khasanovich Sirazhdinov, UzSSR Acad. Sci., ul. Gogolia, 70, Tashkent

Dr. Anatol' Oles'evich Slisenko, Institute of Mathematics, Leningrad Branch, USSR Acad. Sci., nab. Fontanki, 27, 191011 Leningrad

Prof. Boris Avraamovich Trakhtenbrot, Institute of Mathematics, Siberian Branch USSR Acad. Sci., 630090 Novosibirsk

Dr. Sci. Grigorii Samuilovich Tseitin, Faculty of Mech.-Math., LOGLU, 10 liniia V.O., 33, 199178 Leningrad

Dr. Sci. Enn Kharaldovich Tyugy, Institute of Cybernetics, EstSSR Acad. Sci., bul'var Lenina, 10, 200104 Tallinn

Prof. Vladimir Andreevich Uspenskii, Dept. of Mathematical Logic, Faculty
  of Mech.-Math., Moscow State University, Leninskie gory, 117234
  Moscow V-234

Scientific translators

Dr. Anatolii Vasil'evich Anisimov, Dept. of Theoretical Cybernetics,
  Kiev State University, ul. Vladimirskaia, 64, 252017 Kiev-17
Dr. Sci. Vadim Evgen'evich Kotov, Computing Center, Siberian Branch USSR
  Acad. Sci., 630090 Novosibirsk
Sergei Borisovich Pokrovskii, Computing Center, Siberian Branch USSR
  Acad. Sci., 630090 Novosibirsk
Dr. Viktor Karlovich Sabel'fel'd, Computing Center, Siberian Branch USSR
  Acad. Sci., 630090 Novosibirsk

SUPPLEMENT 5

PHOTOILLUSTRATIONS

OFFICERS

R.I. Ishchanov, Chairman
Khorezm Region Executive Committee
PATRON

Acad. S.Kh. Sirazhdinov, Vice-President
Uzbek SSR Academy of Sciences
CHAIRMAN, Organizing Committee

Acad. V.K. Kabulov, Director
Inst. of Cybernetics, UzSSR Ac. Sci.
CO-CHAIRMAN, Organizing Committee

Dr. K.Sh. Babamuradov, Laboratory Head
Inst. of Cybernetics, UzSSR Ac. Sci.
DEPUTY CHAIRMAN, Organizing Committee

479

OFFICERS

Donald Knuth, Andrei Ershov
CO-CHAIRMAN, Technical Program

SPEAKERS

Georgy Adelson-Velsky

Anatoly Anisimov

Anatoly Buda

Jan Barzdin

Andrei Ershov

Yuri Ershov

Anvar Kabulov

Julia Kapitonova

481

SPEAKERS

Stephen Kleene

Don Knuth

Sviatoslav Lavrov

Alexander Letichevsky

Yuri Matijasevich

Nikolai Nagorny

Nikolai Nepeivoda

Mike Paterson

SPEAKERS

Alexei Semenov

Nikolai Shanin

Anatoly Slisenko

Volker Strassen

Boris Trakhtenbrot

Grigory Tseytin

Enn Tyugu

Vladimir Uspensky

483

SPEAKERS

Aad van Wijngaarden

Heinz Zemanek

PARTICIPANTS

Vladimir Kurochkin

Tursun Rashidov

Oleg Ryzhov

Valentin Semik

Ernst Specker

484

GUESTS

Jeanne Kleene

Jill Knuth

Baldabay Kurmambaev

A. Mukhamedjanov

Khalil Sidikov

Benedicte Zemanek

Georg Zemanek

Maria Zemanek

STAFF

Ikram Atabekov
(housing)

Vadim Kotov
(translation)

Ludmila Kotova
(secretary)

Sergei Pokrovsky
(translation)

Viktor Sabelfeld
(translation)

Sarsen Shushbaev
(meeting room)

Jaschin Uzakov
(liaison)

1. N. Mukhitdinov
2. V. Buzurkhanov
3. V. Buzurkhanov
4. I. Atabekov
5. H. Zemanek
6. S.S. Shushbaev
7. M. Viakhodzhaev
8. G.M. Adel'son-Velskii
9. V.A. Uspenskii
10. V.M. Kurochin
11. A.V. Anisimov
12. R. Akramov
13. G.S. Tseitin
14. Iu.V. Matiiasevich
15. Georg Zemanek
16. S. Tuliaganov

17. H. Kaufmann
18. O.S. Ryzhov
19. Ludmila Kotova
20. Benedicte Zemanek
21. S.S. Lavrov
22. Jill Knuth
23. Maria Zemanek
24. V.P. Semik
25. V.E. Kotov
26. V.K. Sabelfeld
27. B.A. Trakhtenbrot
28. A.O. Buda
29. D.E. Knuth
30. Jeanne Kleene
31. S.B. Porkrovskii
32. A.L. Semenov

33.
34. S.C. Kleene
35. E.H. Tyugu
36. A.P. Ershov
37. J. Uzakov
38.
39. A. Pulatov
40. J.V. Kapitonova
41. N.M. Nagornyi
42. Kh. R. Ishchanov
43. M. Israilov
44. A. van Wijngaarden
45. Kh. Israilova
46. Iu.I. Manin
47. N.N. Nepeivoda
48. R. Salikhova

49. A.O. Slisenko
50. A. Gudiev
51. A.A. Letichevskii
52. Mrs. Gudieva
53. V. Strassen
54. A. Mazurkiewiecz
55. Iu.L. Ershov
56. E. Specker
57. G.N. Salikhov
58. Z. Pawlak
59. J.M. Barzdin
60. D. Akhmedóv
61. A. Kreczmar
62. N.A. Shanin
63.
64. A.V. Kabulov